Perspectives on India's Political Economy

This volume contains some of the core foundational contributions on the broad theme of the political economy of India's development. These have been culled from the numerous writings of public personages, thinkers and academic writers over the past century. The extant collections of readings on development economics usually contain readings from academic economists like Sen, Bhagwati, Bardhan, Dreze, Basu, etc. The purpose of this collection is to point out to the lay reader that there is a world of writing on development that is outside the realms of academia. Accordingly, we look at the contributions of figures like Mahatma Gandhi, Jawaharlal Nehru, Babasaheb Ambedkar, Ram Manohar Lohia, etc., who too had thought hard and deep about the process of India's development.

The present volume is a purposive selection of 23 articles out of the 75 pieces published earlier in four volumes with the title *Economic Development of India*, by Routledge in 2015. This selection is brought out with the aim of retaining the flavour of the theme under discussion in a succinct single cover volume with a new introduction that ruminates on the recent developments.

Pulin B. Nayak is presently at the Centre for Development Economics, Delhi School of Economics. He was formerly Professor of Economics and Director of the Delhi School of Economics. He has written on issues pertaining to public finance and economic development.

Perspectives on India's Political Economy

Edited by Pulin B. Nayak

Routledge
Taylor & Francis Group
LONDON AND NEW YORK

First published 2018
by Routledge
4 Park Square, Milton Park, Abingdon, Oxon OX14 4RN

and by Routledge
605 Third Avenue, New York, NY 10017

First issued in paperback 2023

Routledge is an imprint of the Taylor & Francis Group, an informa business

Publisher's Note
The publisher has gone to great lengths to ensure the quality of this reprint but points out that some imperfections in the original copies may be apparent.

British Library Cataloguing-in-Publication Data
A catalogue record for this book is available from the British Library

Library of Congress Cataloging-in-Publication Data
A catalogue record has been requested

ISBN-13: 978-1-138-50178-2 (hbk)
ISBN-13: 978-1-03-265297-9 (pbk)
ISBN-13: 978-1-351-26616-1 (ebk)

DOI: 10.4324/9781351266161

Typeset in Bembo
by Swales & Willis Ltd, Exeter, Devon, UK

For Nalini, Nandini and Supriya

Contents

Acknowledgements

It was Ms Nitasha Devasar who first suggested that I come out with a volume of readings on the political economy of India's development which should be affordable for students and the lay public. I acknowledge my grateful thanks to her. Ms Aafreen Ayub then took charge of the editorial and production processes and I am deeply grateful to her for all her editorial inputs as well as for helping me to work to a time schedule.

P. N.

**

The publishers would like to thank the following for permission to reprint their material:

Narajivan Trust for permission to reprint Mohandas Karamchand Gandhi, 'Unto This Last: Sarvodaya—Non-violent Social Transformation', in Raghavan Iyer (ed.), *The Moral and Political Writings of Mahatma Gandhi* (Oxford: Clarendon Press, 1987), pp. 410–33.

Jawaharlal Nehru Memorial Trust and Smt. Sonia Gandhi for permission to reprint Jawaharlal Nehru, 'The National Planning Committee and the Congress and Industry: Big Industry versus Cottage Industry', *The Discovery of India* (New Delhi: Oxford University Press, 1982), pp. 395–409. First published 1946 by The Signet Press, Calcutta.

The Estate of Sukhamoy Chakravarty for permission to reprint Sukhamoy Chakravarty, 'Development Economics and the Indian Experience', in Kaushik Basu and Pulin Nayak (eds), *Development Policy and Economic Theory* (New Delhi: Oxford University Press, 1994), pp. 1–13

The author for permission to reprint Benjamin Zachariah, 'The Debate on Gandhian Ideas', *Developing India: An Intellectual and Social History* (New Delhi: Oxford University Press, 2005), pp. 156–210.

Indian Economic Review for permission to reprint Baldev Raj Nayar, 'Nationalist Planning for Autarky and State Hegemony: Development Strategy under Nehru', *Indian Economic Review*, Vol. 32, No. 1 (January–June 1997), 13–38.

Disclaimer

The publishers have made every effort to contact authors/copyright holders of works reprinted in *Perspectives on India's Political Economy*. This has not been possible in every case, however, and we would welcome correspondence from those individuals/companies whom we have been unable to trace.

Introduction

The political economy of India's development

Pulin B. Nayak

I

India has just completed 70 years of her Independence from nearly two centuries of colonial rule. This is a point in time of no small significance. Seventy years is a period of substantial length. It should be possible to take stock of what our aspirations were when Pandit Jawaharlal Nehru had addressed the midnight session in the central hall of Parliament on the eve of 15 August, 1947, and how we have measured up to them in these intervening years. Pandit Nehru's eloquent and stirring words were:

> Long years ago we made a tryst with destiny and now the time comes when we shall redeem our pledge, not wholly or in full measure, but very substantially. At the stroke of the midnight hour, when the world sleeps, India will awake to life and freedom.

This speech is justifiably regarded as one of the greatest made in the twentieth century. Moving on, in the same address, Pandit Nehru had said:

> The achievements we celebrate today is but a step, an opening of opportunity, to the greater triumphs and achievements that await us . . . It means the ending of poverty and ignorance and disease and inequality of opportunity. The ambition of the greatest man of our generation has been to wipe every tear from every eye.

To what extent have we been able to realise the expectations we had set for ourselves seven decades back? This is the momentous question for India today.

More than a century and a half after the French Revolution, when Chairman Mao had apparently been asked what its impact had been on world affairs, Mao seems to have quipped: 'It is too early to tell.' In the long civilisational history of five thousand years of this great sub-continent, seven decades form possibly too insignificant a time span but one would like to argue here that this period has salience because after a long period of foreign rule Indians were in charge of their own destiny. There is no gainsaying that even the most basic modicum of material well-being had been denied to the vast bulk of this country for too long a period, especially when Western Europe and North America were marching ahead at a rapid pace in the wake of the Industrial Revolution. India today is home to more than a sixth of the world's population and, even now, seventy years after Independence, in terms of per capita income, India's is barely 15 per cent of the world average. There is a lot of catching up to do and there is a long way to go.

The purpose of the readings in this collection is to understand and appreciate the crucial issue of India's economic development. We need to make three points right away. First, it must be stated up front that the process of economic development is necessarily something that always needs to be understood within the given historical context, and within the contextual social and political milieu. It is usually a grave error to conceive of the economic realities and processes in a country purely in narrow economistic terms; terms that are independent of the historical, political and social milieu. So, when we speak of development or economic development, we are here necessarily adopting a holistic approach.

The second point to note is that contemporary thinking on economic matters in India has a rich and hoary lineage. There is no doubt that the field of study of economic development in its modern form is essentially a post second world war development. Yet, it must be emphasised that serious thinking on development matters in the Indian context was systematically articulated at least as early as the first decade of the twentieth century in the writings of major figures such as Dadabhai Naoroji and Mohandas Karamchand Gandhi (Naoroji 1901; Gandhi 1909). During India's freedom struggle there were several major figures other than Gandhiji who had certain well developed views regarding the issue of India's economic development. The most consistently prominent and cerebral among them, by a long margin, was Pandit Jawaharlal Nehru, but there were many others, including, Jayaprakash Narayan, Achyut Patwardhan, Subhash Chandra Bose, Ram Manohar Lohia, Minoo Masani, Babasaheb Ambedkar, J. C. Kumarappa, to name a few. Quite clearly, for all of them, the Independence of the country was a prerequisite before there could be any consideration of actual implementation of any policy.

Third, soon after India's Independence in 1947, a large swathe of countries in Asia and Africa gained independence from colonial rule. The immediate task for the political leadership in these countries clearly was rapid economic development. Somewhat prior to this, many of the war-ravaged economies of Europe were also, at that time, engaged in the task of urgent reconstruction. The basis for the emergence of the field of development economics certainly had a lot to do with the confluence of both these factors. Some of the early writings in development economics appeared in the 1940s and 1950s (see, for example, Rosenstein-Rodan 1943; Mandelbaum 1945; Nurkse 1953; Lewis 1954; Myrdal 1957 and Hirschman 1958), most of which had a Euro-centric flavour. However, very soon, an impressive list of Indian authors joined this group, and these included, notably, A. K. Dasgupta, V. K. R. V. Rao, Bhabatosh Datta, B. N. Ganguly, K. N. Raj, Amartya Sen, Jagdish Bhagwati, Sukhamoy Chakravarty and many, many others. The latter authors were all formally trained economists and they wrote in a language and used the idiom that was familiar to Western scholars writing on the same theme.

It is possible to argue that by the 1960s development economics was already emerging as an important field within economics, much like international trade or public finance. Interestingly, a lot of the theorising was beginning to take shape with India as the reference country. There were several reasons for it. China too had embraced a new political dispensation under Chairman Mao in 1949. China and India were, and are, the two most populous countries, together accounting for more than a third of the world's population. Both were low wage economies and both had large swathes of deep poverty. The key difference was the political systems in place: China under a Communist regime, and India with a Westminster type parliamentary democracy, as a link to its colonial past with Britain. Between the two countries, clearly, it was India with a relatively free political system, an active media and a vibrant democracy, that evinced greater interest from the thinking public across the globe. Indeed, for the early scholars of development economics India seemed to be the natural laboratory to theorise on.

It would not be incorrect to state that the first group of writers looked at the problem of underdevelopment as being associated with inadequacy of capital. The focus, therefore, first and foremost, was on capital formation. A necessary requirement of this was to mobilise adequate savings from the nation's income which would need to be used for capital formation (see, for example Lewis 1955). The crux of the matter was to raise the savings rate of low income economies from the usual range of about 4 to 5 per cent of GDP to the range of 12 to 15 per cent, or more, in the medium term. This was expected to break the stasis and automatically help an economy 'take off' into a path of self-sustained growth.

The great Cambridge economist Alfred Marshall (1890) firmly believed that the subject and the principal concern of economics can be best described in the phrase 'Natura non facit saltum', i.e., nature does not make a jump. It would be no exaggeration to say that ever since the first edition of his book appeared in 1890, the language of discourse for economists everywhere in the world began to be framed very much in Marshallian terms. Yet, barely a quarter century after Marshall's death in 1924, the new development theorists were daring to think of the exact obverse of the Marshallian proposition. Trying to capture the spirit of its early proponents, Rosenstein-Rodan (1984) went to the extent of describing the concerns of development economics in a manner that he thought would be more consistent with 'Natura facit saltum', i.e. nature makes jumps.

The reason for this contrary description should not be difficult to fathom. In the three decades after the Second World War, the Western capitalist world experienced the most consistent and stable run of economic progress, thanks to a Keynesian management of the macro economy in those countries. Western Europe and North America achieved unprecedented levels of real incomes, and capitalism for the common man and woman was now defined by mass consumption of goods. The contrast with the developing countries of Asia and Africa grew sharper and more stark with each successive year. With poverty and hunger stalking a large swathe of the world, it was logical to think in terms of constructing social and economic systems that would necessarily have to take jumps, if not leaps, for there were limits to which deprivation could be endured in the world of the 1980s and 1990s. It was too much of a luxury to think in terms of being content with gradualism.

To be fair to the founding fathers of India's freedom movement, many of the notable ones among them – certainly Gandhi, Nehru, Jayaprakash Narayan, Lohia and Ambedkar – were deeply concerned with the abysmally poor condition of Indian peasants – especially the ones among them who were in the category of landless labourers – and factory workers. The condition of scheduled caste and scheduled tribe population across the length and breadth of the country often comingled with the above categories and was no better either. Rapid intervention was the need of the hour. But for this a prerequisite was the independence of the country.

The average growth rate of the gross domestic product (GDP) of India in the last half century prior to Independence was under one percentage point. For Pandit Nehru, the first Prime Minister of the country, planning by the state was to be the sheet anchor of the government's social and economic policy. Nehru was intellectually attracted to Fabian socialism and was known to be a believer in planning from the 1920s. In 1927 he had been invited by the Soviet Union to attend the festivities to celebrate the completion of ten years of the October Revolution. Nehru was impressed with what he saw. He was no doctrinaire Communist himself and was never in favour of any bloodshed in a social and economic revolution. Politically Nehru was firmly wedded to a liberal parliamentary form of democracy while in terms of his economic ideology he was grudgingly accommodative of the market mechanism as long as the commanding heights of the economy were firmly under the control of the state.

Nehru was a modernist and he believed that after gaining Independence India had to immediately chart out a path of rapid industrialisation under the overarching control of the state. This was fundamentally at variance from the formulation that Gandhi (1909) had enunciated in Hind Swaraj in the first decade of the twentieth century, at a juncture when he was still in South Africa, and yet thinking deeply about the basic problems confronting the Indian economy. On his return to

India for good in 1915, Gandhi not only picked up the mantle of the political leadership, but also articulated his social and economic thoughts quite vigorously in the pages of Young India and Harijan. In their essence, these were elaborations of his core ideas already articulated in the Hind Swaraj.

Gandhiji was keen to place emphasis on the rural, agricultural, sector because one could verily say that India lived in its villages. He firmly wished to eschew the Western capitalist mode of development, which gave rise to widening inequities between capitalists and workers. For him the key issue for the Indian economy was to ensure meaningful employment for one and all. Both Gandhi and Nehru held on to their core beliefs quite zealously. Gandhiji's assassination in less than six months of Independence automatically made Nehru the final arbiter of India's development process. The Planning Commission came into being on 15 March 1950.

II

The purpose of this collection of readings is to give a panoramic view of the thinking on the development process in India. It should be underlined that presenting a comprehensive or complete picture of the issue at hand is beyond the scope of a single volume. There are various views and collections of readings on India's economic development and the present compilation is therefore just one view of the saga of India's development experience from the beginning of the twentieth century. One of the recent collections is Nayak (2015) that contains 75 readings in four volumes. The present work culls out a subset of 23 readings from this previous collection in order to give a myriad yet succinct view of the development problem in India.

As mentioned in the previous section, rather than confine oneself to the writings of only economists, we have chosen to consider contributions of other prominent personages who came from other walks of life and were not necessarily trained economists. Mahatma Gandhi and Pandit Jawaharlal Nehru were the leading political figures of the country for some three decades prior to India's Independence. They were both trained lawyers, who were totally devoted to leading, in both cases, astonishingly active public lives. They were both highly cerebral beings who have left behind, in each case, a massive volume of written work.

Both Gandhi and Nehru had original economic formulations of their own. There is a body of economic thought that has already been christened as 'Gandhian Economics', by J. C. Kumarappa (1951). There is now already a considerable body of writing around this theme. There has as yet been no special school of economic thought attributed to Jawaharlal Nehru, but it would not be inappropriate to say that Nehru too had a distinct notion of economic development that he articulated in his various speeches and his not inconsiderable writings, and one need not be too diffident in introducing the notion of 'Nehruvian Economics' to denote a system of economic management that is essentially characterised by a 'mixed economy' framework, where the market has the important role of resource allocation while the state plays the key role of looking after the commanding heights, or the core, sectors of the economy.

Nehruvian economics was very much consistent with the ideas advocated by Friedrich List, a forerunner of the German historical school (see Chakravarty 1994, in this volume). Writing in the first half of the nineteenth century List questioned Adam Smith's idea of laissez-faire and made a strong case for the nation-state to engage actively in the task of economic development. List also made a reasoned case for protecting German industries against the onslaught of British mill made goods. Nehru's position was very similar. He was sceptical of the benefit of the Indian economy being opened up to international market forces and was of the view that this would hurt the prospects of the nascent domestic industries which needed protection from established foreign, read British and American, multinationals. Thus the Indian economy necessarily adopted an 'autarkic' mode. This was not without its problems either. This privileged certain business houses – think 'Ambassador' and 'Fiat' cars – to have untrammelled monopoly powers. In terms of their international standing the goods produced were sub-standard in quality and were also priced unreasonably high.

But, to be fair, Nehru's economics and his developmental vision was much more than an insistence on state controlled investment planning that gave enormous clout to bureaucrats and politicians, who did not balk at extensive rent seeking. Very early on, Nehru was insistent on giving a massive push to institutions of higher learning such as the IITs and the IIMs, as well as institutions of scientific research such as CSIR, all of which were fully funded by the state. Nehru was also keen about funding institutions in the medical sphere such as the AIIMS (All India Institute of Medical Sciences), and in the sphere of theoretical physics and mathematics, institutions such as the TIFR (Tata Institute of Fundamental Research).

Institutions in the sphere of the social sciences were not to be left behind. In the late 1940s Pandit Nehru agreed to be the Chairman of the Delhi School of Economics Society, of which the Secretary was the well-known economist V. K. R. V. Rao. The Delhi School of Economics was established in 1949 and it moved into its own building in 1956. The DSE soon became a part of Delhi University and in the years to come, in addition to economics, the DSE also encompassed the disciplines of sociology and geography as well. Nehru had already shown his own intellectual calibre in his many substantial works, including, especially, The Discovery of India (1946), and was very keen to have top rung institutions devoted to research in the area of the social sciences. If India today has a reasonable supply of home trained natural scientists, engineers, doctors, as well as social scientists, we need to acknowledge the visionary spirit and leadership of Pandit Nehru behind this.

If India today, during 2015–17, has achieved growth rates in the range of about 7 to 7.5 per cent of GDP, which made it the fastest growing major economy of the world, one must ask whether this could have been achieved in a vacuum. In other words, did the institutions of higher learning established in the first decade after Independence, not have some role in building up the human capital that has provided the base for this impressive achievement at the present juncture? This is not an empty question, because under the present dispensation there seems to be a systematic effort at denigrating the yeoman contributions of Jawaharlal Nehru who, for good or bad, was at the helm of the country's affairs for the first 17 years of Independence.

The readings contained in this volume seek to present a broad picture of the discourse on the political economy of development from the beginning of the twentieth century up until the present times. Around two decades after India's Independence, in the mid 1960s, the economic conditions prevailing in the country were rather precarious. There had been the Chinese debacle in 1962, which had sullied the reputation and stature of Nehru, from which he was never able to recover till his demise in 1964. The country had gone to war with Pakistan on the western border in 1965, and with two successive droughts the agricultural situation was bleak in 1966. India knocked at the doors of a number of Western countries for food grains, and had to suffer a considerable degree of humiliation in the process. Writing in the *Times*, London, Neville Maxwell, their India correspondent, had stated in 1967: "the great experiment of developing India within a democratic framework has failed." He went on to add that Indians would soon vote in the "fourth – and surely last – general election".

It is around this conjuncture that Gunnar Myrdal came up with his monumental work, entitled *The Asian Drama*. The work was extraordinarily ambitious and comprehensive in its scope. Myrdal was a major Swedish economist, a social democrat, who, other than his theoretical contributions, had earlier studied the condition of the American blacks, and in the 1960s turned his attention on the issue of social, political and economic development in South Asia. Clearly the country that automatically occupied the bulk of the attention had to be India for its sheer size, complexity, as well as the large volume of literature that already existed on the Indian context regarding matters of economic development.

The 1950s were years of the Cold War between the capitalist world led by the US and the communist bloc led by the USSR. Most of South Asia had been under colonial domination for long stretches of time. India had been steadfast in its commitment to a parliamentary form of democracy but the same was not true of many of the other countries of the region, some of which had embraced totalitarian forms of government. In terms of its foreign policy India had scrupulously positioned itself away from both the American or the Soviet blocs and Prime Minister Nehru had been instrumental in forging a non-aligned movement, which found a measure of support from Gamal Abdel Nasser in Egypt, Sukarno in Indonesia and Josip Broz Tito in Yugoslavia.

The common feature characterising the economies of South Asia was low per capita levels of income, fragile political structures and highly unequal and stratified societies. A vast mass of humanity, ill fed, poorly educated and in poor health, resided in this part of the world. Myrdal's purpose was to examine what the prospects of these economies were in the years to come. At the point of time when this was being considered, the late 1960s, a large of part of South Asia, namely Vietnam and Cambodia, were in deep political and military turmoil, and continuing warfare against the military might of the US was sapping the reserves of this poor region of the world. The prognosis for South Asia was, in a word, bleak.

Myrdal's first chapter in his three-volume opus, the *Asian Drama*, was titled 'The Beam in Our Eyes' which appears as the first piece in this volume (Reading 1). Coming from the Western mode of thinking on social and economic matters, Myrdal was trying to make sense of these deeply traditional Eastern societies. Myrdal pleads for a holistic approach to study the problem of economic development, being mindful of traditions, customs, and what he calls a 'sociology of knowledge'. He underlines the fact that circa the 1960s the world was in deep conflict of ideology, and he makes a plea to Western scholars to eschew their concepts and theories, and also, very importantly, their biases, if they are really keen to understand South Asia.

Myrdal emphasises that the approach he has tried to adopt is 'institutional'. He has also tried to resist the typically hegemonistic thinking of economists and tried to emphasise the importance of historical, sociological and cultural factors that might have a telling effect on the development process. Well before institutional economics became an acknowledged branch of economic analysis, Myrdal was mindful of its significance and it is possible to hold that the *Asian Drama* might be regarded as one of the important representative works in the area, following in the tradition of Veblen and Galbraith and adding to the essential corpus of the later work of scholars such as Douglas North. At one point Myrdal observes: "Behind all the complexities and dissimilarities we sense a rather clear-cut set of conflicts and a common theme as in a drama. The action in this drama is speeding towards a climax. Tension is mounting: economically, socially, and politically" (Myrdal 1968, Vol. I, p. 34).

III

A half century after Gunnar Myrdal's *Asian Drama*, it would be no exaggeration to say that the situation in the South Asian region has indeed changed in a rather dramatic fashion! Through the 1990s and subsequently, most of the countries of the region have picked up much developmental steam. During the Nehruvian years of planned economic development the growth rate of the Indian economy was stuck at the Hindu rate of around 3.5 to 4 percentage points, and this continued beyond Nehru's time till the late 1970s, i.e., for another decade and a half. The old style autarkic management of the economy came up for some serious questioning by the beginning of the 1980s. Shrimati Indira Gandhi was now again back at the helm after a brief Janata interregnum. Some of the ills and the utter inefficiencies of the licence-permit raj were apparent even to erstwhile adherents of planning. Some opening up of the economy was brought during Shrimati Gandhi's tenure which was continued further after her tragic assassination when Rajiv Gandhi was called upon to carry her mantle. The growth rate of the Indian economy moved up to the 5 to 5.5 per cent range in the decade of the 1980s.

The late 1980s and beginning 1990s saw some of the most worrying years of political economic instability in India. The old supremacy of the Congress Party was long over and several regional political party formations had come into being. Added to the Mandal and mandir issues that had almost totally consumed the political space, the economy seemed to be in a deep crisis in the fiscal and foreign trade spheres. It is at this conjuncture that Shri Narasimha Rao assumed the reins of power as Prime Minister with Dr Manmohan Singh was brought in as the Finance Minister. Government finances were in such dire straits that Mr Rao had no option but to bring in big sweeping economic reforms. He possibly figured that the situation could not get much worse anyway, and seemed to be sure that some transformative reforms were the need of the hour.

The idea was to allow a greater play to market forces and create an environment for private entrepreneurship and innovation to flourish. The old style mind set associated with planning was now underplayed, and reform was in the air. Both Rao and Singh fundamentally believed that a more open and market friendly economy would enable India to reclaim its true potential. Presenting his first budget in Parliament in 1991 Dr Manmohan Singh quoted Victor Hugo who had said: 'no power on earth can stop an idea whose time has come.' Dr Singh went on to add:

> I suggest to this august House that the emergence of India as a major economic power in the world happens to be one such idea. Let the whole world hear it loud and clear. India is now wide awake. We shall prevail. We shall overcome.

The average growth rate in the decade of the 1990s inched up further to the range of around 6 to 6.5 percentage points. But there were two major nagging points of concern. Commensurate with a step up in the growth rate hardly any new jobs were being created, particularly in the organised sector, giving rise to the phenomenon of 'jobless growth'. Further, there was very little dent on the extent of poverty reduction. What seemed to be happening is that even while the reform process was helping push up the overall growth rate, the benefits were confined to the top quarter of the population, and the bottom half seemed to be getting completely bypassed. An additional worry was that income and wealth inequalities were getting accentuated. This has been noted as an extensive worldwide phenomenon and India was no exception to it (Piketty 2014).

By the turn of the century, economic reforms were about a decade old, and what was significant was that there was broad consensus across the political spectrum of the need to maintain the pace. This was a significant new development. The political alliances grouped under UPA and NDA certainly had some differences on the exact stance on a particular issue such as, say, expenditure on the social sector, or the policy on the telecom sector, but there was unanimity on the necessity of reform. The material difference lay elsewhere, namely, in the political sphere, whether India should remain a secular democratic country, or, should Hindutva define the social and political fabric of this diverse country.

The episode that suddenly catapulted India into the imagination of the world at large was the dramatic step up in the GDP growth rate to the 9 per cent plus range during 2005–08. Dr Manmohan Singh had now assumed the helm of Prime Ministership under a UPA government. The key drivers of this growth rate were the IT sector as well as the open policy towards globalisation. Much of the gain was simply due to arbitrage in wages: an A4 page could be typeset in Bengaluru at one fifth the cost as in the Netherlands or the US and, thanks to improved means of IT connectivity, there was plenty of work coming India's way. This growth rate figure of 9 per cent plus for India was no small matter. China was the only other major country that had achieved such breakneck speed over a much longer period, from around 1979–80, which had already put the Chinese per capita income vastly ahead of India's, even though both countries were more or less evenly matched around 1979–80.

A very significant aspect of this growth achievement was that it was not a one-off affair. It lasted for three continuous years till the onset of the world financial crisis of 2008 put a stop to it. There was one important spin-off of this episode. The naysayers were confronted with a reality that for the first time demonstrated that India does have the potential to grow fast on a sustained basis. And at least one school of thought contended that as long as growth is ensured, poverty, hunger, illiteracy and ill health would ultimately be sorted out. But, as with everything else in dealing with societal change, unless the growth was to be necessarily inclusive, and specially cognisant of the needs of the weaker and more disadvantaged sections, one could easily have a situation where the bottom half would be bypassed in the development process.

The second reading (Reading 2) in this volume is a definitive account of Indian development in a comparative perspective from the joint work of Drèze and Sen (2013). This work marked nearly a quarter century of sustained collaborative work by these two outstanding scholars. One of their early joint works (Drèze and Sen 1989) had found a mention in the citation of the Nobel award to Amartya Sen. Drèze and Sen compare India's position in terms of several key indicators of development – such as per capita income level, life expectancy at birth, infant mortality rate, literacy rate, access to improved sanitation, public expenditure on health and education, etc. – with a number of countries such as Vietnam, Uzbekistan, Pakistan, Sri Lanka, China, Brazil, Cambodia, Burma, Bangladesh, Nepal and Afghanistan. The reference year for their study is 2011.

There are a number of very important takeaways from this important study. We learn that even though a country such as Bangladesh has about half the per capita income of India (in PPP, constant 2005 international $ terms) – 1,569 as against 3,203 – in terms of a number of some of the other key human development indices, say, infant mortality rate, Bangladesh outperforms India. Further, very importantly, the percentage of households practising open defecation in India was as high as 55 (2005–06 data) whereas the figure for Bangladesh was 8.4 (2007 data). In addition to polluting virtually all water sources, open defecation is known to have severe impact on stunting in children with lifelong adverse consequences. The other important point of difference is the considerably more advantageous status of women in Bangladesh vis-à-vis their Indian counterparts.

Another very important takeaway of the Drèze–Sen study is that India's public expenditure on health as a fraction of GDP is a miserable 1.2 per cent, which has since inched to barely 1.3 per cent now. The rate for China is around 3 per cent, while most countries in Western Europe are in the range of around 8 to 10 percentage points. It needs hardly be emphasised that education and health are in the nature of merit goods and a substantial role of the state is a prerequisite for both efficiency and equity in the delivery of both these key sectors.

Within India, too, there is a picture of considerable variation across states. Median per capita income is as high as Rs 9,987 per year in Kerala (data for 2004–05), while the figure for Odisha is a mere Rs 3,450. Much of the income in Kerala owes its origin to remittances from the Middle East, however, and Kerala could well do with a stronger industrial base, given its high quality of human resources. But there is little doubt that in terms of social sector indicators pertaining to education, health and the role of women, Kerala is a remarkable outlier, and as Drèze and Sen remind us, it would be at the top of the South Asian comparisons if it were to be treated as a separate country. Due to its high educational achievements, and high female educational achievements in particular, the level of public awareness in Kerala is of a higher order. Government schemes such as the public distribution system (PDS) work with a much greater degree of efficiency and success as compared to a number of other less fortunate states such as Bihar and Uttar Pradesh. There are important lessons here for all of us.

Subsequent to the magisterial contribution of Drèze and Sen who used data up till 2011, the ground reality in India has changed in several significant ways. First, the UPA government gave way, in 2014, to the new BJP government under the Prime Ministership of Shri Narendra Modi. Under India's first past the post system, the Bhartiya Janata Party got barely 31 per cent of the popular votes, but was able to get a clear majority in the Lok Sabha. Among the first major decisions of Prime Minister Modi was to disband the

Planning Commission. The Commission was dissolved on 17 August 2014. In its place we now have the NITI (National Institution for Transforming India) Aayog, which has now completed its third year. It is too early to tell whether we are better or worse off due to this decision.

But certain other developments need to be mentioned here. During 2015–16, India's growth rate of GDP was recorded at 7.6 per cent. This was the fastest among the major economies of the world. What was particularly important to note was that in the same year growth rates of most West European countries and the US were in the range of about 2.5 to 4 per cent, and Brazil and Russia in fact experienced negative growth. Further, very significantly, the Chinese growth rate, at 7.1 per cent, had been tipped by India. This was clearly no small achievement, though it must immediately be admitted that there are many aspects of the development process that still put India at the unenviable position of 130 in a listing of 188 countries in terms of the human development indicator compiled by the UNDP.

For reasons best known to the Prime Minister, he announced a demonetisation measure on 8 November 2016, which delegitimised 86.7 per cent of currency, in the form of Rs 500 and 1,000 notes, in circulation. The ostensible purpose was to eliminate black money, or 'kala dhan', in the economy and to strike out terrorism. Unfortunately, the intended purpose could scarcely be achieved, and the withdrawal of currency of this magnitude in fact crippled the economy in the short term. The only other experience of demonetisation in independent India was in 1978, when Morarji Desai was the Prime Minister. Currency notes of Rs 1,000, 5,000 and 10,000 denominations were delegitimised, altogether amounting to merely 1.6 per cent of the total value of currency in circulation. The common man was not even aware that such a step had been taken because these high value notes were never in regular use. By contrast, in 2016, currency notes of 500 and 1,000 denominations were in regular usage by common people.

The negative impact of demonetisation on the Indian economy was immediate and extensive. The entire informal sector of the Indian economy works on a cash basis. There was massive disruption in the livelihoods of common daily wagers. The sector that was possibly hit the most was the agriculture sector, where all wage payments and all transactions in grain and vegetable markets, or 'mandis', are in terms of cash. Short of liquidity, prices of all farm products crashed in most mandis across the length and breadth of the country, causing severe grief to farmers, and, in some situations, adding to the already disturbing situation of farmers' suicides. It is quite clear that even nine months after the demonetisation measure the economy as a whole has not quite recovered from the trauma. As per the CSO (Central Statistical Organisation) the GDP growth rate in the year 2016–17 is estimated at 7.1 per cent, and despite official reports to the contrary, the proximate reason for the dip is most likely to have been the disruption due to demonetisation. Indeed the figures for the quarterly growth rate of India's GDP during April–June 2017 have been put at an even lower 5.7 per cent.

IV

It is not our purpose here to offer any detailed recap of the various contributions that are contained in this collection of readings. Yet some brief comments might not be out of place. Gandhiji's 'Sarvodaya: non-violent social transformation' (Reading 3) is a translation of John Ruskin's *Unto This Last* into Gujarati. This appeared in the form of nine articles published in the Indian Opinion in South Africa between 16 April and 18 July in 1908. Gandhi had been given the book *Unto This Last* by his friend Henry Polak in 1904. He read this book on a long train journey from Johannesburg to Durban and as he has said, this book changed his life for ever. In this book Ruskin had challenged the formulations of the classical economists, chiefly Adam Smith, David Ricardo and John Stuart Mill. The foundation stone of Smith's formulation was built on the premise that individuals naturally pursue their self-interest and it is this pursuit by millions of atomistic agents which would, via the 'invisible hand', paradoxically result in social cohesion and harmony.

Ruskin believed that just as important as the pursuit of self-interest were the affections of human beings which constitute an inner force. He believed that classical economic theory is employed to deduce the laws of demand and supply that result in misery for workers. Ruskin, on the contrary, believed that 'only that economy is good which conduces to the good of all' (see Fischer 1951, p. 91). Ruskin fundamentally believed that the underprivileged must find protection in the morality of the well to do. Gandhi went further and believed that the work of all 'has the same value'. For Gandhi the enduring lesson of 'Unto This Last' was the famous aphorism, 'that the life of labour, that is, the life of the tiller of the soil and the handicraftsman, is the life worth living'. It is this moral view of the material world – the world in which goods and services are being produced from scarce factors of production – that forms the core of what we today know as Gandhian economics. And it is this that forms the base of Gandhi's *Hind Swaraj* (1909) which was to be penned a year later on board a ship from England to South Africa.

'Hovering about' London during 1910–12, studying for his Bar examinations, and then finally being called to the Bar in 1912, Jawaharlal Nehru, then 23 years of age, was already getting 'vaguely attracted to Fabians and socialistic ideas' (Ganguli 1964). However, his practical orientation to socialism owed its origin to his deep involvement with the peasants of Oudh in the early 1920s. The oppressed tenants recounted to him their stories of the crushing burden of rent, illegal exactions, ejectments from land and beatings; of the oppression of the zamindar's agents, the money lenders and the police; and of 'kicks and curses and a hungry stomach'. Nehru was perceptive enough to understand that the peasant movement of Eastern Uttar Pradesh was running parallel to the political movement in the rest of the country led by Gandhiji.

Nehru was a keen student of history and contemporary world events and had already familiarised himself with the Marxist mode of analysis. He had keenly followed the deep crisis of Western capitalism when the Wall Street crash occurred in 1929, leading to the Great Depression. He was also a keen follower of the Keynesian remedies which were adopted by Franklin Roosevelt in the US in his New Deal. At the age of 49, Nehru was called upon, in 1938, by Subhash Chandra Bose, the then Congress President, to chair the 'National Planning Committee', which was to provide a blueprint of the economic strategies to be adopted when the country would be free of foreign rule. The working of the NPC is contained in Reading 4 of this volume which is extracted from Nehru's (1946) *Discovery of India*.

The next essay (Reading 5) is by Rajani Palme Dutt (1896–1974), who was a leading theoretician of the Communist Party of Great Britain. Born to a Bengali father and Swedish mother, he was a brilliant student of history and was deeply concerned about the future of India. Palme Dutt's (1940) book *India Today* draws a vivid picture of the bankruptcy of British imperialism in India. He was keenly aware of the rich civilisational history of India and was confident that there would be an awakening in India after the country gained Independence. He believed that this would come about when the working class and the democratic and progressive forces took the reins of India into their own hands to chart out a better and fairer future for themselves.

Ram Manohar Lohia (1910–1967) was one major political figure among the socialists who was known for his exceptional originality of thought. He had a brilliant academic career in India before he went on to Humboldt University, Berlin, to do his doctorate in economics. He wrote his dissertation on 'Salt Taxation in India' and did an analysis of Gandhi's socio-economic theory. The essay by M. Arumugam (Reading 6) on 'Socialist Strategy of Development' presents an account of Lohia's socio-economic formulations.

Among the founding fathers of India's social and economic policy, one of the key concerns was the need for self-reliance. There was an understandable background to this. After years of colonial subjugation, the idea of being dependent on any country, particularly from the capitalist West, was anathema to most of our leaders, especially Nehru. Accordingly, self-reliance was enshrined as one of the key objectives of planning. This is brought out by Reading 7, which is a chapter from the draft outline of the Fourth Five Year Plan. The contribution by B R Ambedkar (Reading 8) is a critical account of the caste structure of India. Sukhamoy Chakravarty (Reading 9) presents a critical account of the subject of development economics and the Indian experience. Benjamin Zachariah (Reading 10) offers a rich picture of the pre Independence debate on Gandhian ideas, while Baldev Raj Nayar (Reading 11) presents a critical account of the Nehru–Mahalanobis approach to planning in India.

A very important question pertains to the issue of the role of the relative roles of the state and the market in economic development. Mrinal Datta-Chaudhuri, in a conceptually seminal paper (Reading 12), re-examines the old issue of market failure which calls for government intervention, possibly by way of taxes and subsidies, or by helping organise markets that would not ordinarily exist on their own. But to this, Datta-Chaudhuri adds another category of failure, namely government failure. It should be understood that the government is not necessarily and always an institution that only does good to society or the economy, and there can indeed be situations when the visible arm of the government is used to promote sectional or private interests, generating undesirable rents. A cruder term for this is corruption that may well seep into the bureaucratic–political machinery and may ultimately be welfare reducing.

Pulin Nayak (Reading 13) addresses the issue of the role of the state in the writings of economists from the pantheon of all-time greats: Adam Smith, Friedrich List, Karl Marx, John Maynard Keynes, Joseph Schumpeter and Michal Kalecki, among others. It is argued that even though the state, from time to time, is found to acquiesce to the bidding of specific interest groups, it is nevertheless the case that the democratic state is the final repository of the hopes and aspirations of the poor, the downtrodden, the women, the dispossessed and religious minorities. When everything else fails, it is the weak via their collective action who would have no option but to take the matter into their own hands and redress their own grievances by using the political fiat of the state. This would call for a wider social and political mobilisation. At the final stage of development Marx had posited that the state would wither away, but it is safe to say that the contemporary world, and certainly today's India, is too far away yet from that home of bliss.

Syed Nawab Haider Naqvi (Reading 14) examines the entire scope of the study of development economics, which, while engaging with issues of poverty reduction, growth and distribution, must also address the ethical aspects of development as well. Rosenstein-Rodan's contribution (Reading 15) addresses the issue of the big push theory, making a case for disequilibrium growth, as a counter poise to the balanced growth theory of Ragnar Nurkse. Deepak Lal's piece (Reading 16) is a contribution to a festschrift volume for Dr Manmohan Singh. Published seven years after economic reforms were initiated in 1991, it underlines the importance of frontally addressing the issue of poverty and, very importantly, he advises Indian policy makers to eschew the institution of a Western style welfare state in India.

In a distinctly original piece Amit Bhaduri (Reading 17) cautions the growth and development enthusiasts to beware of heightened inequality and blatant biases against the poor. He makes a strong plea for those alternative development strategies that pay attention to the basic dignity of the have-nots in the development process. Prabhat Patnaik (Reading 18) takes a critical look at the globalisation process which creates a segmentation between the North and the South, whereby the advanced countries continue to benefit from higher labour productivity whereas the third world wallows in barely subsistence living conditions.

Even though India has eschewed planning only in the past three years, there was a long period after Independence, when the Planning Commission was an extraordinarily powerful body entrusted to channelise massive funds to the states for purposes of investment, as well as to spend substantial amounts as part of the Central plan. A K. Dasgupta's piece (Reading 19) provides an intellectual framework for understanding the planning process in India that we had in place for almost two thirds of a century.

V. K. R. V. Rao's piece (Reading 20) on the multiplier is an important conceptual piece on the applicability of the Keynesian concept in the context of developing countries. Rao cautions the reader against a blind application of trying to increase consumption to bolster aggregate demand and argues, quite emphatically, that the old virtues of working hard and saving more are still very pertinent in the context of a developing country such as India.

One of the big paradoxes of economic reform and the modernisation process is the corollary that the impact on labour is oftentimes adverse. This is a paradox because the whole purpose of the development process, presumably, ought to be to improve the lot of the workers and enhance their capabilities. Katrin Uba's important study (Reading 21) examines why there have been so many protests from labour against privatisation in India. Supriya Roy Chowdhury's study (Reading 22) examines the struggle of labour over wages in Pepsi, Bata and Toyota Kirloskar Motors and the role of trade unions in the changing environment. The contestation between the multinational capitalist owners, the labourers, and the state – as a guarantor and protector of the weak – needs to be carefully worked out without seriously compromising the interests and welfare of labour.

While one of the most commonly used words in the recent discourse of planning and economic development has been 'inclusion'; the ground level reality in many cases would appear to be exactly the opposite. Jan Breman's seminal work (Reading 23) on the life of the poor at the bottom of the rural economy in Gujarat is an eye opener. While economically the government comes up with 'new deals' in various development projects, there continues to be a bitter contestation for local power and, as usual, at the receiving end are the poor and the dispossessed, in this case the Halpati farm labourers. Along with the officially proclaimed economics of inclusion there seems to be, in reality, a more divisive politics of exclusion, and the more we develop, the more we seem to be descending into brutality against the already weak and defenceless.

***

The issues of development necessarily have a wide canvas. It would be impossible for any collection of readings to adequately address all conceivable concerns of the society, economy and polity. Yet there is need to take stock and attempt some broad appraisal from time to time. Having completed seven decades of her Independence, as India races on to become the most populous country of the world in less than a decade, both the challenges and the opportunities are, in a word, epochal. The essays collected in this volume will hopefully acquaint the reader with some the core concerns of poverty, hunger, destitution, malnutrition, employment, health and education with some degree of coherence. It must be underlined that this is merely one particular view, the view of the editor. It has therefore all the shortcomings of the editor, and there is no claim to proclaiming the final truth here. Possibly more than any other country in the world, India continues to be a work in progress.

References

Chakravarty, Sukhamoy (1994), 'Development Economics and the Indian Experience', in Kaushik Basu and Pulin Nayak (eds), *Development Policy and Economic Theory*, Oxford University Press, New Delhi, pp. 1–13.

Drèze, Jean and Amartya Sen (1989), *Hunger and Public Action*, Oxford University Press, Oxford.

Drèze, Jean and Amartya Sen (2013), *An Uncertain Glory: India and Its Contradictions*, Allen Lane, New Delhi.

Fischer, Louis (1951, 2008), *The Life of Mahatma Gandhi*, Harper Collins, London.

Gandhi, Mohandas Karamchand (1909), *Hind Swaraj (Indian Home Rule)*, Navjivan Publishing House, Ahmedabad.

Ganguli, B. N. (1964), Nehru and Socialism, *The Economic Weekly*, Special Number, July.

Hirschman, Albert O. (1958), *The Strategy of Economic Development*, Yale University Press, New Haven, CT.

Kumarappa, J. C. (1951), *Gandhian Economic Thought*, Vora Publishers, Bombay.

Lewis, William Arthur (1954), *Economic Development with Unlimited Supplies of Labour*, Manchester School, vol. *22*, pp. 139–91.

Lewis, William Arthur (1955), *The Theory of Economic Growth*, Allen & Unwin, London.

Mandelbaum, Martin K. (1945), *The Industrialization of Backward Areas*, Oxford, Basil Blackwell.

Marshall, Alfred (1890), *Principles of Economics*, London, Macmillan.

Myrdal, Gunnar (1957), *Economic Theory and Underdeveloped Regions*, London, G. Duckworth.

Myrdal, Gunnar (1968), *The Asian Drama: An Inquiry into the Poverty of Nations*, Penguin Books, Harmondsworth.

Naoroji, Dadabhai (1901), *Poverty and Un-British Rule in India*, Swan Sonnenschein & Co., London.

Nayak, Pulin B. (ed.) (2015), *Economic Development of India: Critical Concepts in Economics*, in 4 volumes, London, Routledge.

Nehru, Jawaharlal (1946), *The Discovery of India*, The Signet Press, Calcutta.

Nurkse, Ragnar (1953), *Problems of Capital Formation in Underdeveloped Countries*, Oxford, Basil Blackwell.

Palme Dutt, Rajani (1940), *India Today*, Victor Gollancz Ltd, London.

Piketty, Thomas (2014), *Capital in the Twenty-First Century*, Harvard University Press, Cambridge, MA.

Rosenstein-Rodan, Paul N. (1943), 'Problems of Industrialization of Eastern and South-Eastern Europe', *Economic Journal*, 25, 202–11.

Rosenstein-Rodan, Paul N. (1984), *Natura Facit Saltum: Analysis of the Disequilibrium Growth Process, in Gerald Meier and Dudley Seers (eds), Pioneers in Development*, The World Bank, Washington, DC.

Part I

Thinking about development

1

The beam in our eyes

Gunnar Myrdal

Source: *Asian Drama: An Inquiry into the Poverty of Nations*, Vol. 1 (Harmondsworth, England: Penguin Books, 1968), pp. 5–35.

1 A plea for a sociology of knowledge

Through the pursuit of social study, human beings and their interrelations in society, like other natural phenomena, are increasingly brought under scientific observation and analysis. What is scientific about this scrutiny and can justify its being called "social science" is its underlying assumption that the way an individual in a society feels, thinks, and acts is not a singular and haphazard phenomenon but one with definite causes and effects. Contained in this assumption is the idea that if we had complete knowledge, every state or change of mind and body could be fully explained and related to every other phenomenon in the world. We would know not only *how* people feel, think, and behave, but *why* they feel, think, and behave as they do, and *with what consequences* for themselves and for others. Without ever approaching such total knowledge, we attack our problems on that assumption and organize our findings accordingly, in terms of observed regularity and causal necessity.

Proceeding along these lines, the social sciences are now penetrating every corner of society and every phase of human life. Taboos are gradually being broken down. Their destruction in order to rationalize common sense has become a major aim of Western social science. We realize that all problems of living are complex; they cannot be fitted into the pigeonholes of our inherited academic disciplines, to be dealt with as economic, psychological, social, or political problems. Sometimes—for teaching purposes and for greater efficiency in research, through specialization—the old disciplines have been retained and even separated into subdisciplines; however, we do not attach the same significance to these divisions as in earlier times. Today, for instance, no one would draw inferences about social reality from the concepts of economics alone, although this was done frequently two generations ago. To avoid a superficial and one-sided approach, the specialized social science disciplines cooperate in research. In addition, one discipline, sociology, focusses on the totality of social relations and takes special responsibility for those fields of social reality that are less closely scrutinized by the other disciplines. This development has been prominent in America for some time.

Thus we economists and other social scientists are now studying intensively how people behave, and how they are motivated and then conditioned both by their inherited constitution and by their environment. We are interested in the selective processes operating on the young as they find their way in life and are guided into different occupations. We are examining the formation of opinions and attitudes, especially decision-making by public administrators, business managers, employers and employees in the labor market, and political leaders and their followers. We are observing how people spend their leisure time, how they marry and pursue family life, how some become criminals, vagabonds, or prostitutes. In short, we are concerning ourselves with human behavior and motivations, in whatever profession, social class, or geographical location.

Only about the peculiar behavior of our own profession do we choose to remain naive. How we as scientists operate in seeking to establish knowledge is largely shielded from the searchlight of social study. But, surely, though we are seeking truth, we are not less conditioned by our mental make-up and the society in which we live and work than are other men. Social scientists are human; some, as we know well, are "all too human"; and they are part of a social system and a culture. Our research interests, the particular approach we choose, the course we follow in drawing inferences and organizing our findings, are not determined by facts and logic alone. We are not automatons like the electronic machines we increasingly use to master large masses of data. And yet, although literature and art have long been considered in relation to the psychology and the environment of their creators, our writings have not been.

Our lack of curiosity about our own peculiar behavior as researchers should be surprising. As a group we are certainly as interesting and important to the dynamics of the social system as are maladjusted girls, new immigrants, and other special groups in society that we are studying more and more intensively; we perhaps even rank with business managers, professional politicians, or creative artists. Our behavior can be easily ascertained from our writings. A deeper study would, of course, entail investigation of our personal history and our present inclinations as these are influenced by our relation to the class structure and our cultural and social milieu.

The desire to make money is naturally a strong determinant of the behavior of men in business and of all of us when we are acting in the "economic" sphere; so the desire to find truth affects the behavior of scientists and, indeed, of all men when they try to form a correct view of reality. As scientists we are not blind to the fact that in the economic sphere there are also other motives. No longer do we assume that in their economic pursuits people have the singlemindedness of the "economic man" of classical economic theory. Recognizing that even in their economic choices people are conditioned by their total mental make-up and, in particular, by the community in which they live, that they are motivated in a variety of ways as are all human beings in all their behavior, we are directing our attention more and more to the interplay of all these forces. But the "scientific man," thought to be conditioned by nothing except his desire to discover the true nature of things, is still commonly taken much for granted. No great effort is made to spell out that abstraction itself, and thereby give it a precise meaning, as the classical economists tried to do for the "economic man." The concept of the "scientific man" exists simply as an observed taboo.

It is clear, of course, that with few exceptions, we want to make scientific study as "pure" as possible, in the sense that it should render as accurate a picture of reality, when looked at from a particular viewpoint, as is attainable. Other influences, external to this objective, acting on our minds during scientific inquiry are irrational: they cause us to take a view that is biased in some direction. There are devices of logic by which we can attempt to purge our research of biases. But as part of the naiveté we retain about our own behavior in social study, those problems of the philosophy of knowledge, of the logic of social study, are usually kept in the shadow. We shall return to them in Sections 7 and 9.

Our main interest in this Prologue is in the sociology of knowledge, which is concerned with causation. The point is that we could better avoid biases, and could therefore expect more rapid progress in the social sciences, if we were a little less naive about ourselves and our motivations.

A minimal desideratum is that we be always aware of the problem and attain some degree of sophistication about the operation of the personal and social conditioning of our research activity.[1] From this should rationally follow systematic inquiry into this important part of social reality. That would require the firmer establishment of a hitherto much neglected discipline: the sociology of knowledge.

These forces working on our minds, which cause irrationality if not recognized and controlled, are exceptionally strong and insidious in our approach to the problems of underdevelopment, development, and planning for development in the underdeveloped countries of South Asia. On this fact rests the defense for beginning our book with the general observations just made.

2 The spurt of interest in the problems of underdeveloped countries

There was little scientific interest in the underdeveloped countries of South Asia, or elsewhere, almost until the Second World War. Since then a swelling flood of research has been devoted to their problems. Many of our resources in the social sciences are now employed in the study of underdeveloped countries. The tide is still rising, and we economists are riding the crest of the wave. Before the war the most intensive work in the underdeveloped world was done by the cultural anthropologists, sent out from centers of learning in the rich Western countries. They described for us, usually in static terms, the structure of institutions and attitudes by which people in those countries live, work, and survive. Now the lead is taken by economists, studying the dynamic problems of underdevelopment, development, and planning for development.

This tremendous re-direction of our work has not been an autonomous and spontaneous development of social science, but a result of vast political changes. Three changes, closely interrelated, stand out sharply: first, the rapid liquidation of the colonial power structure; second, the emergence of a craving for development in the underdeveloped countries themselves, or rather among those who think, speak, and act on their behalf; and, third, the international tensions, culminating in the cold war, that have made the fate of the underdeveloped countries a matter of foreign policy concern in the developed countries. So far as Western countries, scholars, and scholarly institutions are concerned, it is clear that the third cause has been foremost in arousing interest in the problems of the underdeveloped countries. In the underdeveloped countries themselves it is fairly well understood by their intellectuals—and has occasionally given rise to slightly cynical comments—that the readiness to give aid and, more fundamentally, the interest of both the West and the Soviet Union in their conditions and problems were largely due to the world tensions that give significance to their internal affairs abroad.

It should be remembered that the economic and social conditions of the South Asian countries today are not very different from those existing before the disintegration of the colonial power system. The only major change has been the recent rapid acceleration in the rate of population increase. But the outburst of scientific interest in their economic problems preceded this acceleration, and, even more, our full awareness of it. On the whole, the masses in South Asia in prewar times were as poor and their lives as miserable as they are now. Their poverty and misery did not, however, induce economists to take any great interest in their situation, let alone concentrate attention on the practical problems of how to engender development through economic planning and coordinated large-scale state intervention. Practical action along such lines was then not within the realm of political feasibility. Still less was there a feeling of urgency about such action.

The lack of interest among social scientists, particularly economists, in the extreme poverty and economic stagnation in the underdeveloped countries and in their problems of economic development was clearly a reflection of the existing world political situation. More specifically, this lack of interest reflected the character of the colonial regimes and their effect on us as well as on the subject peoples: these regimes were not such as to call forth large-scale research on economic underdevelopment by giving political importance to these problems.

What has happened in this field of study is, of course, a glaring indication of a much more general relationship. For social scientists it is a sobering and useful exercise in self-understanding to attempt to see clearly how the direction of our scientific exertions, particularly in economics, is conditioned by the society in which we live, and most directly by the political climate (which, in turn, is related to all other changes in society). Rarely, if ever, has the development of economics by its own force blazed the way to new perspectives. The cue to the continual reorientation of our work has normally come from the sphere of politics; responding to that cue, students turn to research on issues that have attained political importance. Theories are launched, data collected, and the literature on the "new" problems expands. By its cumulative results, this research activity, which mirrors the political strivings of the time, may eventually contribute to a rationalization of these strivings and even give them a different turn.

So it has always been. The major recastings of economic thought that we connect with the names of Adam Smith, Malthus, Ricardo, List, Marx, John Stuart Mill, Jevons and Walras, Wicksell and Keynes were all responses to changing political conditions and opportunities. Of these great scholars not only List and Marx but also Smith and Keynes, even, to an extent, John Stuart Mill, were aware of the political background of their contributions. The expanding volume of literature on development problems represents a more profound re-direction of economic science, indeed of all social science. A collective effort involving many workers, it cannot be ascribed to any one man or group of men. We are almost all participants in this revolutionary reorientation of research interests.

3 Sources of bias: the world conflict

To obtain a more sophisticated picture of research in the social sciences, we must first acknowledge that the changed world political situation is responsible for our shift of emphasis to the problems of the underdeveloped countries. Once we admit the importance of this influence, we must ask whether it does not affect the manner in which research is conducted as well as the field of research chosen. Although this shift of *field* represents a rational adjustment of our work to the needs of our society, we must suspect that the effect on the *approach* used in our research efforts may be to introduce irrational biases. The epistemological implications of the latter type of influence are quite different from those of the former. The merely selective—negative or positive—conditioning of the choice of research problems does not, in itself, invalidate the research that is done; the fact of such conditioning, however, should make us wary of less tangible influences on the content of our research.

One source of bias is the involvement of our society in the political changes referred to and the tensions they generate, along with our personal involvement. As mentioned above, the world political situation since the Second World War has been characterized by the almost complete liquidation of the colonial power system. The colonies have been replaced by independent nation-states in which influential groups are pressing, with varying success, for state planning to bring about economic development that would lift their countries out of stagnation and poverty. Concomitant with these two major changes has been another set of changes: the rise to power of the Soviet Union; the staggering gain in the size of territories and populations under Communist governments, especially the emergence of Communist China; and the ensuing cold war. To both sides in the world conflict the political allegiance—or at least the neutrality—of the underdeveloped countries has become a stake in the struggle for security and power. Concern is not restricted to the foreign policy of the underdeveloped countries. Their attempts at national consolidation and economic development have also become aspects of the cold war in the sense that the effectiveness, the speed, and, even more, the direction of their reforms have become politically important to the contending power blocs.

The current international political situation bristles with tensions and emotions of the most violent kind. Governments and nations feel their vital interests to be involved. And quite apart from any formal or informal pressures from the authorities or from public opinion, the individual scientist is himself usually deeply engaged in these momentous events. As an American, a European, or a national of one of the underdeveloped countries, he is bound to be anything but indifferent to the theoretical and practical findings of his research. This must have an influence on his inclinations in research and on how he presents his results to the public—unless he exercises the utmost care to avoid a biased view.

In the Communist countries, bias is massively and systematically incorporated in the approach to all social, economic, and political problems and has been hardened into a stale dogma. In these countries, scientific as well as literary writings are programmatically expected to contribute to the fight for Communism.[2] This limitation has virtually eliminated social science as we know it. It has stifled even that sophistication with which laymen approach social problems and which in democratic countries is continually fed by, and in turn stimulates, social research. Another sobering thought for social scientists is that there can be rapid economic development and flourishing progress in the natural sciences and in technology while the social sciences are represented by little more than a crude, teleological doctrine plus a highly developed economic technocracy.

The cramped situation of the social sciences in the Communist countries is explained, of course, by the absence of democracy. In order to exist and function, the social sciences more than other sciences require the freedom of thought and expression that we associate with democracy. At the same time, they themselves fulfill an essential function in a democracy and, on a level of highly trained rationality, they actually represent the democratic way of thinking and living. It is no accident that we may search in vain for important and original contributions by social scientists in the Communist countries to the scientific discussion of development problems in the poor countries.

Gradually, as the degree of personal security and independence is heightened, such contributions may and probably will be forthcoming. The trend toward greater freedom of expression seems sure to continue, as it is spurred by the rapid rise of educational levels in these countries, which is the real force behind de-Stalinization in its broad sense. There have been signs both in the Soviet Union and in some of the East European countries, though not as yet in poverty-stricken China, of greater willingness to allow objective research in the social sciences. Until now, however, the significant modern contribution to the scientific discussion of underdevelopment and development has come from students in the Western democracies and in the underdeveloped countries themselves, a very large part of it from the United States. It is in relation to these research efforts in the non-Communist world that the problem of biases is raised here.

This is not to say that bias arises in the perception of national interest only when it is raised to the pitch of cold war. It stems also from internal interests and pressures exerted by the dominant social strata. In retrospect we can see that even economic studies conducted during the long and carefree era of nineteenth-century liberalism were not free from biases.[3] The present world tension must be expected to be a powerful additional source of bias, particularly in the study of the underdeveloped countries.

4 Political strategy and diplomacy in research

Impelled by the immense interests at stake, it is natural that the national authorities, the institutions sponsoring and financing research, and, indeed, public opinion in the West all press for studies of the problems of the underdeveloped countries. This clamor for research is entirely justified, as these problems are of increasing political importance to the Western countries themselves. But the studies are also expected to reach opportune conclusions and to appear in a form that is regarded as advantageous, or at least not disadvantageous, to national interests as these are officially and popularly understood. Such community pressure for opportunistic research operates in all Western countries, especially in the larger ones actively involved in the cold war. It operates also, though occasionally in a different direction, in the underdeveloped countries themselves. Their institutions and authorities and their educated class—whose views are commonly referred to as "public" opinion—are becoming more and more touchy about most questions dealt with in social study.

The most perceptible political influence on the research approach in Western countries to the problems of South Asian countries is the predominant role given to considerations of national power and international power relations. In a world full of perils to national security and survival, this tendency is understandable; it is often asserted to be a more realistic direction of social research. The implication is, however, that studies of the problems of underdeveloped countries are now undertaken, not with a view to the universal and timeless values that are our legacy from the Enlightenment, but with a view to the fortuitous and narrow political or, narrower still, military–strategic interests of one state or bloc of states. All sorts of studies are now justified by, or focussed on, their contribution to the "security" of Western countries. This officious accommodation by the scholarly profession to a new political "realism" in research often borders on the ridiculous. Even a respectable biologist's compilation of available research on the influence of climatic factors on organisms in the tropics may be introduced by and interspersed with glib and, understandably, inexpert reflections concerning the political effect on the "free world" of economic development there.

Often this is no more than a confession of faith by a troubled soul. At other times it may be intended to provide a mantle of respectability in an emotional environment dominated by nonprofessionals. Most of the time it turns out that the political or even the military–strategic interests of one's own country are taken to consist in the preservation of very general values. The "best interests of the United States," for instance, dictate the establishment and growth in the underdeveloped countries of what many people there themselves strive for: a stable and, where possible, democratic regime in a consolidated nation capable of economic development. This would be an interesting and, we believe, a broadly valid formulation of how American democracy evaluates the underdeveloped countries in the long run. Applied, as it frequently is, to a contemporary short-term perspective on American foreign policy at a time of fluid conflicts and tactical alliances, the proposition is less evidently valid in the policies pursued and is often clearly belied by them. In any case, it is difficult to see the relevance of this assumption about American society, or American interests, to the scientific study of an underdeveloped country's own experiences and problems. If, nevertheless, it *is* given relevance, the door is opened to all sorts of extraneous influences on research approaches, in other words, to biases.

A major source of bias in much economic research on poor countries is thus the endeavor to treat their internal problems from the point of view of the Western political and military interest in saving them from Communism. Sometimes this intention is stated, though not in the form of a reasoned presentation of specific value premises logically related to the definition of the concepts used.[4] More often it remains implicit in the approach, though the study is interspersed with suggestive formulations. This type of reasoning must often make the public and scholars in the underdeveloped countries suspicious and irritated, as they naturally want their problems analyzed from the point of view of their own interests and valuations. The taking of an outside view does not in itself constitute a fault in the methodology of scientists, whose criterion of validity cannot be the acceptability of approaches and conclusions to the people concerned. What is important is that the practice usually goes hand in hand with a retreat from scientific standards, which permits the entrance of uncontrolled biases—and this, of course, gives substance to the suspicion and irritation in underdeveloped countries.

Consideration of Western political and military interests in saving the underdeveloped countries from Communism invites inhibitions, for instance, about observing and analyzing the shortcomings of political regimes in those countries—provided, let it be noted, that they are not friendly with the enemy in the cold war. An indication of such tortuous reasoning, which lends itself to opportunistic arrangement of the facts, is the use even in scholarly writings of labels like "the free world" or "the free Asian countries" to denote, not that people are free in the ordinary sense of the word, but the purely negative fact that a country's foreign policy is not aligned to that of the Communist bloc or blocs. This is not an innocent terminological matter; such practice hides shifts in the meaning of concepts. And, as the literature abundantly proves, this kind of reasoning tends to give strength by association to an assortment of loosely argued and inexplicitly stated value preferences even in matters of internal policy—economic policy in regard to foreign trade and exchange, public versus private enterprise, and so on.

This opportunistic approach to a research task is not necessarily, or even ordinarily, egoistic and hard-hearted in its conclusions. A study may have as its purpose to discover better based and politically appealing reasons for giving more generous aid to the underdeveloped countries. The political influences on Western social research do not usually encourage unkind treatment of underdeveloped countries—as long as they are not hopelessly lost to the enemy bloc. On the contrary, what national communities more or less overtly demand from their social scientists are essays in practical diplomacy pleading certain directions of external and internal policy and giving a more solid and scholarly foundation to such pleas. When, as often happens, social scientists resist having their work turned into diplomacy, the pressures on them may nevertheless force them to engage in research on particularly innocuous problems in an underdeveloped country that have less immediate connection with political issues. They become accustomed to bypass facts that raise awkward problems, to conceal them in technical terminology, or to treat them in an "understanding" and forgiving manner. These are also biases in research. Conditioning that results in omissions rather than commissions nonetheless erodes the basis for objective research. The scholar should not be made to speak with tongue in cheek.

These remarks are not intended to isolate the economic problems of underdeveloped countries from the ideological and power constellations of world politics. The cold war has, of course, considerable bearing on events in the underdeveloped countries of South Asia; and their political allegiance to a power bloc, or their neutrality, is worth studying. Most certainly, the drift of its economy and the social and economic policies it pursues can affect such a country's alignment in the cold war, though this problem is often oversimplified. An underdeveloped country that, for whatever reason, comes under Communist rule will apply Soviet methods of planning for economic development, and this will bring about a major change in the situation under study. In the same way a country's dependence on credits and gifts from the Western bloc may influence its internal policies and thereby affect the social reality we are studying. But to recognize these causal relations is not to say that the Western interest in winning the underdeveloped countries as allies or at least keeping them neutral is an appropriate value premise for the study of their development problems. If it *is* chosen as a value premise, it should be chosen openly and operate in a logical way that does not detract from scientific objectivity.[5] Diplomacy is essential to national policy, but it is disastrous when it dominates the work of social scientists.

The tendency to think and act in a diplomatic manner when dealing with the problems of the underdeveloped countries of South Asia has, in the new era of independence, become a counterpart to the "white man's burden" in colonial times. No one with any critical sense can be unaware of this trend. I can myself testify that British and American and other Western scholars confess and defend as a principle—when speaking "among ourselves," that is, among us who are from the rich and progressive countries—the necessity to "bend over backwards." Not only politicians but also scholars, in public appearances, will apologize for making even slightly derogatory remarks and suggest that as foreigners they should not venture to express a view on the matter. In the literature such discretion leads to the avoidance of certain problems and the deliberate understatement of negative findings. I have often heard writers explain that they did this in order not to hurt feelings. A Russian scholar addressing a South Asian audience is equally tactful now that the policy of the Soviet Union has become friendly to the "bourgeois-nationalist" regimes in the region.

I am here not arguing against diplomacy, except in scientific research. A scholar should work and express himself identically at home and in a foreign country. As a scientist he should, of course, have no loyalty other than that to the truth as he perceives it. When speaking in a wealthy, powerful country like the United States this is easy, as I know from experience. The situation is apparently felt to be different in the underdeveloped countries. But it should be understood that diplomacy of this kind is tantamount to condescension, while to speak frankly is to treat the nationals of these countries as equals. If South Asians realized this, they should be offended by such diplomacy.

An example of how our thinking has become biased in this direction is the escape into terminology that is thought to be more diplomatic than the ordinary usage, as when one or another euphemism is preferred to "underdeveloped countries." For a discussion of the logical embarrassment into which such attempts lead, see Appendix 1, "Diplomacy by Terminology."

5 Another source of bias: transference of western concepts and theories

Another primary source of bias of special importance to the study of the underdeveloped countries of South Asia may appear to be more mechanical, a function merely of the rapidity with which we have undertaken massive research in a previously almost uncultivated field. As research must of necessity start from a theory, a set of analytical preconceptions,[6] it was tempting to use the tools that were forged in the West and that, in the main, served a useful purpose there,[7] without careful consideration of their suitability for South Asia. Thus a Western approach became incorporated into the mainstream of the discussion of development problems in South Asia, both within the region and outside it. Indeed, Western theoretical approaches have assumed the role of master models. For reasons we shall go into at considerable length in the body of the book, a Western approach must be regarded as a biased approach. Let us attempt to understand how this transfer came to pass.

Economic theorists, more than other social scientists, have long been disposed to arrive at general propositions and then postulate them as valid for every time, place, and culture. There is a tendency in contemporary economic theory to follow this path to the extreme. For such confidence in the constructs of economic reasoning, there is no empirical justification. But even apart from this recent tendency, we have inherited from classical economics a treasury of theories that are regularly posited with more general claims than they warrant. The very concepts used in their construction aspire to a universal applicability that they do not in fact possess. As long as their use is restricted to our part of the world this pretense of generality may do little harm. But when theories and concepts designed to fit the special conditions of the Western world—and thus containing the implicit assumptions about social reality by which this fitting was accomplished—are used in the study of underdeveloped countries in South Asia, where they do *not* fit, the consequences are serious.

There is a conservatism of methodology in the social sciences, especially in economics, that undoubtedly has contributed to the adherence to familiar Western theories in the intensive study of underdeveloped countries. Economists operate to a great extent within a framework that developed early in close relationship with the Western philosophies of natural law and utilitarianism and the rationalistic psychology of hedonism. Only with time has this tradition been adapted to changing conditions, and then without much feeling of need for radical modifications. That economists work within a methodologically conservative tradition is usually not so apparent to the economists themselves, especially as the tradition affords them opportunity to display acumen and learning and, within limits, to be inventive, original, and controversial. Even the heretics remain bound by traditional thought in formulating their heresies.[8] As circumstances, particularly political ones, changed, there was room for a shifting of emphasis and approach. When theoretical innovations lagged far behind events, such adjustments sometimes took on the appearance of definite breaks, as in the so-called Keynesian "revolution." The new thoughts were soon integrated into the traditional mold, slightly modified to better suit the environment, the changes in which were themselves largely responsible for inspiring fresh thinking.

Occasionally a breakthrough established new lines of thought that contrasted more sharply with tradition. The most important challenge came, of course, from Marx and his followers. But Marx, at the base of his constructs, retained much of classical economic theory. And gradually economists remaining within the fold incorporated large parts of what was or seemed novel in Marx's approach, not least in regard to the problems of development, as we shall see. For both these reasons we should not be surprised to find that the biases operating on Western economists often tend to converge with those conditioning economists in the Communist countries. These assertions will be exemplified in various contexts in this book.

When we economists, working within this tenacious but variegated and flexible tradition of preconceptions that admittedly are not too badly fitted to our own conditions, suddenly turn our attention to countries with radically different conditions, the risk of fundamental error is exceedingly great.[9] This risk is heightened by the dearth of empirical data on social realities in the underdeveloped countries of South Asia, which enables many biases to be perpetuated that might be questioned and corrected if concepts and theories could be exposed to the challenge of concrete facts. The problem is compounded by another consequence of the Western-biased approach. When new data are assembled, the conceptual categories used are inappropriate to the conditions existing: as, for example, when the underutilization of the labor force in the South Asian countries is analyzed according to Western concepts of unemployment, disguised unemployment, and underemployment. The resulting mountains of figures have either no meaning or a meaning other than that imputed to them. Empirical research then becomes faulty and shallow, and, more important in the present context, less valuable for testing the premises latent in the Western concepts that have guided the production of new statistics. The very fact that the researcher gets figures to play with tends to confirm his original, biased approach. Although it is the confrontation with the facts that ultimately will rectify our conceptual apparatus, initially the paucity and flimsiness of data in underdeveloped countries leave ample opportunity for biases, and the continuing collection of data under biased notions only postpones the day when reality can effectively challenge inherited preconceptions.

The danger of bias does not necessarily arise from the fact that students from the rich countries in the West inevitably face the problems of underdeveloped countries in South Asia as strangers. If anything, the outsider's view has advantages in social research. There are two ways of knowing a toothache: as a patient or as a dentist, and the latter is usually not the less objective. The white Southerner's conviction that he, and he alone, "knows" the American Negroes because of his close association with them has been proved erroneous. The stranger's view may be superficial, it is true, but superficiality is not the monopoly of strangers; it is a matter of the intensity and effectiveness of research. There is thus no necessary connection between superficiality and the extent of bias. Indeed, biases in research have no relation to superficiality *per se*. They emanate from the influences exerted by society, from our personal involvement in what we are studying, and from our tendency to apply approaches with which we are familiar to environments that are radically different. Biases can be present or absent as much when we are strangers to the country we are studying as when we are its nationals and as much when the research undertaken stretches over long periods and is conducted with a huge apparatus as when it is simply a journalist's attempt to put his impressions and reflections in order.

Nor are Western economists uniquely subject to the specific biases emanating from our methodological conservatism. Our confreres in the South Asian countries are afflicted as much, if not more, with them. Many have been trained at Western centers of learning or by teachers who acquired their training in the West. All have been thoroughly exposed to the great economic literature in the Western tradition. Familiarity with, and ability to work in accordance with, that tradition is apt to give them status at home. Their motivations for sharing in this bias are fairly independent of their political attitudes. Part of the explanation, as will be shown in the next section, is that application of the Western approach serves both conservative and radical needs for rationalization in the South Asian countries.

That the use of Western theories, models, and concepts in the study of economic problems in the South Asian countries is a cause of bias seriously distorting that study will be a main theme of this book. For the moment a few *obiter dicta* must suffice to outline this general criticism.

The concepts and the theory of unemployment and underemployment rest on assumptions about attitudes and institutions that, though fairly realistic in the developed countries, are unrealistic in the underdeveloped countries.

The neat division of income into two parts, consumption and saving, is realistic in Western societies where the general levels of income and a stratified system of income redistribution by social security policies and other means have largely abrogated any influence of consumption on productivity. This is not the case in the underdeveloped countries.

Marx's assumption, so widely adopted by Western economists, that the effects of industrialization and, indeed, of investment generally—in the final instance Marx's changes in the "modes of production"—spread quickly to other sectors of the economy and to institutions and attitudes, may be fairly realistic for Western countries, both now and when they started their rapid economic development. But as these "spread effects" are a function of the level of living and of the general culture, the assumption is not valid for most underdeveloped countries, particularly when the sectors of change are small in comparison with the total community. This should be obvious after many decades of colonial history during which the modern enterprises remained enclaves in a largely stagnating economy, but it is seldom given the recognition it deserves, either in economic analysis or in planning for development.

The lack of mobility and the imperfection of markets in underdeveloped countries rob the analytical method of aggregation of magnitudes—employment, savings, investment, and output—of much of its meaning. This conceptual difficulty is in addition to the statistical one already pointed out: that the data aggregated are frail and imperfect, partly because their categories are unrealistic.

The list could be made much longer, as will be seen in this book. Our main point is that while in the Western world an analysis in "economic" terms—markets and prices, employment and unemployment, consumption and savings, investment and output—that abstracts from modes and levels of living and from attitudes, institutions, and culture may make sense and lead to valid inferences, an analogous procedure plainly does not in underdeveloped countries. There one cannot make such abstractions; a realistic analysis must deal with the problems in terms that are attitudinal and institutional and take into account the very low levels of living and culture. The newest attempts to analyze education (and health) in terms of "investment in man" do not even state the problem in a rational way. The "non-economic" facts do not adjust smoothly to economic changes, but set up inhibitions and obstacles to them, so that often the "economic" terms cannot even be given a clear meaning. A practical corollary is the much greater need for coordination of planning in the "economic" and the "non-economic" fields.[10] Acknowledgment of this important difference is frequently made by way of qualifications and reservations. But the basic approach, not least in regard to the problems of economic planning, has remained a rather simple application of Western concepts and theories.

6 The western approach serves deeper inclinations to bias

The temptation to apply the Western approach was said above to be almost mechanical, a function of the speed with which research was begun in a nearly untouched field and our natural inclination to utilize research methods with which we were familiar. The urge to do so was the more impelling as no other kit of tools was available for bringing a semblance of order into the analysis of the complex conditions in South Asian countries. But the matter is not so uncomplicated. The appeal of the Western conceptual approach draws further strength from the fact that it is well fitted to the rationalization of opportunistic interests both in the developed Western countries and among the influential intellectual elite in the underdeveloped countries themselves.

Generally speaking, the Western approach abstracts from most of the conditions that are peculiar to the South Asian countries and are responsible for their underdevelopment and for the special difficulties they meet in developing. These conditions and difficulties are all of a type that South Asians and their foreign well-wishers must desire to forget. They were the features of the social structure that were prominent in the thoughts of the European colonial masters, both in their stereotypes and in their more sophisticated reasonings. Exaggerated emphasis on these impediments to development served their need for rationalization. It explained away their responsibility for the backwardness of colonial peoples and their failure to try to improve matters. Both the post-colonial ideologies and the ideologies of the liberation movements were deeply stamped by protest against that thinking.[11] And so the pendulum of biases swung from one extreme to the other. The intellectuals in these countries want to rationalize in the contrary sense, and it serves their needs to make the abstractions implied by Western economists. Genuine sympathy, in addition to reasons of diplomacy, brought Western economists under the same spell of opportunism. The fact that what they were applying was established theory, which had been successfully used in the Western countries, made the entrance of this systematic bias the easier.

It was an approach that appealed to both radicals and conservatives in South Asia. The radicals, partly under the impact of Marx's thinking, were prone to exaggerate the rapidity of adjustment of the entire social system to changes in the "economic" sphere; conservatives, averse to direct policy intervention in modes and levels of living, attitudes, and institutions, welcomed an approach that placed these matters in the shadow. Concerning the radicals, we must also remind ourselves of the similarities, particularly in basic concepts, between Marx's and Western economic theorizing. These have already been referred to and are illustrated in many contexts in the ensuing chapters.

There are also differences in approach, however, and it should be clear that certain elements of Marx's economic speculation often seem to fit situations in South Asia much more closely than those in the rich modern welfare states of the West: for instance, the apparent existence of a "reserve army" of idle, or largely idle, workers; the existence and the increase of a dispossessed proletariat; the often frank exploitation of workers by employers; and the big and widening gap between a few rich individuals or families and the masses of very poor people. It is remarkable that very little fresh analysis of the problems of the region in Marx's terms is forthcoming, while essays in the Western pattern are abundant. We thus often find at the universities in South Asia economists who are strongly anti-Western in their sympathies and politically far to the left, even avowed Communists or fellow-travellers, but who are yet eager and proud to place the emphasis of their teaching on the latest abstract and formal growth models developed at Cambridge or Yale, and whose ambition is to write articles resembling those in the Western journals and, hopefully, to publish them there.

In attempting to understand this bent of mind of the radicals we must take into account the virtual bombardment of massive Western research on the underdeveloped countries in recent times, while the literary output on their problems in Communist countries has been small, polite, but uninspiring. An additional factor is, however, that pursuit of Marx's particular approach referred to above would inevitably have led to a consideration of "non-economic" factors. The competitive strength of the Western approach is, at bottom, that its abstractions give an optimistic slant to the thinking about the development problems in the underdeveloped countries of the region.

Optimism, and therefore approaches that make optimism seem more realistic, is itself a natural urge for intellectuals in South Asia. That all planning in the region tends to err on the side of optimism is rather palpably clear.[12] The leaning toward diplomatic forbearance in the Western countries fits equally well with biases toward unwarranted optimism among their economists. In Western countries, especially America, optimism is even prized, as a foundation for enterprise and courage; it is almost part of the inherited cultural pattern—what George F. Kennan once called "the great American capacity for enthusiasm and self-hypnosis."[13] In the contest for souls, it is felt to be to the interest of the West that the underdeveloped countries outside the Communist sphere have development and be made to believe in it. In the West there is also a natural wish, and so a temptation to believe, that the underdeveloped countries in South Asia will come to follow policy lines similar to those of the Western countries, and that they will develop into national communities that are politically, socially, and economically like our own. For this reason, too, there is a normal tendency to use a Western approach in studying these countries, as to do so is to play down the initial differences and make such development appear more feasible.

The two main sources of bias in the Western countries thus strengthen each other in that their influences tend to converge. As we saw, the international power conflict and the tensions and emotions associated with it have influenced the study of the problems of the underdeveloped countries in South Asia in the general direction of diplomatic kindness and tolerance—again, provided that these countries are not on the wrong side in that conflict. Many of the conditions peculiar to these countries are highly undesirable; indeed, this is what is meant by their being underdeveloped.[14] Therefore, the other source of bias with which we dealt in the last section—the tendency to use the familiar theories and concepts that have been used successfully in the analysis of Western countries—exerts influences in the same direction. For when using the Western approach one can more easily soften the bite of these peculiar and undesirable conditions.

We have wanted to stress the political urges behind these tendencies that affect research on underdeveloped countries in the region. But these tendencies have at their core a compassion that makes them almost irresistible. Quite aside from the cold war and the opportunistic tendencies to bias emerging from it, we of the West are by tradition disposed to be friendly to peoples in distress, once we begin to take an interest in their condition. And it is our earnest hope, apart from all selfish interests, that they will succeed in their development efforts. That we wish them to develop into national communities as similar to our own as possible is a natural ethnocentric impulse that would make itself felt in the calmest world situation. Perhaps it should be stressed again that the concern of the West about the possibility of Communist expansion in underdeveloped countries is also understandable, and from the viewpoint of our own interests valid. And these interests justify using our influence to stop it. Still less can one criticize the human sympathy that characterizes the Western attitude toward these countries.

Nevertheless, we must not let these understandable and genuine feelings influence our perception of the facts. It is the ethos of scientific inquiry that truth and blunt truth-speaking are wholesome and that illusions, including those inspired by charity and good will, are always damaging. Illusions handicap the pursuit of knowledge and they must obstruct efforts to make planning for development fully effective and successful. For this reason, the present book is intended to be undiplomatic. In our study we want to step outside the drama while we are working. We recognize no legitimate demand on the student to spare anybody's feelings.

Facts should be stated coldly: understatements, as well as overstatements, represent biases.[15]

One more point should be mentioned before we leave this attempt to characterize briefly the forces tending to create biases in research on development problems in South Asia. As these biases engender an over-optimistic view of development prospects, they sometimes provide encouragement; but mainly they are apt to create undue complacency. In any case, a more realistic view makes it clear that *development requires increased efforts: speedier and more effective reforms in South Asia and greater concern in the West.*

7 A note on the unavoidable *a priori*

Our criticism of the tendency to take the Western approach in studying the conditions and problems of the underdeveloped countries in South Asia should not be understood as a denial of the right to start out with a theoretical preconception about how things are or, indeed, of the necessity of doing so. Questions are necessarily prior to answers, and no answers are conceivable that are not answers to questions. A "purely factual" study—observation of a segment of social reality with no preconceptions—is not possible; it could only lead to a chaotic accumulation of meaningless impressions. Even the savage has his selective preconceptions by which he can organize, interpret, and give meaning to his experiences. On a fundamental level modern social science is no different from the magical thinking of primitive man. Scientific data—facts established by observation and classification—have no existence outside the framework of preconceptions. Generalizations about reality, and their organization within an abstract framework of presumed interrelations, precede specification and verification. They constitute "theory" in research.

In strict logic a non-theoretical approach in scientific work is thus impossible; and every theory contains the seed of an *a priori* thought. When this theory is stated explicitly, we can scrutinize its inner consistency. This immanent criticism does not take us beyond the sphere of abstract logical relationships; it conveys nothing about empirical reality. But it is also a first principle of science that facts are sovereign. Theory, therefore, must not only be subjected to immanent criticism for logical consistency but must constantly be measured against reality and adjusted accordingly.

The two processes go together. As we increase the volume of observational data to which we are led by our analytical preconceptions, our original theories are refitted in order to make sense of the data and explain them. This is the crux of all science: It always begins *a priori* but must constantly strive to find an empirical basis *for* knowledge and thus to become more adequate to the reality under study. This is also the reason why we can never achieve perfection—merely an approximate fitting of theory to facts. But there are differences in how close we can come to the facts. In the underdeveloped countries of South Asia, most of the crucial data are deficient in scope and reliability. Moreover, such data as exist are heavily prejudiced by inadequate preconceptions, and we must always be on guard against biases arising from this source.

Theory is thus no more than a correlated set of questions to the social reality under study. Theory always has its essential function in relation to research still to be carried out. As greater realism is approached, theory becomes better equipped to fulfill this function. "Pure" and unrestricted model-building *pro exercitio* may have its aesthetic or pedagogical value, but it is a diversion from serious research.

What must be emphasized is that *all knowledge, and all ignorance, tends to be opportunistic,*[16] and becomes the more so the less it is checked and reconditioned by solid research directed to the empirical facts. Through wide and arduous traveling, which seldom means taking the shortest route, students undoubtedly will be forced gradually to correct their preconceptions, however deeply rooted in opportunism these may be. Until the approach is better tailored to reality, the data fail to fall into place, the facts rebel, and the logic is strained. In the longer time perspective I see no reason for pessimism about the study of the underdeveloped countries in South Asia. Inherent in all honest research is a self-correcting, purifying force that in the end will affirm itself.

An interesting parallel comes to mind—namely, the history of research on inherited group differentials in aptitudes, especially intelligence. This to me has always stood as one of the great monuments to the ethos of truth-seeking and its intrinsic quality of leading, in the end, to truer knowledges. The psychologists who more than half a century ago set out to measure innate differences in intelligence between whites and Negroes, men and women, rich and poor, had no doubt that such differences existed and that they were pronounced. There is truth in the biblical saying that "he that seeketh, findeth"; but if a scientist seeks what isn't there he will find it only as long as empirical data are scanty and the logic is allowed to be forced. As the researchers amassed their observations and as they refined their tools for observation and analysis, they found what they had *not* been seeking and what, indeed, was contrary to their preconceptions: the differences disappeared, or at least could not be scientifically established.

We shall in time come to see a similar change in the approach to the study of the underdeveloped countries in South Asia. The more we labor with these problems, the more evident will become the necessity to modify the analytical preconceptions that are now dominant. But this process of improvement can be speeded up if we help by scrutinizing our approaches for irrational influences that are working on our minds. This is why I have asked for greater interest in the sociology of knowledge. Such an inward turn of research interests would pay large dividends in more rapid scientific progress.

8 A plea for an institutional emphasis

As we are far from satisfied with the conventional approach to the development problems in South Asia, it is incumbent upon us to sketch an alternative theory that can serve as an analytical framework for the conduct of this study.

We shall use as a starting point the incontrovertible fact that the basic social and economic structure of the countries of South Asia is radically different from that existing in advanced Western countries. Conditions in the rich Western countries today are such that, broadly speaking, the social matrix is permissive of economic development or, when not, becomes readily readjusted so as not to place much in the way of obstacles in its path. This is why an analysis in "economic" terms, abstracting from that social matrix, can produce valid and useful results. But that judgment cannot be accurately applied to South Asian conditions. Not only is the social and institutional structure different from the one that has evolved in Western countries, but, more important, the problem of development in South Asia is one calling for induced changes in that social and institutional structure, as it hinders economic development and as it does not change spontaneously, or, to any very large extent, in response to policies restricted to the "economic" sphere.

This view, of course, has been implicit in our criticism of the adequacy of Western conceptual approaches and it forms the essential preconception running through the body of this study. We do not preclude the possibility that, at a future date, the institutional structure of the South Asian countries may be such that some of the Western tools of analysis, at present woefully inadequate, will come into their own. Neither this possibility nor a defense sometimes offered for the current use of Western concepts—their potentiality for defining the targets these countries are seeking to hit—justifies the use of modern Western preconceptions now. The essential first step toward an understanding of the problems of the South Asian countries is to try to discover how they actually function and what mechanisms regulate their performance. Failure to root analysis firmly in these realities invites both distortions in research and faults in planning.

So our approach is broadly "institutional," and we plead for greatly intensified research efforts along these lines. We should remember that to be really fruitful this new approach cannot be restricted to the insertion of qualifications and reservations meant to take into account the things left out by conventional economic analysis along Western lines. As the very theories and concepts utilized in that analysis guide it away from those "non-economic" factors, what is needed is a different framework of theories and concepts that is more realistic for those societies.[17]

Building such a framework, however, is a very large order; it is understandable why it has not been met and why, perhaps, its demands will not be satisfied until much more solidly based empirical work has been done. In this situation even the negative accomplishment of demonstrating the inadequacy of our inherited economic theories and concepts, and thereby discovering that we know much less than we pretend to know, is worthwhile. But, of course, our goal is also the more ambitious one of replacing conventional theories and concepts by other, new ones better fitted to the reality of these countries. And we need not only to establish the mechanisms that can explain the unique properties of these economies but also to build an analytical structure fitted to the dynamic problems of development and planning for development.

In the latter respect the Western economic approach has an alluring appearance of superiority, as it provides a simple system permitting generalizations and, more particularly, one that can fit the needs of dynamic analysis in terms of planning for development. In addition to the influences of theoretical conservatism and of opportunistic interests of various types, as analyzed in Sections 4–6 above, these properties seem to provide more objective reasons for adhering to the Western approach and accounting for its lack of realism by means merely of qualifications and reservations. One might have expected the behavioral disciplines, particularly social anthropology and sociology, to provide the more broadly based system of theories and concepts needed for the scientific study of the problem of development. Unfortunately, they have not done so. The tradition of social anthropology has been to work in static terms, attempting to explain the structure and internal relations of societies in what we now call a state of stagnation or "low-level equilibrium." Much sociological research has remained within this tradition. It is, for instance, surprising how little attention has been devoted in village surveys to the effects of population increase on social stratification. And when studies in these disciplines are focussed on change, as they increasingly are, the emphasis is not often placed on development, much less on framing a more comprehensive system of theories and concepts suited to the needs of the planner.

For this there may seem to be an obvious explanation, that the factors abstracted from in the economic analysis—attitudes, institutions, modes and levels of living, and, broadly, culture—are so much more difficult to grasp in systematic analysis than are the so-called economic factors. They undoubtedly are. But if the view propounded in this book is correct, it simply follows that the problems of under-development, development, and planning for development in South Asia are themselves exceedingly difficult and that they have yet to be mastered. An artificial restriction of "reality" to that which is seemingly easier to grasp misses the central point. For in the South Asian countries the "economic" facts cannot be studied in isolation from other social facts.

To the economists belongs the credit for spearheading the attack on the dynamic problems of underdevelopment, development, and planning for development. Economists have always been the cavalry of the social scientists and have enjoyed the status corresponding to this role. It is to us the politicians turn for advice; it is to us they listen. The doctrine of the preponderance of economic factors has been blamed on Marx. However, it was devised before his time and, as is obvious from national and international political debate, it is adhered to with few reservations by politicians in all countries. Economists dominate fact gathering and planning in every country, and when an international organization is set up, everyone agrees that it must have an economic research unit. For more than two hundred years economists have advised both those in power and those in opposition; some of us have been members of parliaments and governments. By comparison, the other social sciences have been "poor relations."

Our strength in all generations has been our singular sensitivity to the political needs of the time and our courage in offering theories that, though sufficiently complicated to flex our intellectual muscles and to impress the multitude, have been communicable in essence to the public and capable of suggesting solutions to practical, political problems. We have been a fighting church with a message, albeit one with much disputing among sects. When we turned decisively to the dynamic problems of underdeveloped economies after the Second World War, problems that were at the same time of great political significance, this was in keeping with our traditions. Our confreres in the other social sciences noted, as they often have, our impetuous sweep and occasionally warned us that we ought to consider certain matters excluded from our framework of analysis. Administrators and other men of practical affairs also went outside our framework when dealing with such issues as community uplift, educational advance, or land reform. But seldom, and never effectively, did either of those two groups, both of which were in closer touch with reality, formulate their skepticism as a challenge to our fundamental approach. And they had, in any case, no other system of theories and concepts to offer for tackling a problem as political and dynamic as that of development.

In this book we argue that there is a need not merely for qualifications and reservations, but for a fundamental change in approach. If we are correct, there is room for more interdisciplinary research, and we should welcome efforts by sociologists and others to improve our system of theories and concepts. The fact is, however, that a political and dynamic point of view is embedded in the tradition of economics, and less so in the other social sciences. As it is we economists who have inherited that viewpoint, the main hope must be that the economics profession will gradually turn to remodelling our framework of theories and concepts in the direction characterized above as institutional. Just as general philosophy failed to provide economics with a ready-made methodology, with the consequence that economists were left very much on their own to cleanse the metaphysical conception of value (a task they have far from accomplished), so the responsibility for working out a more realistic approach to the problems of underdevelopment, development, and planning for development must rest with economists. Despite the strivings for "cross fertilization" and interdisciplinary research, the barriers hampering transmission of ideas among our disciplines remain considerable. And the new approach must concentrate on the dynamic problem of development, an emphasis that does not come naturally to those brought up outside the tradition of economics.

Certainly we hope to gain support from the practitioners of behavioral research. With strong ideological influences and vested interests working to retain the Western approach of economic analysis, as shown in the foregoing sections, attempts to change it will meet resistance from a majority of both the producers and the consumers of economic research in South Asia, as well as in the West. If the present study, by placing the economic problems in their wider setting, can stimulate researchers in other disciplines to focus their work more directly on issues relevant to economic research, planning, and development, it will have made a contribution.

In the body of this book, we attempt to plot the course in which we believe further research efforts can most profitably be steered. The difficulties in formulating a satisfactory alternative theory of the processes of underdevelopment and development are immense. We are seriously handicapped by the dearth of relevant empirical data; many important matters that we would like to qualify have not yet been measured. The general pattern of preconceptions underlying, our approach—namely, that the institutional environment of South Asian countries is radically different from the one familiar in the West and that "economic" facts cannot be dealt with in isolation—is, however, firmly grounded in observation of life in the region. In attempting to fill out an alternative theoretical scheme, one aim is naturally to develop a broad set of generalizations about conditions in the region and about the mechanism of causal relations between them. Ideally, we should like to support each of these generalizations with a solid body of empirical data. Unfortunately, given the present state of knowledge, this is rarely possible.

For this reason, many of the specific generalizations advanced stem from what Marshall once described as "staple general reasonings." While we are confident that this approach leads us closer to the essential realities of economic processes in South Asia than does one inspired by current analytical preconceptions in the West, we make no claim to infallibility in the substantive content of our generalizations. At this stage, the fundamental merit claimed for an alternative approach is not that it yields answers to the urgent development problems of South Asian countries, but that it raises the right questions.

We regard the generalizations making up our "theory" as highly tentative and often conjectural. Many will challenge them; it is healthy that they should. For an essential ingredient to progress toward an understanding of the complexities of the development process is the dialogue in which generalizations are advanced, challenged, and then modified and corrected. In this fashion, the sources of differing interpretations and conclusions can be isolated and inspected. This function of generalizations should be borne in mind by readers of this book. That the text is not splashed with question marks but, for convenience, is largely written in declarative form should not obscure the role and function of the generalizations contained in it.

A few remarks on what an institutional approach is *not* have their place at the end of this section. It is not an indulgence in "loose thinking," as some of the conventional economists would be apt to think; on the contrary, it imposes the demand that theories and concepts be logically consistent as well as adequate to reality. Anyone who reads this book, especially the methodological appendices, will find that considerable effort is devoted to clarifying the concepts used. Indeed, a major general criticism launched against the conventional approach of economists is that they have generally been very careless in their reasoning. Paradoxically enough, loose thinking is most often found when they have pretended to be strict and rigorous in their reasoning, but have not scrutinized it as they should by submitting it to transcendental and immanent criticism.

Neither can an institutional approach be characterized as reasoning in "qualitative" terms. If anything, his approach induces the institutional economist to press harder for research that can give quantitative precision to his theories and bring them to the empirical test. In our view, the idea that there is a sphere where "qualitative" reasoning can substitute for thinking in quantitative terms is mistaken. The goal must always be to quantify facts and the relationships between facts, and until we can measure them our knowledge has not proceeded far from the initial *a priori*. Moreover, the institutionalist, since he is basically more critical than the conventional economist, regularly finds the latter's claims to quantitative precision unwarranted, often on logical grounds.

Finally, the conventional economist, whose models we shall frequently have to criticize for loose thinking and unwarranted precision, should not conclude that the institutionalist is "adverse to models." Model-building is a universal method of scientific research, in the same way that quantifying knowledge is a necessary aim of research. As research proceeds, models can be made ever more useful tools in our work. Even if as yet we are in most respects far from the stage where algebraic master models for the whole economy, or large sections of it, have meaning, there are many specific relationships where, to the great advantage of further intensified empirical research, an algebraic statement of the problem can be useful. But to construct such models in the air, out of uncritically conceived concepts that are inadequate to reality and usually not logically consistent, and so pretend to knowledge when none has been established, does not represent scientific progress; it comes near to being an intellectual fraud.

9 Valuations and their inevitability in scientific study

This is the point when at last we have to raise the question of objectivity in research as a problem of logic.

In principle, it would seem easy to lay down the rules for objective research on the South Asian countries. The student should have no ulterior motives. He should confine himself to the search for truth and be as free as possible from both the pressures of tradition and of society around him and his own desires. More particularly, he should in his research have no intention of influencing the political attitudes of his readers, either inside or outside the countries whose conditions he is studying. His task is to provide factual information that will help them all reach greater rationality in following out their own interests and ideals, whatever those are. In his scientific work he should have no loyalties to any particular country or group of countries or any particular political ideology, whatever his own preferences. Indeed, he should have no loyalties at all except to the professional standards of truth-seeking.

These are laudable principles well worth expressing. But they do not solve the methodological problem of how to avoid biases. The problem of objectivity in research cannot be solved simply by attempting to eradicate valuations. Just as the fault with our general views is not that they are general but that often they are logically untenable and not adequate to reality, the fact that valuations are implied cannot be condemned as unscientific. On the contrary, every study of a social problem, however limited in scope, is and must be determined by valuations.[18] A "disinterested" social science has never existed and never will exist. For logical reasons, it is impossible. A view presupposes a viewpoint. Research, like every other rationally pursued activity, must have a direction. The viewpoint and the direction are determined by our interest in a matter. Valuations enter into the choice of approach, the selection of problems, the definition of concepts, and the gathering of data, and are by no means confined to the practical or political inferences drawn from theoretical findings.[19]

The value premises that actually and of necessity determine approaches in the social sciences can be hidden. The student himself may be unaware of them. In fact, most writings, particularly in economics, remain in large part simply ideological. Some two centuries ago, the modern social sciences branched off from the metaphysical philosophies of natural law and utilitarianism. As our heritage from these philosophies, we continue to attempt to "objectify" and "neutralize" the valuation viewpoints and the value- loaded concepts used in scientific analysis. Such attempts are, for instance, plainly visible in the so-called welfare economics, which has lately had a new efflorescence, but they are a much more general phenomenon. Throughout the history of social studies, the hiding of valuations has served to conceal the inquirer's wish to avoid facing real issues. As, for logical reasons, no one can approach a social problem and analyze it without valuations, the result of remaining unaware of these valuations by leaving them implicitly assumed is a concealed *non sequitur*, and thus a space for uncontrolled influences from the valuation sphere. I have seen few efforts in recent years by economists to reform themselves on this score, least of all among those devoting themselves to abstract economic theory.[20]

Efforts to run away from the valuations are misdirected and foredoomed to be fruitless and damaging. The valuations are with us, even when they are driven underground, and they guide our work. When kept implicit and unconscious, they allow biases to enter. The only way in which we can strive for objectivity in theoretical analysis is to lift up the valuations into the full light, make them conscious and explicit, and permit them to determine the viewpoints, the approaches, and the concepts used. In the practical phases of a study the stated value premises should then, together with the data—established by theoretical analysis with the utilization of those same value premises—form the premises for all policy conclusions.

We have argued here for making the value premises explicit that research may be objective. But we also need to specify them for a broader purpose: clarity and conclusiveness in scientific reasoning. Here we touch on the main problem of the philosophy of knowledge. There is this relation between that problem and the problem of the sociology of knowledge, which has been the focus of interest in this Prologue: that the elucidation of our general views and the definition of our specific value premises are more obviously imperative, and at the same time are made easier, once we realize that we must not naively expect our ideas, even in scientific research, to be unconditioned by anything other than our urge to find the truth.

In Chapter 2 we shall follow up this train of thought by attempting to define the value premises applied in the present study.

10 The conception of Drama

The title of the book, *Asian Drama*, was chosen in order to express the conception of events in South Asia held by the author at the beginning of his work and fortified in the course of study. Behind all the complexities and dissimilarities we sense a rather clear-cut set of conflicts and a common theme as in a drama. The action in this drama is speeding toward a climax. Tension is mounting: economically, socially, and politically.

To some degree all of us are participants in this drama. It is as if the stage, set for South Asia, were enlarged and drew onto itself the entire world, so that no one could be merely a spectator. The growing Western literature on the problems of the underdeveloped countries in South Asia since the Second World War, to which this book is another contribution, is due to a heightened awareness of our stake in the dramatic happenings in these countries. As was pointed out in Section 2 the spurt of interest of the social sciences in their problems is not a spontaneous widening and deepening of research, but is politically determined. Despite the increased interest in South Asian problems in other parts of the world, the leading figures in this drama are the people of South Asia themselves, above all their educated class. The participation of outsiders through research, provision of financial aid, and other means is a sideshow of rather small importance to the final outcome.

This drama has its unity in a set of inner conflicts operating on people's minds: between their high-pitched aspirations and the bitter experience of a harsh reality; between the desire for change and improvement and mental reservations and inhibitions about accepting the consequences and paying the price. Such conflicts are a part of human life in all times and places; but in the countries under study, they have an exceptional, mounting intensity and assume a unique form.

Urged on by aspirations but curbed by material conditions and their own inhibitions, articulate individuals and groups in all these countries continually take decisions with the objective of resolving or accommodating the conflicts. The drama gains its fast pace from the terrific strength of the forces creating the conflicts. The lofty aspirations of the leading actors are separated by a wide gap from the abysmal reality—including the unreadiness of leaders, followers, and the more inert masses to accept the consequences of attempting to attain these aspirations. And that gap is widening. The movement of the drama is intensified as, through time, aspirations are inflated further by almost everything that is printed and preached and demonstrated, be it planned or not, while positive achievements lag. Meanwhile populations are increasing at an ever faster pace, making the realization of aspirations still more difficult.

This conception of the problems in South Asia is not a mere artifice but an image that comes naturally to an observer of the present life of these nations. No one who listens to the public proclamations, reads the papers, talks to people in various walks of life, watches the moves and countermoves in private and public affairs, compares pretensions with reality and declared aspirations with achievements, appraises the efforts and the fulfillments, contemplates the extraordinary disparities, discrepancies, and outright contradictions woven into that half-intentional or unintentional confusion present in almost everything that meets the eye, can fail to sense a fateful constellation of explosive potentialities for extremely rapid change and stubbornly formidable external difficulties and internal obstacles and inhibitions to change. One cannot escape feeling that what one is observing is precisely the unfolding of a drama in the classic sense. It is exceptionally intense, as well as immense in its involvement of hundreds of millions of people, but through its complexities and dissimilarities, as through a classical drama, runs an essentially simple theme.

Indeed, the whole public discussion, whenever it transcends the particulars, runs in terms of a momentous drama. Even debates on particular issues are readily cast in terms of a country's destiny. Wrapped up in the dramatic conception of the life of these nations is also the recognition, shared at bottom even by those who assert the opposite, that the outcome is anything but certain. The student knows, of course, that at some future date a backward glance will be taken, and today's choices will then seem necessary under the circumstances. For this is the way history is explained; everything that happened had its causes and exerted further effects in unending sequence.

In the classic conception of drama—as in the theoretical phase of a scientific study—the will of the actors was confined in the shackles of determinism. The outcome at the final curtain was predetermined by the opening up of the drama in the first act, accounting for all the conditions and causes of later developments. The protagonist carried his ultimate fate in his soul, while he was groping for his destiny. In life, while the drama is still unfolding—as in the practical phase of a study, when policy inferences are drawn from value premises as well as from premises based on empirical evidence—the will is instead assumed to be free, within limits, to choose between alternative courses of action. History, then, is not taken to be predetermined, but within the power of man to shape. And the drama thus conceived is not necessarily tragedy.

Notes

1 The American novelist, Richard Wright, who in his book *White Man Listen!* tried to deal with a problem in general terms, was conscious of the need to watch the way he was conditioned in his views: "I state that emotion here precedes the idea, that attitudes select the kind of ideas in question. . . . We are human; we are the slaves of our assumptions, of time and circumstances, we are the victims of our passions and illusions, and . . . our critics can ask of us . . .: Have you taken your passions, your illusions, your time, and your circumstances into account? This is what I am attempting to do." (Richard Wright, *White Man Listen!*, Doubleday and Company, New York, 1957, p. 64.)
A social scientist should not be less humble and assume that he is purely "factual and objective." He cannot, in any case, escape valuations, as he needs explicit, or implicit, value premises even to ascertain the facts; see below in Section 9.

2 In Khrushchev's words: "The impact of the social sciences will increase steadily in the study of mankind's historical path to Communism . . . in moulding the materialist world outlook in people, in the education of the man of Communist society and in the struggle against bourgeois ideology . . . . Literature and art will play a big part in moulding the new man. By asserting Communist ideas and genuine humanism, literature and art instil in Soviet man the qualities of builders of the new world . . ." (Nikita S. Khrushchev, "Report on the Programme of the Communist Party of the Soviet Union," as delivered to the Twenty-second Congress of the C.P.S.U., *Soviet Weekly*, Supplement, October 18, 1961, p. 15.)

3 Gunnar Myrdal, *The Political Element in the Development of Economic Theory*, Routledge & Kegan Paul, London, 1953; cf. two other works by the same author: *Economic Theory and Under-developed Regions*, Duckworth, London, 1957, Part II (in America: *Rich Lands and Poor*, Harper, New York, 1957); and *Value in Social Theory, A Selection of Essays on Methodology*, Paul Streeten, ed., Routledge & Kegan Paul, London, 1958.

4 Chapter 2, Section 1.

5 Chapter 2, Section 1.

6 Section 7 below.

7 Throughout this book I am making the generous assumption that the Western approach is fairly adequate to Western conditions. This might be an overstatement. In any case, this is a book on South Asia, and I have not felt it to be my task to go into a critical analysis of the use of Western concepts and theories outside the region I am studying.

8 See Myrdal, *Economic Theory and Under-developed Regions*, pp. 129 ff.

9 "One ever-present problem is the possibility that a conceptual scheme will imprison the observer, allowing him to see only what the scheme directs him to see and ruling out other Interpretations of data. It is readily admitted that this danger is implicit in all a priori thinking." (Richard C. Snyder and Glenn D. Paige, "The United States Decision to Resist Aggression in Korea: The Application of an Analytic Scheme," in *Administrative Science Quarterly*, Vol. 3, No. 3, December, 1958, p. 358.)

10 See Appendix 2, Section 19.
"For all practical purposes growth and development in the less developed parts of the world seem to depend rather upon the speed and efficiency with which given attitudes and institutions can be and actually are modified and changed. Viewed in its truly dynamic dimension the process of economic growth and development is and always has been a problem of political and socio-cultural change." (K. William Kapp, *Hindu Culture, Economic Development and Economic Planning in India*, Asia Publishing House, Bombay, 1903, p. 69.)

11 Chapter 21, Section 7 *et passim.*

12 India's First Five Year Plan would seem to be an exception, as it underestimated the growth of output. But the surpassing of estimates was largely due to unexpectedly favorable monsoons and other accidents. The targets in regard to the policy measures actually making up the plan, and in particular the investments, were not met.

13 In the Soviet Union uncritical optimism is programmatic, and realism, when it does not lead to optimistic conclusions, is considered a "bourgeois" deviation; this constitutes one of the many similarities in cultural situation between the United States and the Soviet Union.

14 Appendix 2, Section 5.

15 In regard to issues that have been felt to be awkward and threatening—for instance, the Negro problem in America—biases toward forbearance and optimism have been quite general in the social sciences. A "balanced view" on such issues tends to be a view that soft-pedals difficulties and causes for worry. Understatements, though in principle just as damaging to the establishment of truth as overstatements, are considered more "objective" and certainly give more respectability. When working without explicit value premises, "the optimistic bias becomes strengthened, paradoxically enough, by the scientist's own critical sense and his demand for foolproof evidence. The burden of proof is upon those who assert that things are bad in our society; it is not the other way around. Unfortunate facts are usually more difficult to observe and ascertain, as so many of the persons in control have strong interests in hiding them. The scientist in his struggle to detect truth will be on his guard against making statements which are unwarranted. His very urge to objectivity will thus induce him to picture reality as more pleasant than it is." (Gunnar Myrdal, *An American Dilemma, The Negro Problem and Modern Democracy*, Harper, New York, 1944, p. 1039.)

"I have often observed that social scientists who are responsible for the publication of other authors' works or who utilize them in their own writings, when they apprehend biases, believe that these can be 'edited away,' by modifying certain expressions used or cutting out or revising certain practical conclusions drawn. Similarly, a general tendency toward understatement is observable in most social science literature. When an author has set down something which he feels to be unfavorable about a social class or a region, he looks for something favorable to say in order to 'balance the picture.' A 'balanced view,' a colorless drawing, is considered to be more 'scientific.' Particularly in governmental investigations great care is usually taken to spare the readers. The deliberate attempt that is made in such reports not to offend anyone will often make them difficult to use for scientific purposes. This tendency is, of course, not only ineffective in mitigating biases, but, even worse, it is itself one of the main types of bias in research." (Ibid., p. 1043.)

Concerning the general problem of bias, see the same work, pp. 1035–1045.

16 Myrdal, *An American Dilemma*, pp. 40–42 et passim.

17 "We all agree that the basic requirement of any model is that it should be capable of explaining the characteristic features of the economic process as we find them in reality. It is no good starting off a model with the kind or abstraction which initially excludes the influence of forces which are mainly responsible for the behavior of the economic variables under investigation; and upon finding that the theory leads to results contrary to what we observe in reality, attributing this contrary movement to the compensating (or more than compensating) influence of residual factors that have been assumed away in the model .... Any theory must necessarily be based on abstractions; but the type of abstraction chosen cannot be decided in a vacuum: it must be appropriate to the characteristic features of the economic process as recorded by experience." (Nicholas Kaldor, "Capital Accumulation and Economic Growth," in *The Theory of Capital*, Macmillan & Co. Ltd., London, 1961, pp. 177–178.)

18 For substantiation of the views expressed in this section, see Myrdal, *Value in Social Theory, Essays on Methodology*, and earlier works cited therein. See also Myrdal, "'Value-loaded' Concepts," in Hugo Hegeland, ed., *Money, Growth, and Methodology and Other Essays in Honor of Johan Akerman*, Glerup, Lund, 1961, pp. 282 ff.

19 The terms "theoretical" and "practical" (or "political") are used in this book as they are in the discipline of philosophy. The former word refers to thinking in terms of causes and effects, the latter words to thinking in terms of ends and means.

To stress the subjectivity of the valuation process we deliberately use the word "valuations" rather than "values"—except in the combination "value premises," where certain valuations have been defined and made explicit for use in research. The common use of the term "values" invites confusion between valuations in the subjective sense, the object of these valuations, and indeed the whole social setting of valuations. The use of the term "values" also usually contains a hidden value premise, that a "value" *eo ipso* is valuable in some objective sense; this implies a bias of the "laissez-faire" variety. See Myrdal, *An American Dilemma*, p. 1031.

Concerning the relations assumed between valuations and beliefs, see ibid., Appendix 1.

20 The situation is aptly described by Paul Halmos, who rightly stated that "all social science is 'action research' no matter how etherealized." See "Social Science and Social Change," *Ethics*, January, 1959, p. 108.

He continues a few pages later (p. 117): "One may expect that the efforts of social scientists aimed at 'immunising' their communication from injunctive-normative tendencies will continue. The esoteric, highly speculative and often incomprehensible conceptual systems, the frantic search for specially coined terms free from associated 'value-dross,' the tendency towards explicit neutralism and relativism and the pretence that scientific honesty and loyalty do not belong to a wider context of values—all these and some other aspirations will not stop the positive social sciences from their fact-moulding and object-altering function, a function which the non-social sciences do not possess. There is no way of escaping from the issue of moral responsibility in social science communication, and there is no way of lowering an 'iron curtain' between social science and moral philosophy."

And he quotes David Riesman: "Some social scientists have sought escape from terms which common usage has loaded with values, escape into manufactured symbolism so lacking in overtones as to avoid connotations of praise or blame. In the spirit of certain schools of logical positivism, they want to make only 'meaningful' statements and only purely denotative ones. But, in my opinion, the relation of social science to its subjects, who are also its audience, forbids any such easy undialectical answer to the problem of the researcher's ethical judgments. Terminological opacity will itself be taken as a judgment upon the world, perhaps a manipulative, frightened or unsympathetic one. . . . Literate peoples are going to read what is said about them, no matter how many verbal formulae are set up as barriers, and what they cannot understand they may aggressively misunderstand. Communication involves 'noise,' redundancy—and overtones." (David Riesman, *Individualism Reconsidered*, Free Press, Glencoe, Illinois, 1954, pp. 12–13.)

2

India in comparative perspective

Jean Drèze and Amartya Sen

Source: *An Uncertain Glory: India and its Contradictions* (Allen Lane, 2013), pp. 45–80.

'The first thing I ever learned about India,' Anand Giridharadas notes in his excellent book *India Calling*, 'was that my parents had chosen to leave it.' 'My parents had left India in the 1970s, when the West seemed paved with possibility and India seemed paved with potholes. And now, a quarter century after my father first arrived as a student in America, I was flying east to make a new beginning in the land they had left.'[1] That perspective of a rapidly changing India, re-establishing itself on the world stage, is both engaging and exciting. It is not only that the ancient – and dilapidated – land, traditionally short of opportunities for young men and women, is humming with new and exciting things to do in business and professional lives, but also that the country is full of new energy in the creative fields of literature, music, films, science, engineering, and other areas of intellectual and artistic pursuits. India is certainly calling, with much to offer.

Life can indeed be exciting in the rapidly reshaping India, and the picture of a new and dramatically changed India is both accurate and important. And yet, as was discussed in the earlier chapters, the majority of Indian people have been left behind in the enhancement of living standards. Many of the new freedoms and fresh opportunities can be enjoyed only by a minority of Indians – a very large number of people but still only a minority. In comparing India with the rest of the world to see how India is doing, the results depend greatly on which sections of the Indian population we look at.

Comparisons of India with other countries are often made for the purpose of checking where the country fits in the international 'league'. The focus, quite often, is on India's 'rank' (for example, in terms of GDP per capita). That is not a bad way to proceed, and the Indian obsession with the rank of the country in the world league can be a useful way to start. But much depends on the variable chosen for the ranking. As should be clear from the hype around the growth rate of GDP or GNP per head, this is one league in which India is doing rather well. That high-achievement story, however, conflicts somewhat with India's mediocre performance in the progress of quality of life, as reflected in the standard social indicators.

The minority of people in India who have been prospering well enough is large in absolute numbers. Even though estimates of the size of this minority vary, they certainly far exceed 100 million or so – making them a larger group than the population of most countries in the world. And yet in the statistics involving the total Indian population of more than 1.2 billion, the fortunate group is still too small to swing the average figures for the Indian population as a whole in terms of most social indicators. In what follows we shall compare the Indian average with the averages of other countries, but we must bear in mind the fact that even the low averages reflected in the Indian numbers exaggerate what the Indians not in the privileged group actually enjoy. This would apply to other countries too, but it is particularly relevant for India, given the enormity of class, caste and gender inequalities in Indian society – we shall return to this issue in Chapters 8 and 9.

Comparisons with the non-African poor

In a previous book, we noted that human deprivation was heavily concentrated in two regions of the world: South Asia and sub-Saharan Africa.[2] That has been true for many decades now, and it is still largely true today. For instance, most of the countries with a low 'human development index' are in South Asia or sub-Saharan Africa. Cambodia, Haiti, Papua New Guinea and Yemen are among the few exceptions of countries with high levels of extreme poverty in other global regions.

Even though South Asia and sub-Saharan Africa share problems of high incidences of poverty, they are not, of course, similarly placed in every respect. Living conditions are now, in many ways, considerably better in South Asia (including India) than in sub-Saharan Africa, partly reflecting a faster rate of improvement during the last twenty years or so. For instance, per capita income is now about 50 per cent higher in South Asia than in sub-Saharan Africa, unlike in 1990, when it was much the same in the two regions. More importantly, life expectancy is estimated to be about ten years longer in South Asia than in sub-Saharan Africa, and child mortality is almost twice as high in sub-Saharan Africa compared with South Asia.[3]

It is worth noting, however, that the advantage of South Asia over sub-Saharan Africa in living standards is by no means uniform: indeed some social indicators are not much better – if at all – in South Asia than in sub-Saharan Africa. For instance, female literacy rates are still much the same in both regions, not only among adult women (50 per cent and 55 per cent respectively) but also in the younger age groups (e.g. 72 per cent and 67 per cent, respectively, in the age group of 15–24 years).[4] Despite some progress in recent years, both regions continue to share a severe problem of mass illiteracy and lack of school education, especially among women, which sets them apart from all other major regions of the world. Further, in at least one field – that of nutrition and especially child nutrition – South Asia fares, distinctly worse than sub-Saharan Africa. More than 40 per cent of South Asian children (and a slightly *higher* proportion of Indian children) are underweight in terms of standard WHO norms, compared with 25 per cent in sub-Saharan Africa (the corresponding figure, incidentally, is less than 12 per cent in every other region of the world).[5]

Leaving sub-Saharan Africa aside, India is not well placed at all in international comparisons of living standards. Contrary to the increasingly used rhetoric which suggests that India is well on its way to becoming an economic 'superpower', this is far from the real picture, even in terms of per capita income. In fact, despite rapid economic expansion in recent years, India remains one of the poorest countries among those outside sub-Saharan Africa. According to the World Bank, only fifteen countries outside sub-Saharan Africa had a 'gross national income per capita' lower than India's in 2011: Afghanistan, Bangladesh, Burma, Cambodia, Haiti, Kyrgyzstan, Laos, Moldova, Nepal, Pakistan, Papua New Guinea, Tajikistan, Uzbekistan, Vietnam and Yemen. India does indeed have a large gap in world living standards to overcome, as was discussed in the last chapter. What is disturbing, given the past, is not India's comparatively low position in terms of income per head among the countries in the world outside sub-Saharan Africa, but how badly India does in terms of *non-income* features of living standards even within this group of poorest non-African countries, as can be readily seen in Table 1.

India has, by the choice of our cut-off point, the highest GDP per capita in this particular group, with the rank of being number 1 among these sixteen countries. Aside from GDP per capita, as the last column indicates, India's rank among these sixteen poor countries is 10th or worse in most cases. Not only are India's figures worse than the average for the other fifteen countries for all social indicators presented here (except for the total fertility rate and male literacy rate), its rank in this group is an inglorious 10th for child mortality, 11th for female literacy and mean years of schooling, 13th for access to improved sanitation and DPT immunization, and absolutely the worst (along with Yemen) in terms of the proportion of underweight children.[6]

We argued in the last chapter that the common characterization of India's current economic growth rate of around 6 per cent per year as 'dismal' is hard to justify because India's rate of economic growth, though reduced, is still among the fastest in the world (as it would still be, even if the prediction of a 5 per cent growth rate by some agencies proved to be true). But 'dismal' would indeed be a very good adjective to describe the picture of comparative living standards, as Table 1 reveals.

Table 1 Selected indicators for the world's 16 poorest countries, outside sub-Saharan Africa

	India	*Average for other poorest countries*[a]	*India's rank among 16 poorest countries*[b]
GDP per capita, 2011 (PPP, constant 2005 international $)	3,203	2,112	1
Life expectancy at birth, 2011 (years)	65	67	9
Infant mortality rate, 2011 (per 1,000 live births)	47	45	10
Under-5 mortality rate, 2011 (per 1,000 live births)	61	56	10
Total fertility rate, 2011 (children per woman)	2.6	2.9	7
Access to improved sanitation, 2010 (%)	34	57	13
Mean years of schooling, age 25+, 2011	4.4	5.0	11
Literacy rate, age 15–24 years, 2010 (%)			
Female	74[c]	79	11
Male	88[c]	85	9
Proportion of children below five years who are undernourished, 2006–10[d] (%)			
Underweight	43	30	15
Stunted	48	41	13
Child immunization rates, 2011 (%)			
DPT	72	88	13
Measles	74	87	11

[a] Population-weighted average of country-specific indicators. In two cases of missing data for a particular country (e.g. literacy rates for Afghanistan), the average was taken over the remaining countries.
[b] Based on ranking from 'best' to 'worst'. In case of 'ties', India was ranked first.
[c] 2006.
[d] Latest year for which data are available within 2006–10.

Sources: See Table 2. This table focuses on 16 countries with per capita GDP lower than or equal to India's, outside sub-Saharan Africa. These are: Afghanistan, Bangladesh, Burma, Cambodia, Haiti, India, Kyrgyzstan, Laos, Moldova, Nepal, Pakistan, Papua New Guinea, Tajikistan, Uzbekistan, Vietnam and Yemen.

Table 2 gives the detailed information on which the summary presented in Table 1 is based. Some of these comparisons are quite instructive. For instance, Vietnam fares enormously better than India in terms of all these indicators, in spite of being poorer than India. So, incidentally, does Nicaragua, with virtually the same per capita GDP as India (just a little higher, so that Nicaragua is not included in Table 2). Uzbekistan, too, is far ahead of India in many respects, with, for instance, universal literacy in the younger age groups, universal access to improved sanitation, and (nearly) universal immunization of children – all goals that are nowhere near being achieved in India. Another striking contrast is between India and Nepal, which has much the same social indicators as India, with barely *one third* of India's per capita income (the last makes Nepal one of the very poorest countries outside Africa, along with Afghanistan and Haiti).

It could be argued that one would expect India not to fare as well, in many ways, as other countries at a similar level of per capita income, because India is growing quite fast and it takes time for higher per capita incomes to translate into better social indicators. In a country growing at 7 per cent per year in per capita terms, per capita income would double in ten years, but it could quite possibly take longer, even with significant efforts, to bring social indicators level with those of countries that were once twice as rich. That is a point worth noting, and is itself a good reason not to rely on income growth alone to bring about a transformation of living conditions (which is one of the main points we are trying to make). The basic concern remains that, for whatever reasons, India is not doing well at all in many respects even in comparison with some of the poorest countries in the world. This is not to disparage India's achievements, but to put them in perspective, and to focus on the deficiencies that plague India most and which have to be overcome.

India's decline in South Asia

One indication that there is something defective in India's 'path to development' arises from the fact that India is falling behind every other South Asian country (with the exception of Pakistan) in terms of many social indicators, even as it is doing spectacularly better than these countries in terms of the growth of per capita income. The comparative picture is presented in Table 3.

Table 2 Poorest countries, outside sub-Saharan Africa (part 1)

	India	*Vietnam*	*Moldova*	*Uzbekistan*	*Laos*
GDP per capita (PPP), 2011	3,203	3,013	2,975	2,903	2,464
Life expectancy at birth, 2011	65	75[d]	69	68[d]	67
Infant mortality rate, 2011	47	17	14	42	34
Under-5 mortality rate, 2011	61	22	16	49	42
Total fertility rate, 2011	2.6	1.8[d]	1.5	2.5[d]	2.7
Access to improved sanitation, 2010 (%)	34	76	85	100	63
Mean years of schooling, age 25+, 2011	4.4	5.5	9.7	10	4.6
Literacy rate, age 15–24, 2010 (%)					
Female	74[a]	96	100	100	79[b]
Male	88[a]	97	99	100	89[b]
Undernourishment among children below 5, 2006–10[e]					
Underweight	43	20	n/a	4	31
Stunted	48	31	n/a	19	48
Child immunization rates, 2011 (%)					
DPT	72	95	93	99	78
Measles	74	96	91	99	69

Table 2 Poorest countries, outside sub-Saharan Africa (part 2)

	Pakistan	*Papua NG*	*Kyrgyzstan*	*Cambodia*	*Yemen*	*Tajikistan*
GDP per capita (PPP), 2011	2,424	2,363	2,119	2,083	2,060	2,052
Life expectancy at birth, 2011	65[d]	63	69[d]	63	65	68
Infant mortality rate, 2011	59	45	27	36	57	53
Under-5 mortality rate, 2011	72	58	31	43	77	63
Total fertility rate, 2011	3.4[d]	3.9	2.9[d]	2.5	5.1	3.2
Access to improved sanitation, 2010 (%)	48	45	93	31	53	94
Mean years of schooling, age 25+, 2011	4.9	3.9	9.3	5.8	2.5	9.8
Literacy rate, age 15–24, 2010 (%)						
Female	61[c]	72	100[c]	86[c]	74	100
Male	79[c]	65	100[c]	88[c]	96	100
Undernourishment among children below 5, 2006–10[e] (%)						
Underweight	31	18	2	28	43	15
Stunted	42.	43	18	40	58	39
Child immunization rates, 2011 (%)						
DPT	80	61	96	94	81	96
Measles	80	60	97	93	71	98

Table 2 Poorest countries, outside sub-Saharan Africa (part 3)

	Burma	*Bangladesh*	*Nepal*	*Haiti*	*Afghanistan*
GDP per capita (PPP), 2011	n/a	1,569	1,106	1,034	1,006
Life expectancy at birth, 2011	65	69	69	62	48[d]
Infant mortality rate, 2011	48	37	39	53	73
Under-5 mortality rate, 2011	62	46	48	70	101
Total fertility rate, 2011	2.0	2.2	2.7	3.3	6.3
Access to improved sanitation, 2010 (%)	76	56	31	17	37
Mean years of schooling, age 25+, 2011	3.9	4.8	3.2	4.9	3.1
Literacy rate, age 15–24, 2010 (%)					
Female	96	78	78	70[a]	n/a
Male	96	75	88	74[a]	n/a
Undernourishment among children below 5, 2006–10[e] (%)					
Underweight	23	41	39	18	33
Stunted	35	43	49	29	59
Child immunization rates, 2011 (%)					
DPT	99	96	92	59	66
Measles	99	96	88	59	62

[a] 2006.
[b] 2005.
[c] 2009.
[d] 2010.
[e] Latest year for which data are available within 2006–10.

Source: *World Development Indicators* (online, 1 January 2013). Mean years of schooling from *Human Development Report* 2013 and child undernutrition data from UNICEF (2012). The countries in the table (other than India) are all those with per capita GDP lower than India in 2011, ranked in descending order of per capita GDP. In the absence of updated data, Burma (or Myanmar, as the military rulers of Burma now insist on calling it) has been placed in the same position as that in which it appears (in terms of per capita GDP) in *World Development Indicators* 2011.

The comparison between Bangladesh and India is a good place to start. During the last twenty years or so, India has grown much richer than Bangladesh: India's per capita income, already 60 per cent higher than Bangladesh's in 1990, was estimated to be about double that of Bangladesh by 2011. However, during the same period, Bangladesh has *overtaken* India in terms of a wide range of basic social indicators, including life expectancy, child survival, enhanced immunization rates, reduced fertility rates, and even some (not all) schooling indicators. For instance, life expectancy was more or less the same in both countries in 1990, but was estimated to be four years higher in Bangladesh than in India by 2010 (69 and 65 years respectively). Similarly, child mortality, a tragic indicator, was estimated to be about 20 per cent higher in Bangladesh than in India in 1990, but has fallen rapidly in Bangladesh to now being 25 per cent *lower* than in India by 2011. Most social indicators now look better in Bangladesh than in India, despite Bangladesh having less than half of India's per capita income.

Table 3 South Asia: selected indicators (1990 and latest)

		South Asia						*China*
		India	*Bangladesh*	*Bhutan*	*Nepal*	*Pakistan*	*Sri Lanka*	
GDP per capita, PPP:	1990*	1,193	741	1,678	716	1,624	2,017	1,121
(constant 2005 international $)	2011	3,203	1,569	5,162	1,106	2,424	4,929	7,418
Life expectancy at birth:	1990*	58	59	53	54	61	70	69
(years)	2011	65	69	67	69	65[f]	75[f]	73[f]
Infant mortality rate:	1990*	81	97	96	94	95	24	39
(per 1,000 live births)	2011	47	37	42	39	59	11	13
Under-5 mortality rate:	1990*	114	139	138	135	122	29	49
(per 1,000 live births)	2011	61	46	54	48	72	12	15
Maternal Mortality Ratio:	1990	600	800	1,000	770	490	85	120
(per 100,000 live births)	2010	200	240	180	170	260	35	37
Total fertility rate:	1990*	3.9	4.5	5.7	5.2	6.0	2.5	2.3
(children per woman)	2011	2.6	2.2	2.3	2.7	3.4[f]	2.3[f]	1.6[f]
Access to improved sanitation (%):	1990	18	39	n/a	10	27	70	24
	2010	34	56	44	31	48	92	64
Infant immunization (DPT) (%):	1990*	59	64	88	44	48	86	95
	2011	72	96	95	92	80	99	99
Infant immunization (measles) (%):	1990*	47	62	87	57	50	78	95
	2011	74	96	95	88	80	99	99
Mean years of schooling, age 25+:	1990	3.0	2.9	–	2.0	2.3	6.9	4.9
	2011	4.4	4.8	2.3[e]	3.2	4.9	9.3	7.5
Female literacy rate, age 15–24	1991[a]	49	38	–	33	–	93	91
(%):	2010[b]	74	78	68	78	61	99	99
Proportion (%) of underweight	1990[c]	59.5	61.5	34	–	39	29	13
children:	2006–10[d]	43	41	13	39	31	21	4

* Three-year average centred on the reference year (e.g. 1989–91 average when the reference year is 1990).

[a] 1990 for China; the Sri Lanka figure is an interpolation between 1981 and 2001 figures.

[b] 2006 for India, 2005 for Bhutan, 2009 for Pakistan.

[c] 1988 for Bhutan, 1991 for Pakistan, 1987 for Sri Lanka.

[d] Latest year for which data are available within this period.

[e] 2002–2012.

[f] 2010.

Sources: Mean years of schooling from ***Human Development Report 2013***, online; other indicators from ***World Development Indicators***, online (1 January 2013). Some of the country-specific figures for 1990 are subject to a significant margin of error; the focus is best kept on broad patterns rather than exact numbers.

No less intriguing is the case of Nepal, which – with all its problems of politics and governance – seems to be catching up rapidly with India, and even overtaking India in some respects. Around 1990, Nepal was far behind India in terms of almost every development indicator. Today, as Table 3 illustrates, social indicators for both countries are more similar (sometimes a little better in India still, sometimes the reverse), in spite of per capita income in India being about three times as high as in Nepal.[7]

Even the comparison with Pakistan, though favourable to India in general, is not comprehensively flattering. Between 1990 and 2011, real per capita income at constant prices increased by about 50 per cent in Pakistan and 170 per cent in India (see Table 3, first row). But the gap in social indicators (initially in favour of India in some respects, but in favour of Pakistan in others) has not been fundamentally altered in most cases. And in some respects, such as immunization rates, things seem to have improved more in Pakistan than in India.

To look at the same issue from another angle, Table 4 displays India's 'rank' among South Asia's six major countries respectively around 1990 and today (more precisely, in the latest year for which comparable international data are available as we write this book). As expected, in terms of the absolute level of per capita income, India's rank has improved – from fourth (after Bhutan, Pakistan and Sri Lanka) to third (after Bhutan and Sri Lanka). In terms of the rate of expansion of income per head, India is now at the top of this group (as it is of most groups of countries in the world). But in most other respects, India's rank has worsened, in fact quite sharply in many cases. Overall, only one country in South Asia (Sri Lanka) clearly had better social indicators than India in 1990, but now India looks second worst, ahead of only trouble-torn Pakistan.

The comparative perspectives in South Asia tend to be commonly overlooked in development studies, especially in India. Yet there is a great deal to learn from looking around us within South Asia. For instance, many development experts in India, increasingly keen on using the private sector for school education, would be interested to learn that in Sri Lanka, with its huge lead over India in social indicators and particularly schooling and literacy (see Table 3), private schools are virtually absent – and have in fact been prohibited since the 1960s. A similar remark applies to the fact that in Sri Lanka 'few people live more than 1.4 km away from the nearest health centre'.[8] Many other

Table 4 India's rank in South Asia

Indicator		*India's rank among six South Asian countries (Top = 1, Bottom = 6)*	
		In 1990	*Around 2011*
1	GDP per capita	4	3
2	Life expectancy	4	5
3	Infant mortality rate	2	5
4	Under-5 mortality rate	2	5
5	Maternal mortality ratio	3	4
6	Total fertility rate	2	4
7	Access to improved sanitation	4–5[a]	5
8	Child immunization (DPT)	4	6
9	Child immunization (measles)	6	6
10	Mean years of schooling, age 25+	2–3[a]	4
11	Female literacy rate, age 15–24	2–3[a]	4
12	Proportion of underweight children	4–5[a]	6

[a] Ambiguous rank due to missing data for Bhutan (or Nepal, in the case of 'underweight children').

Source: See Table 3. The six countries considered here are Bangladesh, Bhutan, India, Nepal, Pakistan and Sri Lanka.

policies and achievements in neighbouring countries merit attention from Indian planners – and the Indian public generally. Notwithstanding its enormous size and rapid economic growth compared with its neighbours, India may have much to learn from them.

Bangladesh's progress and the role of women

Bangladesh has come a long way in the last four decades. In the first half of the 1970s, the country endured a lethal cyclone (estimated to have killed up to half a million people in 1970), a popular rebellion and a fully fledged 'war of liberation' (eventually leading to the country's independence in 1971), and a large-scale famine (in 1974, when 6 per cent of the population had to depend for their survival on the distribution of free food in *langarkhanas*, or feeding centres). Few observers at that time expected Bangladesh to make rapid social progress in the next few decades. In fact, the famine of 1974 appeared to vindicate the prophets of doom, some of whom had even dismissed Bangladesh as a 'basket case' country that should not even be assisted because it was sure to lose in the race between population and food.

Today, Bangladesh is still one of the poorest countries in the world, and large sections of its population continue to lack many of the bare essentials of good living. And yet Bangladesh has made rapid progress in some crucial aspects of living standards, particularly in the last twenty years – overtaking India in terms of many social indicators in spite of its slower economic growth.

Some particular features of the Bangladeshi experience are of special relevance to India. Bangladesh is not a model of development by any means. In spite of much recent progress, it remains one of the most deprivation-ridden countries in the world, and many of the policy biases discussed in this book with reference to India apply to Bangladesh as well. With per capita GDP half as high in Bangladesh as in India, and public expenditure a mere 10 per cent or so of GDP in Bangladesh (again about half as much as in India), public services in Bangladesh are inevitably restrained, and whatever is already in place suffers from serious accountability problems, much as in India.[9] Democratic institutions in Bangladesh are also in some trouble, maintaining a tradition by which opposition parties do not seem to attend Parliament. And yet there are also features of astonishing achievement in Bangladesh that cannot but excite interest, curiosity and engagement.

The roots of Bangladesh's social achievements are not entirely transparent, and deserve much greater scrutiny than they have received so far.[10] However, some likely clues are immediately worth noting. Perhaps the most important clue is a pattern of sustained positive change in gender relations. As Table 5 shows, many gender-related indicators are now much better in Bangladesh than in India. For instance, women's participation rate in the workforce is almost twice as high in Bangladesh as in India (57 per cent and 29 per cent, respectively). This, along with greater female literacy and education, is recognized across the world as a powerful contributor to women's empowerment, and Bangladesh has made much greater use of this avenue of change than has India.[11] In the field of elementary education, Bangladesh has made remarkable strides towards gender equality, so much so that school participation rates and literacy rates of Bangladeshi girls are now *higher* than those of boys, in contrast with India where a substantial gender bias (against girls) persists. Indeed, Bangladesh is now one of the few countries in the world where the number of girls exceeds the number of boys in school. Even the share of women in Parliament, while much below one half in both countries, is higher in Bangladesh than in India.[12]

To what extent women's agency and gender relations account for the fact that Bangladesh has caught up with, and even overtaken, India in many crucial fields during the last twenty years calls for further investigation. But it certainly looks like an important factor, in the light of what we know about the role of women's agency in development. For instance, the fact that both female literacy and women's participation in the workforce play an important role in the 'demographic transition' (from high to low mortality and fertility rates) is

Table 5 Gender-related indicators in India and Bangladesh

	India	*Bangladesh*
Female labour force participation rate, age 15+, 2010 (%)	29	57
Female-male ratio in the population, 2011 (females per 1,000 males)		
All ages	940	997
Age 0–6 years	914	972[a]
Ratio of female to male death rates, 2009[b]		
Age 0–1	1.01	0.89
Age 1–4	1.55	1.25
Ratio of female to male school enrolment, 2010 (%)		
Primary	100[c]	104[d]
Secondary	92	113
Literacy rate, age 15–24 years, 2010 (%)		
Female	74[e]	78
Male	88[e]	75
Proportion of adults (age 25+) with secondary education, 2010 (%)		
Women	27	31
Men	50	39
Women's share of seats in national Parliament, 2011 (%)	11	20
Total fertility rate, 2011 (children per woman)	2.6	2.2

[a] Age 0–4 years.
[b] 2007 for Bangladesh.
[c] 2008.
[d] 2009.
[e] 2006.

Sources: *World Development Indicators* (online, 1 January 2013), unless started otherwise. ***Human Development Report 2011***, p. 141, for adults with secondary education. Female-male ratios in the population from Census of India 2011 (Government of India, 2011b, p. 88) and Population and Housing Census 2011 (Bangladesh Bureau of Statistics, 2011, p. 7); ratio of female to male death rates from ***Sample Registration System Statistical Report 2009*** and Bangladesh Demographic and Health Survey 2007 (National Institute of Population Research and Training, 2009, Table 8.3, p. 104).

fairly well established.[13] The subjugation of women in South Asia has also been plausibly invoked in the past as a major explanation for the 'South Asian enigma' – the fact that child undernutrition rates are higher in this region than in many countries that are much poorer. It is thus entirely plausible that Bangladesh's recent progress has been significantly driven by positive changes in gender relations and by the new role of women in Bangladeshi society. Some of its achievements, in fact, build in a fairly direct and transparent way on women's agency. For instance, very large numbers of Bangladeshi women have been mobilized as front-line health workers (both by NGOs and by the government).[14] In this and in many other areas of activity involving Bangladeshi women, it looks as if the country would have been a very different place – and far less successful – but for the positive role played by its women.

No comparable change can be observed in India as a whole, and especially in its 'northern heartland'.[15] There, women's participation in the workforce has been stagnating at very low levels for decades, in sharp contrast not only with Bangladesh but also with many other Asian countries, where large numbers of women have entered remunerated employment. Similarly, India continues to have a serious problem of gender bias in childcare (reflected for instance in much higher mortality rates and lower school participation rates for girls than for boys), which has even acquired new manifestations in the recent past, such as sex-selective abortion. As will be discussed in Chapter 8, these biases against the girl child are reflected in a low female–male ratio among children: only 914 girls per 1,000 boys in India in 2011, compared with 972 in Bangladesh, suggesting much less gender discrimination in childcare there as well as a relative absence of sex-selective abortion (see Table 5).[16] None of this detracts from the fact that Bangladesh, like India, is a traditionally male-dominated society and continues to be very patriarchal in many ways even today. But at least there are strong signs of transformational change in Bangladesh, much more so than in India as a whole.

A second pointer, particularly relevant to health achievements, is Bangladesh's apparent ability to focus on the basic determinants of health care and elementary education in ways that have not happened in India. Bangladesh's endeavours have been helped by flourishing NGO activities, from comprehensive development efforts to specialized micro-credit initiatives (led by organizations such as BRAC and Grameen Bank). There have also been sensible moves in the public sector with an eye to basic living requirements. Even though the overall size of public expenditure on health is still very low in Bangladesh, and many of the governance issues that have plagued India's health care system also seem to apply to Bangladesh, nevertheless the country has made very substantial progress with essential, low-cost measures, particularly related to public health. The point is easily seen in the information presented in Table 6. Taking the data in Tables 5 and 6 together, the contrast between the two countries is very sharp: elementary good-health practices such as the use of sanitation facilities, full immunization of children, and oral rehydration therapy (to treat diarrhoea) have become widely accepted social norms in Bangladesh, but are still confined to only a section of the Indian population, leaving large gaps in coverage.

The sanitation figures are worth noting. Only 56 per cent of Bangladeshi households have access, at their homes, to facilities – such as modern toilets – that meet the World Development Indicators' standards of 'improved sanitation' (with an even lower figure, 34 per cent, for India – see Table 3). However, a much higher proportion – more than 90 per cent – of households in Bangladesh do have access to some sanitation facilities, including rudimentary latrines and washing facilities, so that only 8.4 per cent have to resort to 'open defecation' (see Table 6). In India, a full 50 per cent of households had to practise open defecation in 2011, according to the latest population census – a higher proportion than in almost any other country for which data are available. Open defecation is not only a major health hazard, but also a source of enormous hardship, particularly for women who are often constrained to rise before dawn and have no convenient way of relieving themselves after that.[17] This hardship passes largely unnoticed, and indeed, the need for universal access to basic sanitation

Table 6 India and Bangladesh: selected indicators of public health

	India (2005–6)	*Bangladesh (2007)*
Proportion of households practising open defecation (%)	55	8.4
Proportion of children aged 12–23 months who are fully immunized (%)	44	82
Proportion of children who started breastfeeding within 24 hours of birth (%)	55	89
Proportion of children aged 9–59 months who received Vitamin A supplements[a] (%)	18	88
Proportion of the population with sustainable access to an improved water source (%)	88	97
Proportion of diarrhoea-affected children treated with 'oral rehydration therapy' (%)	39	81

[a] Age 6–59 months for India.

Sources: Bangladesh Demographic and Health Survey 2007, for Bangladesh; National Family Health Survey 2005–6, for India. These two surveys (DHS and NFHS respectively) are very similar in terms of questionnaires and survey methods – both are variants of the worldwide DHS household surveys.

facilities has not been a major concern in Indian planning until very recently. Bangladesh, meanwhile, has been quietly building toilets around the country over the years, sparing the vast majority of the population from the hardships and hazards of open defecation. Even if some of these facilities are quite rudimentary, they are at least laying foundations for adequate sanitation.[18] This is also a good illustration of the possibility of effective health initiatives even with a great shortage of public resources.

Another area of particular interest is family planning in the two countries. Bangladesh has implemented a fairly effective, non-coercive family planning programme which has led to a dramatic reduction of fertility in a relatively short time – from around 7 children per woman in the early 1970s to 4.5 in 1990 and 2.2 in 2011 (very close to the 'replacement level' of 2.1). As one commentator put it to us, family planning is now as familiar to Bangladeshi women as 'dal-bhat' (rice and lentils – the staple foods of the country). This is also reflected in survey data (e.g. from the Bangladesh Demographic and Health Survey), showing high levels of awareness of family planning matters among Bangladeshi women, and a much higher use of modern contraceptive methods than in India. Just to cite one more example, Bangladesh has also made early strides in the development and distribution of low-cost generic drugs through public or non-profit institutions.[19] It is partly by focusing on these and other 'basics' that the country has been able to improve people's health in spite of its very low per capita income.

A third pointer relates to the importance of social norms in health, education and related fields, and to the role of public communication and community mobilization in bringing about changes in social norms. Most of Bangladesh's relatively successful programmes in these fields have built in one way or another on these social factors.[20] Tens of thousands of grass-roots health and community workers (mobilized by the government as well as by NGOs) have been going from house to house and village to village for many years facilitating child immunization, explaining contraception methods, promoting improved sanitation, organizing nutrition supplementation programmes, counselling pregnant or lactating women, and much more. India, of course, has also initiated programmes of this sort, but it still has much to learn from Bangladesh, both about the required intensity of these communication and mobilization efforts, and about the need to overcome the social barriers that often stand in the way of such initiatives.

India among the BRICs

While the South Asian perspective has been much neglected in India, another group of countries is commonly seen as comprising its 'peer group': Brazil, Russia, India and China (also known as the BRIC countries). These nations do have some important features in common, starting with their gigantic populations.

As Table 7 illustrates, however, India is actually an exception within this group, in important ways. For instance, while every country in the set has achieved universal or near-universal literacy in the younger age groups, India is still quite far from this elementary foundation of participatory development: one fifth of all Indian men in the age group of 15–24 years, and one fourth of all women in the same age group, were unable to read and write in 2006. Similarly, child immunization is almost universal in every BRIC country except India. In fact, as we saw earlier, India's immunization rates are abysmally low even in comparison with those of other South Asian countries including Bangladesh and Nepal. India also stands out dramatically in terms of the extent of undernourishment among children. This terrible problem has largely disappeared in other BRIC countries, but is still rampant in India, where more than 40 per cent of all children below the age of five are underweight, and an even higher proportion (close to 50 per cent) are stunted.

To some extent, this pattern reflects the fact that India is still much poorer than other BRIC countries: India's per capita GDP (adjusted for 'purchasing power parity') is less than half of China's, one third of Brazil's, and one fourth of Russia's.

Table 7 Selected indicators for 'BRIC' countries

	India	*China*	*Brazil*	*Russia*
GDP per capita (PPP, 2005 constant international $), 2011	3,203	7,418	10,279	14,821
Life expectancy at birth, 2010				
Female	67	75	77	75
Male	64	72	70	63
Infant mortality rate, 2011	47	13	14	10
Under-5 mortality rate, 2011	61	15	16	12
Total fertility rate, 2010	2.6	1.6	1.8	1.5
Access to improved sanitation, 2010 (%)	34	64	79	70
Mean years of schooling, age 25+, 2011	4.4	7.5	7.1	11.7
Literacy rate, age 15–24, 2010 (%)				
Female	74[a]	99	99[c]	100
Male	88[a]	99	97[c]	100
Undernourishment among children below 5, 2006–10[b] (%)				
Underweight	43	4	2	n/a
Stunted	48	10	7	n/a
Child immunization rates, 2011 (%)				
DPT	72	99	96	97
Measles	74	99	97	98
Public expenditure on health, 2010:				
As a proportion of total health expenditure (%)	29	54	47	62
As a proportion of GDP (%)	1.2	2.7	4.2	3.2
Per capita (PPP, 2005 constant international $)	39	203	483	620
Public expenditure on education as a proportion of GDP, 2010 (%)	3.3	n/a	5.6[c]	4.1[d]

[a] 2006.
[b] Latest year for which data are available within this period.
[c] 2009.
[d] 2008.

Source: *World Development Indicators* (online, 1 January 2013). Mean years of schooling from ***Human Development Report*** 2013 and child undernutrition from UNICEF (2012). Countries are ranked in increasing order of GDP per capita.

But clearly, much more needs to be done to fill these massive gaps than just 'catching up' in terms of per capita income. For instance, rapid economic growth has not achieved much on its own, during the last twenty years or so, to reduce India's horrendous levels of child undernourishment, or to enhance child immunization rates. Similarly, making a swift and decisive transition to universal literacy in the younger age groups would take more than just waiting for the growth of per capita incomes to make it easier for parents to send their children to school.

In others words, the required 'catching up' pertains not only to per capita incomes but also – very importantly – to public services, social support and economic distribution. It is, in fact, worth noting that among these four countries, India is the only one that has not (at least not yet) gone through a phase of major expansion of public support or economic redistribution. China made enormous progress (especially in comparison with India) very early towards universal access to elementary education, health care and social security – much *before* embarking on market-oriented economic reforms in 1979. While there were some setbacks in some of these fields in the 1980s and 1990s, notably in the field of health care, China's growth-oriented policies during that period benefited a great deal from the solid foundations of human development that had been laid earlier, and also retained that commitment in many ways, for instance through guaranteed and equitable access to land in rural areas. Further, as discussed in Chapter 1, the undoing of socialized health care in the 1980s and 1990s, for which China paid a heavy price, was reversed again from around 2004.[21] The principle of universal health coverage has reappeared in China's health planning, and rapid progress has been made in that direction: it appears that nearly 95 per cent of the people are now covered by the revamped, publicly funded health system.

Russia, too, had put in place a comprehensive system of social protection and public services during the Communist period. As in China, the system came under heavy stress after economic reforms – of a more extreme variety – were introduced in the early 1990s. In Russia, however, the breakdown was far more serious, and compounded by an economic catastrophe (possibly the worst economic recession in modern history, lasting for the best part of a decade), not unrelated to the lethal advice of Western experts who kept predicting an imminent 'economic miracle' in a newly marketized Russia even as the economy kept sinking.[22] There was, eventually, an economic take-off of a limited sort (in the 2000s), but only after the economy and social infrastructure had been substantially ruined, or handed over to business magnates. This prolonged economic crisis was associated with an equally catastrophic deterioration of the health of the Russian population, particularly men, who now have the same sort of life expectancy as Indian men (see Table 7). Even then, some of the social achievements of the earlier period remained, including universal basic education, involving schooling well beyond literacy. And as in China, there have been major efforts to rebuild public services and the social security system in Russia in recent years, with help from sustained economic growth from the turn of the century.[23]

To some extent, similar events have taken place in various parts of the former Soviet Union and Eastern Europe. It is often forgotten that, before the break-up of the Soviet Union in 1991, patterns of social spending in Western and Eastern Europe were not vastly different – most countries in both regions had a well-developed welfare state and spent a large proportion of their GDP on health, education, social security and related purposes.[24] It was after the break-up of the Soviet Union, and the economic catastrophe that followed in much of Eastern Europe, that social spending also came under enormous strain in many countries of that region (especially those with weak democratic institutions). The damage still remains partially unrepaired.

In Brazil, progressive social policies are comparatively recent, and followed a period of rapid economic growth, instead of preceding it as in China; it is perhaps interesting that the social indicators of Brazil and China look quite similar today (see Table 7), even though they reached a similar situation through very different routes. For a long time, Brazil combined rapid economic growth with repressive governance, massive inequality and endemic deprivation. However, as discussed in the next section, this picture has radically changed during the last twenty years, a time of ambitious and wide-ranging initiatives in the fields of health, education and social security (largely driven by the democratic upsurge that followed the end of military dictatorships), and the results have been impressive.

The old and new Brazil

Along with our analysis of the scope for 'growth-mediated' development, in an earlier book, we also discussed the pitfalls of 'unaimed opulence' – the indiscriminate pursuit of economic expansion, without paying much attention to how it is shared or how it affects people's lives.[25] At that time (in the late 1980s), Brazil was in many ways a fitting illustration of this pattern. In the 1960s and 1970s, it had one of the fastest-growing economies in the world, but living conditions remained deplorably low for large sections of the population. Commenting on this again in the mid-1990s, in contrast with a more equitable and participatory growth pattern in South Korea, we wrote that 'India stands in some danger of going Brazil's way, rather than South Korea's'.[26] Recent experience vindicates this apprehension about the path that India might be following – there is a fair amount of unaimed opulence in India today.

Interestingly, over the last couple of decades, Brazil has substantially changed course, and adopted a more inclusive approach based on active social policies. This change has been largely driven by the flourishing of democracy that followed the promulgation of a democratic constitution in 1988, soon after the end of a long spell of military dictatorships. Notable aspects of this new orientation include a strong commitment to free and universal health care, bold programmes of social security and income support, and major efforts to expand the reach and quality of elementary education. It is, of course, the case that many significant imperfections remain, but these problems are subjects of powerful critiques and public discussions in Brazil today.[27]

The right to health was included in the new democratic constitution, not in the non-binding mode of the 'directive principles' of the Indian constitution, but as a matter of justiciable right. In pursuance of this state obligation, Brazil created the 'Unified Health System', aimed at providing free health care to everyone without discrimination, and also launched an ambitious Family Health Programme. The system involves both public and private health care providers, but is publicly funded. It has led to a major expansion of access to health care, particularly for the underprivileged – according to the World Health Organization, 75 per cent of the population 'rely exclusively on it for their health care coverage'.[28] Today, Brazil's health indicators are reasonably good, with, for instance, universal immunization of children, an infant mortality rate of only 14 per 1,000 (compared with 47 in India), and only 2 per cent of children below five being underweight (compared with a staggering 43 per cent in India).

A special feature of Brazil's new health care project is that it is rooted in strong popular movements. The Unified Health System itself was largely conceived by health activists as part of a larger 'social policy project designed by social movements', strongly associated with 'the transformation of the state and society into a democracy'.[29] Interestingly, this project is known in Brazil as 'health sector reform' – a useful reminder that 'reform' has many possible connotations, and need not be taken to mean, as it is often assumed in India, a retreat from state action. Brazil's experience also reminds us that, in a democracy, health care can be a lively political issue, as it is in the experience of Western Europe (and to some extent, more recently, even of the United States). As discussed in Chapter 6, there is a very important lesson here for India, where health care is still way down on the list of issues that catch the imagination of political leaders, opposition parties or talk-show hosts.

Programmes of income redistribution and social security, also in line with Brazil's new democratic constitution, have had substantial results as well. In an insightful study, Martin Ravallion (2011) compares the speed and causes of poverty reduction in Brazil, India and China between 1981 and 2005. During the second half of this period (between 1993 and 2005), Brazil's per capita GDP grew at just 1 per cent or so, compared with nearly 5 per cent in India. Yet, the rate of poverty reduction (in terms of annual percentage reduction of the 'head-count ratio') was much larger in Brazil, where this was also a period of substantial redistribution, in contrast with India where economic inequality went up.[30] Further investigations, based on updated data series extending to the late 2000s, corroborate the role of economic redistribution in Brazil's recent experience of poverty reduction.[31]

The redistribution initiatives relevant to poverty included various social assistance programmes (including large pension schemes), minimum wage policies, and, from 2003 onwards, the well-known *Bolsa Familia* programme of targeted cash transfers, which covers about one fourth of the population – mainly those outside the formal sector of the economy.[32] These programmes have had a limited impact on the extent of *inequality* in Brazil – indeed, Brazil is still one of the most unequal countries in the world (along with India, China and South Africa). But they certainly had a major impact on poverty, especially extreme poverty.[33]

Less well known than *Bolsa Familia* or *Fome Zero* (Zero Hunger, Brazil's food security initiative), but no less important, is the sustained expansion and improvement of Brazil's schooling system during the last twenty years or so.[34] Even in Brazil's highly unequal society, the proportion of children attending private schools at the primary level (about 10 per cent) is much smaller than in India (nearly 30 per cent), and unlike in India, it does not seem to be growing.[35] Government schools, for their part, have gone through major reforms. For instance, municipalities have started assuming the main responsibility for school management; a 'funding equalization law' has been enacted to ensure a fair distribution of education funds; pupil achievements have been carefully monitored through regular, standardized country-wide school tests; conditional cash transfers (initially *Bolsa Escola*, and later *Bolsa Familia*) have been used to promote school attendance; and (very importantly) Brazil has invested heavily in pre-school education, which has been extended to more than 80 per cent of young children.[36]

The results have been impressive. At least three major educational improvements have been well documented. First, there was a large increase in school attendance and schooling attainment in the younger age groups. By 2009, school attendance in the age group of 6–14 years was 98 per cent, and literacy in the age group of 15–24 years was also 98 per cent.[37] Second, this period also saw a sharp reduction in educational *inequality*. For instance, the Gini coefficient of years of schooling dropped from 0.41 in 1995 to 0.29 in 2009.[38] Education reforms, including the funding equalization policy, also helped the lagging regions (such as the north-east) to catch up with the rest of the country. Third, pupil achievements (as measured by test scores) dramatically improved, albeit from what was, in an international perspective, a low base. In fact, between 2000 and 2009, Brazil had one of the fastest rates of improvement of student test scores among all those included in the Programme of International Student Assessment (PISA).[39] To view the speed of progress in these different dimensions from another angle, by 2009 the average schooling opportunities of children from the *poorest* income quintile in Brazil were not far from those enjoyed by children from the *richest* income quintile just 16 years earlier.[40]

Social spending as a proportion of GDP is now higher in Brazil (about 25 per cent) than in any other Latin American country except Cuba (about 40 per cent), and about four times the corresponding ratio in India (a measly 6 per cent or so).[41] As in many other Latin American countries, a substantial proportion of this social expenditure (especially social security expenditure) has regressive features, in the sense that it disproportionately benefits comparatively well-off sections of the population.[42] But recent initiatives have firmly extended the reach of social support to the underprivileged, and corrected the earlier biases to a significant extent. These achievements and the speed of change – most of this happened within twenty years of a democratic constitution being promulgated – are important facts from which encouraging lessons can be drawn.

Comparisons within India and the internal lessons[43]

While India has much to learn from international experience, it also has a great deal to learn from the diversity of experiences *within* this large country. The regional records are very diverse indeed, and if some states were separated out from the rest of India, we would see a very different picture from the average for the country taken together. A number of Indian states – Kerala and Tamil Nadu, for example – would be at the top of the South Asian comparisons if they were treated as separate countries, and others – Uttar Pradesh and Madhya Pradesh, for example – would do enormously worse. But what is most powerfully apparent from these interstate comparisons within India is just how much this diverse country can learn from the experiences of the more successful states within it.

These contrasts are indeed sharp. For instance, whereas female life expectancy is 77 years in Kerala, it is still below 65 years in many of the large north Indian states. Further, these contrasts reinforce, in many ways, the lessons of comparative international experiences for development strategy. In particular, the Indian states that have done well tend to have been those which had laid solid foundations of participatory development and social support early on, and actively promoted the expansion of human capabilities, especially in terms of education and health.

Table 8 Selected indicators for major Indian states, 2005

	Education-related indicators			*Health-related indicators*			*Poverty-related indicators*		
	Female literacy, age 15–49 years, 2005–6 (%)	*Proportion of children aged 6–14 attending school, 2005–6 (%)*	*Proportion of children aged 8–11 who pass a simple reading test, 2004–5 (%)*	*Under-5 mortality rate, 2005–6 (per 1,000)*	*Proportion of young children fully immunized, 2005–6 (%)*	*Proportion of adult women with low BMI, 2005–6 (%)*	*Proportion of population below the poverty line, 2004–5 (%)*	*Proportion of population in India s lowest wealth quintile, 2005–6 (%)*	*Median per capita income, 2004–5 (Rs/ year)*
Andlira Pradesh	49.6	81.4	50	63.2	46.0	33.5	29.6	10.8	6,241
Assam	63.0	84.4	72	85.0	31.4	36.5	34.4	19.8	6,000
Bihar	37.0	62.2	44	84.8	32.8	45.1	54.4	28.2	3,530
Chhattisgarh	44.9	81.1	61	90.3	48.7	43.4	49.4	39.6	5,306
Gujarat	63.8	83.0	64	60.9	45.2	36.3	31.6	7.2	6,300
Haryana	60.4	84.1	65	52.3	65.3	31.3	24.1	4.1	9,443
Himachal Pradesh	79.5	96.2	83	41.5	74.2	29.9	22.9	1.2	9,942.
Jammu & Kashmir	53.9	87.8	40	51.2	66.7	24.6	13.1	2.8	8,699
Jharkhand	37.1	71.7	59	93.0	34.2	43.0	45.3	49.6	4,833
Karnataka	59.7	84.0	53	54.7	55.0	35.5	33.3	10.8	5,964
Kerala	93.0	97.7	82	16.3	75.3	18.0	19.6	1.0	9,987
Madhya Pradesh	44.4	89.1	46	94.2	40.3	41.7	48.6	36.9	4,125
Maharashtra	70.3	87.2	66[a]	46.7	58.8	36.2	38.2	10.9	7,975[a]
Odisha	52.2	77.5	58	90.6	51.8	41.4	57.2.	39.5	3,450
Punjab	68.7	85.3	66	52.0	60.1	18.9	20.9	1.4	9,125
Rajasthan	36.2	75.4	55	85.4	26.5	36.7	34.4	24.2	6,260
Tamil Nadu	69.4	93.9	79	35.5	80.9	28.4	29.4	10.6	7,000
Uttar Pradesh	44.8	77.2	39	96.4	23.0	36.0	40.9	25.3	4,300
Uttarakhand	64.6	90.4	63	56.8	60.0	30.0	32.7	6.0	6,857
West Bengal	58.8	79.7	51	59.6	64.3	39.1	34.2	25.2	6,250
India	55.1	79.6	54	74.3	43.5	35.6	37.2	20.0	5,999

[a] Including Goa.

Sources: Figures with 2005–6 as reference year are from the third National Family Health Survey (International Institute for Population Sciences, 2007, and state reports for school attendance); poverty estimates for 2004–5 are from the Tendulkar Committee Report (as reprinted in Government of India, 2012c); reading proficiency and median per capita income are from the India Human Development Survey (Desai et al., 2010). For further details, see Drèze and Khera (2012a).

The interstate disparities are illustrated in Table 8, which presents a sample of basic development indicators relating to education, health and poverty.[44] We also present in Table 9 two summary indexes of deprivation: a standard 'human development index', which gives equal weight to the nine indicators given in Table 8, and the proportion of the population estimated to be living in 'multi-dimensional poverty'.[45]

Seven major states (with a combined population of 545 million in 2011, about half of India's population) have had poor social indicators for a long time, as well as high levels of poverty: Bihar, Chhattisgarh, Jharkhand, Madhya Pradesh, Odisha, Rajasthan and Uttar Pradesh.[46] The dismal nature of living conditions in these states, for large sections of the population, is evident from Table 8. These figures show, for instance, that less than half of all children aged 8–11 years are able to pass a very simple reading test (going a little beyond liberal definitions of 'literacy') in some of these states, only 23 per cent of young children are fully immunized in Uttar Pradesh, and more than half of the population in Bihar lives below the Government of India's extremely low poverty line.

In international perspective, some of these states are not very different from the poorer countries of Africa in the intensity of human deprivation. This is reaffirmed by the recent work on multi-dimensional poverty. For instance, computations of the 'multi-dimensional poverty index' (MPI) place states like Bihar and Jharkhand in the same category as some of the poorest African countries – countries like Mozambique and Sierra Leone.[47] Further, in terms of MPI, the seven states mentioned earlier (Bihar, Chhattisgarh, Jharkhand, Madhya Pradesh,

Table 9 Human development and multi-dimensional poverty: summary indexes for major Indian states

	Human Development Index, 2005[a]	*Proportion of population 'multi-dimensionally poor', 2005–6*[b] *(%)*
Kerala	0.970	12.7
Himachal Pradesh	0.846	29.9
Tamil Nadu	0.749	30.5
Punjab	0.742	24.6
Haryana	0.670	39.3
Jammu & Kashmir	0.655	41.0
Uttarakhand	0.612	39.5
Maharashtra	0.601	37.9
Gujarat	0.520	41.0
Karnataka	0.500	43.2
Andhra Pradesh	0.458	44.5
West Bengal	0.446	57.4
Assam	0.441	60.1
Rajasthan	0.301	62.8
Chhattisgarh	0.271	69.7
Madhya Pradesh	0.230	68.1
Odisha	0.229	63.2
Uttar Pradesh	0.212	68.1
Jharkhand	0.170	74.8
Bihar	0.106	79.3
India	0.400	53.7

[a] Based on National Family Health Survey (NFHS) data for 2005–6, National Sample Survey (NSS) data for 2004–5, and India Human Development Survey (IHDS) data for 2004–5.
[b] Based on National Family Health Survey (NFHS) data for 2005–6.

Sources: The human development index presented here is an unweighted average of normalized values for each of the 9 indicators presented in Table 8 (see Drèze and Khera, 2012a). On the multidimensional poverty figures, see Alkire and Seth (2012). The states are ranked in decreasing order of HDI for 2005.

Odisha, Rajasthan and Uttar Pradesh) are more or less on a par – taken together – with the 27 poorest countries of Africa, and have roughly the same population.[48] What the multi-dimensional poverty figures suggest, roughly speaking, is that *living conditions in the poorer half of India are not much better, if at all, than in the poorer half of Africa.*

Looking at the other end of the scale, in Table 9, three major states distinguish themselves with relatively high levels of human development: Kerala, Himachal Pradesh and Tamil Nadu. Punjab and Haryana are not very far behind; in fact, in terms of 'multi-dimensional poverty', Punjab actually does a little better than both Himachal Pradesh and Tamil Nadu. There are, however, two particular reasons to give special attention to Kerala, Himachal Pradesh and Tamil Nadu. First, they do much better than Punjab and Haryana by gender-related and child-related indicators. Second, Kerala, Himachal Pradesh and Tamil Nadu are all states that were very poor not so long ago (say in the 1950s and 1960s) – unlike Punjab and Haryana, which have been relatively prosperous regions of India for a long time.[49] This adds to the interest of their recent achievements – their performance in enhancing living conditions as well as their success in raising per capita income along with the expansion of human capability.

Kerala's social achievements have a long history and have been widely discussed – including in our earlier work.[50] What is interesting is that Kerala continues to make rapid progress on many fronts, and that its lead over other states shows no sign of diminishing over time. Since the 1980s there have been regular warnings – coming mainly from commentators suspicious of state intervention – that Kerala's development achievements were unsustainable, or deceptive, or even turning into a 'debacle'.[51] As it turns out, however, the improvement of living conditions in Kerala has not only continued but even accelerated, with help from rapid economic growth, which in turn has been assisted by Kerala's focus on elementary education and other basic capabilities.

Like Kerala, Himachal Pradesh launched ambitious social programmes, including a vigorous drive toward universal elementary education, at a time when it was still quite poor – the early 1970s.[52] The speed of progress has been truly impressive: as Table 8 illustrates, Himachal Pradesh is now on a par with Kerala as far as elementary education is concerned, and other social indicators are also catching up. Within forty years or so, Himachal Pradesh has made the transition from severe social backwardness and deprivation (as the region was seen then) to a relatively advanced state with a widely shared freedom from abject deprivation.

Tamil Nadu is another interesting case of a state achieving rapid progress over a relatively short period, though it started from appalling levels of poverty, deprivation and inequality. Throughout the 1970s and 1980s official poverty estimates for Tamil Nadu were higher than the corresponding all-India figures, for both rural and urban areas (about half of the population was below the Planning Commission's measly poverty line).[53] Much as in Kerala earlier, social relations were also extremely oppressive, with Dalits (scheduled castes) parked in separate hamlets (known as 'colonies'), generally deprived of social amenities, and often prevented from asserting themselves even in simple ways like wearing a shirt or riding a bicycle. It is during that period that Tamil Nadu, much to the consternation of many economists, initiated bold social programmes such as universal midday meals in primary schools and started putting in place an extensive social infrastructure – schools, health centres, roads, public transport, water supply, electricity connections, and much more. This was not just a reflection of kind-heartedness on the part of the ruling elite, but an outcome of democratic politics, including organized public pressure. Disadvantaged groups, particularly Dalits, had to fight for their share at every step.[54] Today, Tamil Nadu has some of the best public services among all Indian states, and many of them are accessible to all on a nondiscriminatory basis. Tamil Nadu's experience will be discussed again in Chapter 6, with special reference to health and nutrition.

While each of these experiences tends to be seen, on its own, as some sort of confined 'special case', it is worth noting that the combined population of these three states is well above 100 million. Tamil Nadu alone had a population of 72 million in 2011, larger than most countries in the world. Further, the notion that these states are just 'outliers' overlooks the fact that their respective development trajectories, despite many differences, have shared features of much interest. First, active social policies constitute an important aspect of this shared experience. This is particularly striking in the vigour of public education, but it also extends to other domains, such as health care, social security and public amenities.

Second, these states have typically followed universalistic principles in the provision of essential public services. This is especially noticeable in the case of Tamil Nadu, as will be further discussed in Chapter 6, but the point also applies to Himachal Pradesh and Kerala. The basic principle is that facilities such as school education, primary health care, midday meals, electricity connections, ration cards and drinking water should as far as possible be made effectively available to all on a non-discriminatory basis, instead of being 'targeted' to specific sections of the population. In fact, in many cases the provision of essential services and amenities has not only been universal but also free.[55]

Third, these efforts have been greatly facilitated by a functioning and comparatively efficient administration. The governments involved have delivered their services in traditional lines, and there has been little use of recently favoured shortcuts such as the use of para-teachers (rather than regular teachers), making conditional cash transfers, or reliance on school vouchers for private schools (rather than building government schools). The heroes in these successful efforts have been 'old-fashioned' public institutions – functioning schools, health centres, government offices, Gram Panchayats (village councils) and cooperatives. These traditional public institutions have left much room for private initiatives at a later stage of development, but they have laid the foundations of rapid progress in each of these cases.

Fourth, dealing with social inequality has also been an important part of these shared experiences. In each case, the historical burden of social inequality has been significantly reduced in one way or another. In Kerala and Tamil Nadu, principles of equal citizenship and universal entitlements were forged through sustained social reform movements as well as fierce struggles for equality on the part of underprivileged groups – especially Dalits, who used to receive abominable treatment and have to continue their battle to reverse the old handicaps altogether.[56] Himachal Pradesh benefited from a more favourable social environment, including relatively egalitarian social norms and a strong tradition of cooperative action. While substantial inequalities of class, caste and gender remain in each case, the underprivileged have at least secured an active – and expanding – role in public life and democratic institutions.

Fifth, these experiences of rapid social progress are not just a reflection of constructive state policies but also of people's active involvement in democratic politics. The social movements that fought traditional inequalities (particularly caste inequalities) are part of this larger pattern.[57] These social advances, the spread of education, and the operation of democratic institutions (with all their imperfections) enabled people – men and women – to have a say in public policy and social arrangements, in a way that has yet to happen in many other states.

Last but not least, there is no evidence that the cultivation of human capability has been at the cost of conventional economic success, such as fast economic growth. On the contrary, these states have all achieved fast rates of expansion, as indeed one would expect, both on grounds of causal economic relations and on the basis of international experience (including the 'east Asian' success story). While many of their big social initiatives and achievements go back to earlier times, when these states were not particularly well-off, today Kerala, Himachal Pradesh and (to a lesser extent) Tamil Nadu have some of the highest per capita incomes and lowest poverty rates among all Indian states (see Table 8). Economic growth, in turn, has enabled these states to sustain and consolidate active social policies. This is an important example of the complementarity between economic growth and public support, discussed earlier.

Not so long ago, Kerala was considered as an anomaly of sorts among Indian states. Its distinct social history and political culture appeared to set it apart, and to make it difficult for any other state to follow a similar route. Today, the situation looks a little different. Kerala is still ahead in many ways, but some other states have also made great strides in improving the quality of life – not in exactly the same way but in ways that share many interesting features with Kerala's own experience. Other states have good reason to learn from these positive experiences, even as India also learns from the successes and failures in the rest of the world.

Notes

1 Anand Giridharadas (2011), p. 1.
2 See Drèze and Sen (2002), Chapter 3.
3 The figures cited in this section are taken from the World Bank's *World Development Indicators* (online, 1 January 2013). This is also the main source used throughout the book for purposes of international comparisons of development indicators. For India, we are using the WDI for international comparisons, and the latest figures available from national statistical sources otherwise. For further discussion, see the Statistical Appendix.
4 *World Development Indicators*, online. Age-specific literacy rates from the Census of India 2011 are not available at the time of writing, and it is quite possible that India's (and therefore South Asia's) literacy figures will improve somewhat after they are released.
5 See Chapter 6, Table 6.3.
6 Similarly, in terms of the 'multi-dimensional poverty index' (MPI), discussed further in this chapter, India ranks 11th out of 14 countries for which estimates are available in this group (Sabina Alkire, personal communication).
7 Recent work on multidimensional poverty indexes, partly presented in *Human Development Report* 2013, suggests astonishingly rapid progress in Nepal between 2006 and 2011 (Sabina Alkire, personal communication). This new development is yet to be fully investigated.
8 OXFAM International (2006), p. 9.
9 See e.g. Chaudhury and Hammer (2004), with reference to health facilities.
10 For useful contributions to a better understanding of these achievements, see S. R. Osmani (1991, 2010), Simeen Mahmud (2003), B. Sen et al. (2007), World Bank (2007), Wahiduddin Mahmud (2008), Begum and Sen (2009), Naila Kabeer (2011), Koehlmoos et al. (2011), David Lewis (2011), Rehman Sobhan (2011), Chowdhury et al. (2012), among others.
11 On this connection see Drèze and Sen (1989, 2002) and Sen (1999). According to World Bank data, 'women's participation in economic activity [in Bangladesh] increased from 9% in 1983 to 57% in 2011' (Chowdhury et al., 2012). Even allowing for a substantial margin of error in the earlier estimates, this points to an astonishing increase in the participation of women in the economy, which has absolutely no parallel in India.
12 The last point should be read in light of the fact that there is some reservation of parliamentary seats for women in Bangladesh; see e.g. P. K. Panday (2008). In India, a constitutional amendment proposed for this purpose (the 'Women's Reservation Bill') has been held up in the Indian Parliament for many years.
13 See Drèze and Sen (2002), and the literature cited there; also Chapter 8 of this book.
14 See e.g. Chowdhury et al. (2012).
15 For further discussion, see Chapter 8.
16 There are major contrasts in gender relations, including the prevalence of sex-selective abortion, among different regions within India, and the comparison of Bangladesh's figures with the average numbers for India can be rather deceptive (some of the regional contrasts will be discussed later on in this chapter and in Chapter 8). However, for the same reason, some regions of India compare much more unfavourably with Bangladesh than the comparison between country averages indicates.
17 There is also a possibility that lack of sanitation facilities is playing a major role in the persistence of exceptionally high levels of child under-nutrition in India; on this, see Dean Spears (2012a, 2012b, 2013). In a few countries such as Chad and Eritrea, the incidence of open defecation is as high as (or even a little higher than) in India. But no country seems to come close to India in terms of the intensity of open defecation per square mile, which – it has been argued – is what really matters from the point of view of health hazards, including child undernutrition (Dean Spears, personal communication).
18 In some Indian states, the use of toilets is difficult to promote because of inadequate water supply facilities. Bangladesh, where there is abundant groundwater, may have a 'comparative advantage' in this respect. But even Indian states that are well endowed with groundwater (West Bengal, Uttar Pradesh, Bihar, among others) have much higher rates of open defecation than Bangladesh, e.g. 39 per

cent in West Bengal and 63 per cent in Uttar Pradesh; see Statistical Appendix, Table A.3.

19 See e.g. Zafrullah Chowdhury (1995).

20 See Mahmud (2008), Chowdhury et al. (2012), El Arifeen et al. (2012), among others.

21 The proportion of the rural population covered by the cooperative medical system crashed from 90 per cent to 10 per cent between 1976 and 1983 (the period when market-oriented reforms were initiated), and stayed around 10 per cent for a full 20 years. From 2004, when the 'new cooperative medical scheme' was launched, it rose again to more than 90 per cent within a few years; see Shaoguang Wang (2008), Figure 6. On China's new cooperative medical scheme, see also Yip and Mahal (2008), Lin Chen et al. (2012), Qun Meng et al. (2012), Yip et al. (2012), among others.

22 On this, see e.g. Joseph Stiglitz (2002), Chapter 5.

23 See e.g. Alfio Cerami (2009). On 'postcommunist welfare states' in the former Soviet Union and Eastern Europe, see Mitchell Orenstein (2008) and the literature cited there.

24 See e.g. Barr and Harbison (1994). As the authors observe (p. 17), based on 1991 data: 'What is noteworthy about social spending in Central and Eastern Europe is that it does not differ greatly as a proportion of GDP from spending in the highly industrialized economies, whose per capita incomes are much higher.'

25 See Drèze and Sen (1989), particularly Chapter 10; also Drèze and Sen (1995).

26 Drèze and Sen (1995), p. 183.

27 See Cataife and Courtemanche (2011), da Silva and Terrazas (2011), Comim (2012), Comim and Amaral (2012), among other critiques.

28 Jurberg and Humphreys (2010), p. 646. Another recent study (Cataife and Courtemanche 2011) suggests that access to public health care in Brazil is now more or less independent of income within localities, even though regional disparities persist. On Brazil's health system, see also the collection of papers published in *The Lancet* on 21 May 2011, particularly Paim et al. (2011), and the literature cited there.

29 Sonia Fleury (2011), p. 1724.

30 See Martin Ravallion (2011), Tables 1 and 2. For further discussion of economic inequality in India, see Chapter 8.

31 See e.g. Ferreira de Souza (2012), and the literature cited there.

32 For a helpful introduction to *Bolsa Familia*, see Fabio Soares (2011); see also Francesca Bastagli (2008, 2011), Soares et al. (2010), Ferreira de Souza (2012) and the literature cited there. Bolsa Familia is, however; only one programme (though it has received enormous attention abroad), and Brazil's social security system extends much beyond this particular scheme.

33 Partly due to social assistance programmes, the incomes of the poor in Brazil grew quite rapidly during this period, in spite of the near-stagnation of per capita GDP (Ferreira et al., 2010). This is in sharp contrast with the situation in India, where, as we noted in Chapter 2, the growth of per capita expenditure among the poor was just a fraction of the growth of per capita GDP during the last twenty years or so.

34 On this see e.g. Bruns et al. (2012), and earlier work cited there.

35 Bruns et al. (2012), Figure 1, p. 5, showing that the proportion of Brazilian children enrolled in private schools at the primary level hovered around 10 per cent between 1991 and 2009. In India, the proportion of children studying in private schools at the elementary level (roughly corresponding to Brazil's primary level) was already as high as 28 per cent in 2004–5 (see Statistical Appendix, Table A.3), and is growing rapidly. For further discussion of India's schooling system, see Chapter 5.

36 Bruns et al. (2012).

37 Ferreira de Souza (2012), Table 3, p. 9.

38 Ferreira de Souza (2012), Figure 5, p. 10.

39 Bruns et al. (2012). On the PISA study, see also Chapter 5.

40 Based on data reported in Bruns et al. (2012), p. xxii. This statement applies not only to years of schooling (about eight on average, for a 20-year-old in the poorest income group in 2009), but also, to a large extent, to pupil achievements as measured by PISA test scores, at least in mathematics.

41 See Gastón Pierri (2012), Graphic 2, p. 11 (the reference year is 2008); see also Ferreira and Robalino (2010), Table 2, p. 37. Brazil and Cuba have similar levels of public expenditure on health and social security, as a proportion of GDP (close to 20 per cent in both cases). However, Cuba spends much more on education, and therefore, on the social sectors (health, education and social security) as a whole.

42 On this point, see Lloyd-Sherlock (2009).

43 This section draws on more detailed analyses of the development experiences of Kerala, Himachal Pradesh and Tamil Nadu in our earlier work (Drèze and Sen, 2002), as well as on more recent studies of these experiences. On Tamil Nadu, see also Chapter 6.

44 A wider range of state-specific indicators are presented in the Statistical Appendix, Tables A.3 and

A.4, not only for the major states but also for the smaller states of the north-eastern region. Some of these smaller states, such as Sikkim (and, in some respects, Manipur, Mizoram and Tripura), have done comparatively well in various dimensions of human development. These experiences deserve more attention than they have received so far.

45 The idea of multi-dimensional poverty is that poverty manifests itself in multiple deprivations, such as poor health, lack of education, absence of sanitation facilities, and various kinds of material deprivations. A person is counted as 'multi-dimensionally poor' if he or she experiences at least a certain proportion (say one third) of these deprivations. This approach can help to make detailed comparisons of living standards across countries, regions or communities, going beyond income-based criteria such as the World Bank's universal benchmark of 'two dollars a day' (adjusted for purchasing power parity). For further examination and use of this approach, see Alkire and Foster (2011).

46 These states – minus Odisha – used to be known by the unflattering acronym of BIMARU (*bimar* means 'ill' in Hindi), which referred to undivided Bihar (including Jharkhand), undivided Madhya Pradesh (including Chhattisgarh), Rajasthan and Uttar Pradesh. The acronym was sometimes modified to BIMAROU, to include Odisha.

47 See Alkire and Santos (2012) and Alkire and Seth (2012). The 'multi-dimensional poverty index' (MPI) is the percentage of multi-dimensionally poor persons in the population multiplied by the average number of deprivations they have.

48 These 27 countries are (in descending order of MPI): Niger, Ethiopia, Mali, Burkina Faso, Burundi, Somalia, Central African Republic, Mozambique, Guinea, Liberia, Angola, Sierra Leone, Rwanda, Benin, Comoros, DR Congo, Senegal, Malawi, Tanzania, Uganda, Madagascar, Côte d'Ivoire, Mauritania, Chad, Zambia, Gambia and Nigeria. Their combined population is around 600 million, of which 71 per cent are estimated to live in multi-dimensional poverty. In the seven Indian states mentioned in the text, 70 per cent of the population are estimated to live in multi-dimensional poverty. For further details of the basis of these calculations, see Alkire and Santos (2012).

49 According to Gaurav Datt and Martin Ravallion's time series of state-specific poverty estimates (analysed in Datt et al., 2003), Kerala was the poorest Indian state in the 1950s and 1960s, in terms of the proportion of the population below the poverty line. Tamil Nadu was also among the poorest states (more or less on a par with Bihar), while Punjab and Haryana already had much lower poverty levels than any other major state at that time. We are grateful to Gaurav Datt for sharing these unpublished poverty estimates.

50 See Drèze and Sen (1989, 1995, 2002), V. K. Ramachandran (1996), and the literature cited there; also Patrick Heller (1999, 2000, 2009), M. A. Oommen (1999, 2009), Achin Chakraborty (2005), Prerna Singh (2010a, 2010b), among others. The term 'Kerala model' has often been used in this literature, and more distressingly has occasionally been attributed – entirely erroneously – to our analysis. We have never used this particular rhetoric. There is much to learn from scrutinizing the experience of Kerala – and of the other high-performing states – but there is little evidence for seeing Kerala as a model to be mechanically emulated.

51 See e.g. Isaac and Tharakan (1995) and Tharamangalam (1998). While some of these warnings were simple prophecies of gloom, others proved to be useful enough in that they drew attention to some deficiencies in Kerala's approach, including the need for more constructive economic policies with attention paid to the role of markets, and may have contributed to the policy revisions that happened later, contributing to the rapid economic growth complementing and sustaining the state's active social policies.

52 On the 'schooling revolution' in Himachal Pradesh, see PROBE Team (1999) and De et al. (2011). On Himachal Pradesh's development experience, see Kiran Bhatty (2011) and the literature cited there.

53 See e.g. Government of India (1993) and World Bank (2011a).

54 On this see particularly Vivek Srinivasan (2010).

55 This approach is consistent with growing evidence of the strongly adverse incentive effects of 'user fees' (that is, charging beneficiaries) in the context of essential public services, especially related to health and education. These and other aspects of the delivery of supportive public services are discussed more fully in Chapter 7.

56 See M. A. Oommen (2009), Harriss et al. (2010), Prerna Singh (2010a, 2010b), Vivek Srinivasan (2010), among others.

57 See e.g. M. A. Oommen (2009), with reference to Kerala, aptly described by the author as 'a movement society par excellence; not only political, but also social, cultural and environmental movements' (p. 31).

References

A substantial proportion of the publications listed here are available online. Hyperlinks are given in cases of publications that appear to be available only on the Internet.

Alkire, S. and Foster, J. (2011), 'Counting and Multidimensional Poverty Measurement', *Journal of Public Economics*, 95.

Alkire, S. and Santos, M. E. (2012), 'Acute Multidimensional Poverty: A New Index for Developing Countries', *mimeo*, Oxford Poverty and Human Development Initiative, University of Oxford.

Alkire, S. and Seth, S. (2012), 'Multidimensional Poverty Index (MPI) Rates in Rural and Urban Indian States', *mimeo*, Oxford Poverty and Human Development Initiative, University of Oxford; available at http://ophi.qeh.ox.ac.uk.

Bangladesh Bureau of Statistics (2011), *Population and Housing Census: Preliminary Results July 2011* (Dhaka: Ministry of Planning, Government of the People's Republic of Bangladesh).

Barr, N. and Harbison, R. W. (1994), 'Overview: Hopes, Tears, and Transformation', in *Barr (1994)*.

Bastagli, Francesca (2008), 'The Design, Implementation and Impact of Conditional Cash Transfers Targeted on the Poor: An Evaluation of Brazil's *Bolsa Familia*', PhD thesis, London School of Economics.

Bastagli, Francesca (2011), 'Conditional Cash Transfers as a Tool of Social Policy', *Economic and Political Weekly*, 21 May.

Begum, S. and Sen, B. (2009), 'Maternal Health, Child Well-Being and Chronic Poverty: Does Women's Agency Matter?', *Bangladesh Development Studies*, 32.

Bhatty, Kiran (2011), 'Social Equality and Development: Himachal Pradesh and its Wider Significance', M.Phil. thesis, London School of Economics.

Bruns, B., Evans, D. and Luque, J. (2012), *Achieving World-Class Education in Brazil* (Washington, DC: World Bank).

Cataife, G. and Courtemanche, C. (2011), 'Is Universal Health Care in Brazil Really Universal?', *Working Paper 17069*, National Bureau of Economic Research, Cambridge, MA.

Cerami, Alfio (2009), 'Welfare State Developments in the Russian Federation: Oil-Led Social Policy and "The Russian Miracle"', *Social Policy and Administration*, 43.

Chakraborty, Achin (2005), 'Kerala's Changing Development Narratives', *Economic and Political Weekly*, 5 February.

Chaudhury, N. and Hammer, J. (2004), 'Ghost Doctors: Absenteeism in Rural Bangladeshi Health Facilities', *World Bank Economic Review*, 18.

Chowdhury, M., Bhuiya, A., Chowdhury, M. E., Rasheed, S., Hussain, A. M. Z. and Chen, L. C. (2012), 'The Bangladesh Paradox: Exceptional Health Achievement despite Economic Poverty', mimeo, International Centre for Diarrhoeal Disease Research, Bangladesh; to be published in *The Lancet*.

Chowdhury, Zafrullah (1995), *The Politics of Essential Drugs: The Makings of a Successful Health Strategy: Lessons from Bangladesh* (London: Zed).

Comim, F. (2012), 'Poverty and Inequality Reduction in Brazil throughout the Economic Crisis', *ISPI Analysis, no. 106*, Instituto per gli Studi di Politica Internazionale, Milan.

Comim, F. and Amaral, P. (2012), 'The Human Values Index: Conceptual Foundations and Evidence from Brazil', background paper for Brazil's Human Development Report; to be published in *Cambridge Journal of Economics*.

da Silva, V. A. and Terrazas, F. V. (2011), 'Claiming the Right to Health in Brazilian Courts: The Exclusion of the Already Excluded?', *Law and Social Enquiry*, 36.

Datt, G., Kozel, V. and Ravallion, M. (2003), 'A Model-Based Assessment of India's Progress in Reducing Poverty in the 1990s', *Economic and Political Weekly*, 25 January.

De, A., Khera, R., Samson, M. and Shiva Kumar, A. K. (2011), *Probe Revisited: A Report on Elementary Education in India* (New Delhi: Oxford University Press).

Drèze, J. P. and Khera, R. (2012a), 'Regional Patterns of Human and Child Development', *Economic and Political Weekly*, 29 September.

Drèze, J. P. and Sen, A. K. (1989), *Hunger and Public Action* (Oxford: Oxford University Press).

Drèze, J. P. and Sen, A. K. (1995), *India: Economic Development and Social Opportunity* (Oxford: Oxford University Press).

Drèze, J. P. and Sen, A. K. (2002), *India: Development and Participation* (Oxford: Oxford University Press).

El Arifeen, S. et al. (2012), 'Community-based Approaches and Partnerships: Innovations in Health Service Delivery in Bangladesh', *mimeo*, International Centre for Diarrhoeal Diseases Research, Dhaka.

Ferreira de Souza, Pedro H. G. (2012), 'Poverty, Inequality and Social Policies in Brazil, 1995–2009', *Working Paper 87*, International Policy Centre for Inclusive Growth, Brasilia.

Ferreira, F., Leite, P. and Ravallion, M. (2010), 'Poverty Reduction without Economic Growth? Explaining Brazil's Poverty Dynamics 1985–2004', *Journal of Development Economics*, 93.

Ferreira, F. and Robalino, D. (2010), 'Social Protection in Latin America: Achievements and Limitations', *Policy Research Working Paper 5305*, World Bank, Washington, DC.

Fleury, Sonia (2011), 'Brazil's Health-Care Reform: Social Movements and Civil Society', *The Lancet*, 377.

Giridharadas, Anand (2011), *India Calling: An Intimate Portrait of a Nation's Remaking* (New Delhi: Fourth Estate).

Government of India (1993), *Report of the Expert Group on Estimation of Proportion and Number of Poor* (New Delhi: Planning Commission).

Government of India (2011b), 'Provisional Population Tables', *Census of India 2011, Series 1 (India), Paper 1 of 2011* (New Delhi: Office of the Registrar General).

Government of India (2012c), *Press Note on Poverty Estimates, 2009–10* (New Delhi: Planning Commission).

Harriss, J., Jeyarajan, J. and Nagaraj, K. (2010), 'Land, Labour and Caste Politics in Rural Tamil Nadu in the 20th Century', *Economic and Political Weekly*, 31 July.

Heller, Patrick (1999), *The Labor of Development: Workers and the Transformation of Capitalism in Kerala, India* (Ithaca, NY: Cornell University Press).

Heller, Patrick (2000), 'Degrees of Democracy: Some Comparative Lessons from India', *World Politics*, 52.

Heller, Patrick (2009), 'Democratic Deepening in India and South Africa', *Journal of Asian and African Studies*, 44.

International Institute for Population Sciences (2007a), *National Family Health Survey (NFHS-3), 2005–06: India* (Mumbai: IIPS).

Isaac, T. and Tharakan, M. (1995), 'Kerala: Towards a New Agenda', *Economic and Political Weekly*, 5 August.

Jurberg, C. and Humphreys, G. (2010), 'Brazil's March Towards Universal Coverage', *WHO Bulletin*, 88.

Kabeer, Naila (2011), 'Between Affiliation and Autonomy: Navigating Pathways of Women's Empowerment and Gender Justice in Rural Bangladesh', *Development and Change*, 42.

Koehlmoos, T. P., Islam, Z., Anwar, S., Hossain, S. A. S., Gazi, R., Streatfield, P. K. and Bhuiya, A. U. (2011), 'Health Transcends Poverty: The Bangladesh Experience', in *Balabanova et al. (2011)*.

Lewis, David (2011), *Bangladesh: Politics, Economics and Civil Society* (Cambridge: Cambridge University Press).

Lin Chen, de Haan, A., Zhang, X. and Warmerdam, W. (2012), 'Addressing Vulnerability in an Emerging Economy: China's New Cooperative Medical Scheme (NCMS)', *Canadian Journal of Development Studies*, 32.

Lloyd-Sherlock, P. (2009), 'Social Policy and Inequality in Latin America', *Social Policy and Administration*, 43.

Mahmud, S. (2003), 'Is Bangladesh Experiencing a Feminization of the Labor Force?', *Bangladesh Development Studies*, 29.

Mahmud, W. (2008), 'Social Development in Bangladesh: Pathways, Surprises and Challenges', *Indian Journal of Human Development*, 2.

Meng, Q., Xu, L., Zhang, Y., Qian, J., Cai, M., Xin, Y., Gao, J., Xu, K., Boerma, J. T. And Barber, S. L. (2012), 'Trends in Access to Health Services and Financial Protection in China between 2003 and 2011: A Cross-Sectional Study', *The Lancet*, 379.

National Institute of Population Research and Training (2009), *Bangladesh Demographic and Health Survey 2007* (Dhaka, Bangladesh, and Calverton, MD, USA: National Institute of Population Research and Training, Mitra and Associates, and Macro International).

Oommen, M. A. (ed.) (1999), *Rethinking Development: Kerala's Development Experience* (New Delhi: Concept).

Oommen, M. A. (2009), 'Development Policy and the Nature of Society: Understanding the Kerala Model', *Economic, and Political Weekly*, 28 March.

Orenstein, M. A. (2008), 'Postcommunist Welfare States', *Journal of Democracy*, 19.

Osmani, S. R. (1991), 'Social Security in South Asia', in S. E. Ahmad, J. P. Drèze, J. Hills and A. K. Sen (eds.) (1991), *Social Security in Developing Countries* (Oxford: Oxford University Press).

Osmani, S. R. (2010), 'Towards Achieving the Right to Health', *Bangladesh Development Studies*, 33.

OXFAM International (2006), *Serve the Essentials: What Governments and Donors Must Do to Improve South Asia's Essential Services* (New Delhi: OXFAM India Trust).

Paim, J., Travassos, C., Almeida, C., Bahia, L. and Macinko, J. (2011), 'The Brazilian Health System: History, Advances, and Challenges', *The Lancet*, 377.

Panday, Pranab Kumar (2008), 'Representation without Participation: Quotas for Women in Bangladesh', *International Political Science Review*, 29.

Pierri, Gaston (2012), 'Development Strategies and Law in Latin America: Argentine, Brazilian and Chilean Conditional Cash Transfer Programs in Comparative Perspective', *Documentos de Trabajo 05/2012, Institute Universitario de Analysis Económico y Social, Universidad de Alcala.*

PROBE Team (1999), *Public Report on Basic Education* (New Delhi: Oxford University Press).

Ramachandran, V. K. (1996), 'Kerala's Development Achievements', in *Drèze and Sen (1996)*.

Ravallion, Martin (2011), 'A Comparative Perspective on Poverty Reduction in Brazil, China and India', *World Bank Research Observer*, 26.

Sen, Amartya (1999), *Development as Freedom* (New York: Knopf, and Oxford: Oxford University Press).

Sen, B., Mujeri, M. K. and Shahabuddin, Q. (2007), 'Explaining Pro-Poor Growth in Bangladesh: Puzzles, Evidence, and Implications', in T. Besley and L. J. Cord (eds.) (2007), *Delivering on the Promise of Pro-Poor Growth* (New York: Palgrave Macmillan).

Singh, P. (2010a), 'We-ness and Welfare: A Longitudinal Analysis of Social Development in Kerala, India', *World Development*, 39.

Singh, P. (2010b), 'Subnationalism and Social Development: A Comparative Analysis of Indian States', PhD thesis, Princeton University; to be published as a monograph.

Soares, F. V. (2011), 'Brazil's Bolsa Familia: A Review', *Economic and Political Weekly*, 21 May.

Soares, F. V., Ribas, R. P. and Osório, R. G. (2010), 'Evaluating the Impact of Brazil's Bolsa Familia: Conditional Cash Transfers in Perspective', *Latin American Research Review*, 45.

Sobhan, Rehman (2011), 'Bangladesh at 40: Looking Back and Moving Forward', *mimeo*, Centre for Policy Dialogue, Dhaka.

Spears, Dean (2012a), 'Effects of Rural Sanitation on Child Mortality and Human Capital: Evidence from India's Total Sanitation Campaign', *Working Paper, Research Institute for Compassionate Economics*.

Spears, Dean (2012b), 'How Much International Variation in Child Height Can Sanitation Explain?', *Working Paper, Research Institute for Compassionate Economics*.

Spears, Dean (2013), 'The Long and Short of Open Defecation', *The Hindu*, 14 March.

Srinivasan, Vivek (2010), 'Understanding Public Services in Tamil Nadu: An Institutional Perspective', PhD dissertation, *University of Syracuse, NY; to be published as a monograph*.

Stiglitz, J. E. (2002), *Globalization and its Discontents* (New York: Norton & Co.).

Tharamangalam, J. (1998), 'The Perils of Social Development Without Economic Growth: The Development Debacle of Kerala, India', *Bulletin of Concerned Asian Scholars*, 30.

UNICEF (2012), *The State of the World's Children 2012* (New York: UNICEF).

Wang, S. (2008), 'Double Movement in China', *Economic and Political Weekly*, 27 December.

World Bank (2007), *Whispers to Voices: Gender and Social Transformation in Bangladesh* (Washington, DC: World Bank).

World Bank (2011a), *Perspectives on Poverty in India: Stylised Facts from Survey Data* (Washington, DC: World Bank).

Yip, W. and Mahal, A. (2008), 'The Health Care Systems of China and India', *Health Affairs*, 27.

Yip, W. C. M., Hsiao, W. C., Chen, W., Hu, S., Ma, J. and Maynard, A. (2012), 'Early Appraisal of China's Huge and Complex Health-Care Reforms', *The Lancet*, 379.

3

Unto this last

Sarvodaya—non-violent social transformation

Mohandas Karamchand Gandhi

Source: Raghavan Iyer (ed.), *The Moral and Political Writings of Mahatma Gandhi* (Oxford: Clarendon Press, 1987), pp. 410–33.

§ I. Unto this last *180.* Sarvodaya[1] / Unto this last/

Preface

People in the West generally hold that it is man's duty to promote the happiness—prosperity, that is—of the greatest number.[2] Happiness is taken to mean material happiness exclusively, that is, economic prosperity. If, in the pursuit of this happiness, moral laws are violated, it does not matter much. Again, as the object is the happiness of the greatest number, people in the West do not believe it to be wrong if it is secured at the cost of the minority. The consequences of this attitude are in evidence in all western countries.

The exclusive quest for the physical and material happiness of the majority has no sanction in divine law. In fact, some thoughtful persons in the West have pointed out that it is contrary to divine law to pursue happiness in violation of moral principles. The late John Ruskin[3] was foremost among these. He was an Englishman of great learning. He has written numerous books on art and crafts. He has also written a great deal on ethical questions. One of these books, a small one, Ruskin himself believed to be his best. It is read widely wherever English is spoken. In the book, he has effectively countered these arguments and shown that the well-being of the people at large consists in conforming to the moral law.

We in India are much given nowadays to imitation of the West. We do grant that it is necessary to imitate the West in certain respects. At the same time there is no doubt that many western ideas are wrong. It will be admitted on all hands that what is bad must be eschewed. The condition of Indians in South Africa is pitiable. We go out to distant lands to make money. We are so taken up with this that we become oblivious of morality and of God. We become engrossed in the pursuit of self-interest. In the sequel, we find that going abroad does us more harm than good, or does not profit us as much as it ought to. All religions presuppose the moral law, but even if we disregard religion as such, its observance is necessary on grounds of common sense also. Our happiness consists in observing it. This is what John Ruskin has established. He has opened the eyes of the western people to this, and today, we see a large number of Europeans modelling their conduct on his teaching. In order that Indians may profit by his ideas, we have decided to present extracts from his book, in a manner intelligible to Indians who do not know English.

Socrates gave us some idea of man's duty. He practised his precepts. It can be argued that Ruskin's ideas are an elaboration of Socrates'. Ruskin has described vividly how one who wants to live by Socrates' ideas should acquit himself in the different vocations. The summary of his work which we offer here is not really a translation. If we translated it, the common reader might be unable to follow some of the Biblical allusions, etc. We present therefore only the substance of Ruskin's work. We do not even explain what the title of the book means, for it can be understood only by a person who has read the Bible in English.[4] But since the object which the book works towards is the welfare of all—that is, the advancement of all and not merely of the greatest number—we have entitled these articles *'Sarvodaya'*.

Roots of truth

Man suffers from many delusions; but none so great as his attempt to formulate laws for the conduct of other men disregarding the effects of social affection, as if they were only machines at work. That we cherish such an illusion does us no credit. Like other forms of error, the laws of political economy also contain an element of plausibility. Political economists assert that social affections are to be looked upon as accidental and disturbing elements in human nature; but avarice and the desire for progress are constant elements. Let us eliminate the inconstants and, considering man merely as a money-making machine, examine by what laws of labour, purchase and sale, the greatest amount of wealth can be accumulated. Those laws once determined, it will be for each individual afterwards to introduce as much of the disturbing affectional elements as he chooses.

This would be a convincing argument if the social affections were of the same nature as the laws of demand and supply. Man's affections constitute an inner force. The laws of demand and supply are formulations concerning the external world. The two, therefore, are not of the same nature. If a moving body is acted upon by a constant force from one direction and a varying force from another, we would first measure the constant force and then the inconstant. We will be able to determine the velocity of the body by comparing the two forces. We can do this because the constant and the inconstant forces are of the same kind. But in social dealings the constant force of the laws of demand and supply and the accidental force of social affection are forces that differ in kind. Affection has a different kind of effect on man and acts in a different manner. It changes man's nature, so that we cannot measure its effect with the help of laws of addition and subtraction, as we can the effects of different forces on the velocity of a body. A knowledge of the laws of exchange is of no help in determining the effects of man's social affections.

I do not doubt the conclusions of the science of economics if its premises are accepted. If a gymnast formulated laws on the assumption that man is made only of flesh without a skeleton, those laws might well be valid, but they would not apply to man, since man has a skeleton. In the same way, the laws of political economy may be valid but they cannot apply to man, who is subject to affections. A physical-culture expert may suggest that man's flesh be detached from the skeleton, rolled into pellets, and then drawn out into cables. He may then say that the re-insertion of the skeleton will cause little inconvenience. We should describe such a man as a madcap, for the laws of physical culture cannot be based on the separation of the skeleton from the flesh. In the same manner, the laws of political economy which exclude human affections are of no use to man. And yet the political economists of today behave exactly like the gymnastic instructor. According to their mode of reasoning, man is a mere body—a machine—and they base their laws on this assumption. Though aware that man has a soul, they do not take it into account. How can such a science apply to man, in whom the soul is the predominant element?

Every time there is a strike, we have a clean proof that economics is not a science, that it is worse than useless. In such situations, the employers take one view of the matter, the workers another. Here we cannot apply the laws of supply and demand. Men rack their brains to prove that the interests of the employers and the employees are identical.

These men know nothing of such matters. In fact, it does not always follow that because their worldly interests—economic interests—are at variance men must be antagonistic to each other. Let us suppose that the members of a family are starving. The family consists of a mother and her children. They have only one crust of bread between them. All of them are hungry. Here, the interests of the two—of the mother on the one hand, and the children on the other—are mutually opposed. If the mother eats, the children will starve; if the children are fed, the mother will go hungry. There is no hostility between the mother and the children for that reason; they are not antagonistic to one another. Though the mother is the stronger, she does not eat up the bread. The same is true of men's relations with one another.

Let us suppose that there is no difference between men and animals, and that we must fight like animals in pursuit of our respective interests. Even so we can lay down no general rule either way on whether or not the employer and the employee will always remain hostile to each other. Their attitudes change with circumstances. For instance, it is in the interest of both that work should be well and properly done and a just price obtained for it. But in the division of profits, the gain of the one may or may not be the loss of the other. It does not serve the employer's interests to pay wages so low as to leave his men sickly and depressed. Nor does it serve the worker's interests to demand a high wage irrespective of whether the factory pays its way or not. If the owner does not have enough money to keep the engine-wheels in repair, it will obviously be wrong for the worker to demand full wages or to demand any wages at all.

We can thus see that we are not likely to succeed in constructing a science on the basis of the principle of supply and demand. It was never God's intention that the affairs of men should be conducted on the principle of profit and loss. Justice must provide the basis. Man must give up, therefore, all thought of advancing his interests by following expediency regardless of moral considerations. It is not always possible to predict with certainty the outcome of a given line of conduct. But in most cases we can determine whether a certain act is just or unjust. We can also assert that the result of moral conduct is bound to be good. We cannot predict what that result will be, or how it will come about.

Justice includes affection. The relation between master and operative depends on this element of affection. Let us assume that the master wants to exact the utmost amount of work from his servant. He allows him no time for rest, pays him a low wage, and lodges him in a garret. In brief, he pays him a bare subsistence wage. It may be argued that there is no injustice in all this. The servant has placed all his time at the master's disposal in return for a given wage, and the latter avails himself of it. He determines the limits of hardship in exacting work by reference to what others do. If the servant can get a better place, he is free to take it. This is called economics by those who formulate the laws of supply and demand. They assert that it is profitable to the master thus to exact the maximum amount of work for the minimum wage. In the long run, the entire society will benefit by it and, through the society, the servant himself.

But on reflection we find that this is not quite true. This method of calculation would have been valid if the employee were a mere machine which required some kind of force to drive it. But in this case the motive power of the servant is his soul, and soul-force contradicts and falsifies all the calculations of the economists. The machine that is man cannot be driven by the money-fuel to do the maximum amount of work. Man will give of his best only when his affections are brought into play. The master–servant nexus must not be a pecuniary one, but one of love.

It usually happens that, if the master is a man of sense and energy, the servant works hard enough, under pressure; it also happens that, if the master is indolent and weak, the performance of the servant is not of the best in quality or quantity. But the true law is that, if we compare two masters of equal intelligence, the servant of the one who is sympathetically inclined will work better than that of the other who is not so inclined.

It may be argued that this principle does not quite hold, since kindness and indulgence are sometimes rewarded with their opposites. The servant becomes unmanageable. But the argument is nevertheless invalid. A servant who rewards kindness with negligence will become vengeful when treated harshly. A servant who is dishonest to a liberal master will be injurious to an unjust one.

Therefore, in any case and with any person, this unselfish treatment will yield the most effective return. We are here considering affections only as a motive power. That we should be kind because kindness is good is quite another consideration. We are not thinking of that for the present. We only want to point out here that not only are the ordinary laws of economics, which we considered above, rendered nugatory by the motive power of kindness—sympathy—but also that affection, being a power of an altogether different kind, is inconsonant with the laws of economics and can survive only if those laws are ignored. If the master is a calculating person who shows kindness only in expectation of a return, he will probably be disappointed. Kindness should be exercised for the sake of kindness; the reward will then come unsought. It is said that he who loses his life shall find it, and he who finds it shall lose it.[5]

Let us take the example of a regiment and its commander. If a general seeks to get his troops to work in accordance with the principles of economics, he will fail. There are many instances of generals cultivating direct, personal relations with their men, treating them with kindness, sharing their joys and hardships, ensuring their safety—in brief, treating them with sympathy. A general of this kind will be able to exact the most arduous work from his troops. If we look into history, we shall rarely find a battle won where the troops had no love for their general. Thus the bond of sympathy between the general and his troops is the truest force. Even a band of robbers has the utmost affection for its leader. And yet we find no such intimate relation between the employer and the employees in textile mills and other factories. One reason for this is that, in these factories, the wages of the employees are determined by the laws of supply and demand. Between the employer and the employee there obtains, therefore, the relation of disaffection rather than of affection, and instead of sympathy between them we find antagonism. We have then to consider two questions: one, how far the rate of wages may be so regulated as not to vary with the demand for labour; second, how far workmen can be maintained in factories, without any change in their numbers irrespective of the state of trade, with the same bond [between workmen and employer] as obtains between servants and master in an old family, or between soldiers and their commander.

Let us consider the first question. It is surprising why economists do nothing to make it possible for standards of payment for factory workers to be fixed. We see, on the other hand, that the office of the Prime Minister of England is not put up to auction, but that whoever the incumbent, the remuneration remains the same. Nor do we offer the job of a priest to anyone who agrees to accept the lowest salary. With physicians and lawyers, too, we do not generally deal in this manner. Thus we observe that in these instances a certain standard of payment is fixed. It may be asked, however, whether a good workman and a bad one must both be paid the same wage. In fact, that is as it should be. In the result, the rate of wages for all workers being the same, we shall engage only a good bricklayer or carpenter as we go only to a good physician or lawyer—the fees of all physicians or lawyers being the same. That is the proper reward of a good workman—to be chosen. Therefore, the right system respecting all labour is that it should be paid at fixed rates. Where a bad workman finds it possible to deceive employers by accepting a low wage, the eventual outcome cannot but be bad.

Let us now consider the second point. It is that, whatever the state of trade, the factories must maintain the same number of workers in employment. When there is no security of employment, the workers are obliged to ask for higher wages. If, however, they can be assured of continued employment for life, they will be prepared to work for very low wages. It is clear, therefore, that the employer who assures security of employment to his workers will find it profitable in the long run. The employees also stand to gain if they continue steadily in the same job. Large profits are not possible in factories run on these lines. Big risks cannot be taken. Gambling on a large scale will not be possible. The soldier is ready to lay down his life for the sake of his commander. That is why the work of a soldier is considered more honourable than that of an ordinary worker. The soldier's trade is really not slaying, but being slain in defence of others. Anyone who enlists as a soldier holds his life at the service of the state. This is true also of the lawyer, the physician and the priest. That is why we look up to them with respect. A lawyer must do justice even at the cost of his life. The physician must treat his patients at the cost of inconvenience to himself. And the clergyman must instruct his congregation and direct it along the right path, regardless of consequences.

If this can happen in the professions mentioned, why not in trade and commerce? Why is it that trade is always associated with unscrupulousness? We shall see on reflection that it is always assumed that the merchant is moved solely by self-interest. Even though he has a socially useful function, we take it for granted that his object is to fill his own coffers. Even the laws are so drafted as to enable the merchant to amass wealth with the utmost speed. It is also accepted as a principle that the buyer must offer the lowest possible price and the seller must demand and accept the highest. The trader has thus been encouraged in this habit, yet the public themselves look down on him for his dishonesty. This principle must be abandoned. It is not right that the merchant should look only to self-interest and amass wealth. This is not trade, but robbery. The soldier lays down his life for the state and the trader ought to suffer a comparable loss, ought even to lose his life in the interests of society. In all states the soldier's profession is to defend the people; the pastor's to teach it; the physician's to keep it in health; the lawyer's to enforce pure justice in it; and the merchant's to provide for it. And it is the duty of each on due occasion to die for the people. The soldier must be prepared to die at his post of duty rather than desert it. During a plague epidemic, the physician must not run away from his task but instead attend to the patients even at the risk of infection. The priest must lead people from error to truth even if they should kill him for it. The lawyer must ensure, even at the cost of his life, that justice prevails.[6]

We pointed out above the proper occasions for members of the professions to lay down their lives. What, then, is the proper occasion for the merchant to lay down his life? This is a question which all, the merchant included, must ask themselves. The man who does not know when to die does not know how to live. We have seen that the merchant's function is to provide for the people. Just as the clergyman's function is not to earn a stipend but to instruct, so the merchant's function is not to make profits but to provide for the people. The clergyman who devotes himself to preaching has his needs provided for, and in the same manner the merchant will have his profits. But neither of them must have an eye only on the main chance. Both have work to do—each a duty to perform—irrespective of whether or not they get the stipend or the profit. If this proposition is true, the merchant deserves the highest honour. For his duty is to procure commodities of high quality and distribute them at a price which people can afford. It also becomes his duty at the same time to ensure the safety and well-being of the hundreds or thousands of men working under him. This requires a great deal of patience, kindness and intelligence. Also, in discharging these several functions he is bound, as others are bound, to give up his life, if need be. Such a trader would not sell adulterated goods or cheat anyone, whatever his difficulties or even if he was going to be reduced to utter poverty. Moreover, he will treat the men under him with the utmost kindness. Very often a young man taking up a situation with a big factory or commercial house travels a long way from home, so that the master has to accept the role of his parents. If the master is indifferent, the young man will be like an orphan. At every step, therefore, the merchant or the master must ask himself this question, 'Do I deal with my servants as I do with my sons?'

Suppose a ship's captain places his son among the common sailors under his command. The captain's duty is to treat all sailors as he would treat his son. In the same manner, a merchant may ask his son to work alongside of those under him. He must always treat the workers as he would then treat his son. This is the true meaning of economics. And as the captain is bound to be the last man to leave his ship in case of shipwreck, so in the event of famine or other calamities, the trader is bound to safeguard the interests of his men before his own. All this may sound strange. But the really strange thing about the modern age is that it should so sound. For anyone who applies his mind to it will be able to see that the true principle is as we have stated it. Any other standard is impossible for a progressive nation. If the British have survived so long, it is not because they have lived up to the maxims of economics, but because they have had many heroes who have questioned them and followed instead these principles of moral conduct. The harm that results from the violation of these principles and the nation's consequent decline from greatness, we shall consider on another occasion.

Veins of wealth

Economists may reply in the following manner to what we said earlier concerning 'roots of truth': 'It is true that certain advantages flow from social affection. But economists do not take these advantages into their reckoning. The science with which they are concerned is the science of getting rich. Far from being fallacious, it has in experience been found to be effective. Those who follow it do become rich, and those who disregard it become poor. All the millionaires of Europe have acquired their wealth by following the laws of this science. It is futile to seek to controvert this. Every man of the world knows how money is made and how it is lost.'

This is not quite true. Men of business do indeed make money but they do not know whether they make it by fair means and if their money-making contributes to the national wealth. Very often they do not even know the meaning of the word 'rich'. They do not realize that, if there are rich men, there must also be poor men. People sometimes believe, mistakenly, that by following certain precepts it is possible for everybody to become rich. But the true position can be compared to a water-wheel where one bucket empties out as another fills. The power of the rupee you possess depends on another going without it. If no one wants it, it will be useless to you. The power it possesses depends on your neighbour's lack of it. There can be wealth only where there is scarcity. This means that, in order to be rich, one must keep another poor.

Political economy consists in the production, preservation and distribution, at the fittest time and place, of useful and pleasurable things. The farmer who reaps his harvest at the right time, the builder who lays bricks properly, the carpenter who attends to woodwork with care, the woman who runs her kitchen efficiently are all true political economists. All of them add to the national income. A science that teaches the opposite of this is not 'political'. Its only concern is with individuals merely accumulating a certain metal and putting it to profitable use by keeping others in want of it. Those who do this estimate their wealth—the value of their farms and cattle—by the number of rupees they can get for them, rather than the value of their rupees by the number of cattle and farms they can buy with them. Furthermore, men who thus accumulate metal—rupees—think in terms of the number of workmen whose services they can command. Let us suppose that a certain individual possesses gold, silver, corn, etc. This person will require a servant. And if none of his neighbours is in need of gold, silver or corn, he will find it difficult to get one. He will then have to bake his bread, make his clothes and plough his field all by himself. This man will find his gold to be of no greater value than the yellow pebbles on his estate. His hoard of corn will rot. For he cannot consume more than his neighbour. He must therefore maintain himself by hard labour as other men do. Most people will not want to accumulate gold or silver on these terms.

Careful reflection will show that what we really desire through acquisition of wealth is power over other men—power to acquire for our advantage the labour of a servant, a tradesman or an artisan. And the power we can thus acquire will be in direct proportion to the poverty of others. If there is only one person in a position to employ a carpenter, the latter will accept whatever wage is offered. If there are three or four persons who need his services, he will work for the person who offers him the highest wage. So that growing rich means contriving that as large a number of men as possible shall have less than we have. Economists generally assume that it is of advantage to the nation as a whole if the mass of people are thus kept in want. Equality among men is certainly not possible. But conditions of scarcity, unjustly created, injure the nation. Scarcity and abundance arising naturally make, and keep, the nation happy.

Thus the circulation of wealth among a people resembles the circulation of blood in the body. When circulation of blood is rapid, it may indicate any of these things: robust health, effects of exercise, or a feeling of shame or fever. There is a flush of the body which is indicative of health, and another which is a sign of gangrene. Furthermore, the concentration of blood at one spot is harmful to the body and, similarly, concentration of wealth at one place proves to be the nation's undoing.

Let us suppose that two sailors are shipwrecked on an uninhabited coast. They are then obliged to produce food and other necessaries of life through their own labour. If they both keep good health and work in amity, they may build a good house, till the land and lay by something for the future. All these things would constitute real wealth. If both of them work equally well, they will have equal shares. Therefore, all that economic science would have to say about their case is that they had acquired a right to an equal share in the fruits of their labour. Let us suppose now that after a while one of them feels discontented. So they divide the land and each one works on his land by himself and on his own account. Let us suppose that at a critical time one of them falls ill. He would then approach the other for help. The latter might reply: 'I shall do this work for you, but on condition that you do the same amount of work for me when required. You must undertake in writing to work on my field when required for the same number of hours that I work for you now.' Suppose further that the disabled man's illness continues and that every time he has to give a written promise to the other, healthy person. What will be the position of the two men when the invalid recovers? They will both of them have been reduced to utter poverty. For, during the time that the invalid was laid up, his labour was unavailable. Even assuming that the friend was very hard-working, it is obvious that the time which he devoted to the ailing man's land was at the expense of work on his own. This means that the combined property of the two would be less than it would have been otherwise.

Also, the relation in which the two stood to each other has altered. The sick man becomes a debtor, and can only offer his labour as payment towards the debt. Suppose now that the healthy man decided to make use of the documents in his possession. He would then find it possible wholly to abstain from work—that is, be idle. If he chose, he could exact further pledges[7] from the man who has recovered. No one can attribute any illegality to such a transaction. If now a stranger were to arrive on the scene, he would find that one of the two men had become wealthy and the other had lost his wellbeing. He would also see one of them passing his days in idle luxury and the other in want, though labouring hard. The reader will note from this that claiming the fruits of another's labour as of right leads to a diminution of real wealth.

Let us consider another illustration. Suppose that three men established a kingdom and then they all lived separately. Each of them raised a different crop which the others could also avail themselves of. Suppose, further, that one of them, in order to save the time of all the three, gave up farming and undertook to arrange the transfer of commodities from one to the other, receiving in return a quantity of food-grains. If this man provided the required commodity[8] at the right time, all of them would prosper. Now suppose that he kept back some of the grain he was to transfer. Then suppose there set in a period of scarcity, and the middleman offered the stolen corn at an exorbitant price. In this way he could reduce both the farmers to poverty and employ them as labourers.

This would be a case of obvious injustice. This is, however, the way the merchants of today manage their affairs. We can also see that in consequence of this fraudulent practice the wealth of the three, taken collectively, will be less than it would have been if the middleman had behaved honestly. The other two farmers have done less work than they could have. Because they could not obtain the supplies they wanted, their labour did not fructify to the fullest, and the stolen commodities[9] in the hands of the dishonest middleman were not put to the most effective use.

We can therefore reckon with mathematical accuracy how far the estimate of a nation's wealth depends on the manner in which that wealth has been acquired. We cannot estimate a nation's wealth on the basis of the quantity of cash it possesses. Cash in the hands of an individual may be a token of perseverance, skill and prosperity, or of harmful luxuries, merciless tyranny and chicanery. Our way of estimating wealth not only takes into account the moral attributes of the different modes of acquiring it but is also sound mathematically. One stock of money is such that it has created ten times as much in the gathering of it. Another is such that it has annihilated ten times as much in the gathering of it.

To lay down directions for the making of money without regard to moral considerations is therefore a pursuit that bespeaks of man's insolence. There is nothing more disgraceful to man than the principle 'buy in the cheapest market and sell in the dearest'. Buy in the cheapest market? Yes, but what made your market cheap? Charcoal may be cheap among roof timbers after a fire and the bricks of buildings brought down by an earthquake may be cheap. But no one, therefore, will make bold to assert that fire and earthquake redound to the nation's benefit. Again, sell in the dearest market? Yes, but what made your market dear? You made good profit today from the sale of your bread. But was it by extorting the last cowrie from a dying man? Or, did you sell it to a rich man who will tomorrow appropriate all that you have? Or did you give it to a bandit on his way to pillaging your bank? Probably you will not be able to answer any of these questions, for you do not know. But there is one question you can answer, namely, whether you sold it justly and at a reasonable price. And justice is all that matters. It is your duty to act so that no one suffers through your actions.

We saw that the value of money consists in its power to command the labour of men. If that labour could be had without payment, there should be no further need of money. Instances are known where human labour can be had without payment. We have considered examples which show that moral power is more effective than the power of money. We also saw that man's goodness can do what money cannot do. There exist men in many parts of England who cannot be beguiled with money.

Moreover, if we admit that wealth carries with it the power to direct labour, we shall also see that the more intelligent and moral men are, the greater is the wealth amassed. It may even appear on a fuller consideration that the persons themselves constitute the wealth, not gold and silver. We must search for wealth not in the bowels of the earth, but in the hearts of men. If this is correct, the true law of economics is that men must be maintained in the best possible health, both of body and mind, and in the highest state of honour. A time may also come when England, instead of adorning the turbans of its slaves with diamonds from Golkonda and thus sporting her wealth, may be able to point to her great men of virtue, saying, in the words of a truly eminent Greek, 'This is my wealth.'

Even-handed justice[10]

Some centuries before Christ there lived a Jewish merchant, Solomon[11] by name. He had made a large fortune and earned great fame. His maxims are remembered in Europe even today. He was so beloved of the Venetians that they erected a statue in the city to his memory. Though his maxims are known by rote, very few persons actually practise them. He says: 'Those who make money through lies are afflicted with pride, and that is a sign of their death.' At another place, he adds: 'Treasures of wickedness profit nothing. It is truth which delivers from death.'[12] In both these maxims Solomon asserts that death is the outcome of wealth unjustly acquired. Nowadays, people tell lies or perpetrate injustice so cleverly that we cannot find them out. For there are misleading advertisements. Things bear attractive labels, and so on.

Again the wise man says: 'He that oppresseth the poor to multiply his riches shall surely come to want.' And he adds: 'Rob not the poor because he is poor. Oppress not the afflicted in the place of business. For God will corrupt the soul of those that torment them.' At present, however, it is the practice in business to administer kicks to those who are already dead. We are eager to take advantage of a needy man. The highwayman robs the rich, but the trader robs the poor.

Solomon says further: 'The rich and the poor are equal. God is their maker. God gives them knowledge.'[13] The rich and the poor cannot live, the one without the other. They always need each other. Neither of them can be regarded as superior or inferior to the other. But evil consequences follow when the two forget that they are equal, and that God of their light.

Wealth is like a river. A river always flows towards the sea, that is, down an incline. So, as a general rule must wealth go where it is needed. But the flow of wealth, like the course of a river, can be regulated. Most of the rivers run out their courses unregulated, their marshy banks poisoning the wind. If dams are built across these rivers to direct the water flow as required, they will irrigate the soil and keep the atmosphere pure. Similarly the uncontrolled use of wealth will multiply vices among men and cause starvation; in brief, such wealth will act like a poison. But the selfsame wealth, if its circulation is regulated and its use controlled, can, like a river whose stream has been properly harnessed, promote prosperity.

The principle of regulating the circulation of wealth is ignored altogether by economists. Theirs is merely the science of getting rich. But there are many different ways of getting rich. There was a time in Europe when people sought to acquire wealth by poisoning owners of large estates and appropriating their possessions. Nowadays, merchants adulterate the food sold to the poor, for example, milk with borax, wheat flour with potato flour, coffee with chicory, butter with fat and so on. This is on the same level as getting rich by poisoning others. Can we call this either an art or a science of getting rich?

Let us now, however, assume that by 'getting rich' economists merely mean 'getting rich by robbing others'. They should point out that theirs is a science of getting rich by legal or just means. It happens these days that many things which are legal are not just. The only right way, therefore, to acquire wealth is to do so justly. And if this is true, we must know what is just. It is not enough to live by the laws of demand and supply. Fish, wolves and rats subsist in that manner. Bigger fish prey on smaller ones, rats swallow insects and wolves devour even human beings. That for them is the law of Nature; they know no better. But God has endowed man with understanding, with a sense of justice. He must follow these and not think of growing rich by devouring others—by cheating others and reducing them to beggary.

Let us examine what then the laws of justice regarding payment of labour are.

As we stated earlier, a just wage for a worker will be that which will secure him the same labour, when he needs it, as he has put in for us today. If we give him a lower wage, he will be underpaid, and if more, overpaid.

Suppose a man wants to engage a worker. Two persons offer their services. If the man who offers to accept a lower wage is engaged, he will be underpaid. If there is a large number of employers and only one worker, he will get his own terms and will very likely be overpaid. The just wage lies between these two points.

If someone lends me money which I have to repay after a time, I shall pay him interest. Similarly, if someone gives me his labour today, I must return him an identical quantity of labour and something more by way of interest. If someone gives me an hour of labour today, I should promise to give him an hour and five minutes or more. This is true of every kind of worker.

If, now, of two men who offer me their services, I engage the one who accepts the lower wage, the result will be that he will be half-starved while the other man will remain unemployed. Even otherwise, if I pay full wages to the workman whom I employ, the other man will be unemployed. But the former will not starve, and I shall have made just use of my money. Starvation really occurs only when the due wages are not paid. If I pay due wages, surplus wealth will not accumulate in my hands. I shall not waste money on luxuries and add to the poverty. The workman whom I pay justly will in turn learn to pay others justly. Thus the stream of justice will not dry up; instead it will gather speed as it flows. And the nation which has such a sense of justice will grow happy and prosper in the right direction.

According to this line of reasoning, economists are found to be wrong. They argue that increased competition means growing prosperity for a nation. This is not true in fact. Competition is desired because it reduces the rate of wages. The rich become richer thereby and the poor poorer. Such competition is likely to ruin a nation in the long run. The right law of demand and supply should ensure the payment of a just wage to a workman according to his worth. This, too, will mean competition, but the result will be that people will be happy and skilful, for, instead of being obliged to underbid one another, they will have to acquire new skills to secure employment. It is for this reason that men are drawn to government service. There, salaries are fixed according to the gradation of posts. The competition is only with regard to ability. A candidate does not offer to accept a lower salary but claims that he is abler than others. The same is the case with the Army and the Navy, and that is why there is much less corruption in these services. But only in trade and commerce is there unhealthy competition, as a result of which corrupt practices, such as fraud, chicanery, theft, have increased. Furthermore, goods of poor quality are manufactured. The manufacturer wants a lion's share of the price for himself, the workman to throw dust in the eyes of others and the consumer to exploit the situation to his own advantage. This poisons all human intercourse, there is starvation all round, strikes multiply, manufacturers become rogues and consumers disregard ethical considerations. One injustice leads to numerous others, and in the end the employer, the operative and the customer are all unhappy and meet with ruin. A people among whom these corrupt practices prevail comes to grief in the end. Its very wealth acts like a poison.

This is why men of wisdom have held that where Mammon is God, no one worships the true God. Wealth cannot be reconciled with God. God lives only in the homes of the poor. This is what the British profess, but in practice they place wealth above everything else, estimate the prosperity of the nation by the number of its rich, and their economists formulate precepts for everyone to get rich quickly. True economics is the economics of justice. That people alone will be happy which learns how to do justice and be righteous under all conditions of life. All else is vain, a kind of moral perversity that presages doom. To teach the people to get rich at any cost is to teach them an evil lesson.

What is just?

We saw in the three preceding chapters that the generally accepted principles of economics are invalid. If acted upon, they will make individuals and nations unhappy. The poor will become poorer and the rich richer; neither will be any the happier for it.

Economists do not take men's conduct into account but estimate prosperity from the amount of wealth accumulated and so conclude that the happiness of nations depends upon their wealth alone. Hence they advocate greater accumulation of wealth through more and more work in factories. In England and elsewhere factories have multiplied because of the spread of these ideas. Large numbers of men leave their farms and concentrate in cities. They give up the pure and fresh air of the countryside and feel happy breathing the foul air of factories. As a result, the nation grows weaker, and avarice and immorality increase, and if someone suggests measures for eradicating vice, the so-called wise men argue that vice cannot be eliminated, that the ignorant cannot be educated all at once and that it is best to let things alone. While advancing this argument, they forget that it is the rich who are responsible for the immorality of the poor. The wretched workers slave for them day and night so that they may be kept supplied with their luxuries. They have not a moment to themselves for self-improvement. Thinking about the rich, they also want to be rich. When they fail in this, they become angry and resentful. They then forget themselves [in their anger], and having failed to gather wealth by honest means, turn in desperation to fraud. Both wealth and labour are thus wasted, else they are utilized for promoting fraud.

Labour, in the real sense of the term, is that which produces useful articles. Useful articles are those which support human life. Supporting human life means provision of food, clothing, etc., so as to enable men to live a moral life and to do good while they live. For this purpose, large-scale industrial undertakings would appear to be useless. To seek to acquire wealth by establishing big factories is likely to lead to sin. Many people amass wealth but few make good use of it. If the making of money is likely to lead a nation to its destruction, that money is useless. On the contrary, present-day capitalists are responsible for widespread and unjust wars. Most of the wars of our times spring from greed for money.

We hear people say that it is impossible to educate others so as to improve them, and the best course would be to live as well as one could and accumulate wealth. Those who hold these views show little concern for ethical principles. For the person who values ethical principles and does not yield to avarice has a disciplined mind; he does not stray from the right path, and influences others merely by his example. If the individuals who constitute a nation do not observe moral principles of conduct, how can the nation become moral? If we behave as we choose and then point the accusing finger at an errant neighbour, how can the result of our actions be good?

We thus see that money is no more than a means which may make for happiness or misery. In the hands of a good man, it can be used for cultivating land and raising crops. Cultivators will find contentment in innocent labour and the nation will be happy. In the hands of bad men, it is used for the production, say, of gun-powder, and bringing utter ruin on the people. Both those who manufacture gun-powder and those who fall victims to it suffer in consequence. We thus see that there is no wealth besides life. That nation is wealthy which is moral. This is not the time for self-indulgence. Everyone must work according to his ability. As we saw in the illustrations earlier, if one man remains idle another has to labour twice as hard. This is at the root of the starvation prevalent in England. There are men who do little useful work themselves because of the wealth that has accumulated in their hands, and so force others to labour for them. This kind of labour, being unproductive, is not beneficial to the workers. In consequence, the national income suffers diminution. Though all men appear to be employed, we find on closer scrutiny that a large number are idle perforce. Moreover, envy is aroused, discontent takes root and, in the end, the rich and the poor, the employer and the workman violate the bounds of decency in their mutual relations. As the cat and the mouse are always at variance with each other, so the rich and the poor, the employer and the workman become hostile to one another, and man, ceasing to be man, is reduced to the level of beasts.

Conclusion

Our summary of the great Ruskin's book is now concluded. Though some may have been bored by it, we advise those who have read the articles once to read them again. It will be too much to expect that all the readers of *Indian Opinion* will ponder over them and act on them. But even if a few readers make a careful study of the summary and grasp the central idea, we shall deem our labour to have been amply rewarded. Even if that does not happen, the reward of labour, as Ruskin says in the last chapter, consists in having done one's duty and that should satisfy one.

What Ruskin wrote for his countrymen, the British, is a thousand times more applicable to Indians. New ideas are spreading in India. The advent of a new spirit among the young who have received western education is of course to be welcomed. But the outcome will be beneficial only if that spirit is canalized properly; if it is not, it is bound to be harmful. From one side we hear the cry for *swarajya*; from another, for the quick accumulation of wealth by setting up factories like those in Britain.

Our people hardly understand what *swarajya* means. Natal enjoys *swarajya*, but we would say that, if we were to imitate Natal, *swarajya* would be no better than hell. The Natal whites tyrannize over the Kaffirs, hound out the Indians, and in their blindness give free rein to selfishness. If, by chance, Kaffirs and Indians were to leave Natal, they would destroy themselves in a civil war.

Shall we, then, hanker after the kind of *swarajya* which obtains in the Transvaal? General Smuts is one of their leading figures. He does not keep any promise, oral or written. He says one thing, does another. The British are disgusted with him. Under the guise of effecting economy, he has deprived British soldiers of livelihood and has been replacing them with Dutchmen. We do not believe that in the long run this will make even the Dutch happy. Those who serve only their own interests will be ready to rob their own people after they have done with robbing others.

If we observe happenings all over the world, we shall be able to see that what people call *swarajya* is not enough to secure the nation's prosperity and happiness. We can perceive this by means of a simple example. All of us can visualize what would happen if a band of robbers were to enjoy *swarajya*. In the long run they would be happy only if they were placed under the control of men who were not themselves robbers. America, France and England are all great States. But there is no reason to think that they are really happy.

Real *swarajya* consists in restraint. He alone is capable of this who leads a moral life, does not cheat anyone, does not forsake truth and does his duty to his parents, his wife, his children, his servant and his neighbour. Such a man will enjoy *swarajya* wherever he may happen to live. A nation that has many such men always enjoys *swarajya*.

It is wrong normally for one nation to rule over another. British rule in India is an evil but we need not believe that any very great advantage would accrue to the Indians if the British were to leave India. The reason why they rule over us is to be found in ourselves; that reason is our disunity, our immorality and our ignorance.

If these three things were to disappear, not only would the British leave India without the rustling of a leaf, but it would be real *swarajya* that we would enjoy.

Many people exult at the explosion of bombs. This only shows ignorance and lack of understanding. If all the British were to be killed, those who kill them would become the masters of India, and as a result India would continue in a state of slavery. The bombs with which the British will have been killed will fall on India after the British leave. The man who killed the President of the French Republic was himself a Frenchman and the assassin of President Cleveland of America was an American.[14] We ought to be careful, therefore, not to be hasty and thoughtlessly to imitate the people of the West.

Just as we cannot achieve real *swarajya* by following the path of evil—that is by killing the British—so also will it not be possible for us to achieve it by establishing big factories in India. Accumulation of gold and silver will not bring *swarajya*. This has been convincingly proved by Ruskin.

Let it be remembered that western civilization is only a hundred years old, or to be more precise, fifty. Within this short span the western people appear to have been reduced to a state of cultural anarchy. We pray that India may never be reduced to the same state as Europe. The western nations are impatient to fall upon one another, and are restrained only by the accumulation of armaments all round. When the situation flares up, we will witness a veritable hell let loose in Europe. All white nations look upon the black races as their legitimate prey. This is inevitable when money is the only thing that matters. Wherever they find any territory, they swoop down on it like crows upon carrion. There are reasons to suggest that this is the outcome of their large industrial undertakings.

To conclude, the demand of *swarajya* is the demand of every Indian, and it is a just demand. But *swarajya* is to be achieved by righteous means. It must be real *swarajya*. It cannot be achieved by violent methods or by setting up factories. We must have industry, but of the right kind. India was once looked upon as a golden land, because Indians then were people of sterling worth. The land is still the same but the people have changed and that is why it has become arid. To transform it into a golden land again we must transmute ourselves into gold by leading a life of virtue. The philosopher's stone which can bring this about consists of two syllables: *satya*. If, therefore, every Indian makes it a point to follow truth always, India will achieve *swarajya* as a matter of course.

This is the substance of Ruskin's book.

Sarvodaya [9 articles] (G.)

Indian Opinion, 16 Apr–18 July 1908

Notes

1 The Advancement of All.

2 The reference is to Bentham's maxim of 'the greatest good of the greatest number'. Gandhi opposed it on moral grounds. Ruskin, too, criticized the construction of a 'science' of economics on the Newtonian model from which 'social affections' had been wholly abstracted. Ruskin argued that the greatest art or science was that which aroused 'the greatest number of the greatest ideas'.

3 (1819–1900); a Scotsman and author of many books on architecture, painting, social and industrial problems, the place of women in society, etc.; Slade Professor of Art in Oxford for some time; later became opposed to vivisection and usury and interested in workers' education and co-operative industrial settlements. Together with *Munera Pulveris, Unto This Last*, which was published as a series of articles in *Cornhill Magazine*, expounds Ruskin's social utopia. Gandhi describes Ruskin as 'one of the three moderns ... who made a deep impress on me'. *Unto This Last* 'brought about an instantaneous and practical transformation. ... I arose with the dawn, ready to reduce these principles to practice.' Polak commended this book to Gandhi, who read it on the train journey between Johannesburg and Durban. See *Autobiography*, Part IV, Ch. XVIII.

4 Parable of the Labourers in the Vineyard, St Matthew, Ch. XX, v. 14. 'I will give unto this last, even as unto thee.'

5 St Matthew. Ch. X, v. 39.

6 Ruskin found Beauty in 'the appearance of felicitous fulfilment of function in living things, more especially of the joyful and right exertion of perfect life in man'. (*Modern Painters*, Vol. II, Part III, Sec. I, Ch. 3.) Gandhi, too, speaks of the beauty of *satyagraha*, which is 'suffering undergone to exemplify Truth'.

7 Pledges of bonded labour in return for the provision of the debtor's current needs.

8 Farming implements, seeds, etc.

9 The food-grains and farming implements withheld by the middleman.

10 This corresponds to Ruskin's chapter '*Qui Judicatis Terram*.' 'Ye that be judges of the earth, love righteousness.'

11 (993–953 BC); believed in Ruskin's day to have been the author of Proverbs in the Old Testament.

12 Cf. Proverbs, Ch. XXI, v. 6, and Ch. X, v. 2.

13 Cf. Proverbs, Ch. XXII, v. 2: 'The rich and poor meet together: the Lord is the maker of them all', and Proverbs, Ch. XXIX, v. 13: 'The poor and the deceitful man meet together: the Lord lighteneth both their eyes.'

14 President Cleveland died a natural death. Gandhi may have had Lincoln in mind.

4

The National Planning Committee and the Congress and industry

Big industry versus cottage industry

Jawaharlal Nehru

Source: *The Discovery of India* (New Delhi: Oxford University Press, 1982), pp. 395–409. First published 1946 by The Signet Press, Calcutta.

Towards the end of 1938 a National Planning Committee was constituted at the instance of the Congress. It consisted of fifteen members plus representatives of provincial governments and such Indian states as chose to collaborate with us. Among the members were well-known industrialists, financiers, economists, professors, scientists, as well as representatives of the Trade Union Congress and the Village Industries Association. The non-Congress Provincial Governments (Bengal, Punjab and Sind), as well as some of the major states (Hyderabad, Mysore, Baroda, Travancore, Bhopal) co-operated with this committee. In a sense it was a remarkably representative committee cutting across political boundaries as well as the high barrier between official and non-official India—except for the fact that the Government of India was not represented and took up a non-cooperative attitude. Hard-headed big business was there as well as people who are called idealists and doctrinaires, and socialists and near-communists. Experts and directors of industries came from provincial governments and states.

It was a strange assortment of different types and it was not clear how such an odd mixture would work. I accepted the chairmanship of the committee not without hesitation and misgiving; the work was after my own heart and I could not keep out of it.

Difficulties faced us at every turn. There were not enough data for real planning and few statistics were available. The Government of India was not helpful. Even the provincial governments, though friendly and co-operative, did not seem to be particularly keen on all-India planning and took only a distant interest in our work. They were far too busy with their own problems and troubles. Important elements in the Congress, under whose auspices the committee had come into existence, rather looked upon it as an unwanted child, not knowing how it would grow up and rather suspicious of its future activities. Big business was definitely apprehensive and critical, and probably joined up because it felt that it could look after its interests better from inside the committee than from outside.

It was obvious also that any comprehensive planning could only take place under a free national government, strong enough and popular enough to be in a position to introduce fundamental changes in the social and economic structure. Thus the attainment of national freedom and the elimination of foreign control became an essential pre-requisite for planning. There were many other obstacles—our social backwardness, customs, traditional outlook, etc.—but they had in any event to be faced. Planning thus was not so much for the present, as for an unascertained future, and there was an air of unreality about it. Yet it had to be based on the present and we hoped that this future was not a distant one. If we could collect the available material, co-ordinate it, and draw up blue-prints, we would prepare the ground for the real effective future planning, meanwhile indicating to provincial governments and states the lines on which they should proceed and develop their resources. The attempt to plan and to see the various national activities—economic, social, cultural—fitting into each other, had also a highly educative value for ourselves and the general public. It made the people come out of their narrow grooves of thought and action, to think of problems in relation to one another, and develop to some extent at least a wider co-operative outlook.

The original idea behind the Planning Committee had been to further industrialization—'the problems of poverty and unemployment, of national defence and of economic regeneration in general cannot be solved without industrialization. As a step towards such industrialization, a comprehensive scheme of national planning should be formulated. This scheme should provide for the development of heavy key industries, medium scale industries, and cottage industries. . . .' But no planning could possibly ignore agriculture, which was the main stay of the people; equally important were the social services. So one thing led to another and it was impossible to isolate anything or to progress in one direction without corresponding progress in another. The more we thought of this planning business, the vaster it grew in its sweep and range till it seemed to embrace almost every activity. That did not mean we intended regulating and regimenting everything, but we had to keep almost everything in view even in deciding about one particular sector of the plan. The fascination of this work grew upon me and, I think, upon the other members of our committee also. But at the same time certain vagueness and indefiniteness crept in; instead of concentrating on some major aspects of the plan we tended to become diffuse. This also led to delay in the work of many of our sub-committees which lacked the sense of urgency and of working for a definite objective within a stated time.

Constituted as we were, it was not easy for all of us to agree to any basic social policy or principles underlying social organization. Any attempt to discuss these principles in the abstract was bound to lead to fundamental differences of approach at the outset and possibly to a splitting up of the committee. Not to have such a guiding policy was a serious drawback, yet there was no help for it. We decided to consider the general problem of planning as well as each individual problem concretely and not in the abstract, and allow principles to develop out of such considerations. Broadly speaking, there were two approaches: the socialist one aiming at the elimination of the profit motive and emphasizing the importance of equitable distribution, and the big business one striving to retain free enterprise and the profit motive as far as possible, and laying greater stress on production. There was also a difference in outlook between those who favoured a rapid growth of heavy industry and others who wanted greater attention to be paid to the development of village and cottage industries, thus absorbing the vast number of the unemployed and partially employed. Ultimately there were bound to be differences in the final conclusions. It did not very much matter even if there were two or more reports, provided that all the available facts were collected and coordinated, the common ground mapped out, and the divergencies indicated. When the time came for giving effect to the Plan, the then existing democratic government would have to choose what basic policy to adopt. Meanwhile a great deal of essential preparation would have been made and the various aspects of the problem placed before the public and the various provincial and state governments.

Obviously we could not consider any problem, much less plan, without some definite aim and social objective. That aim was declared to be to ensure an adequate standard of living for the masses, in other words, to get rid of the appalling poverty of the people. The irreducible minimum, in terms of money, had been estimated by economists at figures varying from Rs. 15 to Rs. 25 *per capita* per month. (These are all pre-war figures.) Compared to western standards this was very low, and yet it meant an enormous increase in existing standards in India. An approximate estimate of the average annual income *per capita* was Rs. 65. This included the rich and the poor, the town-dweller, and the villager. In view of the great gulf between the rich and the poor and the concentration of wealth in the hands of a few, the average income of the villager was estimated to be far less, probably about Rs. 30 *per capita* per annum. These figures bring home the terrible poverty of the people and the destitute condition of the masses. There was lack of food, of clothing, of housing and of every other essential requirement of human existence. To remove this lack and ensure an irreducible minimum standard for everybody the national income had to be greatly increased, and in addition to this increased production there had to be a more equitable distribution of wealth. We calculated that a really progressive standard of living would necessitate the increase of the national wealth by 500 or 600 per cent. That was, however, too big a jump for us, and we aimed at a 200 to 300 per cent increase within ten years.

We fixed a ten-year period for the plan, with control figures for different periods and different sectors of economic life.

Certain objective tests were also suggested:

1 The improvement of nutrition—a balanced diet having a calorific value of 2,400 to 2,800 units for an adult worker.
2 Improvement in clothing from the then consumption of about fifteen yards to at least thirty yards *per capita* per annum.
3 Housing standards to reach at least 100 square feet *per capita*.

Further, certain, indices of progress had to be kept in mind:

(i) Increase in agricultural production. (ii) Increase in industrial production. (iii) Diminution of unemployment. (iv) Increase in *per capita* income. (v) Liquidation of illiteracy. (vi) Increase in public utility services. (vii) Provision of medical aid on the basis of one unit for 1,000 population. (viii) Increase in the average expectation of life.

The objective for the country as a whole was the attainment, as far as possible, of national self-sufficiency. International trade was certainly not excluded, but we were anxious to avoid being drawn into the whirlpool of economic imperialism. We neither wanted to be victims of an imperialist power nor to develop such tendencies ourselves. The first charge on the country's produce should be to meet the domestic needs of food, raw materials, and manufactured goods. Surplus production would not be dumped abroad but used in exchange for such commodities as we might require. To base our national economy on export markets might lead to conflicts with other nations and to sudden upsets when those markets were closed to us.

So, though we did not start with a well-defined social theory, our social objectives were clear enough and afforded a common basis for planning. The very essence of this planning was a large measure of regulation and co-ordination. Thus, while free enterprise was not ruled out as such, its scope was severely restricted. In regard to defence industries it was decided that they must be owned and controlled by the state. Regarding other key industries, the majority were of opinion that they should be state-owned, but a substantial minority of the committee considered that state control would be sufficient. Such control, however, of these industries had to be rigid. Public utilities, it was also decided, should be owned by some organ of the state—either the Central Government, provincial government, or a local board. It was suggested that something of the nature of the London Transport Board might control public utilities. In regard to other important and vital industries, no special rule was laid down but it was made clear that the very nature of planning required control in some measure, which might vary with the industry.

In regard to the agency in state-owned industries it was suggested that as a general rule an autonomous public trust would be suitable. Such a trust would ensure public ownership and control and at the same time avoid the difficulties and inefficiency which sometimes creep in under direct democratic control. Cooperative ownership and control were also suggested for industries. Any planning would involve a close scrutiny of the development of industry in all its branches and a periodical survey of the progress made. It would mean also the training of the technical staffs necessary for the further expansion of industry, and the state might call upon industries to train such staffs.

The general principles governing land policy were laid down: 'Agricultural land, mines, quarries, rivers, and forests are forms of national wealth, ownership of which must vest absolutely in the people of India collectively.' The co-operative principle should be applied to the exploitation of land by developing collective and co-operative farms. It was not proposed, however, to rule out peasant farming in small holdings, to begin with at any rate, but no intermediaries of the type of talukdars, zamindars, etc., should be recognized after the transition period was over. The rights and title possessed by these classes should be progressively bought out. Collective farms were to be started immediately by the state on culturable waste land. Co-operative farming could be combined either with individual or joint ownership. A certain latitude was allowed for various types to develop so that, with greater experience, particular types might be encouraged more than others.

We, or some of us at any rate, hoped to evolve a socialized system of credit. If banks, insurance, etc., were not to be nationalized they should at least be under the control of the state, thus leading to a state regulation of capital and credit. It was also desirable to control the export and import trade. By these various means a considerable measure of state control would be established in regard to land as well as in industry as a whole, though varying in particular instances, and allowing private initiative to continue in a restricted sphere.

Thus, through the consideration of special problems, we gradually developed our social objectives and policy. There were gaps in them and occasional vagueness and even some contradiction; it was far from a perfect scheme in theory. But I was agreeably surprised at the large measure of unanimity achieved by us in spite of the incongruous elements in our Committee. The big business element was the largest single group and its outlook on many matters, especially financial and commercial, was definitely conservative. Yet the urge for rapid progress, and the conviction that only thus could we solve our problems of poverty and unemployment, were so great that all of us were forced out of our grooves and compelled to think on new lines. We had avoided a theoretical approach, and as each practical problem was viewed in its larger context, it led us inevitably in a particular direction. To me the spirit of co-operation of the members of the Planning Committee was peculiarly soothing and gratifying, for I found it a pleasant contrast to the squabbles and conflicts of politics. We knew our differences and yet we tried and often succeeded, after discussing every point of view, in arriving at an integrated conclusion which was accepted by all of us, or most of us.

Constituted as we were, not only in our Committee but in the larger field of India, we could not then plan for socialism as such. Yet it became clear to me that our plan, as it developed, was inevitably leading us towards establishing some of the fundamentals of the socialist structure. It was limiting the acquisitive factor in society, removing many of the barriers to growth, and thus leading to a rapidly expanding social structure. It was based on planning for the benefit of the common man, raising his standards greatly, giving him opportunities of growth, and releasing an enormous amount of latent talent and capacity. And all this was to be attempted in the context of democratic freedom and with a large measure of cooperation of some at least of the groups who were normally opposed to socialistic doctrine. That co-operation seemed to me worth while even if it involved toning down or weakening the plan in some respects. Probably I was too optimistic. But so long as a big step in the right direction was taken, I felt that the very dynamics involved in the process of change would facilitate further adaptation and progress. If conflict was inevitable, it had to be faced; but if it could be avoided or minimized that was an obvious gain. Especially as in the political sphere there was conflict enough for us and, in the future, there might well be unstable conditions. A general consent for a plan was thus of great value.

It was easy enough to draw up blue-prints based on some idealist conception. It was much more difficult to get behind them that measure of general consent and approval which was essential for the satisfactory working of any plan.

Planning, though inevitably bringing about a great deal of control and co-ordination and interfering in some measure with individual freedom, would, as a matter of fact, in the context of India today, lead to a vast increase of freedom. We have very little freedom to lose. We have only to gain freedom. If we adhered to the democratic state structure and encouraged co-operative enterprises, many of the dangers of regimentation and concentration of power might be avoided.

At our first sessions we had framed a formidable questionnaire which was issued to various governments and public bodies, universities, chambers of commerce, trade unions, research institutes, etc. Twenty-nine sub-committees were also appointed to investigate and report on specific problems. Eight of these sub-committees were for agricultural problems; several were for industry; five for commerce and finance; two for transport; two for education; two for public welfare; two for demographic relations; and one for women's role in planned economy. There were in all about 350 members of these sub-committees, some of them overlapping. Most of them were specialists or experts in their subjects—businessmen, government, state, and municipal employees, university professors or lecturers, technicians, scientists, trade unionists, and policemen. We collected in this way much of the talent available in the country. The only persons who were not permitted to co-operate with us, even when they were personally desirous of doing so, were the officials and employees of the Government of India. To have so many persons associated in our work was helpful in many ways. We had the advantage of their special knowledge and experience, and they were led to think of their special subject in relation to the wider problem. It also led to a greater interest in planning all over the country. But these numbers were disadvantageous also, for there was inevitable delay when busy people spread out all over a vast country had to meet repeatedly.

I was heartened to come into touch with so much ability and earnestness in all departments of national activity, and these contacts added to my own education greatly. Our method of work was to have an interim report from each sub-committee, which the planning committee considered, approving of it or partly criticizing it, and then sending it back with its remarks to the sub-committee. A final report was then submitted out of which arose our decisions on that particular subject. An attempt was being made continually to co-ordinate the decisions on each subject with those arrived at on other subjects. When all the final reports had been thus considered and disposed of, the Planning Committee was to review the whole problem in its vastness and intricacy and evolve its own comprehensive report, to which the sub-committees' reports would be added as appendices. As a matter of fact that final report was gradually taking shape in the course of our consideration of the sub-committees' reports.

There were irritating delays, chiefly due to some of the subcommittees not keeping to the time-table fixed for them, but on the whole we made good progress and got through an enormous amount of work. Two interesting decisions were made in connection with education. We suggested that definite norms of physical fitness for boys and girls be laid down for every stage of education. We also suggested establishment of a system of compulsory social or labour service, so as to make every young man and woman contribute one year of his or her life, between the ages of eighteen and twenty-two, to national utility, including agriculture, industry, public utilities, and public works of all kinds. No exemption was to be allowed except for physical or mental disability.

When World War II started in September, 1939, it was suggested that the National Planning Committee should suspend its activities. In November the Congress governments in the provinces resigned and this added to our difficulties, for under the absolute rule of the Governors in the provinces no interest was taken in our work. Business men were busier than ever making money out of war requirements and were not so much interested in planning. The situation was changing from day to day. We decided, however, to continue and felt that the war made this even more necessary. It was bound to result in further industrialization, and the work we had already done and were engaged in doing could be of great help in this process. We were dealing then with our sub-committees' reports on engineering industries, transport, chemical industries, and manufacturing industries, all of the highest importance from the point of view of the war. But the Government was not interested in our work and in fact viewed it with great disfavour. During the early months of the war—the so-called 'phoney' period—their policy was not to encourage the growth of Indian industry. Afterwards, the pressure of events forced them to buy many of their requirements in India, but even so they disapproved of any heavy industries being started there. Disapproval meant virtual prohibition, for no machinery could be imported without government sanction.

The Planning Committee continued its work and had nearly finished dealing with its sub-committees' reports. We were to finish what little remained of this work and then proceed to the consideration of our own comprehensive report. I was, however, arrested in October, 1940, and sentenced to a long term of imprisonment. Several other members of the Planning Committee and its subcommittees were also arrested and sentenced. I was anxious that the Planning Committee should continue to function and requested my colleagues outside to do so. But they were not willing to work in the Committee in my absence. I tried to get the Planning Committee's papers and reports in prison so that I might study them and prepare a draft report. The Government of India intervened and stopped this. No such papers were allowed to reach me, nor were interviews on the subject permitted.

So the National Planning Committee languished, while I spent my days in jail. All the work we had done which, though incomplete, could be used to great advantage for war purposes, remained in the pigeon-holes of our office. I was released in December, 1941, and was out of prison for some months. But this period was a hectic one for me, as it was for others. All manner of new developments had taken place, the Pacific war was on, India was threatened with invasion, and it was not possible then to pick up the old threads and continue the unfinished work of the planning committee unless the political situation cleared up. And then I returned to prison.

The Congress and industry: big industry versus cottage industry

The Congress, under Gandhiji's leadership, had long championed the revival of village industries, especially hand-spinning and hand-weaving. At no time, however, had the Congress been opposed to the development of big industries, and whenever it had the chance, in the legislatures or elsewhere, it had encouraged this development. Congress provincial governments were eager to do so. In the twenties when the Tata Steel and Iron Works were in difficulties, it was largely due to the insistence of the Congress party in the Central Legislature that government aid was given to help to tide over a critical period. The development of Indian shipbuilding and shipping services had long been a sore point of conflict between nationalist opinion and government. The Congress, as all other sections of Indian opinion, was anxious that every assistance should be given to Indian shipping; the government was equally anxious to protect the vested interests of powerful British shipping companies. Indian shipping was thus prevented from growing by official discrimination against it, although it had both capital and technical and managerial ability at its disposal. This kind of discrimination worked all along the line whenever any British industrial, commercial, or financial interests were concerned.

That huge combine, the Imperial Chemical Industries, has been repeatedly favoured at the expenses of Indian industry. Some years ago it was given a long term lease for the exploitation of the minerals, etc., of the Punjab. The terms of this agreement were, so far as I know, not disclosed, presumably because it was not considered 'in the public interest' to do so.

The Congress provincial governments were anxious to develop a power alcohol industry. This was desirable from many points of view, but there was an additional reason in the United Provinces and Bihar. The large numbers of sugar factories there were producing as a by-product a vast quantity of molasses which was being treated as waste material. It was proposed to utilise this for the production of power alcohol. The process was simple, there was no difficulty, except one—the interests of the Shell and Burma Oil combine were affected. The Government of India championed these interests and refused to permit the manufacture of power alcohol. It was only in the third year of the present war, after Burma fell and the supplies of oil and petrol were cut off, that the realization came that power alcohol was necessary and must be produced in India. The American Grady Committee strongly urged this in 1942.

The Congress has thus always been in favour of the industrialization of India and, at the same time, has emphasized the development of cottage industries and worked for this. Is there a conflict between these two approaches? Possibly there is a difference in emphasis, a realization of certain human and economic factors which were overlooked previously in India. Indian industrialists and the politicians who supported them thought too much in terms of the nineteenth century development of capitalist industry in Europe and ignored many of the evil consequences that were obvious in the twentieth century. In India, because normal progress had been arrested for 100 years those consequences were likely to be more far-reaching. The kind of medium-scale industries that were being started in India, under the prevailing economic system, resulted not in absorbing labour, but in creating more unemployment. While capital accumulated at one end, poverty and unemployment increased at the other. Under a different system, with a stress on big scale industries absorbing labour, and with planned development this might well have been avoided.

This fact of increasing mass poverty influenced Gandhi powerfully. It is true, I think, that there is a fundamental difference between his outlook on life generally and what might be called the modern outlook. He is not enamoured of ever-increasing standards of living and the growth of luxury at the cost of spiritual and moral values. He does not favour the soft life; for him the straight way is the hard way, and the love of luxury leads to crookedness and loss of virtue. Above all he is shocked at the vast gulf that stretches between the rich and the poor, in their ways of living, and their opportunities of growth. For his own personal and psychological satisfaction, he crossed that gulf and went over to the side of the poor, adopting, with only such improvements as the poor themselves could afford, their ways of living, their dress or lack of dress. This vast difference between the few rich and the poverty-stricken masses seemed to him to be due to two principal causes: foreign rule and the exploitation that accompanied it, and the capitalist industrial civilization of the west as embodied in the big machine. He reacted against both. He looked back with yearning to the days of the old autonomous and more-or-less self-contained village community where there had been an automatic balance between production, distribution, and consumption; where political or economic power was spread out and not concentrated as it is today; where a kind of simple democracy prevailed; where the gulf between the rich and the poor was not so marked; where the evil of great cities were absent and people lived in contact with the life-giving soil and breathed the pure air of the open spaces.

There was all this basic difference in outlook as to the meaning of life itself between him and many others, and this difference coloured his language as well as his activities. His language, vivid and powerful as it often was, drew its inspiration from the religious and moral teachings of the ages, principally of India but also of other countries. Moral values must prevail, the ends can never justify unworthy means, or else the individual and the race perish.

And yet he was no dreamer living in some fantasy of his own creation, cut off from life and its problems. He came from Gujarat, the home of hard-headed businessmen, and he had an unrivalled knowledge of the Indian villages and the conditions of life that prevailed there. It was out of that personal experience that he evolved his programme of the spinning-wheel and village industry. If immediate relief was to be given to the vast numbers of the unemployed and partially employed, if the rot that was spreading throughout India and paralysing the masses was to be stopped, if the villagers' standards were to be raised, however little, *en masse*, if they were to be taught self-reliance instead of waiting helplessly like derelicts for relief from others, if all this was to be done without much capital, then there seemed no other way. Apart from the evils inherent in foreign rule and exploitation, and the lack of freedom to initiate and carry through big schemes of reform, the problem of India was one of scarcity of capital and abundance of labour—how to utilize that wasted labour, that manpower that was producing nothing. Foolish comparisons are made between manpower and machine-power; of course a big machine can do the work of a thousand or ten thousand persons. But if those ten thousand sit idly by or starve, the introduction of the machine is not a social gain, except in long perspective which envisages a change in social conditions. When the big machine is not there at all, then no question of comparison arises; it is a nett gain both from the individual and the national point of view to utilize manpower for production. There is no necessary conflict between this and the introduction of machinery on the largest scale, provided that machinery is used primarily for absorbing labour and not for creating fresh unemployment.

Comparisons between India and the small highly industrialized countries of the west, or big countries with relatively sparse populations, like the U.S.S.R. or the U.S.A., are misleading. In western Europe the process of industrialization has proceeded for 100 years, and gradually the population has adjusted itself to it; the population has grown rapidly, then stabilized itself, and is now declining. In the U.S.A. and the U.S.S.R. there are vast tracts with a small, though growing, population. A tractor is an absolute necessity there to exploit the land for agriculture. It is not so obvious that a tractor is equally necessary in the densely populated Gangetic valley, so long as vast numbers depend on the land alone for sustenance. Other problems arise, as they have arisen even in America. Agriculture has been carried on for thousands of years in India and the soil has been exploited to the utmost. Would the deep churning up of the soil by tractors lead to impoverishment of this soil as well as to soil erosion? When railways were built in India and high embankments put up for the purpose, no thought was given to the natural drainage of the country. The embankments interfered with this drainage system and, as a result, we have had repeated and ever-increasing floods and soil erosion, and malaria has spread.

I am all for tractors and big machinery, and I am convinced that the rapid industrialization of India is essential to relieve the pressure on land, to combat poverty and raise standards of living, for defence and a variety of other purposes. But I am equally convinced that the most careful planning and adjustment are necessary if we are to reap the full benefit of industrialization and avoid many of its dangers. This planning is necessary today in all countries of arrested growth, like China and India, which have strong traditions of their own.

In China I was greatly attracted to the Industrial Co-operatives—the Indusco movement—and it seems to me that some such movement is peculiarly suited to India. It would fit in with the Indian background, give a democratic basis to small industry, and develop the co-operative habit. It could be made to complement big industry. It must be remembered that, however rapid might be the development of heavy industry in India, a vast field will remain open to small and cottage industries. Even in Soviet Russia owner–producer co-operatives have played an important part in industrial growth.

The increasing use of electric power facilitates the growth of small industry and makes it economically capable of competing with large-scale industry. There is also a growing opinion in favour of decentralization, and even Henry Ford had advocated it. Scientists are pointing out the psychological and biological dangers of loss of contact with the soil which results from life in great industrial cities. Some have even said that human survival necessitates a going back to the soil and the village. Fortunately, science has made it possible today for populations to be spread out and remain near the soil and yet enjoy all the amenities of modern civilization and culture.

However that may be, the problem before us in India during recent decades has been how, in the existing circumstances and restricted as we were by alien rule and its attendant vested interests, we could relieve the poverty of the masses and produce a spirit of self-reliance among them.

There are many arguments in favour of developing cottage industries at any time, but situated as we were that was certainly the most practical thing we could do. The methods adopted may not have been the best or the most suitable. The problem was vast, difficult, and intricate, and we had frequently to face suppression by government. We had to learn gradually by the process of trial and error. I think we should have encouraged cooperatives from the beginning, and relied more on expert technical and scientific knowledge for the improvement of small machines suitable for cottage and village use. The co-operation principle is now being introduced in these organizations.

G. D. H. Cole, the economist, has said that 'Gandhi's campaign for the development of the home-made cloth industry is no mere fad of a romantic eager to revive the past, but a practical attempt to relieve the poverty and uplift the standard of the village.' It was that undoubtedly, and it was much more. It forced India to think of the poor peasant in human terms, to realize that behind the glitter of a few cities lay this morass of misery and poverty, to grasp the fundamental fact that the true test of progress and freedom in India did not lie in the creation of a number of millionaires or prosperous lawyers and the like, or in the setting up of councils and assemblies, but in the change in the status and conditions of life of the peasant. The British had created a new caste or class in India, the English-educated class, which lived in a world of its own, cut off from the mass of the population, and looked always, even when protesting, towards its rulers. Gandhi bridged that gap to some extent and forced it to turn its head and look towards its own people.

Gandhiji's attitude to the use of machinery seemed to undergo a gradual change. 'What I object to,' he said, 'is the craze for machinery, not machinery as such.' 'If we could have electricity in every village home, I shall not mind villagers plying their implements and tools with electricity.' The big machines seemed to him to lead inevitably, at least in the circumstances of today, to the concentration of power and riches: 'I consider it a sin and injustice to use machinery for the purpose of concentration of power and riches in the hands of the few. Today the machine is used in this way.' He even came to accept the necessity of many kinds of heavy industries and large-scale key industries and public utilities, provided they were state-owned and did not interfere with some kinds of cottage industries which he considered as essential. Referring to his own proposals, he said: 'The whole of this programme will be a structure on sand if it is not built on the solid foundation of economic equality.'

Thus even the enthusiastic advocates for cottage and small-scale industries recognize that big-scale industry is, to a certain extent, necessary and inevitable; only they would like to limit it as far as possible. Superficially then the question becomes one of emphasis and adjustment of the two forms of production and economy. It can hardly be challenged that, in the context of the modern world, no country can be politically and economically independent, even within the framework of international interdependence, unless it is highly industrialized and has developed its power resources to the utmost. Nor can it achieve or maintain high standards of living and liquidate poverty without the aid of modern technology in almost every sphere of life. An industrially backward country will continually upset the world equilibrium and encourage the aggressive tendencies of more developed countries. Even if it retains its political independence, this will be nominal only, and economic control will tend to pass to others. This control will inevitably upset its own small-scale economy which it has sought to preserve in pursuit of its own view of life. Thus an attempt to build up a country's economy largely on the basis of cottage and small-scale industries is doomed to failure. It will not solve the basic problems of the country or maintain freedom, nor will it fit in with the world framework, except as a colonial appendage.

Is it possible to have two entirely different kinds of economy in a country—one based on the big machine and industrialization, and the other mainly on cottage industries? This is hardly conceivable, for one must overcome the other, and there can be little doubt that the big machine will triumph unless it is forcibly prevented from doing so. Thus it is not a mere question of adjustment of the two forms of production and economy. One must be dominating and paramount, with the other as complementary to it, fitting in where it can. The economy based on the latest technical achievements of the day must necessarily be the dominating one. If technology demands the big machine, as it does today in a large measure, then the big machine with all its implications and consequences must be accepted. Where it is possible, in terms of that technology, to decentralize production, this would be desirable. But, in any event, the latest technique has to be followed, and to adhere to out-worn and out-of-date methods of production, except as a temporary and stop gap measure, is to arrest growth and development.

Any argument as to the relative merits of small-scale and large-scale industry seems strangely irrelevant today when the world, and the dominating facts of the situation that confront it, have decided in favour of the latter. Even in India the decision has been made by these facts themselves, and no one doubts that India will be rapidly industrialized in the near future. She has already gone a good way in that direction. The evils of unrestricted and unplanned industrialization are well recognized today. Whether these evils are necessary concomitants of big industry, or derived from the social and economic structure behind it, is another matter. If the economic structure is primarily responsible for them, then surely we should set about changing that structure, instead of blaming the inevitable and desirable development in technique.

The real question is not one of quantitative adjustment and balancing of various incongruous elements and methods of production, but a qualitative change-over to something different and new, from which various social consequences flow. The economic and political aspects of this qualitative change are important, but equally important are the social and psychological aspects. In India especially, where we have been wedded far too long to past forms and modes of thought and action, new experiences, new processes, leading to new ideas and new horizons, are necessary. Thus we will change the static character of our living and make it dynamic and vital, and our minds will become active and adventurous. New situations lead to new experiences, as the mind is compelled to deal with them and adapt itself to a changing environment.

It is well recognized now that a child's education should be intimately associated with some craft or manual activity. The mind is stimulated thereby and there is a co-ordination between the activities of the mind and the hands. So also the mind of a growing boy or girl is stimulated by the machine. It grows under the machine's impact (under proper conditions, of course, and not as an exploited and unhappy worker in a factory) and opens out new horizons. Simple scientific experiments, peeps into the microscope, and an explanation of the ordinary phenomena of nature bring excitement in their train, an understanding of some of life's processes, and a desire to experiment and find out instead of relying on set phrases and old formulae. Self-confidence and the co-operative spirit grow, and frustration, arising out of the miasma of the past, lessens. A civilization based on ever-changing and advancing mechanical techniques leads to this. Such a civilization is a marked change, a jump almost from the older type, and is intimately connected with modern industrialization. Inevitably it gives rise to new problems and difficulties, but it also shows the way to overcome them.

I have a partiality for the literary aspects of education and I admire the classics, but I am quite sure that some elementary scientific training in physics and chemistry, and especially biology, as also in the application of science, is essential for all boys and girls. Only thus can they understand and fit into the modern world and develop, to some extent at least, the scientific temper. There is something very wonderful about the high achievements of science and modern technology (which no doubt will be bettered in the near future), in the superb ingenuity of scientific instruments, in the amazingly delicate and yet powerful machines, in all that has flowed from the adventurous inquiries of science and its applications, in the glimpses into the fascinating workshop and processes of nature, in the fine sweep of science, through its myriad workers, in the realms of thought and practice, and, above all, in the fact that all this has come out of the mind of man.

5

India in the modern world

Rajani Palme Dutt

Source: *India Today* (Calcutta: Manisha Granthalaya (Pvt) Ltd., 1986), pp. 1–18. First Published 1940 by Victor Gollanz, London.

> When in the course of human events it becomes necessary for one people to dissolve, the political bonds which have connected them with another, and to assume among the powers of the earth the separate and equal station to which the laws of nature and a nature's God entitle them, a decent respect of the opinions of mankind requires that they should declare the causes which impel them to the separation.
>
> —American Declaration of Independence.

The future of India is today one of the big questions of world politics.

The four hundred millions of India comprise close on one-fifth of the human race. For two centuries they have been subject to foreign rule. Today that foreign rule is approaching its end.

On a world scale the subjection of India has been the largest and most important basis of empire domination in the modern world. For centuries the wealth and resources of this vast territory, and the life and labour of its people, have been the object of Western capitalist penetration, aggression and expansion, and finally of absolute domination and intensive exploitation. The ending of this system will not only open up a new future for one-fifth of the human race. It will also mean a decisive change in the balance of world relations, a further weakening in the world system of imperialism, and a strengthening of the advance of freedom of the peoples throughout the world. The liberation of India, alongside free China, will open the way for the liberation of all the peoples of Asia and of all the colonial peoples.

All the problems and conflicts of the modern world find their focus in India. Here amid the ruins of an old historic civilisation, which has been submerged and has stagnated under the crushing weight of modern conquerors, the lowest levels of primitive economy, poverty and servitude exist alongside the most advanced forms of finance-capitalist exploitation. Chronic agrarian crisis, famine, debt-slavery, the shackles of caste and of the outcaste, industrial exploitation without limit, contrasts of wealth and poverty more appalling than in any country in the world, social and religious conflict, class conflict, emergent national issues within India—all these problems reflecting in many respects the backwardness and retarded development of a subject country, and intensified by foreign domination, force themselves to the front today alongside the central problem of liberation from imperialist rule, and complicate the conditions of the struggle for liberation.

India today is entering into an era of profound economic social and political revolution. The first step in that revolution will be liberation from foreign rule and the winning of complete independence. But that liberation, which is drawing close, will only release the gigantic internal problems, social strains and conflicts which have accumulated through centuries of foreign domination and arrested development, and which today clamour for solution. The Indian people today stand before a vast task of national and social renovation.

1. India on the eve of freedom

The new world situation following the victory of the United Nations over the fascist Powers has brought the question of Indian freedom to the forefront of world politics.

The first world war of 1914–18 and the revolutionary wave which swept over the world in its train inaugurated an era of great changes in India, as in all colonial countries. Powerful mass struggles shook India in 1919–22, and again with even greater intensity (after the world economic crisis which affected India most profoundly) in 1930–34. British rule sought to counter the rising national movement with alternating reforms and repression. Promises of future self-government were accompanied by constitutional concessions which left the real relations of power unchanged. These constitutional concessions, which resulted in the formation of Provincial Ministries of the National Congress in 1937 in eight of the eleven provinces, did not stem the rising unrest, but rather gave it new impetus. The onset of war in 1939 found India already in the ferment of a sharpening struggle for independence against the Federal Constitution which the British Government was preparing to impose. The dragging of India into the war without any pretence of consultation or popular endorsement, and the establishment of an emergency war dictatorship only emphasised the gulf between the rulers and the ruled.

The second world war brought new urgency to the question of Indian liberation. The alliance of the United Nations officially proclaimed the aim of "the right of all peoples to choose the form of Government under which they will live." In contrast, to the first world war, the alliance of the United Nations constituted a coalition led by four Powers which included not only the two imperialist Powers—Britain and the United States—but two non-imperialist Powers—National China and the Socialist Soviet Union. All over the world powerful national liberation movements were fighting for national freedom against fascism. It was not surprising that in this world situation the Indian people should demand with all the greater intensity the same national freedom which was being fought for by so many peoples and for which Indian soldiers were being called on to lay down their lives.

The special circumstances of the war in Asia increased this urgency. British imperialist domination in Asia which had so long with suicidal folly encouraged and assisted Japanese aggression and expansion, was shaken to its foundations by the headlong advance of that aggression after Pearl Harbour. The bankruptcy and inner rottenness of the old colonial system was exposed in the sight of all, as the vast territories of South East Asia collapsed before the invader almost without resistance, save for the unsuccessful defence by imported troops, with the foreign rulers totally incapable of mobilising the populations over whom they ruled.

This exposure produced its profound effect on popular sentiment in India. The myth of British invincible power was broken. Japanese armies reached and overran the borders of India. The Axis Powers made a skilful use of the former Congress President, Subhas Bose, who had placed himself in their hands, and of the "Indian National Army" to mask their aims of aggression and conquest behind a hypocritical pretence of concern for India. Against a free India such a propaganda could have had no effect. In relation to an India held subject it had a certain measure of inevitable effect.

Thus, the second world war produced a situation in which not only the principles of democracy, but the vital interests equally of the defence of India and of the whole battlefront of the United Nations required speedy Indian liberation. India's national leaders had from the outset recognised

India's common interests with the democratic peoples against the world alliance of fascism. They had recognised that common interest and actively campaigned against the reactionary policies of support for fascism at a time when the rulers of Britain were still aiding and abetting fascist aggression. They recognised that in the war of the United Nations against the Axis the interests of India were bound up with the defeat of fascism and victory of that camp which included National China, the Socialist Soviet Union and the democratic liberation movements in Europe. But they demanded, and rightly demanded, that India must be free, under the control of an Indian National Government with full and effective powers in order to mobilise the full strength of the Indian people as a voluntary partner in the alliance of the United Nations. This demand corresponded to the interests of the United Nations. It was supported not only by democratic opinion in all countries of the United Nations but also by representations from official quarters of the Allies of Britain, notably by President Roosevelt and Marshal Chiang Kai-shek.

Nevertheless, the close of the second world war did not bring India freedom. Toryism was in the saddle in Britain and obstinately resisted every proposal for Indian independence or even for any temporary wartime compromise which would put effective power in the hands of India's popular leaders. Churchill's motto that he "had not become the Prime Minister of Britain in order to preside over the liquidation of the British Empire" remained the guiding line of British policy even in the most critical days of danger and difficulty. The Cripps negotiations of 1942 broke down. The national movement, frustrated and torn by the dilemmas of the situation in which they found themselves, became bogged in the impasse following the August Resolution. India's national leaders were thrown into prison and the sporadic unofficial movement and disorders which followed the arrests of the leaders were easily suppressed.

The end of the war found India still a subject nation and the political situation one of deadlock.

But the victory of the United Nations over fascism brought a new situation. All over the world the military defeat and utter collapse of the fascist Powers represented the heaviest blow against reaction since the days of 1917. The popular movements surged forward in all countries. Imperialism was heavily weakened. German, Italian and Japanese imperialisms had vanished from the map of the world. There remained only two major imperialist Powers—Britain and the United States—together with the subordinate colonial empires of France, Belgium, Holland, and Portugal. In Europe, new democratic governments replaced the old conservative regimes which had surrendered to or allied themselves with fascism. In Britain, Toryism experienced an overwhelming electoral debacle and was replaced by the first majority Labour Government. All over Asia the colonial liberation movements pressed forward; and the Indonesian Republic held out against the military assault of Anglo-Dutch imperialism and its Japanese troops. Within India, the universal demand for independence and the movement for national revolt rose to new heights in the winter of 1945–46 and found expression in mass demonstrations of Hindu Moslem unity and in the extension of the national revolt to the armed services.

This situation compelled a speedy turn in British policy under the direction of the new Labour Government. On February 19, 1946, the Labour Prime Minister, Mr. Attlee, announced the decision to send the Cabinet Mission to India. On March 15, on the occasion of the departure of the Mission, Mr. Attlee declared:

> It is no good applying the formula of the past to the present position. The temperature of 1946 is not the temperature of 1920, 1930 or even 1942 . . .
>
> "Nothing increases the pace and movement of public opinion more than a great war. Everyone who had anything to do with this question in the early days between the wars knows what effect the war of 1914–18 had on Indian aspirations and ideas. The tide that runs comparatively slowly in peace, becomes vastly accelerated in wartime, and especially directly afterwards, because that tide is to some extent banked up during war. I am quite certain that at the present time the tide of nationalism is running very fast in India and indeed all over Asia . . .

India herself must choose as to what will be her future situation and her position in the world. Unity may come through the United Nations or through the Commonwealth, but no great nation can stand alone by herself without sharing what is happening in the world.

I hope that India may elect to remain within the British Commonwealth. I am certain that she will find great advantage in doing so, but if she does, she must do so of her own free will, for the British Commonwealth and Empire is not bound together by chains of external compulsion. It is a free association of free peoples.

If on the other hand she elects for independence—and in our view she has a right to do so—it will be for us to help make the transition as smooth and as easy as possible.

It was universally noticed that for the first time in British official expression the term "independence" was used as a possible goal for India.

Nevertheless, the too easy expectations which were widely spread in many quarters, both within and outside India, that the dispatch of the Cabinet Mission subsequent to the proposals of the British Government already meant Indian freedom, were premature. The history of the negotiations of the Cabinet Mission and the subsequent new constitutional proposals will be examined later in these pages. The final outcome of these negotiations and measures will only be shown in practical experience. But it is probable that the historical verdict will reach the conclusion that these proposals were in reality the last of the long series of attempts at constitutional adaptation and compromise by British imperialism rather than the beginning of Indian freedom.

In 1946, India is still a part of the British Empire. The formal concession of the right of a future choice to independence is largely vitiated by the pre-determined and far from representative character, composition and procedure of the constitution-making body which alone is to exercise the right.

The coming period may thus still show for a certain term a further lease of life of imperialism and continuance of effective imperialist domination even within new forms. The fight for Indian freedom has still to be won.

But today there can be no longer any doubt in any quarter that the whole current of historical development is driving towards Indian freedom, and that this full freedom will be won in the near future.

This is the context of any examination of India today, of the last days of imperialist rule and the outcome of that long record of domination, and of the rising advance of the Indian people.

2. Imperialism and India

India has for centuries been the main base of modern imperialist expansion and domination.

The area of India is 1,808,679 square miles, or fifteen times the area of the British Isles, and twenty times the area of Great Britain. The population of India was 389 millions in the last 1941 census, and is estimated to be now approaching 400 millions, or nearly one-fifth of the human race.

The 400 millions of India constitute three-quarters of the total population of the British Empire, four-fifths of the overseas population of the British Empire and nearly nine-tenths of the subject colonial population of the British Empire.

If we compare the extent of the eight leading colonial empires on the eve of the present war, the Indian population subject to British rule represented in 1938 more than half the total colonial population of the world, and more than one and a half times the combined colonial population of the French, Japanese, Dutch, American, Belgian, Italian and Portuguese empires—that is, of the remaining colonial empires.

India is not only far and away the largest of the direct colonial possessions of imperialism. It is also the oldest, the longest dominated and exploited over many generations and, therefore, the most complete demonstration of the workings and outcome of the colonial system.

The European colonising powers all directed their first efforts towards India and the wealth of India: they stumbled across America and the West Indies in the course of searching for the new sea route to India; it was only in the later period that they extended their expansion to Africa, Australia, China and the rest of Asia.

If we look at the map, it is easy to see how India has been the central region of imperialist domination.

Around the vast expanse of the Indian Ocean, with India as the commanding centre, stretches the Persian Gulf, the new Middle Eastern empire and Arabia on the west; then the Red Sea and Egypt, and all Africa to the south-west; to the east, Burma, the Malay States and the East Indies; to the south-east, Australia; and through the gates of Singapore, as well as more recently through the new Burma–Yunnan Road, the route to China.

With the impenetrable mountain barriers to the north (open only to invasion on the north-west) and with command of the sea, India constitutes the central fortress and base for the domination of this whole region, as well as itself comprising the richest source of wealth and exploitation.

European capitalist penetration into India began with the Portuguese establishment of their factory at Calicut in 1500 and their conquest of Goa in 1506, more than four centuries ago. The British East India Company was founded in 1600, the Dutch East India Company in 1602 and the French Compagnie des Indes in 1664. British direct territorial rule in India, beyond the trading settlements which were already the initial outposts of conquest, dates from the middle of the eighteenth century. The traditional starting-point from the Battle of Plassey in 1757 gives close on two centuries of British rule in India.

The conquest of India by Western civilisation has constituted one of the main pillars of capitalist development in Europe, of British world supremacy, and of the whole structure of modern imperialism. For two centuries the history of Europe has been built up to a greater extent than is always recognised, on the basis of the domination of India. Behind the successive struggles of Britain with Spain and Portugal, with Holland, with France, with Russia and with Germany, may be traced the issue of the route to India and the domination of India. Behind the inner course of politics in England, and directly under-propping the whole social and political structure laboriously and precariously built up in England, may be traced the role of this same domination.

India has long been recognised as the pivot of the British Empire. As the last outstanding Viceroy of still expanding imperialism in India, Lord Curzon wrote in 1894 (before his viceroyalty):

> Just as De Tocqueville remarked that the conquest and government of India are really the achievements which have given to England her place in the opinion of the world, so it is the prestige and the wealth arising from her Asiatic position that are the foundation stones of the British Empire. There, in the heart of the old Asian continent, she sits upon the throne that has always ruled the East. Her sceptre is outstretched over land and sea. "Godlike," she "grasps the triple fork, and kinglike, wears the crown."
>
> (Hon. G. N. Curzon, "Problems of the Far East", 1894, p. 419.)

Four years later, in 1898, this intoxicated panegyrist of imperialism was sounding a new note:

> "India is the pivot of our Empire . . . If the Empire loses any other part of its Dominion we can survive, but if we lose India the sun of our Empire will have set."

In this often-quoted rhetorical flight, the forebodings of the approaching end were already beginning to make themselves felt.

The economic and financial significance of India to Britain and to the whole development and structure of British capitalism has been very great through the historical record. It is now weakening but is still considerable. The old monopoly of the Indian market reaching to over four-fifths in the 19th century and two-thirds even on the eve of the war of 1914–18 has now vanished never to return. Since 1929 India is no longer the largest single market for British goods and had fallen to the third place by 1938. But the lion's share of Indian trade is still in British hands. The volume of British capital holdings in India was estimated at £1,000 million in 1933 (estimate of the Indian Chamber of Commerce) or one-fourth of the total of British overseas capital investment. This total is now reduced, though no authoritative estimate of the effects of changes during and since the second world war has yet been made. It is notable that while British overseas investments in other countries were freely sold under the stress of war, those in India were tenaciously retained. The present total is, on paper, more than offset by the Indian sterling balances accumulated during the war through the drawing of goods from India without payment. But the future fate of those sterling balances has still to be settled. The value of the annual tribute drawn from India to Britain, in one form or another, has been estimated at £150 million (calculation based on the year 1921–22 in Shah and Khambata, "Wealth and Taxable Capacity of India", p. 234), or more than the total of the entire Indian Budget at the same date, and equivalent to over £3 a year per head of the population in Britain, or nearly £1,700 a year for every super-tax-payer in Britain at the time of the estimate.

No less important is the strategic significance of India to British imperialism, both as the basis from which the further expansion of the Empire has been in great part undertaken, the exchequer and source of troops for innumerable overseas wars and expeditions, and also as the centre-point to which strategic calculations (control of the Mediterranean, the Suez Canal and the Red Sea, the Persian Gulf and the Middle Eastern empire, and Singapore) have been continuously directed. This strategic significance was further demonstrated in the second world war.

3. Bankruptcy of imperialism in India

What has been the outcome of imperialist rule in India?

Whatever the divergent social and political viewpoints of observers, on one point all, whether of the right or the left, are agreed. After two centuries of imperialist rule, India presents a spectacle of squalid poverty and misery of the mass of the people without equal in the world.

This is not a question of natural poverty of the country or deficiency of resources. The vast territories occupied by the Indian people enjoy a great natural wealth and resources, not only in respect of the fertility of the soil and potentialities of agricultural production, which; as further examination will show, could, if brought into full use, provide abundant supplies for a, much greater population than the existing, but also in respect of the raw materials for highly developed industrial production, especially coal, iron, oil and water-power, alongside the intelligence and technical aptitude, and dexterity (not wholly lost from the time when India enjoyed technical primacy among nations, before imperialist rule), of the population.

Yet these resources and possibilities are mainly undeveloped, if capitalism in general is characterised by waste and relative failure to utilise the full potentialities of production, then this failure reaches an absolute degree in India, which makes it basically different in type from any imperialist country.

A recent American observer, Professor Buchanan, after a monumental survey of economic and industrial development in India up to 1934 reaches the melancholy conclusion:

> Here was a country with all the crude elements upon which manufacturing depends, yet during more than a century, it has imported factory-made goods in large quantities and has developed only a few of the simplest industries for which machinery and organisation had been highly perfected in other countries. With abundant supplies of raw cotton, raw jute, easily mined coal, easily mined and exceptionally high-grade iron ore, with a redundant population often starving because of lack of profitable employment, with a hoard of gold and silver second perhaps to that of no other country in the world, . . . with an excellent market within her own borders and near at hand in which others were selling great quantities of manufactures; with all these advantages India, after a century, was supporting only about two per cent of her population/ by factory industry.
>
> (D. H. Buchanan, "The Development of Capitalist Enterprise, in India", 1934, p. 450.)

The standard British authority on Indian economics, Dr. Vera Anstey, Lecturer in Commerce at London University, finds in India a picture of arrested economic development which is felt to be

> the more strange because up to the eighteenth century the economic condition of India was relatively advanced, and Indian methods of production and of industrial and commercial organisation could stand comparison with those in vogue in any other part of the world . . .
>
> It is not, of course, asserted that no economic progress has been made under British rule. The results of the British connection have been to provide India with cheap imported manufactures, to increase the demands for many types of Indian produce, and to introduce public works and administrative methods which have enabled India to produce (especially by means of extended irrigation) and to transport (by rail and steamship) vastly increased quantities of crops and other goods. During the second half of the nineteenth century in particular, India's total production and trade advanced by leaps and bounds.
>
> But these changes brought about a peculiar interdependence between India and the West, whereby India tended to produce and export in the main raw materials and foodstuffs, and to import textiles, iron and steel goods, machinery and miscellaneous manufactures of the most varied description. Moreover, the concurrent increase in population counterbalanced the increase in total production so that no considerable increase in production per head could be traced. These facts certainly lend colour to the view that economic development had been "arrested" in India. . . .
>
> Up to the end of the nineteenth century the effects of British rule on the prosperity of the people were undoubtedly disappointing.
>
> (V. Anstey, "The Economic Development of India", 3rd Edition, 1936, Introduction, p. 5.)

What of the more recent period in which it is sometimes alleged that this situation has changed and that industrialisation is now well on its way? The same authority examines the figures revealed by the census of 1931 and readies a negative conclusion:

> It is difficult to reconcile these figures with a picture of rapidly progressing industrialization. . . . Not only is industrial development insignificant in comparison with agricultural, but India still depends excessively upon foreigners for the provision of many goods and services that are essential for any materially advanced country. . . . A well-balanced economic life has not yet been attained and the standard of life of the masses remains miserably low.
>
> (*ibid.*, p. 8.)

What is the explanation of this paradox of extreme, indescribable poverty amidst potential plenty (far exceeding the same paradox in ordinary capitalist countries), of arrested, stunted economic development after two centuries of rule by the most technically advanced and highly developed industrial power?

In order to understand this paradox it is necessary to come closer to the real working of imperialism in relation to the social-economic situation of the Indian people.

For *it is this failure to develop the productive resources of India that finally sounds the death-knell of imperialism in India today*, just as it was the relative economic superiority of the British bourgeois invaders to the system of rule of the feudal princes (despite the wholesale destruction and spoliation involved in that invasion) which caused the victory of their rule two centuries ago.

The social-political expression of this bankruptcy of the old order in India and rise of the new is the gathering revolt of the Indian people against imperialist rule which has more and more dominated the Indian scene in the twentieth century.

There is no doubt that the conditions have matured for a transformation which will end the stagnation of imperialist decay in India and replace it by a modern advancing India of the people.

4. The awakening of India

It is against this declining and bankrupt system of imperialist rule that the Indian people have risen in ever-extending and universal revolt.

The Indian national movement[1] has developed through many stages over the past century and in its modern forms since the third quarter of the nineteenth century. It has developed in many forms, legal and illegal, constitutional and revolutionary. It has comprised many currents—conservative and racial, and in the modern era, socialist and communist. Half a century ago, the demands of the legal movement were still only for moderate reforms within the imperialist structure. The organised movement was confined to a handful of the educated middle-class. But from the twentieth century the scope and aims of the movement have continuously extended. After the first world war, the national movement took on a full mass character, the demands advanced to full self-government which was finally defined from 1929 onwards as complete independence and separation from the British empire.

India is awakening. India, for thousands of years the prey of successive waves of conquerors, is awakening to independent existence as a free people with their own role to play in the world. This awakening has leapt forward in our lifetime. In the last 25 years a new India has emerged. Today India's advance to freedom, whatever the obstacles still to be overcome, is universally recognised as approaching victory in the near future. But the freeing of India removes the main base of modern imperialist domination of subject peoples.

Over the whole past period British policy has sought, with every weapon in its armoury—whether of violent repression, or by constitutional concession, by skilfully playing on the divisions or by approaches to the upper leadership of the movement—to counter, check, divide, corrupt or oppose the national movement and stem its advance. British imperialist policy, the most skilful, flexible and experienced expression of imperialist policy, has endeavoured by every means and resource, combining coercion with reforms, to adapt itself to the new situation and to maintain the reality of its power and exploitation while making far-reaching concessions in form. The liberal imperialist and reformist theories of the possibility of gradual and peaceful advance and progress of a colonial people to self-government and freedom within imperialism have here been brought to the test of practice. History will determine the final outcome of this conflict which will be decisive, not only for the future of the Indian people, but for the future of the British Empire.

The record of the past quarter of a century has shown that all the efforts of imperialism at adaptation to the new conditions, all the alternating waves of coercion and concession which have characterised this period, have not succeeded in damming the advancing tide of the national movement, nor have they brought any solution to the problem of India.

The rising contradictions, rooted in the social and economic, no less than the political conditions of India under imperialist rule, again and again defeat the attempts at harmony. The two levels, of the most advanced and elaborate finance-capitalist exploitation and domination above, and of the lowest levels of social misery and backwardness below, are closely intertwined in a network of cause and effect. In between these two levels—between the two opposing extremes of the imperialist exploiters at the apex of the pyramid and the destitute producing masses at the base—exist a host of transitional forms, intermediary parasitism, subordinate mechanisms of exploitation, old decomposing forces and new advancing forces. Through it all, extending every year, develop the rising national consciousness of the Indian people and the rising economic demands of the hungry Indian masses. This is a situation packed at every turn with social dynamite.

The basic problem of India is not only national but social. The challenge of the Indian people to imperialism is in its simplest sense a claim of one-fifth of humanity to freedom from foreign domination. But this demand for freedom inevitably strikes deeper than a claim for political independence in which it finds its political expression. It is at root a challenge to a deeply entrenched system of exploitation which has its seat in the City of London, but which is closely bound with a subordinate system of privilege and exploitation within India. The one cannot be touched without the other.

In this sense the Indian question is in the last analysis a social question. The basic problem of India is a problem of four hundred million human beings who are living under conditions of extreme poverty and semi-starvation for the overwhelming majority, and are at the same time living under a foreign rule which holds complete control over their lives and maintains by force the social system leading to these terrible conditions. These hundreds of millions are struggling for life, for the means of life, for elementary freedom. The problem of their struggle and of how they can realise their aims is the problem of India.

The immediate aim of the struggle of the Indian people is national liberation, the conquest of national independence and the democratic right of self-government. But this aim represents the first stage of a deeper social struggle, of a moving social revolution within India. The national and social issues are closely intertwined, and the understanding of this interconnection is the key to the understanding of the Indian situation.

Social conservatism is still deeply rooted in India and profoundly affects the problems and character of the national movement. The effects of such social conservatism and reactionary tendencies weaken and disorganise the advance of the national movement. Just as imperialism has produced its mythology to cover up its real predatory record with the conventional picture of its "civilising mission" so we need to be on guard against corresponding presuppositions and conventional mythologies in the opposite direction.

For, in opposition to the conventional imperialist mythology some backward-looking sections in India have endeavoured to build up a counter-mythology. In reaction against the evils of imperialist domination, they have endeavoured to paint a picture of a golden age of India in the past before British rule. They seek to slur over the evils of the rotting social system which went down before the British onset. They seek, not only to explain historically, but to idealise and glorify just those reactionary survivals of India's past which hamper progress, weigh down the consciousness of the people and prevent unity. On the basis of these reactionary survivals they seek to build up national consciousness. In this way they have sought to turn the fight against imperialism into a fight against "Western civilisation" in general. They turn their gaze backwards, not forwards.

This is not to strengthen the national front, but to weaken it. Nothing is to be gained by failing to face those evils of Indian society, which are not only derivative from imperialist rule, but also inherited from India's historical past. On the contrary, the national front grows strong precisely in proportion as it can show itself more capable than imperialism to fight those evils which imperialism, from the very nature of its role and social basis, is compelled to tolerate and even foster.

So long as imperialism was able to stand out as the representative of a more advanced social and economic order, for so long, whatever its attendant cruelties and waste, it was bound to dominate. Today, the more clearly the forces of the national front become identified with the advanced social forces of the Indian people, and can stand out as the representatives of a superior social and economic order to imperialism, the more certain becomes their future victory.

The Indian people, through the profound inner social conflicts and problems which are being brought to the front in the gathering crisis, stand before some of the most basic revolutionary tasks of any section of humanity. The deeper problems of the backwardness of India, of the task to clear away the dirt and filth of ages of subjection, arrested development and conservative social custom, will not reach their solution in the moment of national liberation, but will only then reach their full amplitude and the first approach to the conditions for their solution. By the resolution of these conflicts and problems, as the working masses of India advance to consciousness and to control of their own destiny, by the bringing forward of India from its present economic and cultural backwardness to the level of the most advanced nations, the people of India is marked out to play a foremost role in the future advance to world socialism and the final overcoming of the distinctions between East and West, between advanced and backward nations.

Every stage of civilisation and culture within class-society, from the most primitive to the most advanced, exists in India. The widest range of social, economic, political and cultural problems thus find their sharpest expression in Indian conditions. The problems of the relations and co-existence of differing races and religions; the battle against old superstitious and decaying social forms and traditions; the fight for education; the fight for liberation of women; the question of the reorganisation of agriculture and of the development of industry, and of the relationship of town and country; the issues of class conflict in the most manifold and acute forms; the problems of the relationship of nationalism and socialism; all these varied issues of the modern world press forward with special sharpness and urgency in India.

The solution of these manifold problems cannot be realized in isolation, but is necessarily bound up with the central immediate issue of national liberation, releasing the material and human forces for the creation of a new India. The solution of the problems of India means the solution of the most typical and sharpest problems, in their most complicated form, that confront in common the peoples of the world.

The people of India have already played a great part in world history, not as conquerors but in the sphere of culture, thought, art and industry. The national and social liberation of the Indian people will bring great new wealth to humanity.

Note

1 The terms "Indian Nation" and "Indian National Movement" are here and in subsequent pages used to describe the unity of the struggle of the people of India against British imperialism and for shaping their own political future. No judgment is implied by this term on the question of the future political forms a free India may adopt, or the signs of emergence of the multi-national character of a future free India with the significance which this may carry for political institutions. This special question will be separately considered later.

6

Socialist strategy of development

M. Arumugam

Source: *Socialist Thought in India: The Contribution of Rammanohar Lohia* (New Delhi: Sterling Publishers, 1978), pp. 91–123.

Lohia's approach

Government regulation of economy gained wide practice in the capitalist economies after the depression of the 1930s. Its impact on the policy development of the newly liberated countries during the period which started with the end of the Second War has been regarded as pragmatic in approach.

In India, for instance, Nehru defined it in 1949 that in the context of the conflict between capitalist and communist or socialist ideologies it was to be "some middle way". That method, to put it in his words, need not necessarily be an extreme method belonging to either of these two rival ideologies. It may be something in between. He pointed out that there was an attempt in most countries "to find other ways which certainly are completely divorced from the old style capitalism and which go towards what is normally called Socialism."[1] In the sweep of such an attempt, concepts of 'economic growth' as related to 'rate of investment', and of a complementary relation between the mature economies of the West and the underdeveloped countries in terms of foreign aid became pervasive in the growing economic literature.[2] In the words of Gunnar Myrdal, it was a "reflection of the fundamentally changed international political situation."[3]

The now oft-spoken desire in advanced economies to help retarded economies, Lohia commented in 1949, is a ritual and at best a scratch on the problem. In his view, as has been referred to earlier, the doctrine of full employment now being used for theories of world trade and social security has to yield place to the doctrine of relatively equal productivity. Colonialism, although reducing to a marginal phenomenon, was affecting human relationships in devious ways.[4] He further put forth the concept to the Third Camp based on the principle of Equal Irrelevance. He held very firmly that the conflict between the two power blocs was not relevant to the problem of creation in the new states of Asia. Capitalism and communism were according to him two forms of the same civilisation except in respect of the property question. They are essentially doctrines of political and economic centralisation and of force. The division of the world into the communist and non-communist blocs is causing a complete subordination of idea to force. Thinking becomes propagandist and not creative. Hence, he ruled out ideological preference between the two.[5]

He conceived of the Third Camp in view of the States of the newly liberated peoples, who want progress. 'A camp, in the international sense of today, consists of a bloc and a force, a bloc of governments and a force of peoples.'[6] Lohia distinguished it from the capitalism of *status quo* and the communism of chaos, as the camp of socialism for peaceful revolution and economic reconstruction.[7] In the following pages, an attempt is made to grasp the dimensions of the concepts he formulated in this direction.

'Small-unit' machine for industrialisation

"The large-scale machine, high rationalization, etc. may give a few Kanpurs and Calcuttas," Lohia pointed out, "but it will create around these islands of frenzied activity colossal unemployment and poverty." In an oft-quoted statement, he posed it as follows. To turn a peasant of India, Java, or China into a worker, a cultivator into a tractor driver, or to provide a factory worker with the concentrated capital of modern technology may or may not be a high endeavour, but its achievement is impossible and it shall stay a barren and cruel effort. Lands averaged around 15 acres for every agricultural worker in Russia before collectivisation and the tractor brought them on somewhat at a level with American agriculture. Where lands average between one acre and one and a half as in India and China, the communist modernisation would throw tons of crores of people out of work.[8] In Europe and America, the workers have tools and machines worth somewhere between 5,000 and 10,000 rupees.[9] According to such rational standards, Lohia stated, no less than seven crores of persons are unemployed in India.[10] The same consideration has been stressed later on by Reddaway that the problem of unemployment here should not be conceived of merely in 'numbers' as in the developed West but necessarily in its 'productivity' dimension.[11]

In another forthright statement, Lohia said that both communism and capitalism are doctrines of centralisation and mass production that shatter against the stone walls of a high density of population jutting upon an infernally low productive equipment. Asia's density of population varies from 300 persons per square mile of India to Java's 600 persons, while its productive equipment averages at Rs. 150 per person. To provide Asia with a rational economic existence, this huge density together with a totally inadequate capital equipment must be faced. These two factors taken together make it impossible for any scheme of industrialisation on the Ford or Stalin basis to succeed.[12]

Lohia found it an imperative need of socialism to disintegrate the premises of capitalism and communism. Capitalism is a doctrine of the individual and of free enterprise that leads to ever-changing application of science to industry and agriculture. Communism is a doctrine of social ownership and of release of means of production from their relations of private property. However, it inherits from capitalism its technique of production.[13] Similarly in regard to socialism in Europe, he stated that it had a reservoir of massed forces of production. Socialism in the rest of the world must build the reservoir as much as it has to distribute the contents. Hence he suggested the need for a different strategy of Revolution.

The advance of backward Russia to a position of comparative equality, Lohia wrote, has somewhat obscured the fact that benefits of industrial age are local and uniquely historical and may be reproduced. He noted two significant points in this connection: (1) Russia did not start from scratch, and (2) the exceedingly low density of her population which provided great scope for methods of mass production.[14] Just as communism at one time fought feudalism as well as capitalism and went beyond them both, Lohia affirmed, socialism today fights capitalism as well as communism and goes beyond them both.[15]

Noting the derisive remark of Krushchev against the Chinese Communists, viz., "Socialism" of "high-minded but hungry people sitting around an empty table in complete equality," Richard Lowenthal stated, "it would lack one of the main attractions hitherto exerted by the communist bloc on intelligentsia of the underdeveloped countries—the attraction of a model for quick modernisation."[16] He has further commented,

"Communism of the Chinese type would then become not a model for development but a model for accepting its failure and reacting by a final extrusion of the influence of Western civilisation." Lohia had posed this problem in the following words in 1952: "The choice for Asia's planners is between lifting up region or an industry to acknowledged rational levels while keeping the rest of the economy depressed and an all-round, although slower, lifting up of the whole economy with all its occupation and regions. Asia needs more tools and machines, new industries and occupations; it needs to cultivate new lands and make the old yield more."[17]

The economic trends of the nineteenth century in Western Europe and North America are, as observed by Alice and Daniel Thorner, "no longer adequate guides to the path lying before India. In absolute terms, the strength of the male working force in manufacture in India remained at about 7 million from 1911 through 1931, and doubled between 1931 and 1961. From 1911 to 1931 the number of manufacturing workers for every 100 men at work dropped from 9 to 8, by 1961 the figure had risen to 11. But thenceforward, "India's progress toward modernisation is unlikely to be reflected in a sizeable increase in the percentage of workers engaged in manufacture."[18] To get out of this troublesome situation, Lohia stressed the need for a small machine technology. The new technology should be such as not to demand the high capitalisation of Western standards and would give rational employment to ten times the number possible by Western standards of rationalisation for a given annual investment. He was thinking of an economy in which the capitalisation will rise up sufficiently so as to enable a decent living without the specific strains of rationalisation and unrationalisation. It would be possible to re-equip the economy of two-thirds of the world with a tool that will make an advance upon the existing situation but will not make such crushing demands upon our general economy as to cause dislocations, as to give the benefits of rationalisation only to a small sector and to deny it to the rest.[19]

To make a distinction between Marxism and Socialism, so far as this analysis is concerned, Lohia said in 1952, "one would have to admit that Marxism and Communism construe their task by one-half. They think alone in terms of destroying the relations of capitalist production, whereas a genuine socialism would have to think in terms of destroying both the capitalist relations of production and the capitalist forces of production, or at least vastly remodelling them."[20] The only way to rationalise the existing occupations is through the invention of a pervasive technology that needs small unit, and will not require concentration, and will go into the village and the town.[21] "The small-unit machine need not necessarily be less efficient than the heavily capitalised machine, for," Lohia added, "apart from social gains, there is no way yet to compare the accountancy of 'round-about' production, with that of immediate production. Furthermore, the advocates of the small-unit machine do not totally reject mass production where it is inescapable."[22]

It is interesting to read in this connection the view of C.L. Barbar, Professor of Economics, University of Manitoba: "The kind of equipment which would be most suited to the needs of the most underdeveloped countries simply does not exist because the necessary techniques have never been invented. While it would undoubtedly be possible to develop types of equipment which would be both labour intensive (capital-saving) and sufficiently efficient to compete with the equipment currently available, until this development takes place it can be confidently predicted that underdeveloped areas will continue to adopt the labour-saving equipment now being produced in the West.[23] Therefore, the aim of a new technology policy would be to select and "develop techniques" that can be employed by small producing groups, and to make them available at a cost which they can afford.[24] The scientific problem in India, as in all undeveloped economics, is more stubborn than what a mere transplanting of Western methods of manufacture would occasion. If a student of economics and politics is at all competent to advise scientists and technicians, Lohia said in 1950 that he would request them to direct their energies into the invention of small-unit machinery. Villages and towns of our country have abundant raw material of various kinds. It is being wasted. Its processing and manufacture would be possible only when small machinery is available. He was visualising the time "when over all our country, in towns and villages, will be spread millions of little power-driven machines for producing wealth and easing the pressure on land."[25]

The basic problem of development in the underdeveloped countries, as Frankel has put it, consists precisely in the fact that it is essential to utilise more adequately and fully the labour resources as they now are in those countries, so as gradually to build up new forms of capital. The way to accumulate in these countries is to make the best use of labour—not to displace it by capital, which is relatively scarce, and has to be imported at considerable cost. So postulate a capital intensity in them akin to that which is found in the more advanced countries is unwarranted. For what is really involved is the evolution of a different art of living and working.[26]

A capital export to, or import by, an underdeveloped country—a capital outlay or input—is not necessary investment at all—it may well represent only capital consumption, i.e. its use in situations where it is impossible to expect economic activity sufficient to maintain or replace the capital and provide for its further accumulation. The great growth of capital in the eighteenth and nineteenth centuries in Europe was due not to mechanical forces but to the evolution of new patterns in social relationships. 'Saving', he defines, was not a mechanical act but the result of new attitudes in social behaviour.[27]

Lohia's agrarian plan of food army

Lohia attached great importance to the organisation of peasant movement in developing latent powers of the country and the peasants. The peasant orientation of the socialist movement in India was already discussed in chapter three. It was especially marked in the revolutionary role assigned by Acharya Narendra Dev in his speeches at the Kisan Sabha in 1930s. Lohia affirmed in 1950, "Our task is to break the shackles of society, to bring flow to the waters that have grown stagnant. This is possible only when there is a real flowering of the social forces that are now dormant."[28] He noted in his programme to end poverty, "At the core of every problem in the country is the stupendous poverty of the people and it is directly traceable to the dearth of productive occupations, the denial of social justice and an increasing population."[29] A couple of years back, he noted, as a member of the Foodgrain Policy Committee (1948), as follows : "A purpose and a plan, with of course, adequate equipment dissipate the inertia that has numbed our minds and altogether disabled us . . . when there is land and there are men, no reasoning can ever justify lack of food."[30]

Lohia categorically observed that the Socialist Plan of Indian Agriculture will consist of (1) improvement in existing cultivation and (2) extension of new farming.

Extension of new cultivation will be undertaken either through a department or an autonomous organisation. Of the available 15 crores which yet are not under cultivation, he ascertained that nearly 100 million acres of cultivable tracts lie largely in mass, away from settled villages and are not likely to yield immediate harvest.[31] It would be idle to expect private initiative to cultivate these tracts. For this purpose, he advocated recruitment of a Food Army by the State, citing the instance of the land army in Britain which brought in the year 1942 nearly four million acres of new land under the plough. Lohia thus stated in 1950 that with immeasurably greater resources in manpower and land, the food army in India should be able to bring at least 10 million acres of land under the plough per year for a period of two years.

On the basis of the capital outlay of Rs.150 per acre and at an annual working expenditure of Rs. 1,000 each person, over a period of two years the food army will cost Rs. 250 crores in the first year, and Rs.150 crores in the second year. An additional Rs. 50 crores as emergency or miscellaneous expenditure may be budgeted for. The test for the food army "shall not be that of efficiency but that of attainability". Whatever is attainable by way of agricultural tools in our present condition of manufacture should be brought to the aid of the food army. At the end of two years, the food army will have started paying its way, as the additional cultivation will have begun to yield around four million tons of food. At this time, the major portion of the food army will have turned into farmers of model villages, which will be changed into cooperatives of various kinds and degree in consultation with the people concerned. A trained technical personnel of over 10,000 persons, in addition to various types of land-machines, will also become available to the Republic.[32] Use will undoubtedly be made of such machinery as bulldozers and tractors wherever absolutely necessary.[33]

The following may be regarded as the advantages of the food army:

1 additional employment to one million persons who, in course of time, may well become the nucleus for the livelihood of four or five million persons;
2 increase of food production by four million tons annually;
3 breaking down of barriers of class and caste and to the approach to economic equality;
4 founding of new villages whose joyous life may impel and support neighbouring villages towards activity;
5 encouragement to the industries of clothing and housing materials, particularly artisan manufacture.

Thus in Lohia's view the benefits accruing from the "food army" would be not only the solution of immediate problems of food and employment but also the introduction of dynamic elements into the social structure and agricultural economy of our people.[34]

In this connection a reference may be made to the details of a district level land army outlined by C. T. Kurien. The workers should live in barracks in four or five centres within the district with provision to visit their families once a week. By providing part of the wages in the form of food, the food surplus is utilised. By moving the men into different parts of the district and through other organised efforts it widens the horizons of the workers. And yet because the programme is flexible and related to the ongoing activity in the villages, it does not constitute a sudden disruption of the village economy. It has also additional advantages such as the job opportunities and impetus to a growing number of service entrepreneurs in the rural areas and in the suburbs. This may entail a reduction of the availability of labour in agriculture. Some marginal farmers may leave farming also. These two developments will change the characteristics of the rural economy and the rural structure itself. "A controlled transformation of property relations will therefore become necessary almost along with the mobilisation of manpower; a land policy will have to accompany the Land Army programme."[35]

On land question and food problem

Lohia regarded redistribution of land not alone as an act of social justice, but primarily as a measure to increase production through voluntary development. He conceived voluntary labour as a third item of capital formation. He pointed out that a major part of the reconstruction in Yugoslavia has been achieved through voluntary effort. According to him, if the 4 crores of adults in the country volunteered an hour's labour every day, the tasks accomplished would equal those which the Government of India gets done by a year's budget.[36] Such voluntary activity is only possible through socialism, which will accomplish a sense of communal ownership. He emphasised the point that reconstruction of the country is impossible through the ordinarily known ways. Utilisation of idle hours of the people who have not sufficient work to do will perhaps be the greatest objective of successful government. This is impossible of accomplishment on the basis of money payment. Increase in money supply, he has cautioned, has great dangers in an impoverished country like ours. Funds through taxation could also never suffice for this huge task. It could only be done on a voluntary basis.[37]

If people would feel themselves the owners of fields and factories, this feeling would bring them the realisation that their personal gains are possible through social activity alone. Of the existing agriculture of 27 crore acres over 20 crore acres of land remain victim of the vagaries of weather. It is imperative to lay main emphasis on minor irrigation while river-training schemes together with major irrigation projects will be continued. As it is not a feasible proposition to undertake such colossal development of irrigation on the basis of hired labour, Lohia put it emphatically, "voluntary labour of almost the entire adult population now engaged in agriculture could alone undertake such a gigantic task." If the bulk of them could be moved to give an hour's free labour to dig for canals, bunds, and other reservoirs, it would be possible to programme for earthworks irrigation of such magnitude.[38]

Lohia viewed the structure of land ownership in the village as the stubborn obstacle to the achievement of such a mass voluntary labour. The structure of land ownership in the Indian village has split it wide open of disunities of behaviour, corruption of mind, and a general absence of collective will. The division of land workers into landlords of various removes and holdings, agricultural labourers of registered and insecure holdings and landless labourers and artisans has in conjunction with the insupportable pressure on land, produced in the village a war of each against all.[39] Under such circumstances—while a vast section in the village is landless, or owns a nominal strip of land, a few on the top possess extensive tracts—voluntary labour would be another name for forced labour or begar.[40] The only solution for the land problem in India with regard to its aspect of ownership would be to think boldly and act courageously. "Those who actually till the land must be made secure masters of their harvest. This simple principle has to be legislated. Further legislation may come in its own time."[41]

With regard to the Government's approach to the land question, it would suffice to quote the following comment. "Land reforms have been legislated but ingenious ways of avoiding them have been found. Defective legislation and the delay in giving effect to land ceiling law enabled the big landlord to keep his holding intact. He is able to distribute his land to relatives each getting a share within this ceiling limit."[42] This is a monumental failure of the Government in view of the fact that the Indian rural scene, as Daniel Thorner has put, is ready to yield to any sustained pressure for change, "In this setting, the agrarian legislation must come first. Only then there can be a proper footing for the long needed rationalisation of agricultural production."[43] In the long run what holds out the best hope is any programme that will set the rural mass into motion, make them into a self-propelling force, generating their own energy.[44]

After acceptance of the principle that the tiller is the master of his harvest, Lohia had stated, redivision of land becomes inevitable.[45] In another statement, he noted: redistribution of land will be completed throughout the country in the five-year period of a socialist government.[46] A family of five persons engaged in agriculture will be left with a maximum of three times the unit of land that a family can cultivate without employing hired labour or mechanisation.[47] "Land available for cultivation is around 40 crore acres, while the number of families depending on agriculture may at present be estimated between 4 and 5 crores."

Ceiling fixation becomes meaningful, Lohia stated forthright by way of comment on the Congress resolution of 1959 at Nagpur on Land Reforms, only when viewed in the background of: (1) The acute land hunger of the landless agriculturists, (2) Abolishing landlordism both direct and indirect, and (3) The question of compensation. The Congress resolution shies away from making any concrete formulation on any of the three parts. Its policy regarding compensation while on the one hand, retarding land reforms, and putting an extra burden on the people has on the other hand tended to create new privileged classes in the village community. Payments of fabulous amounts to big landlords and the creation of different categories of holdings on the basis of the peasants' ability to pay, have tended to make existing inequalities even more acute.[48]

Lohia's categorical propositions go to counter the facile argument that there is no surplus land for redistribution, and give a new vigour to the land question. He criticised the Zamindari Abolition Fund as a Tughlakian blunder and that the

Congress aligned itself with landlords and capitalists. He urged for a change in the Constitution for effecting a redivision of land and recommended only a rehabilitation compensation in respect of the smaller landholders.[49] In Lohia's perspective, redivision of land on the principle of 'land to the tiller' together with the item of food army would relieve the pressure on agricultural land.

"All cultivable and uncultivable land," Lohia stressed, "must be brought under the control of the central government. Regional prejudices and separatism must not be allowed to play ducks and drakes with the food of the people, the unity of the country and glorious prospects of a revitalised and democratic social structure."[50] He remained a staunch critic of the policy of food control. Instead he laid emphasis on an expanding economy, increasing production and better distribution. In his note separate to the interim report of the Government of India's Foodgrain Policy Committee (1948) he recommended cooperative sales and purchase mechanism in place of the Food Administration. In order that the private trader might not fill the picture again, he suggested the institution of grain banks. These grain banks would be owned by the Panchayats, run by trained officers under the general control of the Panchayat, and the Central government would have first right over sales apart from the minimum quantities which members of such banks could draw. A significant feature of this proposition consisted in the prospect of "very fruitful interaction between the Panchayat and its grain cooperatives so that democracy and economic reconstruction draw vigour from each other."[51] He was opposed to any system of permits and licenses since it tends to degenerate into scramble for money all over; to restriction of the movement of foodgrains from one state to another, and to the imports of foodgrain from outside the country. He also pointed out that controls have helped the bigger ones to the detriment of the small men.[52] He believes that with the instituting of grain cooperatives, it would be easier for the government to look after regions of scarcity than under the present system of controls.

India being essentially an agricultural country the problem of land and of the peasants needs a careful understanding for proper solution. The problem of food is also linked up with it. Lohia stated that redivision of land, volunteers for village construction, major projects and dams and food army for cultivating waste lands are four interrelated items of Socialist Food Policy.[53] Referring to Nehru, Lohia further said that he had accepted item number three alone, viz., major projects and dams. He commented that the measures taken by the government were halting and inadequate.

He always emphasised the need of policy in respect of uncultivated land. He had stated that the two virgin states Vindhya and Rajasthan, could develop themselves under such planning to the benefit of the country as a whole.[54] He also struck a warning note that except a plan to end poverty, nothing—not even the exercise of all available force—can prevent the dissolution of India.

With regard to his view on Colombo Plan, Lohia stated in his reply, "it is not only a question of extending assistance or granting small sums for capital investments to those countries. What is more important is the development of local capital in those countries."[55] He thought that the advanced countries could help best by getting their inventors to construct small machines and placing them at the disposal of underdeveloped countries. Unassisted by machines, he reminded, no amount of hard labour can produce wealth in the world of today. Such machines have to be manufactured in the state owned factories alone, which run not for profit but for capital formation. Agricultural tools should be among the top priorities for iron and steel and, they will be increasingly refined as manufacture proceeds.

Socialism and peasantry

He further stressed that the three aims of the food army, small-unit industries and redivision of land as a complex unit, and hence to be taken together as three items of capital formation.[56] After land has been redivided on an egalitarian basis, the hunger for land and the sense of possessing will disappear. What will remain is initiative and independence of spirit coupled with the desire of collective well-being.

As to the fact of property in land which the farmer uses, Lohia stated categorically, the principle must be recognised that no denial of socialism takes place if the property used does not entail employment of another's labour.

He also commented that European socialism and communism drew their main strength from the vast masses of factory workers and they have disliked the farmer, both because he is an owner of property and an exactor of high prices for their food. "This absurd theory, universalised from a partial European and American experience, has done some damage to the cause of socialism among the peasantry."[57]

The vast majority of the agrarian population of India consists of small landlords, tenants of various types, unregistered tenants and share-croppers and landless labourers. A further complication is caused by the factor of caste. He saw a number of group tensions, rather than the class struggle, in the relationships of this vast agrarian population. Hence he regarded organisation of agricultural labourers as an auxiliary to the wider peasant movement. Lohia categorically stated that in India the social stratification was more defined by caste.[58] And to him the principle of 'class' consisted in the struggle for equality, and that of 'caste' lay in a fixed social design meant for stability and against change.[59]

He saw the efficacy of Gandhi's technique in that 'Satyagraha' could be the fighting weapon irrespective of an organisational backing. He wanted organisation of the peasantry through fight against unjust laws and constructive work, and to eliminate the caste basis. Any strategy of development in India which is meant to make it a genuinely people's movement, as C.T. Kurien has put it, must have our rural areas as the centre of attention and action.[60] Lohia proposed that "spade" is to socialist movement what the "spinning-wheel" was to the freedom movement.[61] It symbolised mass action as well as the direction of organising the farmers. Lohia viewed farmer as the co-builder of a new social order in Indian economy. Lohia differed from other socialists who believed in the efficacy of Westernisation as a cure for the problem of caste. Instead he proposed institutional remedy together with involvement of the mass in the political process through fragmentation of state power. This means a decentralised framework in which village, district, state and the Centre should function as "four pillars of the state." This is the type of constitution Lohia envisaged for introducing change and activity in the Indian social context, wherein caste was all prevailing as an obstruction to political change.

He sought to forge an approach in which the "general aims" of society (freedom and equality) and its "economic aims" (bread and technology) are inter-related. Lohia's emphasis on constructive action as denoted by "spade" underlines this approach vis-à-vis his perception of caste. Caste is immobile class; it is a socio-psychological framework. While class signifies the social motivation toward equality; caste leads to stability as against change. Caste, in Lohia's hypothesis, must have arisen out of a declining society or economic stagnation.[62] Capitalism fostered class in European society due to expanding forces of production; that is, a free play of struggle for equality took place. On the contrary capitalism was externally imperialistic. As it meant impoverishment, the caste was reinforced; that is to say, group inequality and poverty had grown together in India. In such a context, Lohia was seized of the need to create unity of mind and instil a sense of large social objective among the masses. This implies a difference on two points i.e., diagnosis and prescription from the concept of Western Socialism.

As regards the diagnosis, the forces of production are neither developed nor the relations of production are socialised to have class consciousness. Therefore as regards policy prescription, socialism in India had to seek for a mode of action which will help achieving both construction of productive and development of social consciousness and integration. A move for such an organisation of the agrarian population is symbolised by "spade" for socialism in opposition; and is expressed as land army, redivision of land, etc., in the governmental programme of socialism.[63] In Lohia's perspective, this is the first step in a series of developmental processes which include the rise of leadership from all the downtrodden castes who constitute four-fifths of the population in India.

The role of party and socialist mode of action

To Lohia's mind, "A consistent, worthwhile sociological or economic theory must be able to face the problems of a backward economy like the Indian economy."[64] Socialism was defined in the West as the transformation of relations of production to make it consonant with the developed forces of production. Its historical scaffolding was one of changing classes. The serf bound to his master has been replaced by the free peasant or the hired labourer on farms. Guilds of artisans with their caste rules of apprenticeship and admission were steadily broken down and have been replaced by the industrial factory with its labourers moving up and down the scale. As a consequence of democracy, political power has somewhat drained from its earlier receptacles to parties of the common man, trade unions and the like. Eventually economic equality has become a common element of all ideologies.[65]

This view is inadequate for an underdeveloped economy which requires creation of forces of production, a new technology consistent with socialism. That is, socialism needs to be defined by constructive as well as combative aspects.[66] Class struggle, Lohia reaffirmed, is the dynamics of social change.[67] It hastens and matures the destruction of capitalism. In the undeveloped areas where a productive apparatus has yet to be created, it cannot always adhere to the slow processes of constitutionalism. Lohia urged that socialism in India must be drastic, instead of being gradual, and unconstitutional whenever necessary, and lay the accent on production.[68] The people express their will through their vote, and this expression prevails for five years. In that sphere there is "no challenge to the ballot." But with regard to injustices and oppression, where they have assumed unbearable proportions, the alternative is "between the bullet and civil disobedience."[69] Thus the course of action, formulated by Lohia comprised the principles of constructive action resistance against injustice and democracy symbolised by "Spade-prison-and-Vote".

"By Communist reasoning itself, fullness of freedom shall come after the achievement of fullness of bread but, as communism shows no way to rationalise underdeveloped economies," in the terse words of Lohia, "what tend to become permanent are the general aims it adopts in the process and not those it preaches as an ideal. The centralised party and state and all that they give birth to seem to be the only achievable general aims of communism. Communism can provide neither bread nor freedom to two-thirds of the world."[70] Europe had accepted violence as the midwife of social change; but this aspect has to be understood against the background of the French Revolution and the subsequent radical movement which had adopted armed struggle. Later with the overall rise in the standard of living and the introduction of universal franchise, the Western socialists began to debate on the proposition "democracy versus violence". The Indian socialist could easily call this a wrong proposition. He was well aware of the efficacy of civil disobedience or satyagraha. Therefore, he saw a third course of action, beyond the two alternatives of parliament and insurrection, with the advent of Gandhi. He added that it should be open for the people to violate unjust laws and to resist injustice through peaceful struggle when constitutional methods have proved incapable of achieving redress. He firmly believed that organisation of violence inevitably leads to concentration of power.[71]

In a reference to the common belief that Gandhism means the change of heart, he recollected, "Gandhi himself probably spent six months or a year of his lifetime in changing the heart of foreign satraps or native oligarchs and devoted a full fifty-six years to changing the heart of his people from cowardice into bravery."[72] As Gandhi himself has put it, "no man can be actively non-violent and not rise against social injustice, no matter when it occurred. Unfortunately Western socialists have, so far as I know, believed in the necessity of violence for enforcing socialistic doctrines." "Agitation against every form of injustice is," in his judgement, "the breath of political life." It is rewarding to note that the assertions in quote were made by Gandhi in regard to Jayaprakash and

Lohia respectively.[73] To Lohia's mind, there is no contradiction between satyagraha and class struggles which are but two names of a single exercise in power—reduction of the power of evil and increase in the power of the good.

Throughout the world, and more so in the underdeveloped territories, a doctrine and a party is judged not alone by what it professes but also by the extent to which it can struggle and suffer. Apart from the political advantages of a struggle, it is difficult to believe that a genuine doctrine can stay unmoved in the face of an injustice. He added, "Whoever refuses to resist injustice, when other forms of agitation are not available or exhausted, becomes a party to it." "Various issues such as famine, land ownership, high prices, dismissal and unemployment, and, on top of them, police repression are daily acquiring such proportions that the whole of India may well become a vast stage for intermittent practices in satyagraha. A day may come later, in Lohia's prophetic words, "when the whole nation is summoned to organise resistance against injustice and for the achievement of a new order."[74]

With regard to the argument that there is no place for satyagraha in a free country, Lohia in 1950, exhorted the people to fight injustices. According to him, this will bring strength to the people and they will also get over the habit of tolerating everything. He had further pointed out that it will take time for the distinction between state and government to get established. After this tradition has been established, the need for satyagraha will diminish. In a comparatively mature democracy, people have acquired a political mind. The Indian people do not yet have a political mind. They are increasingly turning away from the Congress, but they stand at the crossroads and refuse to move towards any other organisation. In order to move them on toward the effort for creating a new order, he proposed constructivism and combatism and criticised electionism and insurrectionism. The cynicism born out of a sense of betrayal must be combatted by purposeful action, both while in opposition and in government.[75]

Lohia had struck a note of warning in 1950 that "they easily construe dissatisfaction with the Congress Party as support of the Socialist Party, which it certainly is not. An unbelievable self-deception occurs."[76] This was confirmed by the results of the first general elections of 1952. At the Pachmarhi conference of the Party, Jayaprakash referred to it as "moment of political and ideological confusion."[77] At this conference Lohia advised his partymen in the course of his famous presidential address against being led away by the incipient polarisation between the Congress Party and the Communist Party and also against seeking easy solutions. He put it in unmistakable terms that a policy of support to the Congress "would disable the party from organising the people's will and combating injustices." He urged for intensifying its own constructive action and peaceful struggles and initiating political moves in a big way.[78] But, on the contrary, Nehru-Narayan talks on cooperation with the Government were held subsequently in 1953. The rank and file of the Socialist Party disapproved such an approach at the Betul Convention of 1953. The crisis in the party at Betul in 1953 was averted by the bold mediation of Lohia whose sole concern was the unity in the party.[79] However, Lohia's efforts came to naught since the process of disintegration of the party was not to be arrested. Jayaprakash Narayan who contemplated cooperation with the "Government" in 1953 declared however at the Bodh Gaya Sarvodaya Conference (1954) that he was dedicating himself to Bhoodan movement and renouncing party-politics. He contended that he was disenchanted with the party system as all the parties were concerned with the capture of power.

It may be noted here that following the complete defeat of his Radical Democratic Party in the 1946 spring elections, M. N. Roy had also subjected the party system to scathing criticism for its lustful pursuit of power. For some time to come, he stated, one or the other parties may still manage to usurp power ; we shall not compete in the practice, which is a denial of democracy.[80] Democracy can never be practised through the intermediary of party-politics, since a party is bound to be exclusive.[81] If human freedom is not to be sacrificed in the scramble for power, according to Roy, we shall have to explore the possibility of political practice without the interpolation of political parties between the people and their sovereign power.[82] It is not important, however, for our purpose, as to whether this kind of approach was philosophical or one of defeatism. Whatever that be, it is evident that both M. N. Roy and Jayaprakash Narayan denied the role of party system in India.

In contrast, Lohia was firm that "party" is an essential element of politics having a definite place in democracy. He was critical of the cynical tendency on the part of a party to deride the vote in the event of an electoral reverse. He advocated a two-way relationship between the people and the party so as to look upon an electoral reverse as a spur to further efforts in organised action.[83] He was quite categorical that there was no alternative to vote. He held democracy as absolutely necessary; he was equally emphatic that constitutionalism alone was not a sufficient condition for democracy. The periodical elections must be supplemented by peaceful struggles to resist injustice. Thus in Lohia's formulation both "vote" and "prison" constitute the twin symbols of democracy denoting the roles of elections and civil disobedience movements, in the constitution of government, and the method of social struggles, respectively.

In Roy's humanist political approach, there would be some people throughout the country who would "begin the task of awakening the urge for freedom in the individuals" and they would "act as a powerful catalyst" and enable the people "to examine election promises in a critical spirit."[84]

Commenting on this Lohia has said, "I fail to see how this work can be done by a group of people who stay outside of and above political parties. Even if such a group should come into existence which is itself almost impossible, it will soon turn into a political party with its own promises or a pack of highbrow and superior people whose capacity for action is completely blocked. In such a situation, they would either become cynical or seek for an adjustment and accommodation with all kinds of important people." In Lohia's perspective, "Some day the electorate will examine programmes . . . not because of the doings of non-party people but because of an honest political party that assists them to this critical spirit as also to the enthusiasm needed for all political action. Enthusiasm and criticality must go together if they are to be effective and useful."[85]

Lohia was averse to the proposition that good people must come together and blur the outlines of the parties, for such an accent can only end in a political dictatorship. He laid stress on three factors for the success of a programme: concrete and timebound items, suitable agency, and appropriate popular atmosphere. He regarded top adjustments and manoeuvres in search of power, rather than change in people's thinking and creation of appropriate organisations, as *status quoist* methods. He criticised Asoka Mehta's recommendation of areas of agreement with the government party—such as nationalism, secularism and democracy—as faulty and mechanical reasoning.[86] He clarified the issue as a party inevitably arises when the existing ways have lost their value and a new way becomes necessary. He was inclined to think that the less deserving a government is of people's cooperation, the more frequently does it extend invitation for cooperation. As a consequence of the search for areas of agreement, the party will only stultify itself by shutting its eye to the sweeping areas of disagreement with the government party. In a country, where ejectments, police repression, unemployment and other injustices continually prevail, it would mean sharing only of the discredit of the administration rather than substantial reconstruction of the country.[87] In his view, the people have to be roused "on the move," and they must become seized with hunger for equality and prosperity just as they were moved by the thirst for freedom in the earlier years.[88]

A short note on planning in India

The present planning in India, Lohia observed in 1956, has chosen to adopt the course of raising the standard of life of small select portions of the population to the minimum European, if not American, standards of living. Again the aim may be to keep on enlarging these sectors, but let us think of the consequences of this course which would raise portion of the population to an European standard of living. The greatest single consequence would be increasing bureaucratisation of the people.[89] This foresight is now being appreciated.

Later many economists began to consider that the orientation of the plans is responsible for "the concentrations of economic power in the hands of a few and the lowering of the standard of life of the majority of the people."[90] To quote A.K. Chanda, "In the last parliament, the late Dr Ram Manohar Lohia made an abrasive attack on government's economic performance. Armed with an array of facts and figures, he sought to prove that 270 million people live on only 3 annas a day. Replying on behalf of government, Mr Gulzarilal Nanda, the then Home Minister and previously the Vice-Chairman of the Planning Commission, could only say that it was not quite so bad that the per capita spending in rural areas was 4.3 annas and in urban areas 5.3 annas. This was a damaging admission to make and did no credit to our planning or its priorities."[91]

The ideal would be an integrated society with power decentralised whereas the prevailing phenomenon of Indian life is social disintegration accompanied by centralisation of political power.[92] It will be possible to diffuse economic power through spreading social ownership over the "four pillars of the state" and not through the fixed economy.

Lohia has also criticised the government plans for their unique relation to external dependence. All that remains is the desire to get money from other countries, to balance income and expenditure. Somehow, build a factory or two anyhow, while the country lives in a state of continuing famine." He has pinpointed the fantastic increase in our debts and its burden on the future generation. It is interesting to note that he did not believe in theory of cold war as an explanation for the "foreign aid" in international relations. According to him, "The Cold War after 1950 was more play-acting than reality. Russia and America came to tacit agreement to preserve the *status quo* in the rest of the world."[93] He has instead regarded trade relation as the pertinent factor. He marks the fact, "Even now, eighty or seventy per cent of India's trade relations is with the Atlantic bloc." To quote further, Lohia has stated, "The adverse balances during the first plan was Rs. 300 crores, but now it has reached the figures of Rs. 6,300 crores . . . I would like to say to men like Mr Masani that Americans do not like planning in their own country, but like it elsewhere. . . . Without a plan, it becomes difficult for them to give loans or aid. For Indian government also, it becomes difficult to justify things without a plan."[94]

There is indeed sufficient ground to generalise that the leaven of India's industrial growth has worked on the adjunct of Western economic dynamics. The steel expansion programme although originating from Indian demands and preoccupations, Ragnar Nurkse has put it in mild terms, may have been partly due to the fact that foreign capital became available for this particular purpose.[95] Ryuizo Yamaizaki has observed in 1957 that the advanced countries have been aiming at "securing markets on a long-range basis through various forms of economic cooperation, including technical guidance, extension of credit, etc., rather than merely resorting to simple forms of export. This tendency sharply reflects itself in the recent trend of world trade, as evidenced by German participation in the establishment of the Rourkela Mill in India, Britain's rendering technical guidance and loan to the India Durgapur Steel Mill."[96] Western aid took on a quasi-institutional form in August 1958 with the inauguration of an 'Aid India Club'—a creditor's consortium. The point to be noted is that India's imports from the industrially advanced countries of Europe were facilitated with her programmes for industrialisation.

Addressing a public meeting at Rourkela in 1960, Lohia wanted the German people to change their policies with regard to the Rourkela steel plant and to treat it as a centre from where Germany would help train Indian technician worksmen to industrialise their land. He stated that over 400 Indian officers were drawing salaries above Rs. 1,000 per month and amenities at a minimum of Rs. 4,000 a month while the salary and amenities of the highest office in the steel plant was estimated by him at Rs. 25,000 a month, and also that over 500 German workers were each drawing a minimum of Rs. 10,000 a month as salaries and amenities, the 6,000 regular workers were receiving each Rs. 100 as salaries and amenities, and 24,000 irregular workers less than Rs. 60 or Rs. 70 a month. He also observed that industrialisation was impossible unless these disparities were removed which only a revolution could achieve.[97]

Lohia has noted in 1952 that a new middle class of politicians and bureaucrats is appearing with the emergence of various Asian countries into freedom.[98] He co-related the phoney talk of socialism in India to the fact that the bureaucrat who is a pseudo-radical is derived largely from the caste of learning. Although the bourgeoisie and the bureaucrat are inter-related in their economic interests he disclosed the schism between the two on grounds of caste affiliation.[99] He has further referred to the striking difference between the standard of our administrators and that of Mao Tsetung, Chou En-lai or Ho Chi Minh, especially the last mentioned. He stated, "a chief reason why China's pace of development was greater than India's was this narrowing down of the difference between the rulers and the ruled in their language, dress and ways of living, whereas in India the estrangement has been ever on the increase."[100] In Lohia's propositions limitation on personal expenditure needs to be imposed for twenty to thirty years. Such a step would save from Rs. 1,000 crores to Rs. 2,500 crores for investment expenditure.[101] He has also emphasised that equality of incomes and expenditure should be directly sought, "for even under social ownership of means of production, a class of bureaucrats, managers, and political leaders with high salaries and allowances, for comfort and luxury may grow."[102] He was quite specific that a programme for equality should comprise both levelling up and levelling down. In fact, the levelling down will take place somewhat earlier than levelling up, although this unavoidable chronological sequence must not lead to a logical sequence in the mind. He regarded such of those who talk alone of levelling up as reactionary, and those who restrict to levelling down as irrelevant.[103] A proportion of lowest and highest incomes in the range of one to ten was meant to be a concept of immediate attainability as well as preconditions of social conscience, of comparative disciplining of wants, of comparative multiplication of produce.[104]

The four-pillar state: framework of socialist planning

Gandhism meant to Lohia's mind the principle of immediacy in action. He found it not only in civil disobedience but also in "Charkha" and the concept of "village republic". In his view Gandhi's proposition pointed to the need of a new direction of thought. He was aware of the limitations of Gandhian propositions. However, he believed that a rationalistic applications of them will invigorate the cause of socialism.[105] The only way to diversify the occupations and rationalize the existing ones is through the invention of a pervasive technology that will be a small unit, that will not require concentration, and will go into the village and the town. This decentralised technology will provide the framework which will make it possible to have a government of the community, by the community, for the community.[106]

The significance of Lohia's concept can be seen in the following excerpt from the letter of Mr Yashiki Hoshino, a socialist leader of Japan to the Indian socialist leader Dr Ram Manohar Lohia,: ". . . I knew that Gandhiji had emphatically taught us decentralisation of power. But you are a leader of the Socialist Party so I rather expected that you would express us centralists ideas. But contrary to my expectations I found that you were a developed successor of Gandhism rather than its antagonist with the European formalistic socialism."[107]

While Lohia wanted the doctrine of socialism to be enriched by Gandhi's contribution, he was clear in his mind that superimposition of non-violence on socialism or democracy on socialism would be infructuous.[108] He was emphatic that there should be harmony in the socialist integration of its economic and general aims. He stated that socialism in Asia must increasingly become the doctrine of maximum attainable equality through redivision of land and social ownership over industry. Its political structure must arise out of the decentralised state and it must seek its technological framework in the small machine.[109]

He categorically rejected the idea of "restricted capitalism and mixed economy."[110] Lohia expressed his concern over the fact that the bureaucratic and the capitalist minority in the country were imitating the Western standard of consumption even before reproducing their productive equipment. As C.T. Kurien has observed, "Under the influence of the doctrines and patterns of both the West and the East the development problem in our country has always been presented as an academic economic problem. If a breakthrough is desired, a new orientation to development is the first requirement. Development has to be seen as a major transformation of society where the decision-making processes are genuinely participatory. Refusal to see this connection between development and mass movement has been the greatest weakness of the development efforts in our country."[111]

Decentralisation of state power

Lohia stressed that small-unit industries have to be taken together with the other aims such as food army and redivision of land. These items must also fit in the framework which he called the "four-pillar state."[112] According to this concept the centre must have power enough to maintain the integrity and unity of the State and the rest of it must be fragmented. The idea underlying the four-pillar state is not that of the self-sufficient village but of the intelligent and vital village. This is a path-breaking concept inasmuch as the existing principles of federalism divide state power between a centre and the federating units and provide the local framework with limited powers as a "conferment from the top."[113]

The four-pillar state is both a legislative and executive arrangement. The state is to be so organised and sovereign power so diffused that the active participation of village community is achieved in the affairs of the country. Such an advance is possible when the country frames its constitution on the basis of "the village, the district, the province and the centre being the four pillars of state."[114] He suggested that several departments, for example, those for cooperative societies, rural and agricultural development, a substantial part of irrigation, seeds, revenue collecting, and the like may be transferred to the village and the district. A substantial part of state revenues, between one-third or a fourth of the total revenue should belong by right to the village and the district. It can be seen that the four-pillar state rises above the issues of regionalism and functionalism.[115]

The necessity of such an arrangement is better appreciated in the light of the following observation of D.R. Gadgil. "As chairman of the Bombay-Poona Planning Committee," he found that "the investment that may be necessary in the next few years for just improving Bombay's roads would be the sort of investment that the Government of Maharashtra would be prepared to provide for all the roads in the rest of Maharashtra."[116] If the development process is to become a mass movement, as C.T. Kurien has put it, the power of decision-making on many important matters must belong directly to the people exercised through their immediate representative bodies. Decision-making power will become effective only if it is accompanied by the power to implement as well. He has aptly pointed out the two way relation between a structure of multi-level decision making units and the evolution of such a system from the movement itself."[117]

The structure of administration will undergo corresponding changes. Several welfare and development departments, particularly in relation to agriculture, which are now being run by State governments through a bureaucracy, will be transferred to local bodies in their own right.[118] The four-pillar state may indeed occasion numerous errors and upsets in the beginning because of the special conditions of India, its illiteracy and above all its castes. And yet to give power to the village representative seems the only way, to Lohia's mind, to deliver the people from inertia as well as an administration that is both top-heavy and corrupt. For instance, the only way to purify controls is to leave their administration to the village, town and district Panchayats and to take them out of the hands of legislators and government servants. It will clean up the administration in the end by the process of forcing the vast mass to judge and act.[119]

A literate army of three to four lakhs of educated young men, alongside of the food army of one million persons recruited from all over India, will also help to liquidate illiteracy within a period of ten years. Lohia stated reassuringly that a master campaign of literacy can easily be undertaken in a four-pillar state which has been rid of landed and capitalist relationship.[120]

Social policy on caste and mass education

The four-pillar state was regarded by Lohia as the effective way of introducing change and activity into Indian life.

He was aware that castes have stratified Indian society. He saw caste essentially as immobile class. Everybody struggles for increasing his or his group's share in the national income. This struggle is indeed universal to man, but where national income grows an expansive mentality prevails. A restrictive mentality goes with caste and poverty, for everyone's primary aim is to secure his own share. Caste resulting in greater group inequalities and poverty grow together.[121]

He perceived a new sociological law that shrinkage and contraction of opportunity and ability is a necessary accompaniment of caste. Hence he made a strong plea : the narrowing selection of abilities must now be broadened over the whole, and that can only be done if for two or three or four decades backward castes and groups are given preferential opportunities.[122] Preference will be given to scheduled castes and tribes in the matters of land distribution, employment, and educational opportunities.[123]

The system of education in the country, he suggested, needs drastic changes. It neither trains the person's mind nor equips him for living. He strongly believed that the prevalence of a foreign language has given an air of imitativeness to the whole country. He wanted the educational system to be given new foundations. The entire country should have a network of polytechnics and people's Universities for the benefit of peasants, workers and the poor middle class. He cited that countries like Germany and Sweden have been developed by workers and peasants who have, off and on, been to polytechnics.[124] Expensive schools of snobbery must be closed, for they obstruct social cohesion and add misery to life of middle classes, who try beyond their means to send their children to them. Structural changes in economy are a necessary accompaniment for such reforms in education.

High caste, English education and wealth as three characteristics distinguish India's ruling class. The combination of any two of these three factors makes a person belong to the ruling class.[125] The presence of the factor of high caste freezes the whole into an almost improbable immobility, for over 90 per cent of country's ruling classes belong to the high castes. He has described the political inter-play of castes as sectional elevation. For instance, in Maharashtra the Brahmin began to lose his monopoly of political power and the Maratha did not share his new found authority with the other downgraded castes. The phenomenon of caste exclusion was witnessed again, with the roles changed. A sectional elevation changes some relationships within the caste system, but it leaves the basis of castes unaltered. Moreover, the exclusion of the high-caste from political power does not necessarily imply their exclusion from economic and other types of power.[126] Lohia viewed the system of castes as a terrifying force of stability and against change.[127] "It renders nine-tenths of the population into onlookers, in fact, listless and nearly completely disinterested spectators of national tragedies."[128] In an economy where there is very little to go round, the scramble is hard, farsight almost impossible and group cohesiveness an inescapable need.

From the political attack on caste, in the sense of drawing the nation's leadership from all the castes in the country in Lohia's prophetic words, may come that revolution which gives to all Indian society the solidarity and reinsurance now given to smaller groups by caste.[129]

Conclusion

To sum up, the socialist approach to development postulates a new orientation in the constitution of the state. While the liberal and communist constitutions depend on two institutions, viz., the Centre and the federating units, Lohia's concept of "four-pillar state" incorporates the principle of mass participation and decentralisation of power so as to impart dynamics into local units and to work for an integrated society. This concept represents a rationalistic application of Gandhian principles. The decentralisation of power by means of the "four-pillar state" will provide the social framework of economic planning, which will generate development process conducive to a new technology, and which will take industry and power to the village.

Such a process is based on a programme of redivision of land—consisting of the principle "land to the tiller" which will enable utilisation of rural labour on a voluntary basis; employment of surplus workers in Food or Land Army into which is built a mass literacy campaign; and establishment of polytechnic schools in villages. Progress of planning in this direction would broaden the opportunities which alone could break the inertia and release social forces on to the development path through measures of equality. In short, according to Lohia, socialist policy for prosperity lies through equality with four-pillar state as its bed-rock and small-machine technology, its technical basis.

It is necessary to underline the point that Lohia's formulation stems from what he has called the principle of Equal Irrelevance. According to this, capitalism and communism, being systems of political and economic centralisation, are not relevant to the Asian problem of progress with large populations and low capital equipment. Lohia has therefore endeavoured a new approach by assimilation of Gandhian 'principle of immediacy' into the triple tasks of industrialisation, people's revolution and decentralisation of power.[130]

Notes

1 "We should pull together," *Independence and After* (A collection of the more important speeches of Jawaharlal Nehru from September 1946 to May 1949), 1949, pp. 181–98.
2 "Trade and Employment," *The Economist*, January 15, 1944. Kenneth Kurihara, "International Capital Movements and National Economic Growth," *Economic Internationale*, November 1966, pp. 597–603.
3 Gunnar Myrdal, "Preface," *Economic Theory and Underdeveloped Regions*, 1957, p. v.
4 "Some Fundamentals of a World Mind," (1949), *Fragments of a World Mind*, 1952, pp. 1–5, *Marx, Gandhi and Socialism*, 1963, pp. 283–88.
5 "The Third Camp in World Affairs" (1950) *Fragments of a World Mind*, 1952, pp. 8–16. See also "Principle of Equal Irrelevance," *Marx, Gandhi and Socialism*, pp. 242–57.
6 "The Third Camp in World Affairs," op, cit., p. 19.
7 "Asia and World Order" 1952, *Will to Power*, 1956, p. 72.
8 Ram Manohar Lohia, "The Doctrinal Foundation of Socialism," 1952, *Marx, Gandhi and Socialism*, 1963, p. 324.
9 Lohia, "Marxism and Socialism," 1952, in *Marx, Gandhi and Socialism*, 1963, p. 97.
10 Lohia, "The Approach to Socialist Planning," *Mankind*, Vol. I, No. 4 November 1956, p. 384.
11 W. B. Reddaway, *The Development of the Indian Economy*, 1962, p. 24.
12 Ram Manohar Lohia, "An Asian Policy"—Speech; Rangoon, March 1952, *Fragments of World Mind*, 1952, pp. 246–47.
13 Lohia, "The Doctrinal Foundation of Indian Socialism," 1952, *Marx, Gandhi and Socialism*, 1963, pp. 322–24.
14 Lohia, "Materiality and Spirituality," 1953, *ibid.*, p. 203.
15 Lohia, "An Asian Policy," 1952, *Fragments of a World Mind*, 1952, p. 250.
16 Richard Lowenthal, "Prospects of Pluralistic Communism," in Milord M. Drachkovitch (ed.). *Marxism in the Modern World*, 1965, pp. 247–48.
17 *ibid.*, p. 246.
18 Alice and Daniel Thorner, "The Twentieth Century Trend in Employment in Manufacture in India—As illustrated by the case of West Bengal," in C.R. Rao (ed.). *Essays on Econometrics and Planning*, 1963, pp. 301–05.
19 Ram Manohar Lohia, "Marxism and Socialism," (August 1952), *Marx, Gandhi and Socialism*, 1963, p. 107.
20 Lohia, "Marxism and Socialism," 1952, in *Marx, Gandhi and Socialism*, 1963, p. 110.
21 Lohia, *Marx, Gandhi and Socialism*, 1963, p. 406.
22 Lohia, "A New Integration," 1952, in *Marx, Gandhi and Socialism*, 1963, p. 378.

23 C.L. Barber, "The Capital-Labour Ratio in Underdeveloped Areas," *The Philippine Economic Journal*, First Semester 1969, Vol. VIII, No. 1, p. 86.
24 Raj Krishna, "Human Values and Technological Change," *Mankind*, Vol. I, No. 3, October 1956, P. 233.
25 "The Farmer in India," *Fragments of a World Mind*, 1952, pp. 62–65.
26 S. Herbert Frankel, *The Economic Impact on Underdeveloped Societies—Essays on International Investment and Social Change*, 1953, pp. 98–99.
27 *ibid.*, p. 69.
28 "The Farmer in India," *Fragments of a World Mind*, 1952, p. 85.
29 "Thirteen-point Programme of the Hind Kisan Panchayat," *Fragments of A World Mind*, 1952, p. 108.
30 Ram Manohar Lohia, "Separate Note (No. 11)," *Foodgrains Policy Committee—Interim—Report*, 1948, p. 52.
31 "The Farmer in India," (1950), in Ram Manohar Lohia, *The Fragments of a World Mind*, 1952, p. 59.

cf :	Million acres	Percentage
Forests	93.39	15
Net area sown	268.43	43
Current fallows	59.36	10
Cultivable waste	102.67	16
Not available for cultivation	99.57	16
Total	623.42	100

Source: *Census of India, 1951, Part I-B*, pp. 32–33.

32 "Statement of Policy" (1953), *Marx, Gandhi and Socialism*, 1963, pp. 403–04.
33 *Fragments of a World Mind*, 1952, pp. 59–60. "Statement of Policy," 1953, *Marx, Gandhi and Socialism*, 1963, pp. 403–04.
34 *Fragments of a World Mind*, 1952, p. 61. *Marx, Gandhi and Socialism*, 1963, p. 404.
35 C.T. Kurien, "New Development Strategy," *Seminar* [149, India 1971] January 1972, p. 44.
36 Ram Manohar Lohia, "The Farmer in India," 1950, *The Fragments of a World Mind*, 1952, p. 81.
37 *ibid.*, p. 80.
38 "The Farmer in India," *Fragments of a World Mind*, 1952, p. 81. "Statement of Policy" (1953), *Marx, Gandhi and Socialism*, 1963, pp. 401–02.
39 Ram Manohar Lohia, "The Farmer in India," 1950, *Fragments of a World Mind*, 1952, p. 57.
40 Lohia, "Statement of Policy," 1953, in *Marx, Gandhi and Socialism*, 1963, p. 402.
41 Lohia, "The Farmer in India," 1950, *Fragments of a World Mind*, p. 58.
42 *Papers for the Conference on Agricultural Labour*, National Commission *on* Labour, 1968, p. 100. Also, see, Daniel Thorner, *Agrarian Prospect in India*, 1956, pp. 4, 21, 36, 43, 72.
43 Daniel Thorner, *Agrarian Prospect in India*, 1956, p. 83.
44 *ibid.*, p. 84.
45 Ram Manohar Lohia, "The Farmer in India," (1950), *Fragments of a World Mind*, 1952, p. 65.
46 Lohia, "Statement of Policy," 1953, *Marx, Gandhi and Socialism*, 1963, p. 402.
47 *ibid.*, p. 402.
48 "Congress Strategy and Socialism: Lohia" (1959), *Mankind*, September 1969, pp. 60–61.
49 "The Farmer in India" (1950). op. cit., p. 58.
50 *ibid.*, p. 61.
51 *ibid.*, p. 54.
52 *ibid.*
53 *Janata*, Vol. V, No. 49, January 6, 1951.
54 *Janata*, Vol. V. No. 1, January 26, 1950.
55 *Janata*, Vol. VI, No. 30, August 26, 1951.
56 Ram Manohar Lohia, "The Farmer in India," 1950, *Fragments of a World Mind*, 1952, p. 66.
57 *ibid.*, p. 88.
58 Ram Manohar Lohia, "The Farmer in India," 1950, *Fragments of a World Mind*, pp. 87–88.
59 Lohia, *Wheel of History*, 1955, p. 58.
60 C.T. Kurien, op. cit., p. 43.
61 Ram Manohar Lohia, "The Farmer in India," 1950, *Fragments of a World Mind*, 1952, p. 103.
62 Lohia, *Wheel of History*, 1955, pp. 36 and 58.
63 Lohia, "A New Integration," 1952, *Marx, Gandhi and Socialism*, 1963, p. 377.
64 Lohia, "Marxism and Socialism," 1952, *ibid.*, p. 102.
65 Lohia, "The Meaning of Equality," 1956, in *Marx, Gandhi and Socialism*, 1963, pp. 227–28.
66 Lohia, "The Farmer in India," 1950, *Fragments of a World Mind*, p. 82.
67 Lohia, "On Doctrine," 1952, *Marx, Gandhi and Socialism*, 1963, p. 368.
68 "The Doctrinal Foundation of Socialism," 1952, *Marx, Gandhi and Socialism*, 1963, pp. 329–30.
69 "Gandhism and Socialism," 1952, *Marx, Gandhi and Socialism*, 1963, pp. 127–28.
70 "The Doctrinal Foundation of Socialism," 1952, op. cit., p. 327.
71 *ibid.*, pp. 125–27, 347.
72 Ram Manohar Lohia, "A New Chapter," 1955, *Marx, Gandhi and Socialism*, 1963, p. 426.
73 See p. 81–82 above.

74 "The Doctrinal Foundation of Indian Socialism (1952)," *Marx, Gandhi and Socialism*, 1963, pp. 344–45.
75 "The Farmer in India" (1950), *Fragments of a World Mind*, 1952, pp. 86, 100, 105, "An Asian Policy," *ibid.*, p. 241.
76 "The Farmer in India" (1950), op. cit., p. 100.
77 *Report of the Special Convention held at Pachmarhi, Madhya Pradesh*, The Socialist Party, 1952, p. 3.
78 *ibid.*, pp. 166–67, and in *Marx, Gandhi and Socialism*, pp. 358–59.
79 *Report of the Special Convention of the Praja Socialist Party, Betul* (Madhya Pradesh), 1953, pp. 73–87.
80 Speech of M.N. Roy at the Political Study Camp, Dehradun, May 17–25, 1947, "A Party Disclaims Power," *Politics, Power and parties*, 1960, p. 85.
81 "Politics Without Party" (1949), *Politics, Power and Parties*, p. 95.
82 *ibid.*, p. 76.
83 "The Doctrinal Foundation of Indian Socialism" (1952), op. cit., p. 349.
84 M.N. Roy, "Humanist Politics (1949)," *Politics, Power and Parties*, 1960, pp. 125–26.
85 Letter to Ravela dated 24th January, 1965, Reproduced under "M.N. Roy's Humanist Politics." *Mankind*, Vol. XIV No. 2, February–March, 1970, pp. 85–86.
86 Asoka Mehta, "Political Compulsions of Backward Economy," *Report of the Special Convention of the Praja Socialist Party held at Betul*, June, 14–18 1953, pp. 167–70. For Lohia's position, *ibid.*, pp. 39–47.
87 Ram Manohar Lohia, "To the Betul Convention," (1953), in *Will To Power*, 1956, p. 141.
88 Resolution "On the Move," *Report of the Seventh Annual Conference of the Socialist Party held at Patna*, March 6–10, 1949, pp. 138–41.
89 "The Approach to Socialist Planning," *Mankind*, Vol. I, No. 4, November 1956, p. 383.
90 A.K. Chanda, "The Public Sector: Is it a Mirage," in *The Bombay Plan and Other Essays*, 1968, p. 72.
91 *ibid.*, p. 72.
"One cannot easily forget the Socialist leader, Dr Ram Manohar Lohia's powerful speech in Parliament on August. 21, 1963 . . . ." V.B. Kulkarni, *British Dominion in India and After*, 1964, p. 375.
See also, *India Lok Sabha Debates (3rd Series)*, Vol. 19, (Col. 1835), August 21, 1963. For Nehru's position on the issue, *ibid.*, Vol. 19, (Col. 2204–05), August 22, 1963. For Nanda's classification, *ibid.*, Vol. 19, (Col. 2609–10), August 26, 1963. For Lohia's "Discussion Re-Distribution of National Income," *ibid.*, Vol. 20, (Col. 4875–88), September 6, 1963.
92 Ram Manohar Lohia, "The Farmer in India," 1950, *Fragments of a World Mind*, p. 84.
93 "Plea for a Budget Without Foreign Aid," *Mankind*, Vol. XI No. 5, July 1967, p. 24.
94 *ibid.*, p. 25.
95 Ragnar Nurksc, "Reflections on India's Development Plan," *Quarterly Journal of Economics*, May 1957, p. 197.
96 Trade Bureau, Ministry of International Trade and Industry, Japan, "Japan's Economic Cooperation with Asian Countries and its Problems," *Asian Affairs* (Tokyo), September 1957, pp. 246–47.
97 "Industrialisation, Disparities and Germany," *Mankind*, Vol. 5, No. 5, December 1960, p. 52.
98 "An Asian Policy" (1952), *Fragments of a World Mind*, p. 236.
99 "Economic Disparities Among Nations," Seminar at Athens in Oct. 1961, organised by the Centre for the Study of Democratic Institutions, *Mankind* June 1968, p. 9.
100 "India, China, Congressism and Communism," *Mankind*, Vol. 4, No. 6, January 1960, pp. 27–28.
101 Ram Manohar Lohia during a discussion held at the University of Arizona USA on May 1, 1964. Reproduced in "Indian Politics Today," *Mankind*, Vol. XII, No. 2, March-April 1968, p. 7.
102 "Statement of Principles of the Socialist Party adopted at its Foundation Conference," Hyderabad, January 1956, in Ram Manohar Lohia, *Marx, Gandhi and Socialism*, 1963, p. 481.
103 Ram Manohar Lohia, "The Meaning of Equality," 1956, in *Marx, Gandhi and Socialism*, pp. 230–31.
104 "Materiality and Spirituality," 1953, *ibid.*, pp. 205–06.
105 Lohia, "Gandhism and Socialism," 1952, *Marx, Gandhi and Socialism*, p. 121.
106 Lohia, "Statement of Policy," 1953, *Marx, Gandhi and Socialism*, 1963, p. 406.
107 Reproduced in *Janta*, Vol. VI, No. 36, October 7, 1951.
108 Ram Manohar Lohia, "Marxism and Socialism," 1952, *Marx, Gandhi and Socialism*, 1963, pp. 115–16.
109 Lohia, "An Asian Policy," 1952, *ibid.*, pp. 307–08.
110 Lohia, "The Doctrinal Foundation of Indian Socialism," 1952, *ibid.*, 327.
111 C.T. Kurien, "New Development Strategy," *Seminar*, January 1972, pp. 39, 42.
112 Ram Manohar Lohia, "The Farmer in India," *Fragments of a World Mind*, 1952, pp. 66–94.
113 *ibid.*, p. 70.
114 *ibid.*
115 *ibid.*, pp. 70–72.
116 "Planning and Social Policy" (An address delivered by Dr. D. R. Gadgil, Deputy Chairman,

Planning Commission on the foundation day of the University of Gujarat, November, 23, 1968). Ministry of Information and Broadcasting, December 1968, p. 8.

117 C.T. Kurien, "New Development Strategy," *Seminar* January 1972, p. 45.

118 Ram Manohar Lohia, "Statement of Policy," 1953, *Marx, Gandhi and Socialism*, 1963, pp. 408–09.

119 Ram Manohar Lohia, "The Farmer in India," 1950, *Fragments of a World Mind*, 1952, p. 73.

120 *ibid.*, p. 95.

121 Ram Manohar Lohia, "Preface" *Marx, Gandhi and Socialism*, 1963, pp. xxxiv–xxxv.

122 Lohia, "Caste and Shrinking Opportunities," October 1960; "Anti-Caste," December 1961; *The Caste System*, 1964, pp. 119 and 127.

123 Lohia "Statement of Policy," 1953, *Marx Gandhi and Socialism*, 1963, p. 408.

124 Lohia, "The Farmer in India," 1950, *Fragments of a World Mind*, 1952, pp. 82–83, 95.

125 Lohia, "A Note on India's Ruling Classes," 1959, *The Caste System*, 1954, p. 106.

126 Lohia, "Towards the Destruction of Castes and Classes," 1958, *The Caste System*, 1964, p. 91.

127 *ibid.*, p. 83.

128 *ibid.*, *p.* 81.

129 *ibid.*, pp. 85, 90.

130 "Gandhism and Socialism" (1952), *Marx Gandhi and Socialism*, 1963, pp. 120–28.

7

Self-reliance and the perspective for development

Planning Commission

Source: *Fourth Five Year Plan – A Draft Outline* (New Delhi: Government of India, 1996), pp. 24–38.

Implications of self-reliance

A major objective of our economic planning is the achievement of self-reliance. Self-reliance not only means freedom from dependence on foreign aid but also involves the establishment of an acceptable minimum standard of living for the masses and a continuing rise in this standard. With self-reliance, therefore, has been linked the capacity for self-sustaining growth. This means that the objective is not only to take the country towards freedom from dependence on external aid for its economic development but also to generate domestic capacities that will enable it to have a steady and satisfactory rate of economic growth without dependence on external aid. This does not mean that we aim at economic autarky or that we shall be able to dispense with all imports. No country in the world is able to do so. What it does mean is that the country's requirements will be met from within to the maximum possible extent, and that what it must obtain from abroad will be limited to what it cannot produce within its borders or finds it uneconomic to do so in terms of comparative advantage and, even more important, that it is able to pay for these imports with its export earnings. A self-reliant and self-sustaining economy, therefore, cannot do without imports; and it must have exports sufficient to meet the cost of these imports. To the extent that its economic development has been facilitated with external credits, the country must also have an export surplus that will be adequate for the purpose of meeting its interest and re-payment commitments. In other words, self-reliance and balance of payments gap cannot go together nor is it consistent with dependence on external credits of a continuing character for meeting its normal imports or imports necessary for the full and effective utilisation of its capacity as well as imports that may be necessary for facilitating the continued growth of the economy. Nor should self-reliance be contemplated within the framework of a low level of economic development.

2. It is not necessary to emphasise the magnitude of the implications of the objective in the context of an economy like India's, which started her economic planning from a low base of production, investment, and savings, a low base of the physical capacity needed for capital formation, and a low base of exports from the stand-point of meeting the requirements of a self-reliant and self-sustaining economy. It was natural, therefore, that Indian economic planning should have postulated an increasing rate of domestic resource mobilisation, a higher rate of investment, and the use of

external credits to bridge the gap in the early years of the country's development. The Third Plan document set out a perspective of 15 years for the achievement of the goal of economic self-reliance and self-sustenance and stressed the imperative need for ensuring that over the next three plan periods all the possibilities of economic growth should be fully and effectively mobilised. The Third Plan was to be treated as "the first stage of a decade or more of intensive development leading to a self-reliant and self-generating economy".

The perspective of development

3. This perspective has now to undergo some change in the light of the performance of the economy during the Third Plan period, the circumstances following the devaluation of the Indian rupee, and the outlook for the immediate future as it emerges from our Fourth Plan proposals. Three imperatives, however, stand out from any review of the current position. First, the need for closing the balance of payments gap as early as possible and the speedy termination of *dependence* on external credits for the continuing economic growth of the country. Second, the need for the speedy building up of the country's capacity for both capital formation and adequate consumption. Third, the need for achieving both these objectives consistently with price stability and absence of inflationary finance. The revised perspective that we may formulate must reconcile these three objectives and set out clearly the changes it may involve in the time horizon as well as in the conditions necessary for its achievement. It goes without saying that the realisation of the perspective is wholly conditioned by the fulfilment of the required conditions. It would, therefore, be necessary to have a realistic view of the feasibility of these conditions and take a deliberate decision on the action programme necessary for their fulfilment before the perspective can be embodied as an integral part of our proposals for planned development.

4. In any revision of the perspective, it is the Planning Commission's considered opinion that the balance of payments gap in terms of maintenance imports and debt servicing charges (including both interest and repayment commitments) should be met during the Fifth Plan period, and that external credits (except for inflow through normal commercial channels or international agencies) should completely cease during the Sixth Plan period. In other words, the economy should reach self-reliance by the beginning of the Sixth Plan period. The Commission is also of the opinion that in view of the increased rupee cost of external credits following devaluation and in order to close the balance of payments gap during the Fifth Plan period, and the continuance of balance of payments equilibrium in subsequent periods, external credits envisaged for the Fifth Plan should undergo an appropriate sharp reduction. What is referred to of course is governmental credits and not credits obtained from international agencies or commercial channels. If this is taken as a constraint, the revised perspective has to undergo suitable alteration in terms of targets and time horizon, depending upon the view taken of the realistic and practical feasibility of the conditions regarding (1) domestic resource mobilisation in terms of exports, domestic capacity for capital formation and operational maintenance of the economy, and domestic savings and investment, and (2) maintenance of price stability. Attention will also have to be paid to changes in distribution policy as may be necessary to bring nearer the achievement of the objective of minimum income than would be feasible on the basis of a revised perspective of production and the earlier policy formulations regarding distribution.

5. In drawing up a revised perspective, it has to be recognised that the position has changed somewhat not only on account of the higher cost of imported equipment and materials and of the debt burden and debt servicing charges resulting from devaluation but also on account of failure of the Third Plan in achieving fully its original targets of production. Thus, national income in 1965–66 is estimated to be only Rs. 15,930 crores at 1960–61 prices as compared to the Third Plan target of Rs. 19,000 crores. 1965–66, however, was an abnormal year because of the severe drought we had during the year and unforeseen interruptions in the flow of imports for the maintenance of the

economy. If we take 1964–65 or the fourth year of the Plan as a base, the national income reached is Rs. 16,630 crores (at 1960–61 prices), which is about Rs. 1100 crores less than was implied in the Third Plan targets of income. We are not likely to reach in 1970–71 a national income of Rs. 25,000 crores (at 1960–61 prices) as set out in the perspective contained in the Third Plan. In turn, this would perhaps cast doubts on the feasibility of attaining in 1975–76 the target of Rs. 33,000 to Rs. 34,000 crores given in that document.

6. It would, however, be unduly pessimistic to jump to such a conclusion. While the Third Plan has not been satisfactory in its performance and the final year of that Plan period has been particularly unsatisfactory in this respect, there are certain other factors that must be taken into account before coming to a judgement on this question. Thus, it must not be forgotten that a major cause of the unsatisfactory record of the Third Plan, apart from the two conflicts and other disasters, is the delay in the achievement of its targets. These delays have pushed into the first and second year of the Fourth Plan some of the target capacities and outputs in key sectors. What must be remembered is the significant growth-orientation that has taken place in the structure of the economy by the end of the Third Plan and the further growth that is bound to take place from the action taken during this period. The production potential already built up or in sight will be further augmented by the programme we have included in the Fourth Plan, a more explicit and deliberate priority for agriculture, export promotion and import substitution, and within the limits of what appears to be feasible resource mobilisation during the period.

7. In considering the extent, if any, to which the perspective set out in the Third Plan document should undergo revision, it must be remembered that it is generally undesirable to lower one's sights, especially, when one is thinking of a period as distant as ten years from now rather than of the immediate future. Planning in the immediate future has necessarily to be strictly realistic in the sense of taking due note of the constraints on growth and the extent to which the time span involved would permit a relaxation or elimination of these constraints. But when one is visualising the targets at the end of the Fifth Plan or beyond, one must never forget the objective of planning which is not merely the establishment of a self-reliant and self-sustaining economy but also the achieving of a satisfactory and rising standard of living for the masses of the people. Constraints which loom large in the immediate present tend to diminish or even disappear, given timely decisions and prompt action in the present, and a deliberate strengthening of the national will towards social and economic growth. Economic development is not merely a function of material investment and physical inputs but also of the way in which the human factor functions, and this means technical skills, involvement, motivation and organisation. The pull which an understanding and acceptance of the need for creating a socialist society can give in terms of mass involvement in the developmental process, will be enormously strengthened if the perspective for development includes the material and institutional ingredients for a significant betterment of mass welfare. In fact, the perspective can itself be an active element in accelerating the process of economic growth by the effect it has on the national will for the reduction and elimination of constraints based on current attitudes to consumption, savings, work, *swadeshi*, and exports. Hence, the reluctance of the Commission to lower the sights of perspective planning below the targets previously proposed except in terms of a minimum allowance for the effects of recent happenings in the economy.

8. It may be recalled that the perspective presented in the Third Plan document was as under:

9. It has not so far been possible to study the full implications of the lower output levels of the Third Plan and the revised programmes of the Fourth Plan consequent on devaluation on the scope and strategy of the Fifth Plan. This is proposed to be done in the course of the next few months, after which requisite advance action for the Fifth Plan will be considered. For the same reason, it is not possible to indicate at this stage the extent of revision required in the perspective. What is clear, however, is that we cannot afford to slacken our efforts during the Fifth Plan period.

	1960–61	*1965–66*	*1970–71*	*1975–76* *33,000 to*
national income (at 1960–61 prices, Rs. crores)	14500	19000	25000	34000
population (millions at the end of year, i.e., in March)	438	492	555	625
per capita income (Rs. per annum)	330	385	450	530
net investment as percentage of national income	11	14–15	17–18	19–20
domestic savings as percentage of national income	8.5	11.5	15–16	18–19

Indeed it may well have to increase in both magnitude and intensity. In any case, our perspective for development is based on reaching by the beginning of the Sixth Plan, a stage when further economic growth will no longer require any net increase in our foreign indebtedness. This would mean that, as contrasted with the figures given in the table above, both savings and investment rates will have to be higher in the revised perspective. Further, if we are to reduce our indebtedness, the savings rate will have to be higher than the investment rate, as savings have not only to be sufficient for creating maintenance imports but also the balance of payments gap arising from interest and debt repayment charges in the Fifth Plan period. It would also mean a stepping up of exports at a rate higher than during the Fourth Plan period simultaneously with a slower rate of increase in commodity imports, whether for maintenance or for projects. In turn, this would also mean not only the full utilisation of the physical capacity for capital formation created during the Fourth Plan period but also sufficient additions to the same to offset the reduction in the rate of growth of imports and largely eliminate net dependence on foreign sources for further increase in growth capacity during the Sixth Plan period. Concretely, this could mean by the end of the Fifth Plan period, an investment rate of 19–20 percent, a savings rate of 20–21 percent, a reduction in the rate of population growth by 20 to 30 percent, and the creation of a domestic economic structure capable of meeting the physical requirements of capital formation, maintenance needs, and a substantial increase in mass consumption availabilities. A substantial export surplus should also be achieved by the beginning of the Sixth Plan period.

10. As regards distribution, the perspective has to provide for a reduction in inequalities of income and property not only by income groups but also by urban and rural areas, developed and backward regions of the country, and by the subsections within the agricultural communities like the large holders, small holders, and agricultural labourers. Steps must also be taken to reduce concentration of economic power and resort to monopolistic practices, while simultaneously extending the field for new comers and fresh talent in all fields of enterprise. The scope for equalisation of opportunities must be expanded by a more comprehensive system of scholarships and other opportunities for individual betterment. Above all, it is necessary to move in the direction of bringing about a significant rise in minimum incomes both by increase in employment and increase in the social services provided by the State.

The tasks

11. Can this perspective be realised or is it merely a matter of setting the sights high in order to urge the nation to greater effort? The answer depends upon what will be done by the people; and what the people do will depend upon the leadership, the clarity and definiteness of the measures it proposes to follow for the development objective, and the determination and drive with which it operates these measures. Leadership not only includes the realm of politics, but also the professions, the administration, and those in charge of production and distribution in the private sector. The task is not impossible. But it cannot be achieved by mere wishful thinking or ardent desire divorced from effort.

12. It is now necessary to spell out in concrete terms the details of the task the country has to undertake if we want to achieve the revised perspective set out in this document.

13. To begin with, every effort has to be made to see that the Fourth Plan is implemented in full. There should be no question of shortfalls or unscheduled spillovers into the next plan if we want to reach the perspective envisaged for 1975–76. The building up of the structure of the Indian economy in the terms envisaged in this document for the Fourth Plan is a 'must', if we want to achieve self-reliance in the Fifth Plan period consistently with a continuing improvement in mass welfare and satisfactory rate of economic growth. If we are to do this, then special attention must be paid to certain key programmes which taken together constitute the core of the Plan. While these have been spelt out in detail in subsequent chapters, it is worthwhile drawing attention to them in this chapter because of their intimate relation to the realisation of self-reliance and the successful achievement of the revised perspective of development.

14. To begin with, and claiming the highest priority, is the programme for increasing agricultural production. Necessary financial outlays have been provided, industrial planning has built into it a high priority for the physical inputs needed by agriculture such as fertilisers, pesticides, agricultural implements, etc., and the necessary provision is being made for imports to make up the balance of demand not met by domestic production. Other programmes such as minor irrigation works, rural electrification, expansion and better utilisation of irrigation potential created by major and medium irrigation schemes, better implementation of land reforms, adequate provision of credit facilities and integrated approach to agriculture production by area planning have been specially emphasized in the Plan. What must be stressed here is the vital role of administration and of peasant involvement. There has to be proper allocation of ministerial and official responsibilities. Cabinet Ministers who have the highest drive and organising capacity should be in charge of agriculture and the necessary coordination should be provided with the relevant activities of other Ministries. Similarly, the most efficient among the officials should be in charge of the production programmes in agriculture and allied activities. Panchayati Raj institutions and cooperative societies should be more actively involved in both the planning and implementation of production programmes. Above all, it must be recognised that the investment needed in agriculture is not merely in financial outlays and physical inputs, but also in the intensity of human effort and the supply of efficient organisation. Success in this field will promote self-reliance by doing away with the need for food imports and increasing our exports of agricultural and agriculture-based commodities, raise living standards by increasing domestic availabilities and supply the raw material requirements of the country's growing industrial activity.

15. An almost equally important programme that would not only determine freedom from external credits but also promote the rate of capital formation is machine building, as domestically produced machinery will have to become more or less the whole base for expansion of productive capacity from the end of the Fifth Plan period. If the programme put forward in this Plan is implemented, the country would have, by 1970–71, the capacity to build its own steel mills, fertiliser plants, equipment for power generation, transmission, transport and a variety of other equipment. This will require concentrated effort both in the public sector and in the private sector.

16. Associated with this programme for machine building is the need for decreasing our dependence on imports of spare parts and components. This involves not only greater care in settling the details of foreign collaboration but also much greater emphasis on standardisation of specifications etc., such as will enable the country to build up domestic supplies of spare parts and components. The phased production programme we are now insisting on in licensing imports for actual producers will also help in this development. Success in this field will enable us to reduce the volume of our maintenance imports in the future, and also help the export of capital goods by creating facilities for servicing and supply of spare parts and components.

17. Linked with this is also the expansion and diversification of consultancy and design services in the country. What is needed is not so much an increase in the supply of technical skills but a bolder and more extensive utilisation of the capacity that is already in existence. The process will be materially assisted by a firm policy of not going in for turn-key jobs in cases of foreign participation or financing. Designing and consultancy can grow only by use. This cardinal fact must be given more operational recognition by both public and private sectors.

18. Another important key to self-reliance is export promotion and import substitution. The opportunities created by devaluation cannot be exploited to the full unless export supplies are built into production planning in the Fourth Plan period and fiscal and administrative measures are fully implemented for assisting the procurement of export supplies and motivating producers and traders to show preference for exports over the domestic market. State participation in the export trade may have to be extended for ensuring the needed increase in exports and preventing possible leakages in foreign exchange. As for import substitution, action must be taken to ensure that every industrial and other import-using enterprise in the country undertakes a phased programme for reducing its dependence on imports. It is also necessary to see that import liberalisation does not act as a disincentive to import substitution but is used for the speedy promotion of capacity for import substitution as well as export promotion. It will be helpful if the annual reports of these enterprises are required to contain information on the progress achieved in this respect.

19. Self-reliance also requires that the policy outlined in the Fourth Plan of linking education more directly with developmental and manpower requirements is faithfully implemented. Similarly, the need for giving technical education a more practical bias and linking it closely with industry and its existing as well as expanding and diversifying requirements has to be given concrete and detailed recognition in our programmes for technical education.

20. Resource mobilisation is in some ways the kingpin in the Fourth Plan as a prelude to self-reliance. This is so because, for the first time, our plan is based on a definite and complete eschewal of deficit financing. Deficit financing not only emerges from budgetary deficits but can also arise in many other ways, including credit. It is, therefore, imperative that a close watch is kept on all avenues of deficit financing and prompt action taken. While price stability in a total sense is neither possible nor desirable in a developing economy, as explained elsewhere, monetary and credit policy should be so conducted as not to lead to any general rise in prices. On the positive side, the following programmes need special attention:

(a) improvement of the tax collecting machinery;
(b) plugging the loopholes in the tax system that lead to legal avoidance of tax liability, and taking prompt action to close new loopholes as they emerge;
(c) a closer look at the items allowed as deductions for taxable income, and especially the scale on which they are allowed, in order to prevent functionally avoidable lowering of tax receipts;
(d) a more imaginative and efficient attempt at locating and preventing tax evasion, which is now assuming a formidable form in the Indian economy, leading to the emergence of illegal markets, speculative and non-priority investments, and reckless spending with inflationary consequences. Legislation must contain stringent penalties for tax evasion, action taken against tax evaders must be prompt and public; and necessary institutional changes made to prevent tax evasion;
(e) new incomes generated as a result of economic development have to bear their share of the fiscal burden of development. This is possible only by a bold re-structuring of the tax system and a greater resort to tax at the source;
(f) the small savings target in the Fourth Plan needs a more active and imaginative policy of motivating, identifying and mobilising small savings. Extension of the provident fund system to the maximum possible number of employed workers, devising a similar savings system for the self-employed, linking up

savings with felt needs for the future such as housing, education and marriage of children, these and other measures need to be taken for getting the required increase in small savings;

(g) capital gains especially in urban land values, monopolistic and *rentier* elements in income, incomes from speculative activity and incomes divorced from functions, all these are appropriate fields for additional taxation and need greater attention in the Indian financial system.

21. Another kingpin of the Fourth Plan, and in some ways the most difficult of achievement, is family planning. Action has to be voluntary and all that the State can do is to motivate and provide supplies. Hence the importance of showing the greatest understanding and imaginativeness in the drawing up of this programme and securing the involvement of voluntary agencies and public opinion at local levels for ensuring its success. Failure in this field will give a set back to our attempt at self-reliance.

22. Another programme that needs more attention than it has received so far in our planned development is the securing of public cooperation. Planning for a continental and economically under-developed economy like that of India needs mass understanding, mass support, and mass involvement. Clarity and definite-ness in objective and confidence that the steps being taken are in the right direction are essential for securing public cooperation; and so also are conspicuously visible programmes for improvement in the social and economic conditions of the masses of the people. In addition, we need a more purposive and effective use of the entire machinery of mass communication, including press, radio, films, and literature.

23. One of the weakest areas in Indian planning is the regulation and direction of the private sector. We need to devise, therefore, a suitable machinery for the progressing and implementation of developmental programmes in the private sector. Non-priority diversions have to be discouraged and priority items have to be adequately serviced and speeded up in both formulation and execution. Fiscal, administrative, and other methods of regulation, inducement, deterrence, vigilance and evaluation have all to be harnessed for ensuring the fulfilment of Plan targets in the private sector.

24. Not the least important among the Fourth Plan programmes is the maximisation of employment. On present estimates, increase in employment opportunities during this period will not be sufficient to absorb the addition to the labour force. It will, therefore, be necessary to undertake a large rural works programme in several parts of the country to ensure work, specially during the slack agricultural seasons. Adequate provision of employment opportunities is essential for ensuring a minimum income. Therefore, along with programmes for industrial and economic development, there must be continuous emphasis on the full use of the manpower resources available in rural areas and a high degree of priority should be attached to labour intensive programmes.

25. The programmes referred to above need for their implementation certain administrative and management reforms. They have been dealt with in a subsequent chapter. There are, however, some items which need special mention. Thus, the agricultural programme needs more efficient implementation of land reforms for securing land to the tiller, and where this may not be possible in terms of ownership, it needs security of tenancy, restriction of rents, and availability of credit on the basis of crop production programmes. The co-operative movement also needs strengthening especially in the fields of crop loans, and credit linked with marketing, processing of agricultural products, and cooperative farming in the case of small and uneconomic holdings. Alternative credit arrangements of a transitional character have to be provided where the cooperatives are yet unable to serve this function. There has to be some machinery for enforcing plan priorities in the industrial sector in respect of the production of agricultural inputs while, simultaneously, the supply organisations for agricultural inputs should be strengthened in their functioning. The necessary machinery must also be created for enforcing Plan priorities in the agricultural sector in regard to high yielding varieties of food crops and increasing the yield of export crops. It is also necessary to undertake a greater measure of both decentralisation and

localisation of agricultural planning and its implementation taking down to blocks and villages and using the panchayati raj and cooperative institutions for this purpose. This will also involve more emphasis on inter-departmental coordination and public participation in terms of area development. In particular, coordination at the district and block levels is required between the departments of agriculture, cooperation, community development, irrigation, rural electrification, rural works, and rural education.

26. As regards industry, the necessary machinery has to be created for the direction and regulation of the private sector in accordance with Plan priorities. It is also necessary to have a specific machinery for dealing with the problems of cost reduction, and improve the machinery for preparation, scrutiny, and clearance of projects in the industrial sector. Some machinery is also required to watch and speed up progress in machine building in both the private and the public sector. Public enterprises need a special machinery for improving their profitability, increasing their competitive strength, and streamlining their administration.

27. Plan targets in regard to foreign trade also require to be dealt with by a special machinery for their implementation. Problems of import substitution have to be identified and dealt with, export industries have to increase their competitive capacity, and supplies have to be assured for exports. Public sector enterprises should have special cells for export promotion, and the machinery of state trading in imports and exports has to be strengthened.

28. The administration also needs strengthening to cope with the large increase in Plan effort that is now contemplated, particularly in the realms of decision-making, disposal, and sympathetic identification with the economic and social ethos of planning. The machinery for watching progress and evaluating performance in Plan implementation has to be strengthened both at the Central and State levels, and more attempts should be made to link up earnings with productivity, including where possible an extension of the principle of payment by piece work and incentive payments. Improvement is needed in machinery for Plan publicity and mass education in the objectives of planning and implication in terms of the effort involved to achieve them. There is also need for a review and subsequent improvement in the machinery for economic intelligence, trade intelligence, and short-term forecasting by the use of modern methods of data collection, analysis, and communication. Manpower planning is another field where the relevant machinery needs coordination and strengthening at the Central and State levels and also in the private sector.

29. Research is an important tool both for the implementation of the Fourth Plan and the eventual achievement of self-reliance. There is need for an efficient machinery for the better coordination of basic scientific research and technological research specially oriented towards industrial (including small industries) and agricultural growth, and for the utilisation of the results of such research. Social science research not only needs more support but also better coordination with developmental problems and requirements. Training programmes should pay special attention to the personnel requirements of scientific, technological and social research.

30. Planning is intended for the enlargement of material benefits, as well as to meet social requirements. Indian planning has not only an economic objective but also contains a social ethos. It is necessary, therefore, to strengthen the machinery for the enforcement of constitutional and legislative provisions for the maintenance of human dignity and the avoidance of social discrimination. The implementation of land reforms for the securing of ownership by the actual tiller is also another step in the recognition of human dignity, apart from its economic implications. Special attention needs to be paid for implementing and extending the benefits of Plan programmes for the amelioration of the conditions of the handicapped and weaker sections of the society.

Attitudes and behaviour patterns

31. Changes and improvements in machinery and institutions outlined above are not in themselves

sufficient to bring about the implementation of the Fourth Plan programmes or take the country towards self-reliance and rising standards of living. Attitudes and behaviour patterns have to change for meeting the needs of our developing economy. In the words often used by the late Prime Minister Jawaharlal Nehru, it is a war against poverty that the country is engaged in, and planning is the strategy used for the purpose. Attitudes and behaviour patterns, therefore, have to undergo as much of a fundamental change as they do when a country gets engaged in war. These changes have to be such as to maximise work, efficiency, savings and resource mobilisation. They must motivate and move the people in the direction of economic development. For this purpose, specific measures in terms of policies, machinery, and communication must be undertaken to bring about or strengthen the following changes in attitudes and behaviour patterns in the country.

32. To begin with, there has to be a change in the attitude of the well-to-do sections of the community towards consumption. Austerity to the extent possible should be encouraged not only in daily life but also extended to the conspicuous expenditure that now takes place on ceremonial occasions. This would also have to be accompanied by limiting the disposable incomes of the better-off sections of the community in the direction of reaching a desired range between minimum and maximum personal incomes. Resources thus released from consumption could then be made available for investment in Plan priority channels.

33. Along with this it is also necessary to get a change in the public attitude towards taxation. Taxation should be recognised as an instrument of resource mobilisation for the promotion of economic development and not as a means for financing wasteful and unproductive expenditure. While promoting the recognition of taxation as a necessary social obligation attendant upon the receipt of income, public opinion should also be built up to frown upon all wasteful and nonfunctional expenditure and encourage the necessary internal discipline whether in the public or the private sector. Social displeasure should also be brought to bear on tax evaders and dealers in unaccounted money.

34. To encourage the mobilisation of external resources, it is also necessary to stimulate in the people a general willingness to put up with the reduced availabilities caused by the imperative claim of exports on the domestic output of exportable commodities together with a corresponding obligation on the part of public authorities to bring about an equitable distribution of the incidence of such hardships. Simultaneously, there has to be a deliberate building up of an attitude of preference for *swadeshi* products on the part of consumers and producers in both the public and private sectors in order to give support to import substitution. Import substitution applies not only to commodities but also to skills. For this purpose, there should be a deliberate building up of public opinion for the encouragement of indigenous talent in the scientific, technical and consultancy fields on the part of both public and private enterprises.

35. For the promotion of productive efficiency on the part of both individuals and enterprises, it is necessary to secure the economy against interruptions to production or transport by promoting a climate of industrial peace and effective operation of the machinery for the identification and speedy settlement of legitimate grievances. Full utilisation of existing capacity and getting the maximum return from past investments should become a ruling norm for productive enterprises and be given, generally speaking, first preference over the establishment of additional units of production. Along with this there should be a stimulation of a sense of pride in work leading to the fulfilment of targets in terms of output, quality, and time phasing, and public recognition and appreciation of such personal achievements. It is also necessary to create cost consciousness on the part of all producers and encourage competitive emulation in terms of cost reduction and quality improvement. Productivity would be also stimulated by the acceptance of the principle of merit, as against that of mere seniority, in filling key posts and specialised appointments and promotions in both the public and the private sectors.

36. Public opinion must also be mobilised for the support of the general objectives of the Plan such as price stability, family planning, and

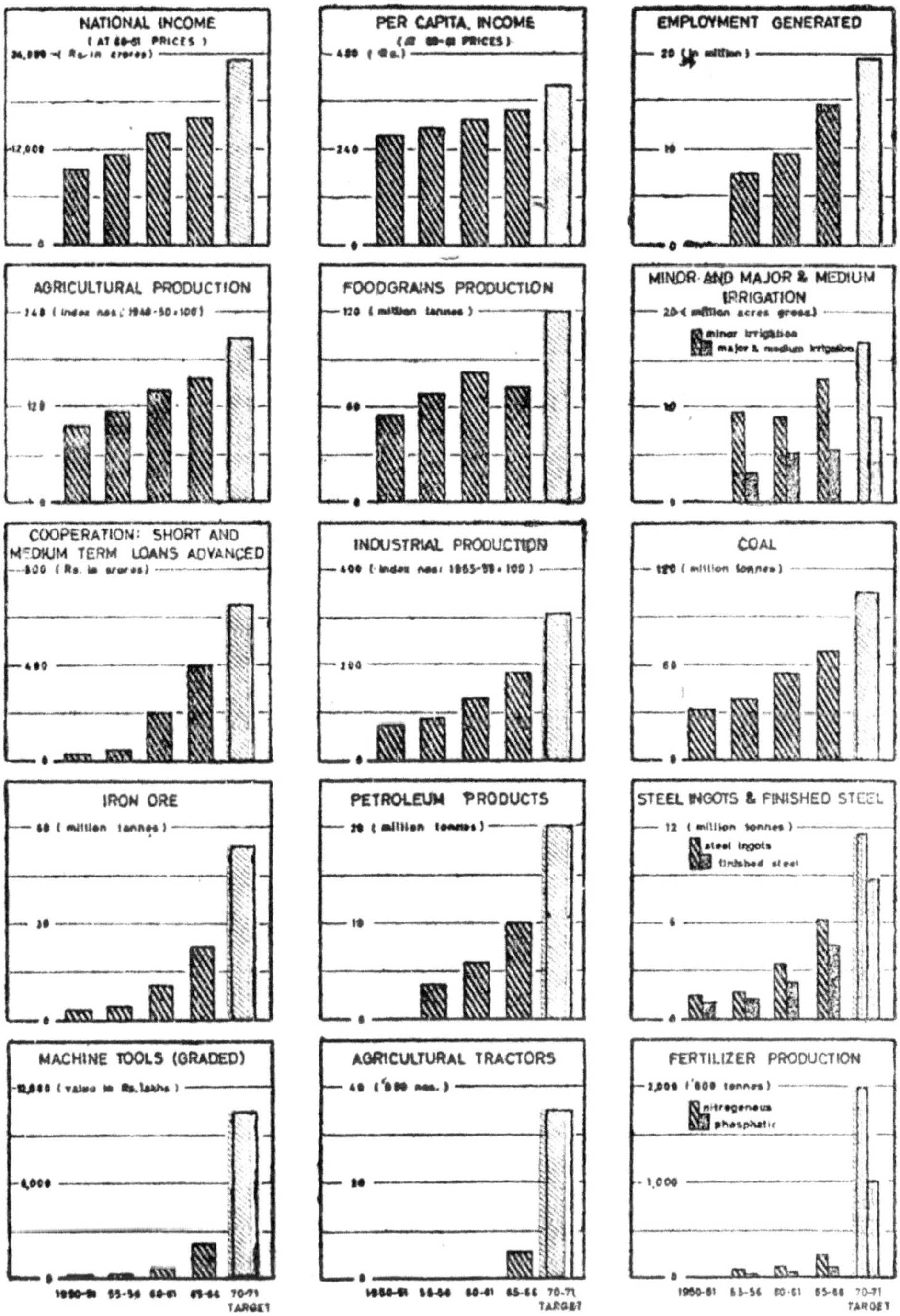

SELECTED FIRST, SECOND AND THIRD PLAN ACHIEVEMENTS AND FOURTH PLAN TARGETS

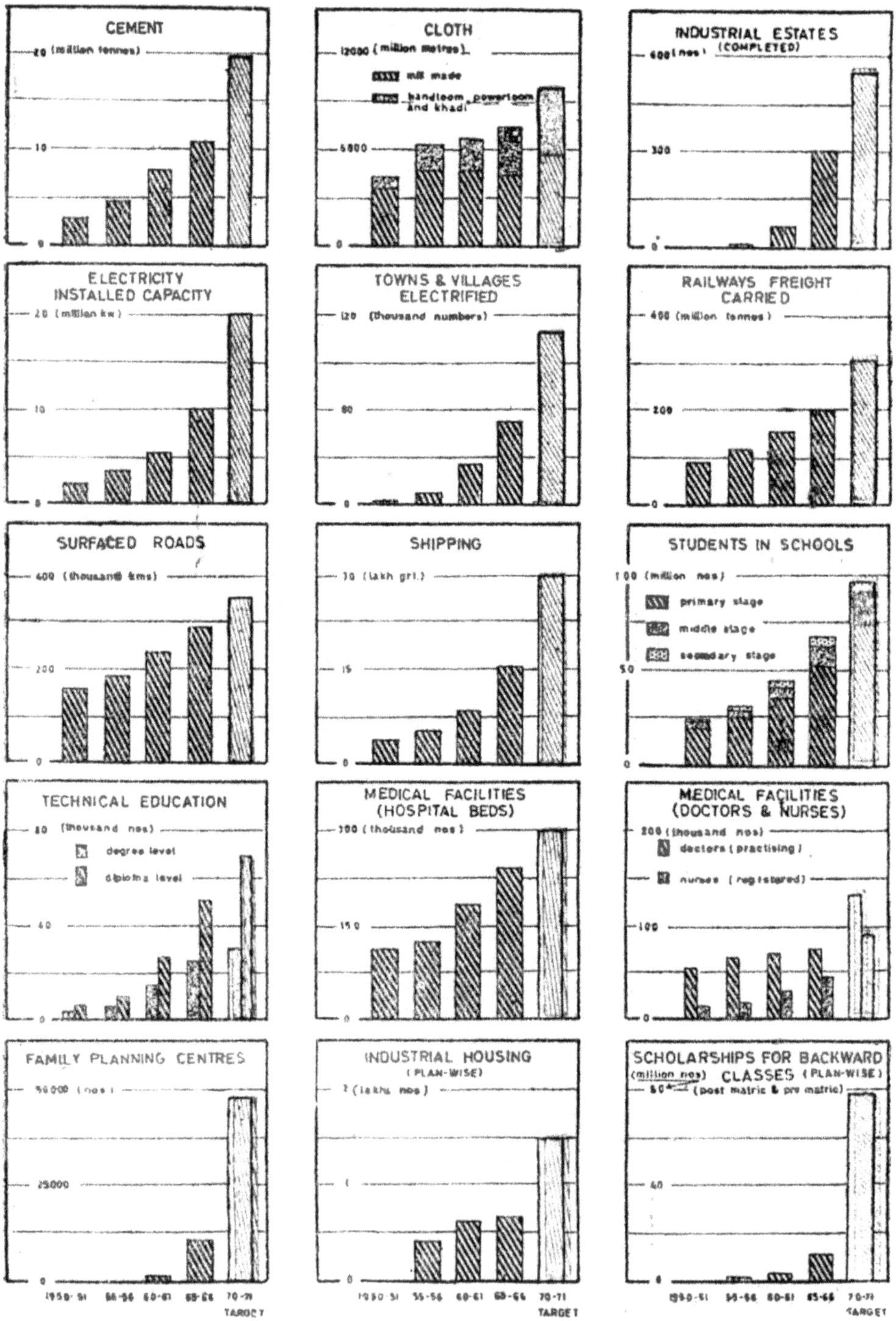

SELECTED FIRST, SECOND AND THIRD PLAN ACHIEVEMENTS AND FOURTH PLAN TARGETS

equalisation of opportunities. Thus, a positive public opinion should be brought to bear on hoarders, blackmarketers and profiteers, while simultaneously public support should be encouraged for consumer cooperative stores, fair price shops, and private traders who observe price regulations. It is also necessary to bring about a preference for small families and promote willingness to make full use of the facilities provided for family limitation, spacing of births, and reduction in the growth rate of population. Public opinion must be built in favour of common educational facilities in place of the current trend of going in for private schools with differential advantages for the higher income groups.

37. Finally, it must not be forgotten that the administration forms a partnership with the people for the promotion of economic development. While this requires on the part of public officials a spirit of identification with the Plan and a deliberate effort on their part to cut down red tape and speed up action, it also involves on the part of the public an attitude of understanding of the difficulties of administrators and of creating the confidence that they will not be penalised for bonafide mistakes of judgement that may result from their functioning in a more decisive and dynamic manner.

38. What has been said above demands a great deal of effort on the part of the government and the people. But all this is capable of achievement. What is needed is the national will to do so. The results of the planning efforts undertaken so far have enabled the formulation of a Fourth Plan of the size and pattern set out in the following pages. If the Fourth Plan is implemented, implementation of an appropriate Fifth Plan becomes less strenuous of achievement. The Fourth Plan constitutes the real challenge in our planning endeavour. If the challenge is followed by response—and the details of what constitutes this response have been spelt out in this chapter—there can be no doubt about our success in reaching the desired goal of self-reliance and continuing economic and social betterment.

8

Evidence before the Southborough Committee:[1] 27 January 1919

B.R. Ambedkar

Source: *Dr. Babasaheb Ambedkar: Writings and Speeches*, Vasant Moon (ed.) (The Education Department, Government of Maharashtra, Vol.1, 1979), pp. 247–77. Reprinted in *B.R. Ambedkar: Perspectives on Social Exclusion and Inclusive Policies*, Sukhdeo Thorat and Narender Kumar (eds) (New Delhi: Oxford University Press, 2008), pp. 65–87.

'The most difficult and the most momentous question of Government (is) how to transmit the force of individual opinion and preference into public action. This is the crux of popular institutions.' So says Professor A. B. Hart. But this is only half the definition of popular Government. It is therefore necessary to emphasize the other half which is equal if not more in importance. As the Government is the most important field for the exercise of individual capacities, it is in the interest of the people that no person as such should be denied the opportunity of actively participating in the process of Government. That is to say popular Government is not only Government for the people but by the people. To express the same in a different way, representation of opinions by itself is not sufficient to constitute popular Government. To cover its true meaning it requires personal representation as well. It is because the former is often found without the latter that the Franchise Committee has to see in devising the franchises and constituencies for a popular Government in India, it provides for both, that is, representation of opinions and representation of persons. Any scheme of franchise and constituency that fails to bring this about fails to create a popular Government.

Success in this task will ultimately depend upon the accuracy of the *de facto* conception of the society which is to be given the popular form of Government. *De facto* India was well portrayed by Lord Dufferin when he described it as a:

> Population . . . composed of a large number of distinct nationalities, professing various religions, practicing diverse rites, speaking different languages, while many of them . . . still further separated from one another by discordant prejudices, by conflicting sources of usages, and even antagonistic material interests. But perhaps the most patent characteristic of our Indian cosmos is its division into two mighty political communities as distant from each other as the poles apart—On the one hand the Hindus—with their elaborate caste distinctions—on the other hand, the Mohammedans—with their social equality. To these must be added a host of minor nationalities most of them numbering millions—almost as widely differentiated from one another by ethnological or political distinctions as are the Hindus from the Mohammedans, such as Sikhs, with their warlike habits and traditions and their enthusiastic religious beliefs, the Rohillas, the Pathans, the Assamese, the Baluchis and other wild and martial tribes on our

> frontiers, the hillmen dwelling in the folds of the Himalayas, our subjects in Burma, Mongol in race and Buddhist in religion, the Gonds, Mhars, Bheels and other non-Aryan people in the centre and south of India, and the enterprising Parsees, with their rapidly developing manufactures and commercial interests. Again, amongst these numerous communities may be found, at one and the same moment, all the various stages of civilization through which mankind has passed from the pre-historic ages to the present days.

Englishmen have all along insisted that India is unfit for representative Government because of the division of her population into castes and creeds. This does not carry conviction with the advanced wing of Indian politicians. When they say that there are also social divisions in Europe as there are in India they are amply supported by facts. The social divisions of India are equaled, if not outdone, in a country like the United States of America. Corresponding to those in the former, we have in the latter men bonded together in a criminal conspiracy and trust or combinations that prey upon the public. Not only are there political sub-divisions but also industrial, scientific, and religious associations, differing in their aims and their attitudes towards each other. Apart from political parties with diverse ends, social sets, cliques and gangs we find in the United States of America more permanent divisions of the population such as the Poles, Dutch, Swedes, Germans, Russians, etc., each with its own language, religious and moral codes and traditions. If social divisions unfit a country for representative Government, it should unfit the United States of America as much as India. But if with all the social divisions, the United States of America is fit for representative Government, why not India? Ask the Indian politicians, so entrenched, it is difficult to dislodge them, and show that the social divisions of India are of a different kind or grant them their contention. Without these two there is no third alternative possible.

In my opinion their contention cannot be granted for the social divisions of India do matter in politics. How they matter can be best shown by understanding when they don't matter. Men live in a community by virtue of the things they have in common. What they must have in common in order to form a community are aims, beliefs, aspirations, knowledge, a common understanding; or to use the language of the Sociologists, they must be like-minded. But how do they come to have these things in common or how do they become like-minded? Certainly, not by sharing with another as one would do in the case of a piece of cake. To cultivate an attitude similar to others or to be like-minded with others is to be in communication with them or to participate in their activity. Persons do not become like-minded by merely living in physical proximity, any more than they cease to be like-minded by being distant from each other. Participation in a group is the only way of being like-minded with the group. Each group tends to create its own distinctive type of like-mindedness, but where there are more groups than one to be brought into political union, there would be conflict among the differently like-minded? And so long as the groups remain isolated the conflict is bound to continue and prevent the harmony of action. It is the isolation of the groups that is the chief evil. Where the groups allow of endosmosis they cease to be evil. For endosmosis among the groups makes possible a resocialization of once socialized attitudes. In place of the old, it creates a new like-mindedness, which is representative of the interests, aims, and aspirations of all the various groups concerned. Like-mindedness is essential for a harmonious life, social or political and, as has just been shown, it depends upon the extent of communication, participation or endosmosis. Applying this test to the divisions in India, we must pronounce upon them as constituting an obstacle in the path of realizing a harmonious political life.

The groups or divisions each with its set like-mindedness that are sure to be in conflict may be given as follows: (1) Hindus (2) Mohammedans (3) Christians (4) Parsees (5) Jews, etc.

Except the Hindus the rest of the divisions are marked by such complete freedom of communication from within that we may expect their members to be perfectly like-minded with respect to one another. Regarding the Hindus, however, the analysis must be carried on a little farther. The significant fact about the Hindus is that before they are Hindus they are members of some caste. The castes are so exclusive and isolated that the consciousness of being a Hindu would be the chief guide of a Hindu's activity towards non-Hindu. But as against a Hindu of a different caste his caste-consciousness would be the chief guide of activity. From this, it is plain that as between two Hindus, caste-like-mindedness is more powerful than the like-mindedness due to their both being Hindus. Thus from within the Hindus, as from without, there is likely to be a conflict of like-minded persons. There are some who argue that this conflict runs through the whole gamut of the caste system. But this is protesting too much. From the point of view of communication the Hindus, in spite of castes, divide themselves into two significant groups—the touchables and the Untouchables. The touchables have enough communication between them to enable us to say that the conflict of like-mindedness so far as they are concerned is not much to be dreaded. But there is a real difference and consequent conflict between the like-mindedness of the touchables and the Untouchables. Untouchability is the strongest ban on the endosmosis between them. Their complete isolation accounts for the acuteness of the difference of like mindedness.

The real social divisions of India then are:

1 Touchable Hindus
2 Untouchable Hindus
3 Mohammedans
4 Christians
5 Parsees
6 Jews

It will not do good to ignore these real divisions in devising a system of policy, if the policy is to take the form of popular Government. But if the success of popular Government depends upon how well the constituencies and franchises transmit the social forces and how well they secure personal representation; we must first study the form which the conflict between these groups will assume in an election.

In a territorial constituency, which will group together voters belonging to the above groups, a majority of votes will declare a candidate to be a representative for the constituency in question. Now the question arises: is such a candidate, a true representative of the groups, covered by the territorial constituency? Is he a true mirror of the mind of the constituency? Is he a representative of all the interests in the constituency? To be concrete, will a Hindu candidate represent Mohammedan interests? At this stage it must be recalled that the various divisions described above are held together by a community of interests which are non-secular or purely religious. We cannot say that each division is held together by a community of interests which are secular or material. If so, then for secular purposes the groups will be broken up. From the point of view of material interests, there are no such people as Mohammedans, Parsees, Hindus, etc. There will be in each of these groups landlords, labourers, capitalists, free traders, protectionists, etc., each of the groups having community of interests which are material will be composed of Hindus, Mohammedans, Parsees, etc. Consequently, a Hindu candidate can very well represent the material interests of the Mohammedans and *vice versa*. There is thus no conflict of material interest in the main among the communities as such. If we suppose that religious interests in future will occupy a subordinate place in the affairs of men, the secular interests of a group can be well represented by a candidate from another group.

From this point of view a territorial constituency will be sufficient for a popular Government. A little more consideration will show that it will be sufficient for only one-half the definition of popular Government. How true it is, will be shown presently. In an electoral fight between the various groups in a territorial constituency the voters will discriminate in favour of a candidate with whom they are in sympathy. But with whom they will be in sympathy is determined for them in advance. Given two candidates belonging to different groups but purporting to represent the same interest, the voters will mark their votes on the person belonging to the same community. Any group yielding a large number of electors will have its own candidate elected. This discrimination on the part of the voters, though it may not leave unrepresented the interests of the members of the minor groups, leaves them without any chance of personal representation.

To those who are busy in devising schemes for the proper and adequate representation of interests and opinions dilating on the importance of personal representation is likely to seem idle. But personal representation is not therefore unimportant; in recent times 'Government for the people' has claimed more attention than 'Government by the people'. In fact there are instances to show that 'Government for the people' can exist in the best sense of the phrase without there being a 'Government by the people'. Yet all political theorists will unanimously condemn such a form of Government. And the why of it is important to know. It will be granted that each kind of association, as it is an educative environment, exercises a formative influence on the active dispositions of its members. Consequently, what one is as a person is what one is as associated with others. A Government for the people, but not by the people, is sure to educate some into masters and others into subjects; because it is by the reflex effects of association that one can feel and measure the growth of personality. The growth of personality is the highest aim of society. Social arrangement must secure free initiative and opportunity to every individual to assume any role he is capable of assuming provided it is socially desirable. A new rule is a renewal and growth of personality. But when an association—and a Government is after all an association—is such that in it every role cannot be assumed by all, it tends to develop the personality of the few at the cost of the many—a result scrupulously to be avoided in the interest of Democracy. To be specific, it is not enough to be electors only. It is necessary to be law-makers; otherwise who can be law-makers will be masters of those who can only be electors.

Territorial constituencies are therefore objected to, and rightly, on the ground that they do nothing to prevent this absurd outcome. They erroneously suppose that electors will vote on the programmes of the candidates without any regard for their persona. As a matter of fact, the electors before they are electors are primarily members of a group. The persona of the candidates does matter with them. Naturally, therefore, as members of a group they prefer the candidate who belongs to their group to another candidate who does not belong to their group though both of them claim to represent the same interest. As a result of this preference the electors of a large group are destined to rise to a higher position of becoming eventual law-makers, while the electors of a smaller group for no fault of theirs are doomed to a lower position of remaining electors. One crux of popular Government is the representation of interests and opinions. The other crux is personal representation. Territorial constituencies fail to create popular Government because they fail to secure personal representation to members of minor groups.

If this is a correct analysis as to how the social divisions operate to the prejudice of the political life of some communities, never was a more improper remedy advocated to meet the situation than proportional representation. Proportional representation is intended to give proportionate representation to views. It presupposes that voters vote for a candidate because of his views and not because of his persona. Proportional representation is ill-suited for the purpose in hand.

We have therefore two possible methods of meeting the situation; either to reserve seats in plural constituencies for those minorities that cannot otherwise secure personal representation or grant communal electorates. Both have their usefulness. So far as the representation of the Mohammedans is concerned, it is highly desirable that they should participate in a general election with seats reserved for them in plural constituencies. The angularity of the division that separates the Hindus and Mohammedans is already sharp and communal representation, it may be urged, sharpens it the more. Communal election, however, seems to be a settled fact, so far as the Mohammedans are concerned and nothing is likely to alter it, even though alteration is likely to be beneficial.

But this argument is mainly intended to concern itself with the representation of the Hindus in general, and of the Untouchable Hindus in particular. The discussion of the representation of the Hindus may be best introduced by a quotation which expresses the newer consciousness that has arisen in the various Hindu groups. It is said:

> A community may claim representation only on the ground of separate interests which require protection. In India, such interests are of three kinds only: either they arise out of religious antipathies which are pretty strong in India, or out of the backward state of a community in educational matters, or out of the socio-religious disabilities to which a community may be subject. Confining ourselves to the Hindu communities there are certain communities who, besides being very Backward, are suffering under a great social tyranny. The Untouchable classes must have their own men in the Council Hall to fight for the redress of their grievances. The non-Brahmins as a class are subjected to the social and intellectual domination of the Brahmin priesthood and may therefore rightly advocate separate representation.

From this it will be seen that the new consciousness among the Hindus while acknowledging the separate interests of the Untouchables does not accept the position that the touchable Hindus form a group by themselves. The new consciousness insists on dividing the touchable group into Brahmins and non-Brahmins each with its own separate interests. Separate electorates or reserved seats in mixed electorates are demanded for the three groups in which the Hindus are divided. Before dealing with the problems of the representation of the Untouchables something will be said on the question of the Brahmins and non-Brahmins.

That the non-Brahmins are 'backward in educational matters' cannot be said in any way to be their special interest. It is the general interest of all even of those Brahmins who are educationally backward. 'The intellectual domination of the Brahmins' is not a matter that affects the non-Brahmins alone. It affects all and it is therefore the interest of all. What remains then as a special interest for the non-Brahmins to require their protection?

The case for separate representation for non-Brahmins fails because they cannot prove to have a common non-Brahmin interest.

But do they fail to secure personal representation? This can be best shown by reference to the figures in the table below.

Reducing the above figures to the basis of a thousand we have the following interesting result:

So arranged, the conclusions to be drawn from these figures are highly important.

1 The Brahmins, given a uniform franchise for all, though a small minority so far as numbers are concerned becomes a majority so far as the total of voters is concerned as is the case in Group II.
2 Though with a uniform franchise the non-Brahmin communities like the Lingayats and

Caste of voters Local Board	*Group I*		*Group II*	
	No. of voters for the Local Boards of the districts of Belgaum, Bijapur and Dharwar	*Total population of the three districts*	*No. of voters for the Local Boards of the districts of Ratnagiri and Kolaba*	*Total population of the two districts*
1	*2*	*3*	*4*	*5*
Brahmins	4600	85739	4477	89786
Lingayats	12730	933123	–	–
Marathas	1074	255526	3667	446077
Mahars	22	196751	33	138738
Mohammedans	661	295838	1169	106273
Others	4241	1065821	2837	1016930
Total	23328	2832798	12183	1797804

Marathas do not fail to figure on the voters' list, the proportion of their voters to their population is insignificant as compared with the proportion which the Brahmin voters bear to the Brahmin population.

The proportion of the Brahmins to their voters is really extravagant. It is justified neither by faith in them nor by their own numbers. The Lingayats though they can legitimately complain that the proportion of their voters is small will succeed in securing personal representation. The Marathas though larger in numbers than the Brahmins, besides the very small proportion of their voters suffer on the voters' list and very likely will fail to secure personal representation for themselves. So argued, the case for special provision of the Marathas can be sustained and should be admitted.

The question is what form the provision should take. In my opinion such provision instead of taking the form of Separate Electorates of reserved seats should take the form of a low pitched franchise. The franchise for the non-Brahmin should be lower than that for the Brahmin. By this arrangement the Marathas would improve their position on the voters' list and the altogether favoured position of the Brahmin would be equalized. It is in the interest of all that the Brahmin should not play such a preponderant part in politics as he has been doing hitherto. He has exerted a pernicious influence on the social life of the country and it is in the interest of all that his pernicious influence should be kept at a minimum in politics. As he is the most exclusive he is most anti-social.

Even the authors of the report on constitutional reforms are not in favour of a limited or uniform franchise. They say, 'We consider that the limitations of the franchise, which it is obviously desirable to make as broad as possible, should be determined rather with reference to practical difficulties than to any prior considerations as to the degree of education or amount of income which may be held to constitute a qualification. It is possible that owing to unequal distribution of population and wealth it may be necessary to differentiate the qualifications for a vote not merely between provinces, but between different parts of the same province' (p. 147). To this I should like to add that we should differentiate the qualifications for a vote not merely between provinces or parts thereof but between communities of the same provinces. Without this differentiation some communities with a small but wealthy or educated population will secure more votes than a large community consisting of poor and uneducated members. Uniformity in franchise should be dispensed with. An important result will be that communal representation or reservation of

Name of Castes	*Group I*			*Group II*		
	Proportion of population of a caste thousand of the population covered	*Proportion of voters of a caste to every thousand of the population of the same caste*	*Proportion of voters of a caste to every thousand of voters*	*Proportion of population of a caste to every thousand of the population covered*	*Proportion of voters of a caste to every thousand of the population of the same caste*	*Proportion of voters of a caste to every thousand of voters*
1	*2*	*3*	*4*	*5*	*6*	*7*
Brahmins	30.2	53.7	197.2	50.8	49.8	367.4
Lingayats	329.4	13.6	545.7	–	–	–
Marathas	90.2	4.2	46.0	248.8	8.2	300.9
Mahars	69.5	0.1	0.9	74.5	0.2	2.7
Mohammedans	104.4	2.2	28.3	59.2	10.9	95.9
Others	376.2	3.9	181.3	562.2	2.8	232.8

Note: Compiled by Ambedkar

seats for some non-Brahmin communities who are now clamouring for it would be avoided.

The Untouchables are usually regarded as objects of pity but they are ignored in any political scheme on the score that they have no interests to protect. And yet their interests are the greatest. Not that they have large property to protect from confiscation. But they have their very *persona* confiscated. The socio-religious disabilities have dehumanized the Untouchables and their interests at stake are therefore the interests of humanity. The interests of property are nothing before such primary interests.

If one agrees with the definition of slave as given by Plato, who defines him as one who accepts from another the purposes which control his conduct, the Untouchables are really slaves. The Untouchables are so socialized as never to complain of their low estate. Still less do they ever dream of trying to improve their lot, by forcing the other classes to treat them with that common respect which one man owes to another. The idea that they have been born to their lot is so ingrained in their mind that it never occurs to them to think that their fate is anything but irrevocable. Nothing will ever persuade them that men are all made of the same clay, or that they have the right to insist on better treatment than that meted out to them.

The exact description of the treatment cannot be attempted. The word Untouchable is an epitome of their ills and sufferings. Not only has untouchability arrested the growth of their personality but also it comes in the way of their material well-being. It has also deprived them of certain civil rights. For instance, in Konkan the Untouchables are prohibited from using the public road. If some high caste man happens to cross him, he has to be out of the way and stand at such a distance that his shadow will not fall on the high caste man. The Untouchable is not even a citizen. Citizenship is a bundle of rights such as (1) personal liberty, (2) personal security, (3) rights to hold private property, (4) equality before law, (5) liberty of conscience, (6) freedom of opinion and speech, (7) right of assembly, (8) right of representation in a country's Government and (9) right to hold office under the State. The British Government by gradual growth may be said to have conceded these rights at least in theory to its Indian subjects. The right of representation and the right to hold office under the State are the two most important rights that make up citizenship. But the untouchability of the Untouchables puts these rights far beyond their reach. In a few places they do not even possess such insignificant rights as personal liberty and personal security, and equality before law is not always assured to them. These are the interests of the Untouchables. And as can be easily seen they can be represented by the Untouchables alone. They are distinctively their own interests and none else can truly voice them. A free trade interest can be voiced by a Brahmin, a Mohammedan or a Maratha equally well. But none of these can speak for the interests of the Untouchables because they are not Untouchables. Untouchability constitutes a definite set of interests which the Untouchables alone can speak for. Hence it is evident that we must find the Untouchables to represent their grievances which are their interests and, secondly, we must find them in such numbers as will constitute a force sufficient to claim redress.

Now, will a general territorial electorate provide for the adequate return of the Untouchables to the law-making body? Referring back to the figures we find that the Untouchables (represented in the table by the Mahars), though they formed 69.4 in every thousand of the population, did not claim even a voter from their class. Under such circumstances it is impossible for them to elect their own man in a general electorate. On the other hand they must despair of any votes being cast by the touchable Hindus for an Untouchable candidate. The gradation of castes produces a certain theological basis which cuts the Untouchables both ways: in the minds of the lower orders it creates a preference for the higher orders while it creates contempt for the lower orders in the minds of the higher orders. Thus the ascending scale of preference and the descending scale of hatred and contempt beggars the Untouchables both ways. Without giving a single vote to the Untouchables, the touchables are sure to make a large draft on the already meagre voting strength of the Untouchables.

So situated, the Untouchables with the largest interests at stake will be the greatest sufferers in a general territorial electorate. To give them an opening special provision shall have to be made for their adequate representation . . ..

The total population of the Bombay Presidency by the Census of 1911 (British districts only) is 19,626,477. Of this the Untouchable population is 1,627,980 or 8 per cent of the total. Assuming for the present the Bombay Legislative Council to consist of 100 elected members, the Untouchables should have 8 representatives to represent them in the Council. If we distribute one representative to every 200,000 of the people (which is just the ratio of 100 representatives to the 20 millions of the population), then the Untouchables can by right claim 8 representatives to themselves. But the Untouchables of the Bombay Presidency may be allowed to elect 9 members in all . . ..

It may be objected that though 8 representatives are not in excess to the Untouchable population it may be in excess to the voting strength of Untouchables. That the Untouchables are a poor community and that under the same franchise they yield per thousand a smaller proportion of voters than other communities is a fact. But if the grave position of the Untouchables is admitted instead of restricting their number of representatives, the aim should be to increase the number of their voters, i.e., we must aim at lowering the franchise so far as the Untouchables are concerned.

What the franchise should be is a very important question. There is a line of argument which urges that franchise should be given to those only who can be expected to make an intelligent use of it. As against this view it can be said in the words of Prof. L. T. Hobhouse that it is true that 'the success of democracy depends on the response of voters to the opportunities given to them. But conversely the opportunities must be given in order to call forth the response. The exercise of popular Government is itself all education . . . enfranchisement itself may precisely be the stimulus needed to awaken interest. The ballot alone effectively liberates the quiet citizen from the tyranny of the shouter and the wire-puller. An impression of existing inertness alone is not a sufficient reason for withholding responsible Government or restricting the area of suffrage.' Taking into consideration that suffrage is an education and that there are groups with unequal distribution of wealth and education among them and that these groups are not sympathetically like-minded, the authors of the reports rightly argue that the case for uniformity of franchise cannot be sustained.

But in the case of the Untouchables there are as few reasons for curtailing the number of their representatives as the reasons for widening their electorate are many. If under a given franchise the Untouchables do not muster strong as electors, it is not their fault. The very untouchability attached to their person is a bar to their moral and material progress. The principal modes of acquiring wealth are trade, industry or service. The Untouchables can engage in none of these because of their untouchability. From an Untouchable trader no Hindu will buy. An Untouchable cannot be engaged in lucrative service. Military service had been the monopoly of the Untouchables since the days of the East India Company. They had joined the Army in such large numbers that the Marquis Tweedledale in his note which he submitted to the Indian Army Commission of 1859 wrote, 'It should never be forgotten that India was conquered with the help of the low-caste men.' But after the mutiny when the British were able to secure soldiers from the ranks of the Marathas, the position of the low-caste men who had been the prop of the Bombay Army became precarious, not because the Marathas were better soldiers but because their theological bias prevented them from serving under low-caste officers. The prejudice was so strong that even the non-caste British had to stop recruitment from the Untouchable classes. In like manner, the Untouchables are refused service in the Police Force. In a great many of the Government offices it is impossible for an Untouchable to get a place. Even in the mills a distinction is observed. The Untouchables are not admitted in Weaving Departments of the Cotton Mills though many of them are professional weavers. An instance at hand may be cited from the school system of the Bombay Municipality. This most cosmopolitan city ruled by a Corporation with a greater freedom than any other Corporation in India has two different sets of schools . . . one for the children of touchables and the other for those of the Untouchables. This in itself is a point worthy of note. But there is something yet more noteworthy. Following the division of schools it has divided its teaching staff into Untouchables and touchables. As the Untouchable teachers are short of the demand, some of the Untouchable schools are manned by teachers from the touchable class. The heart-killing fun of it is that if there is a higher grade open in Untouchable school service, as there is bound to be because of few Untouchable trained teachers, a touchable teacher can be thrust into the grade. But if a higher grade is open in the touchable school service, no Untouchable teacher can be thrust into that grade. He must wait till a vacancy occurs in the Untouchable service!!! Such is the ethics of the Hindu social life. Under it if the Untouchables are poor, the committee, it may be hoped, will not deny them representation because of their small electoral roll but will see its way to grant them adequate representation to enable the Untouchables to remove the evil conditions that bring about their poverty. At present when all the avenues of acquiring wealth are closed, it is unwise to require from the Untouchables a high property qualification. To deny them the opportunities of acquiring wealth and then to ask from them a property qualification is to add insult to injury. Just what sort of franchise and just what pitch are required to produce sufficient voting strength from the Untouchables? In absence of data, I leave it to the Committee to decide. It would be better to pitch the franchise so low as to educate into political life as many Untouchables as possible. They are too degraded to be conscious of themselves. I only wish to emphasize that in deciding upon the representation of the Untouchables the Committee looking to their interests at stake will not let the extent of the electorate govern the number of representatives, but will rather let the number of representatives govern the extension of the electorate.

In this connection it would not be improper to remind the Committee of Lord Morley who is reported to have said that 'the object of Government was that the Legislative Councils should represent truly and effectively with reasonable approach to the balance of real social forces, the wishes and needs of the communities concerned. This could not be done by Algebra, Arithmetic, Geometry or Logic, but by a wide outlook. He saw no harm as to a compromise that while numbers should be the main factor in determining the extent of representation modifying causes might influence the number of representatives.' It is therefore proposed that the Untouchables of the Bombay Presidency should be allowed to elect 9 members through the constituencies made up as above. These 9 members will further form a constituency to elect one member from among themselves to represent the Untouchables in the Imperial Legislative Council leaving 8 members to represent the Untouchables in the Bombay Legislative Council.

Besides communal electorates there are other schemes in the field for the representation of the Untouchables. It would not be proper to close this statement without a word of comment on those Schemes.

The Congress has denied communal representation except in the case of Mohammedans and it also denies the extensive use of nomination; the only way then left open to the Untouchables is to fight in a general electorate. Now this is as it should be if all were equally free to fight. To educate the Untouchables by Shashtras into pro-touchables and the touchables into anti-Untouchables and then to propose that the two should fight out at an open poll is to betray signs of mental aberration or a mentality fed on cunning. But it must never be forgotten that the Congress is largely composed of men who are by design political Radicals and social Tories. Their chant is that the social and the political are two distinct things having no bearing on each other. To them the social and the political are two suits and can be worn one at a time as the season demands. Such a psychology has to be laughed at because it is too interested to be seriously taken into consideration either for acceptance or for rejection. As it pays to believe in it, it will die a hard death. Starting from this unnatural premise the Congress activities have been quite natural. Those who attend the Congress do not care to attend the National Social Conference held in the same pandal. In fact those who attend the Congress had once started a campaign to refuse the use of the pandal to the Conference which was once refused the pandal in the city of Poona, the roosting place of the intelligentsia of our Presidency. As the Congress is a non-national or anti-national body, its views on communal electorates are worthy of no serious consideration.

The moderates in their separate meeting have been more kindly than just. They proposed the reservation of seats for backward communities in plural constituencies. They have not specified the number of seats for the Untouchables. But the general sense of many enlightened moderates and others kindly inclined is that one or two representatives of the Untouchables in the Legislative Council would suffice. It is impossible to agree with these gentlemen though they are entitled to gratitude for this much sympathy. One or two representatives of the Untouchables are as good as having none. A Legislative Council is not an old curiosity shop. It will be a Council with powers to make or mar the fortunes of society. How can one or two Untouchables carry a legislative measure to improve their condition or prevent a legislative measure worsening their state? To be frank, the Untouchables cannot expect much good from the political power to be given over to the high caste-Hindus. Though the power may not be used against the Untouchables and one cannot be altogether sure of this, it may not be used for their betterment. A Legislative Council may be sovereign to do anything it likes, but what it will like to do depends upon its own character. The English Parliament, we may be certain, though it is sovereign to do anything, will not make the preservation of blue-eyed babies illegal. The Sultan will not, though he can, change the religion of Mohammed just as the Pope will not, though he can, overthrow the religion of Christ. In the same way Legislature, mainly composed of high caste men, will not pass a law removing untouchability, sanctioning intermarriages, removing the ban on the use of public streets, public temples, public schools; in short, cleansing the person of the Untouchables. This is not because they cannot, but chiefly because they will not. A Legislature is the product of a certain social condition and its power is determined by whatever determines society. This is too obvious to be denied. What may happen in future can be guessed from what has happened in the past. The high caste men in the Council do not like any social question being brought before the Legislature, as may be seen from the fact of the Resolution introduced by the Honourable Mr. Dadabhoy in 1916 in the Imperial Legislative Council. That it was adversely criticized by many who claimed to evince some interest in the Untouchables is too well known to need repetition. But what is not well known is that though the resolution was lost the mover was not pardoned; for the very moving of such a nasty resolution was regarded as a sin. At a subsequent election the mover had to make room for the Honourable Mr. Khaparde, who once wrote in an article: 'Those who work for the elevation of the Untouchables are themselves degraded.'

Isn't this sympathy of the higher castes for the Untouchables, sympathy with a vengeance?

Those who tell that one or two members would suffice for the Untouchables fail to grasp the true import of political right. The chief import of a political right though technically summed up in the power to vote does lie either in voting upon laws or for those who make laws; neither does it consist in the right to speak for or against a certain measure nor in being able to say 'yea or nay' upon roll-call; to be able to put into a ballot-box a piece of paper with a number of names written thereon is an act which, like those mentioned above, of itself possesses no value which stamps it as inherently superior to many of the most ordinary transactions of daily life. They are educative but as much as any transaction is. The chief significance of suffrage or a political right consists in a chance for active and direct participation in the regulation of the terms upon which associated life shall be sustained. Now the terms upon which the associated life between the touchables and Untouchables is carried on today are the most ignominious to the former and highly detrimental to the latter. To make effective the capacities of a people there must be the power to fix the social conditions of their exercise. If the conditions are too obdurate, it is in the interest of the Untouchables as well as of the touchables that the conditions should be revised. The Untouchables must be in a position to influence the revision. Looking to the gravity of their interests, they should get their representation as proposed in proportion to their population. One or two is only kind but neither just nor sufficient. As Lord Morley says in an earlier quotation, 'needs not numbers should govern the extent of representations.'

Recently there is brought into the forefront a rival scheme for the representation of the Untouchables by the Depressed Class Mission. The scheme is known as co-option. The scheme proposes that the representatives of the Untouchables should be nominated by the cooption of the elected members of the Council. Whether one should laugh or cry at the solicitude of the Mission for the Untouchables it is rather 'difficult to decide'. To cry is to believe that such a silly scheme would ever be adopted. The best way is to laugh it out. From the scheme can be easily seen that what is sometimes called benevolent interest in others may be an unwilling mask for an attempt to dictate to them what their good shall be, instead of an endeavour to agree with them so that they may seek and find the good of their own choice. The Mission, it must be said, was started with the intention of improving the condition of the Depressed Classes by emancipating them from the social tyranny of their high caste masters. But the Mission has fallen on such bad times that it is forced to advocate a scheme by which its wards or their representatives will be bounden slaves of their past masters. The masters and the mission have thus met and evolved a scheme which will keep the Depressed Classes eternally depressed without any hope of deliverance. Such tactics do not deceive the Untouchables ignorant as they are; less will they deceive the Franchise Committee. From another point of view the scheme of the Mission is unacceptable. It is aggravating to see the Mission proposing a scheme for the representation of the Untouchables while persistently refusing to admit an Untouchable in its governing council. Interested and officious as it is, its scheme must be rejected.

Nomination even though by Government in itself to be preferred to the former kind of nomination, is to be objected to from the standpoint of the Untouchables. Apart from restricting the freedom of the representatives it fails to give political education which is the urgent need of all communities, much more of the Untouchables.

At this stage we must consider the argument against communal representation. The first argument raised by the authors of the report is to the effect 'that the history of self-government among the nations who have developed it is decisively against' communal representation. But on an earlier page the authors say that the difference of caste and creeds must be taken 'into account as presenting a feature of Indian Society which is out of harmony with the ideas on which elsewhere in the world representative institutions rest.' (page 97). In writing the former the later analysis of the situation must have vanished from their minds, else we must say that the authors could hold two opposing views at the same time. Presented in juxtaposition, the authors must be expected to agree to communal representation on the score of an exceptional remedy required to meet an exceptional situation.

Another and chief argument against communal representation is that it will perpetuate social divisions. The fun of it is that those who uphold the social divisions are the loudest in their expression of this adverse argument. The committee will please note that those who are the opponents of communal representation on this score are also the staunchest opponents of Mr. Patel's Inter-Caste Marriage Bill as a caste-breaking bill. The sincerity of those who bring forward this argument is seriously to be doubted. But as even the authors of the report have put it as a second count against communal representation, this particular argument must be met if possible.

Does communal representation perpetuate social divisions? If you look upon communal representation as making electoral Colleges of social divisions, the criticism may be said to be valid. This is true only if it is presupposed that the divisions are no real divisions and that they don't matter. This is as false a presupposition as that of inviting India which is made when it is said that Englishmen are unsocial. Communal Representation is a device to ward off the evil effects of the divisions. To those who, while agreeing to this particular benefit of communal representation, object to it on the score that it perpetuates the divisions it can be shown that there is another perspective from which it can be said that communal representation instead of perpetuating the social divisions is one of the ways of dissolving them.

While communal electorates will be co-terminous with social divisions their chief effect will be to bring together men from diverse castes who would not otherwise mix together into the Legislative Council. The Legislative Council will thus become a new cycle of participation in which the representatives of various castes who were erstwhile isolated and therefore anti-social will be thrown into an associated life. An active participation in an associated life, in its turn, will not leave unaffected the dispositions and attitudes of those who participate. A caste or a religious group today is a certain attitude. So long as each caste or a group remains isolated its attitude remains fossilized. But the moment the several castes and groups begin to have contact and co-operation with one another the resocialization of the fossilized attitude is bound to be the result. If the Hindus become resocialized with regard to their attitude towards Mohammedans, Christians, etc., and the Mohammedans, Christians, etc., become resocialized with regard to their attitudes towards the Hindus, or the touchable Hindus with regard to the Untouchables, caste and divisions will vanish. If caste is an attitude and it is nothing else, it must be said to be dissolved when that particular attitude symbolizing the caste is dissolved. But the existing set attitude representing the diverse castes and groups will be dissolved only if the diverse groups meet together and take part in a common activity. Such changes of disposition and attitudes will not be ephemeral but will, in their turn influence associated life outside the Council Hall. The more opportunities are created for such conjoint activities the better. The resocialization will then be on a larger scale and bring about a speedier end of caste and groups. Thus those who condemn communal representation on the score of perpetuating the existing divisions will welcome it, on reflection, as a potent solvent for dissolving them.

The importance and necessity of communal and adequate representation of Untouchables is beyond question. The depth of emotion with which the Untouchables speak on this topic must have been easily gauged when the Untouchables of the Madras Presidency told Mr. Montagu that there would be bloodshed if Home Rule for India was not accompanied by communal representation to the Untouchables. The authors of the Report however are actuated by a faith in the intelligentsia to effect all reforms for the elevation of the Untouchables from permanent degradation and ostracism. They say 'they find the educated Indian organizing effort not for political ends alone but for various forms of public and social service.' As the authors have connived at the demands of the Untouchables on this score it is but proper to investigate whether their faith is well grounded. On education and its social value the words of Joseph Addison are not too stale to be recalled. He said, 'There can be no greater injury to human society than that good talent among men should be held Honourable to those who are endowed with them without any regard how they are applied. The Gifts of Nature and the Accomplishments of Art are valuable but as they are exerted in the interest of virtue or governed by the Rules of Honour, we ought to abstract our minds from the observation of an excellence in those we converse with, till we have taken some notice or received some good information of the Disposition of their Minds, otherwise they make us fond of those whom our reason and judgment will tell us we ought to abhor.'

Statistics will show that the intelligentsia and the Brahmin caste are exchangeable terms. The disposition of the intelligentsia is a Brahmin disposition. Its outlook is a Brahmin outlook. Though he has learned to speak in the name of all, the Brahmin leader is in no sense a leader of the people. He is a leader of his caste at best, for he feels for them as he does for no other people. It is not intended to say that there are no Brahmins who feel for the Untouchables. To be just, there are a few more moderate and rational Brahmins who admit the frightful nature of the institution of untouchability in the abstract and perceive the dangers to society with which it is fraught. But the great majority of the Brahmins are those who doggedly deny the horrors of the system in the teeth of such a mass of evidence as never was brought to bear on any other subject and to which the experience of every day contributes its immense amount; who, when they speak of freedom, mean the freedom to oppress their kind and to be savage, merciless and cruel, and whose inalienable rights can only have their growth in the wrongs of the Untouchables. Their delicate gentility will neither bear the Englishmen as superior nor will it brook the Untouchables as equal. 'I will not tolerate a man above me, and of those below none must approach too near' sums up the true spirit of their social as well as political creed. Those who speak against the anti-social spirit of the Brahmin leaders are often cautioned that in their denunciation they do not pay sufficient regard to the existence of the first class of Brahmin leaders. This is no doubt the case. Noble but very rare instances of personal and pecuniary sacrifice may be found among them just as may be found to be tender in the exercise of their unnatural power. Still it is to be feared that this injustice is inseparable from the state of things with which humanity and truth are invoked to deal. The miserable state of the Untouchables is not a bit more tolerable because some tender hearts are bound to show sympathy, nor can the indignant tide of honest wrath stand still because in its course it overwhelms a few who are comparatively innocent among a host of guilty.

The trend of nationalism in India does not warrant us to believe that the few who are sympathetic will grow in volume. On the other hand it is the host of guilty that time is sure to multiply. With the growth of political agitation, the agitation for social reform has subsided and has even vanished. The Prarthana Samaj, the Brahmo Samaj with their elevating influence have become things of the past. The future has few things like these in store. The growth of education if it is confined to one class, will not necessarily lead to liberalism. It may lead to the justification and conservation of class interest; and instead of creating the liberators of the downtrodden, it may create champions of the past and the supporters of the *status quo*. Isn't this the effect of education so far? That it will take a new course in future *ceteris paribus*, there is no ground to believe. Therefore, instead of leaving the Untouchables to the mercy of the higher castes, the wiser policy would be to give power to the Untouchables themselves who are anxious, not like others, to usurp power but only to assert their natural place in society.

This gigantic world war, however motivated, has yielded what is known as the principle of self-determination which is to govern international relations of the future. It is happy to note that the pronouncement of the 20th August 1917 declared the application of the principle to India—a principle which enunciates the rule that every people must be free to determine the conditions under which it is to live. It would be a sign of imperfect realization of the significance of this principle if its application were restricted to international relations, because discord does not exist between nations alone, but there is also discord between classes from within a nation. Wittingly our Indian politicians in their political speeches and harangues hold on to 'the *de jure* conception of the Indian people'. By the *de jure* conception they conceive of the Indian people as by nature one and emphasize the qualities such as praiseworthy community of purpose and welfare, loyalty to public ends and mutuality of sympathy which accompany this unity. How the *de jure* and *de facto* conceptions conflict, it is hoped, the committee will not fail to realize. As an instance the following may be noted. The moral evil to the Indian people of their conquest and subjugation by the British is a theme which is very attractive to the Brahmin politicians, who never fail to make capital out of it. The moral evils were once portrayed by John Shore in his 'Notes on Indian Affairs' written in 1832. The late Honourable Mr. Gokhale once voiced the same feeling when speaking about the 'excessive costliness of the foreign agency'. He said:

> There is a moral evil which, if anything, is even greater. A kind of dwarfing or stunting of the Indian race is going on under the present system. We must

> live all the days of our life in an atmosphere of inferiority and the tallest of us must bend, in order that the exigencies, of the existing system may be satisfied. The upward impulse, if I may use such an expression, which every schoolboy at Eton and Harrow may feel, that he may one day be a Gladstone or Napoleon or a Wellington, and which may draw forth the best efforts of which he is capable, is denied to us. The full height to which our manhood is capable of rising can never be reached by us under the present system. The moral elevation which every self-governing people feel cannot be felt by us. Our administrative and military talents must gradually disappear, owing to sheer disuse till at last our lot as hewers of wood and drawers of water in our own country, is stereotyped.

I beg to invite the attention of the Committee whether these sentiments which have been voiced by a Brahmin (a noble Brahmin to be sure) to the disgrace of the British bureaucracy cannot be more fittingly voiced by the Untouchables to the disgrace of the Brahmin oligarchy? May it be said to the credit of the bureaucracy, that it has disproved the charge of being wooden and shown itself susceptible to feeling by proposing changes in the system of the Government which has dwarfed the personality of those for whom it was devised. But can the oligarchy claim anything half as noble? Their belief is that the Hindu social system has been perfected for all time by their ancestors who had the superhuman vision of all eternity and supernatural power for making infinite provision for future ages. This deep ingrained ethnocentrism has prevented a reconstruction of Hindu Society and stood in the way of a revision of vested rights for the common good. A farce of a conference for the removal of untouchability was enacted in March 1918 in Bombay. Doctor Kurtakoti, the Shankaracharya of Karvir fame, though promised to attend, left for Northern India just a day or two before the conference met, on some urgent business. Mr. Tilak is credited with a short speech at the conference which has for the good luck of Mr. Tilak remained unreported. But this was only lip sympathy shown to hoodwink the Untouchables for when the draft of the proclamation removing untouchability was presented to Mr. Tilak, it is known on creditable evidence that he refused to honour it with his signature.

Here is disclosed a patent disharmony within a nation and therefore a proper field for the application of the principle of self-determination. If the advanced classes are clamouring for its application to India and if the powers that we have sanctioned it, however partially, to ward off the future stunting and dwarfing of the Indian people, may not the Untouchables with justice claim its benefit in their own interest? Admitting the necessity of self-determination for the Untouchables communal representation cannot be withheld from them, for communal representation and self-determination are but two different phrases which express the same notion.

Note

1 *BAWS* 1979, vol. 1: 247–77.

9

Development economics and the Indian experience

Sukhamoy Chakravarty

Source: Kaushik Basu and Pulin Nayak (eds), *Development Policy and Economic Theory* (New Delhi: Oxford University Press, 1994), pp. 1–13.

I

The subject of this paper may appear a forbiddingly ambitious one. At the start, it is best to disabuse readers of any notion that I am going to offer a comprehensive overview of either development economics or of the Indian experience.

Nearly a decade ago, it became quite fashionable to proclaim the demise of development economics. I thought news of its death, like that of Mark Twain, was highly exaggerated. As a long-time student of the subject I felt obliged to deny such reports. My denial was published in the June 1987 issue of *The Manchester School* under the heading, 'The State of Development Economics'. It is not my purpose to extend the argument presented in that paper.

Meanwhile, as evidence of the continued state of 'good health' of this subdiscipline, I refer readers to the *Handbook of Development Economics* edited by H.B. Chenery and T.N. Srinivasan, and to a volume edited by T.P. Schultz and G. Ranis on the same subject.

My task on the present occasion is the modest one of trying to present an analytic sketch of the evolution of development economics in the Indian context. This implies a need to look not only at the period with which we are most familiar, that is to say the years since independence, but also at the period since the late 1890s. Despite the fact that the Zeitgeist shows a great preference for algebraic manipulation, regression analysis, etc., over reasoned verbal discourse, I have not been able to discern any significant 'epistemological break' between what an economist like M.G. Ranade had to say on problems facing the Indian economy in the late nineteenth century and what the authors of the First Five Year Plan had to say on most issues of substantive importance. In fact, the ease with which a particular policy planning mix was adopted in India in the fifties appears to me in a significant way explainable by what had been argued at length in the first two decades of the twentieth century. In a way this is not surprising because the structural characteristics of the Indian economy had not significantly altered in the years between approximately 1918 and 1947, the period between the end of World War I and the year India gained independence. Furthermore, even within the domain of economic thinking, discussion of development thought had not seen any great elaboration during the intervening period comparable with what James Stewart, A. Smith, and D. Ricardo had presented during England's industrial transition, or what Mill had to say during the heyday of Victorian capitalism. The authorities mentioned earlier, with the exception of Stewart, had been read and absorbed by the first generation of Indian development theorists, as even a quick look at their major writings shows. The neo-classical writers, by and large, had not much to offer on development issues; Schumpeter's major achievement was largely ignored, along with the isolated, though brilliant, achievements of Allyn Young. Marx had much to say that was vitally important, but he was hardly read, let alone adequately comprehended, during this period, when the import of Marxist works into India was treated as subversive.

The situation in India was, in this respect, strikingly different from what happened in Russia, where even a 'legal Marxist' like Tugan-Baranovski had a lot to say on the structural changes taking place in Russia, utilizing the Marxist analytical framework; and Professor Sieber was held by Marx himself as a great authority on his work and on the work of classical economists. Lenin was at this time championing the 'cause' of capitalism, in contrast with Mihailovski, who represented a populist ideology of rural development. Even during the first decade of India's planning, Marxist ideas were less in evidence amongst the professional writings of Indian economists, although some aspects of the Soviet industrialization debate of the twenties were quite influential.

In more recent years, there has been a growing realization of the complexity of the development process, and people are rediscovering 'facts' or 'quasi-facts' which were already well known to students of economic history, especially to those who studied the experiences of the peripheral countries of Europe, such as the prewar Balkans or the Iberian peninsula. Meanwhile, there has also emerged a neo-Marxist perspective on the development question which has been accompanied, interestingly enough, by a more free-market oriented mode of reasoning. This can be seen as a conservative counterpoint to the neo-Marxian political economy. Undoubtedly, the eighties, and to a lesser extent the second half of the seventies, raised issues which go beyond the framework of a reasoning which was largely accepted during the preceding two and a half decades of the post-independence experience. I can, therefore, differentiate three stages of development thinking in India. While the first stage, pre-independence thought, is largely uncharted, I shall try to show its pertinence to what came immediately after. Equally important, the two stages of post-independence thinking need a differentiated approach, if a clearer treatment of the policy issues facing us today is to be adequately pursued. The changed conditions also imply the need to explore currently emerging areas of socio-economic enquiry.

II

Three phases of development thinking and experience in India

Phase A

Phase A, which may be called 'pre-independence thinking', was not entirely homogeneous. There are three major strands in pre-independence thought.

(1) One major strand pertaining to the pre-independence thinking phase is best represented by Ranade's early and important essays on Indian economic problems, including especially his very important essay, 'Indian Political Economy'.[1] Ranade's ideas were further elaborated and in part implemented by M. Visvesvaraya, who was a successful dewan of the state of Mysore, and who influenced the thinking of the Indian National Planning Committee, set up by Subhash Chandra Bose when he became President of the Congress Party.

Briefly stated, the Ranade position contains the following major arguments.

(a) The inapplicability of the Ricardian theories of rent and, more generally, of the Ricardian theories of value and distribution to the Indian situation. Ranade here relies on the work of Richard Jones for his intellectual orientation. Jones was an economist much admired by Marx, although he was treated in negative terms by the immediate disciples of Ricardo, and he vanished from discussions of economic problems during the heyday of neo-classicism. With hindsight, we can look upon Jones as an important precursor of evolutionary reasoning in economics.

(b) A Listian perspective on the cumulative inequalizing tendencies of free trade between countries which are at very different stages of development. Ranade was very clear that the Ricardian prescriptions, in their actual application, were dynamically flawed, as he was clearly thinking in terms of processes rather than one-point solutions.

(c) Advocacy of a state-promoted policy of industrialization based on protection, which goes beyond Mill's 'infant industry' argument.

(d) The need to expand technical education and other accompanying institutional changes as a necessary concomitant of a policy of sustained industrialization.[2]

Ranade was followed by many economists, e.g. G.V. Joshi. I will mention here one relatively little-known figure, P.A. Wadia who, along with K.T. Merchant, was the author of a textbook on the Indian economy.[3] It appears that Wadia provided an early version of what came to be known much later as 'dependency theory'. In an article called 'The True Basis of Protection', published in the *Economic Journal* when Keynes was an active editor, Wadia put the problem of protection in a perspective which considerably transcended the typical 'protectionist formulation' by bringing in issues of unequal exchange, which Prebisch and Latin American authors were to later popularize.[4]

(2) As against this modernizing position, a rural-communitarian perspective was represented in the work of Mahatma Gandhi. It was also developed by professional economists such as Radhakamal Mukherji, J.J. Anjaria, and several others who were sensitive to the institutional specificities of Indian rural life and its eroding material foundation. Basically, the idea was to restore the unity between 'industry' and 'agriculture' which had been greatly ruptured by the British impact and the concomitant process of commercialization. Space prevents me from dealing with the evolution of Gandhiji's ideas, especially on 'machinery', but it is important to realize that his ideas evolved in this area over a period of time, and not in a negative direction, as is indicated by his high praise for the Singer sewing machine.

(3) Ranade's approach was heavily influenced by his reading of Jones, Cliffe Leslie, and the writings of the German historical school, whose main contention rested on accepting the relativity of economic laws, in contrast with the deductive bias of the Ricardian school. However, a Marshallian point of view was developed by economists such as J. Coyajee (a pupil of Marshall), H.L. Dey, and others who were critical of the protectionist models of industrialization on grounds which are not significantly different from what is often heard in critiques of the inward-looking industrialization policy these days. Dey, in particular, criticized industrial protection as it imposed an additional burden on Indian agriculturists. In addition, these economists preached Marshallian virtues such as family-based thrift, a changed attitude towards work, and a very cautious policy of tariff protection if the facts of the matter so warranted.

These three theoretical positions are by no means of antiquarian interest, as it is possible to trace a line of continuity between the policy advocated by Ranade and the policy mix as it evolved in the course of the first two decades of post-independence development, especially under the leadership of Nehru. While Nehru brought in some socialist ideas, which increasingly diluted over the years, his lineage as a practising economic statesman runs from Ranade via Visvesvaraya. This is also evident from the generous tributes that Nehru paid to Visvesvaraya as the 'father of Indian Planning'. While, during the earlier pre-independence phase, development issues were largely discussed in the context of Indian problems, the hiatus between the theoretical courses taught at most Indian universities and the most pressing issues of the day was distressingly large.

This was largely because the treatment of value theory contained in Marshall's Principles, Book V, though posing sufficient conundrums which were to occupy the best minds of the Anglo-Saxon world for nearly forty years, had little to say to Indian students interested in development problems. Marshall's penetrating comments on the process of economic change, interspersed throughout his life—which were inconsistent with his value-theoretic foundations—had an effect only on those who were inclined in an institutionalist direction. The first generation of Indian economists, in contrast, had the benefit of reading John Stuart Mill, who is unduly neglected in the field of economic theory, and who devoted a lot of attention to the development dimension of the economic problem in his Principles of Political Economy.

Phase B: The planning period 1950–75

On the level of formulation, Phase B involves a quantum jump in analytical terms. But closer inspection conveys a much greater feeling of continuity with the ideas which had been developed by Ranade, Joshi, Wadia, and others.

The main point of continuity, and a very important one, was an assumed consensus on the character of the state in the dominant formulations of this period. Much of the policy-based theorizing attributed a relatively independent role to the state in shaping the contours of a development strategy. A *nation state* was no longer only a 'concept' which List and others had talked about; it also formed the basis of actual policy-making. Similarly, Listian ideas on the primacy of growth of 'productive forces' over current production are amply reflected in the Nehru-Mahalanobis strategy of long-term investment planning. Both Nehru and Mahalanobis were willing to sacrifice some incremental gain in near-term consumption for a long-term increase in the growth rate.

While, therefore, the broad conceptual underpinning was Listian, the changed nature of discourse was represented by the use of post-Keynesian growth models, including an elegant but somewhat simplified formulation of Marx's two-sector model of expanded reproduction, developed by Mahalanobis, which dealt with the problem of capital accumulation in a structural sense.

Indian discussion, at this point, dovetails with discussion emanating from Western, non-Marxist sources. This was, incidentally, a period when 'underdevelopment' was discovered as a major fact of international life, requiring an explanation in *economic* terms.

It is not always realized that *facts* of scientific discourse are not simply 'out there', but require a process of discovery, sometimes a very prolonged one.[5] Thus, while it would be inaccurate to say that underdevelopment was not noticed before by Western scholars writing on Eastern problems, we are justified in saying that much analysis ran in terms of racial characteristics, climatic factors and/or religious motivations. Weber, in particular, regarded both Hinduism and Confucianism as incompatible with the requirements of economic development.[6] While some of the early Indian analysts had discovered 'underdevelopment' as the major fact of our national life, we have noted already that, even within India, there was not complete agreement about how to develop a set of analytic categories to deal with the problem with any degree of precision. The fifties saw a change in this respect, the magnitude of which can, however, be overestimated.

The development of a concept of 'planning' as a societal response to problems of underdevelopment was not altogether a new thing, as the concept already existed in List's writings. Its acceptance as a subject for closer economic exploration and implementation was based on the changed climate of opinion, as well as on the changed political environment. Here again List, rather than Marx, was more important, although only discerning commentators like E.H. Carr explicitly noted this point. Incidentally, the argument of 'balanced growth' as a theoretical underpinning to planning exercises is also to be found in List, even though, for obvious reasons, no attempt at quantification was made by him.

During this period even those who had earlier subscribed to the Marshallian position found it possible and necessary to change to a planning viewpoint because of their general acceptance of a broad Keynesian framework regarding the limitations of the market mechanism, although the strict applicability of Keynes' policy model was rejected by many on the ground that it was largely demand-oriented.[7] A supply-oriented view, reminiscent in some sense of classical economics, was considered an appropriate analytical framework—as is evident from the work of Rao, A.K. Dasgupta, and several others.

The discovery of an *elastic* capital supply in overpopulated agrarian economies, making it possible for higher levels of real investment to fructify without the prior increase of a savings fund (i.e. 'wages fund' in the classical sense) was first noted by Kalecki in a pre-war review of the influential book by M. Manoilesco, although Kalecki himself became somewhat doubtful about the emphasis given to it by Nurkse and others in the absence of large-scale institutional changes in agriculture.[8]

Terms-of-trade pessimism in the Prebischian sense was generally congenial to the Indian point of view as it meshed well with India's own experience in the context of the post-Korean world depression of commodity prices. Export substitution was hardly considered a feasible option in the short run, even though long-term substitution in the export basket in terms of high-valued products was clearly envisaged as one of the basic rationales for investment planning in the Second Five Year Plan.

Phase C

The dating of Phase C may differ from one economist to another. Some may want to trace it back to 1965. I think 1975 is a more pertinent date.

The major differences of perception that characterize this period are outlined below.

(1) Constraints on 'state action' were seen as not merely due to extraneous factors such as droughts, unfavourable international developments, etc., but as stemming from the character of the 'state' itself. Increasingly, the state was being seen more as a locus for accommodating conflicting class/group interests, and less as a source of legitimate authority when it came to determining the contours of the capital process.

(2) Coupled with this shift, there was also a generally growing feeling that India was developing in a quasi-autarkic fashion, a process seen by many as subject to serious inefficiencies in matters relating to the utilization of scarce resources.

(3) While the earlier literature viewed the intersectoral planning of growth rates as the major solution to the poverty problem, opinions in recent years have been divided into two positions, one favouring higher growth rates, leaving the details to be sorted out by the market, and the other proposing a direct attack on 'poverty'. While these two positions imply in many ways very different political perceptions, as well as make different assumptions about the character of binding constraints, they seem to agree on the need to shift attention away from investment planning by a central authority as providing the basic design for economic management.

The reasons behind the shift of perception are due to several factors. Briefly, they reflect objective processes at work as well as the changed climate of opinion in the developed West.

Objective factors include the inability to restrain the growth of consumption in upper income brackets, based in part on the large initial inequality of asset distribution, and in part on the differential ability of certain segments of Indian society to bend the 'rules of the game' to their own advantage. Earlier assumptions regarding the efficacy of certain policy instruments have, therefore, been held up as overly facile, perverse or, at best, unduly optimistic, depending on one's inclination.

As regards the climate of opinion, the resurgence of a conservative outlook on matters relating to social and economic inequality in Britain and the US has, in recent years, had a noticeable impact on the thinking of the Indian elite, which increasingly views a taste for high living as a productive phenomenon.

This last phenomenon, which may be described as the 'aspiration effect', was first described by the eighteenth century economist James Stewart as a beneficial influence but was rejected by classical economists, such as Smith and Say. During the revived classicism of the fifties, it was roundly condemned by Nurkse and others who talked about the negative influence of the 'demonstration effect' on the development process.

There is little doubt that in fashioning development strategy today, Indian economists and policymakers cannot simply ignore these perceptions for reasons which are already too obvious to discuss here.

In my opinion, it would, however, be unwarranted to infer from these changed perceptions that a radically different 'development paradigm' has been discovered as providing an answer to our most pressing problems, which still centre around the following economic imperatives.

(1) The need for maintaining macroeconomic stability, in particular maintaining a policy frame which safeguards the balance of payments as well as non-inflationary growth.
(2) The urgent necessity of improving the level of living of the broad masses of India's people through the generation of adequate employment opportunities, and otherwise.
(3) Ensuring the greater overall efficiency of resource use.
(4) Maintenance of suitable ecological conditions which are not excessively costly, taking into account also the changed demographic environment in which we operate these days.

III

In the final analysis, the crucial problem that I see is the old one, first seen clearly by Marx at a great distance, and since then talked about by all leading Indian thinkers, that is—how to restore the rupture between agriculture and industry that was introduced by the implantation of an alien mode of production on Indian soil.

Obviously, the restoration of this unity is neither possible nor desirable on an old basis. It cannot be done on the basis of the old system of social relationships, nor can it be done on a primitive technological base. On the other hand, the developments of the last forty years have highlighted the increasing distance between rural and urban areas; this is currently described as the internal dualism of Indian society.

One can clearly see that, left to itself, the market mechanism today will integrate much more easily the developing metropolitan centres in India with the developed nations abroad. Although conventional measures such as GNP growth rates, even adjusted on a per capita basis, may show some acceleration as a result, this process will not solve the problem of 'dualism' in the foreseeable future. Here, the nature of the technological changes taking place today is of some importance, as they do not have the labour-attracting characteristics of the earlier periods, which were marked by epochal innovations of a different type. Nonetheless, suitably directed, some of the present changes may provide for a greater degree of spatial dispersal of productive activities. I refer here to certain aspects of new information technology, interpreted in the widest sense of the term. I believe that the area of interface between technology and institutional change has been inadequately explored in Indian development literature. It is not true to say that it was altogether ignored: Mahalanobis, Pant, and other planners were well aware of the problem. However, they operated on the paradigm of an earlier technological epoch where 'coal and iron' provided the material embodiment of technological change. We have now entered a different epoch with new problems, possibilities, and perplexities.

The central question that is *new* is how best to steer technological change. Here, possibly problems of strategic control and intervention by the state deserve careful attention rather than large-scale public investment as such.

I am well aware that there is no completely painless way of absorbing large-scale technical changes, which essentially involves 'creative destruction', to use a Schumpeterian expression. From the institutional angle, as things stand today, the ones who are likely to be asked to pay a high price are the ones who are least able to afford it. Hence, social direction is essential, stemming from certain basic limitations of the market mechanism.

In sectoral terms, sectors which need maximum attention need to be clearly identified, and training and redeployment in some areas have to be combined with augmented investments in areas such as irrigation and energy, in regions where the production potential still remains largely untapped.

Our conventional analysis of the development process has largely run in terms of the replication of existing capital stocks. Compositional shifts have been generally predicted on the basis of known intersectoral linkages. What is needed is a certain measure of suitable technology forecasting and plans for absorption.

Classical complete input–output tables may need to be supplemented and/or substituted by a theory of 'development block'. In this respect, some ideas of the Swedish economist Erik Dahmen, who provided a penetrating analysis of Swedish industrial change, deserve to be carefully noted.

To avoid a Latin American type disruption of the growth process, Indian policy-makers must pay careful attention to the planning of consumption. Amongst economic historians, Werner Sombart paid a lot of attention to the role of major shifts in demand in producing economy-wide changes in the pattern of resource allocation. I believe that demand issues need to be carefully looked into, especially the dynamics of demand changes.

It is essential to make sure that the modernization of the consumption basket maintains some appropriate relationship to changes in the production pattern. Given the nature of India's persistent poverty problem, it is clear that the country can ill afford to concentrate on the potential demand emerging from the top decile. Indian sectoral planning cannot, accordingly, be guided by the revealed preferences of the market: a large majority of Indian people do not have the capacity to register their effective preferences. This poses major problems of control and management. While suggesting the need for an overall step-up in the level of investment, a mere acceleration in the growth rate of the gross national product will not do the job. We need to ensure a suitable composition as well.

Notes

1 See Ranade (1903).
2 Ranade, as an economist, was discussed at a special session of the Indian Economic Association where Professor Bhabatosh Datta, then teaching at Ripon College, Calcutta, criticized him for showing 'a singular lack of appreciation of socialist ideas'. See B. Datta (1941–2), pp. 260–75.
3 Some readers may wonder why I have not included in the text a reference to Dadabhai Naoroji's influential theory of the external drain of resources imposed by the British colonial administration. This is because the logical structure of the entire argument, especially that pertaining to the magnitude of the drain is not completely clear to me. For a generous interpretation of Dadabhai's theory, I can recommend to the reader the book by the late Professor B.N. Ganguli (1965). It is, however important to note here that there were interesting differences between Dadabhai and Ranade on the question of the drain. Ranade's early ideas on this question were formulated only in Marathi, but as early as 1872–3. A reissue of these lectures was brought out by the Gokhale Institute in 1963. Ranade's subsequent reformulation and partial repudiation of his earlier position was given in the course of his inaugural address to the First Industrial Conference in Poona in 1890. Why Ranade changed his position is an interesting question and requires more study. Some light is thrown on this question by N.V. Sovani (1985).
4 See P.A. Wadia (1924).
5 The first serious effort in this direction was put forward by L. Fleck in his major but greatly neglected work. Thanks to the work of Thomas Kuhn, his ideas have recently gained considerable currency. See Fleck (1979).
6 We may note that Weber's position on Confucianism has been recently turned around by M. Morishima.
7 See especially the important article by V.K.R.V. Rao (1952). Dasgupta's contributions are included in his volume (1965).
8 See M. Kalecki (1938).

References

Chakravarty, S. (1987), 'The State of Development Economics', *The Manchester School*, June.
Chenery, H.B., and T.N. Srinivasan (eds) (1988), *Handbook of Development Economics*, Amsterdam: North Holland.

Dasgupta, A.K. (1965), *Planning and Economic Growth*, London: Allen & Unwin.

Datta, Bhabatosh (1941–2), *Indian Journal of Economics*, vol. *22*.

Fleck, Ludwik (1979), *Genesis and Development of a Scientific Fact*, University of Chicago Press.

Ganguli, B.N. (1965), *Dadabhai and the Drain Theory*, Bombay: Asian Publishing House.

Kalecki, M. (1938), 'Review of Manoilescio', *Economic Journal*.

Ranade, M.G. (1903), *Essays in Indian Economics*, Madras: G.A. Valesion & Co.

Rao, V.K.R.V. (1952), 'The Multiplier', *Indian Economic Review*.

Schultz, T.P., and G. Ranis (1988), *State of Development Economics*, Oxford: Blackwell.

Sovani, N.V. (1985), 'The Drain Theory: Naoroji and Ranade', in K. Prasad and R.K. Sinha (eds.), *Perspectives on Economic Development and Thought*, Bombay: Somaiya Publications.

Wadia, P.A. (1924), 'The True Basis of Protection', *Economic Journal*.

10

The debate on Gandhian ideas

Benjamin Zachariah

Source: *Developing India: An Intellectual and Social History* (New Delhi: Oxford University Press, 2005), pp. 156–210.

This chapter seeks to examine the ways in which Gandhian ideas on India's future socio-economic order, centred on the self-sufficient, or nearly so, village, were sought to be justified by Gandhians before an audience of intellectuals who were the main protagonists in debates on 'development' in the 1930s and the 1940s. This was a period of relative marginalization of Gandhian ideas in the Congress and, more generally, in the Indian nationalist movement. The chapter traces the origins in earlier debates of some of the ideas brought into play in such justifications, and how they were sought to be expressed in terms of the general concerns with 'development' which were being articulated at the time by intellectuals. In so doing, it examines the ideas of Mohandas Karamchand Gandhi, who remained, throughout the period, a pre-eminent moral and political leader despite the rejection of his ideas in many circles, and with the interpretation of Gandhi on the subject of a desirable socio-economic order for India provided by J.C. Kumarappa who, as secretary of Gandhi's All-India Village Industries Association (AIVIA), conducted most of its propaganda and publicity drives.

Gandhi's ideas, as they were extended and popularized in this field (with regard to a desirable socio-economic order), were not part of an alternative discourse separate from British imperialist or 'Western' discourse or, indeed, from nationalist replies from within that discourse (which, as I have observed, shared some of the beliefs and/or discursive conventions of imperialist arguments but reworked them into quite different arguments). Nor were they in some sense more 'popular'. On the contrary, they were variations on those replies, elitist in origin and didactic in intent and tone.

Gandhian ideas have been seen by many later commentators as subordinate to, or less important than, the much discussed debates on socialism, capitalism, and industrialization which have been taken to be at the core of Indian debates on 'development'; and indeed were at the core of debates in the field of 'development economics' until quite recently, when ideas of 'sustainable development', environmentalism, and decentralization pushed previously marginalized ideas, among them Gandhian ones, back into centrestage. Consequently, much attention has been claimed recently by 'Gandhian economics' which, since the late 1960s or the early 1970s has continued to find supporters.[1] Current alternative positions, however, in seeking to recover marginalized ideas of development such as the Gandhian, often conduct unhistorical readings based on present day concerns and, thereby, attribute to those ideas meanings which they could not have had in their contemporary context.[2]

The main outlines of what has come to be known as 'Gandhian economic thought' are well known—a decentralized, village-based economic order which was as self-sufficient as possible, of rural small-scale agriculture, and industries which employed low technology—but the neatness and consistency of this position is more the contribution of later writers than of Gandhi himself.[3] Gandhi's several versions of his antimachinery doctrine show that they were modified over the years to accommodate the use of some machinery. In 1924 Gandhi claimed he was not against all machinery, but was against the 'craze' for labour-saving devices while men went about unemployed. He called the Singer sewing machine 'one of the few useful things ever invented'; and when it was pointed out to him that these machines had to be made in factories with power-driven machinery, Gandhi replied that this was true, but he was 'socialist enough to say that such factories should be nationalised, State- controlled'.[4] In 1933 Gandhi praised the Nazis for reviving village industries and for de-mechanizing certain industries to create more employment, arguing that even a technically advanced country such as Germany recognized the need for limiting the use of machinery.[5]

Another aspect of Gandhi's thinking on the economic order which has not received attention from his retrospective supporters is his idea of the 'trusteeship' role of the wealthy: the rich would hold their wealth in trust for society in general, for which they would be expected, according to Gandhi's argument, to feel a moral responsibility.[6] This lack of attention is understandable; if the latter is treated together with the former, it is difficult to construct of 'Gandhian economic thought' the alternative to capitalism which many of its supporters claim for it.

'Gandhian economic thought' must, therefore, be recognized as a gradual and retrospective creation. Aspects of it were defined and articulated first as a political weapon against the economic domination of Lancashire, with precedents in the Swadeshi movement following the first partition of Bengal in 1905; other aspects were connected to Gandhi's concern for the moral and ethical education of Congress members and the Indian people; further aspects were articulated later, partly in response to the growing critique of Gandhi's ideas of village industries and 'constructive work'. The debate on Gandhi's ideas of a village-centred social, political, and economic order as a possible path to Indian 'development' began in earnest from the 1930s, and grew through the 1940s, and after his death. By the Second World War, these ideas seemed to have been successfully marginalized, but they came together in different forms after independence, with Acharya Vinoba Bhave's Sarvodaya movement claiming surprising converts, possibly the most surprising being one of Gandhian ideas' most articulate critics, Jayaprakash Narayan.[7] The forms in which post-Independence incorporations of economic and social ideas referred to as 'Gandhian' took place could, however, only partially be attributed to Gandhi—such as, the incorporation of Gandhi as a central legitimizing icon in 'community development' schemes in the 1950s.[8]

The 'Gandhian' approach, in its own time, concentrated not on the details along which to work out practical economics, 'picturesque descriptions of such things as sanitary devices, sinking and cleaning of wells, utilisation of waste, hygienic precautions to be taken etc.'. These were considered necessary; but 'much more important is the spirit of the approach'.[9] This chapter examines the manoeuvres and strategies of argument adopted in attempting to clear a discursive space for Gandhian ideas from the 1930s. In dealing with the arguments thus put forth as 'manoeuvres' or 'strategies' I do not mean to suggest that these were merely strategic ploys; they were, most of them, part of a larger world view, whose rationale and philosophical underpinnings needed to be explained before the more specific ideas that followed could persuasively be put forth.

In dealing with the strategic placement of Gandhian arguments, I argue that contrary to many interpretations, contemporary and hostile, present day and favourable, Gandhi and the Gandhians did not operate through claims to being anti-modern. They claimed, on the contrary, to offer solutions which were more modern than industrialization-based models of society, and to challenge the criteria of modernity which they saw as being somewhat uncritically borrowed from the 'West'. They based themselves on an equation of socialism and capitalism, both being 'Western' systems, as systems which paid too much attention to material needs, consequently neglecting the moral and ethical basis for society. This basis was sought in certain aspects of 'traditional' Indian society, which often meant a creative borrowing from and reinterpretation of 'Hindu' traditions as being 'modern' before the 'West' was 'modern'.

It was not possible, however, to base an argument at the time on a rejection of 'modernity'. Unlike in much present day writing, in which 'modernity' and the 'West' are equated and regarded as negative (this equation being projected into the past), 'modernity' was viewed as extremely empowering, and carried with it extremely positive connotations for a people called 'primitive' and 'backward'. The terms of the 1930s and 1940s—the modern, modernizers, modernity; Western, the West, and so on—were generally assumed to be intelligible in similar terms to the audiences before whom they were placed. They did not need to be defined; precision might perhaps weaken their effectiveness. In the political discourse of the time, their emotive significance had already been well established; of the two sets of terms, the first was desirable, the second to be avoided. A legitimate position, therefore, had to be based on something which was 'modern', but not 'Western'.

A major, if not the decisive, role in this process of formulating 'Gandhian economic thought' in these terms was played by J.C. Kumarappa. Kumarappa's major statement of the philosophy of the village movement was formulated in a book entitled *Why the Village Movement?*.[10] According to Kumarappa this was meant to clarify the ideals of the All-India Spinners' Association and the AIVIA;[11] the book, nonetheless, grew with each subsequent edition, addressing wider debates on socialism and capitalism, nation building, centralization, development, and planning, as they emerged.[12] This book largely succeeded in being an annotated commentary, from a Gandhian perspective, on development debates in India in the 1930s and the 1940s. Kumarappa was the best possible commentator among the Gandhians, given his early training in economics and finance and his consequent ability to place his arguments in the conventionally respected language of economics.[13] But it was a lot more than that as well; in it, Kumarappa undertook the rather ambitious project of enunciating an entire social philosophy on which his economic arguments were to be based. *Why the Village Movement?* is, after *Hind Swaraj*, the closest example we have to a manifesto of Gandhism. Kumarappa could be expected to interpret Gandhi to middle-class audiences and seek to persuade them with intellectual tools readily assimilable to mundane, rational thinking; he elaborates a series of arguments with a keen sense of the specifics of the issues with which he has to contend, centralizing, communist, socialist or capitalist. This chapter, consequently, deals in some detail with the social and intellectual genealogy of Kumarappa, his relationship with Gandhi, his writings, and the reception or potential impact of his writings.

In the sections that follow I attempt the following: to place Gandhi in the political and socio-intellectual currents of the times; to examine the positions being articulated in opposition to Gandhi and the consequent need for a further effective intervention in the debates on Indian 'development' from a Gandhian perspective; to examine that intervention; and to place the position so articulated in the perspective of the positions against which it contended.

Placing Gandhi

Gandhi has often been seen as standing outside the main currents of political debate in colonial India. Thus, while imperialists and nationalists both spoke of Indian 'backwardness', Gandhi apparently refused to join a debate with the colonial government on terms he understood to be their own terms: the solution to problems of 'backwardness' was to reject definitions of 'backwardness' which depended on a conception of 'civilisation' based on making 'bodily welfare the object of life',[14] founded on material rather than spiritual values. One of the ways in which the Gandhian attack on development through industrialization functioned was through an equation of industrial modernity with the 'West', which by implication or by direct accusation could be considered alien, immoral and culturally disruptive. Although this could remain, in Gandhi's own writings, within a universalist rather than a nationalist particularist philosophical position (the 'West' had deviated from its own spiritual roots, and, could potentially return to them and, thereby, overcome its spiritual degradation)[15] this distinction could, nonetheless, be lost in dissemination. Gandhi's interventions, therefore, tended to operate within a recognized convention of political argument in colonial India, in terms of a simple distinction between 'East' and 'West'.

It has also been said of Gandhi's writings and statements that they were essentially moral in character; though Gandhi was capable of putting forward arguments in which his idea of the village as economic unit was defended on essentially economic grounds—the wisdom of village industries in a largely agrarian economy with an abundance of underemployed labour—this was not his main argument. According to this view, it was only reluctantly that Gandhi expressed himself in terms of capitalism, socialism, law, and so on; but the terms of the debates on 'development' that emerged strongly from the 1930s forced him occasionally to do so. Here, this was in terms of the possibility of applying 'our own distinct Eastern traditions' in finding a 'solution to the question of capital and labour', or to the organization of the national economy around village-centred production by self-sufficient small producers.[16] Otherwise, Gandhi is said to have conducted a 'total moral critique of the fundamental aspects of civil society', of the 'dubious virtues of modern civilisation', without an appeal to history or precedent, outside 'the bounds of post-Enlightenment thought'.[17]

Starting from this point, Gandhian ideas, economic or otherwise, can be seen in several ways: as a more 'authentic' articulation of the Indian situation, through a critique of 'post-Enlightenment modernity' and its socio-cultural standards, and the reading of Gandhian ideas as 'cultural resistance',[18] an 'alternative vision'. They may also be seen as emanating from the debate within 'Hindu' tradition regarding the need to revitalize Hindu society and to defend it against colonial assaults;[19] or as a necessary stage in nationalist thought, its 'moment of manoeuvre', in which decrying the 'modern' (colonial capitalism) serves to consolidate the 'national' and pave the way for (Indian) expanded capitalist production, 'the development of the thesis by incorporating a part of the antithesis'.[20]

If viewed retrospectively, or from present-day perspectives, Gandhian ideas might indeed be interpreted as serving any or all these purposes. Whether he stood outside 'the bounds of post-Enlightenment thought' (an ambiguous phrase, since post-Enlightenment thought can be interpreted as thought which rejects some of the Enlightenment's tenets—illustrating some of the dangers of the prefix 'post-') or appealed to history and precedent only in exceptional circumstances seems more doubtful.[21] There are other interpretations as well, matters not being made much easier by his refusal to be consistent and his 'aphoristic' language.[22] It seems unproductive to quibble about the essential character of Gandhian thought; nor does it seem possible to arrive at a consensual description of Gandhism; instead, an attempt to unravel its specific meanings in relation to different contexts and audiences might prove to be more meaningful. Perhaps the strength of Gandhi's language was the multiple interpretations to which it could lend itself: it could acquire different meanings to different audiences—the Gorakhpur peasantry, Marwari businessmen, or militant Chitpavan Brahmins.[23]

This seems also to have been Gandhi's intention (he presumably recognized this as his strength); he was capable of switching register quite dramatically, arguing from several different standpoints. It is, therefore, better to recognize the equivalence of moral and political arguments in Gandhi's thought;[24] and, moreover, the strategic nature of Gandhi's uses of these arguments, switching 'abruptly . . . from a religious idiom to a secular humanist one';[25] or indeed to the idiom of scientific expertise. The strategic placement of an argument within a discourse from which it was most likely to be effective was a consideration which often played an important role in Gandhi's thinking; he was prone to asking advice on the technical aspects of economic problems from businessmen before writing articles in which they would appear transformed into his characteristic style of presenting ethical dilemmas.[26]

Gandhi's own mysticism on economic matters has, unfortunately, often been mistaken for a mysticism of approach rather than of rhetoric. Gandhi was fully aware of the need for straightforward rational approaches to such matters; and although he did not usually take such a line himself in a sustained argument (perhaps he felt this would undermine his position as a spiritual leader), he believed it was important that somebody should. Gandhi, consequently, made certain demands on his authorized interpreters, demands which were rather empiricist in their approach to the problems of persuasion. Dissatisfied with one of the latter's efforts, Gandhi wrote sternly to Kumarappa in 1941,

> Your article on industrialisation I consider weak. You have flogged a dead horse. *What we have to combat is socialisation of industrialism.* They instance the Soviet exploits in proof of their proposition. You have to show, if you can, *by working out figures* that handicrafts are better than power driven machinery products. You have almost allowed in the concluding paragraphs the validity of that claim.[27]

The political context

'Modernist' debates regarding models of 'development' explicitly positioned themselves against Gandhian ideas. 'Socialist' alternatives for India began to be confidently articulated and presented to professional and intellectual audiences from the 1930s; socialist and communist activity previously having been mainly confined to organizing the urban working class. A less than systematic engagement with the possibilities opened out by the Russian Revolution for oppressed peoples had also begun among nationalist leaders, but this fell well short of an understanding of or sympathy with the goals of early Bolshevism.[28] The 1930s saw a second wave of socialism. The period after 1931 was one of intense soul-searching and the quest for alternative tactics and ideology to the Gandhian within the Congress and among Congress sympathizers, as a consequence of Gandhi's tendency to order retreats, and of the anticlimax of the 1931 Round Table Conference. There was, gradually, a turn to socialism among a small but articulate group within the Congress—less through a thorough theoretical understanding, or through actual work among the peasantry, rural agricultural labour or the urban working class, than through an admiration of the most spectacular achievements of that other 'backward' country emerging from backwardness—an empowering experience—the Soviet Union. This was a late wave, corresponding to the news of Soviet miracles and the good press the Soviet Union was beginning to get even among the respectable left in Britain.[29]

Capitalists, who often cast themselves as inheritors of the traditional economic nationalist positions of opposition to government economic policies,[30] also failed until quite late to articulate their vision of a future Indian economy and society—possibly deliberately. As G.D. Birla pointed out, it was not a good idea for businessmen themselves to come up with a defence of capitalism, it looked too much like self-interest.[31] Moreover, a far more effective justification of capitalism was provided by Gandhi himself, through his theory of the 'trusteeship' of business which was, for Gandhi, perfectly compatible with his dislike of capitalism: the possessing class, Gandhi argued, held property in trust for the nation and for their less fortunate fellow beings, and they had a duty to use their wealth for the common good.[32] It was, therefore, useful for businessmen to restrict themselves to a more limited agenda of stressing the need for 'national' enterprise—thereby shifting the confrontational aspects of the debate outwards, directing them against colonial rule and, thereby, claiming allies on the basis of business demands being national ones—rather than turning the matter into an internal quarrel as a defence of Indian capitalism against either 'Gandhism' or 'socialism'.[33] As for the contradiction of claiming to be supporters of Gandhi and at the same time being large-scale machinery users, this was a dichotomy to be lived with. As Birla, the businessman who was perhaps closest to Gandhi, put it, the Mahatma was his spiritual leader, but as a businessman there were certain things which he simply had to do although he knew Gandhi did not approve.[34]

Gandhi's success in turning the Congress into a mass movement notwithstanding, many of his ideas were accepted by his political associates as politically expedient rather than out of conviction. Gandhi's frequent retreats, at times when mass movements seemed to be gathering pace and showing signs of independence from his leadership, were also prone to demoralize or disillusion some members.[35] Many of his ideas regarding the economic and social organization of a future India seemed particularly clouded in moral rhetoric and were regarded as far from practicable as the basis of national economic policy, although a 'constructive programme' of spinning and weaving *khadi* could be accommodated without much trouble. With the advent of a strong school of thought which regarded planning for industrialization as the basis for national development, opposition to Gandhi's economic ideas grew more explicit. This coincided, from the mid-1930s, with Gandhi's own relative eclipse in national politics. In 1934, after the anticlimax of the Gandhi–Irwin Pact, the failure of Gandhi to secure any gains from the Round Table Conference, and the failure of the second Civil Disobedience Movement, a group of younger Congressmen, who had been doing some serious rethinking decided to make explicit their socialist approach to politics and society and their differences with Gandhian politics. They still stressed the need to remain within the Congress, the most important anti-imperialist platform in the country, and the priority as the demand for independence from imperialism, but declared their goal of campaigning for a more socialist orientation, the mobilization of peasants and workers and an eventual goal of socialism after the immediate goal of freedom had been achieved.[36] Jayaprakash Narayan advocated left unity, anticipating the Comintern's United Front line, and urged socialists of all kinds to enter the Congress to strengthen its left wing.[37] Meanwhile, Gandhi retired from active membership of the Congress and declared it to be his intention to concentrate on 'constructive work' for the uplift of the masses. This did not mean that he was a peripheral figure in politics: on the contrary, he often crucially intervened, staking his personal integrity and image against those he considered recalcitrant or opposed to what he felt desirable.[38]

This was the background against which the great debate on Gandhian economic ideas took shape: the disillusion with, and self-imposed exile of Gandhi, and (against the backdrop of the Great Depression, the collapse of prices and consequent impoverishment of peasants) the great excitement caused by the economic successes and technological progress of the 'backward' Soviet Union. In this context Gandhi's statements about the importance of 'constructive work' in the villages and the immorality of machine civilization were often met with impatience. Socialists attempted both to bring Gandhi round to their point of view and to point out the flaws in his arguments so as to wean away his supporters and to gain more supporters themselves. Implicitly or explicitly, it was recognized by socialists that the main obstacle to a wider acceptance of (or, at least, a wider sympathy with) socialist principles, was Gandhi's insistence that socialism and capitalism were both foreign solutions to Indian problems; both were materialist and based on the violence of machinery. Capitalists, meanwhile, were able to hide behind the rhetoric of Gandhism.

As a result a great many socialists who attacked Gandhian positions were convinced that the route to an attack on Indian capitalism lay through a weakening of the Gandhian position. However, many who approached the problems of 'development' from a more technological perspective also attacked Gandhi, with arguments which were sometimes not clearly distinguishable from the socialists' arguments. Of this latter group, many were not opposed to or were supporters of private enterprise, although some thought of themselves as socialists. The organized critique of Gandhian ideas was thus conducted both by socialists and by those who considered themselves men of science; for reasons mentioned above, capitalists felt it desirable to pull their punches, reserving their energies to combat the socialist strand of thought. Those businessmen not explicitly 'nationalist', or only contingently so, also refrained from entering this debate with any intensity.[39]

Against Gandhi

The main lines of criticism of Gandhi were on the lines of his ideas inadvertently serving capitalism by providing legitimation for the capitalists through the idea of the 'trusteeship' role of the wealthy; that his ideas were 'backward' and not conducive to modern life; and that contrary to Gandhi's claims, they were not 'indigenous'. On this last point, unlike the other points, it was his opponents who felt more defensive. Gandhi's claim that his opponents' positions were not in keeping with Indian traditions or conditions; that they were 'Western', was the main strength which Gandhian arguments could rely on, as it drew on old anxieties regarding cultural disruption or what constituted legitimate borrowings from the 'West'.[40] The response of 'modernisers' to accusations of 'Westernisation' or a lack of respect for 'tradition' was based on a strategy which claimed that there was nothing wrong with the principles of science and the benefits of technology on which industrialization was based per se; if it appeared that they were not universally valid, this was due to their misuse, which had distorted the results obtained. In the hands of a nationalist government with due regard for Indian conditions they could be put to the best possible use.

The Gandhian voice seemed to represent an unfortunate commitment to 'backwardness'—it was admitted by 'modernisers' that village industries might have a place in an economically rational scheme to provide employment at the local level, and for this purpose might even be worthy of government protection, but, as the journal *Science and Culture* put it, to place a commitment to 'the philosophy of spinning wheel and bullock cart' at the centre of national economic life could only be a denial of the progress of science, of the 'techniques of modern civilisation'.[41] This was an unviable approach '[i]f India is to grow into a powerful world-entity like the U.S.A., Soviet Russia, and the countries of Western Europe . . . A nation, however great its moral and spiritual qualities may be, cannot hope to win battles with bows and arrows against tanks and artillery. In this world of strife and competition, if a nation wants to survive, it must develop the latest techniques of civilised existence'.[42] This, it might be noted, was a view of the state and of state power being conflated with the nation.

This was, moreover, a scientist's or a technologist's critique; it assumed a good deal in terms of the transformative capacity of technology. The Congress Socialists' critique was more subtle, and took Gandhian ideas more seriously, while still maintaining a strong polemic against them. The CSP were always careful to preface their criticism of Gandhian ideas with the assertion that they had no doubts as to Gandhi's own good intentions—it was merely the logic of his ideas that they questioned. Asoka Mehta, addressing the Gandhian question of whether machines caused unemployment, accepted that this was indeed the case in many countries of the world at present, but concluded that this was only the case under capitalism—'the logic of capitalism demands an army of unemployed as its reserve force, and it will not eliminate it'. Under socialism, 'there will be planned economy and work will be so evenly distributed that all will have their share of work and leisure'.[43] This rebuttal was conducive to confusions on an important point: planning under private ownership of technology could also lead to the replacement of workers by machines. Mehta had made the point clear elsewhere, when he argued, describing the initiatives of the New Deal, that planning under capitalism merely strengthens capitalism.[44] In the above passage, it was possible to interpret planning and socialism as somehow necessarily connected. This was a conflation of terms often made, with a planned economy and a large state sector being allowed to masquerade as socialism.

Another point of necessary attack on Gandhian ideas was on the claim that it presented a truly 'indigenous' solution. While pointing out that the logic of Gandhi's ideas often was of great help in justifying capitalists, the CSP maintained that

Gandhi was not a supporter of capitalism. Jaya Prakash Narayan, while accepting this, expressed himself forcefully in a rather polemical piece of writing. Pointing out that Gandhi's idea of the 'trusteeship' of the wealthy was not 'indigenous', he quoted William Godwin's *Political Justice*: 'The most energetic teachers of religion . . . have taught the rich that *they hold their wealth only as a trust* . . . The defect of this system is that they rather excite us to palliate our injustice than to forsake it'.[45] Narayan continued, in ironic mode:

> He [Gandhi] says: "The Ramarajya of my dreams ensures the rights alike of the prince and the pauper". This is the keynote to the entire philosophy of Mahatma Gandhi. . . . Even in his *dream* Ramarajya there will be paupers.
>
> A Ramarajya of paupers and princes! Why not? How else will the noble soul get an opportunity to practise deeds of high-minded philanthropy and thus prove the Hindu conception of human nature![46]

A two-part article in the *Congress Socialist* by Nirmal Bose, a writer sympathetic to Gandhi, and not himself a socialist, examined Gandhi's ideas and asked the question, 'Is Gandhi a Nationalist?' (referring to the Hindu chauvinist Madan Mohan Malaviya's newly-formed party within the Congress, and excluding from its ambit socialists and Gandhians), coming up with interesting answers.[47] The Nationalists, according to Bose, wanted to build up a state which would 'primarily protect and foster the industries and the culture of India'. Gandhi, on the contrary, 'does not divide the human race into classes or nations. For him, humanity is one. In this respect, his sympathies are more with the Socialists than the Nationalists'.

> But Gandhi is not a Communist . . . Gandhi is in fact a philosophical anarchist. But as a practical idealist, he aims at building up little village states, as well as a feeble confederation of them in the form of a centralised State. That requires a certain use of violence, which he thinks, is unavoidable under the circumstances. He is eager to drop even that centralisation as early as possible. As such, Gandhi's Varnashrama, in its practical form, is another form of Socialism, but approaching Anarchism more closely than most prevalent forms of Socialism. It approaches Kropotkin's idea of an anarchistic socialism more closely than anything else'.[48]

This was a more gentle engagement with Gandhi than the more direct assaults on his ideas often found in socialist circles and elsewhere; it seemed to make Gandhism intelligible within (though not compatible with) the framework of socialist thinking, assimilating it to debates with which a reader of past and present socialist debates would be familiar, in particular the Narodnik-Marxist debates in Czarist Russia. In such a view, although Gandhi was regarded as wrong, he represented a stage through which many Marxists had passed.

Gandhi, according to this argument, had been appropriated by the Nationalists largely against his better judgement.

> Time and again, the nationalists gave promises of support to Gandhi and wrenched out from him victories on their own behalf. Gandhi had to support the fostering of the mill-industry, disapprove of movements against the propertied classes as such, state that a rich man could become a trustee on behalf of the poor; but deep down he knew that trusteeship was a legal fiction necessary for an approximation in practice as long as the masses were not strong enough to bring the rich to their senses through non-co-operation. These leases of Gandhi to the capitalists did not form part of his creed; they merely represented Gandhi in retreat and, to that extent, the stabilisation of capitalism in India.[49]

Bose believed, however, that 'Gandhi's alliance with the nationalists was now at an end with the formation of the AIVIA, far closer to Gandhi's own heart than anything he had done before, which represented Gandhi's 'anarchistic socialism', and which Bose described as 'an experiment in the theory of Varnashrama made suitable to modern conditions'—he did not address the charge that the AIVIA was not 'modern'. Despite this, and despite his claim of Gandhi's affinity to socialism, Bose was not optimistic about an alliance between Gandhians and socialists—he dismissed such hopes as unrealistic; instead, he foresaw the probability of 'competition' between 'Gandhi's village organisation' and socialism—he referred to the two as 'Socialism both of the Gandhian and the Communistic type'.[50] This expression separated Bose from the socialists—few socialists would have accepted that a Kropotkinist view was compatible with theirs—intelligible, perhaps, but not compatible. Moreover, his interpretation of Gandhi as anti-capitalist depended on dismissing Gandhi's 'trusteeship' ideas as an inessential and irrelevant part of Gandhi's political creed. This was something many socialists wanted to believe; Gandhi's own good intentions were to be separated from the logic of his ideas and from the uses to which they could be put.

Gandhi's earlier intervention

The difficulties faced by contemporaries in the 1930s in placing Gandhi's ideas in the intellectual landscape of their time should not be taken to imply that Gandhi was so exceptional as to be unclassifiable. The key to the understanding of Gandhi's ideas is hinted at by the interpretations, both contemporary and retrospective, which placed him in a late nineteenth century context. This context has so far never been effectively analysed. Raghavan Iyer makes several remarks in passing, in what is essentially a sympathetic account of Gandhi's moral and political thought, which provide important directive guidelines: Gandhi's formative years were before his years in India (he returned to India from South Africa at the age of 45, in 1914); and he 'was more at ease with writers of the late nineteenth century . . . than with twentieth-century thinkers like Freud'.[51]

Gandhi's main political statement in coherent form was the text which continues to be regarded as his political manifesto, *Hind Swaraj*. Over the years, Gandhi continued to defend this text as the key to his ideas.[52] *Hind Swaraj* was first published in South Africa in the Gujarati section of *Indian Opinion* in two instalments, on 11 and 19 December 1909. It was first published in book form in January 1910, and in English (the translation being Gandhi's own) in March 1910, the first Indian edition not appearing before 1919.[53] Although written in his South African period, it intended to address Indian audiences concerned about the state of India and of the correct path to be taken by nationalism in the context of the issues thrown up by the then ongoing *Swadeshi* Movement; and from the political commentary it provided along with its attempted philosophizing, it was apparent that Gandhi felt the need to address these general concerns. The historical context he provides in the text suggests this (and would have been taken for granted by his readers at the time).[54] However, *Hind Swaraj* did not reach India till 1919—it was banned as seditious by the Government of India in 1910[55]—and perhaps missed its chance to make its most profound impact. Although many read it in the 1920s as a manifesto of the Non-Cooperation Movement, this was in many ways a matter of strategy rather than conviction.[56]

At a time when the burning issues, in the aftermath of the first partition of Bengal in 1905, related to what constituted a swadeshi approach to politics and society—'constructive *swadeshi*', as one historian put it[57]—'national' committees and bodies of various kinds strongly debated what constituted appropriate borrowings from the 'West', and how to indigenize them. Gandhi's was an extreme position on the question of the acceptability and possible assimilation of cultural borrowings. His position on those debates as to how far 'Western' science, technology, or education was relevant to India was to reject all of modern industrial civilization. His resolution of the problems of how to arrive at a pure nationalism, without the distortions caused by machinery and modern civilization (which had tainted the spiritual nature of the West's own Christian traditions), fit closely with the discussions on the nature of technology and science, of the East and the West, which had been taking place from the late nineteenth century among intellectuals and practitioners of science, though they were usually resolved differently. There was a perceived need for reconciliation of science as 'Western' and science as 'Eastern' or 'universal'[58]—a reconciliation which was sometimes effected in strange ways: in his later life, Bankimchandra Chattopadhyay was to claim that he found Darwin's theory of natural selection close to the Hindu concept of trinity; Ramendra Sunder Trivedi concluded his discussion on Darwin by saying that ultimately the world is *Maya*.[59] Gandhi, however, came up with a position of stronger rejection than anyone else of the dangers of modern civilization, which in *Hind Swaraj* is still identified closely, though contingently, with 'Western' civilization.

Ironically, in doing so, he often drew far more strongly on so-called 'Western' trends than many of those who sought to direct and guide the discussions which crystallized around the Swadeshi movement. Gandhi was an up-to-date and subtle user of various eclectic elements from 'Western' learning in his own philosophy. His European and North American influences have been traced in some detail by now.[60] Two aspects of these influences need to be highlighted, however. First, Gandhi's attraction to anti-industrialization and anti-technology ideas needs to be seen against the background of late nineteenth and early twentieth century reactions to industrialization, critiques of or discomfort with capitalism and market forces among thinkers in the 'West'—important to the understanding of Tolstoy, Thoreau, Edward Carpenter, or Ruskin, for instance. Second, many of Gandhi's other sources were equally inflected with British writings on India from the mid-nineteenth century or earlier, either directly or at second hand; and as a corollary to this, it needs to be noted that his interest in the philosophy and practices of 'Hinduism' and of 'Indian tradition' were also directed by his encounter with the 'West', and by 'Western' interest in 'Hinduism'. A good example of the second point is Gandhi's reading of Henry Maine's *Village Communities of the East and West*, included in the short bibliography of *Hind Swaraj*. Maine's comparative jurisprudence, which Gandhi came across in the course of his legal training, drew on the former's Indian experiences and on accounts of the 'Indian village community' which had been influential in early Orientalist accounts.[61] Gandhi was far from being the only Indian to come up with a romanticized account of 'village India'; the rural community ordered as an ideal and harmonious society, and the consequent privileging of an indigenous past shorn of colonial impurities appears, for instance, in the works of Radhakamal Mukerjee and Radhakumud Mookerji.[62]

But there is, of course, a further twist to the debates on the 'East' and the 'West' in this tale. The debates with which Maine was concerned—the origins of the Teutonic Mark and the Russian *Mir*, could, he felt, be illuminated by a study of the Indian village community, already shown to be closely related to a common 'Aryan' past through the comparative philology begun by William Jones, and popularized, in the Oxford of Maine's day (Maine himself was at Cambridge), by Max Mueller.[63] This academic debate, transported to Russia, became the scholarly basis of 'populism', to use a somewhat inadequate translation, which today means something quite different, in the Narodnik movement. This, ironically, spawned its own debate on the 'East' and the 'West': in this case, the Russian East had to avoid employing non-indigenous categories imported from the developed West.[64] There was thus a certain circularity of arguments: Tolstoy, familiar with the Russian debates, and glorifying his peasants, would have had access to the same intellectual source-material which debated the question of the East and the West with such vigour in different contexts. Upon reading Gandhi's *Hind Swaraj*, which the latter had sent him as a token of respect for his spiritual and intellectual influence, Tolstoy wrote in his diary, 'Read Gandhi about civilisation, wonderful'.[65]

Of the corollary to the second point, that Gandhi returned to his version of 'Indian tradition' through his agonized encounters with England, evidence can most directly be sought in his own story of his 'experiments with truth'. In Pretoria in 1893, he did 'not know much of Hinduism', and knew 'less of other religions', but he intended to rectify this error through study.[66] In London, he was introduced to what was later to be his main source of religious and philosophical inspiration, the *Bhagavad Gita*, by the Theosophists, and the first version he read was Sir Edwin Arnold's translation, *The Song Celestial*, though he was acquainted with the *Ramayana* through his family tradition.[67] He read, in South Africa, Max Mueller's *India—What*

Can it Teach Us? and the Theosophical Society's translations of the *Upanishads;* also Edwin Arnold's *Light of Asia*, Washington Irving's *Life of Mahomed and his Successors* as well as 'Carlyle's panegyric on the prophet', and a book entitled *The Sayings of Zarathustra*,[68] His nationalist sympathies were acquired and philosophically moulded, by his own account, through very specific experiences: in South Africa; his initial contacts were with the Meman community from his native Porbandar; by extension he came to see the unity of Indians, but (perhaps in keeping with the spatial delinking of life in South Africa) his nationalism never extended as far as the Kaffirs.[69] His own attempts at 'playing the English gentleman', which he so successfully ridiculed later, tell a familiar tale of Indian attempts to conform to European civilizational values.[70] Gandhi carried his renunciation of these attempts to their extreme logical conclusion; true civilizational values were not to be found in 'modern civilisation'—therefore both India and Britain should reject it and return to their respective spiritual roots. The reason for highlighting these arguments is to stress the point that for Gandhi, as for many professionals and intellectuals in colonial India, the route to a discovery of India lay through Britain. To read Gandhi as an outsider to 'colonialist discourse' (as many do now) is to miss the point which Gandhi himself tried extremely hard to make: it is through indirections that he found his directions. This, it might justifiably be said, was the keynote of his intellectual and spiritual quest, of whose validity he sought to convince others.

I have argued so far that Gandhi's claims to 'indigenism' have been overdrawn. Gandhi, far from refusing to engage with 'Western' intellectual traditions, had himself had a long, intense and painful period of engagement with 'Western' values. Through this engagement he had negotiated a personal identity, and begun to discover and elaborate a moral, social, and, ultimately, political philosophy for Indians who sought to overcome both physical and mental colonialism. At a more distant level, and through his engagement with the writings of thinkers involved in a romantic rejection of capitalism, based on a rejection of materialistic values and a privileging of rural life, he appears to have absorbed and internalized Orientalist writing on India and, in particular, on the ancient Indian village republic, in some cases at second remove.[71]

It may also be argued that Gandhi himself played on a theatrical imagery of the quintessential Eastern holy man in his political style of functioning: the 'fakir', with powers beyond the comprehension of the European mind,[72] was a useful image to project before his imperialist opponents, his life and person thereby standing as evidence of the real possibilities of opposing colonialism. It was also an image that the Congress deliberately set out to create for Gandhi in the 1920s: Jawaharlal Nehru, then a loyal follower of Gandhi, and other Congress leaders, addressed the peasantry and told them that not all men in saffron were holy men: the real holy man was Gandhi; consequently, it was Gandhi who ought to be obeyed.[73]

But while this was important in his style of political functioning, it was hardly useful in an argument regarding how best to order the economic life of a country, which had to persuade quite a different audience. This is where Kumarappa came in; addressing the strategic problems of persuading an educated middle-class audience of the validity of Gandhi's economic ideas for India. Personal conviction being taken for granted, how could the ground best be laid for the communication of ideas to which the intellectual environment of the time was sceptical, if not downright hostile? This called for an intervention of an altogether different order, so as to claim for Gandhi's ideas a relevance in the political and intellectual environment of the 1930s.

Gandhi's economic *Avatar* and the coming of J.C. Kumarappa

By the 1930s, Gandhi was aware that the battle for 'his' way—that of the village community, decentralized village-based production, and economic self-sufficiency of the locality—would also have to be fought on a measurable and 'scientific' basis: on the basis of arguments which were communicable and persuasive also on grounds recognized by contemporaries as economic–rational. This was especially so as he knew he was seeking to communicate with the professional intellectuals who were the main advocates of allegedly 'Western' perspectives on development. And as mentioned earlier, there was among them a trenchant opposition to Gandhian ideas, expressed sharply and polemically, and using all the fora at their disposal; much of the criticism was directed at the implications of these ideas: their role in—indirectly—legitimizing capitalists; and the retrogressive nature of his ideas from the point of view of science and/or socialism.

However, Gandhi's economic ideas as a critique of industrialization-as-modernity were not particularly accessible to the people concerned with national development except when interpreted as a kind of modernity. Thereafter, there would, at least, be common terms on which to argue.

At the same time, Gandhi could not be seen to be arguing in such a manner as to treat the moral or ethical arguments as secondary; and also to be too explicitly against his, and the nationalist movement's, main financiers, the capitalists, who had gained legitimation through his 'trusteeship' theory. The main bulk of the 'economic' logic against 'Western' economic systems was provided, therefore, by Gandhi's main deputy in this regard, Kumarappa. 'Gandhian economic thought' was largely Kumarappa's creation; this was cemented as a concept even more after Gandhi's death, when Gandhi himself could make no more interventions.

Kumarappa adopted many of Gandhi's own ideas deriving from 'Hinduism' and Gandhi's debates with 'Hindu' tradition, especially regarding the allegedly moral basis of caste categories, though he systematized them more than Gandhi himself did; but as a Christian Kumarappa adapted these arguments to his interpretation of Christianity as well; and they fit.[74] The moral colouring to Gandhian economic thought, it could, therefore, be argued, was compatible with a vision of God and religious belief, irrespective of particular faiths. Yet Kumarappa used the 'Hindu' version far more than he used the Christian, unless he was specifically addressing Christians, in the knowledge that the Hindu appeal was likely to be wider. It is perhaps a pity that there was no one to provide a version of 'Gandhian economics' compatible with Islam.

The uses of economic argument

A brief digression may be in order here, to demonstrate the use of apparently economic arguments to justify a position which might otherwise be interpreted as moral, communitarian, or obscurantist. In the course of defending the village-oriented economic order, the defence of the cow became an important project. That this was a divisive and potentially explosive project was evident. The attempted creation, from about the late nineteenth century, of a specifically 'Hindu' identity around the issue of the cow and its protection, and the assertion among Muslims of their cultural right to kill cows, is now well known.[75] The issue of the cow was one of the crucial issues regarded as 'communal' and potentially explosive, and was not useful in securing adherents to the nationalist cause among Muslims and other minorities. On the other hand, a great many nationalist leaders who did not see themselves as 'communal' were keen to defuse the issue by finding a way to argue against cow-killing, some feeling strongly themselves that this should be prevented; Gandhi himself was one of them.[76] A version of this argument was also inserted into ideas of a humane, village-based economic and social order, with an economic twist to them.

If the argument against cow-slaughter was framed in economic, terms (which, the public was often being reminded, was a neutral, technical, and therefore non-communal way, of looking at things), the emotionally-charged problem could be dealt with at a more rational level. In 1927, for instance, a book published from Madras examined the economic validity of the argument for cow-protection. The author wrote, he said, as an economist, through which discipline the truth of the matter could be arrived at; the disturbing business of cow-protection riots could be avoided through an economic understanding of the issues involved. The arguments he used were conventional: the importance of the cow in the agrarian economy of India. The optimism of the position is notable in its belief that the problem could be solved through rational arbitration within the rules of the discipline of economics, whose jurisdiction he did not question. The title page stressed that the author was a Fellow of the Royal Economic Society, London.[77]

Most of the arguments in this genre backed an anti-cow-slaughter position. This also became one of Gandhi's approaches to the argument. Situating himself in an argument made about 'national wealth', Gandhi introduced and personally endorsed a number of books published about the cow, several of them from publishers controlled by Gandhian organizations. 'Those who are interested in the preservation of the priceless wealth of India in the shape of the cow through constructive means will find much food for thought in the following well-written pages', he wrote in 1930 in his foreword to one such book.[78] The book itself, though claiming a 'scientific' approach, and providing tables and large quantities of facts and figures, usually from government sources such as the Indian Industrial Commission, the Royal Commission on Agriculture in India, and the Punjab Board of Economic Enquiry, occasionally lapses into a straightforward appeal to sentiment or morality. In one example, this is from a 'humanitarian' point of view (a passage which quotes from the *Brahma Purana* on the virtues of nursing sick cattle in their old age rather than selling them to others who will slaughter them, an argument dangerously close to arguing against selling old cattle to Muslims); in another, the Mughal Emperor Akbar's tolerance in forbidding cow-slaughter is held up to testify to his wisdom. The examples work in a different tone as well; in another passage a livestock officer's testimony before the Royal Commission on Agriculture in India, and Bhishma's views as retold in the *Mahabharata* are both cited as expert opinions—Bhishma having 'realised intuitively what modern science discovers by experiment'.[79]

Another such detailed study, written about twelve years later, ran to two large volumes, and was less eclectic in its selection of sources.[80] In the foreword, Gandhi commended the author, Satish Chandra Dasgupta, as 'one of the first and best pupils of the late lamented Dr P.C. Ray', and the book 'to the lover of the cow as also to every one who would learn that the slaughter of cattle for food is a pure economic waste'; he called the cow the 'Mother of Prosperity'.[81] The work was clearly positioned primarily as a 'scientific' book both by Gandhi and by Dasgupta; Acharya P.C. Ray was widely recognized as a figure who had stood for both science and swadeshi, and was a heroic public figure to whom both a lay public and a scientific community could relate.[82] Dasgupta engaged in a long debate against some of the findings of the Royal Commission on Agriculture in India, which had misled 'the scientific men and the economists'; consequently, he had 'had to quote expert opinion' for the 'findings' he had arrived at.[83] A long section on pharmacology in the second volume, essentially a veterinary tract, betrayed the author's background in chemistry; the drugs he prescribes include 'indigenous' herbs, but far from giving them primacy, he treated them as supplementary—hardly in keeping with Gandhi's *Hind Swaraj* position that 'to study European medicine is to deepen our slavery'.[84] Yet such argument was not to be considered merely scientific: 'The book is no mere collection of formulae for feeding a cow, or directions for obtaining the utmost milk from a cow. Cow-keeping is a *yajna*, and I have tried to show why and how it is so'.[85] The cow, if 'lifted from its downtrodden condition' by the 'constructive workers in the village', would prove a 'most responsive animal'; and, more importantly, the uplift of the cow would 'amount to lifting the nation'.[86]

The tone as well as some of the content of Dasgupta's work matches that of a good deal of the writing of Kumarappa who, by this time, was the established public face of the Gandhian constructive movement.[87] The message is clear: the movement for a village-based social and economic order was morally the correct choice for India; but if the question of the correct social and economic order were addressed scientifically, it would be found that the village-based social and economic order would also be the economically correct choice for India. This was constantly reiterated by Kumarappa in his speeches and articles. But beyond this congruence of the moral and the practical, there was the need for a deeper philosophical argument, on which to base the moral order.

Addressing the intelligentsia

If Gandhism had a weakness, it was that its appeal to the urban professional middle classes and intelligentsia was limited. Gandhi's own appeals to the inherent instincts of the peasants (which he, nonetheless, sought to define, control, and direct to his own satisfaction) deprived many intellectuals of their perceived role in directing the nationalist movement. When dealing with matters of 'development', such ideas were at their weakest: it was important to convince the main protagonists in the debate—intellectuals—that Gandhian ideas deserved a hearing. But the moral rhetoric used by Gandhi was not particularly useful in this regard; though, of course, the ideas of the 'modernisers' also drew on moral principles, the rhetoric was predominantly that of economics, science, and rationality, moral principles being regarded as secondary, merely reinforcing arguments whose validity had already been established. Consequently, in order to effectively join this debate, Gandhism required translators who could dress Gandhian ideas in appropriate forms. Gandhi himself was not particularly well suited to the task; by his own admission, he knew very little about economics, and it was widely felt that he was rather too dependent on the views of industrialists in this regard.[88] It may be suspected that he knew more than he was willing to let on; nonetheless, he preferred to allow his disciples to interpret his economic ideas on his behalf; he was prepared to endorse these views as compatible with his own.

Kumarappa was the most original and interesting of Gandhi's authorized interpreters. Born in 1892, the ninth of ten children, the grandson of a priest, he was himself a devout Christian and an accomplished lay preacher. He wanted to be an engineer, but ended up as an accountant, completing his training in chartered accountancy in London; in 1927, he was invited by his elder brother J.M. Kumarappa (then known as John J.Cornelius) to come to New York. Having arrived in the USA, he obtained a BSc from Syracuse University in business administration, and then an MA in public finance from Columbia University in 1927–8, under the supervision of E.R.A. Seligman[89] (among whose students was B.R. Ambedkar),[90] where he did 'excellent work in the general field of Economics' and wrote 'an unusually able essay on "The Public Finance and Poverty of India"'.[91] The lineage of Kumarappa's choice of subject was rather respectable: finance was a subject which provided, within the framework of the academic discipline of economics, an ideal starting point for a critique (or defence) of the British government in India. An extremely respectable line of Indian academics and political activists wrote on public finance in India.[92]

Kumarappa was a late convert to nationalism, apparently arriving at his views on British exploitation of India in the course of his study of Indian public finance. Thereafter he turned his back on his 'upbringing on English model', as one of his biographers puts it (the similarity of this tale of renunciation with Gandhi's narrative of his own renunciation of English values is notable),[93] met Gandhi (on 9 May 1929), began to wear khadi, and along with his brothers adopted the Hindu family name 'Kumarappa', changing his name from Joseph Chelladurai Cornelius to Joseph Cornelius Kumarappa on 10 May 1929. He remained a bachelor all his life. From 1935 till his death in 1955 he was at the head of Gandhi's AIVIA; in 1938–9 he was involved in conducting an industrial survey of the North West Frontier Province and the Central Province and Berar. As member of the Nehru Committee in 1947–8 he helped formulate the 'Economic Policy of the Congress in Free India'; and was chairman of the Agrarian Reforms Committee of the AICC from 1948–50.[94] He was also a member of the Congress' National Planning Committee which came into being in 1938, but resigned after seven months, as he felt nothing particular could be gained by remaining a member of a body committed to large-scale industrialization.[95]

The Gandhi–Kumarappa partnership began in 1929, when Kumarappa returned from the USA and was searching, as suggested by Professor

Seligman, for a publisher for his manuscript on public finance. He was told that this was a subject in which Gandhi might be interested; Gandhi should be given a first look at it before it was submitted to another publisher. Accordingly, he wrote to Gandhi of his manuscript, which he said 'attempts to trace how the Government Policy of Taxation has impoverished and lessened the productivity of the masses during the last hundred years'.[96] Gandhi was, indeed, interested and said that he proposed to publish it as a series in *Young India*.[97] He also asked Kumarappa whether he would be willing to undertake a rural survey for him in Gujarat for the Gujarat Vidyapith, as Gandhi found Kumarappa's approach to economics to be 'almost exactly the same as his'.[98]

It took slightly longer for Kumarappa to become a full-fledged disciple; he had, for instance, a few misgivings about Gandhi's penchant for vows. In 1930, he wrote, in a passage notable for its views of moral evolution:

> I believe, spiritually and morally all men are not alike. A few are advanced, but most are mainly followers of leaders. We in different stages need different methods of guidance and leadership. I believe this is acknowledged by most religions and especially by Hinduism which approve [sic] of idolatry for those who are at the *lower end of the scale*. If I mistake not, you yourself are not averse to the use of idols by those who are unable to conceive God without material representation. Just as idols are means by which we seek to attain an end and help out those in the *lower stages of development* so are vows means by which leaders strive to hold up the highest resolve [in] the actions of their followers.[99]

The Church, he added, used vows as 'concessions to the weakness of man', which 'find no place in Christ's teachings'. A man should instead rely on 'the higher law of inner voice or his ideals', otherwise he was in danger of being degraded 'to the position of an automaton'. He stressed that he was not criticizing Gandhi's own vows, but 'the effect it will have on the ignorant masses'.[100] Gandhi's reply clarified, 'The vow I am thinking of is a promise made by one to oneself'. Jesus Christ, he added, 'was pre-eminently a man of unshakeable resolution, that is, vows. His yea was yea for ever'.[101] This was apparently convincing; in later years Kumarappa was to get extremely close to equating Gandhi with Jesus—the apotheosis of the Protestant idea of a personal God.[102]

Kumarappa provided for the Gandhian position all the necessary heavy artillery of a political economy education. He was an able pamphleteer not merely on the Gandhian position; he was the main author of the Congress' report on debt repudiation which was to be the basis of the Congress' position at the Round Table Conference in 1931.[103] During the War he voiced nationalist concerns over inflation, the sterling balances and the Bretton Woods Conference in extremely effective polemical pamphlets which managed to simplify complex problems to communicate with a general public.[104] But his main vocation remained the promotion of the ideal of the village movement.

Kumarappa's Village Movement

Kumarappa, beginning his manifesto *Why the Village Movement?* with a narrative of the evolution of the species and of man, sought to establish the basis for two 'types' which were crucial to his arguments: the 'pack type', who 'unite for aggression' (and are usually 'carnivores'); and the 'herd type' who gather together for safety (and are generally 'vegetarian').[105] Good and bad, desirable and undesirable, in this classificatory scheme, correspond to the 'herd' and 'pack' types, respectively.[106]

Evolution, economics, and civilizations

Civilized man's economic organizations still bear marks of earlier forms—the 'herd type' and the 'pack type'. The latter is characterized by a short-term outlook; central control and the concentration of power 'in the hands of individuals or small groups in a personal way' (as opposed to the impersonal); rigorous discipline; 'disregard of the welfare of the actual workers or contributors to the success of the organisation'; the '[s]uppression of individuality of the worker and a spirit of intolerance either in competition or in rivalry'; concentration of benefits among a limited few 'without reference to the altruistic value of service rendered'. Its motive force is 'the prospect of obtaining gains' and its activities 'generally radiate from a limited geographical area such as cities'.[107]

Having proceeded to set up the 'pack type' as a particularly unpleasant and undesirable one, Kumarappa needed only to characterize the forms of economic organization he was opposed to as 'pack type' organizations. Kumarappa was perfectly aware that he had to come up with an argument that undermined the sanctity of the generally held standards set by 'economics' and 'science' (the two terms considered to be intimately linked). Some of the images called upon to describe 'pack type' organizations were reminiscent of existing socialist and communist ideas: capitalism having reduced social relations to a cash nexus, the idea of alienated labour, and the ideal of individual freedom within a consensual community. At the same time, as further reading makes clear, Kumarappa intended these remarks to be a prelude to his attack on the Soviet system, which he also classified as 'pack-type', and bracketed in the same category as capitalism—for Kumarappa, as for many contemporaries whose ideas he opposed, an attack on the Soviet system constituted an attack on socialism.

The advantages of 'herd type' social organizations were: a long-term outlook; social control, decentralization and distribution of power being 'impersonal'; 'directed by a consideration of certain set ideals and social movements'. The object of all this was 'to satisfy needs judged from an altruistic point of view' (the community being, presumably, the custodian of the 'altruistic point of view').[108] The 'herd type' meets Kumarappa's 'test of civilization':

> We must bear in mind that the true test of civilisation is not our material possessions or our manner or mode of life but the thought we bestow on the well-being of others. In predation, which is really barbarism, we cannot expect to find any civilisation, for true culture shifts the emphasis from 'rights' to 'duties'.[109]

On this basis, Kumarappa proceeds to approach the description of 'Western' and 'Eastern' economic organizations. 'Western' economic organizations, predictably, are of the 'pack type'. There follows a bit of European history, in which Western economic organizations are classified, 'according to the personnel of the central controlling group', into five groups: 'the dynasty of might, the dynasty of finance, the dynasty of the machine, the dynasty of labour, the dynasty of the middle classes'. The 'masses, whether of the West or of the East, are of much the same kind' and are, therefore, not a basis for classification.[110]

Kumarappa's classificatory system is based on the assumption that the economically dominant group controls military and political power—a familiar and unobjectionable assumption to his audiences. Yet given that his arguments hinge on a distinction between the West and the East, it is rather elitist that he does not attribute to the 'masses' any capacity for cultural or other differences based on their 'Easternness'.

The first three dynasties—of might, finance, and the machine—taken together, are considered 'capitalist' by Kumarappa; and a combination of the first two—of might and finance—give rise, according to him, to 'Imperialism'. The middle classes' struggle to seize power, represented by Nazism and Fascism, is also described as being 'based on much the same lines as capitalism'.[111] The classification of communism or the dynasty of labour as 'pack type' seems not to be quite so self-evident, so Kumarappa explains:

> Most of the characteristics of the other organisations are represented, *viz.* centralisation of control and power, rigid discipline and suppression of the individual in regard to production and distribution. Whatever good may have been obtained or envisaged by the directing body giving primary consideration to the needs of the community and not so much to the amount of profit obtained, yet the organisation too is a sectarian or class organisation run by the proletariat with special privileges attached to the sect in power.[112]

There are certain features common to all these 'pack type' organizations which Kumarappa tars with the same brush. All of them are 'city-centred' and will lead to the 'degeneration of the producing masses because no initiative is left to them, their functions being merely one of carrying out higher orders'. Kumarappa sees symptoms of this degeneration in the high incidence of 'nervous diseases' in the USA and the consequent 'clamour for "leisure" . . . under their system, leisure is a necessity as their organisation is unnatural'. Consequently, the worker is led to 'resort to drink and other vices'.[113] Leisure, according to Kumarappa, is unnecessary if the worker has a rewarding life; all that is needed is a 'rest period' between spells of work.[114]

Under capitalism, 'every individual gets an opportunity to exercise his talent and energy as he likes', though this may be 'at the cost of injuring society'. Communism takes things to the other extreme: the profit motive is done away with, individualism is suppressed, and 'a small idealistic group plans the work for the nation'. Under both systems 'human values are not fully taken into account . . . We have no right to look upon the common run of human beings, as either gun-fodder as under capitalism, or a cogwheel in a machine as under communism'. Both capitalism and communism, Kumarappa claimed, failed to bring out the best in individuals, and both had led to 'group violence'; while under imperialism this violence was 'directed towards foreigners and strangers', communism directed it internally 'in order to suppress the bourgeois class'.[115] He conceded that '. . . a certain amount of violence will always be involved in any state control, but what matters is the degree and the spirit behind what appears to be violence. Even a loving father chastises his child . . . If the Government is truly democratic the Government will represent the people. In such a Government any regulatory functions that require violence, will be self-inflicted and so it is nothing more than self- discipline'.[116]

It is in the Eastern civilizations, such as India and China, and Japan before she chose to imitate the West, that one finds 'agricultural civilisation influencing economic organisation'.

> Such civilisations are the results of philosophical and conscious social planning. The Western systems are haphazard growths without any thought behind them. In this sense the West can hardly be said to have a civilisation at all. It is more a refined barbarism.

The only exception to this in the Western world is Soviet Russia, 'the first attempt at a well-planned society in the West with a sociological philosophy, good or bad, behind it'. But this system shares with other Western, 'pack-type' forms of social organization, the common characteristic of 'aggression for economic purposes'.[117] In the political sphere, too, this is reflected in the West's lack of 'true democracy': what exists is a system which 'masquerades under the cloak of parliamentary organisation in which real power is vested in a group or in a single dominating personality'; and in religion, even a tolerant religion such *as* Christianity came to vest power and authority in a single person or institution.

By contrast, in India 'village republics managed their own affairs' which continued undisturbed 'even when foreign invaders came'; and in religious life a 'tendency to decentralise the form of worship and views in regard to the Godhead' resulted in 'extreme tolerance'.[118] Oriental systems achieve regulation and decentralization of power by 'hitching the economic machinery either to civil laws or religion or superstition'. Kumarappa conducts a defence of the joint family system, the 'division of labour by caste', and the 'method of distribution to artisans of a share in the products of agriculture'.[119]

Kumarappa conceded that 'exploitation was not altogether absent' in these 'old systems'; but 'the purpose of the organisation' was to minimize such exploitation by erecting 'social barriers' to it. And although they were admitted to be incapable of 'bearing the strain put on them by the tremendous expansion in the field of economic activity', and were now 'decadent', Kumarappa stressed the necessity of modelling 'present-day production' on similar principles: 'a system of economic production best suited to modern conditions and capable of working satisfactorily in India, if industrialisation is not to bring with it all the evils attendant on its development in the West'.[120]

Kumarappa had an ingenious interpretation of the *varnashrama* (the caste system): people in society could be divided into four groups: the idealistic, taking a 'long-range view of life'; the altruistic, whose somewhat narrower view 'is still beyond the span of their own life'; the materialistic; and, finally, 'those who follow in a rut without much imagination'. These corresponded, respectively, to the *brahmin*, *kshatriya*, *vaisya*, and *sudra*, respectively. These categories were, therefore, not dependent on birth; nor, indeed on occupation, but on motives:

> For example an electrician who lives to explore the possibilities of the science without any regard to personal gain is a Brahmin. One who learns the science with the object of helping to industrialise his country and thereby raise the economic standards of his people is a Kshatriya. He who takes contracts or deals in electric supply or goods in consideration of material gain is a Vaisya. But the man who wants to enter the Government electrical department because of the permanency of tenure, economic security and a pension is a Sudra.[121]

In much the same manner, a brahmin or kshatriya by birth could degrade himself by acting contrary to the principles of his caste. The caste system, therefore, '[p]runed of all extraneous growth', is 'graded on a cultural standard of values almost unknown to money economy. Material considerations sink into insignificance when human needs claim our attention. Duty and not our rights determines our position in society'.[122]

Similarly, 'forms of human activity' can be classified, according to dominant motive forces, into four schools: The first, the economy of predation, is the 'lowest type', with life being 'on an animal plane'. The next, the economy of enterprise, ('laissez-faire' and the 'capitalist mentality'), stresses the exercise of the rights of the individual in a 'self-centred' manner. The 'economy of gregarianism' acknowledges certain ties between man and man, but includes imperialism, fascism, nazism, communism and socialism, in that '[t]he higher cultural values are forgotten and man is to live by bread alone'. All these are based on short-term interests: those of the individual's lifespan or that of a group or nation, therefore, are 'economies of transience' and are correspondingly characterized as sudra (predation), vaisya (the 'economy of enterprise and imperialism'); and kshatriya (nazism and communism), where 'individual interests are sacrificed on the altar of altruism'.[123]

The fourth school, the 'economy of permanence', is, however, '*Brahmanical* in its idealism and conception. It is an attempt to get into alignment with the order that prevails in the universe and work in unison and in tune with the Infinite. It is the highest evolution man is capable of'. Principles of economics are framed therein 'in the perspective of eternity': a sparing use of natural resources, the consumption of labour and materials readily creatable by man rather than the drawing on exhaustible resources; and, consequently, an emphasis on distribution.[124]

This view of varnashrama as determined by good intentions and spiritual qualities was not always consistently maintained by Kumarappa; elsewhere, he argued that the caste system constituted 'Indian planning'—it was 'functional planning as opposed to production planning. Under this each person has a definite function to perform taking into consideration his inborn qualities, his environment and his training'. The caste system had now, he admitted, 'gone to seed' in becoming hereditary.[125]

Science, economics, and the eastern modern

The ideas outlined above were the basis for all the distinctions, definitions, and characterizations which the author sought to make in the rest of the book. It is significant that Kumarappa found it necessary to set up this elaborate structure on which to build his arguments. That he was not merely tilting at windmills is evident when his seemingly abstract polemic is viewed against the backdrop of the arguments he sought to oppose.

Apart from positioning his arguments as a better alternative to communism or socialism and, consequently, as an 'Indian', 'non-violent' socialism, Kumarappa was also involved in addressing the arguments of science. Kumarappa's principles were far from self-evident given the prevailing intellectual and economic environment. The desirability of industrialization did not need to be established on theoretical grounds, the possession of power and affluence being so clearly with the industrialized nations. Kumarappa could not, however, be seen to draw merely on extra-economic or moral arguments, given the 'technical' or 'scientific' terms of the debates he sought to enter. He had the dual task of establishing that what he believed was morally correct was also economically rational, in order to establish the validity of his claim that an economics informed by the ethical and moral concerns he articulated was also viable. Conceptions of science were, therefore, brought in to reinforce ideas of the wisdom of the East and the need to 'regain the principles that guided our forefathers'.[126]

Thus, principles of economics framed 'in the perspective of eternity' alone can 'lead to the peace and prosperity of the human race and to a life of peace and goodwill based on culture and refinement'. It is because of this that the 'science' of economics must be studied 'from objective standards' and its application approached 'in relation to laws that govern the universe' rather than to 'man's needs of the moment'. This will '. . . give expression to a mode of life very different from what is considered "modern" in the West . . . The "Modern" world is of Iron and Steel. We cannot afford to draw on our inheritance too freely and extravagantly . . . Strange as it may seem the mud huts of India belong to the Economy of Permanence while the steel and concrete sky scrapers of New York are symbols of the Economy of Transience'.[127]

Kumarappa thus sought to establish the practicability of the village-based economy on the basis of the scientific wisdom of the principles of economics on which it rested. This was not a rejection of 'modernity'; Kumarappa challenged the basis of generally accepted yardsticks of 'modernity', claiming to establish a case for a better yardstick in the consideration of a longer time frame: 'the perspective of eternity'. Far from rejecting conceptions of 'modernity' and, consequently, of 'science' or 'economics', Kumarappa therefore sought to persuade his readers that his standards of 'modernity', 'science', and 'economics' were better than those which had currency.

Practical arguments

This is evident in his other writings. In many of his articles he argued strongly that science and technology should be placed at the disposal of village industries, and denied the charge that the AIVIA was 'against human progress'. The idea that the village should be self-sufficient should not, he argued, be taken to imply that the artisans should be left to themselves: a *chamar*'s expertise in leather-working should not be restricted by the older technologies of tanning to which he was accustomed; rather, the assistance of scientific research should be available to him. Science should, however, be put to such correct uses, to transform the 'crude village economy'. 'We want to yoke science to human progress,' Kumarappa wrote. 'Today, science is being prostituted', its use 'denied to the masses'; it needed to be harnessed to village problems.[128] Stating his economic programme in a speech at Sir M. Visvesvaraya's Mysore Swadeshi Exhibition in 1936, he asserted:

> (1) supply preceding demand is unnatural and leads to imperialism. (2) Production of goods without reference to the market leads to competitive increase of supply. (3) capitalistic production causes deterioration in the personality and the character of the masses engaged in machine feeding. (4) It is not possible to give gainful occupation to crores of people by industrialisation with large scale industry.
>
> The obvious conclusions are: we have to follow demand and produce goods by decentralised methods and not standardise consumption unless we wish to standardise people.[129]

In such practical argument, however, the ethical underpinnings had to be accepted for the argument to retain its persuasive power. This is more explicit in another example: Kumarappa stressed the need for alerting consumers to their social responsibility: the urban buyer had it in his hands to alleviate the condition of the poor villager. Buyers influenced employment patterns and methods of production; therefore, they should not buy foreign or machine-made articles.[130] In *Why the Village Movement?* the buyer's duty is assigned to women:

> The present system of production does not take into consideration the role that is assigned to women by nature. It will be generally admitted that by their very make up they are the custodians of a nation's culture and project into the future the achievements

> of the present generation. In primitive times consumption was controlled by women, while supplies were in the hands of men . . . In the language of economics the woman was the creator of demand and the man's place was that of the supplier.[131]

In India, which was a 'herd type' 'Eastern' culture, women still looked after the home and made decisions which created demand. It followed that women could make or mar a nation's economic life; if uneducated, they would make ill-informed buying decisions, and if educated to 'consumers' duties', they would not fall 'an easy prey to psychological suggestions made by advertisers'.[132] Education, therefore, was Kumarappa's suggested insurance against the proverbial frailty of women.[133]

Kumarappa was at times prone to draw conclusions incommensurate with his observations, or to make implausible claims. In 1946, with India threatened with further food shortages, he made the point that '[t]he basic cause of food shortage is the departure from the village-economy of self-sufficiency'—he did not consider whether in such a situation of self-sufficiency the cities might starve instead.[134] In 1935, he observed that the true Swadeshi spirit which had been engendered by the partition of Bengal in 1905 had now been 'diverted into a support of large-scale industries in India to the exclusion of village crafts which were slowly dying out'.[135] A few years later, he argued that the idea of swadeshi in Bengal had been 'purely political, that is, Indian made articles as against foreign made goods'. It was Gandhi who had, according to Kumarappa, discerned 'that the downfall of India was due more to economic causes than political ones and he bravely shouldered single-handedly the burden, ridicule and ignominy of the charkha movement'.[136] This was an important step towards the reinvention of Gandhi as an economist, at least of a kind.

Conclusions: statement, communicability, (mis?)readings

There are many discrepancies, inconsistencies, and incoherent passages in Kumarappa's arguments, which are not even internally consistent. One of the main opponents in *Why the Village Movement?* is an imagined communism which Kumarappa seems to have read a little about—in Columbia as part of his MA course, as well as afterwards—but had little direct experience of.[137] The ideal state, in his view, would inflict 'discipline' on itself. This self-disciplinary 'violence' is acceptable, he writes, because if a government is 'truly democratic', it 'will represent the people'; this violence is as a 'loving father chastises his child'. Kumarappa stops short of saying that the state will be the people: at best, it can be a sort of extended patriarchal family. He also frankly admits that existing ('Western') states are characterized by the nature of their leadership, and do not in any sense arise organically from society: the 'masses' are the same, Eastern or Western. But his envisaged alternative can think no further than a loving, decentralized patriarchy. This might even be read as a pre-conscious fascist argument, though Kumarappa would probably have been horrified by such a reading.

The defence of caste in terms of its 'directing the various units of economic activity'—as a mechanism for redistributing wealth, preventing falling prices, as a guarantor of subsistence and an obstacle to exploitation—is vulgar economism of a kind most 'Western', by his standards. Again, Kumarappa's (and Gandhi's) argument about the spiritual basis of caste was not particularly appealing at the time. A brahmin might degrade himself, but no one had any difficulty distinguishing the spiritually poor brahmin from the spiritually rich Sudra, the consequences for acting contrary to one's caste being quite different in the two cases. (It must be pointed out that Kumarappa's interpretation of Gandhi's views on caste, in seeking to be consistent, was more dangerously appropriable than Gandhi's less consistent pronouncements. In some cases, Gandhi took caste to be a spiritual state, by doing which he disarmed high-caste claims to being automatically superior; in other cases he denounced caste as having no basis in true religion or in true Hinduism.[138]) Kumarappa's claim to study economics 'in relation to laws that govern the universe' is strongly reminiscent of Stalinist dialectics—history and society follow universal laws that cannot be influenced by human beings or their conscious behaviour. Kumarappa, therefore, gets entangled in the positions he seeks to oppose.

But the defects in his arguments are not the point of this analysis. How if at all was his persuasive strategy meant to work? What ideas did they link up with? The main link in Kumarappa's assimilation of the Gandhian moral discourse with the developmentalist modern one, was the distinction between East and West. This distinction had been used in various ways in constructing a rationale of 'difference' in both colonial and nationalist arguments. In nationalist versions, the West is generally spiritually inferior though materially superior (an argument with which not all colonialists were uncomfortable); in the Gandhian version material superiority is devalued by an assault conducted on the basis of that spiritual inferiority, enabling the East to claim an overall superiority. Gandhi, at least by the 1930s, claimed that his was not a critique of 'Western' culture or religion, 'only a critique of the "modern philosophy of life"; it is called "Western" only because it originated in the West'.[139] Kumarappa maintained this distinction; yet he went a step further, using Gandhi's ideas in seeking to detach modernity from the West and claim it for the East: the former's 'modernity' was only apparently so, as he sought to demonstrate in his descriptions of the 'transience' of Western economic organizations or of the 'barbarism' of Western civilization.

Kumarappa's strategies of argument were substantially different from that of Gandhi's. He made a very definite appeal to history and the process of evolution of human societies—although there was not much historical evidence in it that would be accepted according to the contemporary standards of the discipline. Although in a number of his other writings, he also claimed a more spiritual and religious sanction for this 'Gandhian' order in the Christian scriptures, this was largely before Christian audiences, who Kumarappa had made it his personal task to wean away from collaboration with British rule in India.[140] For general audiences, while discussing the desirability of contending visions of the future development of India, he stuck to less directly religious arguments.

In doing so he was less mystical than Gandhi. Those attracted by Gandhi's moral ideas were often frustrated by the 'exceedingly elusive' nature of his economics,[141] and were constrained to sift through his numerous writings and statements to put together a coherent version. Kumarappa's success lay in his preserving a strong moral content—which, though as much Kumarappa's own as Gandhi's, was compatible with the latter's—while presenting economic matters in such a way as to bring Gandhian ideas into the field of everyday rational discourse, as well as to attempt to fit this moral and economic world view into 'modern' clothes. Kumarappa's writings presented Gandhian ideas in terms of economics, science, socialism, and modernity—terms which, by the 1930s, were crucial to nationalist formulations of 'development'.[142]

Kumarappa's (and Gandhi's) project was in this regard not fundamentally different from that of the 'modernisers': both were engaged in contesting the link between the West and the 'modern'. The latter, as I have said before, stressed the universal character of the 'modern'—and/or, in the version provided by *Science and Culture*, the connection, albeit indirect, of that modernity to the East, where originated 'all those arts and crafts which are responsible for the greatness of the present European civilisation'.[143] Kumarappa, similarly, claimed that a 'science of economics' based on 'Eastern' principles was better deserving of the term 'modern'. Kumarappa's was still the more ambitious project, conducted as a defence of principles, institutions, and customs especially considered opposed to the modern, rather than following the simpler path.

Kumarappa's version of Gandhism fitted more easily into the political discourse of the time. Given the fundamental importance to nationalists of the project of 'modernising' India through economic development, while at the same time appearing to be carving out a path different from that prescribed by colonialism,[144] there was a need to break the link between 'Westernisation' and 'modernity'.[145] It was not desirable to claim that the principles on which Indian development was to be based, despite their 'Western' origins, were perfectly relevant to India—nationalists could not afford to be seen as plagiarist.[146] This would have been seen as a surrender to the British imperialist view of Indian nationalism: nationalists belonged to a tiny elite of Westernized, English-educated urban professionals and intellectuals cut off from the 'real' India, creatures of Macaulay's Minute. This, it might be said, was one of the vital points regarding Indian nationalist thought: 'derivative' or not, whether it succeeded in being different or not, it sought to be different.[147] But it had to seek to be so without seeming to fit British descriptions of 'backwardness'. The search by Indian nationalism for resources of resistance to British rule had long included claims to a better, more civilized, glorious past before British rule. These claims often leaned heavily on early British and European scholarship on the Indian past;[148] yet they did not consciously or directly do so. Kumarappa's appeals to 'regain the principles that guided our forefathers', to 'the perspective of eternity' and to rather selective 'Eastern principles' are not incompatible with his claims to defending a 'modern' position. Kumarappa was, therefore, drawing on a long-standing conventional framework of argument in which nationalist thought sought to be different by claiming a longer tradition, counterpoising Indian antiquity to that of Europe's classical antiquity; recovering the original nature of a now decadent varnashrama; or claiming that Eastern civilizations were 'the result of philosophical and conscious social planning' as opposed to Western systems' 'haphazard growths', were all ways to claim that India was modern before anyone else. This was not an unique claim, but one he shared with predecessors (in, for instance, the Arya Samajists' 'back to the Vedas' ideology, or Rammohun Roy's quest for a more rational religious faith in the ancient scriptures) as well as contemporaries and near-contemporaries.[149] Kumarappa's version of 'Indianness' or 'Eastern wisdom', as opposed to 'Westernisation' thus had something in common with other arguments which similarly looked for solutions to economic or social problems which could either be regarded as 'Indian', or at any rate not un-Indian.

This indicates not a separate trajectory, but a similarity in strategies of argument and possibly also similar anxieties shared by Indians under colonial rule. For some, the modern was more appealing for its being universal, fears regarding 'culture' or 'Indianness' being secondary; for others, modernity was more comforting if it could be Indian. This provides a reminder of the dual purpose which nationalist developmental ideas had to serve: to be modern, not backward (in answer to colonial claims) as well as to be Indian, not Western (in answer, once again, to colonial claims of the progressive aspects of colonial thought, as well as in response to Indian accusations or fears of loss of 'culture'). It is within this shared framework of anxieties and aspirations that the particular manoeuvres of Gandhian ideas were situated.

The question regarding Kumarappa's success or failure in communicating and propagating his ideas, therefore, rests on the persuasive capacity of his ideas within this framework, as possible resolutions to the given problems; in other words, Kumarappa's version of Gandhism fits more easily into the political discourse of the time, but did it actually succeed in making a significant impact on it? It must be said that these manoeuvres were not in the first instance very successful. More philosophically and psychologically satisfying resolutions were available elsewhere, which were also backed by the endorsement of present successes and by the prospect of similar success in India. Although Kumarappa was well within the parameters of conventional nationalist thinking in arguing a case for 'Indian' solutions, he was, as a consequence of his Gandhian training, often arguing a by then not entirely attractive case, which had been resolved and was, therefore, considered relatively uninteresting. By the 1930s, when Kumarappa was writing, questions of whether technology, machinery or 'socialism' could be regarded as 'Indian' or not, had been resolved in other quarters in ways that largely assuaged the anxieties (though some residual anxieties remained) and expressed the aspirations of a leading section of the nationalist intelligentsia: science and technology, though perhaps at present a 'Western' import, were universal achievements, worthy of emulation.[150]

Attacks on the Gandhian position, moreover, continued to base themselves mainly on Gandhi's, rather than Kumarappa's pronouncements—one of the drawbacks of the Gandhians' great dependence on Gandhi's unquestioned moral stature as a leader and, consequently, the great importance attached to his own statements by both opponents and allies. One critic, dismissing Kumarappa's intervention, called the philosophy of the AIVIA a 'cloak of tattered patches', which added to elements of Ruskin, William Morris, Proudhon, Bakunin, and Tolstoy 'an added dose of economic potion poured into it by Mr Kumarappa at the behest of the Bombay Congress—and produced practically to order as a swadeshi alternative to the imported ideas of socialism'.[151]

The tone of this criticism implied that Kumarappa's economics was an ill-conceived front: it was not proper economics at all. Critics continued to stress the fact that Gandhi had no answer to questions of economic exploitation, and the theory of 'trusteeship' came in for much ridicule. Although Kumarappa underplayed the trusteeship idea in his version of the argument, he also avoided questions of ownership of property; and as Gandhi continued through the 1930s and 1940s to make public statements, Kumarappa's special version of Gandhism was often undermined. For instance, Kumarappa claimed that khadi was more expensive because 'there is a greater degree of distribution of wealth included in the price while the apparent cheapness of imported mill made articles is due to a small share in the booty of the manufacturer and his government'. He, therefore, claimed that the urban consumer had a duty to buy khadi, and that Gandhi 'has often repeated that Khadi sales is his barometer'.[152] But Kumarappa's efforts to establish that khadi was economically viable if people took their duties as consumers seriously were undermined by Gandhi's statement, in 1945, that khadi should not be sold, but should only be given in exchange for yarn. This would ensure that the wearing of khadi would maintain its moral meaning, and that spinning would be a universal training in truth and non-violence; for only those who actually spun yarn would then have yarn to exchange for khadi. 'If hand-spun yarn cannot represent non-violence why should I not retrieve the error while I am still alive and save the wood used in the Charkhas?'[153] This was a difficult situation for the AIVIA and, for Kumarappa. Although Kumarappa himself had written widely on the dangers of a money economy which forced peasants to exchange goods that they needed themselves for money which they needed for other purposes,[154] he had barely begun to find wider markets for khadi among people who would not spin themselves. Gandhi's statement effectively undermined his claim that a Gandhian economic order was economically viable. With no clear signal emerging, it was difficult to provide an unambiguous message.

There was also a problem of how to read the message which Kumarappa did provide. Hostile readings of Gandhi's ideas as anarchist were, of course, quite common; a more positive reading was provided in 1949 by R.B. Lotvala, a retired anarchist, of the Libertarian Socialist Institute, Bombay, on the basis of conversations with Kumarappa's brother. Lotvala summarized the Gandhian position as follows:

1 India being an agricultural country, priority should be given to rural development.
2 Decentralisation.
3 Man should be non-economic.
4 State being a class organisation to be replaced by voluntary cooperative associations.

Lotvala said that both men had agreed that these were 'predominantly Anarchistic ideas'; and added, 'Fundamentally, Anarchist position is humanistic and so man has been made herein the centre of all rational and moral values. Gandhism is very near to it.' He regretted that the Congress government had drifted from Gandhism and was 'merged [sic] in power politics', while it was 'exploiting the name of the Mahatma to stabilise its position'.[155] In a later letter, Lotvala wrote:

> I appreciate the work you are doing. But mere writing to the Press or the literature of the type that you bring out will not be sufficiently effective as long as the capitalist system is not replaced by some other social system as would bring about equality of income, opportunity and even status. Fundamental values underlying capitalist system which are based on adoration of money economy as understood and taught by orthodox economists and acted upon by the government should change.

He added that a dependence on 'change of heart' was not enough; 'the truth must be based on scientific inductive research, to be verified on "a priori" method'. Although Gandhi had made great efforts to revive the *charkha* and handicrafts, 'as relations of forces, psychology and environments were against his program[me], he could not succeed in spite of vast energy and money spent after it'.[156] Lotvala had put his finger on the main problems: the hostile reception of Gandhian ideas was partly due to the environment; but also that the 'Gandhian' position did not seek to overthrow capitalism, and could at best be an enclave within it, composed of morally correct, by their own standards, individuals. At the same time, Lotvala's reading indicated the possibilities for selective and creative readings of 'Gandhism', incorporating particular aspects of it. As for the equation of Gandhism with anarchism, Kumarappa seems to have been an agnostic; earlier, he had replied to a hostile critic that he (the critic) would 'search in vain for authorities in Western text books', unless he recognized that the 'Village Industries Movement is an outcome of a desire for non-violence and truth in the economic sphere'. He admitted that 'certain aspects of our reasoning can be paralleled from anarchists and others but that is not sufficient cause to hang us'.[157] Apparently, the description of Gandhians as 'anarchists' could be negative when coming from a hostile critic, and positive, or at least neutral, when coming from a friendly critic.

More serious confusions of reading were also possible. Kumarappa's writing, in seeking to situate itself within a specifically 'Indian' ethos, could lend itself easily to slippages into a culturally defensive, parochial Hindu elitism, or to crudely obscurantist celebrations of a cultural identity which combined Gandhism with varying degrees of religious bigotry or sectarian triumphalism. One correspondent, a Brahmin by the name of T.V. Narayanaswami Iyer, wrote to Kumarappa in May 1947 in praise of *Why the Village Movement?* and paraphrased it in his own terms:

> It [the book] is an unparalleled exposition of the truths of the ancient religion of India. The teachings of the great Rishis Vyasa and Valmiki are there in the English form. I also find same terms Varnashrama Dharma Swadharma. Self discipline and mass welfare. Truth is greatly stressed and non-violence still greater. The Ancient religion of India is a composition of Politics & Economics which is eternal and has got only one interpretation. Islam Christianity and other religions are only diluted forms of this ancient religion . . . The caste system is no more than party systems which exist today. That party which observes most strictly the eternal principles are held high and the others a little below.[158]

The confusion of 'Hindu' with 'Indian' was, of course, not peculiar to Kumarappa; much has been written on the effects of early British imperialist accounts in privileging an ancient 'Hindu' civilization in India, and representing an Islamic period in India as a dark age of violence and oppression from which British rule rescued India.[159] For those who did not altogether accept this schematic partition of Indian history, there was a tendency to reject the idea of a British rescue from tyranny by a description of British rule itself as tyranny; but many of these rejections sought their intellectual resources in the same ancient and classical splendour that was the 'Hindu' India of the Orientalist imagination. A search for truly Indian values worthy of being upheld and carried forward to an age of renewal in independent India, therefore, often depended on accounts of such an ancient civilization. These, unfortunately, slid all too easily into an idiom which imagined India as Hindu.[160]

Iyer's view of a desirable India, taking off from Kumarappa's statements, was that true religion comprised spiritual, moral, and material aspects. Islam and Christianity, in his view, had 'diluted the eternal principles of Brahmacharyam & chastity'. He approved greatly of the AIVIA's paying 'greater attention to the spiritual and moral aspects before entering with full vigour in the material aspect'. He went on to wax lyrical on the subject of how 'village industries & village panchayats flourished in times past'. As symptoms of present decay, he pointed to '[t]he cow sacrifice by Muslims, the selling of vast numbers of cows by Hindus to agents of Slaughterhouses, the class distinction in railway carriages & steamers, the food and drink consumption and the manner of living by the people of High & Low rank'. He wrote at length on the dangers of the loss of the spirit of *brahmacharya*—a word which, it ought to be noted, has connotations of learning and spirituality as well as of celibacy:

> Islam lured away the Kshatriya spirit in the land with their woman [sic] and brought down both their downfall [sic]. The English lured away the brahmanic spirit of the land with their Gold and brought down both their downfall [sic]. Woman & Gold are the negative aspects that attract irresistibly the positive in man and he has to struggle hard to extricate himself out of them and Seek the negative within himself.[161]

Man, Iyer explained, could only be complete unto himself if he contained both positive and negative aspects within himself; this could only happen in the spiritual sphere.

Although such interpretations were not particularly useful in shedding light on a project for the future of India, they also indicated the weaknesses of Kumarappa's playing on anxieties related to the 'West'. It might be argued that Iyer's pouring out his heart to an imagined sympathetic fellow-believer in Kumarappa can hardly be blamed on Kumarappa. On the other hand, Kumarappa's position certainly opens up the discursive space for such an interpretation as Iyer's within the framework of respectable argument. Nothing in Iyer's paraphrase is actually said in Kumarappa's book; but all of Iyer's premises can easily be found in the writing of Kumarappa, and in the writing of other Gandhians: the interpretation of *varna* as the 'brahmanical spirit' or the 'Kshatriya spirit', cow-killing as wrong, or celibacy as desirable. The rest might be extrapolation from what he saw as first principles, driven forward by goals and moulded by anxieties peculiar to him or more widely shared; and in the context of the 1940s, with anxieties regarding religious, regional, national, or other identity corresponding with political uncertainties and forcing those who were uncertain about such choices into making choices, they were more widely shared.[162] This was precisely what 'modernisers' of the Visvesvaraya, Meghnad Saha, and Nehru kind sought to avoid: the implications of arguments which drew on 'tradition' and derided 'Western' modernity were capable of being bent to obscurantist and reactionary arguments, regardless of the intentions of the originators of the argument. Ordinarily, without being linked to conceptions of civilisation and spirituality rather than religion, such a reading would be dismissed as 'communalism' and therefore, as illegitimate. When combined with the justificatory power of an argument endorsed by the Mahatma himself, such views could more comfortably stake their claim for inclusion in the mainstream.

Moreover, Kumarappa, unlike Gandhi, was not particularly careful about ensuring that such readings were avoided. A furious letter from one N.C. Bedekar in Aurangabad, written in 1948, objected strongly to Kumarappa's reply to a question on whether volunteers of the Rashtriya Swayamsevak Sangh (RSS), a Hindu paramilitary organization, could be of help in promoting constructive work. Kumarappa had apparently replied in the affirmative and had 'showered praise on the R.S.S. volunteers and even encouraged them to carry on their activities, which have been professedly antinational & communal in character in face of Govt. opposition & restriction on their activities'. Bedekar found this particularly objectionable in the light of the RSS' dangerous role in the communal violence and propaganda leading up to and after the partition of India in August 1947.[163] Kumarappa's reply seems in retrospect to be either extraordinarily naive or deliberately disingenuous. He wrote:

> All I said were generalisations to which no exception can be taken. If there were young men of ideals, renunciation and firmness of purpose, *wherever we may find them*, they will be of invaluable use to our motherland at this time to build up our nation, if they are properly directed.
>
> I am not concerned with Government policy towards the R.S.S. nor do I know what it is. So it will be futile my writing about it.[164]

This reply seems all the more extraordinary because, by the time this correspondence took place in late 1948, the RSS' active involvement in the assassination of Gandhi, on 30 January of that year, was well known. However, neither correspondent specifically mentioned it.

Despite these peculiarities, however, there were aspects of Kumarappa's interpretation of Gandhi which were clearly more accessible than his justifications in terms of caste or Indianness. Ideas of avoiding class struggle or relying on the goodwill and cooperative spirit of the propertied classes, as well as the significance of opposition to capitalism by advocating responsible buying and careful use of impermanent resources found other formulations. These were individual elements in an unstable and ultimately less than coherent system of thought. As individual elements, however, they were useful in other combinations, especially when they could be associated with the legitimating icon of the Mahatma, and could become free-floating elements in political debates which reappeared at various times in various combinations to justify diverse projects.

Gandhian arguments have, in recent times, been supported for being more culturally sensitive and less elitist than those of the 'socialists' in India, or even claimed by 'socialists' as a form of culturally sensitive and participatory 'socialism'. This view is not borne out by the writings of Gandhi or the Gandhians. Gandhians took upon themselves the task of convincing the 'masses' of what was good for them, and the right to guide the 'masses' to the correct moral and material goals. The execution of this task was to be accomplished at a local level rather than at a centralized level, but this was, nonetheless, to be done based on principles laid out by right-thinking, spiritual Brahmins, and not necessarily or even primarily on precedents derived from local practices—which makes Gandhians' claims, or later academics' claims on their behalf, to cultural sensitivity or anti-elitism seem rather dubious. On the contrary, they shared with more mainstream nationalists similar concerns with directing and disciplining the activities of the ordinary Indian in desired directions.

Notes

1 See, for instance, E.F. Schumacher, *Small is Beautiful* (London, 1973); Madhav Gadgil, 'On the Gandhian Economic Trail', *Gandhians in Action* (April-June 1994); or various statements by Medha Patkar on behalf of the Narmada Bachao Andolan.

2 For instance, Gadgil, 'On the Gandhian Economic Trail'; Madhav Gadgil and Ramachandra Guha, *Ecology and Equity: The Use and Abuse of Nature in Contemporary India* (London, 1995), especially, pp. 38–9, 188; Vasant Kumar Bawa, 'Gandhi in the Twentieth Century: Search for an Alternative Development Model', *Economic and Political Weekly*, Vol. XXXI, No. 47, 23 November 1996, pp. 3048–49; various articles in the journal *Gandhi Marg*.

3 See the chapter on 'Gandhian Economics', in Bhabatosh Datta, *Indian Economic Thought: Twentieth Century Perspectives* (New Delhi, 1978), pp. 150–8, especially, p. 152; Ajit Dasgupta, *Gandhi's Economic Thought* (London, 1996).

4 Mahadev Desai, preface to M.K. Gandhi, *Hind Swaraj* (revised new edition, Ahmedabad, 1939), pp. ix–x. in which he reprints a previous article from the *Harijan*.

5 *Harijan*, 27 October 1933, reprinted in *The Collected Works of Mahatma Gandhi*, Vol. LVI (New Delhi, 1973), pp. 146–8.

6 For an account of Gandhi's various elaborations of this theory, see Ajit K. Dasgupta, *Gandhi's Economic Thought* (London, 1996), chapter six.

7 On Vinoba Bhave, see Shriman Narayan, *Vinoba: His Life and Work* (Bombay, 1970)—Shriman Narayan, formerly Shriman Narayan Agarwal, (and author of the 'Gandhian Plan' of 1944—he later dropped his caste name), was himself a Gandhian; consequently, this is an insider's biography. For Jayaprakash Narayan's own account of his move from socialism to Gandhism, see Jayaprakash Narayan, 'Letter to PSP Associates', 25 October 1957, reprinted in Jayaprakash Narayan, *Towards a New Society* (New Delhi, 1958).

8 See Benjamin Zachariah, *Nehru* (London, 2004), pp. 194–8.

9 J.C. Kumarappa, 'The Economy of the Cross', a summary of three addresses to the Mid-India Conference of Christian Students at Nagpur, 5–7 November 1942, reprinted in *Christianity: Its Economy and Way of Life* (Ahmedabad, 1945), p. 1.

10 J.C. Kumarappa, *Why the Village Movement? (A plea for a village-centred economic order in India)* (fifth edition, Wardha, 1949; first edition, 1936) [hereafter, referred to as Kumarappa, *Village Movement*].

11 Preface to the first edition, reprinted in Kumarappa, *Village Movement*, p. (iii).

12 The second edition in 1937 added material on 'Barter Exchange', 'Education for Life', 'Democracy in the Orient', and 'Centralisation and Decentralisation'. The third, in 1939, added a chapter on 'Surveys and Plans'; the fourth, in 1945, added material on 'Schools of Economics', 'Peoples' Income', 'Moral Issues of Riches, 'Non-violent Standards of Life', and 'Planned Economy'. The book was also translated into several Indian languages.

13 See my point in Chapter 1 of this book on why economics became important as the terms which served to frame arguments, but was seen to include, or to need supplementing by, important non-economic issues. See, also, Chapter 2 on 'moral and material progress' and its importance in British, nationalist, and (the apparent exception) Gandhian conceptions of development; and Chapter 3 for its operation in imperial arguments.

14 M.K. Gandhi, *'Hind Swaraj'*, chapter VI, p. 35, in Anthony J. Parel (ed.), *Gandhi: Hind Swaraj and Other Writings* (Cambridge, 1997).

15 As has been pointed out, for instance, by Partha Chatterjee, *Nationalist Thought and the Colonial World: A Derivative Discourse?* (London, 1986), p. 93, and Parel, 'Introduction', in *Gandhi: Hind Swaraj*, p. xlvii.

16 Partha Chatterjee, *Nationalist Thought*, p. 112.

17 Partha Chatterjee, *Nationalist Thought*, pp. 93–4, 99.

18 See, for instance, Ashis Nandy, *Tradition, Tyranny and Utopias: Essays in the Politics of Awareness* (Delhi, 1987).

19 See Bhikhu Parekh, *Colonialism, Tradition and Reform: An Analysis of Gandhi's Political Discourse* (New Delhi, 1989).

20 Partha Chatterjee, *Nationalist Thought*, pp. 50–2; for the exposition, see chapter four, pp. 85–130.

21 Partha Chatterjee, *Nationalist Thought*; Partha Chatterjee, 'Gandhi and the Critique of Civil Society', in Ranajit Guha (ed.), *Subaltern Studies 111* (Delhi, 1984).

22 Gandhi's own word for his language, quoted in Partha Chatterjee, *Nationalist Thought*, p .85.

23 See Shahid Amin, 'Gandhi as Mahatma', in Ranajit Guha (ed.), *Subaltern Studies 11* (Delhi, 1983); GD. Birla, *In the Shadow of the Mahatma: A Personal Memoir* (Bombay, 1968); Tapan Ghose, *The Gandhi Murder Trial* (New York, 1973).

24 As, for instance, implicitly, in Raghavan Iyer, *The Moral and Political Thought of Mahatma Gandhi* (New York, 1973); and, more explicitly, in Ajit Dasgupta, *Gandhi's Economic Thought*.

25 Ajit Dasgupta, *Gandhi's Economic Thought*, p. 103. Dasgupta observes many such shifts, but does not read them as particularly significant in strategic terms.

26 For instance, he asked Thakurdas about aspects of business views on the British government's 'scorched earth' policy when Japanese invasion was anticipated in 1942. See Thakurdas Papers, NML, File 279 Part I, ff. 12–14, Thakurdas to Gandhi, 12 March 1942, responding to Mahadev Desai's request for Thakurdas to write to Gandhi on his views on 'scorched earth', and Gandhi's version, *Harijan*, 22 March 1942, copy in Thakurdas Papers, File 279 Part I, f. 60.

27 'Bapu' to 'Ku', 12 August 1941, J.C. Kumarappa Papers (JCK), NML, New Delhi. Subject File No. 5, f. 75. Emphasis mine. Significantly, Gandhi did not phrase the intended project in terms of the need to combat the use of machinery, as he was conventionally wont to do, but in terms of the need to combat the 'socialisation of industrialism'—not 'industrialism', but the 'socialisation' thereof. This was certainly an engagement with issues thrown up by the 'Enlightenment'.

28 See, for instance, Karuna Kaushik, *Russian Revolution and Indian Nationalism: Studies of Lajpat Rai, Subhas Chandra Bose and Ram Manohar Lohia* (Delhi, 1984), pp. 38–86, on Lala Lajpat Rai. Lajpat Rai was impressed by the Russian Revolution but remained an Arya Samajist, with the Hindu overtones which went with being a member of that organization.

29 Many people cited accounts such as Sidney and Beatrice Webb, *Soviet Communism: A New Civilisation?*, two volumes, (London, 1935). The Government of India initially contemplated banning the book in India, but decided against it. See IOR: L/P&J/12/493.

30 For an account, see Bipan Chandra, *The Rise and Growth of Economic Nationalism in India* (Delhi, 1966).

31 See Birla's letter to Thakurdas regarding the 'Bombay Manifesto' against Nehru's socialist pronouncements, quoted in Bipan Chandra, 'Jawaharlal Nehru and the Capitalist Class, 1936', *Economic and Political Weekly*, Vol. X, No. 33–35 (August 1975), p. 1319. This is not to suggest that businessmen steered clear of political issues: see Claude Markovits, *Indian Business and Nationalist Politics* (Cambridge, 1985).

32 See Ajit Dasgupta, *Gandhi's Economic Thought*, chapter six, on the Gandhian theory of trusteeship.

33 See Chapter 5 of this book, for further discussion.

34 Birla, *In the Shadow of the Mahatma*, p. xv.

35 For Gandhi's retreats, see, especially, Sumit Sarkar, 'The Logic of Gandhian Nationalism: Civil Disobedience and the Gandhi-Irwin Pact (1930–31)', *Indian Historical Review*, Vol. Ill, No. 1 (1976).

36 See CSP manifesto, reprinted in *Congress Socialist*, 29 September 1934.

37 See Jayaprakash Narayan, *Why Socialism?* (Benares, 1936). Narayan also advertised the Marxist and Leninist approaches of the CSP, which was far from true of all its members, but was *believed* by a large number of members, at least at the time, to be an accurate way to describe their politics.

38 For instance, he crucially intervened to disarm Subhas Bose as Congress president in 1939. On the 'Tripuri crisis', see Sumit Sarkar, *Modern India 1885–1947* (Madras, 1983), pp. 372–5.

39 For the distinctions between groupings of businessmen vis-à-vis nationalism, see Claude Markovits, *Indian Business and Nationalist Politics*.

40 Such anxieties have been chronicled for earlier periods—see, for instance, Sumit Sarkar, *A Critique of Colonial India* (Calcutta, 1985); Partha Chatteijee, *The Nation and its Fragments: Colonial and Post-colonial Histories* (Princeton, 1994), especially, pp. 6–7 on the 'cultural' sphere of 'nationalism'; Dhruv Raina and S. Irfan Habib, 'Bhadralok perceptions of Science, Technology, and Cultural nationalism', *Indian Economic and Social History Review*, Vol. 32, No. 1 (1995); Dhruv Raina and S. Irfan Habib, 'The Unfolding of an Engagement: The Dawn on Science, Technical Education and Industrialisation', *Studies in History*, Vol. 9, No. 1, (January-June 1993); and Ashis Nandy in some of his early essays—see, Ashis Nandy, 'Sati: A Nineteenth Century Tale of Women, Violence and Protest', in Ashis Nandy, *At the Edge of Psychology: Essays in Politics and Culture* (Delhi, 1980)

(Nandy's interpretation is based on what current psychotherapy and social work terminology might refer to as 'reactive ethnicity'—he does not use the term—and his writing indicates that he is possibly suffering from it himself). There are disagreements as to the significance to be attributed to the trends referred to—but the evidence points clearly to anxieties related to disruption of a world and a world-view by British colonial rule, and the search for a world-view compatible with new conditions of existence and with the newly-available intellectual tools as well as what was understood of the old.

41 *Science and Culture*, Vol. IV, No. 10 (April 1939), pp. 534–5. One of the stronger advocates of 'modern' solutions to problems of Indian development was the journal *Science and Culture* ('A Monthly Journal of Natural and Cultural Sciences'), published from Calcutta, founded and edited by Meghnad Saha, eminent physicist and developmentalist.

42 *Science and Culture*, Vol. IV, No. 10 (April 1939), editorial, p. 533.

43 Asoka Mehta, 'The Victory of Socialism over Romanticism', *Congress Socialist*, 3 February 1935.

44 Asoka Mehta, *Planned Economy for India?* (Bombay, 1935), a CSP pamphlet which contains the substance of his articles in the *Congress Socialist;* Mir Alam, 'India's New Deal', *Congress Socialist*, 3 February 1935, p. 15, which includes a review of M. Visvesvaraya's *Planned Economy for India* (Bangalore City, 1934).

45 Quoted in J.P. Narayan, *Why Socialism?* p. 86: JP's italics.

46 J.P. Narayan, *Why Socialism?* pp. 87–8.

47 Nirmal Bose, 'Is Gandhi a Nationalist?', *Congress Socialist*, 10 February 1935, pp. 14–16; and 'Is Gandhi a Nationalist: Alliance with the Socialists', *Congress Socialist*, 24 February pp. 6–8. For the views of the nationalists, see their pamphlet, Madan Mohan Malaviya and M.S. Aney, *The Congress Nationalist Party: What it Stands for: Why Every Indian Should Support It* (Bombay, August 1934), IOR: P/V 119. The main plank of the Nationalists' programme was their rejection of Ramsay MacDonald's 'Communal Award', which they denounced as a British attempt to divide the Indian population, but then fell victim to that logic by asserting that 'Hindus' were not adequately represented considering the strength of their numbers. The Congress Socialists regarded the Nationalists as a 'communal' party: see *Congress Socialist*, 6 October 1934, p. 14. This usage of the term 'Nationalist' was an unusual and specific one: a 'nationalist' was generally considered to be someone who opposed British rule in India, by which meaning 'socialists' and 'Gandhians' were sub-sets of 'nationalists'. It is in the latter sense that I have used the term elsewhere in this dissertation.

48 *Congress Socialist*, 10 February 1935, p. 16.

49 *Congress Socialist*, 24 February 1935, p. 7.

50 *Congress Socialist*, 24 February 1935, p. 8. Looking at the future, Bose predicted: 'So far as Nationalism is concerned, there is no doubt that it will hardly be able to raise its head sufficiently as long as Gandhi is there to work against it. Devoid of any active programme, there is a likelihood that the two branches of Communalism, Hindu and Muslim, will now form a combine against Socialism both of the Gandhian and the Communistic type. But it will be a harmless organisation because it will have no path of direct action of its own. Only the more idealistically inclined nationalists will go over either to the side of Gandhi or the Socialists, and add some strength to those two causes'. This polarization did not take place.

51 Raghavan Iyer, *The Moral and Political Thought of Mahatma Gandhi* (New York, 1973), pp. 9–10, 14. Iyer's classification of Freud as a twentieth century thinker is interesting; most current studies treat the intellectual genealogy of Freud as a nineteenth century Viennese Jewish bourgeois one. Gandhi himself did on occasion refer to psychoanalysis.

52 See Anthony J. Parel, 'Introduction', in Anthony J. Parel (ed.), *Gandhi: Hind Swaraj and Other Writings* (Cambridge, 1997). As late as 1945, Gandhi stated that he stood by what he had written in *Hind Swaraj*: Gandhi to Jawaharlal Nehru, 5 October 1945 (in Hindustani written in the Roman script), Jawaharlal Nehru Papers JNP, NML, Correspondence, Vol. 26, f. 135.

53 See 'A Note on the History of the Text', in Parel (ed.), *Gandhi: Hind Swaraj*, p. lxiii.

54 This point has largely been missed by commentators—it is not mentioned, for instance, by Parel in any of his sections on the historical and intellectual contexts in his introduction—probably because Gandhi's text did not explicitly state its desire to intervene in these debates.

55 Parel (ed.), *Gandhi: Hind Swaraj*, Note 2, p. 5.

56 See, for instance, Naba Choudhuri, Cuttack, to Jawaharlal Nehru, 8 September 1933, JNP, Correspondence, Vol. 12, ff. 49–53: Gandhism, Choudhuri wrote, had 'now outgrown the personal moral ideas, prejudices and Sanskaras of Gandhiji himself. Gandhism as a revolutionary method is quite distinct from Gandhism as a spiritual force for the moral upliftment [sic] of the human personality'. He believed in the value of Gandhism as revolutionary method, but rejected Gandhi's personal views (f. 49). Another more contemporary reading is S.A. Dange, *Gandhi vs Lenin* (Bombay, 1921)—which has been

read as hostile to Gandhi by Anthony Parel (Parel (ed.), *Gandhi; Hind Swaraj*, pp. lviii–lix)—I read it, in fact, as a detailed analysis of the relative strategic value of a 'Leninist' and 'Gandhian' approach to political struggle in the specific case of India, with the tone as well as the content of the text by no means implying that the matter was decided.

57 Sumit Sarkar, *The Swadeshi Movement in Bengal 1903–1908* (Delhi, 1973), pp. 55–7.

58 For a more detailed discussion of this point, see Chapter 5 of this volume.

59 Deepak Kumar, *Science and the Raj 1857–1905* (Delhi, 1995), p. 195.

60 See, for a well-researched short account, Parel, 'Introduction', in *Gandhi: Hind Swaraj*, pp. xxxii–xlvii.

61 Parel, 'Introduction', p. xlii. On Maine, see J.W. Burrow, *Evolution and Society* (1970 edition; first edition Cambridge, 1966), pp. 137–87. Maine had outlined his first major contribution to his field, *Ancient Law*, before he had ever been to India; he elaborated these ideas in his *Village Communities of the East and West*, published in 1871, with his Indian experience behind him.

62 See, for instance, Radhakamal Mukerjee, *The Foundations of Indian Economics* (London, 1916); Radhakumud Mookerji, *Local Government in Ancient India* (London, 1919). An example of the overlapping of the imperial and national uses of the idea of 'development', appears in John Matthai's doctoral dissertation, at the LSE, under Sidney Webb, and published in 1915: John Matthai, *Village Government in British India* (London, 1915). Matthai was often cited by colonial officials: see Chapter 3 of this book—but what he claimed in his dissertation did not seem to be central to his own later thinking.

63 J. W. Burrow, *Evolution and Society*, (Cambridge, 1966), pp. 141, 148–9.

64 Burrow, *Evolution and Society*, p. 159; Clive Dewey, 'Images of the Village Community: A Study in Anglo-Indian Ideology', *Modern Asian Studies*, Vol. 6, No. 3 (1973); for a concise account of the Russian situation, in particular the Narodnik-Marxist divide, see Isaac Deutscher, *The Prophet Armed* (London, 1959), chapter 1. *Narodnaya Volya* defended the 'indigenous' *Mir* as the basis of action, and attacked the emergent Marxists as outsiders and Westernizers. The 'Marxists', on the other hand, referred to the *Mir* as a bulwark of absolutism; the emancipation of the serfs in 1861 had given the responsibility for periodic land redistribution to the *Mir*. Ironically, Marx himself seems to have tended towards accepting the so-called 'indigenist' and 'terrorist' position of Narodnaya Volya and was suspicious of the 'Genevans', as he called the *Cherny Peredel* group of Georgi Plekhanov, who called themselves 'Marxists'. Cyril Smith, *Marx at the Millenium* (London, 1996), pp. 52–9.

65 Tolstoy's diary, entry for 20 April 1910, quoted in Raghavan Iyer, *The Moral and Political Thought of Mahatma Gandhi*, p. 24.

66 M.K. Gandhi, *The Stories of My Experiments with Truth* (Harmondsworth edition 1982; first published in two volumes, 1927 and 1929, Ahmedabad, translated by Mahadev Desai), p. 121.

67 Gandhi, *The Story of My Experiments with Truth*, p. 77.

68 Gandhi, *The Story of My Experiments with Truth*, pp. 156–7.

69 See Maureen Swan, *Gandhi: The South African Experience* (Johannesburg, 1985); Dhruba Gupta, 'Indian Perceptions of Africa', *South Asia Research*, Vol. 11, No. 2 (November 1991), pp. 163–5. Gupta argues persuasively that Gandhi was not inclined to make an argument for equality of 'kaffirs' and Indians.

70 Gandhi, *The Story of My Experiments with Truth*, pp. 60–3.

71 I use the term in its pre-Saidian sense—to denote eighteenth- and nineteenth- century students of 'classical' India, though the post-Saidian meaning might also be useful here: see Edward W. Said, *Orientalism* (London, 1978).

72 That is, Orientalism in its post-Saidian sense—as a stereotype of the non- European in the European imagination. This was somewhat ironic, given that Gandhi had come to such stereotypes through his acquaintance with British thinking on the subject.

73 S. Gopal, *Jawaharlal Nehru: A Biography*, Vol. 1 (London, 1975), p. 53.

74 See Kumarappa, *The Practice and Precepts of Jesus* (Ahmedabad, 1945); and the essays collected in Kumarappa, *Christianity: Its Economy and Way of Life* (Ahmedabad, 1945).

75 See Gyan Pandey, 'Rallying Round the Cow', in Ranajit Guha (ed.), *Subaltern Studies II* (Delhi, 1983). Subho Basu, 'Strikes and "Communal" Riots in Calcutta in the 1890s', *Modern Asian Studies*, Vol. 32, No. 4 (1998) describes the importance for Muslim jute-mill hands of their perceived right to sacrifice cows, and their attacks on the police (though not on their Hindu fellow-workers) because of the police's attempts at preventing cow-sacrifice. In some circumstances it was possible to ensure that Muslims voluntarily gave up eating beef and killing cows out of solidarity with their Hindu brethren. In December 1919, in connection with

the Non-Cooperation and Khilafat movement, the Muslim League asked its followers to give up sacrificing cows at Bakr-Id. Cited in Sumit Sarkar, *Modern India 1885–1947* (Madras, 1983), p. 196.

76 For a reading of Gandhi's opposition to cow-slaughter as an 'animal rights' argument, rather than an opposition dictated by Hindu reverence for the cow, see Ajit K. Dasgupta, *Gandhi's Economic Thought* (London, 1996), pp. 60– 3.

77 L.L. Sundara Ram, *Cow Protection in India* (Madras, 1927).

78 M.K. Gandhi, Foreword to Valji Govindji Desai, *Cow Protection* (Ahmedabad, 1934). Note that Gandhiji's endorsement of the book is dated Sabarmati, 8 March 1930, four years before the book was finally published (by the Navajivan Press, judging by its appearance and design, though the name of the Press, usually present in its publications, is missing here). The delay was presumably due to the Civil Disobedience Movement, the Round Table Conference, and the second Civil Disobedience Movement which intervened.

79 Valji Govindji Desai, *Cow Protection* (Ahmedabad, 1934), pp. 29–30, 101–2, 116.

80 Satish Chandra Dasgupta, *The Cow in India, Vol. I—Breeding—Dairy Industries* (Calcutta, 1945); *The Cow in India, Vol. II: The Body of the Cow— its Diseases and Treatment* (Calcutta, 1945). Both volumes were published by the Khadi Pratisthan, in May and September 1945, respectively.

81 M.K. Gandhi, Foreword, to Satish Chandra Dasgupta, *The Cow in India, Vol. I*, p. (i), dated Mahabaleshwar, 20 May 1945.

82 On P.C. Ray and his influence, see Chapter 5 of this volume. See also P.C. Ray, *Life and Experiences of a Bengali Chemist* (Calcutta and London, 1932), especially, pp. 129–151; and the somewhat ironically-titled *Acharyya Ray Commemoration Volume* (Calcutta, 1932), edited by Satya Churn Law, a *Festschrift* for the Acharya on the occasion of his seventieth birthday, published half a year late, but certainly during his lifetime.

83 Dasgupta, *The Cow in India, Vol. I*, p. (vii). Much of Dasgupta's opposition to the Royal Commission was due to the latter's recommendation that the buffalo was a more useful agricultural animal than the cow; Dasgupta argued strenuously against that position: chapter four, pp. 87–203. This caused Gandhi to emphasize, in his Foreword, that this argument was not intended to imply that the buffalo 'should be killed or starved out', merely that it should 'not be favoured at the expense of the cow'. Gandhi, 'Foreword', p. (i).

84 Dasgupta, *The Cow in India, Vol. II*, Part VI, pp. 291–316; Gandhi, *Hind Swaraj*, in Parel (ed.), *Gandhi: Hind Swaraj and Other Writings*, p. 64.

85 Dasgupta, *The Cow in India, Vol. I*, p. (vii).

86 Dasgupta, *The Cow in India, Vol. I*, p. (viii).

87 He was almost single-handedly editing as well as writing the AIVIA paper, the *Gram Udyog Patrika*, in its early years. Later on, Kumarappa's brother Bharatan Kumarappa was also a frequent contributor; when Kumarappa was in jail during the Quit India Movement, many of the articles were written by Vaikunth L. Mehta.

88 See Benthall Papers, Centre for South Asian Studies, Cambridge, Box II, file on 'Ghandi'; Dietmar Rothermund, *India in the Great Depression 1929–1939* (Delhi, 1992), p. 212.

89 McVickar Professor of Political Economy, Faculty of Political Science, Columbia University.

90 Seligman supervised B.R. Ambedkar's PhD thesis, later published as *The Evolution of Public Finance in British India: a Study in the Provincial Decentralisation of Public Finance* (London, 1925), and appears in the acknowledgements of Gyan Chand's *Essentials of Federal Finance: A Contribution to the Problem of Financial Re-adjustment in India* (London, 1930), Preface, p. viii.

91 Seligman's recommendation letter, dated 29 January 1929, copy in JCK, NML, Subject File No. 1, f. 19.

92 See, for instance, K.T. Shah, *Sixty Years of Indian Finance* (Bombay, 1921); B. R. Ambedkar, *The Evolution of Public Finance in British India*; Gyan Chand, *Essentials of Federal Finance* and *Local Finance in India* (Allahabad, 1947); P. J. Thomas, *The Growth of Federal Finance in India: being a Survey of India's Public Finances from 1833 to 1939* (India Branch, Humphrey Milford, Oxford University Press, 1939).

93 See Gandhi, *The Story of My Experiments with Truth*, pp. 60–3. For Kumarappa's account of the beginnings of his own renunciation, see Kumarappa, 'Our meeting', n.d., p. 1–3, in JCK, NML, Speeches and Writings, Vol. VI, ff. 15–17.

94 Biographical details are taken from K. Muniandi, 'Kumarappa the Man', *Gandhi Marg*, Vol. 14, No. 2 (July-September 1992), pp. 318–26; and Devendra Kumar, 'Kumarappa and the Contemporary Development Perspective', *Gandhi Marg*, Vol. 14, No. 2 (July-September 1992), pp. 294–5, unless otherwise stated.

95 Kumarappa's reason for his resignation—its 'economic aspect'—was laid before the readers of the *Gram UdyogPatrika* in an article entitled 'Out of One's Element'. The priority for the AIVIA, as far as economic organization was concerned, was the

creation of employment for the villages. This was also a correct approach for a country with an abundance of labour and a shortage of capital. The NPC did not appreciate this; instead, they 'seemed to think that all would be well as long as we produced large quantities of standardised goods'. *Gram Udyog Patrika*, September 1939, pp. 1–2.

96 Kumarappa, 'Our Meeting', p. 1; letter to Gandhi dated 22 May 1929 on letterhead 'Cornelius and Davar, Incorporated Accountants and Auditors', in JCK, NML, Subject File No. 5, f. 17.

97 It was serialized in *Young India* over November and December 1929 and January 1930, and published subsequently in book form by the Navajivan Press as J.C. Kumarappa, *Public Finance and Our Poverty: the Contribution of Public Finance to the Present Economic State of India* (Ahmedabad, 1930).

98 Kumarappa, 'Our Meeting', p. 2. The Gujarat Survey was published as J.C. Kumarappa, *A Survey of Matar Taluka (Kaira District)* (Ahmedabad, 1931); when it was reprinted in 1952—without revisions or modifications (Kumarappa's preface to the second edition, p. xi)—it was entitled, significantly, *An Economic Survey of Matar Taluka* (Ahmedabad, 1952).

99 Kumarappa to Gandhi, 25 October 1930, JCK, NML, Subject file No. 5, f. 1. Emphases added.

100 Kumarappa to Gandhi, 25 October 1930, JCK, NML, Subject file No. 5, ff. 3, 5.

101 Gandhi to Kumarappa, 31 October 1930, JCK, NML, Subject file No. 5, f. 5a. The translation of the original term into English, Gandhi said, had been inadequate; Gandhi had not read the translation. He added, 'A life of vow is like marriage, a[s] sacred[.] It is marriage with God[,] is dissoluble [sic] for all time. Come let us marry Him.' The equivalent Sanskrit term was *vrata*, a solemn resolve or a spiritual decision, according to Gandhi. [Raghavan Iyer transliterates this text as '. . . A life of vow is like marriage, a sacrament . . .': *The Moral and Political Thought of Mahatma Gandhi*, p. 82). On the wider parameters of Gandhi's views on the importance of vows, of Gandhi's statement on the connotations of the Sanskrit terms vrata and *yama*, and the debate with Kumarappa, see Raghavan Iyer, *The Moral and Political Thought of Mahatma Gandhi*, pp. 73–81, 164–7.

102 See Kumarappa, *The Practice and Precepts of Jesus*, especially, pp. 3–5. He prefaced his later remarks with the following contextualizing statement: 'It is a common practice among oriental teachers and devotees to identify themselves with the Godhead. This is never understood to signify an exclusive claim to divinity. The fourth gospel depicts Jesus in this mode throughout, (p. 3).

103 See 'Congress Select Committee, Report on the Financial Obligations Between Great Britain and India, official summary issued July 1931', copy in IOR: L/I/1/149. This argued that most of India's public debt was not really India's public debt but Britain's, as it had not been incurred in Indian interests or by a government which was Indian.

104 See Kumarappa, *Currency Inflation: Its Cause and Cure* (Wardha, 1943)—the title is loosely borrowed from the title of Edward Carpenter's book; his collection of essays on imperial wartime finance, Kumarappa, *Blood Money* (Wardha, 1948); and Kumarappa, *Clive to Keynes (A Survey of the History of our Public Debts and Credits)* (Ahmedabad, March 1947), respectively.

105 I have elaborated the details of Kumarappa's classificatory system elsewhere: Benjamin Zachariah, 'Interpreting Gandhi: JC Kumarappa, Modernity and the East', in Tapati GuhaThakurta (ed.), *'Culture' and 'Democracy': Papers from the Cultural Studies Workshops* (Calcutta, 1999). I shall outline the main points here.

106 Kumarappa, *Village Movement*, pp. 1–3.

107 Kumarappa, *Village Movement*, pp. 4–5.

108 Kumarappa, *Village Movement*, pp. 5–6.

109 Kumarappa, *Village Movement*, p. 3.

110 Kumarappa, *Village Movement*, pp. 7–8. Much of Kumarappa's attempted history of 'Western' economic organizations can be omitted; it is a confused and somewhat incoherent account, with several obvious inaccuracies in historical detail—Napoleon is in his account a feudal baron, for instance: '. . . what did Napoleon care how many of his soldiers he left dead on the way so long as he could get to Moscow?' is Kumarappa's example of feudalism. Kumarappa, *Village Movement*, p. 8.

111 Kumarappa, *Village Movement*, p. 10.

112 Kumarappa, *Village Movement*, pp. 9–10.

113 Kumarappa, *Village Movement*, pp. 10–11.

114 Kumarappa, *Village Movement*, p. 62.

115 Kumarappa, *Village Movement*, pp. 12, 15.

116 Kumarappa, *Village Movement*, p. 15.

117 Kumarappa, *Village Movement*, p. 16.

118 Kumarappa, *Village Movement*, pp. 18–19.

119 In the joint family competition is controlled and the weak protected through the 'equitable' sharing of the income of the earning members with non-earning members. The caste system 'aimed at directing the various units of economic activity in consonance with one another and safeguarding the community from overproduction', and payment in kind to artisans such as the carpenter, blacksmith, or chamar ensured everyone a 'minimum subsistence

allowance', the underlying principles being 'the conception that work itself is a method of distribution of wealth', and that the community as a whole was 'a corporate unit', its parts akin to organs of the same body. Kumarappa, *Village Movement*, pp. 16–17.

120 Kumarappa, *Village Movement*, pp. 18–20.

121 Kumarappa, *Village Movement*, p. 22.

122 Kumarappa, *Village Movement*, pp. 22–3.

123 Kumarappa, *Village Movement*, pp. 25–9.

124 Kumarappa, *Village Movement*, pp. 27–8, 30.

125 Kumarappa, 'The Village in Our Economy'. Sent to *India and World Affairs*, n.d., ff. 95–6, Speeches and Writings in Bound Volumes, Vol. II, JCK, NML.

126 Kumarappa, *Village Movement*, p. 21.

127 Kumarappa, *Village Movement*, p. 28. Kumarappa elaborated these ideas in a later work: Kumarappa, *The Economy of Permanence* (Wardha, 1948). (Kumarappa recycled his writing a good deal. As he was also a prolific journalist, a great number of his articles also recycle earlier material; his main arguments remain simple, and the rest is elaboration from first principles.)

128 'Place of Science in the Industrial Development of India: Inaugural lecture to the Science Association of Nagpur University at the Convocation Hall, by Sjt J.C. Kumarappa, Secretary, All India Village Industries Association', n.d., ff. 299–305, Speeches and Writings in Bound Volumes, Vol X, JCK, NML.

129 'Summary of a speech delivered at the Mysore Swadeshi Exhibition of 30th May 1936 by Sjt. J.C. Kumarappa', ff. 189–91, Speeches and Writings in Bound Volumes, Vol X, JCK, NML.

130 Kumarappa, 'Intelligent Buying', *Gram Udyog Patrika*, July 1941, reprinted in *Gram Udyog Patrika, Part I* (Madras, 1971), pp. 191–3; Kumarappa, 'Consumer's Duty', *Gram Udyog Patrika*, April 1946, reprinted in *Gram Udyog Patrika, Part I* (Madras, 1971), pp. 415–16; Kumarappa, *Village Movement*, chapter IX: 'The Place of Women', pp. 70–81.

131 Kumarappa, *Village Movement*, chapter IX: 'The Place of Women', pp. 70–1.

132 Kumarappa, *Village Movement*, pp. 70–3.

133 Women's education was considered especially necessary by Kumarappa for another reason: because women were 'the natural custodians of the generations to come'; at an early stage of a child's life, women were '[b]y temperament and natural endowment' better equipped to deal with it. Kumarappa, *Village Movement*, pp. 182. Such clearly ascribed roles for women were an essential part ofthe public statements of Gandhi or the Gandhians. J.B. Kripalani, while making a speech to popularize khadi, apparently told his audience that he could not understand why women complained that khadi saris were too heavy when they bore the weight of their husbands every night. This was reported to Nehru by a correspondent, who asked him whether this was not overstepping the limits of decent politics: M.N. Chadha to Jawaharlal Nehru, 13 October (1933?), JNP, NML, Part 1. Vol. IX, f. 129. (It might be noted in parentheses that Kripalani's missionary zeal also seems to have assumed the missionary position).

134 Kumarappa, 'Balanced Cultivation', *Gram Udyog Patrika*, June 1946, reprinted in *Gram Udyog Patrika, Part I* (Madras, 1971), p. 423.

135 Typescript of article, 'A Catechism on the All India Village Industries Association', *Contemporary India*, 29/6/1935, f. 9, Speeches and Writings in Bound Volumes, Vol. II, JCK, NML.

136 Outline of speech by Kumarappa on 'Gandhiji's Programme of Village Reconstruction', made at Jinnah Hall, [place not stated], 29 September 1941, f. 293, Speeches and Writings in Bound Volumes, Vol. X, JCK, NML.

137 See JCK: Notebooks, especially, SI. Nos. (2), (4), and (10), NML. Kumarappa seems to have read a number of extremely eclectic critiques of capitalism; and his first encounters with the ideas of Soviet Marxism seem to have been through the accounts of Fabians. His notebook for 1936 contains notes from Sidney and Beatrice Webb's *Soviet Communism*, which he summarized in two pages, apparently without much interest in it—at a time when he had presumably already written much of *Why the Village Movement?*—Kumarappa, Notebooks, SI. No. (4), pp. 55–6, JCK, NML. There is no indication that he had read much more than this, though he ought to have read a fair amount of J.A. Hobson, judging by the course outline provided by Seligman. See Kumarappa, Notebooks, SI. No. (2).

138 See Dasgupta, *Gandhi's Economic Thought*, pp. 100–104.

139 Quoted in Partha Chatterjee, *Nationalist Thought*, p. 93 and Note 28, p. 126.

140 See Kumarappa, 'The Economy of the Cross', a summary of three addresses to the Mid-India Conference of Christian Students at Nagpur, 5–7 November 1942, reprinted in Kumarappa, *Christianity: Its Economy and Way of Life* (Ahmedabad, 1945), and other essays in that volume.

141 J.J. Anjaria, *An Essay on Gandhian Economics* (1944), quoted in Bhabatosh Datta, *Indian Economic Thought*, p. 158.

142 See Chapter 5 of this book.

143 *Science and Culture*, Vol. IV, No. 10 (April 1939), editorial, p. 535.

144 Partha Chatteijee, *Nationalist Thought', The Nation and its Fragments*, chapter eleven.

145 Rather than, as in the version provided by so much 'cold war' developmental rhetoric, maintain a distinction between 'tradition' and 'modernity', with the latter being identified by adherents of the former as 'Western'.

146 Even though, at the level of the particular, British precedent was regularly cited as a reason to introduce a particular measure in India, this was usually by way of accusing the British of inconsistency with proclaimed values.

147 I am referring here to work following from Partha Chatteijee's *Nationalist Thought*, the phrase 'derivative but different', Chatterjee's own, has become, in the work of some subsequent scholars, one which is regarded as an adequate summary of his views on the nature of nationalist thought in the colonial world—rather unfortunately, as it does no justice to the details of his arguments.

148 That is, 'Orientalists' in the pre-Saidian sense of the term.

149 The Indian case was perhaps not unique either; through the nineteenth century and into the twentieth, various nationalisms had claimed that their nation had always existed, while radical strands within them had been anxious to bury the unpleasant and undistinguished past.

150 See Chapter 5 of this volume.

151 P.S. Narayan Prasad, quoted in Kumarappa, 'Violence in Economic Activity', typescript of article for the *Harijan*, n.d., in reply to an article in *Twentieth Century* by Narayan Prasad, f. 56, Speeches and Writings in Bound Volumes, Vol. II, JCK, NML. The phrase 'at the behest of the Bombay Congress' was a reference to the Congress right, which was seen to be an ally of Indian big business.

152 Kumarappa, 'The Message of Khadi', *Gram Udyog Patrika*, April 1940.

153 M.K. Gandhi, 'Why Khadi for Yarn and Not for Money?', *Gram Udyog Patrika*, July 1945.

154 For instance, Kumarappa, 'A Stone for Bread', *Gram Udyog Patrika*, December 1942.

155 R.B. Lotvala to Kumarappa, 21 March 1949, ff. 1–2, Correspondence with Lotvala, JCK, NML. Lotvala is described by Sumit Sarkar as 'a millionaire with socialist leanings', who supplied Marxist literature to S.A. Dange's group of student radicals in Bombay in the 1920s—a connection which led to Dange's writing of *Gandhi vs Lenin* in 1921 (Sumit Sarkar, *Modern India*, p. 212). He was also extremely interested in eugenics, which he sought to promote in India: see Sarah Hodges, 'Indian Eugenics in an Age of Reform', in Sarah Hodges (ed.), *Reproductive Health in India: History, Politics, Controversies* (Delhi, 2003), pp. 123–4.

156 Lotvala to Kumarappa, 31 March 1949, f. 3, Correspondence with Lotvala, JCK, NML. Kumarappa had replied to Lotvala's earlier letter to say that he did not have the time to read Lotvala's writing.

157 Kumarappa, 'Violence in Economic Activity', typescript of article for the *Harijan*, n.d., in reply to an article in *Twentieth Century* by Narayan Prasad, f. 56, Speeches and Writings in Bound Volumes, Vol. II, JCK, NML.

158 Narayanaswami Iyer to Kumarappa, 11 May 1947, Subject File No. 12, JCK, NML.

159 See Thomas Metcalf, *Ideologies of the Raj* (Cambridge, 1994), for a summary.

160 For an overstated case, which argues that all imaginings of India, except for those of the communists, were 'religious nationalist', see Peter van der Veer, *Religious Nationalism: Hindus and Muslims in India* (Berkeley, 1994); see also my review of the book in *Modern Asian Studies*, Vol. 32, No. 1 (1998). A tendency to see 'Hindu' India as an ancient and sophisticated civilization, in opposition to British claims of Indian 'backwardness', I would argue, falls short of constituting a religious nationalism. There were, of course, explicit attempts to push forward the idea of an aggressively 'Hindu' and exclusionary India, but these were by no means universally accepted even by those who drew on the model of a glorious Hindu past.

161 T.V. Narayanaswami Iyer to Kumarappa, 11 May 1947, Subject File No. 12, JCK, NML.

162 The contexts to the 'communalism' of the 1940s must be kept in mind here; but rather than argue that there was such a thing as 'communal consciousness' as a clearly defined and coherent world view, it is more plausible to argue that a variety of factors contributed to a privileging of 'Hindu' or 'Muslim' identities in the 1940s; and that this privileging was neither inevitable nor immutable.

163 N.G Bedekar, Aurangabad, to Kumarappa, n.d., but sometime in late 1948, Subject File No. 12, JCK, NML.

164 Kumarappa to Bedekar, 6 December 1948, Subject File No. 12, JCK, NML. Emphasis mine.

11

Nationalist planning for autarky and state hegemony

Development strategy under Nehru

*Baldev Raj Nayar**

Source: *Indian Economic Review*, 32:1 (1997), 13–38.

The break in economic policy instituted in the mid-1950s under Nehru, with economic planning, autarky and building socialism as its centrepiece, is of historic importance, at least for India. All three elements also lie at the core of economic nationalism. Autarky, of course, is equated with economic nationalism by definition and is used interchangeably with it as well as with economic independence and economic self-sufficiency, involving "a deliberate rejection of external relationships than simply manifesting indifference or ignorance of their possibilities". But no less important is the connection of planning and socialism with economic nationalism. It has been rightly claimed that planning is "an assertion of economic nationalism", "a formal expression of sovereignty by the state, and of an intention to exert ultimate direction and control. It is a symbol of independence". Similarly, "a fairly well-defined position purports that the practical success of economic nationalism is inconceivable without the presence of key components of socialism". Indeed, such a position has been pushed even further to maintain that "in the absence of an appropriate socialist commitment, no claim to be nationalistic can be accepted as valid. Economic nationalism is, then, in some versions and some accounts actually subsumed under socialism" (Burnell, 1986, pp. 37, 78, 209).

Setting aside for the moment the controversies surrounding the question whether the Indian endeavour at policy change was rigorous or authentic enough so as to be dignified by using the terms economic planning, autarky and, particularly, building socialism, these three features can nonetheless be said to define, in some measure, the *Indian development pattern*. A "development pattern" has been considered to have three dimensions: (1) the kind of industries accorded prominence; (2) the orientation of these industries to the world economy (whether they are oriented inward or outward); and (3) the economic agents chosen for development (Gereffi and Wyman, 1990, p. 17). In the Indian development pattern, firstly, the emphasis was placed on capital goods, metal-making and heavy engineering industries, also referred to as heavy, basic or investment goods industries in Indian planning; secondly, these industries were inward-oriented and were expected to make the Indian economy self-sufficient as well as self-reliant for future sustained growth; and, finally, they were to be both owned and managed by the state. While this development pattern was executed with full force only between 1956 and 1965, it can be considered to have lasted in its broader dimensions, at times in intensified form and at others in attenuated form, until 1985 and indeed until 1991.

That much is clear. The important question is what led to the change in economic policy as a historic rupture that resulted in this development pattern. That issue relating to the origins of the particular policy change forms the central focus of this article.

There are two major interpretations in the literature, with the proponents of both referred to here being only illustrative and not exhaustive. One interpretation focuses on economic theory or economic ideas of the time as being influential in the policy change, or at least as theoretically validating the policy stance adopted by Indian economic planners. A key proponent of this view has been the distinguished internationally- renowned economist as well as noted economic planner, the late Sukhamoy Chakravarty. The immediate intellectual basis for the economic strategy that led to the Indian development pattern had been the "plan-frame" for the Second Five Year Plan (1956–1961) and the underlying economic model, both having been put forward by the eminent economic planner P.C. Mahaianobis, and accordingly characterized as the Mahalanobis model. Chakravarty (1987, 1993) justifies the Mahalanobis model by reference to contemporaneous economic theory and economic ideas, referring in different contexts to Harrod and Domar, Hicks, Lewis, Nurkse, Prebisch, and Rosenstein-Rodan. Similarly, another economist and economic planner with a long record of service in high economic positions in the government, Bimal Jalan (1991), also refers to the prevailing economic ideas of the time as influential in determining the economic strategy set out in the Second Plan. These authorities may additionally refer to other factors in justification of the strategy, but the primary thrust of their argument is to place reliance on what may be called "the power of theory", that is, economic theory.

The other interpretation, which is held by Marxist activists and scholars, debunks any claims to building socialism and forthrightly proclaims the intent in the economic strategy as building, instead, capitalism on behalf of the bourgeoisie or capitalist class. The eminent communist leader E.M.S. Namboodiripad (1988, pp. 2, 226) thus declares that Nehru "represented, and acted as the spokesman of a particular class – the Indian bourgeoisie" and that his economic plans "were all in line with the objectives of the bourgeoisie as a class". Similarly, the Marxist scholar Prabhat Patnaik (1994) states that "the class-configuration which prevailed, upon which industrial capitalism was to develop, dictated in broad terms a certain course of action, and the Mahalanobis strategy fitted in with this".

As against the first of these two interpretations, the position taken in the story as it unfolds here is that, while in a proximate sense a case can be made, no doubt, about the affinity between the Mahalanobis model and the then prevailing economic theory, that argument establishes what is only a surface relationship, which serves merely to detract from a deeper analysis into the origins of the model. In a more profound sense, the Mahalanobis model was founded on the historical commitment of the freedom movement to economic nationalism. Without in any way minimizing the theoretical merits of the Mahalanobis model, or its conjunctural importance in the formalizing of the Indian economic strategy, or its intellectual affinity with contemporaneous economy theory, it would be no exaggeration to say that the model simply provided a theoretical scaffolding as it were for an economic architecture already determined on political grounds, without the benefit of or any reference to economic theory. In this perspective, a more appropriate explanation for the strategy is a "theory of power", as will be demonstrated here, instead of the power of theory.

As for the second interpretation, it would seem that it errs in making a mechanical application of the Marxist theory of state power and class agency, derived from the single model of the industrialization of Britain, to the entirely different situation of India. As a consequence, it neglects the specificity of India's class structure, power configuration, and ideological currents. As against this interpretation, the argument here will emphasize the importance of the ideological commitment of certain strategically placed political leaders to socialism in the context of a different balance of class forces that essentially excluded the capitalist class from state power. It is curious why Marxist activists and scholars, who are themselves convinced of the merits of the Marxist mode of analysis and are committed to the ideal of socialism notwithstanding their own petit bourgeois background, deny or fail to see the impact of ideology in the case of others. In the discussion that follows, the first and second sections critically examine each of the preceding two interpretations in that order.

I. The Mahalanobis model and its origins

The Mahalanobis model belongs to the general family of economic models encompassed under the rubric of what is known as the Harrod-Domar model. The latter model had already been employed in the formulation of the First Five Year Plan (1951–1956) though really only redundantly, for the First Plan had in essence little to do with serious economic planning since it was essentially an aggregation of projects already under way or readily available on the shelf. As a renowned statistician of world eminence, but initially without familiarity with the economic literature, Mahalanobis had developed the conceptual foundations of his model independently without any awareness of the Harrod-Domar model, but when the latter was brought to his attention he graciously acknowledged its temporal priority. The Harrod-Domar model is focused on capital accumulation as the engine of economic growth; its aim was to determine for developed economies the rate of investment necessary to assure such increase in national income as to provide full employment. The Mahalanobis model went further, however; going beyond the aggregate requirements of investment, it specified the various sectors within the economy in which investment ought to take place and in what measure in order to make the structural leap from an agricultural underdeveloped economy to an industrial developed economy. The model was nonetheless focused on the operational requirements specifically of the Indian case without any larger claim of contribution to economic theory. It had arrived at that stage not in one blow, but had evolved in several steps.

In 1952, Mahalanobis had developed a model which treated the entire economy as a single sector and, on the basis of empirical data on the growth experience of the US (S. Kuznets) and of the UK (A.R. Prest and L.H. Lenfant), he suggested – in the fashion of Arthur Lewis (1954) later in his article on "Economic Development with Unlimited Supplies of Labour" – that India needed to increase its annual rate of investment as a proportion of national income from 5 per cent to 10 or 11 per cent if it wished to double its per capita income in 35 years (Mahalanobis, 1985, pp. 4, 53, 74, 83–84).[1] In 1953, he went on to elaborate the single sector model into a two-sector one, differentiating the two sectors on the basis of whether they produced investment goods or consumer goods, along with making the implicit assumption of a closed economy. His distinction between the two sectors paralleled, though it did not completely follow, Marx's division between Department I and Department II.

The two-sector model was crucial to the formulation of the final Mahalanobis model; its main conclusion, based on a set of mathematical equations, was that "in the initial stage of development, the larger the percentage [of] investment on consumer goods industries, the larger will be the income generated. But there is a critical range of time and as soon as this is passed, the larger the investment in investment goods industries the larger will be the income generated. Hence, it would be desirable to invest relatively more on the consumer goods industries provided we are interested in the immediate future. If, on the other hand, we are interested in the more distant future, relatively larger investment on investment goods industries would give distinctly better results" (Mahalanobis, 1985, p.15). This stance on investment became of elemental importance in the evolution of India's economic strategy, which had – as had Mahalanobis himself – considerations of long-term development as its foremost preference. The model, with its preference for the investment goods industries sector, was similar to the Feldman model developed in the Soviet Union in 1928.[2]

The final Mahalanobis model – as conceptualized in 1955 in "The Approach of Operational Research to Planning in India", and applied in the "plan-frame" under the prosaic title of "Recommendations for the Formulation of the Second Five Year Plan" – was, unlike his previous two contributions which revolved around growth models, an allocation model intended to determine the broad sectoral outlays. For its time, it was a marvel of ingenuity, sophistication and precision in development planning. For purposes of allocation, the two-sector model was now further elaborated, so that while (1) the basic investment goods industries sector was retained as such, the consumer goods sector was divided into three sectors: (2) factory consumer goods industries; (3) household industries, including agriculture; and (4) services. In this final model, the basic task for the Second Plan was set by the two objectives of (a) an annual increase of 5 per cent in national income, and (b) additional employment for 11 million persons over the plan period (Mahalanobis, 1985, pp. 23–24, 49, 55, 71, 73). Not all the allocations were generated by the variables within the analytical model, however. The process of allocation was initiated with the exogenous injection of a well-reasoned, though in the final analysis arbitrarily determined, allocation of one-third of total investment to sector 1, as against the existing share in investment of one-tenth, "broadly from considerations of long period development" (Mahalanobis, 1985, pp. 78, 86–87, 89, 95). The allocations for sector 2 (17 per cent), sector 3 (21 per cent), and sector 4 (29 per cent) were figured out on the basis of both the expected productivity of investment and the employment generation potential of investment in each sector, in order to arrive at – in combination with the allocation for sector 1 – the annual growth of national income of 5 per cent and additional employment for 11 million persons.

The logic of the differential allocations within the consumer goods sector can be illustrated with reference to the competing claims of factory consumer goods industries and household industries. The former were far more consumptive of capital even as they were far less labour-intensive in comparison to the latter. Accordingly, in order to assure increased employment, Mahalanobis (1985, p. 72) was led to place constraints on the factory production of consumer goods. He was emphatic in his negative and restrictive posture on such production.

> Until employment is brought under control there should not be, therefore, any fresh investments to expand factories which compete with the small and household units of production. In addition, in special cases, it may be also necessary to impose a temporary ban on further expansion of factory production which is competitive with small scale or hand production. This may result in some surplus factory capacity remaining idle temporarily. It may be better to allow machines to remain idle rather than to keep human beings unemployed.

Going even further, he stated:

> The price of hand-made goods would be sometimes higher than the price of factory-made goods of comparable quality. A simple remedy is to levy suitable excise duties on factory-made goods to preserve price parity with hand-made goods at any desired level.

In the final analysis, the entire economic strategy of the Mahalanobis model rested on a single fulcrum, on the one side of which lay what were believed to be strategically required investments for heavy industries – but which in the interim led to new demand – while on the other side were investments on small and household industries that were deemed necessary precisely to satisfy the new demand, with the essential aim of the strategy being to balance the two sides. If in the process the factory consumption goods industries sector – which lay between the state-owned heavy industries sector and the privately-owned small industries sector – was squeezed to meet the requirements of maintaining that balance, no tears needed to be shed for it since restrictions on it, stemming from the technical requirements of the model, additionally met other socially-motivated goals of the planners from the viewpoint of limiting concentration of wealth and power.

In making the case for small-scale and household industries, Mahalanobis did not mean to plan for a technologically dualistic economic structure. His larger objective of achieving a universally modern economy was clear, with the small industry sector meant only for a transitional phase. As Mahalanobis (1985, p. 118) put it:

> The long-term aim would be to use as quickly as possible the most technologically advanced machinery for the production of both investment and consumer goods. This is not immediately possible because of the

> lack of a sufficiently broad base of heavy industries. It is, therefore, necessary to plan for a transition phase, in which preference would be given to capital-light and labour-intensive small scale and household industries to create as much employment as possible in the immediate future and, at the same time, to release capital resources for the heavy industries. However, as the economy expands and employment increases the need of giving preference to labour intensive but low-efficiency production would decrease. As the supply of power, machinery and other capital goods increases, a gradual and steady change-over would be made to more efficient forms of production by the increasing use of machinery driven by power.

The Mahalanobis model was critical to the determination of India's economic strategy, for it not only settled the contours of the Second Plan but more generally for the Indian approach to economic development over the long term; in addition, it by and large determined the final outlays of the Second Plan. Of the three components constituting a development pattern, the Mahalanobis model definitively determined (1) the inward orientation of the economy and (2) the powerful thrust for the basic investment goods industries. In so far as the former was concerned, the closed nature of the economy was simply assumed. No balance of payments considerations entered into the calculations of the model. There was some reference to foreign trade but foreign trade as such did not figure in either the architecture of the model or its details. More importantly, one aim in the thrust for the investment goods industries was not just to assure long-term development but also to cut down, indeed eliminate, dependence on the outside world in the future. This stance of attempted autarky has been attributed to what has come to be characterized as export pessimism or export fatalism on the part of Indian planners. In this view, the markets of the developed world were assumed not to hold any improved prospects for the commodities or products produced by India at that stage in its development. In turn, the resultant poor prospects for exports would have constrained development, because of the consequent inability to obtain capital goods in exchange. Accordingly, India needed to develop its own investment goods industries in order to avoid the trade constraint on its future development.

The third component of the Indian development pattern of (3) state ownership and management of major industry, with the public sector seizing the "commanding heights" of the economy, stood on a different footing as it did not necessarily stem from the Mahalanobis model. As Mahalanobis (1985, pp. 98–99, 113–14) stated it, the model was a technical model and was neutral in regard to ownership. The issue of ownership, he said, was a matter of choice for party and government policy, which had by the time of the formulation of the "plan-frame" already ruled in favour of state ownership of heavy industry. However, Mahalanobis (1985, pp. 116–17) himself endorsed that choice, and indeed advanced instrumental economic reasons for placing the heavy industries in the public sector, maintaining:

> The heavy machinery industry should be in the public sector. For rapid industrialization of an under-developed country it would be desirable to keep the cost of capital goods as low as possible. The further removed the type of capital goods under consideration is from the production of final consumer goods the greater is the need of keeping the price low. Heavy machinery which would manufacture machinery to produce investment goods is the furthest removed from the consumption end. It is essential, therefore, that Government should have complete control over the heavy machinery industry so as to be able to fix prices to suit national needs. Such control would enable Government to shape the future pattern of industrialization through a properly planned programme of production of heavy machinery. If imports are properly regulated it would be also possible to influence the pattern of investment in the private sector through Government policy in respect of the production and price of heavy machinery for that sector.

Economic theory and the Mahalanobis model

What was the bearing of economic theory and economic thinking on the conceptualization of the Mahalanobis model? Neither Chakravarty nor Jalan necessarily trace a direct lineal descent from contemporaneous economic theorists or their thinking to the Mahalanobis model. Nor do they maintain that Mahalanobis was necessarily influenced directly by such economists or their ideas, but what they do demonstrate is that the profound ideas incorporated in the model were widely shared among economists of the time, that indeed there was a consensus over these ideas in development economics, and that Indian economists and planners partook of this consensus. In other words, the Mahalanobis model had a sound basis in economic theory of the time. However, the direct influence of economists, including foreign economists, cannot be altogether excluded. After all, the Indian Statistical Institute, which had been founded in 1931 by Mahalanobis and had been mandated by the government to develop the plan frame, had seen a stream of eminent foreign economists, though mostly of the progressive kind, visit it in connection with the development of the plan-frame. Among them during the winter of 1954–55 were: Ragnar Frisch (Norway); Oskar Lange (Poland); Charles Bettelheim (France); Richard Goodwin (UK); and D.D. Degtyar (Soviet Union) who headed a team of Soviet economists and statisticians. Mahalanobis (1985, pp. 54, 56) himself acknowledged that these visitors "helped us to think clearly; they made constructive criticisms about the logical basis of our thinking" and that the visit of Bettelheim was "particularly stimulating and helpful".

While the relationship of economic theory or ideas can be related to many aspects of the Mahalanobis model, here attention will be focused on the assumption of (1) the closed economy with its inward orientation and (2) the heavy industry strategy. The two were, of course, related and were joined in the assumption of export pessimism. Chakravarty and Jalan differ in their approach to tackling this element, with the former quite sharply focused on the Mahalanobis model while Jalan pays little attention, indeed none, specifically to Mahalanobis. Further, both often advance a multiplicity of factors in the choice of the economic strategy, which makes it difficult to determine what weight they really accord to economic thinking in the choice. However, there is certainly a greater emphasis on the importance of theory in Chakravarty.

In his survey of the Indian planning experience, Chakravarty (1987, pp. 1–2) states his objective to be "to ascertain and evaluate the type of reasoning that has gone into the formulation of Indian plans", and goes on to discuss "the economic theory underlying Indian plans", and indeed figures that *Economic Theory and Indian Planning* could also be a possible title for the book.[3] He goes on to delineate an interactive pattern of influence between early development economics and Indian planning. Not only was Indian planning "in the formulation of its theory, far more self-conscious than that attempted in many third world countries" but most major economists with an interest in development interacted with Indian planners and policy-makers in the 1950s and 1960s. There was as a consequence a two-way exchange: "Dominant ideas of contemporary development economics influenced the logic of India's plans, and correspondingly, development theory was for a while greatly influenced by the Indian case".

While acknowledging that the Second Five Year Plan "was heavily influenced by the work of Mahalanobis", Chakravarty characterizes the Second Plan's strategy as lacking "neither a theoretical rationale nor a measure of empirical plausibility", and underlines – as he approaches the issue of relationship between economic theory and Indian planning – several perceptions then prevalent about the underlying causes of structural backwardness. Chief among these perceptions were: (1) the extreme shortage of material capital as the basic constraint on development; (2) the low level of savings as a factor retarding capital accumulation; (3) the presence of structural limitations on converting savings into investment even if savings could be raised; and (4) the necessity of industrialization in order to employ underemployed rural labour, since agriculture faced long-term diminishing returns. Chakravarty then sees a direct link between these perceptions and planning through the medium of economic theory: "Given all these perceptions, it was felt that economic theory indicated that the basic questions relating to how much to save, where to invest, and in what forms to invest could be best handled with the help of a plan". At the same time, he emphasizes the wide consensus then prevalent on these perceptions:

> It will be noted that the economics profession in the fifties, especially during the early and middle part of the decade, subscribed to most of the perceptions presented above. It is enough to recall Arthur Lewis's famous dictum that the central issue for development economics was to understand how a country which saves 5% of its income is transformed into one which saves 20% of its income. The same view was expressed by A.K. Das Gupta, a prominent Indian economist with a classical bent of mind, who defined India's problem as one of "primary accumulation of capital". . . . On the third proposition, agreement was not so universal. While structuralists like Prebisch would have endorsed it, for most economists it was an empirical question. However, quite a few would have subscribed to Nurkse's "export lag" thesis, especially because of the heavy weight of primary products in India's export basket. Furthermore, the sharp fall in commodity prices after the Korean War also added to the plausibility of that proposition.

Chakravarty avers that "Indian planners operated on the assumption of a low elasticity of export demand accompanied by a system of strict import allocation. Thus they were in reality operating on the assumption of a nearly closed economy". However, he underlines the importance of eluding the savings constraint in the choice of the heavy industry strategy. For, if the economy was closed and savings had to be increased from about 5 per cent to 20 per cent over a 25 year period, then "inter-sectoral consistency over time would demand that the productive capacity of the capital goods sector would have to rise at an accelerated rate to convert growing savings into additional real investment. It was therefore the need to raise the real savings rate that led Indian planners to accord primacy to a faster rate of growth in the capital goods sector". He then speculatively adds: "doubtless there could have been other considerations such as building up defence capability". Similarly, he attributes the reluctance of the Indian state to take to an export strategy, based on India's considerable strength in textiles, to the political factor of not being forced to support a particular region-based group of industrialists.

In sum, the choice of the Indian heavy industry strategy at the time of the Second Plan reflected the thinking in the economics profession, and the key element that led to that choice was apparently export pessimism. Chakravarty cites in support the perception in the Second Plan to the effect that export earnings would increase only after industrialization has gone some distance, but does not enlighten us as to the opinion of Mahalanobis on the issue. That opinion should have been important since the strategy had already been determined in the Mahalanobis model, through a rigorously developed rationale, rather than in the Plan document

In his attempt at understanding the origins of India's economic strategy, Jalan focuses on several aspects: the emphasis on industrialization and the corresponding neglect of agriculture, the inward orientation of the strategy and its relationship to export pessimism, and the activist role of the state as entrepreneur. His multifold explanation is that "the initial choice of the strategy was a response to the prevailing intellectual perception of the initial conditions and the role of the state in development. India's own political and social history also supported the case for an inward-looking strategy of industrialization, with the state in command" (Jalan, 1991, p. 13).[4] Importantly, he underlines that foreign trade had only a small place in Indian planning, because it was believed that the trade regime had a built-in bias against underdeveloped countries "and partly because of the intellectual conviction that export prospects were severely limited".

Jalan then links Indian perception to economic thinking, stating: "The intellectual basis for pessimism about exports, which was widely shared by development economists of the time, was broadly the same as that articulated by Nurkse in his 'export lag' thesis". He repeats the theme by saying: "The conclusions of Prebisch (1950) and Singer (1950) – on the secular tendency of the terms of trade turning against countries exporting primary products and importing manufactures – had *an important impact* on the thinking of planners in developing countries. . . . Equally influential was Lewis's paper. . . . Singer, Prebisch and Lewis's works thus provided a powerful case for import substitution and protection". He then adds: "These perceptions were widely shared by political leaders and Indian intellectuals of the time, and the business of choosing an *economic strategy responded to these perceptions*". Having thus emphasized the impact of these economic thinkers on Indian planners, or at least the affinity between the ideas of the two, Jalan refers to several other factors as strengthening India's determination to build a self-reliant industrial base:

> The colonial experience was sufficient *to reinforce* the belief that the free-trade regime was biased against India and other developing countries and could not be relied upon to generate growth and improve living standards. The call for Swadeshi therefore became an important element in the political struggle against colonial rule. It was inevitable that, after independence, the building of an indigenous manufacturing base should become an important objective of economic policy. This strategy was also an aspect of the struggle for economic and political independence from the UK and other Western powers. The apparent success of the Soviet Union in building up a strong manufacturing base, and its emergence as a superpower within a relatively short period of time, strengthened belief in the efficacy of the state as the primary agent of accumulation.

Since Jalan employs the notion that the colonial experience served "to reinforce", and again reiterates that "these powerful economic arguments were *buttressed by* political perceptions and the ideas of political and intellectual leaders in developing countries", it would be fair to infer that for him it is the economic theory of distinguished thinkers such as Prebisch, Singer, and Lewis that was influential in the determination of Indian economic strategy.

Export pessimism and the Mahalanobis model

In view of the subsequent strong emphasis placed on the link between export pessimism and the heavy industry strategy, it comes as a surprise that there is no reference to such a link in the Mahalanobis model itself. Certainly, such an important premise which would have constituted as it were the very foundation of the model would have merited some reference somewhere in the lengthy over 110-page documentation of the "plan-frame" or the Mahalanobis model. Curiously, Chakravarty had in an earlier article, written jointly with Bhagwati, maintained that the planners gave very cursory attention to the question of the prospective stagnation in external demand for Indian goods, that the subsequent justification of the strategy in terms of stagnant world demand came "somewhat close to a ex *post facto* rationalization", and that "such a *crucial* assumption, if made, would surely have been examined more intensively!" (Bhagwati and Chakravarty, 1969, p. 7). Interestingly, Rosen (1966, p. 126) had already pointed out that exports were not a serious problem at the time of the preparation of the Second Plan and that the theoretical argument on export pessimism was essentially *post facto*.[5] It is noteworthy that Mahalanobis himself articulated five possible limiting factors that could undercut the achievement of the goals of the Second Plan – inadequacy of consumer goods production; inadequacy, equally, of capital goods production; lack of trained manpower; poor mobilization of financial resources; and rigidities of the administrative structure – but none pertained to the external sector.

Indeed, it is evident that the case for the heavy industry strategy was made, not on the basis of a prevailing export pessimism, but on the basis of viewing economic development in the light of a long-term "perspective" of 20 or 30 years (Mahalanobis, 1985, p. 73). Here the crux of the issue for Mahalanobis (1985, p. 75) was that in the single structural weakness of India's national economy – by way of the lack of capacity to produce capital goods, despite the country's abundant resources – lay the explanation for the vast and persistent unemployment; as he saw it:

> India has plenty of iron ore, coal and other natural resources. The long-term aim should, therefore, be to manufacture capital goods within the country rather than to import them. The proper strategy would be to bring about a rapid development of the industries producing investment goods in the beginning by increasing appreciably the proportion of investment in the basic heavy industries. As the capacity to manufacture both heavy and light machinery and other capital goods increases, the capacity to invest

> (by using home-produced capital goods) would also increase steadily and India would become more and more independent of the import of foreign machinery and capital goods.

The argument for the heavy industry strategy rested, not on a negative and reactive posture towards export pessimism, but on more positive foundations, where the foremost interest of long-term development was further conjoined with the related policy-engendered aim of economic independence. Early on, on the basis of the two-sector model of 1952, Mahalanobis (1985, p. 84) had "assumed that, with the progress of planning, the domestic supply of investment goods would become more and more important". Rather than evincing any immediate concern over export pessimism, he simply added: "That is, although in the beginning India will, no doubt, have to depend on imports of capital goods, the policy would be to make India *independent* of such imports as soon as possible. In the present model I have, therefore, assumed that there would be no imports or exports of investment goods" (emphasis in the original). In the "plan-frame", Mahalanobis (1985, p. 24) had asserted: "In the long run, the rate of industrialization and the growth of national economy would depend on the increasing production of coal, electricity, iron and steel, heavy machinery, heavy chemicals, and the heavy industries generally which would increase the capacity for capital formation". He then continued: "One important aim is to make India independent, as quickly as possible, of foreign imports of producer goods so that the accumulation of capital would not be hampered by difficulties in securing supplies of essential producer goods from other countries. The heavy industries must, therefore, be expanded with all possible speed".

Seemingly, then, economic independence had its own intrinsic value for Mahalanobis, without being justified by instrumental reasons such as export pessimism. Not that he was insensitive to external constraints but they belonged to a whole range of possibilities, not immediate pressures and not particularly focused on foreign trade. In a footnote to one statement on economic independence, Mahalanobis (1985, p. 84) explained: "This does not mean that India would not purchase capital goods from other countries. India would make such purchases but India would also manufacture and export capital goods. Secondly, if for any reason (such as lack of foreign currency, shortage of supply or high prices in the world market, state of blockade or war, etc.) there is difficulty in securing essential investment goods from abroad, India should be able to manufacture such goods within the country".

Throughout, Mahalanobis placed emphasis, consistently and persistently, on the long range, asking as to what would advance development over the long term, without any reference to export pessimism. Interestingly, his position on the heavy industry strategy, which constituted the heart of the model – with the aim of making India self-sufficient in capital goods industries – had firmed up before any possible adverse consequences from the end of the Korean war for exports were visible, as is evident from the two-sector model which had been developed by 1952. That position had to do with enhancing the capacity for long-term growth, indeed making India economically independent over the long run, and not with any syndrome of export pessimism. And here there is no hiding his penchant for self-sufficiency and independence from the world economy. As Mahalanobis (1985, p. 116) put it:

> India's present dependence on imports of capital goods is a fundamental structural weakness which must be corrected as quickly as possible. It would be obviously more economical from the national point of view to produce in India as much heavy machinery as possible because this would ensure a supply of capital goods which would make India increasingly independent of imports and would strengthen India's position in the world market. In my opinion, the development of the heavy machine building industry is, so important that, if necessary, targets of even steel, coal, or transport should be reduced to give higher priority to heavy machines because this would facilitate a much quicker rate of industrialization after four or five years.

The penchant for independence emerges also in the discussion on individual industries. Thus, for example, in relation to aluminium, Mahalanobis (1985, p. 77) argued: "The Plan-frame has recommended that the production of aluminium should be progressively increased with a view to replacing copper by aluminium to the largest extent possible. This would be a wise decision because it would increase production through the utilization of Indian resources; and would also make India progressively independent of imports of copper in future. This is the kind of thinking which made us give so much emphasis to the rapid development of the basic industries".

Mahalanobis did not necessarily advocate the necessity or desirability of India becoming "completely self-sufficient in the production of machinery". Nonetheless, he maintained:

> India should, however, acquire both the means of production and technical knowledge to be able, if and when necessary, to manufacture essential investment goods within the country. This is necessary for economic independence.

As he continued, Mahalanobis (1985, p. 117) took a position which was emphatically contrary to expectations of export pessimism:

> But under normal conditions India should continue to purchase abroad such machinery and capital goods as it would not be economic from a national point of view to manufacture in India. On the other hand, India should also develop in the course of time the production of specialized machinery for which there would be an external market. The policy should be to encourage both imports and exports of machinery and capital goods which would be of mutual benefit to India and other countries.

It is obvious from the foregoing that prevailing economic theory or more generally the thinking of economists as regards export pessimism had little to do with the heavy industry strategy as articulated in the Mahalanobis model. On the other hand, equally, there is no doubt that the model was, in a proximate sense, immensely influential in determining the shape of India's economic strategy and, hence, its development pattern. The question arises whether Mahalanobis was the original fountainhead of the heavy industry strategy – with its associated underlying aim of economic independence – on the basis of mathematical model-building, or whether he was simply the agent of other larger social forces emergent on the Indian scene. An answer to that question requires recourse to an exploration of recent history leading up to the formulation of the Second Plan.

The nationalist movement and economic planning

The aim of industrialization goes back to the beginnings of the nationalist movement in India, the organizational expression of which was the Indian National Congress, more commonly referred to as the Congress party. During the liberal or moderate phase of the movement, from 1885 to 1905, the goal of industrialization through large-scale industries was taken to be a self-evident proposition. Indeed, "by the end of the 19th century, the demand for rapid industrialization of the country along modern industries had assumed national proportions" (Chandra, 1966, pp. 65–89). The Congress leadership deemed such industrialization as essential for a variety of reasons: removing poverty and unemployment, eliminating the exclusive dependence on agriculture, developing the productive powers of the nation, achieving a higher level of civilization, and promoting national integration. Toward that end, the moderate leadership endorsed the prescriptions of List for state intervention in the economy for purposes of development, refusing to buy the laissez-faire logic proffered by the British colonial authorities.

By the first decade of the twentieth century, the moderate phase of nationalism had been overtaken by extremism and militancy. In one interpretation, this turn in the course of the nationalist movement sprang in part from the failure of colonial authorities to introduce political reform to meet Indian aspirations, but also importantly in part from the feeling that the authorities had betrayed the trust placed in them about bringing industrialization to India. What is more, it was felt that Britain did not simply fail in actively helping with industrialization, but that in actual fact it thwarted industrialization as a matter of deliberate state policy (Sheel, 1986).

Subsequently, after World War I, Mahatma Gandhi transformed the nationalist struggle into a mass movement of the new middle classes and the rich and middle peasantry, and similarly forged the Congress party into a mass organization. In the process, new leaders rose to the first ranks of the party, among them none more important than Jawaharlal Nehru, second only to Gandhi who later also designated him as his successor. Nehru, however, differed radically from Gandhi on economic policy. Gandhi was against industrialization out of philosophical conviction, believing it to be destructive of traditional civilization and its values. Instead, he wanted a society based on limited wants and organized in self-sufficient villages, relying on agriculture and household or cottage industries. Nehru as a modernizer, on the other hand, favoured nothing less than a full-dress industrialization of the country. In his presidential address to the Congress party at Lucknow in 1936, Nehru declared: "I believe in the rapid industrialization of the country; and only thus, I think will the standards of the people rise substantially and poverty be combated" (Norman, 1965, I, p. 434).

Nehru thereafter repeatedly advocated the case for industrialization and underscored the importance of economic planning. At his urging, the Congress party established in 1938 a National Planning Committee, with Nehru as chairman. With that, Nehru devoted lot of effort to working with industrialists, economists and political leaders on the committee in order to evolve a plan for India's future economic development. In the end, the effort proved abortive because of the drastic change in the political situation following the outbreak of World War II, soon to be followed by his own departure for jail. However, in the meantime, Nehru had already begun to underscore the importance of heavy industry. In a significant article he wrote before the Quit India movement of August 1942, which took him again to jail, Nehru set out the framework for an economic strategy which has an uncanny resemblance with that subsequently associated with the Second Plan. All the key features of the "plan-frame" are present here: the pre-eminent place accorded to heavy industry; the reliance on cottage industries for consumption goods; and the restraint on factory-made consumer goods. What is more, in its reasoning or economic logic for advocating the adoption of these measures, the text reads astoundingly like the Mahalanobis model document, though preceding it by more than a decade. Nehru stated:

> The objective aimed at should be maximum production, equitable distribution and no unemployment. With India's vast population this cannot be achieved by having big industry only, or cottage industry only. The former will certainly result in much greater production of some commodities, but the unemployment problem will remain more or less as it is, and it will be difficult to have equitable distribution. It is also likely that our total production will be far below our potential because of the wastage of labour power. With cottage industries only, there will be more equitable distribution but the total production will remain at a low level and hence standards will not rise. In the present state of India, of course, even widespread cottage industry can raise standards considerably above the existing level. Nevertheless they will remain low. There are other factors also which make it almost impossible for any country to depend entirely on cottage industry. No modern nation can exist without certain essential articles which can be produced only by big industry. Not to produce these is to rely on imports from abroad and thus to be subservient to the economy of foreign countries. It means economic bondage and probably also political subjection.
>
> Therefore it seems essential to have both big industries and cottage industries in India and to plan them in such a way as to avoid conflict. Big industry must be encouraged and developed as rapidly as possible, but the type of industry thus encouraged should be chosen with care. It should be heavy and basic industry, which is the foundation of a nation's economic strength and on which other industries can gradually be built up. The development of electric power is the prerequisite for industrial growth. Machine-making, shipbuilding, chemicals, locomotives, automobiles and the like should follow. All these, and others like them,

> are wealth-producing industries and work-producing industries which do not create unemployment elsewhere. Lighter industries should not be encouraged to begin with, partly because they are likely to come into conflict with cottage industries and thus create unemployment (Norman, 1965, II, p. 114).

It is manifest that the roots of India's economic strategy clearly lie here in the ideas of a man who later as prime minister and chairman of the planning commission presided over the launching of that strategy. Coming as this article did in the midst of World War II it could not have been influenced by export pessimism in relation to the less developed countries, for economic theory then paid no attention to them. Nor could it have been influenced specifically by scholars such as Lewis, Nurkse, Prebisch, or Singer, for Nehru's developmental framework had a substantial chronological priority over their work.

What is impressive about Nehru at this time, however, is not only that he had worked out India's economic strategy this early on and had provided a cogent economic rationale for it, but that his rationale was grounded in a profound understanding of its relationship to power and international politics. An insight into this understanding is provided by his dispute with Gandhi over the relevance of cottage industries to mass welfare. Nehru readily accepted the need for cottage industries as a transitional measure to cope with unemployment; much as Mahalanobis was to express it later, he stated in 1936: "I look upon them more as temporary expedients of a transition stage than as solutions of our vital problems" (Norman, 1965, I, p. 435). However, he absolutely would not countenance making them the sole mechanism of growth in his economic strategy. His reasoning for that posture combined both an economic and a political rationale; in a letter in 1939, he explained:

> But I cannot conceive of the world or of any progressive country doing away with the big machine. Even if this was possible, this would result in lowering production tremendously and thus in reducing standards of life greatly. For a country to try to do away with industrialization would lead to that country falling a prey, economically and otherwise, to other more industrialized countries, which would exploit it. For the development of cottage industries on a widespread scale, it is obvious that political and economic power is necessary. It is unlikely that a country entirely devoted to cottage industries will ever get this political or economic power, and so in effect it will not even be able to push cottage industries as it wants to (Norman, 1965, I, p. 697).

While in jail during World War II, Nehru thought further about the relationship between cottage industries and modern factory industry, and declared that "I am convinced that the rapid industrialization of India is essential to relieve the pressure on land, to combat poverty and raise standards of living, for defence, and a variety of other purposes." Then in a remarkably incisive passage, Nehru (1946, pp. 411–13) laid bare the political logic for his attachment to heavy industry:

> It can hardly be challenged that, in the context of the modern world, no country can be politically and economically independent, even within the framework of international interdependence, unless it is highly industrialized and has developed its power resources to the utmost. Nor can it achieve or maintain high standards of living and liquidate poverty without the aid of modern technology in almost every sphere of life. An industrially backward country will continually upset the world equilibrium and encourage the aggressive tendencies of more developed countries. Even if it retains its political independence, this will be nominal only and economic control will tend to pass to others. This control will inevitably upset its own small-scale economy which it has sought to preserve in pursuit of its own view of life. Thus an attempt to build up a country's economy largely on the basis of cottage and small-scale industries is doomed to failure. It will not solve the basic problems of the country or maintain freedom, nor will it fit in with the world framework, except as a colonial appendage.

What thus underlay the economic strategy of the Second Plan was not the power of economic theory, for Nehru could not have had access to it before it had been formulated for the underdeveloped countries, but a theory of power, to which he gave the fullest expression. Further, the economic nationalism embodied in the strategy was not simply negatively aimed at preventing domination by foreign powers, which India had experienced for some hundreds of years, but also more positively for assuring India a role in the future in the international community commensurate with its perceived importance stemming from its territorial and population size, geographic location and its past as a centre of civilization. These themes continued to be articulated by Nehru before and after the adoption of the economic strategy in the mid-1950s.

The Mahalanobis model was subjected to considerable scrutiny by economists and others immediately after its presentation. Critics called attention to its unreal-ism in respect of the neglect of agriculture and the wage goods constraint as well as the excessive reliance on the household sector to deliver on consumer goods; its irresponsibility in depending on deficit financing to a large extent and in neglecting balance of payments considerations; and its courting political risks by implanting a Soviet-style economic strategy in a representative political system (Shenoy, 1962, pp. 15–26; Vakil and Brahmananda, 1962, pp. 114–19). One critic found it full of inadequacies and asserted that it made sense only in the light of "what you are after. If you are asked (by, say, Pandit Nehru or Khrushchev) whether a particular target, which the government for some reason wants to achieve, can be achieved, you can answer the question with a model of Professor Mahalanobis' sort" (Sen, 1958). This would seem to be a harsh and uncharitable judgement. What is closer to reality is that both Nehru and Mahalanobis shared the same larger orientation in regard to economic strategy, rather than that Mahalanobis simply provided an economic rationale for Nehru's directives. Indeed, it could be argued that this orientation was by and large shared by most Indian intellectuals, either on their own or they had been brought up on it by the constant advocacy by Nehru over the years. As part of the same intellectual classes, most economists in India shared the same value orientation also. So did, in good measure, the capitalist class as well as the right wing of the Congress party, though they would have preferred to follow a strategy modeled after that of the Meiji regime in relying on the private sector rather than state ownership. It is precisely the foundation of the strategy in economic nationalism that explains why when, soon after the Second Plan was launched, many of the economic strains and dislocations that had been predicted for the strategy emerged, India persisted with it even as it made some modifications to cope with the crises.

Even though there developed a widely shared consensus around the strategy, Nehru was the most crucial actor in relation to the strategy since, not only had he first suggested the strategy and propagated it and mobilized support for it, he also held the reins of power in both party and government that implemented the strategy. Of course, in developing his notions about the appropriate economic strategy for India Nehru was himself powerfully influenced by the economic achievements of the Soviet Union precisely through a similar strategy. But the Soviet Union and more importantly the socialist ideology, which purportedly lay at the foundation of the Soviet Union and its economic strategy, were no less influential in the third element of India's development pattern – the state ownership and management of the heavy industries. Indeed, even though for purposes of analysis and discussion, the two elements of the heavy industry strategy and its inward orientation have been separated from state ownership here, for Nehru himself all three elements along with some others constituted a single seamless ensemble encompassed in his vision of a route to an eventually socialist society.

II. The ideological foundations of the public sector

The Marxist case on Nehru's planning as having been intended for building capitalism, rather than socialism, rests on the assertion that the state in India is a capitalist state in which state power is held essentially by a coalition of the bourgeoisie and landlords. In this view, the weakness of the bourgeoisie in the context of an economically backward society and the threat to it from western imperialism results in the reliance by the bourgeoisie on the state – which it controls – to launch a programme of industrialization, particularly in the area of heavy industry, for which it does not have the organizational capacity or the resources to meet the large requirements for investment (Kurian, 1975). It still must remain a mystery, however, how a class too weak to undertake industrialization on its own was strong enough to seize control of the state.

A particularly strong piece of evidence often advanced in behalf of the Marxist case is the extraordinarily ambitious Bombay or Tata-Birla Plan – and Patnaik specifically refers to it – which a group of eminent industrialists developed in 1945, a decade prior to the Mahalanobis plan-frame and model. That plan resembles the Mahalanobis effort in several respects: high ambition in terms of rapid industrialization, recognition of the necessity of centralized planning, emphasis on heavy industry for the explicit purpose of making India economically independent, the reliance on the state for the mobilization of resources, particularly through heavy deficit financing, and the need for strong state interventionism by way of regulation and controls as also for state ownership in certain sectors (Thakurdas, 1945). Although, as should be evident, Nehru's ideas on planning had preceded the Bombay Plan, the resemblance between the Bombay Plan and the Mahalanobis model is taken as sufficient evidence of the state acting on behalf, even if not at the behest, of the capitalist class.

In this argument, state ownership of heavy industries is seen as particularly advantageous for the capitalist class because, apart from the large outlays required for them which are beyond the capacity of private capitalists, such industries have a long gestation period during which no profits accrue and also because of their supposedly low profitability even subsequently, while they would provide state-subsidized inputs for the privately-owned consumer goods industries (Kurian, 1975). Of course, the hypothesis of reliance on state ownership because of the weakness of the capitalist class is held more widely than just by Marxists. Thus, for example, Jalan (1991, p. 22) states matter-of-factly: "Since the investment requirements in these sectors were high, largely beyond the capability of the private sector, and the financial profitability was low, it followed that such investments would have to be undertaken by the state".

The issue, however, is beset with ironies. When the plan-frame document was released, the representative organization of the capitalist' class, FICCI (Federation of Indian Chambers of Commerce and Industry) opposed the kind of economic strategy that was advocated in it. FICCI (1955) found it to be disturbing because of "differences of a basic character" in approaches to planning by government and business, and it took umbrage at "total comprehensive planning". More specifically, FICCI's concern was centred on the plan-frame's near-exclusion of the private sector from large-scale modern industry through the strategy of reliance on cottage and small-scale industry for consumer goods and on the public sector for producer goods. For its part, it advocated pushing forward with large-scale consumer goods industry, and rejected the artificial propping up of village industries "at *the cost of* organized industry". FICCI was dismayed at the diminished role given to the private sector, and challenged the assumption that the private sector did not have the resources for the kinds of projects envisaged in the public sector. It asked the planners "to avoid a doctrinaire approach embodying the prejudices of a few and resulting in viewing the private sector with suspicion or antipathy". However, the government did not budge from its determination to go ahead with the strategy, and the business class had to reconcile itself to the situation.

Of course, it has been suggested by some Marxist scholars that even when the state opposed what the capitalist class wanted and imposed its own programmes on it, the state still reflected the true interests of that class which the class itself was incapable of discerning! Thus, for example, one scholar (Rudra, 1985) states:

> how to explain the Government of India adopting a strategy which turned out to be one for building State Capitalism in the name of Socialism but which was

> initially opposed by the bourgeoisie itself? . . . This is one more instance in history of leaders of a ruling class being much more farsighted than individual members of the same class. The distance between the understanding of ruling class interests as perceived by ordinary individual members of the class and their representatives in the state can be so big that the former may actually oppose the actions of the state until they come to understand the real motive behind the state policies. . . . Nehru and his closest cabinet colleagues were alone crystal clear about what was happening – they alone did not suffer from any delusions.

It would really be futile to attempt to dispute this statement, for framed in the manner that it has been the statement lifts the argument beyond empirical social science.

There is, however, a further irony. As against the strong opposition of the capitalist class to the emphasis in the plan-frame on the public sector and the heavy industry strategy, the Communist Party of India (1977) endorsed the key features of the proposals embodied in the plan-frame, despite its having been the handiwork of a supposedly capitalist state:

> The proposals to build basic industries, if implemented, would reduce the dependence of India on foreign countries in respect of capital goods, strengthen the relative position of industry inside India and strengthen our economic position and national independence. The party, therefore, supports these proposals and also the proposal that these industries should be mainly developed in the public sector. It supports the proposal that the demand for consumer goods should be met, as far as possible, by better utilization of the existing capacity and by development of small-scale and cottage industries so that jobs are provided for an increasing number of people and maximum possible resources are available for the development of basic industries. The party not only supports these proposals but will *expose and combat* those who want them to be modified in a reactionary direction (emphasis added).

It is clear then that the capitalist class opposed the thrust of the plan-frame, while the Communist Party as the representative of the working class supported it. However, the reasons for opposition by the one and for support by the other were fundamentally the same. Both opponents and supporters saw the public sector as excluding important arenas of the economy from private accumulation. More fundamentally, both saw it as reducing the economic and political power of the capitalist class. Again, both saw it as effectively facilitating – to be dreaded by one side and welcomed by the other – the prospect eventually of abolition of capitalism and the capitalist class altogether. Such an outcome would occur either in a unilinear but peaceful fashion through the ever-increasing absolute and relative role of the public sector (as envisaged by Nehru and socialists of his persuasion), or in a dialectical fashion through the eruption of violent conflict between a weakened capitalist class and the strengthened socialist forces cohering around a potent public sector (as envisaged by the communists). What emerges plainly from the entire episode is the fact that, despite the difference in rhetoric and even more in strategy over the question of the mode of transition to socialism, Nehru and the communists essentially shared the same vision of the end of capitalism and the same calculations about the role of an expanding public sector in achieving it.

Contrary to what Marxists asserted, Nehru in the post-independence period was really not taken in by the argument that the Indian capitalist class was incapable of fostering industrialization. Rather, his ideologically-driven aim was to contain, undercut and eventually marginalize the power of the private sector. When he was attacked for excluding the private sector from the basic industries sector, Nehru (1968, p. 130) noted that the private sector already had some basic industries, and then added sharply that private business wanted more of such industries because "not only they might prove to be very profitable but because it gives them economic power". To Nehru that was unacceptable; he found it "highly objectionable that economic power should be in the hands of a small group of persons, however able or good they might be", and he was emphatic that "such a thing must be prevented". It is instructive that

Nehru, if he were truly building capitalism, did not say to the business community in respect of basic industries: "Look, friends, here is a field which is hot profitable for business, you should therefore let the state carry the burden on your behalf." Rather, he declared that this is a field which is apt to add to the economic power of business, and precisely for that reason he meant to pre-empt it for the public sector and to see that business stayed deprived of it.

Nehru, socialism, and the mixed economy

Fundamentally, Nehru's vision of the public sector stood on a different footing from that of the Bombay Plan, in relation to which there really exists a profound misunderstanding or misrepresentation. For the Bombay planners, the role of the state in the economy was only temporary, after the pattern of war-time restrictions, and to be "of limited duration and confined to specific purposes". Their aim was to build a more flourishing industrial capitalism. On the other hand, Nehru envisaged an ever-expanding sector, both absolutely and relative to the private sector, in possession of the commanding heights, fundamentally as a route to a socialist society. Nehru had come to this understanding of the role of an expanding public sector, as a mode of transition to socialism, before independence through self-reflection over a considerable period of time on how to adapt socialism to Indian conditions. Nehru had become an admirer of Marxist ideas by the late 1920s after meeting world revolutionaries in Europe and visiting the Soviet Union. Differing with Gandhi, he proclaimed in his presidential address to the Congress party in 1927 that he was a socialist and that India would have to go the socialist way if it meant to remove its poverty and inequality (Norman, 1965, I, pp. 195–210). In the years subsequent to that, he made it his personal mission to convert the youth and intelligentsia to his socialist creed through a whirlwind of speeches, writing and political campaigns. This effort not only earned him the hostility of the capitalist class but also brought him into conflict with Gandhi and other colleagues in the party, who were irked by what they felt to be his divisive activities that diverted attention from the main goal of independence. Gandhi had to rein him in occasionally, but Nehru nonetheless socialized a whole generation of youth into his ideology, and many from this generation subsequently came to occupy strategic positions in the party, government, media and academia after independence.

After he became chairman of the National Planning Committee in 1938, Nehru increasingly turned his attention to the question of adapting socialism to Indian conditions. He came to the conclusion that the mode of transition to socialism was to be by way of a "mixed economy", though it was not yet termed as such, under which all key industries were to be state-owned and state-managed. As the public sector expanded under a regime of planning in the mixed economy, the private sector would be reduced to an economic appendage, and thus a peaceful transition to socialism would take place. At the same time, in contrast to orthodox Marxists who were votaries of revolution, Nehru was committed to democracy as the political route to the socialist society, and for that commitment to socialism by consent he was ridiculed by them. Having arrived at this model before independence, Nehru had to be quiescent about socialism for several years after independence because of the turmoil of partition and the factional divisions within the party and government. Only in 1954, after he had consolidated his power both in the party and government, did Nehru begin to give public expression to the kind of society he eventually envisioned for India. In November, he made it clear that he rejected capitalism, because "a system which is based purely on the acquisitive instinct is immoral", even as he regarded its days to be numbered. More positively, Nehru ([1957], p. 17) declared:

> The picture I have in mind is definitely and absolutely a Socialistic picture of society. I am not using the word in a dogmatic sense at all. I mean largely that the means of production should be socially owned and controlled for the benefit of society as a whole. There is plenty of room for private enterprise there, providing the main aim is kept clear.

A month later, the Lok Sabha passed a resolution supporting Nehru's vision, and in January 1955 the Congress party in a historic resolution stated that "planning should take place with a view to the establishment of a socialistic pattern of society, where the principal means of production are under social ownership or control, production is progressively speeded up and there is equitable distribution of the national income". Significantly, referring to the two resolutions by parliament and party, Mahalanobis (1985, pp. 28, 56) acknowledged in the model document that "these decisions settled, in principle, the type of economic development of India in future", and in the plan-frame he recommended: "The public sector must be expanded rapidly and relatively faster than the private sector for steady advance to a socialistic pattern of economy".

The Second Five Year Plan (India, 1956, pp. 22–23) repeated the theme: "the basic criterion for determining the lines of advance must not be private profit but social gain. . . . The public sector has to expand rapidly . . . it has to play the dominant role . . . the public sector must grow not only absolutely but also relatively to the private sector". The Industrial Policy Resolution of 1956 then reserved solely for the public sector "all industries of basic and strategic importance, or in the nature of public utility services"; not only that, "other industries which are essential and require investment on a scale which only the State, in present circumstances, could provide, have also to be in the public sector. The State has, therefore, to assume direct responsibility for the future development of industries over a wider area". Even if one supposes that the private sector did not have the capacity to undertake such industries, no purpose other than an ideological one would seem to have been served by this deliberate exclusion by fiat. Meanwhile, the private sector was placed under a rigid system of licensing and strict controls over installation and expansion of industrial capacity. The Third Five Year Plan (India, 1961, pp. 7, 10, 50) later elevated the role of the public sector to a higher level, both practically and ideologically. It posited an "even more dominant" role for the public sector in economic development, and projected it "to grow both absolutely and in comparison and at a faster rate than the private sector". The end purpose in assigning this role to the public sector was the achievement of a socialist society: "In an underdeveloped country, a high rate of economic progress and the development of a large public sector and a cooperative sector are among the principal means for effecting the *transition towards socialism*" (emphasis added). Thus, once the principal means of production would come to be publicly owned while the private sector had been drastically reduced to a relatively insignificant position, the transition to socialism would be completed. Indeed, Nehru (1958, pp. 101–103) believed in respect of the future of the private sector that "gradually and ultimately it will fade away".

Congress party, state power, and socialism

The question arises as to how Nehru was able to prevail in having his plan in respect of heavy industries and the public sector accepted. For, prior to independence, even though Nehru had succeeded in converting a considerable part of the urban intelligentsia to socialism, the Congress party as such refused to accept socialism as its ideology or programme. The party did not accept socialism even during the half-dozen years or so after independence. The movement towards such acceptance began only after the death of Sardar Patel at the end of 1950. With Patel removed by the intervention of fate, Nehru then started the process of assuming supreme leadership within the party and government. The major event in the political conflict that followed was the ouster in a "political coup" of Purshottamdas Tandon from the leadership of the Congress party. Backed by Patel who had for long controlled the party machine, Tandon had earlier been elected as president by an almost evenly divided party split between the followers of Patel and Nehru. Not all those who supported the nominee of the Nehru group necessarily adhered to Nehru's ideology of socialism. Nehru evoked loyalty among the masses and party members the basis of which extended beyond ideology, for he was a political hero to them more for his record of sacrifice for the nationalist movement and his personal charisma. The election revealed that there was no consensus over Nehru's socialist model in the Congress party, as has at times been claimed. The consensus was imposed later by Nehru after he had assumed supreme leadership of the Congress party and consolidated his power in both party and government. Nehru could impose that "consensus" because he was critically important to the Congress party in winning power through elections as a result of his great mass appeal. There was thus an implicit bargain between the party and Nehru, the former exchanging the acceptance of socialism as its ideology for the assurance of power through electoral mobilization in the institutional context of a representative system. In the use of his critical position by Nehru to such powerful effect, Nehru demonstrated the merit of the "strategic contingencies theory", which refers to "the way in which particular participants in an organization can dominate, and influence structure, by their indispensability" (Ham and Hill, 1984, ch. 4).

Even conceding Nehru's strategic importance politically, it is still a marvel that one man could move an organization in a direction that it had refused to countenance in the past. What facilitated Nehru's converting the Congress party to his socialist project was the class configuration within the party. That particular class configuration developed as part of the historical evolution of the nationalist movement. That movement had been launched in the last quarter of the 19th century by the new middle class of the urban areas, which grew out of the impact of western education. The new middle class was later joined by much larger numbers from the middle and rich peasantry in several waves in the 1920s and 1930s. This class alliance between the middle class and the peasantry, but under the leadership of the middle class, finally succeeded in replacing the colonial power. Michal Kalecki (1976, ch. 4), the Marxist economist from Poland, conceptualized as "intermediate regime" precisely such a situation in less developed countries, where the intermediate strata of the new middle class and the rich and middle peasantry held state power. It is noteworthy that during the course of the nationalist movement, this primary alliance was supplemented by a subsidiary alliance which encompassed a largely passive capitalist class and a relatively small working class. Nonetheless, the newly-installed intermediate regime in India was able to adopt or accommodate policies largely consistent with the interests of the primary class alliance.

Some have held that the intermediate regime results in the state fostering an active and dominant public sector, referred to as state capitalism (Sobhan and Ahmed, 1980, pp. 8–9). Such is not necessarily the case. As seen earlier, the Congress party after independence was divided about equally between the Patel and Nehru factions after independence despite some two decades of strenuous missionary effort on the part of Nehru in behalf of socialism. Only the death of Patel enabled Nehru to use the lever of his mass popularity to implement his ideological platform, even if only in part. The structural factor that enabled him to do so was simply that the capitalist class was not in charge of the state. The Indian state was not a state of the bourgeoisie as has often been proclaimed; rather, as the history of the nationalist movement demonstrates, it was an intermediate state. The historically-based exclusion of the capitalist class from state power, even as the existence of that class was tolerated, allowed Nehru to implement his socialist project in relation to the public ownership of the principal means of production.

By the same token, given the nature of state power, Nehru's attempt at building socialism could not but remain incomplete and therefore eventually non-viable. Just as the exclusion of the capitalist class from state power allowed Nehru to act on his ideological platform against the wishes of the capitalist class, the sharing in state power, and indeed the pressure to achieve a dominant position in the coalition, by the rich and middle peasantry prevented Nehru from acting on the rural counterpart to the industrial strategy in his overall socialist programme – agrarian reform and land cooperatives. It is Nehru's failure on agrarian reform and land cooperatives that often results in questioning the very authenticity of his socialist convictions. However, just because one part of the project is thwarted by the particular configuration of power does not make the execution of the other part any less authentic in terms of its ideological origins.

Summary and conclusions

Two dominant features of the Indian economic strategy launched with the Second Five Year Plan in the mid-1950s were the thrust for investment goods industries and their inward orientation in a gigantic programme of import substitution industrialization (ISI). In the postwar period, whether in Latin America or in Asia, ISI seemed like a natural policy for the less developed areas, and accordingly a substantial economic literature developed in the 1950s and 1960s which endorsed that policy. It is quite understandable therefore that economic theorists and planners would detect the influence of economic theory in the Indian economic strategy. The endeavour at discovery of the influence of economic theory seems especially attractive since the economic strategy had its proximate origins in a highly sophisticated theoretical argument developed in the Mahalanobis model. Once the Mahalanobis model had been accepted, the strategy for the Second Plan followed as a matter of course. The Mahalanobis model itself both tempts and facilitates the endeavour to establish the influence of economic theory on it, or at least to find the affinity between it and the economic theory of the time, or at the very least to show the influence of the model as economic theory in its own right on the Second Plan's economic strategy.

Particularly important in the discourse has been the assumed commonality between the prevailing economic theory and the presumed underpinning of Indian economic strategy in respect of export pessimism. However, given that it would have assuredly been a strategic assumption for Mahalanobis in forging a model based on a closed economy, it is surprising that export pessimism does not figure in the model. Rather, that model has its own positive aims of long-term development and economic independence in working out an economic strategy for heavy industries and inward orientation. Thus despite the apparent affinity with ISI programmes elsewhere, the Indian model had its own autonomous origins. Just as there can be several different manufacturing processes for the same product, there can also be different origins for similar economic strategies, and these can be consequential for the economy.

Further investigation reveals, however, that the main features of the Mahalanobis model had all been pre-figured in the pre-independence thinking of Nehru, at whose instance the plan-frame and the Mahalanobis model had been prepared. That only serves to confirm the lack of impact of economic theory on the Indian economic strategy, since such theory was a development only of the 1950s. Rather, in Nehru's thinking the key considerations were sound industrial development, economic independence, and political survival of the nation in a power-driven international system. Mahalanobis can be said to have provided an elegant theoretical structure employing the language of economics for goals which not only Nehru but Mahalanobis himself, as well as most members of the intelligentsia, held in common. These goals had emerged not out of economic theory but nationalism, both economic and political. While historically industrialization has often been driven by economic nationalism (Kitching 1982), India's ISI strategy was rather distinctive in that it emphasized basic and heavy industries instead of consumer goods. The inspiration for that originated in Nehru's understanding of the logic of power in the international system and his admiration for the Soviet model.

The two elements in respect of heavy industries and inward-orientation were joined, in Nehru, with a third one of state ownership in a comprehensive ideology dedicated to the achievement of a socialist society through democratic means. Nehru thus endeavoured through his overall economic strategy to build socialism, and not capitalism as is alleged in Marxist interpretations. The reason he could push through his programme in respect of the heavy industry strategy and the public sector is that, apart from a fairly generalized nationalism, the state was in the control not of the capitalist class but of the intermediate strata consisting of the new middle class and the rich and middle peasantry. However, the class alliance in which the peasantry wielded considerable power also prevented Nehru from enacting agrarian reform and land cooperativization, thus eventually crippling his larger socialist project. In the process, the economic strategy was reduced to building autarky and state hegemony over the economy through a vast far-flung public sector (state capitalism) and a regulatory system of rigid controls over a restricted private sector (state commandism), rather than building socialism which Nehru had aimed for.

Any policy once introduced tends to create structures of support for itself and thus to perpetuate itself. In the case of India, the tendency toward policy inertia was reinforced by the particular origins of policy. India's economic strategy under Nehru issued out of ideology: a widely-supported economic nationalism in respect of heavy industries and their inward orientation, and a somewhat more narrowly-supported socialism in respect of state ownership. The ideological origins of policy favoured a tendency toward persistence in the policy even if it were shown to be less productive. Only crisis could shake the regime out of it.

Notes

* I would like to thank Professor Jagdish Handa, Department of Economics, McGill University, and the readers of the Review for their most constructive suggestions.

1 The important papers of Mahalanobis are available in a single collection: Mahalanobis (1985). The papers of the greatest relevance in the present discussion are those pertaining to (1) the single sector model: "National Income, Investment, and National Development", pp. 1–5; the two-sector model: "Some Observations on the Process of Growth of National Income", pp. 13–18; the "plan-frame": "Recommendations for the Formulation of the Second Five Year Plan", pp. 19–50; and the final Mahalanobis model: "The Approach of Operational Research to Planning in India", pp. 51–129.

2 Indeed, Mahalanobis (1985, p. 257) later pointed out that "a model of exactly this type was developed by Feldman in 1928 in the USSR ... The Indian work, however, was done completely independently of Feldman's findings". That is correct, for the non-Soviet world did not have access to the Feldman model until the late 1950s when Domar (1957) wrote about it. However, it has to be noted that Mahalanobis could not have been unaware of the material consequences of the Feldman model not only in the provisions of the Soviet Five Year Plans but also in the concrete economic performance of the Soviet Union.

3 The discussion of this work in the next few paragraphs relies on pp. 1–19.

4 The discussion in the next few paragraphs relies on Jalan (1991, pp. 13, 22–23, 28–29, 118); emphasis in the citations has been added.

5 See also Manmohan Singh (1964, pp. 153, 338), the burden of whose work was that "India failed to exploit fully even the available opportunities" and that "domestic factors operating in India also played a part in the stagnation of India's export earnings during the last decade", particularly "the rising domestic demand and also ... the stringent import restrictions which have been in force since 1957".

References

Bhagwati, Jagdish N. and Sukhamoy Chakravarty (1969), "Contributions to Indian Economic Analysis: A Survey", *American Economic Review, LIX*, no. 4, Part 2, pp. 1–73, September.

Burnell, Peter J. (1986), *Economic Nationalism in the Third World*, Wheatsheaf Books, Brighton, Sussex, UK.

Chakravarty, Sukhamoy (1987), *Development Planning: The Indian Experience*, Clarendon Press, Oxford.

—— (1993), *Selected Economic Writings*, Oxford University Press, Delhi.

Chandra, Bipan (1966), *The Rise and Growth of Economic Nationalism in India: Economic Policies of Indian National Leadership*, People's Publishing House, New Delhi.

Communist Party of India (1977), "Communist Party in the Struggle for Peace, Democracy and National Advance", pp. 416–40 in Mohit Sen, ed. *Documents of the History of the Communist Party of India*, vol. VIII (1951–1956), People's Publishing House, New Delhi.

Domar, Evsey M. (1957), *Essays in the Theory of Economic Growth*, Oxford University Press, New York.

FICCI (1955), *Second Five Year Plan: A Comparative Study of the Objectives and Techniques of the Tentative Plan-Frame*, New Delhi.

Gereffi, Gary and Donald L. Wyman (1990), eds. *Manufacturing Miracles: Paths of Industrialization in Latin America and East Asia*, Princeton University Press, Princeton, N.J.

Ham, Christopher and Michael Hill (1984), *The Policy Process in the Modern Capitalist State*, Wheatsheaf Books, Brighton, Sussex.

India (1956), *Second Five Year Plan*, Planning Commission, New Delhi.

India (1961), *Third Five Year Plan*, Planning Commission, New Delhi.

Jalan, Bimal (1991), *India's Economic Crisis: The Way Ahead*, Oxford University Press, Delhi.

Kalecki, Michal (1976), *Essays on Developing Economies*, Harvester Press, Hassocks, Sussex.

Kitching, Gavin (1982), *Development and Underdevelopment in Historical Perspective: Populism, Nationalism and Industrialization*, Methuen, London and New York.

Kurian, K. Mathew (1975), ed. *India – State and Society: A Marxian Approach*, Orient Longmans, Bombay.

Lewis, W. Arthur (1954), "Economic Development with Unlimited Supplies of Labour", *Manchester School*, vol. *22*, pp. 131–91.

Mahalanobis, P.C. (1985), *Papers on Planning*, edited by P.K. Bose and M. Mukherjee, Statistical Publishing Society, Calcutta.

Namboodiripad, E.M.S. (1988), *Nehru: Ideology and Practice*, National Book Centre, New Delhi.

Nehru, Jawaharlal (1946), *The Discovery of India*, The John Day Company, New York.

—— (1953), *Speeches: Volume Three: March 1953 – August 1957*, Publications Division, New Delhi.

—— ([1957]), *Planning and Development: Speeches of Jawaharlal Nehru, 1952–56*, Publications Division, New Delhi.

—— (1968), *Speeches: Volume Five: March 1963 – May 1964*, Publications Division, New Delhi.

Norman, Dorothy (1965), ed. *Nehru; The First Sixty Years*, The John Day Company, New York.

Prabhat, Patnaik (1994), "Critical Reflections on Some Aspects of Structural Change in the Indian Economy", ch. 4 in Terence J. Byres, ed. *The State and Development Planning in India*, Oxford University Press, Delhi.

Rosen, George (1966), *Democracy and Economic Change in India*, University of California Press, Berkeley.

Rudra, Ashok (1985), "Planning in India: An Evaluation in Terms of Its Models", *Economic and Political Weekly*, *XX*, no. 17, pp. 758–64.

Sen, Amartya Kumar (1958), "A Note on the Mahalanobis Model of Sectoral Planning", *Arthaniti I*, no. 2, May.

Sheel, Alok (1986), "Peasant Nationalism in India in the Gandhian Era", pp. 67–92 in Amit Kumar Gupta, ed. *Agrarian Structure and Peasant Revolt in India*, Criterion Publications, New Delhi.

Shenoy, B.R. (1962), "The Second Five Year Plan: A Note of Dissent on the Basic Considerations Relating to the Plan Frame", pp. 15–26 in India, Planning Commission, *Papers Relating to the Formulation of the Second Five Year Plan 1955*, Manager of Publications, Delhi.

Singh, Manmohan (1964), *India's Export Trends and the Prospects for Self-Sustained Growth*, Clarendon Press, Oxford.

Sobhan, Rehman and Muzaffer Ahmed (1980), *Public Enterprise in an Intermediate Regime: A Study in the Political Economy of Bangladesh*, Bangladesh Institute of Development Studies, Dacca.

Thakurdas, Purshotamdas et al. (1945). *Memorandum Outlining A Plan of Economic Development for India*, Penguin Books, London.

Vakil, C.N. and P.R. Brahmananda (1962), "Investment Pattern in the Second Five Year Plan", pp. 114–19 in India, Planning Commission, *Papers Relating to the Formulation of the Second Five Year Plan 1955*, Manager of Publications, Delhi.

Part II

Understanding India's development

12

Market failure and government failure

Mrinal Datta-Chaudhuri

Source: Journal of Economic Perspectives, 4:3 (Summer 1990), 25–39.

For several decades a debate has been raging in development economics on the relative virtues of the free market as opposed to state intervention. With the help of analytical models of a market economy, the interventionists demonstrate what they consider serious instances of "market failure"—that is, the inability of a market economy to reach certain desirable outcomes in resource use. The protagonists of free markets, on the other hand, compile impressive lists of ill-conceived and counterproductive policy measures implemented by the governments of different countries at various times, leading to wasteful use of resources in their economies.

This debate inevitably remains inconclusive. The analytical results on "market failure" do not disappear in the face of the evidence that most governments (or for that matter most economies of less developed countries, with or without state intervention) have performed rather badly. When there appears to be scope for improvement over the market outcome, the search for the appropriate corrective measures goes on. Some protagonists of "government failure" question the significance of such market failures; others voice skepticism about the ability of governments to take any action in the economy which is not counterproductive; but none of them seems to be able to explain why a less developed country like India failed to grow during the first half of this century under a non-interventionist colonial administration. Thus, while the debate goes on, neither side succeeds in convincing the other.

While this sterile debate continues, experiences accumulated from research and action in the real world during the last 40 years have led to important new thinking on the roles of market and non-market institutions in the process of economic growth. The planned economies of the socialist world have learned that market institutions are not exclusive to the capitalist mode of production, and that the threat of entry and the fear of exit remain irreplaceable stimuli for cost and quality consciousness in production. Researchers in market economies have learned that price quotations on marketed commodities do not always carry sufficient information for economic decisions, and that institutions matter. This paper pieces together some lessons from the development experiences of the last four decades to enrich our understanding of the role of the state in the process of economic development.

Theories of development

Development economics as we know it today, as a distinct discipline within the economics profession, came into existence in the 1940s. Economists like

Rosenstein-Rodan, Nurske and Kuznets tried to identify the major causes of economic backwardness, and thereby suggest strategies for economic progress for the backward economies. These economists, like many others in the profession, assumed that the state would have to play an important role in raising an economy out of its backwardness. The success of Keynesian activism in fighting the Great Depression in the western countries, the success of the Marshall Plan in engineering the quick reconstruction of the war-damaged economies of western Europe, and the achievements of the Soviet industrialization drive in the 1930s had created a virtual intellectual consensus in the world on the power of the "visible hand."

On the basis of the newly constructed time series data on the national products of different countries, Kuznets (1955) showed that the process of economic development was always accompanied by a shifting of the labor force from low-productivity agriculture to high-productivity manufacturing. But industrialization required a higher rate of capital accumulation. Nurske (1953) wrote about the problem of capital accumulation in a poor country. In his famous doctrine of the "vicious circle of poverty," he said that poor societies remained poor because with low per capita income they could not supply enough savings to increase their stocks of reproducible capital.

Rosenstein-Rodan (1943) analyzed the demand side of capital formation. According to him, the structure of these backward economies was such that there were not enough incentives for investors to choose the right pace or pattern of capital accumulation. Rodan said that in a poor economy the size of the market for industrial products was small and people need to spend most of their incomes on necessities.[1] Moreover, he argued that the production processes in modern industries were subject to great indivisibilities and economies of scale. He particularly identified one category of physical capital for special attention: the social overhead capital like transport, communication, power, urban infrastructure, and so on. These activities were not only bedeviled by nonconvexities, but they had to be in place before private entrepreneurs could decide to install directly productive capital. Borrowing an expression from Allyn Young (1928), Rodan characterized the entire phenomenon as generalized external economies.

It was left to Scitovsky to give a rigorous analytical meaning to Rodan's concept of external economy. Using the framework of the competitive equilibrium and the associated welfare theorems, Scitovsky argued that externalities arose only when interdependence among economic agents was not mediated through market transactions. In his highly influential paper, Scitovsky (1954) concluded that only the externalities arising from intertemporal dependence amongst firms (which he called "pecuniary external economies") presented a serious impediment to the growth of a backward economy, if it were to be propelled by a price-guided system. The implication of the Scitovsky formulation was that the market mechanism could be relied on to take care of the production problems of an economy, but investment allocation required state intervention.[2] Thus, the state emerged in the role of an investment planner in a developing country. It was implicitly assumed that once the productive capacities were created through investment planning, the subsequent problems of getting output, employment and income out of these investments would resolve themselves automatically.

This line of analysis led almost every developing country to set up a planning agency to formulate investment plans based on economy-wide quantitative models. These models varied from country to country in terms of their levels of disaggregation and their computational techniques, but they were similar in certain important aspects. They were rich in their specification of technology and inter-industry linkages, but hopelessly deficient in their specification of behavioral and institutional issues. Therefore, the economic and the statistical analysis embodied in these planning exercises did not provide much guidance as to how these investment plans were to be implemented.[3] It was left to the ingenuity of individual countries to design appropriate mechanisms for implementation, and different countries drew on their own cultural and historical experiences in designing their regulatory systems. It is possible to argue that the performance of the different developing countries can, to a large extent, be explained by the nature of the regulatory mechanisms they adopted.

This body of theory proved deficient both because of deficiencies due to their empirical projections based on historical experiences, and because of the analytical shortcomings of their models of resource allocation. On empirical matters, the assumption that large productivity gains could not be realized in agriculture though technological progress proved to be wrong when the fruits of research in plant genetics became available in the 1960s. Secondly, the stagnant scenario of world trade, experienced throughout the first half of the twentieth century, dramatically changed in the 1950s. The phenomenal economic growth in the OECD countries during the two decades following the Korean war led to massive expansion in world trade. Rising wage rates in the developed countries led to substantial changes in the pattern of the international division of labor. Many poor countries, such as South Korea and Taiwan, could take advantage of the new trade opportunities to become industrialized in a short period of time.

A more lasting consequence arose from the analytical shortcomings of the Nurske-Rodan-Scitovsky framework of development economics. Later researchers in the field of economic growth seriously undermined the importance attached to capital formation in the growth process of an economy. Solow's (1957) seminal contribution demonstrated that only a small part of the growth performance of an economy can be explained by the increment in its stock of reproducible physical capital (or by the employment of a larger number of workers). Most of the economic growth seems to come from technical progress, which is essentially the ability of an economic organization to utilize its productive resources more effectively over time. Much of this ability comes from the process of learning to operate newly created production facilities in a more productive way[4] or more generally from learning to cope with the rapid changes in the structure of production which industrial progress must imply.[5]

Traditional development economics paid little attention to such learning processes and implicitly assumed that whatever technical progress was possible would automatically come with capital accumulation. The development experiences of the last three decades show that economies differ considerably with respect to their abilities to learn how to assimilate new techniques and how to adjust quickly to new lines of production. Moreover, the nature of the industrial organization and the policy environment in which it functions have a considerable impact on the ability to acquire these learning capabilities. To illustrate these points the next section will outline the working of the policy regimes in two economies of Asia—India and South Korea.

Policy regimes in India and South Korea

At a superficial level, there is a great deal of similarity between the planning and the regulatory frameworks adopted by these two countries.[6] Both countries adopted the framework of investment planning with five-year plans computed on the basis of demand projections and interindustry linkages. In the 1970s, the size of the public sector as a percentage share of the gross domestic products of the two countries was roughly the same. The composition of the public sector in both countries was similar: commercial banking, steel, power, and many heavy industries were nationalized in India as well as in South Korea. Both governments intervened heavily in the private sector, using a mixture of direct and indirect controls. However, the manner in which the planning and the regulatory mechanisms worked in the two countries was different in crucial respects. Later, I shall try to explain these differences in terms of the sociopolitical characteristics of the two countries. But before doing that, it is useful to look at the evolution and the working of the two systems.

In the 1950s, India adopted a development strategy which gave investment planning a dominant role. In certain areas the investment targets were implemented by direct public investments; in others, entrepreneurs in the private sector were supposed to be induced to make the required investments. In both fields—managing the public sector as well as regulating the private sector—India relied on the impressive structure of bureaucracy it had inherited from the past. The Mughal empire in the Middle Ages had built an elaborate structure of imperial bureaucracy; the British colonial administration introduced vast improvements in that model of civil administration. In managing the turmoils of Partition during Independence and in the subsequent task of national building, the established bureaucracy had performed in an impressive manner.

This bureaucracy had a good deal of experience in implementing rationing schemes in situations of scarcity. Thus, implementation mechanisms were designed on the logic of rationing a homogeneous commodity to needy users in situations of scarcity.[7] The Five Year Plans produced aggregate investment targets for the different sectors of the economy. A number of choice problems still remained to be solved, such as technique, product mix, location and scale of individual plants, as well as the class of entrepreneurs to be entrusted with the job. Moreover, the choice problems were to be solved while keeping in mind a multiplicity of developmental objectives: growth, employment, interregional equity, self-reliance and control of monopolies. The entire implementation mechanism was based on the hope that civil servants would use their discretion in an enlightened manner, and thereby meet the plan targets while satisfying the various objectives of development.

János Kornai (1982) had spelled out some of the classic syndromes of investment planning under bureaucratic management. Investment planning creates shortages, partly because of the deliberate efforts to raise the overall rate of capital accumulation and partly because of the inevitable uncertainties in synchronizing planned activities. With assured markets, producers step up supplies in certain sectors of the economy. The managers of public sector enterprises produce for the captive market. Given the "soft budget constraint" under which they operate,[8] they are not unduly worried about making losses. Producers in the private sector also have assured markets. With the legal barriers to entry instituted by the licensing system, they do not have much incentive for either cost reduction or quality improvement. Their perceptions, as businessmen, become more and more fixed towards cornering the rents associated with the distribution of licenses.[9] It seems one needs an environment of competition even to design an effective organizational structure within a business enterprise. Over time, the industrial economy becomes wasteful. It neither generates enough surplus for reinvestment, nor is it able to derive sufficient dividends in terms of the growth and the equity objectives of the society on its investments. The industrial economy settles into a modest growth path.

While bureaucratic rationing became the predominant mode of regulation for the manufacturing industries in India's private sector, India adopted a market-oriented form of regulation for agriculture. Since it was not practicable to introduce licensing schemes for the millions of farmers in the country, the Indian state essentially relied on fiscal measures to raise the prices of crops and to lower costs of inputs, thereby increasing the profit opportunities in the farms. This meant giving up on the objectives of interregional and interpersonal equities in the context of agricultural development, because only large farms in favorably located regions could take maximum advantage of these market incentives. This difference is rather ironic, because nearly 80 percent of India's population lives in rural areas and the scope for promoting equity is so much greater in the field of agricultural development than in the context of modern industries.

The Republic of Korea had a different historical experience to draw upon, when it came to designing an implementation mechanism. Under the Japanese occupation before the Second World War, Korea had achieved an impressive level of industrialization. Much of the produce of these industries was sold abroad. In fact, it was only in the late 1960s that South Korea's industrial economy and its export performance (as measured by the shares of manufacturing and of exports in the GDP) reached the levels attained by Korea in 1940. Of course, these industries were then owned and managed by the Japanese; but Koreans at junior levels acquired valuable skills in managing industries and trade. By contrast, the Japanese occupation did not use Korean personnel in running its civil administration. Thus,

President Park Chung Hee had to rely on the new emerging business elite to form his team for development administration in the 1960s. Park and his team used a variety of means—financial incentives, persuasion and sometimes coercion—to influence the behavior of industrialists and traders.[10]

Another important difference between South Korea and India relates to the extent of direct control wielded by the state over the economy's investment resources. With the resources mobilized through the nationalized banks, foreign aid and the public sector, the Korean state in the '70s had direct control over about two-thirds of the aggregate investment funds available to the economy. Korea used credit policy, with differential interest rates ranging from 8 to 34 percent, to channel investments in the desired directions. With this level of command over the capital market, there was not a great deal of need for direct intervention in the sphere of commodity production and exchange. Nevertheless, direct controls, like licensing of production and quantitative restrictions on imports, were widely used. However, the procedures were prompt, and the decisions were made by a high-level committee, a feasible method in a small country (Datta-Chaudhuri, 1981a).

At the enterprise level, the public sector units in Korea had autonomous management, not burdened with a multiplicity of objectives. In the absence of any consideration for regional equity, economies of scale were never sacrificed. Although the producers were given generous protection in the domestic market, the incentive structure encouraged expansion on the basis of export demand. In short, the Korean state was highly interventionist; but the intervention schemes were geared towards developing and supporting the market economy. The market environment encouraged quick learning as well as cost and quality consciousness.

Market institutions and the state

Let us now turn to an aspect of industrial development outside the scope of investment planning. One of India's success stories has been the development of the handloom and other products of cottage industries. This came about largely in response to sales outlets for these products being set up in different Indian cities by the central and state governments. These state-run sales establishments, in addition to providing market outlets for small producers from rural areas, started to interact with their suppliers in a variety of ways. They started disseminating new techniques of production and new designs to the producers. They introduced some quality control, and advanced credit. They also helped to set up a market network which could supply the required inputs (buttons, dyes, and so on) to the producers in a regular manner. Independent producers in remote villages could rely on these organizations for their informational and other market-related needs. To the extent that these organizations handled all the various links with the outside markets (both domestic and foreign) reliably and effectively, small producers had little difficulty in producing the required supply.

In the case of South Korea, the trading companies perform a similar role for independent producers in widely different lines of production. These trading companies integrate (horizontally) a large number of exchange-related activities, such as marketing, transport, communication, credit, insurance and the transfer of technology. In the late 1960s, the government of South Korea took the first initiative in setting up these organizations. It is said that following the Japanese example, the government of South Korea set up exactly ten trading companies as there were in Japan. The phenomenal success of Korea in exporting manufactured goods cannot be fully understood without appreciating the role played by these trading companies.

What these examples suggest is that important externalities do exist in information processing and other exchange-related activities. There also seem to be significant economies of scale and scope in these activities. The emergence of the trading companies in East Asia, which horizontally integrated several exchange-related activities to service the needs of independent producers, explains the greater success of these economies in promoting labor-intensive industrial growth. In many other parts of the world, the typical response of an industrial organization to these externalities has been one of vertical integration, which led to increased supervision costs, which in turn induced a substitution of capital for labor (Datta-Chaudhuri, 1981b). We do not fully know why trading companies do not play as important a role elsewhere as they do in East Asia. However, the case of South Korea suggests that the promotional and supportive role of the state in creating these institutions may be an important factor in their development.

The state-run sales organizations for cottage industry production in India and the state-promoted but privately held trading companies of South Korea provide examples of the need for a certain kind of market organization to support the industrial progress of an economy. These organizations can be said to constitute the "soft" infrastructure of an industrial economy, which is different from the "hard" infrastructure emphasized earlier by Rosenstein-Rodan. The "soft" infrastructure can take a wide variety of institutional forms, with varying degrees of involvement on the part of the state, to serve the function of catering to the informational and marketing needs of an industrial economy (Datta-Chaudhuri, 1981b).

Perceiving and creating new markets

Abba Lerner (1972) warned economists against the dangers of assuming that market institutions sprang up automatically in every place. He correctly saw the modern economy as the end product of a time-consuming process of development. In this development process, societies progressively created appropriate institutions so that interpersonal conflicts could be resolved through economic transactions.

However, producers and traders do not always correctly perceive the various trade or technological possibilities open to them. There is scope for imaginative intervention to alter their perceptions and thereby improve the performance of an economy. Although it is impossible to arrive at general conclusions of universal validity in this field, it is pertinent to examine some instances of noteworthy success with government intervention.

Perhaps the best known examples come from the activities of the Ministry of International Trade and Industries (MITI) in Japan. It is doubtful whether the phenomenal success of Japan in many lines of industrial production would have been possible without the initial promotional efforts of MITI. For example, in the 1950s MITI organized, in collaboration with the Japanese industries, a massive research and development effort aimed at identifying the best areas for future action. These efforts led to the creation of a technological and economic base for the future expansion of industries such as optics, electronics and automobiles. Eventually Japan came to dominate the world market in these lines of production. This example illustrates that foreign trade transformation possibilities are not there for everyone to see and to take advantage of. Sometimes, as in Japan, the state can play a crucial role in shaping the perception of producers and traders leading to hitherto unforeseen possibilities. Without state initiatives such outcomes might have remained beyond the reach of agents in a free market economy.

An even more dramatic example of the effects of this kind of intervention comes from Tanzania in the 1960s (Sabot, 1988). Before Independence in December 1961, most wage-earners in Tanzania were employed in plantations, where wage rates and productivity of labor were low. These wage-earners were migrant workers, who usually returned to their villages after a period of work in the plantations. The plantation owners repeatedly turned down the suggestion that higher wages would create a permanent labor force with higher productivity. They argued that the supply curve of labor was backward-bending and higher wages would make African workers work even less. However, after Independence, the government decreed a drastic increase in wage payments in the organized sector of the economy, which led to a three-fold increase in the wage rate faced by the plantations. This forced the plantation owners to introduce major changes in their system of management. Between

1961 and 1968, aggregate employment in the sisal industry declined from 129,000 to 42,000, but production increased by about 400 percent, without any addition to the stock of physical capital. This dramatic demonstration of the efficiency wage hypothesis was the result of changes forced upon unwilling entrepreneurs from outside.

Naturally, all the various intervention schemes designed by the government of Tanzania did not yield positive results. Neither was the government of Japan successful with all its grand schemes of economic regulation. For example, the New Township Development Scheme of the early '60s, which was to disperse industrial activities away from the Osaka–Nagoya–Tokyo complex, became an expensive failure. Whether a particular government in a particular situation will be able to take the correct course of action is a difficult question, to which, perhaps, there is no context-free answer.

The state and the polity

In an earlier era Mao Zedong had introduced China's statist development strategy with the slogan: "Put politics in command." This formulation is analytically helpful, because it recognizes that the state is a creation of the polity. The point is obvious in the case of a democratic polity, where the activities of a government are circumscribed by the preferences of the dominant interest groups. But even an authoritarian regime can never be indifferent to the questions of legitimacy and popular support.

This point is perhaps best illustrated by an example from Taiwan in the early 1970s (Datta-Chaudhuri, 1981b). At that time, Taiwan had had the lion's share of the lucrative market for bananas in Japan. The production of bananas was organized in small firms using labor-intensive techniques of production. Soon it became obvious that for selling a perishable commodity like bananas to a distant market, large firms (whose production, grading, handling, and packaging were mechanized) had a clear advantage over the traditional methods of production and distribution. A number of multinational farms went to the neighboring country, the Philippines, and established giant mechanized banana plantations, after displacing thousands of small farmers. Taiwan saw this development in the Philippines but prevented any attempt at the creation of large mechanized farms at home, and thereby willingly allowed its market share in Japan to fall drastically.

The example is especially significant because Taiwan was—and still is—one of the most aggressively market-oriented economies in the world and it also had an authoritarian government. Nonetheless, the government of Taiwan did not allow the logic of free market to operate where the livelihood of a large number of farming families were at stake. The usual argument that "sooner or later" the displaced workers would find alternative employment in other efficient industries was politically unacceptable to the society at large.

While political compulsions are important determinants of state action, it is not always easy to recognize the true nature of those compulsions. Actions of a government are never solely dictated by economic considerations, although economic arguments are often employed to legitimize actions which have different intents. Outside observers often reach misleading conclusions because they are unable to see through the strategic behavior of politicians.

For example, the People's Action Party (PAP) of Singapore introduced repressive measures to control trade union activities with the argument that they were necessary for attracting foreign investments and for competing successfully in export markets. But Hong Kong did not repress its labor movement, nor did it suspend the institution of collective bargaining. This did not affect Hong Kong's ability either to attract foreign capital or to perform successfully in export markets. In recent years, South Korea has seen the emergence of active trade unionism, which is often noisy and sometimes militant; but it does not seem to have affected the performance of the South Korean economy adversely. The government of Singapore obviously moved towards a repressive regime to ensure the political survival of the party in power, but it sought legitimacy for its action by invoking economic arguments which had some measure of popular appeal. It, of course, had the unfortunate by-product of confusing many outside economists.

These matters make political economy a difficult subject. Nonetheless, it is possible to identify a few broad features of a polity that crucially influence the relationship between the state and the economy. For example, to explain the evolution of the successful relationship between the state and the economy in South Korea, it is important to consider the land reform imposed on that country (as well as in Japan and Taiwan) from outside after the Second World War. Land reform destroyed the political power of the landed aristocracy and helped the emergence of the commercial and industrial middle classes as the dominant elite in the country. The homogenous social base of the military and the business elite in the early days of President Park paved the way for a system ("Korea Inc.") where the power of the state was brought to control the economy through formal as well as informal channels (Jones and Sakong, 1980).

The importance of this phenomenon becomes apparent when one compares the performance of the South Korean economy with that of the Philippines. The two countries have remarkable similarities geographically as well as in demographic terms. In the early 1960s, per capita incomes in the two countries were very similar."[11] Both countries had close relationships with the United States in military, political and economic matters. The government of each country had a strong ideological commitment to capitalism. Park Chung Hee and Ferdinand Marcos were not dissimilar in their political values and in their willingness to use repressive measures. Yet, the two economies had very different records of economic growth. Social scientists do not as yet have the tool-kit to explain these differences satisfactorily, but it is not difficult to see how the dominance of the landed aristocracy in the political economy of the Philippines hindered the creation of a dynamic capitalist economy. The same factors were also responsible for the Philippines not trying to achieve a greater measure of distributive justice in the society (Datta-Chaudhuri, 1981a).

In the case of India, the size and the heterogeneity of the country prevented a single homogeneous group from dominating the polity and the state. A few dominant classes, fragmented by regional differences, exert collective control over state machinery.[12] Such a coalition had to rest on implicit understandings regarding the manner in which the state could control and regulate the economy. In India, these understandings can be summarized as follows:

First, the affluent peasantry, who constituted perhaps the most powerful group within the Indian coalition, successfully imposed three conditions on economic policies: land reforms should not be pushed beyond a certain point; there should be no taxation of agricultural income and wealth; and the state should maintain high prices for outputs and low prices for major inputs and thereby maintain a budgetary policy with heavy subsidies.

Second, the big industrialists, the second group in the dominant coalition, wanted the state to create profitable opportunities for their expansion in the home market. This meant public sector outlays in social overhead capital, subsidized intermediate goods produced by the public sector, and protection from foreign competition.

Third, the working classes and other employees in the organized sector wanted legal and procedural guarantees ensuring employment security. This reduced the ability of the industrial organization to make quick adjustments in production processes and to create an environment for quick learning.

Fourth, the backward regions of the country demanded a mechanism of investment allocation, whereby new industrial units would be located in those states.

The Indian industrial organization and the policy environment in which it operates are the results of these implicit understandings, which support the equilibrium of group interest in the country's political economy. This is why the Indian state cannot acquire direct control over a larger fraction of the economy's investable resources, as is the case in South Korea. For over a decade, successive governments in New Delhi have tried to reform the existing regulatory mechanisms, which do not encourage either cost and quality consciousness or fast learning and quick adjustments. They have not succeeded, because they could not disturb the old equilibrium in the polity which supports the power of the state.

Summary and conclusions

Market failures present serious obstacles to the growth process of a backward economy. Unfortunately, development economists in the 1940s and 1950s focussed their attention on a rather limited class of market failures; those associated with investment decisions. In the field of development policy, this led to a strong emphasis on investment planning with the naive belief that once the physical capital was installed, the subsequent problems of production and productivity improvement would automatically be resolved.

Subsequent research and development experiences discovered serious market failures associated with the operation of installed capacities. The problems arise from the various facets of the learning process, which is of crucial importance to a developing economy. Learning occurs at several levels: how to operate new techniques of production; how to introduce cost-reducing and quality-improving innovations; how to change the product-mix quickly in response to a changing environment. The state can play an important role in helping the economy to acquire those skills. However, in designing an appropriate role for the state it is important to remember two things.

First, although the market operates inadequately in many spheres, it performs an important function in disciplining producers against wasteful use of resources. Secondly, in a changing world, the required institutional changes in markets do not always take place automatically. The state can play an important role in promoting and supporting the right kind of market institutions.

The principal function of a market organization is to institute rewards and penalties around economic activities. It is important to remember that any economic system must have such schemes of rewards and penalties to guard against wasteful use of resources. Therefore, an activist government needs to strengthen the market institutions so that it can influence the behavior of economic agents effectively. In those spheres where market signals alone are not effective guides to desirable action, appropriate non-market institutions are required to be created. Thus, the market-versus-government dichotomy is a fake one.

The performance of a market economy depends on the perception of economic agents regarding the technological and market opportunities available to them. In some cases, unaided market mechanisms were unable to realize potential economic gains, because economic agents had failed to perceive those options. There are also instances where the state influenced the behavior of producers and traders in a positive direction either through coercive regulations or by cooperative action.

Can a government be relied upon to do the "right" thing and avoid doing the "wrong" thing? It is impossible to give a context-free answer to this question. Economists, as outsiders, tend to believe that it is all a matter of knowing what is right and what is wrong. If that were the case, many tricky problems would have disappeared a long time ago. A government's policies reflect the interests of the dominant social groups which control the state. Changes in the economic policies almost invariably hurt some of these interests, which makes changes difficult within a gradualist framework. Economic analysis can be very useful in identifying areas of potential gains and thereby helping to create new constituencies for change. Such analysis can also identify methods of adjustment which are politically acceptable.

The important question for developing societies is how to develop a mutually supportive structure of market and non-market institutions, which is well-suited to promote economic development. This makes normative development economics a difficult art.

I am grateful to János Kornai, Louis Lefeber, Stephen Marglin, Roderick McFarquhar and Amartya Sen for useful discussions. Pranab Bardhan, Richard Eckaus, Carl Shapiro, Joseph Stiglitz and Timothy Taylor made valuable comments on an earlier draft of this paper. I am, of course, responsible for any errors that may remain.

Notes

1 Although, following Scitovsky, latter-day development economists focussed their attention on externalities and the resultant suboptimality of the competitive equilibria, Rodan himself was primarily worried about the inadequate working of the price mechanism in the absence of strong substitution effects.

2 Externalities occur when a complete set of Arrow-Debreu markets do not exist. Pecuniary externalities result from the absence of future markets. Recent researches on the working of economies with incomplete markets (and imperfect information) show that in such situations even competitive markets fail to optimally perform the required risk-sharing functions. Competitive equilibria for such an economy are not constrained Pareto-efficient and there exist schemes of government intervention which can induce Pareto-superior outcomes (Greenwald and Stiglitz, 1986).

3 In the field of development planning one often hears people talking about "a good plan implemented badly." This dichotomy between the formulation and the implementation of a plan is usually false. If a plan is supposed to be a feasible action program, then it must have been designed on the basis of realistic assumptions regarding the expected behavior of economic agents. Difficulties regarding implementation should arise only from unanticipated exogenous shocks.

4 Arrow (1962) analyzed the implications of acquiring skill through the actual process of operating production capacities over time.

5 Stiglitz (1987) analyzed the importance of "the frame of mind which is associated with asking 'how this task can be performed better?'" This has implications not only for decision-making at the firm and the industry levels, but also for choosing a policy framework in which the industrial economy can learn to take better advantage of its economic environment.

6 Starting from comparable levels of poverty in the early 1960s, the economies of South Korea and India charted widely divergent growth paths for the next three decades. In 1961 India had $73 per capita income at current prices, while the corresponding figure for South Korea was $180. In 1987 the per capita incomes at current prices for these two countries were $300 and $2690 respectively (World Bank, 1989).

7 For example, when a famine occurred in any part of the country, officials in charge of the famine relief instituted rationing schemes for distributing foodgrains to well-defined target groups of victims on the basis of established need-based norms.

8 Losses incurred by the public sector enterprises are automatically borne by the government. As such these enterprises are not disciplined by any fear of bankruptcy. Kornai described this situation as one of decision-making under a "soft budget constraint."

9 Krueger (1974) saw the rent-seeking phenomenon as a shrinking of the production possibility set due to the withdrawal of resources from production to rent-seeking. Perhaps more important than the resource cost of rent-seeking are the effects of the policy environment on the perception of economic agents. In such an environment, producers tend to become obsessed with the short run gains associated with cornering the licenses at the cost of the long run benefits connected with technological and managerial improvements.

10 Jones and Sakong (1980) describe in some detail how President Park forged his alliance with the Korean business community. Under the "Special Law for Dealing with Illicit Wealth Accumulation" most of the country's prominent businessmen were arrested and threatened with confiscation of their assets. Eventually a deal was struck, whereby the government withdrew criminal prosecution and the businessmen agreed to set up some basic industries approved by the government. Later on they were sent abroad under government auspices to negotiate for foreign loans for a number of investment projects. These businessmen later formed the powerful Federation of Korean Industries (FKI) which became a partner of President Park's government in fashioning the growth of the Korean economy.

11 According to the World Bank, per capita GNP at current prices in the Philippines went up from $210 in 1967 to $590 in 1987. During the same period in South Korea it went up from $240 to $2690.

12 For an analysis of India's political economy as a bargaining equilibrium of dominant classes, see Bardhan (1984).

References

Arrow, Kenneth J., "The Economic Implication of Learning-by-Doing," *Review of Economic Studies*, June 1962, *29*, 155–173.

Bardhan, Pranab, *The Political Economy of Development in India*. Oxford: Basil Blackwell, 1984.

Datta-Chaudhuri, Mrinal, "Industrialization and Foreign Trade: The Development Experiences of South Korea and the Philippines." In Lee, E., ed., *Export-Led Industrialization and Development*. Bangkok and Geneva: ARTEP-ILO, 1981a.

Datta-Chaudhuri, Mrinal, "Labor-Intensive Industrialization and the Organisation of Trade," *Indian Economic Review*, July-September 1981b, *16*, 199–212.

Greenwald, Bruce C., and Joseph E. Stiglitz, "Externalities in Economies with Imperfect Information and Incomplete Markets," *Quarterly Journal of Economics*, May 1986, *101*, 229–264.

Jones, L. P., and I. Sakong, *Government, Business and Entrepreneurship in Economic Development: The Korean Case*. Cambridge: Harvard University Press, 1980.

Kornai, János, *Growth, Shortage and Efficiency*. Oxford: Basil Blackwell, 1982.

Krueger, Anne O., "The Political Economy of the Rent-Seeking Society," *American Economic Review*, June 1974, *64*, 291–303.

Kuznets, Simon, "Towards a Theory of Economic Growth." In Levachman, Robert, ed., *National Policy for Economic Welfare at Home and Abroad*, Bicentennial Conference Series. New York: Doubleday, 1955, pp. 12–85.

Lerner, Abba P., "The Economics and Politics of Consumer Sovereignty," *American Economic Review*, May, 1972, *62*, 258–266.

Nurske, R., Problems of Capital Formation in Under-Developed Countries. *Oxford University Press*, 1953.

Rosenstein-Rodan, P. N., "Problems of Industrialization of Eastern and South-Eastern Europe," *Economic Journal*, June–September 1943, *55*, 202–211.

Sabot, Richard H., "Labor Standards in a Small Low-Income Country: Tanzania," *mimeo*, Overseas Development Council, Washington, D.C. 1988.

Scitovsky, Tibor, "Two Concepts of External Economies," *Journal of Political Economy*, April 1954, *62*, 143–151.

Solow, Robert M., "Technical Change and the Aggregate Production Function," *Review of Economics and Statistics*, August, 1957, *59*, 312–320.

Stiglitz, Joseph E., "Learning to Learn, Localized Learning and Technical Progress." In Dasgupta, Partha, and P. Stoneman, eds., *Economic Policy and Technological Performance*. Cambridge: Cambridge University Press, 1987.

World Bank, *World Development Report 1989*, Washington D.C., 1989, pp. 164–165.

Young, Allyn, "Increasing Returns and Economic Progress," *Economic Journal*, December 1928, *58*, 527–542.

13

The state and the market

Pulin B. Nayak

Source: *Economic and Political Weekly*, 31:4 (27 January, 1996), 18–22.

The real issue is not whether to have the market or the state. This is an empty dichotomy and no serious school of political economy would today credibly argue for only one or the other. The question is one of striking the right balance. What one has also to guard against is a new mode of thinking that the market may be entrusted to sort out all the basic problems confronting an economy, even with its manifest incapacity to deal with issues pertaining to income distribution and deprivation.

I Introduction

In much of mainstream neoclassical microeconomics the market looms large and the presence of any state goes almost unnoticed. A market may be thought to be an institution where agents get together to buy and sell goods and services and more generally, to negotiate courses of action. In the perfectly competitive version of it, there are atomistic economic agents who, as consumers, maximise their utilities, while producers, acting as price takers, are engaged in maximising profits. It is well known that under certain conditions governing preferences and technology of production, a competitive equilibrium of the system exists, which means that there exists a balancing price vector at which the demand and the supply of each commodity is matched. Any exogenous change from this position of equilibrium brings about the needed comparative static changes all of which operate through the market system. If, for example, there is an excess demand for some commodity at a given price then its price moves up, or if there is an excess supply of loanable funds at a particular rate of interest then the interest rate falls. Both these operate as part of the inexorable laws that govern the market system. It is also known that a perfectly competitive market system ensures efficiency in the sense of Pareto. It also answers the questions as to what ought to be produced in how much quantity and in what manner and for whom.

While there is a well developed body of literature on market socialism in the Lange-Lerner tradition, it would not be incorrect to say that the overwhelming bulk of the market system paradigm is anchored in the private ownership economy. In such an economy the initial distribution of resources is treated as given and is virtually regarded as sacrosanct. Any tampering with the initial distribution of resources is looked upon as a violation of a certain basic right, viz, the right to private property. Now, if the initial distribution of resources is iniquitous, in terms of certain ethical criteria, there is no presumption that the operation of the market system, left to itself, may bring about equity. Indeed, in a system with unequal bargaining power amongst agents, the operation of market forces may bring about an accentuation of iniquity.

If it were the case that the only difficulty, though this is a serious one, with the market system is its insensitivity to income distributional issues, but that on the other hand it invariably ensures efficiency, then the latter would be a major point in its favour. However, as it turns out, and as is well known, the market system's efficiency property breaks down in the presence of monopoly elements, incomplete or asymmetric information, externalities and public goods, or when we are confronted with decreasing cost industries. Given the pervasiveness of the above features, surely the incidence of market failure and consequent breakdown of efficiency must be equally pervasive. How then can one be sanguine about the overall benign and beneficial effects of the market system?

It turns out that one cannot be. In the presence of public goods or externalities it is clear that it would be necessary to have governmental intervention in order to ensure efficiency of resource use. In the case of pollution, for example, the intervention may take the form of imposition of Pigouvian taxes levied on the polluters, or it may take the form of the government trying to establish markets for named goods in the manner suggested by Arrow (1970).

In this context it is of course well known, and as is argued by Coase (1960), that if there are no transaction costs amongst economic agents in arriving at bargains then no government intervention is called for and that self interested rational agents will arrive at solutions that are consistent with efficiency in resource use. Coase goes on to argue that imposition of Pigouvian taxes may in fact lead to suboptimal outcomes. However the critical assumption here is that transaction costs are zero which is invariably untenable.

Consider the case of financial markets, which are regarded as being the 'brain' of an economic system [Stiglitz 1993]. It is well recognised that the history of modern capitalism has been marked by the linked phenomena of financial crises and economic recessions. Now, in the sphere of financial markets there are several strong reasons for market failure that provide a rationale for government intervention. This is thought to be necessary not only in developing countries but also in the context of industrial countries. The principal reason for the market failure arises from the fact that the assumption of perfect information does not hold, and that markets, left to their own devices do not function efficiently. Now, information differs from conventional commodities in that it is, in a fundamental sense, a public good, in that it is non-rival in consumption and exclusion is very costly. It is well known that competitive market economies provide an insufficient supply of public goods. In order to restore efficiency government may intervene by creating and regulating financial market institutions and intervening directly in the capital market.

One is thus led to the inescapable conclusion that a *laissez-faire* market system must be controlled and regulated by government intervention. There is however nothing new about this conclusion. This has for long been conceded even in the core quarters of neoclassical economics where the market system virtually plays an omniscient role. The crucial feature of this system however is that the ownership of the means of production is necessarily in private hands.

What are the consequences of the means of production being socially owned? It has been demonstrated quite conclusively that there can in fact be rational allocation of resources under socialism, so that at least on theoretical grounds there could be no doubt regarding the efficiency property of a socialist system. However the difficulty with the socialist economy has been at the practical level. The system is perceived to have failed because it does not provide the necessary incentives to economic agents. There is little doubt that if the reward system in any economic organisation is unresponsive to economic effort then the system is bound to face internal contradictions sooner than later.

One ought to draw a distinction between social ownership of the means of production and the role of the state. Indeed in the Marxian blueprint of transition from capitalism to socialism, the role of the state in fact is not large. The ownership of the means of production does in fact get transferred from private to social hands but this does not necessarily entail a large state. In fact Marx had envisaged that in the final stage of socialist transition the state would wither away. In Marx's schemata social ownership of the means of production was consistent with decentralised, co-operative collective action rather than a monolithic and omniscient state.

This may appear somewhat paradoxical, but the conception of the state in the writings of the proponents of the free market, for example, in the writings of Nozick (1974), is one of a minimal state where the state is expected to maintain law and order and to ensure that contracts are carried out. Thus the role of the state in both the right wing libertarian writings of von Hayek and Nozick as well as the Marxian socialist formulations is small.

In which context then is the role of the state large or substantial? It was large precisely in economies of the erstwhile Soviet and East European type, with a large measure of monolithic top heavy centralised planning. And the state is also large in the wide range of mixed economies, spanning the ones like India which are poor developing economies subscribing to development planning, to ones in the developed world which represent welfare states like Sweden and Denmark. It is also well known that in the economic development of countries like Japan, South Korea, Taiwan and Singapore, the state has intervened in strategic areas like credit availability and provision of industrial and export infrastructure to boost the growth rates of those economies.

From the example of the fast growing economies of South-East Asia one may draw an important conclusion. It is that the overwhelming reliance on the market mechanism to maximise economic efficiency, with corrective intervention by the government in the event of public goods and externalities, etc, is based on static notions of resource allocation. The case of the South-East Asian tigers demonstrates that in a dynamic context the state can play a substantially important role. It does so by creating the infrastructure, by making available credit at the appropriate time, by effecting technology transfer and by helping in marketing the products.

II State and market in economic thought

Perhaps a useful reference point of all thinking on the state and the market could be the substantial body of work of Adam Smith (1937, 1804). In the Smithian system the market automatically decides through the price mechanism the basic question of what, how and for whom to produce. The market system operates through the 'invisible hand' of self interest, which leads the entrepreneur to those endeavours where profits are largest while labour seeks those jobs that offer the highest wages. Self interest is held in check by competition, which urges other entrepreneurs to imitate the efforts of the most profitable firms, thereby reducing to 'normal' proportions the short-term profits of entrepreneurs and the high wages of skilled labourers.

The author of the *Wealth of Nations* (1776), for whom self interest was the driving force of all economic activity was also the author of *The Theory of Moral Sentiments* (1759) which stressed sympathy rather than individual gain or utility as the basis of morals. According to Smith, human conduct was actuated by six motives: self love, sympathy, the desire to be free, a sense of propriety, a habit of labour, and the propensity to truck, barter and exchange one thing for another. Left to himself, a moral man would not only attain his own best advantage, but he would also further the 'common good'. Smith argued that since self love was accompanied by other motives, particularly sympathy, the actions resulting from it could not but involve the advantage of others while bringing about one's own gain. It was this fundamental belief in the natural balance of human motives that led Adam Smith to argue that in pursuing one's own advantage each individual is "led by an invisible hand to promote an end which was not part of his intention". Smith was firmly of the view that the common good was paradoxically best served when a person pursues his self interest.

In fact he was suspicious of those who were in the business to exclusively serve the public good, and thought that there is never much good done by such people. Thus the very essence of his ideology was that motives do not have to be intentional and that overall harmony arises out of the spontaneous functioning of human personality.

In the Smithian scheme government interference was the greatest barrier to this spontaneity. Smith held that wherever government had intervened, the outcome was less effective than if it had remained aloof. Yet there were certain areas where Adam Smith was clear about the necessity of state intervention. The first two were defence and justice, which were obvious prerequisites of sovereign power. The third was somewhat more ambiguous. This concerned the erection and maintenance of those public works and institutions which are useful but not capable of bringing in a profit to individuals. These included, for example, bridges and educational institutions. Thus even though Adam Smith has been associated with the doctrine of *laissez-faire*, he in fact tread finely over the relative spheres for the state and the market.

As regards businessmen, Smith in fact had the most caustic comment: "People of the same trade seldom meet together, even for merriment and diversion, but the conversation ends in a conspiracy against the public, or in some contrivance to raise prices." Thus it is far from the case that Smith was an unalloyed champion of the market system.

The background in which Adam Smith wrote was one of the primacy of mercantilism which held that the state should be powerful at home and abroad and the supersession of national royal power over local power was regarded as obviously desirable. Any policy that contributed to an enhancement of the power of the state was thought to be worth pursuing. This was reflected in the approach to impose minute and intricate domestic regulation of manufacturing and commerce. A flourishing domestic economy was regarded as desirable since this would contribute to overall national strength. Even though Adam Smith wrote extensively condemning the restrictive and imprisoning effects of mercantilism and championed *laissez-faire*, he was sufficiently careful to emphasise the importance of sympathy as an essential part of moral conduct, and did envisage a role for the state in areas where private entrepreneurs would have insufficient commercial incentive to have a presence.

Perhaps the strongest argument for a large role of the state has been made in the writings of the German economist Freidrich List (1789–1849). List favoured a strong interventionist government and high tariffs to protect infant industries from British competition. He denied the existence of natural harmony of *laissez-faire* capitalism and rejected the automatic adjustments in the capitalistic model. He emphasised nationalism as the driving force to mobilise human endeavour in underdeveloped countries. List suggested a five-stage theory of economic development and growth where the final stage was one of world commerce, which combined international trade with manufacturing and large-scale commercial agriculture. In his scheme, the task of government was to create through proper legislation the environment that would enable a country to reach the final stage as quickly as possible. List argued that rather than harmony of interest it was conflict and antagonism that was the source of economic as well as political activity.

A fundamental assumption of the economic system outlined by Adam Smith was that *laissez-faire* and minimal governmental control would automatically lead to natural order and the best possible outcome for all. That there was an inherent tendency in a free enterprise system of effective demand falling short of the full output potential of the economy was something that was never considered in the Smith–Say construct. This was first outlined by Malthus in his theory of gluts when he challenged the automaticity of full employment that characterised Say's law and the classical system [see, for example, Roll 1953]. The classical system presumed that general overproduction was impossible. In discussing the possibility of under consumption and unemployment Malthus was a true intellectual precursor to the writings of John Maynard Keynes in the 1930s in the backdrop of the great depression. A low level of effective demand meant unemployment, which assumed alarming proportions in the depression of the 1930s. The way out of this was to have strong intervention by the state, in the form of substantially higher government expenditure.

Thus the case for government intervention may come from two major considerations, viz, those of resource allocation and stabilisation. The allocation arguments, based on externalities, public goods and the like centre on the issue of static efficiency. Government intervention is required either in the form of tax subsidy schemes or in the form of direct intervention to facilitate setting up of markets that would not otherwise be established of their own accord. In the areas of infrastructure and the social sectors like education, health and social security, the government may well have to intervene as an active participant in provisioning these goods and services.

The arguments for a significant and strategic role for the government from the stabilisation angle, especially after the Keynesian revolution, is today regarded as standard received doctrine. The essential basis of this is the recognition that different economic agents are responsible for savings and investment, as a consequence of which there invariably would arise a mismatch between these two variables. If investment falls short of savings it would lead to a contraction of national income and therefore employment. The situation can however be corrected only via corrective-government intervention. Thus the Keynesian construct explicitly recognised the possibility of crises in the capitalist system, and this was something that was virtually ignored by the classical authors in the Smith–Say–Ricardo tradition.

Even though Keynes was essentially a votary of individual initiative operating within the market system, he believed that the state will nevertheless have to exercise a guiding influence. He thought that in particular the state would need to influence the propensity to consume "partly through, its scheme of taxation, partly by fixing the rate of interest and partly, perhaps, in other ways". He goes on to add that a "somewhat comprehensive socialisation of investment will prove the only means of securing an approximation to full employment" [Keynes 1936:378]. In Keynes' scheme this of course did not preclude co-operation between public authority and private initiative. He was emphatic that state socialism ought not to embrace most of the economic life of the community and he was equally emphatic that the state ought not to assume the ownership of the means of production.

Both Keynes and Marx had concluded that the free market capitalist system contained within itself the seeds of instability and crisis. For Keynes the root of the problem resided in a lack of effective demand, whereas in Marx the explanation lay in the fact that while the process of accumulation led to a falling tendency of the rate of profit, the consuming power of society gets limited by the urge for accumulation. This leads to a progressive intensification of the conflict between production and consumption, between the creation of surplus value and its realisation. As regards the suggested remedy, however, whereas Keynes thought in terms of boosting aggregate demand via a programme of active government expenditure, so as to put the economy back onto the full employment path, in the case of Marx the solution was sought in terms of overthrowing the entire capitalist order by the working class and the proletariat. Thus Keynes essentially thought in terms of using the state apparatus to preserve and protect the capitalist order but in the case of Marx, the entire capitalist system had to be violently abandoned in favour of a classless socialist society.

It is somewhat ironic that while Keynes was suspicious of a large role of the state, Keynesianism, which virtually came around to be the creed in the years following the second world war in large parts of the globe, brought in substantially expanded roles for the state. This was as much true of western capitalist democracies which modelled themselves as welfare states as it was true of the newly independent developing countries of Asia, Africa and Latin America.

It is quite well known that about the same time as Keynes was arguing for a policy of counter cyclical government intervention to ensure stability in output and employment, Michal Kalecki too had independently arrived at the same answer. Like Keynes, Kalecki too dismissed the orthodox idea that a market economy is automatically led towards full employment. The task of Keynes and Kalecki was to demonstrate that the capitalist system is essentially demand driven. They demonstrated quite conclusively that in recessionary conditions an active demand expansion policy by the government can raise output and employment without causing serious inflation.

Nature of the state

A very important question pertains to the nature of the state in the context of a developing country like India. This issue has been much discussed in the literature [for a recent review see Byres 1994]. One of the approaches is to adopt a functional view of the state where the state is regarded as a neutral, technocratic and developmentalist state. A second approach is to regard the state as an instrument of class rule, where the state acts at the behest of 'the dominant or ruling class' [Miliband 1973]. A third approach, following Kalecki (1976) and Raj (1973) is to regard the Indian state as an intermediate regime. A fourth view of the state, following Gramsci, seeks to explore the maintenance of class domination through a variable combination of coercion and consent. These do not exhaust the various approaches available in the literature.

It is in fact a truism to assert that the state acts on behalf of the dominant and ruling classes. The point however is that even though the state has invariably been used as a tool to further the interests of the dominant classes, it continues to be a repository of hope for the oppressed classes. This is especially facilitated by widespread political democracy in the form of adult franchise in the developing countries. Thus for the poor and the exploited, the state represents the forces of modernisation and progress, and offers possibilities for improving the living standards of the population at large.

As mentioned earlier, Marx's thoughts on the nature of the state were never explicitly stated. As Poulantzas (1975) has remarked, "in Marx himself this neglect, more apparent than real, is above all due to the fact that his principal theoretical object was the capitalist mode of production, within which the economy not only holds the role of determinant in the last instance, but also the dominant role". Marx thus concentrated on the economic logic of the capitalist mode of production and he did not specifically deal with the other levels such as the state. Schumpeter (1954) had observed that Marx's sociological theory of the state may be summed up in the pithy statement from the Communist Manifesto that a government is a committee for the management of the bourgeoisie. There is therefore no such thing as a socialist state since the state as such dies in the transition to socialism. This is in sharp contrast to the commanding role that the state played in the Soviet system.

With the ownership of the means of production having changed from private to state hands, there now had to be a commanding presence of the state in the management of production and distribution of all manner of goods and services in the Soviet system. But this entailed a huge degree of centralisation, far too unwieldy for quick and efficient decision-making which keeps the wheels of the economy running smoothly. Shortage and surpluses were bound to occur and even though the system somehow delivered over the years, it was never geared to efficiency in the way a system run on the capitalist profit principle could be. Side by side there was the military compulsion of superpower politics during a regime of cold war when substantial funds were diverted to maintain a high level of military preparedness. This took more than its toll on the viability of the Soviet economic system and the system was getting weighed down by its own contradictions.

The world is at present witnessing a decline of the nation-state when a new phase of global corporate capitalism is being championed in several quarters [Kothari 1995]. This is attributable to a general ascendancy of conservative, free market-oriented, thinking and the assault is being spearheaded by multinational conglomerates, principally based in the advanced capitalist countries of Western Europe, North America or Japan. The onslaught is worldwide in its sweep and is undermining of political units and their autonomy especially in developing but also in transitional economies. An important feature of this new trend is the relegation to the background of issues like poverty and income inequality even as great importance is being attached to the expansion and globalisation of markets.

The collapse of the Soviet Union has especially contributed to the growing erosion and marginalisation of the state. Yet while there is increasing scepticism and renewed doubts about the efficacy of the state, there is still a substantial degree of confidence amongst the common masses and especially the poor about the inherent indispensability of the state apparatus which may still be expected to deliver the goods.

III State and market: a reconsideration

As has been mentioned before, in standard welfare economics the case for government action emerges in the event of externalities and public goods, missing markets, imperfect information, existence of entry barriers and increasing returns, among others. The above encompasses a rather large typology of cases and the real world is likely to contain one or more of the above pathologies rather than conform to the ideal version of perfect competition with full information and no externalities. Thus the case for government action may be regarded as the rule rather than an exception.

In addition to the above, the case for state action may be called for to deal with poverty and deprivation. This is an issue of central concern to a developing country like India. Further the state may be looked upon as an agency that acts paternalistically to ensure certain basic rights to its citizens such as the right to basic education and primary health. By the same token the paternal role of the state may be extended to encompass strict legislation and enforcement against drugs and liquor. The state may also intervene to protect the interests of the future generations in terms of issues like environmental degradation and global warming, a concern that is simply unlikely to be addressed by the market [see Stern 1990, for a discussion].

There is however an influential body of opinion that emphasises 'government failure' rather than 'market failure'. This view is held on the ground that most government activities that have to do with regulatory, legislative or administrative functions end up with 'rent seeking' behaviour on the part of government functionaries. Such behaviour reduces the impact of the intended policy intervention and sometimes may even eliminate it altogether. The evidence of rent seeking behaviour is fairly widespread and it can be nobody's case that it can possibly have any beneficial impact.

The real question therefore is one of finding the right balance in trying to avoid the twin evils of market failure and government failure. There are several instances of economies where government action has not been beneficial but by the same token there are several cases where the reverse is the case. It needs no belabouring that China and Korea have performed well with a great deal of government intervention [see Chenery, Robinson and Syrquin 1986, for example] while Hong Kong is an example of a country flourishing with a minimum of government interference. Thus it would be wrong to think in terms of applying the same policy package to all countries. The appropriate prescription undoubtedly has to be based on the history, institutions and ideology prevalent in a country.

Even so there is a broad measure of consensus that there are certain well defined areas where the role of the state is vital, particularly in a developing country. This is especially true of infrastructure, characterised by lumpiness and natural monopoly, and the social sector such as education and health. A major difficulty with the social sector is that it tends not to be self-financing, with limited access to borrowed funds from the market because of the low commercial profitability in these lines. It is therefore invariably in need of budgetary support from the state. Owing to their large commitments in education, health, housing, social security and welfare the share of government expenditure in GNP is as high as 46 per cent in Denmark and 54 per cent in both the Netherlands and Sweden (*World Development Report*, 1995).

A key question pertains to the role of the state in investment activity. Since the private sector is guided principally by the profit motive it would invest in areas where returns come in early and at high rates. This is not likely to be the case in the above-mentioned areas of infrastructure and the social sector. Quite clearly the government has to step in these areas, but the question, as always, is to what extent and in what precise manner. There is an influential view that by making a prior claim on scarce investible resources and pushing up rates of interest public investment in these areas tends to crowd out private investment [see, for example, Sundarrajan and Thakur 1980]. Whether or not there is in fact crowding out in the context of specific economies is an issue of substantial debate and the matter is far from settled. There is however considerable evidence that because public investment is geared towards infrastructure and the core sectors, it in fact acts as a facilitator and presents an enabling environment for the private sector to flourish.

If the ultimate objective of development is to enhance the well-being of human beings, judged in terms of indicators related to life expectancy, adult literacy and universal health care, the role of the public sector in countries as diversely placed as China, Costa Rica, Cuba, Jamaica, Chile and Sri Lanka has been absolutely pre-eminent [Sen 1990]. In a number of countries where a growth-oriented strategy has been adopted, eg, Hong Kong, Korea, Kuwait and Singapore, the results in terms of the above indicators have been remarkable primarily because substantial resources were channelised to the public sector for education, health and social security. In the realm of famine relief it has been seen repeatedly [see Dreze and Sen 1989] that the public sector, through programmes such as cash for work can recreate entitlements lost as a result of disaster and thereby generate income. This can of course be effectively combined with the use of private food trade in the affected region. This combination of public sector based income generation and private sector based food trade can be very effective. In fact it has been seen in several contexts that famine relief work left purely to the public or the private sector is invariably an unmitigated failure.

The effectiveness of public policy to combat famine is intimately related to the issue of political democracy. As Sen has observed, major famines have taken place in market economies and non-market socialist economies, but not in any country with a democratic system, with opposition parties and with a relatively free press. During the major Chinese famine in 1958–61 when nearly 23–30 million people died Chinese newspapers were silent about the disaster. Quite clearly public pressure and the free press have a major role to play in activating the state to intervene purposively in crisis situations.

It is beyond any doubt that the guiding and facilitating role of the state has been central to the development experience of the late industrialisers well as the market economies of east Asia. These states have actively pursued the policy of protecting domestic capitalists from foreign competition, and they have typically pursued both import substitution as well as export promotion. Much more than the invisible hand of the market, it is the pervasive interventionist role of the state that has put economies like that of Korea on a high growth path.

The problem in the context of a developing country like India is substantially more critical, in that there are vast tracts of poverty, low level literacy, poor health care systems and poor infrastructure. The real issue is not whether to have the market or the state. This is an empty dichotomy and no serious school of political economy would today credibly argue for only one or the other. The question however is one of striking the right balance. And one also has to guard against a new mode of thinking that suggests that the market may be entrusted to sort out all the basic problems confronting an economy, even with its manifest incapacity to deal with issues pertaining to income distribution and deprivation. While the profit motive may work well in the sphere of commodity production, in the production of shoes, say, it is fraught with serious problems in the areas of health, education, poverty alleviation and famine relief. There is no alternative other than to have substantial state action in each of these areas.

[This was presented as a theme paper at the Annual Conference of the Indian Economic Association held at Chandigarh in December 1995.]

References

Arrow, K J (1970): 'The Organisation of Economic Activity: Issues Pertinent to the Choice of Market versus Non-Market Allocation' in *Public Expenditure and Policy Analysis*, R H Haveman and J Margolis (eds), Markham, Chicago.

Byres, T (1994): 'State, Class and Development Planning in India' in T Byres (ed). *The State and Development Planning in India*, Oxford University Press, Delhi.

Chenery, H S Robinson and M Syrquin (1986): *Industrialisation and Growth: A Comparative Study*, Oxford University Press. New York.

Coase, R (1960): 'The Problem of Social Cost'. *Journal of Law and Economics*.

Dreze, J and A Sen (1989): *Hunger and Public Action*, Clarendon Press, Oxford.

Kalecki, M (1976): *Essays on Developing Economies*, Harvester Press. Sussex.

Keynes, J M (1936): *The General Theory of Employment, Interest and Money*, Macmillan, London.

Kothari, R (1995): 'Globalisation and 'New World Order': What Future for the United Nations?', *Economic and Political Weekly*.

Miliband, Ralph (1973): 'Poulantzas and the Capitalist State', *New Left Review*, 82.

Nozick, R (1974): *Anarchy. Slate and Utopia*, Basil Blackwell, Oxford.

Poulantzas, N (1975): 'The Problem of the Capitalist State' in R Blackburn (ed). *Ideology in Social Science*. Fontana, Glasgow.

Raj, K N (1973): 'The Politics and Economics of "Intermediate Regimes"', *Economic and Political Weekly*.

Roll, Eric (1953): *A History of Economic Thought*, Faber & Faber, London.

Schumpeter, J A (1954): *History of Economic Analysis*, Oxford University Press. New York.

Sen, A (1990): 'Development Strategies: The Roles of the State and the Private Sector'. *The World Bank Economic Review*, Supplement.

Smith, Adam (1937): *The Wealth of Nations*, Random House, New York.

—— (1804): *The Theory of Moral Sentiments*, Cadell & Davies, London.

Stern, N (1990): 'Development Strategies: The Roles of the State and the Private Sector', *The World Bank Economic Review*, Supplement.

Stiglitz, J (1993): The Role of the State in Financial Markets', *The World Bank Economic Review*, Supplement.

Sundarrajan, V and S Thakur (1980): 'Public Investments, Crowding Out and Growth: A Dynamic Model Applied to India and Korea' *IMF Staff Papers*.

World Bank (1995): *World Development Report*, Oxford University Press, Delhi.

14

Development economics as a paradigm

Syed Nawab Haider Naqvi

Source: *Development Economics – Nature and Significance* (New Delhi: Sage Publications, 2002), pp. 159–89.

This chapter draws together the threads of the main arguments presented so far in this book to highlight both the strengths and the weaknesses of development economics in relation to the major issues of economic development, for example, growth, distribution, employment generation, poverty reduction and enhancing human happiness. The next chapter then evaluates its (net) worth to meet the new challenges of the 21st century, once some of its early shortcomings are remedied. Even at the risk of some repetition, I begin by looking at the founding father's intellectual legacy bequeathed to posterity.

The intellectual legacy

The lineage of development economics has been variously described. Sen (1988) considers William Petty to be 'certainly' the 'founder of development economics' because of his earthshaking observation that 'the French grow too fast' and his concern with measuring economic progress in a broad enough sense to include 'each. Man's particular happiness' (p. 10). Lewis finds the subject buried in the 18th century writings of Hume, Cantillon, Smith and Wallace, among others. 'The theory of economic development established itself in Britain in the century and a half running from 1650 to Adam Smith's *The Wealth of Nations* (1776)' (Lewis 1988: p. 18). Further, he points out that many of the concepts of modern development economics were already in currency in those days.[1] For example, Adam Smith emphasized that economic growth (referred to as 'the Natural Progress of Opulence') is the defining characteristic of the development process. Much later, Marshall (1920) spoke about the 'high theme of economic progress' (p. 461). These observations suggest strong links between the classical economics of the days of yore and modern development economics, which spells out the broader principles of economic development. Further, it suggests that neo-classical economics, by sidelining the growth-related issues, has deviated from the central concern of economics—that is, to explain the reality and to change it for the betterment of humankind.

However, highlighting the continuity of development economics should not be misconstrued as doing 'normal science'; nor should it be seen as old wine in new bottles, though ripened with age. The fact is that development economics, as we understand the term today, was formally inaugurated between Rosenstein-Rodan's 'big-push' conjecture (1943), the Singer Prebisch hypothesis (1950) about the asymmetrical working of international trade, which highlights the dangers of a no-holds barred, export-led growth and Lewis's celebrated two-sector model (1954), whereby growth flows from an unlimited supply of labour in the rural sector, which is drawn to the capitalist urban sector at an unchanged wage rate. Then there were such early lights as Gerschenkron's 'pioneers-latecomers' syndrome (1952); Nurkse's 'balanced-growth' hypothesis (1953); and Mahalanobis's heavy-industry advocacy (1953). A little later in the day came Scitovsky's (1954) dynamic external-economies conjecture, which was followed by Hirschman's (1958) and Streeten's (1959) 'unbalanced-growth' hypotheses. In these contributions we have the first glimpses of a genuine 'paradigm change'—of a change in focus from the off-and-on neo-classical dabbling in the steady-state behaviour of general-equilibrium economic systems, to the full-time occupation of development economics with the central issues of economic development. To this end, the new development paradigm highlighted the growth of the key inputs (labour and capital) over time, and the forces that convert these into a sustained increase in wealth of (poor) nations. It aimed to accelerate the growth process, distribute the fruits of economic progress more equitably and reduce poverty on a durable basis in as short a time as possible.

In this new scientific research programme, the process of economic development appears complex, mysterious and like a many-splendoured thing. Unlike the neo-classical paradigm, its central propositions cannot be straightforwardly deduced from a few simple axioms. It is initiated, and then sustained, by continual economy-wide, inter-sectoral shifts that help capital (saving) accumulation in the capitalist (i.e., manufacturing) sector, where the sun of economic prosperity first rises before lighting up the surrounding environment. These shifting input–output configurations move not into the shadows of a 'stationary state', but towards a more dynamic production structure, helped by a perfectly elastic (or unlimited) supply of labour in the rural sector (resembling the Marxian reserve army of labour), inter-industry linkages, economies of scale, externalities and complementarities. At the center of this process of structural transformation, the rate of growth is determined by the profit rate in the manufacturing activity multiplied by the capitalist's saving, which keeps on rising to finance capital formation and economic growth, while wage income does no better than finance the current consumption of its recipients.

This central tendency of the manufacturing activity racing to the top of the development ladder is by no means inconsistent with agriculture growing at the maximal rate, a point *not* clearly reflected in the development policies of many developing countries. This tendency has been understood as being associated with an initial worsening of the distribution of income between capital and labour, which is expected, however, to work out eventually to everybody's advantage by accelerating capital formation and economic growth. Such a growth would be a 'balanced' one in case of the elastic supplies of the key industrial inputs making maximum use of the horizontal and vertical interdependencies between agriculture and manufacturing sectors. However, it would be an 'unbalanced' one if investment resources were assumed to be fixed with the explicit aim of eventually attaining some kind of a dynamic inter-sectoral balance by exploiting dynamic external economies.[2] The state may have to intervene as a *facilitator* of the development process and also as a *caveat emptor* which conveys correctly the relevant information to consumers and producers efficiently. All of this is of vital importance because factor prices do not reflect opportunity costs when sizeable external economies exist, or when large complementarities bring strange bed-fellows together. The less the opportunities of mutually profitable international trade and investment, the more important will the developmental role of the state be in propelling the development process in more productive directions, especially where free markets fear to tread.

Relationship with neighbours

Development theory and, to some extent, development policy has drawn freely on alternative development paradigms, namely, Keynesian economics and its immediate successor, the Harrod-Domar model, and the Marxian, structuralist and institutionalist explanations of economic reality. From the former, development economics has inherited the courage to declare independence—or, more accurately, autonomy—from mainstream neo-classical economics and to deny the latter's ubiquitous reach and relevance. Indeed, some of the discipline's intellectual armoury consists of concepts which have been directly inspired by Keynesian economics. Examples of such concepts are that of 'rural underemployment'—a 'first cousin' of the Keynesian unemployment equilibrium—and the vision of a mixed economy in which the state plays a dominant role to correct the strategic macro-economic imbalances that the market cannot do much about. However, the cross-fertilization of ideas was the most intense with the Harrod-Domar model and Solow's neoclassical growth model from where development economics has derived some of its key insights—those concerning the centrality of the national savings rate *(s)*, the capital-output ratio *(v)*, the growth of the labour force *(n)*, and technological change *(A)* as the key determinants of the warranted growth rate *(w)*. But it is not enamoured of their neo-classical concerns about the attainability and/or sustainability of the (mythical) steady-state growth paths, which are not amenable to policy manipulations (because these cannot move in a positive direction unless associated with the growth of *n*). Making light of the highly restrictive assumptions on which the Harrod-Domar and Solow models are based, development economics has been more interested in the models' predictions,[3] namely, those relating to the role played by the growth of labour supply as well as its efficiency, which set the upper limit on the sustainable (warranted) growth rate of output; and to the basic result that, given a technological fixed capital–output ratio and growth rate of employment, the economy can be made to grow twice as fast only if the savings rate is twice as high. (Note that 'capital' here mainly denotes physical capital; but with some stretching of the model's labour-efficiency term it can also be interpreted as including human capital.) Also helpful has been Solow's extension of the Harrod-Domar model that a changing capital/output ratio can be an efficient means of achieving the steady-state growth for a while, though not permanently because of the tendency of the diminishing returns to capital, unless arrested or reversed by appropriate technological change (or, more accurately, by an improvement in total factor productivity). This conveyed a message of hope that there is tendency for the low-income economies with a higher rate of return on capital to converge to the high-income economies, where this rate tends to decline with a growing surfeit of capital.

Yet another source of inspiration for development economics has been the Marxist/structuralist analysis, which has informed the former with a sense of history, a sensitivity to the institutional constraints ('fetters') on growth and development, an awareness of the importance of class power and class alliances in the production–distribution nexus, and an attitude of healthy skepticism towards the neo-classical faith in the mutual-benefit claim, which states that notwithstanding the manifold asymmetries in the distribution of political and economic power between competing trading parties, domestic and international exchanges work out to everyone's advantage. Given below are a few examples of such propositions of the Marxist/structuralist origin which are now standard stuff (in duly modified forms) in development economics.

1 An efficient allocation of resources and the fullest development of the production potential (i.e., 'the forces of production') are not independent of the specific configuration of the relationships of ownership and control (i.e., 'the relations of production').
2 The feudal structures—interpreted as 'a type of socioeconomic organization of the society as a whole, a mode of production and of the reproduction of social classes' (Brenner 1990: p. 170)—tend to obstruct the flow of incentives to the direct cultivators, and minimize the 'trickle-down' effects of growth.
3 The adoption in the initial period of certain profitable technologies (i.e., those promising increasing returns to scale) by the vested interests, so that 'the more [these are] adopted the more it is attractive or convenient for others to join the bandwagon', tends to 'lock-in' the future path of economic development (i.e., makes it 'path-dependent') (Bardhan 1988: p. 50).

4 Perhaps the most internalized of the Marxian/institutionalist insights relates to the inevitability of 'unequal exchange' between unequals—between the 'center' and the 'periphery'—which then disqualifies excessive export orientation and an over-reliance on (private) foreign investment as reliable engines of growth, much less development. More generally, within the context of such 'closed loop' unequal relationships, the initial level of social capability casts a long shadow on the subsequent configurations of development trajectories (Abramovitz 1986) and also reinforces the path-dependence of the development process noted in 3.
5 A lasting imprint of the Marxian thought on development theory and policy is the understanding that the development process needs to be guided (though not in as much micro detail as centralized economies attempt to do) in the socially desired directions—that is, in directions where the faint-hearted market forces would never dare to flow.

However, in inducting ideas from competing development paradigms, development economics has sought to leaven them with moderation and, in some cases, even transform their character; but in every case it has stamped them with a mark of its originality. This is especially the case with borrowings from Marxist/structuralist and institutionalist sources. Thus, for instance, historical determinism and the inevitability of class conflict—though not denying such possibilities in cases where a regular venting of popular ire is not allowed—do not appear in its vision of economic development, which, in turn, leaves ample room for individual freedom and rationality (though not necessarily in the narrow neo-classical sense). Thus, even when the 'path dependence' of the development process is emphasized, it is to highlight that its future course can be peaceably altered most effectively by corrective policy interventions in the initial conditions, which are then sustained subsequently (Maddison 1991; Adelman and Morris 1993). A more striking example of such creative adaptation relates to the prescription of the best way out of the Marxian 'contradictions of capitalism'—namely, the inherent incompatibility of the growth of the capitalist system beyond a certain stage, which then acts as a 'fetter' on the fullest development of the forces of production. The Marxian way out is by engineering a social revolution (Baran 1957); but development economics would recommend that the way to save capitalism from itself is by a maximal development of the capitalist modes of production in tandem with far-reaching egalitarian reforms, especially those focusing on the redistribution of assets. This is how its mixed-economy prescription—namely, 'a mixture of free enterprise or market elements with an often considerable element of public intervention in favour of low-income group in the population' (Tinbergen 1985: p. 174) works. Yet another Marxian notion which has been peaceably accommodated in development economics is 'commodity fetishism', which conveys the sense of the historical evolution of social relations within the matrix of commodity exchange. The important Marxian insight here is that the terms and character of commodity exchange are not independent of the mechanism through which the actions of individual economic agents are coordinated (through the market or by conscious planning). This notion carries over into development economics as a criticism of the tendency to over-emphasize 'commodities' at the expense of 'capabilities' and *economic* rather than *human* development—topics which have been discussed at length in Chapters 6 and 7 of this book.

Building up the heritage

Before proceeding any further, it is useful to highlight some of the areas where the 'traditional' development paradigm is improvable. First, it is important to clear up the fog of confusion which is traceable to the centrality it assigns to the savings rate *(s)* per se to raise the growth rate of output (g)—an aspect of the Harrod-Domar model that development economists have accepted uncritically. The correct proposition that a higher rate of growth of savings is a *necessary* condition for the economy to grow at a higher-than-trend growth rate *for some time* was at times confused with the wrong statement that a higher growth of savings is sufficient per se to achieve a sustainable long-run increase in the rate of output.[4] The latter statement is *wrong* because structural transformation (the rising share of the manufacturing activity in GDP) would raise the capital–output *(v)* ratio as well, which is incompatible with the saving to capital–output ratio *(s/v)* remaining equal to the growth rate of labour force *(n)* in steady-state equilibrium (for details see Hahn and Matthews 1965). Also, a lot of saving can go waste due to a rise in the capital–output ratio in case of an inappropriate choice of investment projects, or because inefficient investment may not get translated into a corresponding increase in the (warranted) growth rate. The experience of a number of developing countries, which have attained high rates of saving (i.e., in excess of 20 per cent of the GDP), but not the corresponding high rates of investment and growth (for e.g., India), illustrate such perverse tendencies.

Second, following the Harrod-Domar-Solow models, the centrality of 'endogenizing' population growth in the process of economic development—that is, of the two-way interaction between the economic and demographic variables—was ignored by development economics, which regarded population growth as *exogenous* to the development process. The importance of this neglect can be seen from the fact that development success (failure) in the last 50 years has been due as much to an increase (decline) in the GDP as to a reduction (increase) in the growth rate of population. Thus, the splendid success of East Asia and the modest success (even failure) elsewhere have come about because, unlike the latter, the former could forge a tighter link between the growth rate of output and a decline in the fertility rate flowing from the voluntary decisions of the household. This fact has highlighted the need to achieve Demographic Transition in the shortest period of time—a point explicitly noted by the classical economists, and shown later on by Coale and Hoover (1958) as a precondition of a sustainable growth rate of per capita income.

Third, the critical role of technological process, spurred on by the creation of new ideas—which, because of their non-rivalrous nature, share some aspects of public goods—was highlighted by Schumpeter (1934), in generating a sufficiently high (*ex ante*) rate of investment to raise output on a permanent, rather than on a transitory, basis. However, it was generally not given a central place in his scheme of things. On the other hand, this aspect, though basic to classical growth theories, was not clearly reflected in development *policy*, even when development *theory* recognized it in isolated cases. Looking back, this appears to be a rather surprising omission because Harrod's emphasis on 'technical progress as a built-in propensity in an industrial economy' marked a turning point in the neo-classical doctrine, which treated it as exogenous to the system, 'shocking' it to move on to a higher growth path (Robinson 1967: p. 98). Part of the reason for this neglect may be that most expositions of the Harrod-Domar model have regarded technological progress as exogenous to the model. Further, Solow's model is seen as concerned with rescuing the Harrod-Domar model from its knife-edge predicament by letting the capital–output ratio vary due to technological change (for e.g., Hahn and Mathews 1965: pp. 5–15). However, a more important aspect of the Solow model (1957), which asserts that because of the diminishing returns to capital, the growth rate of output can only be sustained by appropriate doses of technological change, was not given much prominence in development economics. Yet another neglected implication of his model is the possibility of 'convergence', namely, the possibility of the developing countries closing the gap between their per capita incomes and those of the developed countries. This possibility was seldom seriously discussed in the development literature until the East Asian experience (and earlier that of Japan) demonstrated its realism.[5]

Fourth, *human* capital, especially education was assigned only a secondary importance, next to physical capital, in development models—and then too, it was not always explicitly stated. This omission is strange because Solow showed clearly that about seven-tenths of the increase in gross output per hour of work in the US between 1909 and 1945 was due to 'technological progress in the broadest sense', which is now understood as improvements in total factor productivity. What it means is that the contributions of physical capital and labour are considerably less important than development economists would normally have thought—to the chagrin of Lewis and Marx! Later, Denison (1967, 1985) showed in his growth-accounting framework that a full 30 per cent of the per capita growth of output between 1929 and 1982 was accounted for by education per worker, while 64 per cent of it was explained by the advances in knowledge. Thus, the fastest growing countries have been those where the enrolment levels were the highest in the initial period—for e.g., South Korea and Taiwan (IMF 2000a). However, a few caveats may be introduced at this point to explain, though not justify, why development models may not have taken account of human capital:

1 It looked rather odd that the growth phenomenon should almost entirely be explained by factors exogenous to the model, as is the case with the Solow model.
2 It appears that human capital may be a *superior* good, the demand for which increases as higher level of development is reached.

Thus, in sharp contrast to the European experience used by Denison, empirical studies done for developing countries show that 60–70 per cent of the growth in per capita income can be explained by *physical* capital formation caused by inter-sectoral shift of resources, 10–20 per cent is accounted for by education and human capital, with the remaining 20–30 per cent being contributed by the residual (i.e., by improvement in total factor productivity) (Bosworth and Collins 1996: IMF 2000a). In the same vein, it has been shown that faster growth in education and human capital is a necessary, but *not* sufficient, condition for enabling developing countries to catch up with the developed countries (Nelson and Phelps 1996; Barro 1997). It follows that developing countries should not under-emphasize physical capital formation until a fairly advanced level of development is reached and the demand for highly skilled labour sharply increases. In this context, a relevant finding is that the return to education is significantly reduced once it is related to educational *performance* (output) rather than to the increase in inputs to education (for e.g., schools built, etc.), which suggests that the return on educational output may have been over-stated to some extent (Sirageldin 2001).

Fifth, even though Lewis was careful to emphasize the vital importance of a dynamic agriculture to sustain structural transformation of the economy, his two-sector model led to an *extractive* view of agriculture, which tended to grossly underestimate the growth potentialities of the agricultural sector.[6]

Sixth, the original development paradigm has also been criticized for its alleged 'bloody-mindedness' with respect to the distributional aspects of growth.[7] In Lewis's two-sector model with unlimited supplies of labour, economic growth is a function solely of the profit rate: 'the central fact of economic development is that the distribution of income is altered in favour of the saving class' (Lewis 1954), cited in Agarwala and Singh (1963: p. 417). Thus, in this model, the distribution path is completely determined by the growth of capitalist income, with the wage-earners losing out to the capitalists because a rise, for whatever reasons, in the real wage rate signals a weakening of the growth impulse. In the Fei-Ranis model (1963), a less fatalistic scenario is presented—once all surplus labour has migrated and the urban wage starts to rise, the wage-earners will find their lots improved. Thus, in the growth process, no one income group loses out *absolutely*. In this respect, however, one should think that development economists were marching with the spirit of the times. For instance, in the classical savings function, routinely used even by the neo-Keynesians, the rate of growth of income is simply a function of the savings of the profit-earners multiplied by the profit rate. Following them, Lewis (1954), Galenson and Leibenstein (1955), and Kaldor (1955) feature the classical saving function, whereby all saving is done by the capitalist. The empirical studies done by Kuznets (1955) lent respectability to this view by reference to the forces of history, according to which income inequity tends to increase in the initial stages as income rises—following an inverted 'U' pattern—and to be higher in the poor countries than in the rich countries. That may be so, but the fact that growth was accompanied by income inequality should not have been taken to mean that no steps can, or ought to be, taken to remedy this. At any rate, extensive recent research casts doubt on this line of thinking and emphasizes the direct contribution made by low income inequality to economic development. It also points out that growth combined with a more equitable distribution is superior to growth combined with a less equitable distribution (for e.g., Aghion *et al.* 1999; World Bank 2001).

Finally, once again moving with the spirit of the times when logical purity demanded the reduction of a plurality of causes to *one* original cause—for e.g., individual and social welfare measured with respect to the Benthamite metric of utility; of utility *alone* to the exclusion of all else—there has also been a monocentric emphasis in development literature on raising per capita income as the measure of economic progress, while issues like improving the distribution of income, and more generally equity and social justice, may have been sidelined somewhat. Two other reasons for the neglect of the latter set of issues have been: (a) the acceptance by development economics of the finality of the divorce between ethics and economics pronounced by Robbins (1932), which downplayed the distributional and moral aspects of the development process, and (b) the (implicit) acceptance by at least some development economists of the efficiency-oriented Pareto optimality public choice rule, which has banished ethical issues from consideration.

Elements of the development paradigm

The preceding analysis points out some of the defects of our intellectual heritage with respect to our understanding of the development process. But a somewhat defective heritage is better than no heritage at all, and at any rate, it does not mean that we do away with it altogether and opt for an irrelevant (neo-classical) framework of thought. Indeed, with the lively ongoing intellectual debate, such 'defects' have led to a more adequate development paradigm. Contrary to Hirschman's (1981c) assertion that development economics is a 'done thing' because it has not responded creatively to the many challenges it faced both from the Left and the Right, a spate of sympathetic review articles and full length books have appeared at regular intervals to add complexity, rigour, vigour and relevance to the original development paradigm.[8] There are also regular fora—the World Bank, the Asian Development Bank (both pillars of world capitalism)—where development economics is regularly discussed, though mostly with a view to converting it to the neo-classical (market-friendly) point of view! Finally, the UNDP's human development conjecture has led to the inclusion of new ideas and hard data in its annual *Human Development Reports*, which has meant a significant broadening of the conventional development paradigm. With such credentials and vitality, development economics can hardly be faulted for intellectual moribundity. In fact, its response to the changing realities of life in the developing countries and to the new theoretical advances made in mainstream economics has been both positive and creative. We shall pursue these matters in the remaining part of the present chapter. The analysis presented in this book is put in a somewhat holistic framework in order to highlight the distinctive features of development economics and ensure that it does not wilt under the stress of exogenous shocks (for e.g., globalization) due to any lack of self-confidence.

Growth and distribution

The analysis presented so far stresses the need for an integrated approach to economic development, in which some of the tradeoffs between the crucial aspects of the development process are reconsidered and resolved to the extent that it is feasible to do so. Thus, for instance, it is vital to secure both the growth of the GDP *and* its better distribution. This is especially the case when assets, rather than just income, are more equitably distributed (Ferreira 1999). This is important because both are required to enhance people's capabilities, expand their freedom to make choices and raise the economic well-being of the people (and/or to reduce their deprivations). This view of economic development is, however, more comprehensive than that of the founding fathers, who in their enthusiasm to run the engine of growth ever faster, and not seeing the *two-way* positive links between growth and equity clearly enough, did not adequately emphasize the question of an equitable redistribution of income and wealth, though not ignoring it altogether. Their basic idea was not only to do one thing at a time and do it well, but also to reduce the development process to a single causative factor (namely, economic growth), and then let the 'trickle-down effects' take care of income distribution. This faith in the trickle-down effect can be attributed to the alleged success of the Industrial Revolution in raising the share of labour in total output by a secular rise in real wages.[9] But the belief in the trickle-down effect was soon questioned by Singer (1950), Prebisch (1950), Baran (1952) and Myrdal (1956a), among others, who highlighted the forces that limit the size of the trickle-down effect, or the 'spread effect', within countries and between countries.

There is a consensus now that economic growth is likely to be higher with less inequality. Thus, the feudal societies will experience lesser growth than the more industrialized ones where the intra-sectoral linkages are stronger, but this realization has sunk very slowly into development thinking. Kuznet's hypothesis, which on the basis of somewhat skimpy empirical foundations predicts rising inequalities in the early stage of growth, sparked off a series of cross-country studies—for example, those by Adelman and Morris (1973), Papanek and Kyn (1986), and Ahluwalia (1976)—to test the U-shaped relationship between growth and distribution. Kuznet's hypothesis was initially supported, but with the caveat that the relationship may be the accident of history (U-shaped) or the outcome of specific policies (J-shaped). However, more recent evidence is mixed: there is no systematic positive relationship between inequality and a particular stage of economic development (Galor and Zeira 1993; Deininger and Squire 1998; World Bank 2001). Further, the evidence suggests that there is a negative correlation between the average growth rate of income and any known measure of income distribution (Benabou 1996), that when capital markets are imperfect, which is a common occurrence in developing countries, there is *no* absolute trade-off between efficiency and equity, and that there is considerable 'scope for redistributive policies which are also growth-promoting' (Aghion *et al.* 1999). In other words, growth and distribution form an irreducible set of objectives of development policy (Alesina and Rodrik 1994) and these two can together form a mutually reinforcing virtuous circle if proper development policies are implemented (Naqvi 1995).

Not only has the distributional problem been investigated thoroughly, but research has also been done on the ways and means of correcting the de-equalizing biases of growth. One approach has been to reorient the production structure in a labour-intensive manner so that employment can grow faster and raise real wages, especially that of unskilled labour. Leontief (1983) conjectures that such a sequence explains the relatively more equitable industrial growth in Europe in the 19th century. In our own times, Japan and South Korea are the principal examples of such a growth strategy, which seeks to minimize the trade-off between growth and equity (Chow and Papanek's study [1981] on Hong Kong is in the same vein; see also World Bank [1999, 2000]). Another route to enhance the distributional content of growth is to devote an increasing proportion of the increments in national income to the provision of basic needs (Streeten *et al.* 1981), or to the creation of assets owned by the poor (Chenery 1975). In contrast to this 'incrementalist' approach, there are other approaches which focus on the creation of assets for the poor even *before* growth takes place (Adelman 1978). The relationship between growth and inequality is likely to be negative if the initial distribution of income and assets is less, rather than more, unequal (World Bank 2001). An important aspect of the problem is that the people's evaluation of their well-being is essentially a relative matter because they relate their welfare to their location relative to the mean (van Praag *et al.* 1978). Thus, any successful programme of redistribution must ensure that structural reforms aimed at a redistribution of assets are carried out and the rate of increase of income of the poor is kept higher than the rate of increase of income of the rich (Naqvi and Qadir 1985).

The question of sectoral balance

An important, though unfortunate, fallout of the original development model was the development of industry *at the expense of* agriculture. For instance, Lewis's two-sector model was misunderstood as advocating an extractive view of agriculture. In his model, agriculture is seen as home to the 'unlimited supplies of labour', which must be drawn on to serve as an input into industrial production.[10] Not only labour, but also capital would flow to the industrial sector from the agricultural sector to support sustained capital accumulation and accelerated economic growth. The Fei-Ranis model (1963) also popularized the extractive view of agriculture as a self-sacrificing provider of inputs for economic growth. Such a concept of agriculture, emphasizing extraction from it rather than assigning it a positive role with a personality of its own, was mainly responsible in the late 1950s and early 1960s for agricultural stagnation, and increasing rural poverty in the developing countries. As a direct result of underinvestment in agriculture, the productivity of agricultural labour in developing countries has remained significantly lower than that achieved by the developed countries at a similar stage of development on the eve of the Industrial Revolution (Timmer 1988). This view has also been damaging because, as Johnston and Mellor (1961) show, 'economic development is characterized by a substantial increase in the demand for agricultural products, and the failure to expand food supplies in pace with the growth of demand can seriously impede economic growth. The result is likely to be a substantial rise in food prices, leading to political discontent and pressure on wage rates with adverse effects on industrial profits, investment, and economic growth.' Earlier, Kalecki (1971) had echoed the same theme: 'True, the process of development is constrained by the availability of capital; but investment is determined not only by savings but also by the supply of wage goods, which are typically supplied by the agricultural sector'. There is another reason why the development of agriculture is crucial to the aggregate growth rate. It relates to the possibility of varying the capital/output ratio between agriculture and industry to maximize total output in terms of the required capital inputs—an echo of Solow. Recognizing that 'extremely low capital/labour ratio in the dominant rural sector is at the heart of the development problem,' it would clearly be desirable to 'spread the scarce capital resource between the low capital/labour-ratio agriculture sector and the relatively higher capital/labour-ratio industrial sector in order to lower the capital intensity of growth' (Mellor and Johnston 1984).

A vast body of literature has emphasized the dynamic linkages between sectors, especially between the agricultural sector and the manufacturing sector. The central point of these and other contributions to this area is to emphasize the *contributory* role of agriculture to economic development, and the factors which lead to the modernization and growth of the agricultural sector itself.[11] Among such factors, technological change figures prominently because, as Schultz (1964) pointed out, continuing investments in traditional technologies are quickly thwarted by diminishing (marginal) returns. Hence, an 'endogenous' technological change should help agricultural growth, especially food output, which, by the same token, also enlarges the size of the market for urban output. This enlargement of the market takes place by increasing the real income of the rural poor, generating rural employment and lowering food prices through technological change.[12]

Labour markets

Another unfortunate consequence of the original development model has been the rather simplistic view of the labour markets in developing countries, that labour commands very low, or even zero, wages in the agricultural sector because of an unlimited supply. Thus, in this model, the scattered, non unionized labour migrates unidirectionally from the rural backwaters to the urban 'growth poles', where they expect to be fully employed. Indeed, this aspect of development economics, which stresses that the marginal product of labour is zero in agriculture, was used (mistakenly) by Schultz (1964) to deny the very existence of development eco-nomics.[13] (See also, Chapter 9, notes 16 and 17.)

This has provoked a large body of literature examining the peculiarities of the labour market in developing countries, in general, and of the rural market in particular.[14] The research in this area has been helped by the advances made by microeconomic theory about the information and risk problems, by the availability of better and larger data on the labour markets in developing countries, and by learning from the objective reality in these countries. Kalecki (1971) and Mellor (1986) show that a rising real wage in agriculture (caused mainly by a secular decline in the price of foodgrain) plays a critical role in expanding the size of the market for industrial goods and reducing rural poverty. An important theoretical contribution in this area is the Harris-Todaro model (1970) (generalized by Khan [1980]), which explains urban unemployment, and analyses the consequences of government policies to reduce it. In the model, the rural wage is determined competitively but the urban wage is set institutionally. Further, it is typically higher than the rural wage, which starts (and sustains) Lewis's process of rural–urban migration in the *hope* (measured by the relevant probability) of finding (full) employment in the urban sector.[15] Is this hope fulfilled? Lewis said 'yes'; but Harris and Todaro say 'no' because of the labour-market distortion caused by an institutionally set urban wage, which is typically too high. Does it help, then, to provide a wage subsidy to cure the urban unemployment problem? It probably does not, because it only increases the number of the urban unemployed by attracting rural labour in the *expectation* of finding more employment there. It is interesting to note that the Harris-Todaro model, rooted in the realities of the developing countries, not only corrects a defect in the neo-classical model—which conjures up the myth of permanent market-clearing in the labour market—but, as shown by Malinvaud (1984), is also an untenable hypothesis even in the developed countries. Incidentally, this is one of those many instances where development economics has something to give to neo-classical economics.

The market versus the government

The development paradigm discussed in the preceding chapters assigns a complementary, rather than an adversary, role to the market and the government. However, writing when the development process was just beginning to unfold its wings, the founding fathers—Rosenstein-Rodan (1943), Singer (1950), Prebisch (1950), Nurkse (1953), Scitovsky (1954), Hirschman (1958) and Streeten (1959)—may have emphasized government intervention more than would be warranted in today's environment to take care of the then near-ubiquity of cases of market failure, of markets which are far from perfect or too thin, or which simply do not exist. However, an even more fundamental motivation at the time must have been to wean economists away from an uncritical acceptance of classical (and neo-classical) metaphysical *belief*—such as that held by Haberler (1950) and Viner (1952), among others—in universal market clearing as a panacea for all economic problems including those relating to economic development. In particular, due to the perverse working of the terms-of-trade transmission mechanism which undermined the role of trade as an engine of growth, a series of steps *had* to be taken by the government to encourage import-substituting industrialization. This was done with a view to laying a firm foundation for latter-day export expansion and maximizing total output by taking advantage of inter-industry and intra-sector complementarities—an insight that subsequent empirical research has not proved to be mistaken (Bruton 1998). In these situations, investment decisions are required to be taken simultaneously to secure a structure of outputs corresponding to the structure of income elasticities of demand (Nurkse's 'balanced growth' doctrine); or when, due to the shortage of investible resources, investment must be undertaken sequentially to achieve a balanced production structure only gradually (Hirschman's and Streeten's 'unbalanced growth' doctrine). In both these cases, the profit-maximizing private producers could not be relied upon to optimize output without the active support of the government. This is because of the presence of externalities—that is, as *output* expands for one firm, its output-raising consequences for other firms cannot be (fully) internalized, which, in turn, would prevent market prices from summarizing the necessary information required by the profit-maximizing private investor. Of course, if individual firms could have secured information *costlessly* about the strategic responses of the other firms, then profit-seeing behaviour could do the job; but the point is that such information is seldom, if ever, complete, symmetric and costless. In the latter case, the basic propositions of neo-classical economics cease to hold. In particular, 'market equilibrium may not exist . . .; when equilibrium exists, it is, in general, not Pareto efficient; it may not be possible to decentralize efficient resource allocations . . .; market equilibrium may be characterized by an excess demand for credit or an excess supply of labour (that is, the law of supply and demand no longer holds)' (Stiglitz 1988: p. 156).

The intensity of state intervention and its form, however, remains an open issue even though the times have changed greatly. The fact is that, with the tragic exception of Africa (especially, sub-Saharan Africa), a large of number of countries have made significant economic progress, some growing spectacularly (East Asia, China) while others only modestly (South-East Asia, Latin America). Furthermore, information has become much more cheap, spreads at a phenomenal speed and is far too decentralized now than was the case in the past (see Chapter 9). Thus, while it may not be feasible or desirable to centralize information (because that would be too costly), some kind of planning activity is still required, if only to provide a directional focus to economic growth at a time when international inequities of income and wealth are rising rapidly. However, it may have to be only of the indicative type where the markets for such information do not exist, where it is too costly or fragmentary, or where comparative advantage unfolds itself only slowly with the passage of time (Scitovsky 1987). But it may have to be more comprehensive where the strategy of investment emphasizes giving priority to capital goods-producing heavy industries. Such a strategy aims to facilitate the development of downstream industries, expand the industrial base in areas where the country is perceived to have a dynamic comparative advantage and generate 'forced saving'. These industries are also human-resource intensive, with significant spillover effects on the rest of the economy (Bradford *et al.* 1991).

The relevance of the central ideas of development economics in the context of the new realities, now and in the future, is discussed at some length in the next chapter. However, the point to note here is that contrary to the popular notion, there is no evidence of development economics ever going for an all-out *etatisme*. For instance, as noted in Chapter 3, the founding fathers in Pakistan and India explicitly rejected both the (unalloyed) capitalist model and the communist model. Instead, a 'mixed-economy' model has been preferred to the communist model. At any rate, in the modern context, the recommended state intervention need only be, to use Lowe's (1977) terminology, of the 'instrumental-inference type' (which involves setting macro goals and action directives derived from an empirical feasible plan), rather than an 'alternative to the market, based on command and fulfillment'. While the government must remain engaged in economic activities to make the Invisible Hand a little more visible to the naked eye, the productive and the complementary role of the private sector should also be duly accepted. And even when the private initiative is not forthcoming to the extent required, due to too much risk or uncertainty, the government should still, as in the past, establish industries with the explicit aim of eventually selling these to private takers, if and when they are ready to invest. In such circumstances, government intervention is more likely to crowd in, rather than crowd out, private investment (Streeten 1993). The Pakistan Industrial Development Corporation (PIDC) performed this role in the 1960s. The same has been the case in India. In fast-growing East Asia and China, where the government has sought through various means (for e.g., directed credits) to pick the 'winning' producers (i.e., those with the greatest potential efficiency, once firmly put on their feet), such a strategy has been crowned with spectacular success. It is necessary to repeat much of what was done in the past to align the market and government in a productive direction, especially because the market-friendly policies in the last 20 years have not produced the desired results.

True, the government does not always succeed where the market fails, but development experience shows that the government *has* succeeded splendidly in raising agricultural productivity by helping technological change through research institutes, and by ensuring adequate prices both to the producers and the consumers of food—a result that could not have been secured by the private sector. Further, governments have managed to create fairly impressive infrastructures and industrial structures in most of the developing countries (World Bank 1991). If the element of success has been greater in one case (for e.g., South Korea) than in the other (say, India or Pakistan), the difference is attributable to the quality of government, the flexibility of its response to external shocks and to the quality of political leadership in these countries—it does not necessarily hinge on the government being less dominant in the former than in the latter. Reynolds (1977) confirms this point by explicitly attributing the differences in the comparative growth experiences of developing countries to the differences in the managing capabilities of various governments. This, however, also underscores the counterproductive nature of dysfunctional state intervention as much as the limits of the market to maximize social welfare.

Keeping these facts in view, the critics of development economics, who still cite the *dirigiste* practices in developing countries as the prime cause of their failure when many have succeeded mainly *because* of them, appear somewhat ridiculous. First, such arguments commit the error of trying to establish the superiority of a nonexistent phenomenon (free markets in South Korea vs pervasive governments elsewhere) by comparing it with yet another nonexistent situation (i.e., Pareto optimality). Second, it is not logically permissible to infer general 'statements'—the unambiguous superiority of the market-based solutions—from singular statements about the successes/failures of specific countries, due to a variety of reasons. The fact is that the scenario of a generalized market success is sheer neo-classical romanticism, which conveniently blithes over the fact that market success is guaranteed *only* if the most unlikely concatenation of favourable factors occurs—that is, if there are enough markets, if both the consumers and producers behave competitively, and if equilibrium exists. However, the non-satisfaction of *any* of these conditions leads to a withdrawal of the guarantee of market success (Debreu 1959). And, even where the markets do succeed, the outcomes may not be socially desirable. Indeed, the markets may (successfully) 'work by strangulation', to use Joan Robinson's phrase, if the initial distribution of income is highly unequal (for e.g., in the presence of a feudal system). Third, it is hard to understand what to make of such proofs in practice. Should one abolish governments altogether and leave everything to the Invisible Hand? The fact of the matter is that if the government must always fail, then there is no guarantee that the market will always succeed, especially where none exists (Arrow 1974). Also, the fact that government rent-seeking may simply be replaced by private rent-seeking, because the 'agents' in the free market often commit 'fraud' on the 'principals' due to information asymmetry, robs the market-friendly philosophy of much of its 'nearness' (Streeten 1993). As Pack and Westphal (1986) point out, 'the factors responsible for a government's inability to intervene effectively may also preclude its following the neo-classical prescription.'

Ethics and development

There is, however, a more controversial issue which is actually the most fundamental problem, and which has caused considerable 'inner tension' in economics in general, and development economics in particular. It is the failure to synthesize basic economic propositions with a set of universally held ethical norms of behaviour in the society, with a view to healing such tensions.[16] This failure hinders scientific vision because ethical considerations mingle with economic compulsions effortlessly at the level of the economic agents' primary motivation, which then translates into social action. Indeed, in the real world, *the plurality* of *motivations* is the rule rather than the exception, and one would be hard put to prove that either mere self-interest or pure altruism explains a large enough segment of social or individual action.[17] Thus, 'a society of unmitigated egoists would soon knock itself to pieces; a perfectly altruistic individual would soon starve' (Robinson 1973: p. 10). Indeed, it will be highly inefficient to make real-life societies work without generous reinforcement from such moral norms as 'fairness' and 'trust' (Hausman and McPherson 1993). For instance, if each member of the society tries to maximize his/her share of the national cake without regard to what others get, then there may be no democratic way left to remedy the situation, except by rousing people's moral responsibilities to the society. At any rate, even at a purely logical level, the importance of a 'right' moral or value perspective must be clearly recognized due to the fact that objective statements not only become invalid because they are contrary to facts but also because they are based on a wrong value perspective (Harsanyi 1991).

And yet most of development economics has been practised by strictly observing positivism to ensure scientific objectivity—and perhaps also not to annoy the mainstreamers too much by confronting them with two heresies (*etatisme* and ethicalism) rather than just one (*etatisme*). However, it is a case of good intentions paving the way to the hell of total irrelevance: the fact is that by opting to remain positivist, development economics is faced with a motivational vacuum which cannot be filled even by a lot of rudimentary hard-headedness. Thus, if it is true that mainstream economics 'has been greatly impoverished by [its] growing distance' from ethics (Sen 1987: p. 7); then the predicament of development economics will be the more so because of this unnatural separation.

It follows that if the recent attempts to make development economics truly 'positivistic', so that it conforms as closely as possible to the neo-classical prescription of cold-blooded market-oriented efficiency, do succeed, then development economics will become less able to tackle development issues. Indeed it will lose its very identity if it does not yearn for the forbidden apple of morality, because the most fundamental issues of human existence that development economics must explicitly tackle have a clear moral dimension. Such attempts are especially counter-productive now that globalization is crowding out the remaining elements of altruism from economics (UNDP 1999). Fortunately, the recent attempts made by the UNDP's *Annual Human Development Reports* since 1990 to expand the development paradigm and make it more responsive to human concerns like health, literacy, human rights, etc., has made it possible to bring ethical issues within the development economist's calculus (see Chapter 9), Yet the hardcore treatments of the subject continue to feign the Olympian certitude of positivism just to acquire the mesmerizing appeal of being one of the neo-classicals!

What influences, then, explain the neglect of ethics in economics, especially in development economics? Perhaps, once again, it is the spirit of the times; indeed, the same spirit that has moved economists since the time of Adam Smith (1775), a professor of moral philosophy, who was misunderstood as pronouncing the separation of economics from ethics, later formalized by Robbins (1932) into a divorce. More recently, Stigler (1981) laid down: 'Economists seldom address ethical questions as they impinge on economic theory or economic behaviour' because man is 'eternally a utility-maximizer, in his home, in his office—be it public or private—in his church, in his scientific work, in short, everywhere' (p. 176).

However, the fact remains that the extant agnosticism towards ethics should now finally end in order to add greater cutting power to development economics (and also to mainstream economics). To capitulate the highlights of the discussion in Chapters 6 and 7, the following points need to be made. The point of departure for extending the development economists' problematic and making the discipline internally consistent is to de-emphasize—while not discrediting it altogether—the Pareto optimality principle as an operational principle to avoid confusion in the formulation of development policy. The reason is, this positivistic rule is not always efficient, nor is it a preserver of individual liberty. Also it is distributionally neutral, and essentially status quoist by construction. This is because *it cannot even distinguish the rich from the poor*, which is a consequence of the utilitarian and welfarist 'nature' of the principle, and also because it does not allow interpersonal comparisons of utility. As the non-utility indicators of welfare are not admissible in the utilitarian framework, the income levels enjoyed by the rich and the poor can also not provide a basis for setting up a scheme for redistributing income to the poor. But economic development, to make any sense at all, must be concerned with distributional problems, which are inescapably complicated by moral considerations.

Another idea discussed in this book is that development economists must not uncritically accept Nozickian non-consequentialism, with its strictly procedural and negative view of human freedom. From this perspective, state intervention is allowed only to prevent interference with the entitlements of those who pass the test of procedural formalities. However, no intervention is allowed to prevent anyone from the exercise of his her (legal) freedom even if that has extremely adverse consequences for the rest of the society. The state is also not allowed to intervene to redistribute income and wealth, which again is seen as an infringement of individual liberties. It should be obvious that such views cannot be of much use in developing countries, where a non-dictatorial redistribution of income and wealth is the essence of the development process.

What else is there, then, for development economics to draw on from contemporary economics to give it a 'warm heart'? The answer is, there is quite a lot. For instance, as noted at several points in this book, the public choice theory provides an excellent source for thinking about such matters. Thus, for example, especially relevant for development economics is a modified Rawlsian principle (1985) of 'justice-as-fairness', which involves maximizing the welfare of the least privileged in the society, with the explicit proviso that the number of persons so situated is minimized at the same time. However, doing so requires making deep *changes* in the existing social order, which, in general, is neither fair nor just. Another such principle is Sen's capabilities perspective on development issues, which explicitly admits non-utility information to be able to make interpersonal comparisons of individual welfare and relate it to such vital problems as inequity, poverty and human deprivation. These are important issues, which development economics must take cognizance of to repair the damage done to development thinking by unrepentant amorality.

Endogenizing demography

As noted above, development economics must respond creatively to the old–new demographic challenges. A key element of this response is to endogenize demographic variables, such as, fertility, age-composition and migration. We now know that in the (classical) 'magnificent dynamics', population was treated as an endogenous variable—Malthus treated it as one. An example is the wage-fund theory wherein any attempt to improve the worker's lot by increasing wages is only rewarded by an increase in labour supply, which, in turn, reduces wages; the reverse holds true if wages are held below the subsistence level. By the time of Lewis's work, however, population had come to be regarded as an exogenous variable.[18] It was treated as such in the Harrod-Domar model, which, as we have noted, influenced both development theory and practice. However, Lewis did implicitly endogenize population by according centrality to labour surplus, which is continually fed by population growth (apart from the fact that its supply exceeds the demand at the going wage rate) as the primary initiator of the development process. Moreover, population growth would lower the rate of return per capita on capital formation and would slow down the rate of absorption of labour in the urban sector. Yet the dominant tendency in development economics (and also in neoclassical economics) has been to keep it in an exogenous box. Coale and Hoover (1958), however, explicitly showed that a higher population growth would lower savings and capital formation. Coale (1973) duly emphasized the role played by the economic factors explaining the determinants of fertility—namely, the decision to produce more (less) children is an integral part of household decision-making—and of the couple having a clear understanding of the advantages flowing from having a smaller family. If the parents do not do so, they may desire more children than is socially desirable, and the converse is applicable as well. This is a good example of an externality, that is, of market failure—in the absence of the possibility of making profits, the information regarding contraceptives may not be made available by the market. By the same token, it is a case where government intervention can prove very useful. More explicit on this are the fertility models of Becker (1960) and Mincer (1962) which consider the activities of child-bearing and child-rearing as 'internal' to the optimization of decisions taken by households. Further, attempts have been made to measure the effects on fertility behaviour, of the family income, income distribution, labour force participation and wages (Kelly 1980). Some modelling activity has also gone on—the Bachue model is an instance—to relate the economic and demographic variables.

The point of the above-mentioned response of development economics to real-world issues has been to find ways and means to *reduce* the growth rate of population—a programme which has been crowned with success in nearly all the developing countries. Thus, between 1990 and 1998, the population growth rate has declined from an average of 3.4 per cent to 2.4 per cent in low-income countries, and from 2.8 per cent to 1.5 per cent in middle-income countries (World Bank 2000). Indeed, the former are quickly reaching the replacement level of population (of about 1.8 per cent) and may fall below it before long. But success on this score is not going to be achieved without incurring an opportunity cost. Indeed, Nature has already brought to the fore, in both the developed and the developing countries, the opposite issue of 'population ageing'—as if to ensure that humankind does *not* run out of its stock of nagging problems! This new phenomenon has already severely strained the resources of the developed countries, but its next victims are going to be the developing countries. These are fortunately still passing through a phase of Demographic Transition—that is, a passage from a high-fertility–high-mortality to a low-fertility–low-mortality sequence—where a delayed decline in the fertility rates (much later than the decline in mortality rates) will for a time stretch the size of the working-age cohort. This is referred to as a one-time 'demographic gift' before the phenomenon of population ageing begins to drain this working-age pool of labour. The challenge in the 21st century will be to bring about far-reaching organizational reform to make use of this gratuitous gift of Nature. To this end, developing countries must make bigger investments *now* to produce a highly trained and skilled population. However, the problem is that while the successful developers (for e.g., China, East Asia) are taking advantage of the 'demographic gift', most others (including India, Pakistan) have not done much in this regard. This neglect is bound to lead to a decline in their competitiveness and a rise in inter-cohort rivalry (Sirageldin 2001).

Development economics of supply and demand

The (original) development model has been variously described as demand-oriented and supply-oriented. The latter description is supported by the fact that the study of growth '. . . is about accumulation of physical capital, the progress of skills, ideas, innovations, the growth of population, how factors are used, combined, and managed and so on. It is therefore, principally, about the supply-side' (Stern 1991: p. 123). Lewis (1954) also made the supply-side considerations prominent by viewing the insufficient availability of fixed capital (and inadequate saving) as the main constraint on growth. In view of the (allegedly) low supply elasticities, he did not assign significant role to demand-management policies. Thus, for instance, the Keynesian remedy of increasing effective demand to cure unemployment in a developing country would only be penalized by greater inflation. It was thus contended (for e.g., by Lewis) that instead of leaning on the Keynesians, the development economist should learn at the feet of classical economists (especially Ricardo) because of the latter's emphasis on capital accumulation and a greater supply of savings as crucial factors in the development process. However, as noted by Syrquin (1988), the Harrod-Domar model (Harrod 1939; Domar 1946), the two-sector Lewis model (1954), and the balanced-growth model of Rosenstein-Rodan (1943) and Nurkse (1953) are more appropriate instances of greater emphasis on the demand-side factors.

While physical and human capital accumulation continue to be the constraining factors on growth, the inadequacy of effective demand, especially among the rural poor, also limits the growth of output and employment. An even more compelling illustration of this aspect of the problem is the case of famines, which have been caused not only by the short supply of food but more often by a failure of the 'exchange entitlements' of the poor due to a radical decline in their real incomes for a variety of reasons (Sen 1981a; Alamgir 1980). This ailment can also be reversed: the growth-promoting impulses emanating from the demand side will not translate into higher levels of output (and employment) by widening the wage-goods market if the supply elasticities are not high enough (Mellor and Johnston 1984).

However, it would be more fruitful if development economics acquires both blades of the Marshallian scissors, the supply blade as well as the demand blade, to 'enjoy' greater cutting power. In other words, it is more fruitful to think of development economics as an economics both of supply and demand—just as all of economics is. Thus, Klein (1978, 1983) has reformulated the problem as one of linking up the open Keynesian income and product accounts (the demand side), the Leontief input–output framework (the supply side), and the flow-of-funds accounts (the financial side) to get a complete picture of the economic universe, and to devise and implement policies on both the supply and the demand sides of the equation.[19] It is necessary to have such a comprehensive analytical framework to analyse the effects on the economy of an increase in the prices of food and energy, and the costs associated with protecting the environment, controlling population growth and increasing agricultural output. Such information is needed for policy-making both in the developed and the developing countries 'because an adequate explanation of wage income cannot avoid the explicit treatment of physical production involving labour inputs as well as capital inputs' (Klein 1983: p. 2). There is an 'educative' aspect to such an exercise as well, which is also very important. The vast data requirements for building such systems lead to a further strengthening of the database required for development policy. Many developing countries, including Pakistan and India, already have medium-sized macroeconometric models and fairly disaggregated input–output tables, and attempts are also being made to build financial flow-of-funds accounts. Such efforts should continue to enhance the 'empirical content' of the development paradigm.

Notes

1 For example, Lewis (1988) finds in these early writings many of the current development principles—the size of agricultural surplus and the availability of foreign exchange determining the size of the non-farm population; the concept of gains from trade; the distinction between tradeables and non-tradeables; the determination of net saving out of profit rather than wages; and a significant promotional role for the government.

2 There is a historical context to some of these principles. For instance, the experiences of the 'pioneer' (the European) countries, which, according to Rostow (1956), Ohlin (1959) and Gerschenkron (1962), show that they grew by taking advantage of vertical interdependencies between sectors. The 'latecomers' could grow even faster than the pioneers by learning from the latter's experience and by drawing upon their 'book of blueprints' of technical knowledge *free of cost* (Bell 1987).

3 The evaluation of specific theories by reference to the reliability of their predictions rather than by the realism (unrealism) of their assumptions is a Popperian methodological ploy (Popper 1980), advocated by Friedman (1953), and one that is now widely accepted by the economic profession.

4 As Solow (1988) points out, '. . . it is an implication of the diminishing returns that the equilibrium rate of growth is not only not proportional to the saving (investment) rate, but is independent of the saving (investment) rate.'

5 According to IMF (2000a), 24 per cent of the developing countries have managed to converge to the developed countries' (mainly, the US) income levels. However, as noted by Barro (1997), convergence needs to be redefined as 'conditional convergence'—measured by the difference between actual income (y) and long-run (potential) steady-state growth (y*)—to depict a universal growth phenomenon. This redefinition of convergence also explains why a poor country's actual growth may *not* converge *if* its long-run steady-state growth is also low by virtue of a low savings rate, which is true in the case of quite a few developing countries (including Pakistan),

6 Thus, for instance, Hirschman (1958) supported a subservient role for agriculture in the growth process. He wrote: 'Agriculture certainly stands convicted on the count of its lack of direct stimulus to the setting up of few activities through linkage effects—the superiority of manufacture in this respect is crushing'.

7 Lewis, (1955) laid down: 'First, it should be noted that our subject-matter is growth, and not distribution.' However, it should be noted that he was careful enough to point out that inequality of income per se was not enough 'to ensure a high level of saving'. It is 'only the inequality that goes with profits that favours capital formation and not the inequality that goes with rents' (pp. 419–20 in Agrawala and Singh [1963]). It is for this reason that Lewis and others favoured land reforms 'for reasons of equity as well as output (Lewis 1984b: p. 130). At any rate, Singer (1950) and Tinbergen (1959) were explicit about the distributional issues.

8 A two-volume *Handbook of Development Economics* (Chenery and Srinivasan, 1988, 1989) has been published by North Holland, which runs to the impressive length of 1773 pages. It includes comprehensive surveys in as many as thirty-two areas, including such important matters as trade and development, fiscal policy, project evaluation, processes of structural transformation, migration and urbanization, and the economics of health, nutrition and education, to name only a few. An extensive bibliography is appended to each of the surveys.

9 However, the founding fathers were not altogether wrong about the strength of the trickle-down effects. This is because when rates of growth of per capita income exceed 3 per cent per annum, growth does become equalizing. However, the fact is that when growth is slow (say 1.5 per cent per annum) then it need not be equalizing (Naqvi 1995). Thus, based on the 1970 census, Fishlow (1972) found that, in Brazil, income inequalities grew bigger, with the poor losing out even in *absolute* terms, notwithstanding—or, perhaps, as a result of—positive growth rates.

10 Contrary to the popular view, Lewis (1954) strongly argued for a rapid growth of agriculture to accompany, or precede, overall economic growth. He explicitly stated that industrial and agrarian Revolutions always go together, and that 'economies in which agriculture is stagnant do not show industrial development'.

11 Johnston and Mellor (1961) wrote: 'It is our contention that balanced growth is needed in the sense of simultaneous efforts to promote agricultural and industrial development.'

12 Note an important point here; in this view, higher food output leads to *lowering*, instead of a rising, of food prices. This is how it should be because continuously rising food prices would *contract* the size of the market by reducing the real income of the rural poor, who spend an overwhelming proportion of their income on food.

13 This view is mistaken because all that is required for the validity of the Lewis model is that the urban sector attracts rural labour at a *constant* real wage. This constancy may, in turn, be ensured by population growth, greater women participation in the labour force and other such factors (Lewis 1984b; Bell 1987).

14 See, Rozenzweig (1989) for a useful review of the literature on this topic.

15 The unemployment equilibrium condition in this model is denoted by the equality of the rural wage to the expected urban wage.

16 It is interesting to note in this context that the two-volume *Handbook of Development Economics* (Chenery and Srinivasan 1988, 1989) does not include any separate review of the literature on the subject because there is not much understanding of its importance! Only Sen, at the beginning (Chapter 1) and Streeten towards the end (Chapter 22) of the *Handbook*, talk about the subject—the former mostly relating to his 'capability' theory while the latter talking about the role of altruism in cementing international cooperation. The same is true of the most recent survey of literature by Stem (1989). But, of late, the subject is beginning to receive more attention—for e.g., Hausman and McPherson (1993)—even though its impact on the academia is, at best, indeterminate.

17 As Solow (1980) pointed out, without positing some kind of ethical norm of behaviour it is not possible, for example, to explain why some times the labour market should *not* be self-clearing: 'Wouldn't you be surprised if you learned that someone of roughly your status in the profession, but teaching

in a less desirable department, had written to your department chairman offering to teach your courses for less money? Normally, the answer would be in the affirmative: yes, I would be damned surprised if someone did this to me or to you. Although it may not be the economically optimal situation, it would be most desirable that someone did *not* undercut me or you.'

18 Looking back, it is somewhat ironical that Lewis, notwithstanding his many intellectual journeys back in time to 'visit' Adam Smith, Malthus, Mill and the rest, did not take notice of this aspect of the classical growth model.

19 Klein is careful to note that the income-and-product accounts include some very important supply-side elements as well.

15

Natura facit saltum

Analysis of the disequilibrium growth process

Paul N. Rosenstein-Rodan

Source: Gerald Meier and Dudley Seers (eds), *Pioneers in Development* (Washington, DC: The World Bank, 1984), pp. 207–21.

During the Second World War, I proposed in London the formation of a group to study the problems of economically underdeveloped countries instead of the more usual work on current economic problems related to the war. If we were to emerge alive, we should want not to return to the previous status quo but to form a better world. A study group was organized at the Royal Institute for International Affairs (Chatham House) and worked from 1942 till 1945 on problems of "underdeveloped countries." This term appeared then for the first time. My 1943 article in the *Economic Journal* served as a basic document for the group and is now in many anthologies of economic studies of the Third World.[1]

Eastern and Southeastern Europe were selected as a model not because of any special interest in those countries, but because their governments in exile were in London and because Eastern and Southeastern Europe (like Latin America) constitute a group of similar but not identical models. If one compares India, Spain, and Ecuador everything is different. What is cause and what is effect is anybody's guess. When one takes a group of similar countries, they differ from each other in one or two but not in all respects; it is then easier to examine what is cause and what is effect.

Natura facit saltum

If I were to give one characterization to my early thoughts about development, it would be "natura facit saltum"—nature does make a jump, the opposite of the motto "Natura non facit saltum" that Alfred Marshall thought appropriate for economics. Not traditional static equilibrium theory but an analysis of the disequilibrium growth process is what is essential for understanding economic development problems.

The *Economic Journal* article of 1943 attempted to study the dynamic path toward equilibrium, not merely the conditions which must be satisfied at the point of equilibrium. What matters is "the pursuit curve."[2] The pursuit curve shows the dynamic path toward equilibrium—not only the conditions at the point of equilibrium. Equilibrium points are like a compass showing the direction toward the North Pole or South Pole without implying that one is on the North Pole or South Pole. We are therefore concerned not only with the question of the existence of equilibrium, but the possibilities of nonexistence of equilibrium.

The 1943 article introduced four innovations which subsequently became so generally accepted that it is difficult to understand why they originally aroused so much opposition. The first innovation was a concern with "excess agrarian population" (disguised unemployment), which, although a weakness, may represent a source of development and strength. The second was the concept of "pecuniary" external economies, which yielded economies of scale—that is, increasing returns which were fully treated in Alfred Marshall's footnotes but considered to be a "second order of smalls." To take advantage of them, however, planned industrialization comprising simultaneous planning of several complementary industries is needed. The third new idea was that before building consumer goods factories, a major indivisible block of social overhead capital or infrastructure must be built and sponsored because private market initiatives will not create it in time. Low wages should have been a sufficient incentive to create a textile industry in India in the post-Napoleonic era and not in Lancashire, England. Indian wages were 50 or 60 percent lower than the low wages in England. There was no danger of currency manipulation or trade obstacles under British control; the prospect of building a textile mill in Bombay instead of Manchester or Coventry seemed most attractive. Further analysis revealed, however, that in order to build a factory one would have to build a bridge or finish a road or a railway line or later an electric power station. Each of these elements in the so-called social overhead capital requires a minimum high quantum of investment which could serve, say, fifty factories but would cost far too much for one. One cannot build a bridge small enough to allow only a hundred crossings a day. The efficient minimum would be profitable for fifty factories but not for one. The necessary minimum capital outlay outside of the textile mill would more than compensate for the advantage of cheaper labor. Lower wages are not a sufficient incentive for investment.

Industrialization meant (and still means today) urbanization. What are towns compared with rural zones? They are areas of relatively higher wages. Industrialization proceeded by concentrating in areas of high wages (towns), not in the rural areas. The rich countries were the urban zones and the poorer countries the rural zones of the world economy. That was the reason for the widening gap between developed and underdeveloped countries. The market mechanism alone will not lead to the creation of social overhead capital, which normally accounts for 30 to 35 percent of total investment. That must be sponsored, planned, or programmed (usually by public investment). To take advantage of external economies (due to indivisibilities) required an "optimum" size of enterprises to be brought about by a simultaneous planning of several complementary industries. In the process of development, pecuniary external economies play the same role as technological ones.[3]

The fourth innovation was the emphasis on "technological external economies," which are not due to indivisibilities but very largely due to "inappropriability." Under a system of slavery it paid the owner to invest in training a slave because the increase in skills would benefit the investor. When slavery was abolished, a worker trained could contract with an outside employer who did not have to bear the cost of his training. Whoever invested in the training of the worker would run the risk of not being able to appropriate the benefit of increased productivity. The training and education of workers under competitive market conditions would therefore be below optimum. This is a widespread phenomenon, not so rare as the bucolic example in a pastoral economy of not knowing whose bees alight on whose apple trees to produce honey. This example suggested a bias that technological external economies are logically interesting but practically irrelevant. In fact, the process of industrialization of underdeveloped countries was and is largely based on the advantages of training, learning on the job, and the formation of human capital (without using this terminology). In other words, technological external economies are not a second order of smalls, as already stated in 1943 and later on in the theories of human capital (Jacob Mincer and T. W. Schultz).

The market mechanism does not realize the "optimum" either in one nation or between nations because it relies on such unrealistic assumptions as linear homogeneous production functions, no increasing returns or economies of scale or of agglomeration, and no phenomenon of minimum quantum or threshold. This obscures the nature of the development process and the risks involved. Nothing in theology or technology ordains that God created the world convex downwards.

In terms of contemporary theory, the essence of the 1943 article may seem to rest on the basic question whether perfect future markets can exist for all the commodities in the context of a future which is both open-ended and uncertain.[4] Although I recognized that future markets and future prices could provide necessary additional signaling devices, I stated that "It is a moot point whether perfect future markets for all goods can exist. [My] suspicion (without proof) is that they cannot exist for the same reasons for which perfect foresight is impossible. In reality they certainly do not exist."[5]

The seeds of my development analysis had been planted earlier when I became interested in the themes of complementarity and of the hierarchical structure of wants, together with the role of time—that is, the choice of an economic period over which an individual allocates his scarce resources.[6] The dynamics of wants and their interrelatedness were much more important to me than the neoclassical attempt at precise characterization of the properties of the utility function. Consumption complementarities, the role of time, the pursuit curve, plus external economies—all these dynamic factors were not to be considered as a second order of smalls, but even more as pervasive in a less developed country.

Big push

My thinking during the 1940s and 1950s led to the theory of the "big push."[7] "There is a minimum level of resources that must be devoted to . . . a development program if it is to have any chance for success. Launching a country into self-sustaining growth is a little like getting an airplane off the ground. There is a critical ground speed which must be passed before the craft can become airborne."[8] Proceeding bit by bit will not add up in its effects to the sum total of the single bits. A minimum quantum of investment is a necessary—though not sufficient—condition of success.

This theory of the big push contradicts the conclusions of traditional static equilibrium theory in three respects. First, it is based on a set of more realistic assumptions of certain indivisibilities and nonappropriabilities in the production functions. These give rise to increasing returns and to technological external economies. Second, the theory is meant to deal with the path to equilibrium. At a point of static equilibrium net investment is zero. The theory of growth must be very largely a theory of investment. Third, in addition to the risk phenomena and imperfections characterizing investment, the markets in underdeveloped countries are even more imperfect than in developed countries. The price mechanism in such imperfect markets cannot therefore be relied upon to provide the signals that guide a perfectly competitive economy toward an optimum position.

Underlying the need for a big push is the pervasiveness of rural underdevelopment—excess agrarian population. Given that mass migration and resettlement are not feasible, I stated that "The movement of machinery and capital towards labor, instead of moving labor towards capital, is the process of industrialization which, together with agrarian improvement, is the most important aspect of the economic development of the depressed areas."[9]

Industrialization has to be promoted not because of terms of trade, but because external economies are greater in industry than in agriculture alone. Rejecting a strategy of self-sufficiency or an inward-looking strategy of industrialization, I argued for industrialization with the help of international investment and for a pattern of industrialization that would preserve the advantages of an international division of labor and would therefore, in the end, produce more wealth for everybody.

The crucial task of a development program was to achieve sufficient investment to mobilize the unemployed and underemployed for the purpose of industrialization. To reach an optimum size of the industrial enterprises, however, the area of industrialization must be sufficiently large. This calls for planned industrialization by the simultaneous planning of several complementary industries.

These four themes (disguised unemployment, pecuniary external economies, social overhead capital, and technological external economies) were then studied in more detail, first in Italy. Special attention was given to disguised unemployment and consequent dualism as well as the possibility of using welfare-improving policy interventions to realize a rate of growth 60 percent higher than in the previous century (that is, 5 percent a year rather than the previous 3 percent). The studies were followed up in India with special emphasis on analysis of the capital–output ratio, which was assumed to be too low in the India five-year plan, being in reality nearer 3 to 1 than 2 to 1. We also pointed out the importance of shadow pricing, especially the shadow price of capital exemplified by investments in electric power.

General principles of an international aid policy were first studied at the U.N. Economic Commission for Latin America (ECLA) preparatory conference for Quintandinha in the summer of 1954. These principles were used for the doctrine of aid policy in my 1961 paper[10] and later used and applied in the Alliance for Progress. The role of aid policy is ultimately a value judgment but one whose implications were spelled out best in the Alliance for Progress. The philosophy of development remains as valid as ever—it was the real operational manifesto for a New International Economic Order—although it failed by the "trahison des cleres"—that is, the sabotage of the Alliance for Progress by both the U.S. and Latin American bureaucracies.

Disguised unemployment and underemployment

The concept of "agrarian excess" or "surplus population" or of "disguised unemployment in agriculture" emerged in the late 1920s. But it was made one of the cornerstones of the theory of development in the 1940s and 1950s, despite the denial of its existence by such critics as Jacob Viner, Gottfried Haberler, and T. W. Schultz. Schultz had said, "I know of no evidence for any poor country anywhere that would even suggest that a transfer of some small fraction, say 5 per cent, of the existing labour force out of agriculture, with other things equal, could be made without reducing its production."[11]

In contrast to this view, I believed that disguised unemployment of more than 5 percent exists in many—though not all—underdeveloped countries. As proof of this, I offered a description and measurement of disguised underemployment in southern Italy.[12] Focusing on the direct method of measuring the static surplus—that is, an empirical sample enquiry to determine the amount of population in agriculture that can be removed from it (for forty-eight to fifty weeks a year) without any change in the method of cultivation and without any reduction in output—estimated three types of underoccupation: removal, equivalent to true disguised unemployment; irremovable frictional unemployment; and seasonal underemployment.

Disguised underemployment was important for models of dualism. It also placed emphasis on labor-intensive methods of industrialization that involve investing in consumption industries while importing heavy industry products.

Pecuniary external economies

I had been impressed by Allyn Young's analysis that increasing returns accrue to a firm not only with the growth of its size but also with the growth of the industry and of the industrial system as a whole.[13] I believed more emphasis should be given to increasing returns through attention to the indivisibility of demand and indivisibility in the production function.

The indivisibility or the complementarity of demand means that in reality various investment decisions are not independent. Investment projects have high risks because of uncertainty whether their products will find a market. But if investment occurs on a wide front, then what is not true in the case of a single investment project will become true for the complementary system of many investment projects: the new producers will be each other's customers, and the complementarity of demand will reduce the risk of not finding a market. Risk reduction is in this sense a special case of external economies. Reducing such interdependent risks increases naturally the incentive to invest.

The low elasticities of demand in low-income countries make it much more difficult, however, to fit supplies to demands. The difficulty of fitting demand to supply on a small scale constitutes a higher risk in a small market than in a large and growing one. The complementarity of demand will reduce the marginal risk of growing and diversified investments, but it will be below a minimum "sensible" for small doses of investment. There is therefore a minimum threshold at which the complementarity of demand manifests itself. The discontinuity in the complementarity of demand may be called indivisibility of demand. To reach the threshold and take advantage of complementarity in demand, a minimum quantum of investment is required to produce the bulk of additional wage goods on which additionally employed workers will spend their additional income.[14] On the supply side, a high optimum size of firm may be required because of indivisibilities of inputs, processes, or outputs that give rise to increasing returns.

Social overhead capital

A most important instance of indivisibility and externalities is social overhead capital. Although subject to long gestation periods and delayed yields, the provision of social overhead capital creates investment opportunities in other industries. The provision of such "overhead costs" for the economy as a whole requires a large minimum size of investment in each infrastructure project and an irreducible minimum industry mix of different public utilities. A high initial investment in social overhead capital is necessary to pave the way for additional, more quickly yielding, directly productive investments. I considered this indivisibility one of the main obstacles to development.

Indivisibility in the supply of savings was also viewed as a major problem in low-income countries. To provide for a high minimum quantum of investment, the marginal rate of saving out of increased income must become much higher than the average rate of saving. The zero (or very low) price elasticity of the supply of savings and the high income elasticity of savings were somewhat loosely described as a "third indivisibility."

Technological external economies

Another significant source of technological external economies was the training of labor.

> The first task of industrialization is to provide for training and "skilling" of labor which is to transform [Eastern European] peasants into full-time or part-time industrial workers. The automatism of *laissez-faire* never worked properly in that field. It broke down because it is not profitable for a private entrepreneur to invest in training labor. There are no mortgages on workers—an entrepreneur who invests in training workers may lose capital if these workers contract with another firm. Although not a good investment for a private firm, it is the best investment for the State. It is also a good investment for the bulk of industries to be created when taken as a whole, although it may represent irrecoverable costs for a smaller unit. It constitutes an important instance of the Pigovian divergence between "private and social marginal net product" where the latter is greater than the former.[15]

The indivisibilities and the external economies to which they give rise plus the technological external economies of training labor were the theoretical foundations for my advocacy of an integrating, synchronizing "big push" to "jump" over the economic obstacles to development.

The market and programming

The recognition of the complementarity of all investment projects introduced a new set of determinants of optimum investment criteria. They rely on the *delegation* of a "plan" which must be elaborated, while the market mechanism relies on the dispersal of decisions when the program emerges as a *result* not as a previously worked out "plan" of a campaign. A program approach was considered to be logically precedent to project analysis. The dispersal of single investment decisions based on maximization of profit as the only criterion will not lead to the optimum combination. This is for the following reasons:

- The investor maximizes the private, not the social, net marginal product. External economies are not sufficiently exploited. Complementarity of industries is so great that simultaneous inducement rather than hope for autonomous coincidence of investment is called for.
- The lifetime of equipment is so long that the investor's foresight is likely to be more imperfect than that of the buyer and seller or of the producer. The individual investor's risk may be higher than that confronting an overall investment program. The costs of an erroneous investment decision are high; punishment in the form of loss of capital afflicts not only the investor but also the national economy.
- Because of the indivisibility (lumpiness) of capital, large rather than small changes are involved. Yet the price mechanism works perfectly only under the assumption of small changes.
- Capital markets are notoriously imperfect markets, governed not only by prices but also by institutional or traditional rationing quotas.[16]

For these reasons, it was stated that other criteria—especially external economies and diseconomies—had to be added to those considered by the individual investor. Program-using methods of delegation were advocated to supplement the single investor's insufficient knowledge and induce changes in his decisions or supplement them by a set of public investment projects.

Investment programming

The programming of investment in a developing country is necessary to correct for such distortions as indivisibilities, externalities, and information failures. "Programming" is just another word for rational, deliberate, consistent, and coordinated economic policy.[17]

While a development program must be spelled out in projects, it is not a mere sum or shopping list of projects. Single-project analysis cannot simply consider each project in turn, see whether it passes the test, and accordingly decide whether to include it in the program. The various projects constituting a development program are interrelated and reinforce each other. This balance depends on whether complementary activities have been planned on the required scale. A program approach, not a project approach, is therefore necessary to determine the criteria for the productive use of capital. A change in one project may require a reshuffling and change in several other projects. Each investment project's contribution to national income depends on what other investments have been, are being, or will be realized. The complementarities introduce a new set of determinants of optimum investment, and a program approach therefore dominates project analysis.

A shorthand method

A bridge between the two is to establish shadow prices to correct for distorted market prices. In the late 1950s, as we focused on development programs in Italy, India, and Indonesia, our research at the Center for International Studies at MIT emphasized the shadow rate of interest, the shadow rate of foreign exchange, and the shadow rate of wages.[18] These shadow prices were to be used as a computational shorthand method for each project so that it was not necessary to solve each time the optimization problem for the investment program as a whole, of which the project is a part.

Programming is thus to be a supplement to the price mechanism and also an instrument for supplying additional information which the market mechanism cannot supply. The development program is to make use of the market mechanism, but is not to be dominated by it.

International aid policy

The aim of international aid was not to achieve equality of income, but equality of opportunity. Aid should continue to a point at which a satisfactory rate of growth can be achieved on a self-sustaining basis. Ideally, aid was therefore to be allocated where it would have the maximum catalytic effect in mobilizing additional national effort. I suggested that the primary principle is to maximize additional effort, not to maximize income created per dollar of aid.[19]

Major attention was to be given to the absorptive capacity of the developing country and its capacity to repay. The first limit to be determined was the amount of aid. The second was the method of financing it. Where the capacity to repay in low-income countries is below their absorptive capacity, a proportion of aid should be given in grants, in "soft loans" (forty- to ninety-nine-year loans with a ten- to twenty-year grace period and a low rate of interest), or in loans repayable in local currency which will be re-lent for subsequent investment.[20]

The rational strategy is not to reduce a country's foreign indebtedness to zero. The rational question to ask is: How much foreign indebtedness can a country maintain in the long run? Just as any national debt or corporate debt need not be reduced if it is within sound limits, the foreign debt of debtor countries need not be amortized to zero in a sound world economy.

Retrospect and prospect

Looking back, I now see we were overoptimistic in believing that the reservoir of disguised unemployment could be so readily absorbed. A central question that remains for development studies is why the difference between urban and rural wages has remained so high.

A basic restructuring of agriculture—involving far more than agrarian reform—is necessary to reduce the inequality between the rural and urban areas. When assessing the crisis in the Alliance for Progress, I submitted that excessive protectionism had kept the level of industrial prices so high that the domestic terms of trade between agricultural and industrial products were even worse than the world market ones. A thorough reform of tariff policy was advocated. Only when an investment actually materializes should a tariff (or subsidy) be applied. Imperfection in marketing and distribution also had to be reduced. Incentives for modernization of agricultural production must be provided in the form of subsidies for some inputs as well as minimum prices for two or three years at a time—"continuity is as important as the amount"—in order to reduce risks and uncertainty of selling.[21] Such policy reforms are still needed to accelerate agricultural development.

In order to reduce the inequality between the employed and the unemployed, it is necessary to establish a right to work as the minimum of equality of opportunity that modern society must provide. Full employment is an objective that cannot be replaced or compensated by anything else. Yet we are nowhere near its solution in most developing countries. A high rate of growth is necessary to provide an industrial drive sufficient to absorb the present and growing unemployment. Full employment and access to educational facilities undoubtedly remain the fundamental requirements for providing a minimum of equality of opportunity.

It may be asked: If, as we have maintained, the basic purpose of aid is to catalyze additional national effort in developing countries, who then is to judge whether this effect is forthcoming and whether it is adequate? If aid to developing countries is an income tax, the use of the tax should be decided by a consensus of all the parties. Partnership implies a consensus. The Pearson and Brandt reports foresaw both rights and duties—but the discussion stresses rights more than duties.[22]

Another problem neglected in the Pearson report is that of the multinational corporations. They present two aspects: they are very efficient in transferring capital, technology, and management; but their oligopolistic structure raises problems, not because multinationals are foreign—a national shark bites as much as a foreign one—but because they are monopolistic. All guidelines or codes of private international investment are in fact second-best attempts at an antimonopoly law. "The trouble in the past was there was not enough freedom of trade and too much freedom of international movement of capital."[23]

Today's method is unsuitable and often counterproductive; the very discussion by a credit-giving country of what the receiving country should do invariably raises objections that the latter's national sovereignty is being infringed upon. Under such circumstances, the discussion is either incomplete and not explicitly articulated or it is bound to give rise to mutual recrimination.

The only way out of this vicious circle is to establish a committee, which is not appointed by and not responsible to either creditor or debtor governments, to make an independent evaluation of national development effort and a consequent recommendation of the amount of aid to be allocated. It is indifferent whether we call it international arbitration or mediation. It should evolve into a de facto "International Court of Economic Justice." Clearly a new form of impartial international evaluation of that sort must be adopted, which should command confidence and respect on both sides.

Today we have competence, finance, and no democracy in the international banks—and democracy and no finance in the United Nations. The 1954 ECLA report proclaimed the need for a separation of programming and financing. An independent body—not responsible to either creditors or debtors—should evaluate the programs, and resources should be allocated according to that verdict. The World Bank has a good staff (at least in the past twenty-five years), but the developing countries have no confidence in the vote of its board because creditor countries have the overwhelming majority; the developed countries, on the other hand, have no confidence in the United Nations. It is part of national sovereignty for each nation to limit its own rights. There will be no satisfactory solution to this problem without some sort of arbitration. Only an International Development Council—an International Court of Economic Justice—can solve the problem. The Committee of IX of the Alliance for Progress was an attempt to apply such an international arbitration. It failed because of sabotage on both sides, but all great ideas first fail. All progress is first proclaimed to be impossible but is then realized.

Evaluation of the development effort

After some four decades of concerted attention to the challenge of development, we might ask how much economics can explain. Economic theory can determine the necessary, though not the sufficient, conditions of growth. The so-called non-economic factors account for the gap between the necessary and the sufficient. Any evaluation of development can only state that the necessary conditions for growth exist or are being created; it cannot predict with certainty that growth will actually take place. One can learn a lot from past performance, but the criteria of evaluation are ex ante concepts. They yield a probability judgment and have, therefore, to be continually checked.

Most differences of opinion among economists originate from two sources: different interpretation of data, since data are often deficient; and different interpretation of or assumptions about objectives, since the social welfare function is seldom explicitly given or even consistently felt. If both data and objectives were given, there would be a large consensus as to how to apply economic techniques, and few differences of opinion among economists would remain. Data must, however, cover not only available material and human resources, technological possibilities, and psychological preferences but also attitudes of mind and the ability to change them. A good part of the last-named factors (social attitudes) are unknown rather than given quantities, so that the data are never available. And the objectives are largely subconscious—neither quite given nor quite unknown.

A technical problem deals with multiplicity of means and *one* end: for instance, how to cross a river by boat, bridge, or some other way. We can use monetary, fiscal, foreign exchange, and commercial policy in various blends and combinations if the objective is clear. An economic problem consists of a multiplicity of means *and* multiplicity of ends. The "rationalist" assumption that we know what we want and think before making a decision is neither right nor wrong: it is an exaggeration. Our diverse *aims* ("social welfare function") are in partial conflict with each other—we can fulfill more of one and less of the other; moreover we can do it at different rates (more today, less tomorrow or vice versa) in different periods. This system of preferences is like an underdeveloped film: no contour lines are visible, but they are there. Programming (development planning) is the fluid that "develops" them: the contour lines then appear on the film.[24] The different aims—growth, employment, better income distribution—were at once emphasized; growth was only a means to achieve the other ends, since it is easier to reshuffle a growing than a stagnant income. Meeting basic needs and the assault on poverty were implicit but became more explicit in the late 1960s and 1970s.

The development momentum is now passing through a low point. The transfer of financial and technological resources to developing countries has also been disappointing. In the moral crisis of today we see in many developed countries a movement of an international Poujadism: an income tax strike. The richest country in the world, the United States, which pioneered in the field of aid, is the worst offender. When their income per head was merely 40 percent of what it now is, U.S. citizens gave 2 percent of GNP to the Marshall Plan. Today when their income is 2.5 times higher they give less than 0.25 percent for economic aid. The original philosophy of aid is still correct, and present cynics are not justified. People need and want ideals, and ideals are ultimately powerful. A great deal has been achieved in the development effort. The postwar period of development is a history of triumph—not of failure. The increase in life expectancy, the fall in infant mortality, the rates of growth, the achievements in any number of developing countries—nobody at the end of the Second World War would have expected so much. A billion people are still hungry, but it would now be 2 billion without the achievements that have been made.

What got lost, however, in the 1970s was international solidarity. The objective of international full employment disappeared in cynicism after Vietnam. The transition from the national welfare state to the international level must still be made. Not to do enough about inequality of opportunity and poverty when our world resources are sufficient to improve the situation is the real moral crisis of the present world, just as it was at the end of the Second World War. General cynicism is at least as unrealistic as naive idealism. We know what has to be done—we have to mobilize the will to do it.

Notes

1 Paul N. Rosenstein-Rodan, "Problems of Industrialization of Eastern and South Eastern Europe," *Economic Journal*, vol. 53 (June–September 1943), pp. 202–11. This was a chapter from the report of the Economic Group of the Committee on Reconstruction, the Royal Institute of International Affairs. Important predecessors of the theory of development are Harrod-Domar, Joan Robinson, Keynes, and Colin Clark.

2 A dog pursues a hare, without anticipation, along the shortest distance at which he sees him (a straight line). Meanwhile the hare runs from point 1 to point 2. When the dog sees him again in this new position he again runs along the shortest distance (a straight line) in which he sees him. Meanwhile the hare runs to point 3, and so on. The line along which the dog runs is what we want to explain. It is determined by a straight-line distance wherever the dog sees the hare. The overwhelming majority of the points of the pursuit curve are disequilibrium points. It may be called "state of equilibrium" if the dog ultimately catches the hare.
(Pareto had mentioned it but never worked it out.)

3 As Tibor Scitovsky correctly interpreted in his article, "Two Concepts of External Economies," *Journal of Political Economy*, vol. 62, no. 2 (April 1954).

4 See Sikhamoy Chakravarty, "Paul Rosenstein-Rodan: An Appreciation," *World Development*, vol. 11, no. 1 (January 1983), p. 74.

5 Rosenstein-Rodan, "Notes on the Theory of the 'Big Push'" (Cambridge, Mass.: MIT Center for International Studies, 1957), reprinted in *Economic Development for Latin America*, Proceedings of a conference held by the International Economic Association, Howard S. Ellis, ed. (London: Macmillan, 1961).

6 Rosenstein-Rodan, "Grenznutzen," in *Handwörterbuch der Staatswissenschaften*. 4th ed. (Jena, 1927), vol. 4, pp. 1190–1213; translated into English by Wolfgang F. Stolper, in *International Economic Papers*, no. 10 (New York: Macmillan 1960), pp. 71–106; "La Complementarietà: Prima delle Tre Etappe del Progresso della Teoria Economica Pura," *La Riforma Sociale*, vol. 44 (1933), pp. 157–308; "The Role of Time in Economie Theory," *Economica*, New Series (1934), pp. 77–97.

7 "Notes on the Theory of the 'Big Push.'"

8 mit Center for International Studies, Special Committee to Study the Foreign Aid Program, *The Objectives of U.S. Economic Assistance Programs* (Washington, D.C., 1957), p. 70.

9 "The International Development of Economically Backward Areas," *International Affairs*, vol. 20, no. 2 (April 1944), p. 161.

10 "International Aid for Underdeveloped Countries," *Review of Economics and Statistics*, vol. 43, no. 2 (May 1961); and "The Consortia Technique" (Cambridge, Mass.: mit Center for International Studies, 1968).

11 T. W. Schultz, "The Role of Government in Promoting Economic Growth," in Leonard D. White, ed., *The State of the Social Sciences* (Chicago: University of Chicago Press, 1956).

12 "Disguised Unemployment and Underemployment in Agriculture" (Cambridge, Mass.: mit Center for International Studies, 1956); and Food and Agriculture Organization, *Monthly Bulletin of Agricultural Economics and Statistics* (1956).

13 Allyn A. Young, "Increasing Returns and Economic Progress," *Economic Journal*, vol. 38 (December 1928), pp. 527–42.

14 Rosenstein-Rodan, "Notes on the Theory of the 'Big Push,'" section 4.

15 "Problems of Industrialization of Eastern and South-Eastern Europe," pp. 204–05; also, "The International Development of Economically Backward Areas," p. 160.

16 Rosenstein-Rodan, "Programming in Theory and in Italian Practice" (Cambridge, Mass.: MIT Center for International Studies, December 1955), pp. 2–3.

17 "Programming in Theory and in Italian Practice," p. 4.

18 See, for example, Sikhamoy Chakravarty, "The Use of Shadow Prices in Programme Evaluation," India Project C/61–18 (Cambridge, Mass.: mit Center for International Studies, 1961).

19 "International Aid for Underdeveloped Countries," pp. 107–38.

20 "International Aid for Underdeveloped Countries," p. 109.

21 Rosenstein-Rodan, "La Marcha de la Alianza para el Progresso," *Progresso* (Vision), 1966.

22 Lester B. Pearson and others, *Partners in Development*, Report of the Commission on International Development (New York: Praeger, 1969); *North-South: A Program for Survival*, Report of the Independent Commission on International Development Issues, Willy Brandt, chairman (Cambridge, Mass.: mit Press, 1980).

23 Rosenstein-Rodan, "Problems of Private Foreign Investment and Multinational Corporations," in *Multinational Investment in the Economic Development and Integration of Latin America* (Washington, D.C.: International Development Bank, 1968).

24 Rosenstein-Rodan, "Criteria for Evaluation of National Development Effort," *Journal of Development Planning*, vol. 1, no. 1 (1970).

16

Economic reforms and poverty alleviation

Deepak Lal

Source: Isher Judge Ahluwalia and I.M.D. Little (eds), *India's Economic Reforms and Development: Essays for Manmohan Singh* (New Delhi: Oxford University Press, 1998), pp. 231–52.

Introduction

The process of economic liberalization in India, as much as the economic repression that preceded it, has had economists in a leadership position in both the formulation and implementation of the relevant policies. The only one who will however live on as the architect of the Indian reforms is Manmohan Singh, and I am delighted to be able to honour him on this occasion.

Many, though not all the 'government' economists involved in justifying and setting up the dirigiste Nehruvian economic system have now issued some form of *mea culpa*[1]—Manmohan has done much better. As one of the earliest Indian economists to question the export pessimism that underlay the Nehruvian strategy,[2] and particularly after the tragic and untimely death of V.K. Ramaswami, his voice in the government was always geared towards a more liberal economic regime than his other government colleagues and his political masters were willing to stomach. But he bade his time, and most important of all, built up a superb team[3] of young, liberally minded, and technically competent economists under the leadership of another Sikh, Montek Ahluwalia. When as Finance Minister in the Narasimha Rao government he got the opportunity, he boldly began the overdue process of economic liberalization. Despite fears that his departure would lead to a reversal of the reform process, under his successor P. Chidambaram it is still in place, though stalled. But ever since the reform process began, the dirigiste bands have always tried to forestall it by their demands for 'adjustment with a human face'. As this slogan continues to be a thorn in the flesh of reformers in India, the best way in which I can honour Manmohan in this volume is to provide an antidote. A recent comparative study of the political economy of poverty, equity, and growth in 21 developing countries—which did not include India—that Hla Myint and I have recently published provides the means, and much of this contribution is based on our book.[4]

This contribution first briefly identifies the policies that need to be adopted in the next stage of Indian economic reforms. It then notes the continuing philosophical divide between supporters of some form of egalitarianism and those concerned with poverty alleviation. Next, it distinguishes three different types of poverty by their causes, and uses the Lal–Myint findings to show that there need be no conflict between the undoubted need for further and accelerated reform in India and alleviation of all three types of poverty.

I. The next stage of Indian reforms

Even in the areas of past reform there is a great deal of unfinished business: notably to eliminate quotas on consumer goods imports, and to move to full convertibility of the rupee by eliminating exchange controls. There are also whole areas which the reform effort has not yet touched. The common feature of this next phase of reform can be succinctly described as the rescinding of the unviable entitlements to income streams that past dirigisme has created. These have both deleterious macro- and microeconomic effects.

On the macroeconomic front, problems remain in removing the large budgetary subsidies for fertilizers, energy, the public distribution system, and those implicit in carrying loss-making public enterprises and redundant labour in the central and state bureaucracies and parastatals. On the microeconomic side, India's nineteenth century labour laws have hobbled Indian industry for much of this century (see Lal, 1988). They need to be reformed if not repealed. Without the reform of the labour market, the essential privatization of the inefficient and still substantial public sector is well-nigh impossible. Moreover, in the growing global competition for footloose direct foreign investment, these antiquated labour laws pose a serious disincentive for investors in India, when compared to the de facto privatized labour market that now exists in East Asia, most notably in southern China.

These labour market reforms, and the rescinding of other unviable entitlements created by past public interventions is resisted on the grounds that they would worsen either the distribution of income or increase poverty. There is sufficient evidence (see Lal, 1988) that these claims are unfounded. Most of these entitlements have done little to improve income distribution or to alleviate poverty, their most discernible effect being to impair economic efficiency and to corrupt the polity. But precisely for this last reason, politicians will be wary of rescinding them for fear of losing support, thence the politically convenient slogan 'adjustment with a human face'.

II. Egalitarianism vs poverty alleviation

To make sense of this slogan it is first important to note an important difference between improving the distribution of income (an aim favoured by egalitarians) and alleviating poverty (one favoured by most other people). A theoretical case for a link between the two was made on the basis of the so-called Kuznets curve, on which more below. But even if valid, this case for improving income distribution would be as an instrument in alleviating poverty and not in promoting equality per se. Hopefully, after the events of 1989, socialists of various hues in India are at least chastened about the feasibility of promoting egalitarianism, even if they think it is still desirable.

Without entering into the sterile debates about the morality of egalitarianism, and attempts to reconcile so-called 'positive' and 'negative' freedom, all we need note is that the egalitarians have now retreated to a position where they claim that the establishment of fully-fledged Western style welfare states in the Third World *is* required to alleviate its poverty.[5] This is particularly ironical given that the Western welfare state is everywhere on the defensive if not in retreat. It is this contemporary socialist mutation that is now increasingly identified with the term: blank (fill in any economic policy you like) 'with a human face'.

But is this 'social democratic' case for dirigisme any more valid than the old socialist one for planning, and will an acceleration of India's reforms require the simultaneous creation of a Western type welfare state to alleviate poverty? That is the central question I wish to address.

III. Three types of poverty

In answering it, there are two distinctions worth noting. The first is between extensive and intensive growth. Extensive growth has occurred for millennia in most parts of the world with aggregate output rising, pari passu, with the expansion of population that has taken place since our ancestors came down from the trees. Per capita income was however relatively low and stagnant during this phase. By contrast the modern era has been marked by intensive growth with a secular rise in per capita incomes as the growth of output outstripped that of population. There has been a two centuries dispute whether such rises in per capita income will alleviate poverty, that is whether the fruits of intensive growth will 'trickle down' and alleviate poverty.

Answering this question is my first task. In doing so it is useful to distinguish between three types of poverty, based on their causes. These are (i) mass structural poverty, (ii) destitution, and (iii) conjunctural poverty. It is worth noting that though this distinction was well known in the past—for instance in discussions in England since the Elizabethan Poor Law—one strategic linguistic move by socialists was to conflate all of them, so that structural poverty, about which nothing could be done until the era of modern growth, was conflated with destitution—for whose relief most societies have adopted remedial measures. A similar confusion for instance surrounds the whole recent discussion by a distinguished NRI theorist of what he calls An Enquiry into Well-Being and Destitution (Dasgupta, 1993). What he is discussing is mass structural poverty reflected for instance in malnutrition and ill health, which though ubiquitous in the past—and more widespread than it need be in India today—is different from true destitution.

III.1 Mass structural poverty

Mass structural poverty has for most of history been mankind's natural state. Until recently, most economies were agricultural economies, or what the economic historian E.A. Wrigley has called 'organic' economies, whose growth was ultimately bounded by the productivity of land. In such an economy there is a universal dependence on organic raw materials for food, clothing, housing, and fuel. Their supply is in the long run inevitably constrained by the fixed factor—land. This was also true of traditional industry and transportation—depending on animal muscle for mechanical energy, and upon charcoal (a vegetable substance) for smelting and working crude ores and providing heat. Thus in an organic economy once the land frontier has been reached, diminishing returns will take their inexorable toll. With diminishing returns to land, conjoined to the Malthusian principle of population, a long run stationary state where the mass of people languished at a subsistence standard of living seemed inevitable. No wonder the classical economists were so gloomy.

Even in an organic economy there was some hope for intensive growth. The system of market 'capitalism' and free trade outlined and defended by Adam Smith could increase the productivity of an organic economy somewhat from what it was under mercantilism, which together with the lowering of the cost of the consumption bundle, would lead to a rise in per capita income. But if this growth in popular opulence led to excessive breeding, the land constraint would inexorably lead back to subsistence wages. Technical progress could hold the stationary state at bay, but the land constraint would ultimately bite.

The Industrial Revolution led to the substitution of this organic economy by a mineral based energy economy. Intensive growth now became possible, as the land constraint on the raw materials required for raising aggregate output was removed. In particular, coal began to provide most of the heat energy of industry, and the development of the steam engine led to virtually unlimited supplies of mechanical energy. Thus the Industrial Revolution in England was based on two forms of 'capitalism', one institutional, namely that defended by Adam Smith—because of its productivity enhancing effects, even in an organic economy—and the other physical: the capital stock of stored energy represented by the fossil fuels that offered mankind the prospect of eliminating mass structural poverty for the first time in its history. It is possible, as many countries in East Asia for instance have shown, to eradicate mass poverty within a generation, because neither of the twin foundations of the gloomy classical prognostications, diminishing returns, nor the Malthusian principle are any longer secure. A market based liberal economic order that promotes labour intensive growth can cure the age long problem of structural mass poverty.

A crude measure of the extent of mass structural poverty is the so-called 'head-count index' of the proportion of the population below some national but time invariant real poverty line. Using this measure the Lal–Myint country authors found that there was a clear positive effect of per capita income growth on mass poverty redressal in all their countries over the period of study 1950–85. Whilst Gary Fields (1991)—for the same study—found for a larger sample that, in most but not all cases poverty tends to decrease with growth, and that where poverty tends to decrease most the more rapid is economic growth.

For India, Tendulkar and Jain (1995) have recently examined the effects of growth on poverty alleviation—taking account of alternative social welfare orderings—for the period 1970–1 to 1988–9. As they conclude, 'in comparison to the 1970s, the doubling of annual growth rate of per capita GDP in the 1980s was associated with improvement in both the poverty and social welfare situation' (p. 40). In India as elsewhere growth *does* thus alleviate mass structural poverty. In his famous 'tryst with destiny' speech on India's Independence Nehru stated: 'the ambition of the greatest man of our generation has been to wipe every tear from every eye'. The policies he followed however made this impossible because they damaged growth performance. Even the slowly rolling retreat from this past dirigisme has led to higher growth rates and in consonance with all the international evidence, to some sustainable alleviation of India mass poverty. If only India could sustain the spectacular growth rates that East Asia has now shown can be attained even by large economies like China, it is indubitable that mass structural poverty could be eliminated in India within a generation. That is the prize on offer. Nothing stands in the way but political impediments that irrational past dirigisme itself has created.

III.2 Destitution

With mass structural poverty ubiquitous till recently, the problem of 'poverty' has historically been confined to destitution. Most of these traditional organic economies were labour scarce and land abundant. The destitute lacked labour power to work the land because they were physically disabled and had no families. This remains a major source of destitution in land-abundant parts of Africa.[6]

With population expansion and the emergence of land scarce economies in Europe and in many parts of Asia, there arose 'the poverty of the able-bodied who lacked land, work, or wages adequate to support the dependents who were partly responsible for their poverty' (Iliffe, 1987: 5). Their poverty merges with mass structural poverty and growth will, as it has, lead to its amelioration.

No estimates of destitution in India—as far as I am aware—are currently available. Michael Lipton's attempts to find some correlates of destitution, based on village studies, however, show the extremely heterogeneous composition of this group. Thus, for instance, Dasgupta's seemingly reasonable assertion that widows are 'routinely forced into destitution' in India (1993: 323) has been shown to be false by Drèze and Srinivasan (1995) who find 'in terms of standard poverty indices based on household per capita expenditure, there is no evidence of widows being disproportionately concentrated in poor households, or of female-headed households being poorer than male-headed households'.

III.3 Conjunctural poverty

This leaves conjunctural poverty. In organic agrarian economies, climatic crises or political turmoil are its principal cause. Its most dramatic manifestation is a famine. Since the Indian Famine Code was devised by the British Raj in the late nineteenth century, it has been known that to deal with what Sen (1982) labels the 'entitlement failures' precipitating a famine, the government should provide income directly (through public works or food for work schemes) to those suffering a temporary loss of income generating employment. This administrative solution has eliminated famines in India.

Finally, the Industrial Revolution has introduced its own source of conjunctural poverty in the form of the trade cycle and the unemployment that ensues in its downturns. But in India's primarily agrarian economy, the seasonal unemployment of landless labour in rural areas is likely to be of greater importance than urban industrial unemployment. Rural public works schemes like the Maharashtra Employment Guarantee scheme (see Ravallion, 1991), have been effective both in preventing famines and in dealing with problems of short-run income variability. Their success however lies in the self-targeting that is made possible by offering a wage that only the truly needy will accept.

III.4 Income transfers and poverty alleviation

Income transfers are the only way of tackling destitution and conjunctural poverty. Traditionally these have been provided by private agencies—the church, private charity, and most important of all, transfers within extended families.

These private transfers were however replaced in most Western societies by public transfers through the welfare state. In assessing the case for Western style welfare states in dealing with the continuing problems of destitution and conjunctural poverty, it is useful first to distinguish between *social safety nets* and *welfare states*.

The distinction between the 'welfare state' and a 'social safety net' essentially turns upon the universality of coverage of transfers under a welfare state as opposed to the restriction of collectively provided benefits under a social safety net to the truly needy. The World Bank's Poverty Reduction Handbook (PH) noted two essential elements in any design of a social safety net: 'identifying the groups in need of assistance, and the means of targeting assistance to those groups cost-effectively'. It went on to ask: 'Are these questions for public policy, or are they adequately addressed by the traditional family network?' (PH: 2–13)

By contrast, welfare state advocates favour universality as it alone in their view provides a feasible means of achieving the ends sought to be subserved by a social safety net, because of problems concerned with obtaining the requisite information for targeting. Some have argued that, because of the ubiquitousness of imperfect information, markets for risk will be inherently imperfect.[7] Hence, universal welfare states are required as part of an efficient solution to deal with 'market failure'. To deal with this argument would take me too far afield.[8] Suffice it to say that this is a form of 'nirvana economics'[9]—currently fashionable on the Left—but it provides no credible justification for a welfare state.

IV. Two rival philosophies

An implicit objective of those who argue against targeting and in favour of universal welfare states is distributivist. To judge its validity it is useful to contrast two rival ethical and political traditions: the *classical liberal* and the *distributivist egalitarian*, which continue to jostle for our attention and colour the various policies offered for alleviating poverty.

IV.1 Classical liberalism

For the classical liberal it is a contingent fact that there is no universal consensus on what a 'just' or 'fair' income distribution should be, despite the gallons of ink spilt by moral philosophers in trying to justify their particular prejudices as the dictates of Reason. Egalitarianism is therefore to be rejected as the norm for deriving principles of public policy.

This does not mean that classical liberals are immoral! The greatest of them all, Adam Smith, wrote *The Moral Sentiments*. Both the great moral philosophers of the Scottish Enlightenment—Smith and Hume—recognized benevolence as the primary virtue, but they also noted its scarcity. However, as Smith's other great work *The Wealth of Nations* showed, fortunately, a market economy that promotes 'opulence' does not depend on this virtue for its functioning. It only requires a vast number of people to deal and live together even if they have no personal relationships, as long as they do not violate the 'laws of justice'. The resulting commercial society promotes some virtues—hard work, prudence, thrift, and self-reliance—which as they benefit the agent rather than others are inferior to altruism. But, by promoting general prosperity, these lower level virtues do unintentionally help others. Hence, the resulting society is neither immoral nor amoral.

A good government, for the classical liberal, is one that promotes opulence through promotion of natural liberty by establishment of laws of justice that guarantee free exchange and peaceful competition. The improvement of morality is left to non-governmental institutions.

From Smith to Friedman and Hayek, however, classical liberals have also recognized that society or the state should seek to alleviate absolute poverty. On the classical liberal view, as my colleague Al Harberger (1986) has noted, there could be an externality, whereby 'the (poor) recipient's consumption of particular goods or services (food, education, medical care, housing) or his attainment of certain states (being better nourished, better educated, healthier, better housed) that are closely correlated with an "adequate" consumption of such goods' enters the donor's utility function. As it is the specific consumption of these commodities, not the recipient's 'utility' that enters the donor's utility function, there is no 'utility' handle which can be used, as on the alternative distributivist view to allow distributional considerations to be smuggled into the analysis of poverty alleviation programmes.

Thus the indigent and the disabled are to be helped through targeted benefits. For various merit goods—health, education and possibly housing—these involve in-kind transfers. This is very much the type of social policy package that was implemented in Pinochet's Chile, and which succeeded not only in protecting the poor during Chile's arduous transformation to a liberal market economy, but also led to dramatic long-term improvement in its various social indicators.[10]

IV.2 Distributivist egalitarianism

The alternative technocratic approach to poverty alleviation is by contrast necessarily infected with egalitarianism because of its lineage. At its most elaborate it is based on some Bergson-Samuelson type social welfare function, laid down by Platonic Guardians.[11] Given the ubiquitous assumption of diminishing marginal utility underlying the approach, any normative utility weighting of the incomes of different persons or households leads naturally to some form of egalitarian-ism. But this smuggling in of an ethical norm which is by no means universally accepted leads to a form of 'mathematical politics'. Poverty alleviation becomes just one component of the general problem of maximizing social welfare, where given the distributional weighting schema, all the relevant tradeoffs between efficiency and equity, including inter-temporal ones can be derived in terms of the appropriate distribution cum efficiency shadow prices.[12] If the concern is solely with those falling below some normative 'poverty line', this merely implies a different set of weights with the weight of unity say to changes in consumption (income) above the line, and increasing weights to those who fall progressively below the poverty line.[13]

But this is the thin edge of a very big wedge, as far as the defenders of the market economy are concerned. Besides leading to recommendations for all sorts of redistributive schemes, it also leads to a vast increase in dirigisme. To alleviate poverty, an end embraced by classical liberals, they are on this route being led to endorse the creation of a vast Transfer State, which in the long run is incompatible with the preservation of a market economy.

A usual riposte to the classical liberal position of separating questions of alleviating absolute poverty from inequality is that, in theory, a market based growth process could lead to such a worsening of the income distribution, that instead of the poor seeing a rise in their incomes as part of the growth process, they could be further impoverished. This view was strengthened by the so-called Kuznets hypothesis that inequality was likely to worsen in the early stages of development before it declined, as per capita incomes rose towards current developed country levels. All the empirical evidence, to date, is against the Kuznets hypothesis, and its corollary that growth might not alleviate absolute mass poverty.[14]

V. Public versus private transfers

Are public transfers needed, as the welfare state advocates claim, to deal with destitution and conjunctural poverty, and as some assert even to deal with mass structural poverty? We need to briefly examine the relative efficacy of private versus public income transfers.

V.1 Private transfers

Kin based transfers, reciprocity arrangements, and interlinked factor market contracts have been the major way that traditional societies have dealt with income risk. They have been fairly effective.[15] With the inevitable erosion of village communities it is feared that these private insurance arrangements will break down and that no private alternative will be available to counter destitution and conjunctural poverty in increasingly atomistic industrial economies.

It is in this context that the role of private interhousehold transfers is of great importance. Cox and Jimenez (1990) provide evidence to show that they are of considerable quantitative importance.[16]

> For example, among a sample of urban poor in El Salvador, 33 per cent reported having received private transfers, and income from private transfers accounted for 39 per cent of total income among recipients. Ninety-three per cent of a rural south Indian sample received transfers from other households. In Malaysia, private transfers accounted for almost half the income of the poorest households. Nearly three quarters of rural households in Java, Indonesia, gave private transfers to other households. About half of a sample of Filipino households received private cash transfers. [p. 206]

Moreover, since the oil price rise of the early 1970s, the poor in South Asia and parts of South-East Asia have found remunerative employment in the newly rich oil states and their remittances to their Third World relatives has helped to alleviate their poverty.[17]

Private transfers have by now been largely 'crowded out' by public transfers in the West. The potential for such 'crowding out' in developing countries has been estimated for Peru and the Philippines by Cox and Jimenez (1992, 1993). There is potentially a large 'crowding out' effect if public transfer systems were to be instituted in these countries. For example, for the Philippines they find that, if a public transfer programme was instituted that gave each household the difference between its actual income and poverty line income, after private transfers adjust, 46 per cent of urban and 94 per cent of rural households below the poverty line before the programme began would remain below the line after it was implemented!

Moreover, the evidence suggests that private transfers are efficient. By relying on locally held information, and on extra economic motivations like trust and altruism, private transfers overcome many of the problems of adverse selection, moral hazard, etc., which have so exercised the 'nirvana' economics 'market-failure' school. For, as Cox and Jimenez, summarizing the empirical evidence, conclude: 'private transfers equalize income; private transfers are directed toward the poor, the young, the old, women, the disabled and the unemployed' (p. 216).

V.2 Public transfers

Perhaps public transfers can do even better, so that we should not worry if they crowd out private transfers. Public subsidization of the two merit goods—health and education—are the major public transfers in nearly all developing countries. In addition, social security is important in many Latin American countries.[18]

One question on which there is some empirical evidence is the incidence of the benefits from subsidies for merit goods. This overwhelmingly suggests that their incidence is generally regressive, and that they are very imperfect means of helping the poor.[19]

A revealing piece of evidence suggesting that public transfers are not only more inefficient in poverty redressal than private transfers but also crowd them out is provided by a World Bank study. This study

> traced public social sector expenditures for nine Latin American countries in the 1980s . . . [and] found that real per capita public social spending on health, education, and social security fell during some part of the 1980s in every country in the study. The share of health and education expenditures in total government expenditures also fell, even as that of social security rose. In spite of lower funding, and no apparent increases in equity and efficiency, social indicators generally improved in the 1980s. [PH: Box 3.4]

Apart from obvious statistical and other biases that might explain this anomaly, the most plausible explanation provided is that it might be due to 'the growing role of non-governmental organizations, and the response of the market oriented private sector to enhanced expectations and demand'. Thus there was probably a 'crowding in' of more equitable and more efficient private transfers to replace the decline in public ones.[20]

V.3 Political economy of transfer states

The 'middle class capture' of the benefits of social expenditure is not confined to developing countries. It has also been documented for the welfare states of the OECD.[21] A systemic process is clearly at work. It is the political economy of redistribution in majoritarian democracies. In a two party system, politicians will bid for votes by offering transfers of income from some sections of the populace at the expense of others. Models of this political process (which do not need to assume a democracy, but rather the interplay of different pressure/interest groups)[22] show that there will be a tendency for income to be transferred from both the rich and the poor to the middle classes—the so-called 'median voter'. Even if social expenditures are initially intended to benefit only the needy, in democracies such programmes have inevitably been 'universalized' through the political process, leading to what are properly called transfer rather than welfare states, that primarily benefit the middle classes.

The poverty alleviation that may occur as a by-product of the expansion of the transfer state is moreover bought at a rising dynamic cost. With the universalization of various welfare schemes, political entitlements are created whose fiscal burden is governed more by demography than the conjunctural state of the economy. With the costs of entitlements rising faster than the Revenues necessary to finance them, the transfer state, sooner or later, finds itself in a fiscal crisis. This process is discernible both in developing and developed countries.

For developing countries the Lal-Myint study shows how this process is clearly visible in those countries in our sample (Uruguay, Costa Rica, Sri Lanka, and Jamaica) that under the factional pressures of majoritarian democracies have created and expanded welfare states. All four welfare states were financed by taxing the rents from their major primary products. With the expansion of revenues during upturns in the primary product cycle, political pressures led to their commitment to entitlements, that could not be repudiated when revenues fell during the downturn in the price cycle. The ensuing increase in the tax burden on the productive primary sector (to close the fiscal gap) led to a retardation of its growth and productivity, and in some cases to the 'killing of the goose that laid the golden egg'. Thus, whilst there was undoubtedly some poverty redressal as a result of the expansion of these welfare states, over the long run these entitlements damaged the economic growth on which they were predicated, and hence eventually became unsustainable. Similar processes leading to the fiscal crisis of the state are to be found in many other developing countries.[23] Not surprisingly, many of these countries with over extended welfare states are now seeking to rein them back.

Very similar problems are also visible in the more mature welfare states of the OECD.[24] In some countries that had gone furthest down the public welfare route, the late 1980s and 1990s saw a growing questioning of the welfare state in the West, and in some cases its partial or virtual dismantlement.

VI. Policy implications

What are the conclusions for policy that follow from this discussion.

The *first* is that nothing should be done to damage the existing private institutions and channels providing private transfer. 'Forbear' should be the watchword for every proposed scheme that seeks to alleviate poverty through public transfers.

The *second* is that, if for whatever reason, public money is sought to be transferred to the 'needy', this is best done through private agencies. Particularly for 'merit goods'—primary health care and primary education—even if there is a case for public financing there is none for public production.

The *third*, is that the very problems of moral hazard, adverse selection, and monitoring cited by 'nirvana economics' as requiring public insurance, in fact argue for fostering the alternative private route that capitalizes on the comparative informational advantage of private agents with local knowledge. These private welfare channels can be promoted by various methods of co-financing them with public funds.

A radical proposal may be worth considering. This would channel all foreign aid and domestic public expenditure on social programmes and on 'safety nets' to alleviate destitution and conjunctural poverty through NGOs (national and international charities). But to avoid the crowding out of private by public transfers, this public funding should only be provided on a matching basis. The only reservation I would have about such a scheme is the continuing economic illiteracy shown by so many NGOs.

Finally, there is the important question of severance payments that will be needed to slim the over-extended and inefficient public sector and the bureaucracies that were set up to manage controlled economies and are redundant with the move from the plan to the market. Such structural adjustment faces political resistance from the public sector workers who face retrenchment and/or cuts in their real wages. Such workers can exert political pressure to prevent the rescinding of their politically determined entitlements to future income streams that are above what they would be able to obtain in the free market. The capitalized value of the difference between their expected public sector earnings (including pension and other benefits), and those they could get in the private sector (adjusted for the probabilities of being hired and fired in the market), represent the rents public sector workers are currently receiving. If their resistance is to be overcome they might need to be compensated for these rents. This is a political rather than an economic argument for severance payments, over and above those that might already exist in the contractual arrangements that may be in force in the respective labour markets.[25]

Given the heterogeneity of the labour force, the rents derived from public sector jobs will differ for different workers, being highest for the 'bad' workers whose market opportunities relative to their entitlements in the public sector are the worst. With imperfect knowledge of each worker's rents, and the difficulty in devising perfectly discriminating severance payment schemes, if the severance compensation is set to persuade the last 'bad' worker to leave the public sector, the intramarginal workers will be receiving more compensation than the capitalized value of their public sector rents. This could mean a very high cost to the fisc. But in some cases (e.g. where the public enterprise is producing negative value added at world prices), shutting down the enterprise even with this high cost may lead to a gain in net GDP. In others where the enterprise might still be viable after restructuring and privatization that involves retrenchment, the problem of tailoring a severance package remains.[26]

The most attractive plan that would meet both the objectives of limiting political opposition and reducing the fiscal burden would be one limited to workers not hired by the newly privatized enterprise. This tackles the adverse selection problem whereby the 'good' workers take the severance package and the 'lemons' are left with the new firm. The severance package for those made redundant should be based on the principle of tailoring the benefits to the median redundant worker's public sector rents. This would imply that, if the severance package offered uniform compensation at the level of the rents to the median retrenched worker, all those with lower rents would be better off, and they would provide the political support for the scheme to override those workers whose rents were greater than the median and would be worse off. Little more can be said in principle about the specific terms of these programmes that need to be tailored to local conditions, and in particular the relative bargaining power of public sector workers *vis-à-vis* the state.

Conclusion

My conclusions can be brief. There is no case for attempting to institute a Western style welfare state in India. There are feasible ways of dealing with the inevitable pain that the necessary reform of India's labour market will involve, but it is going to require political courage. Lacking that, only a fiscal crisis—that spills over into an inflationary and balance of payments crisis—of the kind that led to the partial reform of Indian commodity and financial markets, is likely to lead to these desperately needed reforms.[27] Without them the accelerated growth required to banish structural mass poverty from the subcontinent in the near future will not occur.

Notes

1 For example Dr I.G. Patel in his 1996 address to the Indian Economic Association, and Dr Bimal Jalan in Jalan (1991).

2 See Singh (1964).

3 My colleague Al Harberger emphasized the importance of the small teams of technocrats who have overseen the reform process in Latin America in his Ely lecture to the 1994 meetings of the American Economic Association.

4 Lal and Myint (1996).

5 See the recent *Human Development Reports* put out by the UNDP.

6 See Iliffe (1987), to whom I owe the threefold classification of poverty.

7 See, e.g., Barr (1992).

8 But see Lal (1993a).

9 The term is due to Demsetz. For an explication in terms of the recent controversy surrounding the minimum wage, see Lal (1995).

10 See Castaneda (1992) for a detailed account of these social policy reforms and their outcome.

11 See Sugden (1993) for a lucid account of the divergent economic traditions that flow from the technocratic and classical liberal viewpoints.

12 See Little and Mirrlees (1974) and Lal (1987).

13 See Ravallion (1992) for a full explication of this approach in the design and evaluation of poverty alleviation programmes in the Third World.

14 See Fields (1991), and Squire (1993).

15 As Platteau (1991) concludes:

Even though empirical evidence is scanty (but not altogether absent), the case can reasonably be made that, barring exceptionally unfavourable circumstances (such as repeated crop failures or crop diseases affecting entire communities), traditional methods for controlling the risk of falling into distress have usually enabled the people to counter natural and other hazards in a rather effective way. [p. 156].

16 Also see Rempel and Lobdell (1978), Knowles and Anker (1981), Collier and Lal (1986), Oberai et al. (1980), Lucas and Stark (1985), on the significant size and effects of remittances within the rural and between the rural and urban sectors in Ghana, Liberia, Nigeria, Pakistan, Tanzania, Kenya, India, and Botswana.

17 See G. Swamy (1981).

18 As social security is currently not an important issue in India, we neglect it here. For a discussion of the highly repressive nature of Latin American social security systems see Mesa-Lago.

19 See Selowsky (1978), Meerman (1979), Jimenez (1989), Deolalikar (1993), Jimenez et al. (1991), Van de Walle (1991).

20 Another piece of evidence is provided by a simple regression I ran on the state level data on per capita public expenditure on health and education between 1976 and 1986, and the changes in literacy rates and life expectancy and infant mortality rates for India, given in Ravallion and Subbarao (1992). In these cross-sections, I found there was no statistically significant relationship between changes on state level health expenditures and health outcomes, and a statistically significant negative relationship between changes in educational expenditure and literacy!

21 See Goodin and Le Grand (1987).

22 See Stigler (1970), Meltzer and Richard (1981), Peltzman (1980).

23 See Mesa-Lago (1983, 1989) for Latin America.
24 See Lal and Wolf (1986), and Lindbeck (1990) for the Swedish case.
25 See Rosen (1985) for a survey of the reasons why many labour market contracts will have various forms of severance terms built into them for efficiency reasons.
26 Papers by Fiszben (1992) and Diwan (1993) provided detailed analyses of the various options, as well as discussions of severance payment schemes in a number of countries.
27 The role of fiscal crises as precipitating reform is outlined in Lal (1987), and empirically substantiated in Lal and Myint (1996).

References

Ahmad, E. (1991): 'Social Security and the Poor: Choices for Developing Countries', *World Bank Research Observer*, vol. 6, no. 1 (Oxford: Clarendon Press), pp. 105–27.

Ahmad, E. et al. (eds) (1991): *Social Security in Developing Countries* (Oxford: Clarendon Press).

Atkinson, A.B. (1987): 'Income Maintenance and Social Insurance', in A.J. Auerbach and M. Feldstein (eds), *Handbook of Public Economics*, vol. 2 (Amsterdam: North Holland), pp. 779–908.

Barr, N. (1992): 'Economic Theory and the Welfare State: A Survey and Interpretation', *Journal of Economic Literature*, vol. xxx, no. 2, June, pp. 741–803.

Castaneda, T. (1992): *Combating Poverty* (International Center for Economic Growth, San Francisco: ICS Press).

Collier, P. and D. Lal (1986): *Labor and Poverty in Kenya 1900–1980* (Oxford: Clarendon Press).

Cox, D. (1987): 'Motives for Private Income Transfers', *Journal of Political Economy*, vol. 95, no. 3, June, pp. 508–46.

Cox, D. and G. Jackson (1989): 'The Connection Between Public Transfers and Private Interfamily Transfers', *mimeo* (Boston: Boston College).

Cox, D. and E. Jimenez (1990): 'Achieving Social Objectives Through Private Transfers: A Review', *World Bank Research Observer*, vol. 5, no. 2, July, pp. 205–18.

—— (1992): 'Social Security and Private Transfers in Peru', *World Bank Economic Review*, vol. 6, no. 1, January.

—— (1993): 'Private Transfers and the Effectiveness of Public Income Redistribution in the Philippines', *mimeo*, World Bank Conference on Public Expenditures and the Poor: Incidence and Targeting.

Dasgupta, P. (1993): *An Enquiry into Well-Being and Destitution* (Oxford: Clarendon Press).

Demsetz, H. (1969): 'Information and Efficiency: Another Viewpoint', *Journal of Law and Economics*, vol. 12, pp. 1–22; rpt in his *The Organization of Economic Activity*, vol. 2 (Oxford: Blackwell, 1988).

Deolalikar, A.B. (1993): 'Does the Impact of Government Health Spending on the Utilization of Health Services by Children and on Child Health Outcomes Differ by Household Expenditure: The Case of Indonesia', *mimeo*, Paper for the World Bank Conference on Public Expenditures and the Poor: Incidence and Targeting.

Diwan, I. (1993): 'Efficient Severance Payment Schemes', *mimeo* May (Washington, DC: World Bank).

Drèze, J. and A. Sen (1989): *Hunger and Public Action* (Oxford: Clarendon Press).

Drèze, J. and P.V. Srinivasan (1995): 'Widowhood and Poverty in India: Some Inferences from Household Survey Data', *Development Economics Research Programme*, Paper No. 62, London School of Economics (mimeo).

Fields, G. (1991): 'Growth and Income Distribution', in G. Psacharopoulos (ed.) (1993).

Fiszben, A. (1992): 'Labor Retrenchment and Redundancy Compensation in State Owned Enterprises: The Case of Sri Lanka', South Asia Region Internal Discussion Paper', Report No. IDP 121 (Washington, DC: World Bank), December.

Goodin, R.E. and J. Le Grand (1987): *Not Only the Poor* (London: Allen & Unwin).

Harberger, A. (1986): 'Basic Needs versus Distributional Weights in Social Cost-Benefit Analysis', *Economic Development and Cultural Change*.

Harris, R. (1988): *Beyond the Welfare State: An Economic, political and Moral Critique of Indiscriminate State Welfare and a Review of Alternatives to Dependency* (London: Institute of Economic Affairs, Occasional Paper No. 77).

Iliffe, J. (1987): *The African Poor* (Cambridge: Cambridge University Press).

Jalan, B. (1991): *India's Economic Crisis* (Delhi: Oxford University Press).

Jimenez, E. (1989): 'Social Sector Pricing Revisited: A Survey of Some Recent Contributions', *Proceedings of the World Bank Annual Conference on Development Economics* (Washington, DC: The World Bank), pp. 109–38.

Jimenez, E., M.E. Lockheed and V. Paqueo (1991): 'The Relative Efficiency of Private and Public Schools in Developing Countries', *World Bank Research Observer*, vol. 6, no. 2, July, pp. 205–18.

Knowles, J.C. and R. Anker (1981): 'An Analysis of Income Transfers in a Developing Country', *Journal of Development Economics*, vol. 8, April, pp. 205–6.
Lal, D. (1987): 'The Political Economy of Economic Liberalization', *World Bank Economic Review*, vol. 1, pp. 273–99, reprinted in Lal (1993).
—— (1988): *The Hindu Equilibrium*, 2 vols (Oxford: Clarendon Press).
—— (1993): *The Repressed Economy*, Economists of the 20th Century Series (Aldershort: Edward Elgar).
—— (1993a): 'The Role of the Public and Private Sectors in Health Financing', *HRO* Working Paper No. 33, Human Resources Development and Operations Policy Dept. (Washington, DC: World Bank).
—— (1994): *Against Dirigisme* (San Francisco: ICS Press).
—— (1995): *The Minimum Wage*, Occasional Paper No. 95 (London: Institute of Economic Affairs).
Lal, D. and H. Myint (1996): *The Political Economy of Poverty, Equity and Growth—A Comparative Study* (Oxford: Clarendon Press).
Lal, D. and M. Wolf (eds) (1986): *Stagflation, Savings and the State* (New York: Oxford University Press).
Lindbeck, A. (1990): 'The Swedish Experience', *Stockholm: Institute for International Economic Studies*, Seminar Paper No. 482.
Little, I.M.D. and J.A. Mirrlees (1974): *Project Appraisal and Planning for Developing Countries* (London: Heinemman Educational).
Lucas, R.E. and O. Stark (1985): 'Motivations to Remit Evidence from Botswana', *Journal of Political Economy*, vol. 93, October, pp. 901–18.
Meltzer, A. and S. Richard (1981): 'A Rational Theory of the Size of Government', *Journal of Political Economy*, vol. 89, pp. 914–27.
Mesa-Lago, C. (1983): 'Social Security and Extreme Poverty in Latin America', *Journal of Development Economics*, vol. 12, pp. 83–110.
—— (1989): *Ascent of Bankruptcy: Financing Social Security in Latin America* (Pittsburgh: University of Pittsburgh Press).
Meerman, J. (1979): *Public Expenditure in Malaysia: Who Benefits and Why* (New York: Oxford University Press).
Mill, J.S. (1948): *Principles of Political Economy*, D. Winch (ed.) (London: Penguin Books, 1970).
Murray, C. (1984): *Losing Ground: American Social Policy 1950–1980* (New York: Basic Books).
Oberai, A.S. and H.K.M. Singh (1980): 'Migration, Remittances and Rural Development', *International Labor Review*, March-April.
—— (1983): *Carnes and Consequences of Internal Migration* (Delhi: Oxford University Press).
Peltzman, S. (1980): 'The Growth of Government', *Journal of Law and Economics*, vol. 25, no. 3, pp. 209–87.
Platteau, J.P. (1991): 'Traditional Systems of Social Security and Hunger Insurance: Past Achievements and Modern Challenges', in E. Ahmad et al. (eds).
Psacharopoulos, G. (ed.) (1991): *Essays on Poverty, Equity and Growth* (Oxford: Pergamon).
Ravallion, M. (1992): *Poverty Comparisons—A Guide to Concepts and Methods*, Living Standards Measurement Study Working Paper No. 88 (Washington, DC: World Bank).
Ravallion, M. and K. Subbarao (1992): 'Adjustment and Human Development in India', *Journal of Indian School of Political Economy*, vol. 4, no. 1, pp. 55–79.
Rempel, H. and R. Lobdell (1978): 'The Role of Urban-to-rural Remittances in Rural Development', *Journal of Development Studies*, vol. 14 (April), pp. 324–41.
Rosen, S. (1985): 'Implicit Contracts—A Survey', *Journal of Economic Literature*, vol. 23, pp. 1144–75.
Selowsky, M. (1978): *Who Benefits from Public Expenditure? A Case Study of Colombia* (New York: Oxford University Press).
Sen, A.K. (1982): *Poverty and Famines* (Oxford: Clarendon Press).
Singh, Manmohan (1964): *India's Export Trends* (Oxford: Clarendon Press).
Squire, L. (1993): 'Fighting Poverty', *American Economic Review*, vol. 83, May, pp. 377–82.
Stigler, G. (1970): 'Director's Law of Public Income Distribution', *Journal of Law and Economics*, vol. 13, no. 1, pp. 1–10.
Sugden, R. (1993): 'A Review of Inequality Re-examined by Amartya Sen', *Journal of Economic Literature*, vol. xxxi, no. 4, December, pp. 1947–86.
Swamy, G. (1981): 'International Migrant Workers' Remittances: Issues and Prospects', World Bank Staff Working Paper No. 481, (Washington, DC: World Bank).
Tendulkar, S.D. and L.R. Jain (1995): 'Economic Growth and Equity: India 1970–1 to 1988–9', *Indian Economic Review*, vol. xxx, no. 1, pp. 19–49.
Van de Walle, D. (1992): 'The Distribution of the Benefits from Social Services in Indonesia, 1978–87', *mimeo*, Policy Research Working Paper, Country Economics Dept. (Washington, DC: World Bank).
World Bank (1992): *Poverty Reduction Handbook* (PH) (Washington, DC: World Bank).
Wrigley, E.A. (1988): *Continuity, Chance and Change: The Character of the Industrial Revolution in England* (Cambridge: Cambridge University Press).

17

Predatory growth

Amit Bhaduri

Source: *Economic and Political Weekly*, 43:16 (19 April, 2008), 10–14.

The much hyped story of India's economic growth hides the truth about heightened inequality, the blatant biases against the poor, the hostility of the state toward welfare, and the misery wrought upon the poorest of the poor. Only an alternative path to development that lays stress on dignity and participation of all sections can be an answer to the ravages of predatory growth.

Over the last two decades or so, the two most populous large countries in the world, China and India, have been growing at rates considerably higher than the world average. In recent years the growth rate of national product of China has been about three times, and that of India approximately two times that of the world average. This has led to a clever defence of globalisation by a former chief economist of the International Monetary Fund (IMF) [Fisher 2003]. Although China and India feature as only two among some 150 countries for which data are available, he reminded us that together they account for the majority of the poor in the world. This means that even if the rich and the poor countries of the world are not converging in terms of per capita income, the well above the average world rate of growth of these two large countries implies that the current phase of globalisation is reducing global inequality and poverty at a rate as never before.

Statistical half truths can be more misleading at times than untruths. And this might be one of them, insofar as the experiences of ordinary Indians contradict such statistical artefacts. Since citizens in India can express reasonably freely their views at least at the time of elections, their electoral verdicts on the regime of high growth should be indicative. They have invariably been negative. Not only did the "shining India" image crash badly in the last general election, even the present prime minister, widely presented as the "guru" of India's economic liberalisation in the media, could never personally win an election in his life. As a result, come election time, and all parties talk not of economic reform, liberalisation and globalisation, but of greater welfare measures to be initiated by the state. Gone election times, and the reform agenda is back. Something clearly needs to be deciphered from such predictable swings in political pronouncement.

Lived experiences

Politicians know that ordinary people are not persuaded by statistical mirages and numbers, but by their daily experiences. They do not accept high growth on its face value as unambiguously beneficial.

If the distribution of income turns viciously against them and the opportunities for reasonable employment and livelihood do not expand with high growth, the purpose of higher growth would be widely questioned in a democracy. This is indeed what is happening, and it might even appear to some as paradoxical. The festive mood generated by high growth is marinated in popular dissent and despair, turning often into repressed anger. Like a malignant malaise, a sense of political unease is spreading insidiously along with the near double-digit growth. And, no major political party, irrespective of their right or left label, is escaping it because they all subscribe to an ideology of growth at any cost.

Unequal growth

What exactly is the nature of this paradoxical growth that increases output and popular anger at the same time? India has long been accustomed to extensive poverty coexisting with growth, with or without its "socialist pattern". It continues to have anywhere between one-third and one-fourth of its population living in subhuman, absolute poverty. The number of people condemned to absolute poverty declined very slowly in India over the last two decades, leaving some 303 million people still in utter misery. In contrast China did better with the number of absolutely poor declining from 53 per cent to 8 per cent, ie, a reduction of some 45 percentage points, quite an achievement compared to India's 17 percentage points. However, while China grew faster, inequality or relative poverty also grew faster in China than in India. Some claim that the increasing gap between the richer and the poorer sections in the Chinese society during the recent period has been one of the worst in recorded economic history, perhaps with the exception of some former socialist countries immediately after the collapse of the Soviet Union.

The share in national income of the poorest 20 per cent of the population in contemporary China is 5.9 per cent, compared to 8.2 per cent in India [Radhakrishna 2008]. This implies that the lowest 20 per cent income group in China and in India receives about 30 and 40 per cent of the per capita average income of their respective countries. However, since China has over two times the average per capita income of India in terms of both purchasing power parity, and dollar income, the poorest 20 per cent in India are better off in relative terms, but worse off in absolute terms. The Gini coefficient, lying between zero and one, measures inequality, and increases in value with the degree of inequality. In China, it had a value close to 0.50 in 2006, one of the highest in the world. Inequality has grown also in India, but less sharply. Between 1993–94 and 2004–05, the coefficient rose from 0.25 to 0.27 in urban, and 0.31 to 0.35 in rural areas. Every dimension of inequality, among the regions, among the professions and sectors, and in particular between urban and rural areas has also grown rapidly in both countries, even faster in China than in India. In short, China has done better than India in reducing absolute poverty, but worse in allowing the gap to grow rapidly between the rich and the poor during the recent period of high growth.

A central fact stands out. Despite vast differences in the political systems of the two countries, the common factor has been increasing inequality accompanying higher growth. What is not usually realised is that the growth in output and in inequality are not two isolated phenomena. One frequently comes across the platitude that high growth will soon be trickling down to the poor, or that redistributive action by the state through fiscal measures could decrease inequality while keeping up the growth rate. These statements are comfortable but unworkable, because they miss the main characteristic of the growth process underway. This pattern of growth is propelled by a powerful reinforcing mechanism, which the economist Gunner Myrdal had once described as "cumulative causation". The mechanism by which growing inequality drives growth, and growth fuels further inequality has its origin in two different factors, both related to some extent to globalisation.

Jobless growth

First, in contrast to earlier times when less than 4 per cent growth on an average was associated with 2 per cent growth in employment, India is experiencing a growth rate of some 7–8 per cent in recent years, but the growth in regular employment has hardly exceeded 1 per cent. This means most of the growth, some 5–6 per cent of the GDP, is the result not of employment expansion, but of higher output per worker. This high growth of output has its source in the growth of labour productivity. According to official statistics, between 1991 and 2004 employment fell in the organised public sector, and the organised private sector hardly compensated for it. In the corporate sector, and in some organised industries, productivity growth comes from mechanisation and longer hours of work. Edward Luce of *Financial Times* (London) reported that the Jamshedpur steel plant of the Tatas employed 85,000 workers in 1991 to produce one million tonnes of steel worth $ 0.8 million. In 2005, the production rose to five million tonnes, worth about $ 5 million, while employment fell to 44,000. In short, output increased approximately by a factor of five, employment dropped by a factor of half, implying an increase in labour productivity by a factor of 10.

Similarly, Tata Motors in Pune reduced the number of workers from 35,000 to 21,000 but increased the production of vehicles from 1,29,000 to 3,11,500 between 1999 and 2004, implying a labour productivity increase by a factor of four. Stephen Roach, chief economist of Morgan Stanley, reports similar cases of Bajaj motor cycle factory in Pune. In the mid-1990s the factory employed 24,000 workers to produce one million units of two-wheelers. Aided by Japanese robotics and Indian information technology, in 2004, 10,500 workers turned out 2.4 million units – more than double the output with less than half the labour force, an increase in labour productivity by a factor of nearly six.[1] One could multiply such examples, but this is broadly the name of the game everywhere in the private corporate sector.

Augmented profit and misery

The manifold increase in labour productivity, without a corresponding increase in wages and salaries, becomes an enormous source of profit, and also a source of international price competitiveness in a globalising world. Nevertheless, this is not the entire story, perhaps not even the most important part of the story. The whole organised sector to which the corporate sector belongs, accounts for less than one-tenth of the labour force. Simply by the arithmetic of weighted average, a 5–6 per cent annual growth in labour productivity in the entire economy is possible only if the unorganised sector accounting for the remaining 90 per cent of the labour force also contributes to the growth in labour productivity. Direct information is not available on this count, but several micro-studies and surveys show the broad pattern. Growth of labour productivity in the unorganised sector, which includes most of agriculture, comes from lengthening the hours of work to a significant extent, as this sector has no labour laws worth the name, or social security to protect workers. Subcontracting to the unorganised sector along with casualisation of labour on a large scale become convenient devices to ensure longer hours of work without higher pay. Self-employed workers, totalling 260 million, expanded fastest during the high growth regime, providing an invisible source of labour productivity growth [the data in Rangarajan et al 2007 could be interpreted this way]. Ruthless self-exploitation by many of these workers in a desperate attempt to survive by doing long hours of work with very little extra earning adds both to productivity growth, often augmenting corporate profit, and human misery.

However, inequality is increasing for another reason. Its ideology often described as neoliberalism is easily visible at one level; but the underlying deeper reason is seldom discussed. The increasing openness of the Indian economy to international finance and capital flows, rather than to trade in goods and services, has had the consequence of paralysing many pro-poor public policies. Despite the fact that we continue to import more than we export (unlike China), India's comfortable foreign reserves position is mostly the result of accumulated portfolio investments and short-term capital inflows from various financial institutions. To keep the show going in this way, the fiscal and the monetary policies of the government need to comply with the interests of the financial markets. That is the reason why successive Indian governments have willingly accepted the Fiscal Responsibility and Budget Management Act (2003) restricting deficit spending. Similarly, the idea has gained support that the government should raise resources through privatisation and so-called public–private partnership, but not through raising fiscal deficit, or not imposing a significant turn over tax on transactions of securities. These measures rattle the "sentiment" of the financial markets, so governments remain wary of them.

The hidden agenda, vigorously pursued by governments of all colour, has been to keep the large private players in the financial markets in a happy mood. Since the private banks and financial institutions usually take their lead from the IMF and the World Bank, this bestows on these multilateral agencies considerable power over the formulation of government policies. However, the burden of such policies is borne largely by the poor of this country. This has had a crippling effect on policies for expanding public expenditure for the poor in the social sector. Inequality and distress grows as the state rolls back public expenditure in social services like basic health, education, and public distribution and neglects the poor, while the discipline imposed by the financial markets serves the rich and the corporations. This process of high growth traps roughly one in three citizens of India in extreme poverty with no possibility of escape through either regular employment growth or relief through state expenditure on social services. The high growth scene of India appears to them like a wasteland leading to the hell described by the great Italian poet Dante. On the gate of his imagined hell is written, "This is the land you enter after abandoning all hopes".

Extremely slow growth in employment and feeble public action exacerbates inequality, as a disproportionately large share of the increasing output and income from growth goes to the richer section of the population, not more than say the top 20 per cent of the income receivers in India. At the extreme ends of income distribution the picture that emerges is one of striking contrasts. According to the *Forbes* magazine list for 2007, the number of Indian billionaires rose from nine in 2004 to 40 in 2007: much richer countries like Japan had only 24, France 14 and Italy 14. Even China, despite its sharply increasing inequality, had only 17 billionaires. The combined wealth of Indian billionaires increased from \$ 106 to \$ 170 billion in the single year, 2006–07 [information from *Forbes* quoted in Jain and Gupta 2008]. This 60 per cent increase in wealth would not have been possible, except through transfer on land from the state and central governments to the private corporations in the name of "public purpose", for mining, industrialisation and special economic zones (SEZs). Estimates based on corporate profits suggest that, since 2000–01 to date, each additional per cent growth of GDP has led to an average of some 2.5 per cent growth in corporate profits. India's high growth has certainly benefited the corporations more than anyone else.

After several years of high growth along these lines, India of the 21st century has the distinction of being only second to the US in terms of combined total wealth of its corporate billionaires coexisting with the largest number of homeless, ill-fed and illiterates in the world. Not surprisingly, for ordinary Indians at the receiving end, this growth process is devoid of all hope for escape. Nearly half of Indian children under six years suffer from under-weight and malnutrition, nearly 80 per cent from anaemia, while some 40 per cent of Indian adults suffer from chronic energy deficit. Destitution, chronic hunger and poverty kill and cripple silently thousands, picking on systematically the more vulnerable. The problem is more acute in rural India, among small children, pregnant females, dalits and adivasis, especially in the poorer states [Radhakrishna 2008], while market-oriented policies and reforms continue to widen the gap between the rich and the poor, as well as among regions.

Income elasticities of demand

The growth dynamics in operation is being fed continuously by growing inequality. With their income rapidly growing, the richer group of Indians demand a set of goods, which lie outside the reach of the rest in the society (think of air-conditioned malls, luxury hotels, restaurants and apartments, private cars, world class cities where the poor would be made invisible). The market for these goods expands rapidly. For instance, we are told that more than three in four Indians do not have a daily income of $ 2. They can hardly be a part of this growing market. However, the logic of the market now takes over, as the market is dictated by purchasing power. Its logic is to produce those goods for which there is enough demand backed by money, so that high prices can be charged and handsome profits can be made. As the income of the privileged grows rapidly, the market for the luxury goods they demand grows even faster through the operation of the "income elasticities of demand". These elasticities roughly measure the per cent growth in the demand for particular goods due to 1 per cent growth in income (at unchanged prices). Typically, goods consumed by the rich have income elasticities greater than unity, implying that the demand for a whole range of luxury goods consumed by the rich expands even faster than the growth in their income. Thus, the pattern of production is dictated by this process of growth through raising both the income of the rich faster than that of the rest of the society, and also because the income elasticities operate to increase even faster the demand for luxuries than income.

Anti-poor

The production structure resulting from this market-driven high growth is heavily biased against the poor. While demand expands rapidly for various up-market goods, demand for the basic necessities of life hardly expands. Not only is there little growth in the purchasing power of the poor, but the reduction in welfare expenditures by the state stunts the growth in demand for necessities. The rapid shift in the output composition in favour of services might be indicative of this process at the macro level [Rakshit 2007]. But specific examples abound. We have state-of-the-art corporate run expensive hospitals, nursing homes and spas for the rich, but not enough money to control malaria and tuberculosis which require inexpensive treatment. So they continue to kill the largest numbers. Lack of sanitation and clean drinking water transmit deadly diseases especially to small children which could be prevented at little cost, while bottled water of various brands multiply for those who can afford. Private schools for rich kids often have monthly fees that are higher than the annual income of an average unskilled Indian worker, while the poor often have to be satisfied with schools without teachers, or class rooms.

Over time an increasingly irreversible production structure in favour of the rich begins to consolidate itself, because the investments embodied in the specific capital goods created to produce luxuries cannot easily be converted to producing basic necessities (the luxury hotel or spa cannot be converted easily to a primary health centre in a village, etc). And yet, it is the logic of the market to direct investments towards the most productive and profitable sectors for "the efficient allocation of resources". The price mechanism sends signals to guide this allocation, but the prices that rule are largely a consequence of the growing unequal distribution of income in the society. The market becomes a bad master when the distribution of income is bad.

Heightened misery for the poor

There are insidious consequences of such a composition of output biased in favour of the rich that our liberalised market system produces. It is highly energy, water and other non-reproducible resources intensive, and often does unacceptable violence to the environment. We only have to think of the energy and material content of air-conditioned malls, luxury hotels and apartments, air travel, or private cars as means of transport. These are no doubt symbols of "world class" cities in a poor country, by diverting resources from the countryside where most live. It creates a black hole of urbanisation with a giant appetite for primary non-reproducible resources. Many are forced to migrate to cities as fertile land is diverted to non-agricultural use, water and electricity are taken away from farms in critical agricultural seasons to supply cities, and developmental projects displace thousands. Hydroelectric power from the big dams is transmitted mostly to corporate industries, and a few posh urban localities, while the nearby villages are left in darkness. Peasants even close to the cities do not get electricity or water to irrigate their land as urban India increasingly gobbles up these resources. Take the pattern of water use. According to the Comptroller and Auditor General report released to the public on March 30, 2007, Gujarat increased the allocation of Narmada waters to industry fivefold during 2006, eating into the share of drought-affected villages. Despite many promises made to villagers, water allocation stagnated at 0.86 million acres feet (MAF), and even this is being cut.

Water companies and soft drinks giants like Coca Cola sink deeper to take out pure groundwater as free raw material for their products. Peasants in surrounding areas pay, because they cannot match the technology or capital cost. Iron ore is mined out in Jharkhand, Chhattisgarh and Orissa leaving tribals without home or livelihood. Common lands which traditionally provided supplementary income to the poor in villages are encroached upon systematically by the local rich and the corporations with active connivance of the government. The manifest crisis engulfing Indian agriculture with more than a hundred thousand suicides by farmers over the last decade according to official statistics is a pointer to this process of pampering the rich who use their growing economic power to dominate increasingly the multitude of poor.

No place for the poorest

The composition of output demanded by the rich is hardly producible by village artisans or the small producers. They find no place either as producers or as consumers; instead, economic activities catering to the rich have to be handed over to large corporations who can now enter in a big way into the scene. The combination of accelerating growth and rising inequality begins to work in unison. The corporations are needed to produce goods for the rich, and in the process they make their high profits and provide well-paid employment for the rich in a poor country who provide a part of the growing market. It becomes a process of destructive creation of corporate wealth, with a new coalition cutting across traditional right and left political divisions formed in the course of this road to high growth. The signboard of this road is "progress through industrialisation".

The middle class opinion makers and the media persons unite, and occasionally offer palliatives of "fair compensation" to the dispossessed. Yet, they are at a loss as to how to create alternative dignified livelihoods for those affected by large-scale displacement and destruction in the name of industrialisation. Talks of compensation tend to be one-sided, as they focus usually on ownership and, at best use rights to the landed. However, the multitude of the poor who eke out a living without any ownership or use right to landed property like agricultural labourers, fishermen, or cart-drivers in rural areas, or illegal squatters and small hawkers in cities, seldom figure in this discussion about compensation. And yet, they are usually the poorest of the poor, outnumbering by far, perhaps in the ratio of 3 to 1, those who have some title to landed property. Ignoring them altogether, the state acquires with single-minded devotion land, water and resources for the private corporations for mining, industrialisation or SEZs in the name of public interest.

With some tribal land that can be acquired according to the PESA (1996) Act only through the consent of the community (gram sabha), consent is frequently manufactured at gun point by the law and order machinery of the state, if the money power of the corporations to bribe and intimidate proves to be insufficient. The vocal supporters of industrialisation never stop to ask, why the very poor who are least able, should bear the burden of "economic progress" of the rich.

It amounts to a process of internal colonisation of the poor, mostly dalits and adivasis and of other marginalised groups, through forcible dispossession and subjugation. It has set in motion a social process not altogether unknown between the imperialist "master race" and the colonised "natives". As the privileged thin layer of the society distance themselves from the poor, the speed at which the secession takes place comes to be celebrated as a measure of the rapid growth of the country. Thus, India is said to be poised to become a global power in the 21st century, with the largest number of homeless, undernourished, illiterate children coexisting with billionaires created by this rapid growth.

An unbridled market whose rules are fixed by the corporations aided by state power shapes this process. The ideology of progress through dispossession of the poor, preached relentlessly by the united power of the rich, the middle class and the corporations, colonises directly the poor, and indirectly it has begun to colonise our minds. The result is a sort of uniform industrialisation of the mind, a standardisation of thoughts which sees no other alternative. And yet, there is a fatal flaw. No matter how powerful this united campaign by the rich corporations, the media and the politicians is, even their combined power remains defenceless against the actual life experiences of the poor. If this process of growth continues for long, it would produce its own demons. No society, not even our malfunctioning democratic system, can withstand beyond a point the increasing inequality that nurtures this high growth. The rising dissent of the poor must either be suppressed with increasing state violence flouting every norm of democracy, and violence will be met with counter-violence to engulf the whole society. Or, an alternative path to development that depends on deepening our democracy with popular participation has to be found. Neither the rulers nor the ruled can escape for long this challenge thrown up by the recent high growth of India.

Note

1 Data collected by Aseem Srivastava, 'Why This Growth Can Never Trickle Down'.

References

Alternative Economic Survey, India (2006–07): *by Alternative Survey Group*, New Delhi, Dannish Books.

Dev, S Mahendra (2008): *Inclusive Growth in India*, Oxford University Press, New Delhi.

Fisher, S (2003): 'Globalisation and Its Challenges', *American Economic Review*, Papers and Proceedings, Vol 93, No 2.

Government of India, *Economic Survey* (2006 07): Ministry of Finance, New Delhi.

Green Left Weekly (2007): Issue No 710, May.

Rakshit, Mihir (2007): 'Service-led Growth', *Money and Finance*, February.

Radhakrishna, R (2008): *India Development Report*, (ed), Oxford University Press.

Rangarajan, C et al (2007): 'Revisiting Employment and Growth', *Money and Finance*, September.

Jain, Anil, Kumar and Parul Gupta (2008): 'Globalisation: The Indian Experience', *Mainstream*, Delhi, February 8–14.

18

Some implications of contemporary globalisation

Prabhat Patnaik

Source: *The Indian Economic Journal*, 59:1 (April–June 2011), 56–68.

The present globalisation differs from all previous globalisation in bringing about a 'de-segmentation' of the world economy. Earlier, while South–North labour movement was restricted, North–South capital movement was free; capital did not however move South except to mines and plantations. The import of manufactures into the North attracted high tariffs; hence the third world capitalists could not utilise low wages to capture metropolitan manufacturing markets. The world economy thus got 'segmented', with a frozen international division of labour, which allowed advanced country wages to rise with labour productivity despite the existence of massive third world labour reserves. Now, with freer trade and hence 'de-segmentation', advanced country wages are being restrained, and even pulled down, by third world labour reserves, which themselves show no tendency to dwindle. This fact unleashes a tendency towards 'underconsumption' in the world economy, which underlies the current world economic crisis.

I. Introduction

The contemporary globalisation is often seen as being qualitatively no different from the earlier, notably pre-first world war, episode of globalisation when the gold standard prevailed, when the world had been coming closer through revolutions in transport and communications, and when there were no juridical restrictions on the global movement of capital under the overall regime of Pax Britannica. This however is a mistake. There is a fundamental qualitative difference between the preceding episode(s) of globalisation and what is occurring now.

Through much of recent history, including the preceding episode(s) of globalisation, the world economy had remained segmented: labour from the south was not free to move to the north; capital from the north, though juridically free to move to the south, did not actually do so, notwithstanding the much lower wages of the south, except to mining and plantations and to railways (to open up those economies), where such movement was in any case unavoidable; and the entrepreneurs from the south, even when they had access to the same technology as those in the north and were hence in a position to out-compete the latter because of the lower wages they had to pay, were prevented from doing so because of northern tariffs on southern manufactured exports (Lewis, 1978) and because of the discriminations they faced within a colonial or semicolonial setting (Bagchi, 1972). The division of the world economy into developed and underdeveloped parts was sustained by this phenomenon of 'segmentation'.

This has greatly changed. The reason lies not so much in the fact of formal 'decolonisation' as in the phenomenon of contemporary globalisation. Capital, both as finance and as direct investment, is far more mobile today than even before, even though labour still is not. And the exports of manufactured goods and services from the south do not face the same hurdles in the north (at least as of now), as they used to earlier. This makes possible the diffusion of a whole range of activities, including manufacturing and services, from the north to the south, for meeting global, especially northern, demand. The world economy in short has become significantly 'de-segmented'. Not that the phenomenon of an enforced pattern of international division of labour has disappeared altogether, but much loosening has occurred in the traditionally-enforced pattern of international division of labour. The 'de-segmentation' in other words is not absolute; but it is substantial, and has profound implications.

The first is that the wages in the north are no longer insulated from the downward drag exercised by the third world labour reserves. The massive third world labour reserves have always kept their wages tied to a certain subsistence level; but in a segmented universe precluding free mobility of labour, of capital, and even of commodities (from the south to the north), these labour reserves could not prevent the wages in the north from increasing as productivity rose, if not *pari passu* then at least significantly. But this becomes impossible when this segmentation is broken, when manufactured goods produced in a third world country like China or services produced in India, can out-compete those produced in the advanced countries, on account of the low, subsistence wages prevailing in the former countries. In this situation, as the workers in the advanced countries compete against the subsistence-earning workers of the third world, there is a tendency for their wages even to fall in absolute terms, or, at the very least, not to rise but to maintain their existing relativity *vis-à-vis* the subsistence wages of the third world. At the same time, the diffusion of activities to the third world entails a rise in labour productivity in the latter, even as wages remain tied to the subsistence level because of the existence of labour reserves. There is, therefore, a decline in the wage share both in the advanced and in the third world economies, in the former because wages tend to fall at the given level of productivity, and in the latter because productivity rises at the given level of wages. These two together entail a rise in the share of surplus in world output.

This tendency towards a rise in the share of surplus in world output is immensely strengthened by the fact that technological progress, entailing an increase in labour productivity in the world economy over time, is unaccompanied by any increase in the vector of real wages in the world economy (as long as the relative magnitude of third world labour reserves remains undiminished). The first significant implication of the current globalisation, therefore, is an increase in the share of surplus in world output.

II

This, it may be thought, is merely a transient phenomenon. As the diffusion of activities to the third world on account of its lower wages gets to absorb more and more workers, its labour reserves would progressively diminish, causing an increase in the bargaining strength not only of third world workers, but, as a consequence, even of the advanced country workers. The tendency towards a rise in the share of surplus in world output would then get restricted.

But, this is an unlikely denouement. The diffusion of activities from the north to the south, even as it raises the rate of growth of output in countries like India and China, which are saddled with massive labour reserves, also raises, necessarily, the rate of growth of labour productivity in these economies. This fact curtails the rate of growth of labour demand. Two other factors also contribute towards this. The first is the tendency on the part of the elites in these countries to adopt increasingly the life-styles of their metropolitan counterparts which are necessarily less employment-intensive than their own earlier life-styles. Since the share of surplus in the output produced within these countries tends to rise over time for reasons discussed above, this tendency on the part of their elites, to whom this growing surplus accrues, to adopt the life-styles of the metropolitan elites, further restricts the rate of growth of labour demand in these economies relative to the rate of growth of output.

The second factor is the tendency unleashed by globalisation to destroy petty production. This is so important that I would call it the second implication of the current process of globalisation. Petty production can survive competition from capitalist production only with the help of the state. In the period immediately following decolonisation, and prior to the triumph of globalisation, the newly independent third world states had provided this support, partly as the fulfilment of the promise of the anti-colonial struggle. The dirigiste regimes that came into existence in most third world countries in the aftermath of decolonisation protected domestic petty production not only from international competition but also from encroachments from domestic capitalist production, often even by reserving spheres for them and putting direct restrictions on the domestic capitalists' capacity to encroach. With globalisation, and the pursuit of neoliberal policies, the state increasingly withdraws from such a protective role. The freeing of trade implies the withdrawal of protection for petty production from international competition. And the dismantling of restrictions on the functioning of capital imposed by the state, which neoliberalism entails, necessarily results in capitalist production encroaching upon petty production.

Bereft of support by the state, petty producers get progressively dispossessed, distressed and compelled to join the ranks of those seeking wage employment, which swells the labour reserves. It follows that there are powerful factors contributing towards a restriction of the rate of growth of labour demand even in high-growth third world economies. This has had the effect of ensuring that the rate of growth of labour demand remains even below the rate of growth of labour supply, and certainly does not exceed it, as far as the third world is concerned. This means that the relative magnitude of labour reserves remains undiminished. Hence the rise in the share of surplus in world output is not a mere transient phenomenon but characterises in an essential sense the era of globalisation.

III

This fact has a crucial bearing upon the movement of world aggregate demand. Since the propensity to consume out of the surplus is lower than the propensity to consume out of wages, a rise in the share of surplus in world output has the effect *ceteris paribus* of lowering the level of world aggregate demand relative to output. And since we are talking about a tendency towards a rising share of surplus in world output rather than a once-for-all increase, there is an *ex-ante* tendency towards overproduction which gets accentuated over time. This growing tendency towards *ex-ante* overproduction, when caused as in the present instance by a declining overall propensity to consume owing to changes in income distribution, is usually referred to as 'underconsumption'.[1] *The* third implication of the current phase of globalisation is this existence of an *ex-ante* tendency towards underconsumption.

This *ex-ante* tendency does not necessarily mean an actual *ex-post* crisis of overproduction; it may be thwarted by increases in government expenditure (which Keynes had suggested), or increases in autonomous credit-financed consumption expenditure (as burgeoning consumer credit in the advanced countries testifies to), or private investment booms promoted by speculative 'bubbles'.

All these countervailing factors have played a role in recent times sustaining growth in the advanced capitalist countries, though the rate of growth in a secular sense has nonetheless come down markedly during the era of globalisation compared to the years of Keynesian demand management that preceded it. But each one of these reaches its limits soon. Speculative 'bubbles' burst, causing financial crisis and recession; and the longer they take to burst, i.e., the more prolonged and pronounced they are, the more severe is the ensuing crisis (a fact that had prompted Dennis Robertson to argue for an increase in the interest rate at the onset of a boom, to nip the boom in the bud and prevent the severity of a depression).[2] The doling out of consumer credit is unsustainable beyond a point as it saddles the financial system with non-performing assets, and even if risks to the system arising from such assets are camouflaged in various ways through 'bundling', they cannot be eliminated. Government expenditure does provide a way out of the tendency towards underconsumption, but in the era of globalisation of finance, the opposition of finance capital to fiscal deficits (an opposition which has little theoretical rationale and which was called by Joan Robinson (1966) 'the humbug of finance'), acquires a spontaneous effectiveness, since finance being internationally mobile can leave the borders of any nation-state that refuses to bow to its caprices. Most nation-states therefore fall in line with the caprices of finance and keep their fiscal deficits restricted, which also restricts the scope for demand stimulation through government expenditure.

But of course there is an exception, namely the leading capitalist country, the United States. Its currency being 'as good as gold' in the eyes of most wealth-holders provides it with the capacity to run fiscal deficits with impunity, in the sense that such deficits in its case, unlike in the case of others, are unlikely to stimulate capital flight. Here, however a different problem arises; let us turn to this problem now.

IV

Just as in the case of an industry a shrinking of demand affects high-cost firms more than it affects low-cost firms, likewise the adverse impact of a reduction in world demand is more likely to be felt by the high-cost advanced capitalist economies, especially the USA, than the low-cost economies like China or East Asia. One could of course argue in textbook fashion that variations in world demand would affect only the high-cost economies, with low-cost economies being forever at their full-capacity output (unless the decline in demand is extraordinarily large). But it is more realistic to believe that variations in world demand affect all economies, with the high-cost ones being more affected than the low-cost ones.

There is however an additional consideration here. When world demand decreases, the low-cost economies can enlarge domestic absorption through larger government expenditure, since the effect of any such increased domestic absorption is likely to be felt mainly upon their own domestic output. But when world demand increases, they would prefer to reduce domestic absorption, make room for exports while preventing profit-inflation (and hence a decline in their real wages even below subsistence level). Of course it may be thought that they have no compulsion to push out larger exports when world demand increases and that their doing so only represents gratuitous mercantile aggressiveness; but this is not true, since any low-cost producer that did not do so would lose its share of the world market to one that did.

In other words, competition between the low-cost producers of the third world ensures that they more or less produce close to capacity output all the time, but absorb more domestically during periods of world recession and less during periods of world boom. Their net exports in other words are positively related to the level of world demand.

But this means that if the leading capitalist economy, the United States, stimulates its own aggregate demand, and hence *ipso facto* world demand, then its own current account deficit also expands. The fourth implication of the current episode of globalisation follows from this, namely that the leading capitalist country cannot expand world demand without increasing its own level of indebtedness.

Looking at it differently, taking the world economy as a whole, we could visualise the tendency towards underconsumption (discussed above) being countered by the interventions of a world state, which could run an appropriate level of fiscal deficit to ensure world full employment. But there is no world state, and the closest approximation to it is a nation-state, that of the United States, which alone has the capacity to run fiscal deficits with some impunity, i.e., without necessarily jeopardising its currency through capital flights as a consequence of such deficits. But the US state is also a nation-state, concerned about the level of indebtedness of its own nation. Since its running a fiscal deficit to stimulate its own level of aggregate demand, and hence *ipso facto* world demand, entails an aggravation of the indebtedness of its own economy, this fact constrains its playing the role of a surrogate world state in thwarting the tendency towards underconsumption.

At the present moment there is much pressure on President Obama to cut back on his stimulus package which is quite unrelated to any concerns about the external indebtedness of the United States. But the point being made here is that even if he could successfully resist such pressure, the issue of the 'leakage' of the stimulus to countries exporting to the United States, and hence the growing indebtedness of the US, would inevitably arise. Hence within the current regime of globalisation where the US eschews protectionism, the fact that its fiscal deficit increases its external indebtedness acts as a constraint upon its state playing the role of a surrogate world state in warding off the tendency towards underconsumption; but of course if the US does go protectionist then the current regime of globalisation comes to an end anyway.

There has been some talk of late about China taking on the role of providing a stimulus to the world economy, or about coordinated action by several nation-states acting in concert to mimic a world state in the matter of stimulating the world economy (a suggestion made by Keynes, among others, during the Great Depression (Kindleberger, 1987)). Neither of these however is practical. The former is impractical since China is still not large enough to play such a role for the world as a whole, even if it were willing to do so, which it is not. Its reluctance arises from the fact that being a low-cost country, and hence with a current account surplus, it is under no obligation to substitute domestic absorption for exports (the same reluctance that had been the bane of the Bretton Woods system under which the surplus countries were not obliged to undertake any adjustment). The second suggestion is also impractical since the group of leading countries that could collectively play the role of a surrogate world state would naturally consist of both high-cost and low-cost countries, which would have divergent interests. Such divergence would work in the direction of preventing any agreement on a coordinated fiscal stimulus.

It follows then that it is only the leading capitalist country, the US, that can at all play at present the role of a stimulator of demand for the world economy; but the US is in no position to do so. The contrast here between the position of the US now and that of Britain during the heyday of Pax Britannica, which incidentally is also a contrast between the earlier episode of globalisation and the current one, may be instructive in this context.

V

It is incumbent on the leading capitalist country that it should keep its doors open for the exports of its emerging rivals, the newly-industrialising countries of the time. If it did not do so, then the global economic regime over which it presides would be torn asunder. It is also the case, however, that accommodating the exports of the newly industrialising countries of the time within its own market inevitably makes the leading country run a current account deficit *vis-à-vis* them, as Britain had to do during the period of its leadership and the US is having to do now. This is simply because the newly industrialising countries of the time are invariably lower-cost producers compared to the leading capitalist country. In Britain's case this was because being an established producer, Britain was saddled with technology that was older on average (an argument sometimes referred to as 'the penalty of the early start'); in the case of the US, as we have seen, this is because *inter alia* the new industrialised countries, saddled with large labour reserves, have lower (near-subsistence) wages compared to the US. Ironically, therefore, leadership of the capitalist world extracts a cost from the leader, namely, it must run a current account deficit *vis-à-vis* the newly industrialising countries of its time. The question is: if it is to maintain its leadership role, then how can it cope with such a deficit?

In the case of Britain the answer was found in the tropical colonies and semi-colonies (Patnaik, 2009). Britain ran a current account deficit *vis-à-vis* continental Europe and (from a later date) with the United States; but it ran a current account surplus *vis-à-vis* colonies like the West Indies and India, which in turn ran a current account surplus *vis-à-vis* continental Europe, the United States and other temperate regions of European settlement, such as Australia, New Zealand, Canada etc. With the current surplus it had with the tropical colonies, Britain not only managed to balance its current deficits *vis-à-vis* all these other countries, but even managed to export vast amounts of capital to some of them.

But the real point lies elsewhere: Britain's current account surplus *vis-à-vis* the tropical colonies and semi-colonies was a deliberately 'manufactured' one. It arose from its exporting cotton textiles and other similar manufactured goods, not wanted anywhere else, to the colonies at the expense of the local petty craft producers, causing what has been called 'industrialisation' there; and it arose also from a unilateral extraction of surplus through taxation from these colonies, without any quid pro quo, and against the fictitious export to these colonies of what was called 'good administration'. Not only was the current account surplus *vis-à-vis* the colonies deliberately 'manufactured', based on an exploitation of their colonial status, but the amount of this surplus was also calibrated in a manner that suited the needs of the British balance of payments. The British economic historian S.B. Saul (1970) calls colonial markets like India 'markets on tap' for Britain.

This was how Britain could maintain its leadership role of the capitalist world, which in turn contributed to the long Victorian and Edwardian boom: it could keep its own markets open for its rival newly industrialising countries; it could run current account deficits *vis-à-vis* them; but it never got indebted because of such deficits, and indeed on the contrary became during the same period a massive capital exporter; it could do all this because it made full use of its domination over its tropical colonies.

The United States today does not have this possibility open to it. And what is more, even if it had colonies, the very prolonged process of exploitation of colonies has reduced them to such a condition that the value of their exports (of primary commodities) to the world market is too insignificant to permit the same solution to its current deficits that Britain could count upon.[3] (Oil no doubt still remains as the one primary commodity which can be used in this manner, but the pitfalls of controlling oil-producing economies are too well-known by now.)

The present globalisation, in short, is globalisation that is not superimposed upon a colonial substructure. Indeed colonial substructures of the old sort can no longer be created; and even if created would no longer suffice. The current leader of the capitalist world therefore does not have the capacity to cope with the cost of leadership that Britain had. And this is one of the major contradictions of the current episode of globalisation.

It follows from the foregoing that the tendency towards underconsumption unleashed by the current phase of globalisation cannot be successfully thwarted by the countervailing factors mentioned earlier. World capitalism therefore appears headed for a protracted period of crisis and stagnation, punctuated perhaps by occasional booms built on the quicksand of speculative 'bubbles' in asset prices.

VI

The tendency towards underconsumption that I have been talking about must be distinguished sharply from the 'savings glut' hypothesis advanced by Ben Bernanke (2005). There is a superficial resemblance between the two but they are vastly different, and indeed belong to irreconcilably diverse theoretical traditions, as the following discussion will clarify.[4]

Bernanke's argument that excess savings over investment in countries like China give rise to a current account surplus in such countries which in turn causes a current account deficit in the United States, appears puzzling at first sight because it does not distinguish between *ex-ante* and *ex-post*. Even if we assume that an excess of savings over investment at near-full capacity output in China does nothing to reduce capacity utilisation in that country but translates itself into a current account surplus, again at full capacity output (presumably because China being a low-cost producer can always export its way out of any demand constraint), it does not follow that the US would not face the contractionary effects of an import surplus. And if it did, then the *ex-post* adjustment to the *ex-ante* excess savings of China could take a range of possible different forms. Bernanke does not discuss these and indeed does not even distinguish between *ex-ante* and *ex-post*, because he assumes 'full employment' (or full capacity) to be prevailing everywhere, i.e., he invokes a Say's Law world. It is only in such a world that excess savings over investment in one country necessarily gets translated into excess investment over savings in another without any income effects, i.e., it is only in such a world that excess of savings over investment in any one country entails only a change in current balances and not in aggregate employment and output.

In fact Bernanke quite explicitly invokes a Say's Law world by postulating that the availability of excess savings from China lowers the interest rate in the United States, which makes the interest rate equilibrate savings and investment as in the pre-Keynesian theory (the so-called 'treasury view' against which Kahn (1931) had written his paper on the 'multiplier'). But since savings, even though a function of the interest rate, are also a function of income, corresponding to different levels of income there are different savings curves (as functions of interest rate). To say that the interest rate equilibrates savings and investment amounts therefore to saying that there is only one such curve, i.e., we are considering only one particular level of income at which interest rate equilibrates savings and investment. It amounts therefore to assuming that output and employment are given, presumably at 'full employment', i.e., that Say's Law is fulfilled.

But if the interest rate is a monetary phenomenon, which Bernanke as a practising banker must acknowledge, then Say's Law cannot hold, and the 'savings glut' hypothesis as advanced by Bernanke cannot hold. The very fact of the current crisis undermines the theory on the basis of which Bernanke advances his argument, since that theory assumes universal full employment. Indeed if one accepted Bernanke's view of the 'savings glut' (which does not reckon with any income effects and hence the possibility of unemployment), then one could not legitimately argue for a fiscal stimulus even in the present context, since such a stimulus is meant precisely to counter unemployment and recession.

The core of the Bernanke proposition, namely that larger domestic absorption by China would work in the direction of correcting world imbalances, which is valid, has got to be located therefore within a different theoretical context that has nothing to do with the assumption of the perennial prevalence of full employment. In this context China's greater domestic absorption would both correct world imbalances, and *ceteris paribus* improve world demand. In fact it would correct world imbalances precisely by improving world demand. The theoretical context sketched in the present paper not only incorporates what is valid in the Bernanke proposition, but also locates the so-called reduced domestic absorption of China within a scenario of changing distribution of income away from the workers and peasants that globalisation has entailed.

In other words the so-called 'excess savings' of China arise not because of any capricious behaviour on the part of the Chinese state, as the Bernanke proposition would entail, but because of certain spontaneous tendencies embedded in the current globalisation process. True, the Chinese state could intervene in this process to step up domestic absorption at the expense of exports, but this would entail losing export markets to low-wage rival countries within the third world itself, which the Chinese state would be averse to doing. Caught in the process of globalisation, the Chinese state itself in other words is part of the spontaneity of the process.

Just as within the universe of a capitalist economy, the individual capitalists are engaged in a Darwinian struggle where each wants to capture as much of the markets as possible in order not to go under, likewise within the universe of capitalist globalisation, each country is engaged in a Darwinian struggle to capture as large a part of the world market as it can. To forego exporting for the sake of enlarging domestic absorption is possible only if the country in question drops out of the process of globalisation, i.e., de-links itself from this process (which is not the same thing of course as autarky), but not otherwise.

This, however, also means that even successful third world economies in the era of globalisation witness growing poverty and distress among their workers and peasants. Let us turn to this now.

VII

There is a pervasive belief that countries like China and India which have witnessed the diffusion of a range of activities from the advanced capitalist countries to their shores as a consequence of globalisation, and have therefore witnessed remarkably high growth rates of output that have even proved resilient to the current crisis, have thus brought down their levels of internal poverty and destitution. This is wrong. The fact that internal poverty and destitution in these countries increases rather than decreases despite high growth follows directly from our analysis of globalisation.

We have seen that the existence of massive labour reserves in these economies, itself the result of the 'drain' of surplus and of 'deindustrialisation' (discussed earlier) which colonialism had inflicted upon them, keeps their wage rates tied to a subsistence level. Unless these reserves start dwindling, the phenomenon of wages being tied to subsistence does not change even though labour productivity increases on account of both diffusion of higher-productivity activities from the advanced countries at the existing levels of technology and of technological progress over time. Within these countries, therefore, the share of surplus increases and income inequalities increase immensely.

At the same time, for reasons we have already discussed, the rate of growth of labour demand at these subsistence wages does not rise sufficiently to keep pace with the rate of growth of labour force, notwithstanding the high rate of growth of output. Hence the relative size of the labour reserves to the total work force does not diminish, but rather increases, perpetuating the situation where workers are absolutely excluded from sharing any part of the productivity gains.[5] Within the work force, however, since the employed part sees no improvement in its absolute wages; the reserve part, consisting of the unemployed, the underemployed and the unemployed-in-disguise, which earns less than the employed part, grows in relative size compared to the latter; and the petty producers, including the peasantry, witnesses a decline in its average income due to the withdrawal of support from the state, there is an absolute worsening in the average condition of the working population.[6]

I shall not say anything about the Chinese situation, but this absolute worsening of the average conditions of the working population is very clear from the Indian data. The most obvious and reliable index of the living standards of the people is the per capita absorption of food grains both directly and indirectly. This is positively correlated across countries with the level of per capita income; this is positively correlated within countries with per capita income across income groups; and this generally rises or falls over time for particular social groups in sync with the movements in their per capita income. At the beginning of the 20th century, the per capita absorption of food grains in 'British India' was 200 kg per annum. By the time of Independence in 1947, it had fallen to around 150 kg per annum, indicating a significant worsening of the living standards of the population in the last half century of colonial rule. After independence with the strenuous efforts of the dirigiste regime it went up to about 180 kg per annum for India as a whole by end-1980s. But in the period of neoliberal policies which began in earnest in India in 1991, it has come down drastically to reach 157 kg in 2008. The decline has been particularly sharp precisely during the period of high growth and because of this decline, the per capita food grain absorption in 2008 has gone back to the same level where it was in 1954. And all this refers to the average for the entire people including the rich and the middle classes; if we look at the bulk of the lower-income population, the worsening in their condition must have been even sharper (Patnaik, 2010).

It is customary to blame governments for such a development. But the governments too, as argued earlier, become part of the spontaneity of the economic processes of globalisation, which usher in increases in both income inequalities as well as in absolute poverty. While this is a general feature of contemporary globalisation, quite independent of whether there is a tendency towards underconsumption and crises, the unleashing of such crises only makes the process of impoverishment even more acute.

VIII

In discussing the implications of globalisation, therefore, we must distinguish between two different points. Assuming that the effects of the *ex-ante* tendency towards underconsumption are thwarted, there is nonetheless a rise in the share of surplus in world output, and the destruction of the viability of petty production which entails an absolute worsening of the conditions of workers and peasants and a swelling of the ranks of the labour reserves. In addition since the tendency towards underconsumption is not thwarted, because there is no nation-state that can play the role of a surrogate world state, this tendency towards absolute impoverishment of substantial sections of the working population gets further accentuated. Since one of our arguments has been that there is no clear end to the current crisis, i.e., that the process of thwarting of the tendency towards underconsumption is unlikely to resume in the foreseeable future, this portends ill for the working people of the world in the coming years.

Notes

1 The classic attempt at postulating a tendency towards 'underconsumption' in the context of an individual advanced capitalist country, exemplified by the United States, is by Baran and Sweezy (1966). But the Baran and Sweezy argument follows analytically simply from a Kaleckian framework where the 'degree of monopoly' is rising. See Kalecki (1971).

2 For Robertson's views and a critique of those views, see Keynes (1946: 327).

3 The proposition that the shrinking value of primary commodity exports in world trade is itself an outcome of a prolonged period of colonial exploitation has been argued in Patnaik (1997).

4 A theoretical critique, more detailed than what is presented below, can be found in Patnaik (2010).

5 In fact one can argue that even if the labour reserves within a particular country get exhausted, this country still cannot witness a rise in wages above the subsistence level, as long as labour reserves exist elsewhere in the third world tying wages there to the subsistence level. In such a case, competition with those countries will entail an attack on trade union rights in the country with dwindling labour reserves, to prevent wages from rising because of local labour scarcity. Something of the sort, it may be claimed, is happening in China. But the argument in the text is based on the presumption, certainly valid in the case of India, that labour reserves are non-dwindling even in relative, let alone absolute, terms.

6 The argument can be stated as follows: let a, b and c be the share in total work force of the petty producers, the reserve army of labour (strictly speaking) and the employed workers in the capitalist sector respectively (a+b+c=l), and let x, y, and z be their per capita real incomes, with $y<x$ and $y<z$ always. If z remains unchanged over time while c is either unchanged or falls, and if a and x fall over time, then ax+by+cz, which is the weighted average real per capita income of the working population, must fall over time, even with a constant y. Of course all this does not consider the middle class. But unless the size of the middle class relative to the working population as defined above increases over time, the proposition about absolute immiseration of the working population still stands.

References

Bagchi, A.K. (1972). *Private Investment in India 1900–1939.* Cambridge: Cambridge University Press.

Baran, P.A. and P.M. Sweezy (1966). *Monopoly Capital.* New York: Monthly Review Press.

Bernanke, Ben (2005). "The Global Savings Glut and the US Current Account Deficit", Sandridge Lecture,

Virgina Association of Economics, Richmond, Virginia.

Kahn, R.F. (1931). "The Relation of Home Investment to Employment", *Economic Journal*, June.

Kalecki, M. (1971). *Selected Essays on the Dynamics of the Capitalist Economy 1933–1970.* Cambridge: Cambridge University Press.

Keynes, J.M. (1946). *The General Theory of Employment, Interest and Money*. London: Macmillan.

Kindleberger, C.P. (1987). *The World in Depression.* Harmondsworth: Penguin.

Lewis, W.A. (1978). *Growth and Fluctuations 1870–1913.* London: George Allen and Unwin.

Patnaik, P. (1997). *Accumulation and Stability Under Capitalism*. Oxford: Clarendon Press.

—— (2009). *The Value of Money*. New York: Columbia University Press.

—— (2010). "The Theory of the Global Savings Glut", www.networkideas.org

Patnaik, U. (2010). "On Some Fatal Fallacies", *Economic and Political Weekly*, November 20–26, Mumbai.

Robinson, J. (1966). *Economic Philosophy*. Harmondsworth: Penguin.

Saul, S.B. (1970). *Studies in British Overseas Trade.* Liverpool: Liverpool University Press.

19

A framework of planning for India[1]

A.K. Dasgupta

Source: *The Indian Economic Journal*, XVI:3 (January–March 1969), 265–76.

I present here a framework of planning for India not with a belief that it will be accepted, far less implemented by the present Government of India. It is not indeed the stage at which the Planning Commission or the Government of India will be in a mood to revise the plan structure in any drastic manner. On the other hand, indications are that thinking in those quarters are away from planning. It is doubtful if there has ever been planning in our country in the strict sense of the term. The experience of the first fifteen years of so-called planning is surely a wide discrepancy between profession and action, between targets and achievements. The result has been, since 1965–66, the emergence of an interregnum for re-thinking. There are two directions in which re-thinking might have moved: to raise questions concerning the reasons for the failure of our plans and to take effective steps to remedy the deficiencies wherever they have occurred, or alternatively to accept the failure as a fact and to take the economy along a path away from planning. The brochure that has been circulated by the newly constituted Planning Commission on Approach to the Fourth Five Year Plan apparently does not take the first line. It gives us a few targets concerning growth in different sectors in the manner the earlier plans did, but it does not even once ask why such targets could not be realized hitherto, nor what special institutional changes would be necessary if the targets set out were to be achieved. On the other hand, it seems clear, considering the omission of the term "socialism"—the declared philosophy of the earlier plans—and the acceptance of a policy of gradual withdrawal of controls, that re-thinking, if there has been any, is rather the other way about.

My own attitude to the problem would be different. I must still say that inadequate planning may be worse than no planning and that bad planning surely is. Yet I am convinced that if we have to have the twin objectives of a reasonably high rate of growth and a high level of employment for an under-developed, over-populated country like India, economic planning is essential. The decision of Jawaharlal Nehru taken eighteen years ago to put our economy under a system of planning was to my mind a correct decision. The plan strategy initiated by the Planning Commission was not also altogether a wrong strategy. Rather the contrary. So far as essentials are concerned, I am still in sympathy with the strategy of increasing the capital stock and of bringing it into line with our labour supply within the quickest possible time. I am thus not allergic, as many people are, to the drive towards the so-called "heavy" industries such as our Planning Commission envisaged. Seeing, however, that the plans have failed, I may seek for an amendment of the strategy. But beyond that, I shall ask why the strategy failed to bear the expected fruit—what weaknesses there are in the setting into which these strategies have been projected. If you take these weaknesses for granted, as the Planning Commission apparently does, you would surely go in for less planning, probably to scrap planning altogether. Personally I would like to go in rather for more planning, on the assumption that sooner or later planning will carry with it measures calculated to remove the weaknesses that have so far inhibited its implementation.

2. Robertson separates economists into two classes—"a class of economic advisers, who must subdue their hand to the material it works in, and never forget that there is nothing either good or bad but thinking makes it so; and a class of pure economists, who are licensed to think dangerous thoughts and even to think them aloud, but who in return must suffer themselves to be burnt at the stake rather than ever to be dragged into giving advice to anybody about anything."[2] Temperamentally I belong to the latter class, "who would not be dragged into giving advice to anybody", except one's own self. I do not believe that I would ever think dangerous thoughts. Yet what I propose to say on planning in India may have implications which will be considered by some of my colleagues on the other side as dangerous. I am not a "defeatist"; but I could assure Robertson, if he were alive, that I am not a "communist" either. For I do not believe, at this time of the day, in spite of Robertson, that an authoritarian state is needed to cope with the problem of transfer and readjustment that planning, in the sense in which I would understand it, would involve.

3. I take employment as the central piece in planning for our country. I recollect having taken this position since our early days of planning. I have always considered the employment target as the most significant element for the determination of the size of investment. But my demand in the earlier stages of planning was rather moderate on this score. For I perceived—not quite correctly, as I now think—that at some stage of the investment process there might arise a contradiction between growth and employment. On the eve of the Second Five Year Plan, I said, as I felt then: "while increased employment certainly adds to national wealth, maximum employment within the available resources of other kinds may not always be compatible with the *maximum* degree of capital formation and maximum income potential".[3] There may be some sense in this assertion. But it seems to me now that it does not contain the whole truth and that it may lend itself to an interpretation suggesting that considerations of employment are subsidiary to considerations of growth. The assertion is surely correct when one is considering the choice of industries, but it is terribly misleading in the context of the choice of techniques.

An employment-oriented approach to planning has a distinct advantage for a country like India. An adequate and judicious use of surplus labour in the economy sets a pace for economic development and also by itself tends to reduce inequality of income in the society. More employment, if the productivity of the marginal unit of labour is at all positive, means higher national income, even though it may mean a fall in average productivity. Further, in so far as a part of the additional employment is directed to the production of capital goods, it makes for higher growth potential. Clearly, also, it is accompanied by a reduction in inequality of incomes between members of the labouring class itself, now that more people belonging to the class come within the income earning category. Whether the process leads to a general reduction in inequality of incomes depends upon the manner in which finance for additional employment is secured. If the finance is secured through inflation, as it has been in our country, and a consequent, reduction in the rate of real wages, it may not. But if it is secured by transfers from higher income groups whose consumption does not enter into the social cost of production, an increase in employment does mean a general reduction in inequality. One essential principle of planning for economic development is to divert resources away from "luxury" goods (i.e., goods which do not help production)[4] partly towards the creation of fixed capital and partly towards such consumption goods as enter into the budgets of the labouring class. Taxing the relatively rich and using the proceeds for investment which promotes growth, through the production of fixed and circulating capital in an appropriate proportion, are measures which tend to reduce inequality and at the same time increase employment.

If the experience of the first fifteen years of planning has taught us anything, it is that we underrated the claim of employment in our framework of planning at our peril. While the rate or capital formation and growth has not been up to expectation— the saving rate is still around a modest 10 per cent of the national income—it cannot be said to be too bad, judged by a normal standard. Leaving out the exceptional years since the end of the Third Plan, the rate of growth has been of the order of about 4%. Even agricultural output, including food production, where our performance has been less satisfactory, has increased more than in proportion to the rate of population growth. Where our plans have failed disastrously is in the field of employment. During the last 10–12 years our unemployment figure has more than doubled, recording a rate of growth which would be at least three times the rate of growth in the labour force. We have thus failed to achieve even the modest target of not permitting the proportion of unemployment to the labour force to increase, let alone the Planning Commission's own target, as set forth in the Second Plan, of not permitting the backlog to expand. The Planning Commission, it will be remembered, proposed for the Second Five Year Plan a target of employment which would match the increase in the labour force consequent on the growth of population. It is true that the growth of population, as revealed in the 1961 Census was more than was anticipated at the beginning of the Plan. Yet the unemployment figure rose so much that in desperation one felt like urging, as a minimum, that the unemployment *percentage* must not be allowed to grow.[5] Even this has not been fulfilled.

4. There seems to be a certain weakness in the model of growth that we have pursued which is responsible for this state of affairs. It is not true that the problem of unemployment has been ignored by the Planning Commission or by the model makers. The reduction in the volume of unemployment has indeed been put up as one of the more important objectives of planning. But the creation of employment has been considered more as a function of the size of investment; techniques have not received in this context the attention that they deserved. Even in the 4–sector model of Mahalanobis, attention has been given to labour-intensive industries, not so much to techniques as such, as counter to capital intensive "heavy" industries that the needs of growth demand. In practice, however, enough attention has not been given to the implementation of the 4–sector model either; it is the two-sector model of Mahalanobis, designed to indicate the condition of growth potential, that has been highlighted in our plans.

Let us then turn to considerations of technique. The problem of choice of techniques, which is essentially a problem of choosing between capital–labour ratios, has been analysed by economists at different levels of abstraction. I shall choose a procedure which has been in vogue in the post-war period in the context of planning, namely a procedure which assumes the stock of capital to be given and labour to be varying with varying techniques. I shall follow Sen.[6] But instead of the integral product curve that he uses, I shall employ the traditional Rent-curve of the text-book variety.

In the diagram quantity of labour is measured along the horizontal axis and the marginal product is measured along the vertical axis. The stock of capital is shown by OK which is below the horizontal line. Following convention, I assume constant returns to scale. Labour is assumed to be homogeneous, so that one labourer working, say, eight hours a day can be taken as a unit. The different points on the horizontal axis denote different capital–labour ratios, as shown by the angle formed by OK and the relevant point. They represent different techniques. The well-known difficulties of measuring capital are set aside, and it is assumed that variation in techniques implies that the same amount of capital assumes different forms. Thus at Lj on the horizontal axis OLj units of labour are employed on OK amount of capital in its appropriate form, yielding a total product OPP_JL_J. If then the wage rate per labourer is OW, the technique that is supposed to maximize surplus is L_2 where OWP_2L_2 is the total wage and WPP_2 is the surplus. In a labour surplus economy, L_2 is, however, not a position of full employment. On the other hand, you cannot go beyond OL_2 without a dent in wage or surplus. If you go up to, say, L, which represents a technique yielding maximum output, and have to offer the same rate of wages, OW, it being the minimum that the labourers are prepared to put up with, there is a loss, at the margin, of wP_2L. The total surplus in this case comes down to WPP_2 minus wP_2L. (See Figure 1 on p. 291.)

It is therefore often argued—and this is indeed the conventional theory—that there is an inevitable clash between maximum surplus and maximum output in the context of a labour surplus economy. If you want to maximize growth, you maximize surplus and choose a technique given by L_2. If you want to maximize employment and hence output, choose the technique given by L. If even then you have got surplus labour, your problem becomes intractable unless you increase the stock of capital.

Those of us who are intuitively inclined towards maximum employment have hitherto argued that strict principles of economy suggest a technique which is nearer L than L_2 on the ground that in a labour surplus economy the shadow rate of wages is zero or near-zero.[7] This certainly is true. But it does not answer our questions; the conflict between maximum growth and maximum employment supposedly still remains. After all, the shadow rate of wages is only a shadow; in real life it does not exist. In real life, if you employ a labourer you have to pay him at the current market rate of wages, the minimum being set by a minimum subsistence, as judged by the labourers. Which means that if the extra L_2L is employed, the total wage will be OWwL, if OW is considered to be that minimum subsistence. And since the total output will be OPL, the surplus will be reduced by wP_2L.

This, however, is not the whole story. In the event of OL_2 labour units being employed on capital OK with a view to "maximum surplus", L_2L labour units remain unemployed. But they cannot remain unemployed and yet exist without being fed. The classical economists, let us remember, did not bother about unemployment because they thought that starvation was a natural cure for it. Starvation deaths are indeed nature's substitute for employment. However, in a society where the unemployed are not permitted to die, where there are institutional obligations that prevent starvation (the joint family system, for example, in India), we have to account for the means of livelihood needed to sustain the unemployed. If, suppose, the unemployed labourers, L_2L, have to be maintained at the minimum subsistence level which, according to our hypothesis is OW, then an extra wP_2L_2L amount of subsistence has to be found. And where can we find it unless we transfer it from WPP_2? And if we do that, our surplus is reduced by wP_2L_2L, whereas if there were full-employment, the reduction would be by only wP_2L.[8] On the other hand, if we assume that the unemployed have to be maintained by the labourers themselves, we have also to accept that they will ask for a rate of wages which is higher than OW, so as to be able to compensate for the extra burden. The concept of minimum subsistence is indeed a flexible concept and cannot be given a precise content; it depends naturally upon the average size of the labourer's family.[9] Here also, therefore, the draft in the ultimate analysis is on WPP_2.

It does seem inescapable that you can maximize surplus only if you maximize output. And in a labour surplus economy you maximize output only when you provide for full employment in the physical sense. Under capitalism, the entrepreneurs will no doubt keep the level of wages down to OW, if they can, not caring perhaps for the problem of loss of efficiency of labour, which after all is a long-run problem. But in a planned economy, where planning is done with a social purpose and where the fear of efficiency deterioration is as much its concern as short-term profit, wages are to be adjusted to a level which takes account of the minimum subsistence of the unemployed. For in such a society, not only starvation but also the under-nourishment, that would follow were wages below subsistence, is an anachronism.

At this stage it seems necessary to mention that although the marginal productivity curve, as drawn in the diagram, is a continuous curve implying an infinitely large variety of techniques, in real life, with known technology, feasible techniques are limited in number. We are told, for example, that in the cotton textile industry in India there are as few as four techniques in vogue. It must be much the same in other industries as well, although it is also probably true that if the production process in an industry were not as integrated as we often find it is even in less developed countries like India, a way could be found to extend the use of labour-intensive techniques. The point that is sought to be emphasized is that, given constant returns to scale, our choice of techniques should move invariably *in the direction of* maximum output.

5. Does the same consideration apply to choice of industries? In allocating resources, do we have to give priority to labour intensive industries, too, so as to ensure full employment? It is sometimes thought that if full employment considerations justify labour-intensive techniques, then by the same token, one has to opt for labour-intensive industries, too. There is indeed a sense in which the argument appears to be valid. The application of a shadow rate of wage and a shadow rate of interest for determining allocation of resources does carry a suggestion to that effect. In an under-developed, over-populated country, the shadow rate of wages, as we have seen, is lower than the actual rate of wages, being zero or near-zero so long as there is unemployment; on the other hand, the shadow rate of interest is higher than the actual rate of interest,—the latter being determined in the money market under institutional pressures. In the circumstances the "shadow" costs of production of commodities turn out to be different from actual costs, being relatively higher in the case of capital intensive industries and relatively lower in the labour intensive industries. Applying the conventional neo-classical competitive model, therefore, we find that in so far as the demands for commodities are at all elastic, the market allocation of resources which follows actual costs tends to yield less than optimum employment; for prices to conform to shadow costs, a shift of resources away from capital intensive industries over to labour intensive industries is thus indicated. The use of shadow rates means in effect alteration in cost curves and a shift in equilibrium position in respect of the allocation of resources. The new equilibrium allocation arrived at on the basis of shadow costs yields larger employment, taking the two groups of industries together. It can be also shown to lead the economy to a more preferred position, given the market valuation.

The argument, however, is too facile and is indeed misleading in the context of planning. If you adopt shadow rates in your cost calculations, why leave demand alone? Demand, which is an expression of peoples' willingness to buy, based on a scheme of income distribution which is itself one of those things which planning purports to alter? The choice of techniques involves considerations of costs only; the choice of industries involves a second variable, demand, which makes our analysis a good deal more complex. Is, for example, the demand for luxury goods, such as exists in our society, justified by the requirements of growth? Secondly in the context of planning, where the primary objective is to stimulate growth via capital accumulation, it would be a wrong procedure to take the shadow rate of interest as static; planning for growth in an underdeveloped economy foresees a declining shadow rate interest.[10] Now there are industries which are growth-stimulating, and they may be relatively more capital intensive; capital goods industries indeed normally are. A shift away from such industries may improve employment, but it will retard growth.

While thus the decision concerning choice of techniques is straightforward, the decision concerning choice of industries is not so. One may therefore, with all his solicitude for employment, go all the way with Mahalanobis in one's emphasis on heavy industries. To ask for a marginal rate of saving of the order of, say, 20 per cent as a first step and bringing it gradually over to, say, 30 per cent in the course of ten years,[11] which is about all that the so-called emphasis on heavy industries implied could not surely be considered too much, if planning were to be taken at all seriously.

Re-thinking on planning is called for not as regards allocation of resources; it is called for in a rather drastic manner as regards "choosing the technique". It is also called for as regards the choice of institutional framework within which such decentralization as is implicit in our choice of labour intensive techniques can be operative. To this we may now turn.

6. There are two questions which we must answer here. How widespread will our labour intensive technique be, and what kind of social organization will be required if we were to avoid a clash between growth and employment?

The answer to the first question appears at first sight to be simple and straightforward. On our assumption of constant returns to scale, a more labour intensive technique will always be preferred to a less labour intensive technique, so long as the marginal product of labour is at all positive. There is thus a strong case for the adoption of small scale and cottage techniques in our economy, in so far as they are feasible in respect of any industry.

Some of our economists, seeing the possibility of a clash between growth and employment, have argued in favour of what they call "intermediate technology" on the ground that it would be a compromise between more productive but less employment-giving higher levels of technology and less productive but more employment-giving lower levels of technology. I suspect that this philosophy of the "middle way", whatever its significance may be in other spheres is utterly inappropriate in economic reasoning. "Intermediate technology" is a myth. If a higher level of technology yields larger output with a given stock of capital and less labour, then you must surely accept it, whatever its implications may be for employment. Let us acknowledge that where there is a possibility of "economies of scale", there our proposition favouring small scale techniques does require revision.

There is, however, one important consideration which is often missed. Economies of scale which arise from a concentration of capital have historically been seen to have resulted from innovations! If capital is diffused and is in many hands, each owning a minute quantity, production is on a small scale. On the other hand, if these small capitals are collected and transformed into a new form which admits of a unified supervision, production is on a large scale. Economies of scale suggest that aggregate output in the latter case is larger than in the former, even though the "quantity" of capital and labour going into production is the same in both. Now, the innovations that have made this possible have largely, if not entirely, been conditioned by the circumstances of the economies wherein they have occurred. The improved technologies that are employed in underdeveloped countries today are imported technologies devised in western countries mainly as an answer to the scarcity of labour relatively to capital. Rather than discarding small scale techniques on the plea that they are not "modern", the underdeveloped countries with surplus labour might try innovations as an answer to the opposite problem of scarcity of capital in relation to labour. Would our scientists and engineers in India take up problems of this kind in our national laboratories, instead of asking for all that is latest in the West? If they did, and possibilities of innovations in the reverse direction are opened up, one could go ahead with labour-intensive techniques even in those fields where, as it is, economies of scale exist. Subsidies to encourage expansion of labour-intensive techniques are thus not as irrational as is often supposed; they can perhaps be considered to be on par with subsidies to "infant" industries.

The answer to the second question will, I am afraid, verge on the "dangerous", at any rate by the standard exhibited hitherto by our planners. The institutional frame-work under which employment with maximum output in our sense can be realized, must have one special feature: *ownership is not to be disassociated from work*. When the owner of capital is himself the producer and does not have to hire labour in the market, the output does not get restricted by considerations of surplus over wage cost; the producer's own interest is to maximize output. Similarly, if all means of production are owned by society, owners as a collective body become themselves the producers. Here again, there is no inhibition in respect of production arising out of considerations of "profit" maximization. For the realization of full employment with maximum output, therefore, you can have two possible social systems. One in which capital, including land, is completely diffused and decentralized, such that production is family-based.

The other is one in which capital, including land, is completely socialized and production is motivated by considerations of common benefit rather than of individual profit. The two systems may have to proceed alongside of one another, permitting the economy, as they say, to "walk on two legs".

7. In agriculture this means by and large an implementation of the sort of agrarian reform that has already been accepted in principle by the Government, with this difference that the ceiling on land holding should be strictly limited to a size which is capable of being cultivated family-wise. One can then depend on individual motivation for the realization of maximum output from agriculture. Where the cultivator is his own master and does not have to engage hired labour, the cost of labour is ruled out of his calculation while he decides how much of labour he should put in towards the cultivation of his land.[12]

There is however one snag here. While the body of small cultivators among whom land is parcelled out may have the motivation to secure maximum output, they may not choose to release the maximum possible surplus for investment. And if they do not, there may yet be a conflict between maximum output and maximum growth. An amendment is thus needed to our reform scheme. And this relates to the surplus land that is released, once a ceiling is placed on land holding. Instead of the surplus land being entirely distributed among the landless labourers, as is contemplated by our land reformers, a certain proportion has to be reserved for state farming. This is to ensure enough agricultural surplus for the needs of industry and of urban population in general. In India, where the urban population forms just about 20% of the total population, it should be enough if some 10–15 per cent of the cultivable land is brought under state farming. For one thing, one should expect the productivity in state farms where inputs are amenable to proper regulation to be higher. For another, one should expect the private farmers, too, to come out to supplement the state farms' surplus, if only to meet their demand for urban goods. State farming surely is a better instrument for the mobilization of agricultural surplus than procurement. A system of land tax is also not to be ruled out, in so far as the ceiling on land is such as yields a measurable surplus to private farmers.

In industry our plan involves, as we have already suggested, an extension of small scale and cottage techniques, wherever they are feasible, and researches to improve the methods of operation in these sectors. Decentralisation of industries is already on the agenda of the Planning Commission; it has only to be given a push and, wherever appropriate, to be linked as ancillary to heavy industries. Our plan also demands, if the logic of our analysis is accepted, the nationalisation of those industries which do not admit of small scale production and where the use of wage labour is inevitable.

The framework of planning outlined here is a kind of a model,—an institutional model designed to secure growth with full employment. To give effect to it we need a strong government and an efficient administration. For it involves problems of transfer and property adjustment which are not easily done. Can such things be in a democracy? My answer is—yes, and no. Yes, if the democracy derives its strength from the people. No, if it derives its strength, as it does in our country today, from vested interests.

Patna, A. K. Dasgupta

Notes

1 An address delivered under the auspices of the Indian Economic Association on the occasion of its Golden Jubilee Celebration held at Hyderabad in December 1968.

2 D. H. Robertson, The Snake and the Worm, *Essays in Monetary Theory* (London, 1940), p. 108.

3 See my Objectives of the Second Five Year Plan in *Papers Relating to the Formulation of the Second Five Year Plan*, Planning Commission, 1955, p. 118.

4 See P. H. Prasad, 'Planning and Growth in India, *Economic and Political Weekly*, September 23, 1967, where, with the help of a three-sector model, the author shows how a reduction in flow of resources to luxury goods sector promotes growth.

5 See my 'A Plea for a Bolder Plan,' *A1CC Economic Review*, Vol. XII, No. 7, 1900, in *Planning and Economic Growth* (London 1965), pp. 74–77. Also ibid., Preface, p. 9.

6 Sen, A. K. *Choice of Techniques*, 3rd ed. (Oxford, 1968) pp. 18–20.

7 See my Choice of Technique, *Economic Weekly*, reproduced in *Planning and Economic Growth* (London, 1965) pp. 111–112.

8 You will notice that in the case of a linear marginal productivity curve, such as we have drawn, the transfer under full employment is just 1/2 of what it would be if only OL_2, number of labourers were employed.
It may be objected that the unemployed do not have the same consumption level as those from whom they derive their sustenance; their level of consumption may well go below minimum subsistence. This is true. Even then our general conclusion remains valid in so far as L_2L number of labourers, when they remain unemployed, consume an amount which is at least equal to wLP_2.

9 The older economists who equated "minimum subsistence" with the "natural price of labour", knew this. Adam Smith, for example, observes in his celebrated chapter on The Wages of Labour: "Thus far at least seems certain, that, in order to bring up a family, the labour of the husband and wife together must, even in the lowest species of common labour, be able to earn something more than what is precisely necessary for their own maintenance; but in what proportion, ... I shall not take upon me to determine." *Wealth of Nations* (Everyman's edition, London), Vol. I, pp. 60–61.

10 This suggests that our model is specifically for a labour surplus economy and that it loses significance as, with increasing accumulation, labour emerges as a scarce factor, Cf. Partha S. Dasgupta, "Unemployment and Optimum Growth", *Economic and Political Weekly*, Vol, III, No. 38, September 21, 1968.

11 In the Mahalanobis model the proportion of investment in capital goods to total investment is assumed to vary over the years from 1/3 to 2/5, so that, given a higher capital–output ratio in capital goods industries, as assumed in the model, the marginal rate of saving would come to very much the same as given in the text.

12 See, for an analysis of agrarian reform in the context of a labour surplus economy, Nicholas Georgescu-Roegen, *Analytical Economics* (Harvard University Press, Cambridge, Mass, 1960), Part IV, p. 369–79.

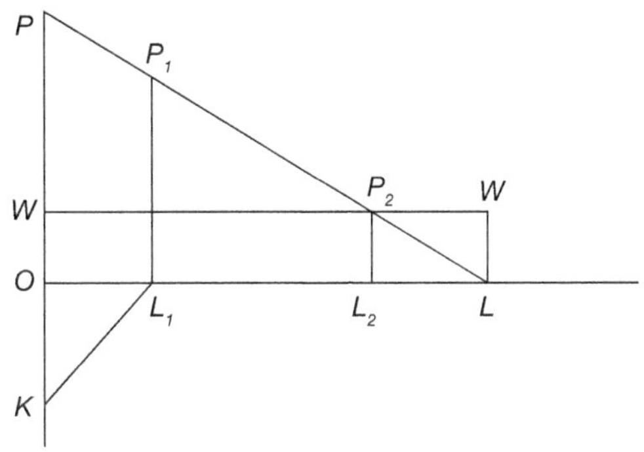

Figure 1 Please see p. 287.

20

Investment, income and the multiplier in an underdeveloped economy

V.K.R.V. Rao

Source: *The Indian Economic Review*, 56:2 (July–September 2008), 56–66.

The paper begins by providing a very cogent and comprehensive account of the main findings and policy implications of the famous Keynesian Multiplier Theory. The author has brought out, through his analytical and perceptive arguments, that the validity of the Keynesian Multiplier Theory depends upon various crucial assumptions, most which are not valid in the case of underdeveloped countries. He argues that these assumptions include, *inter alia*, the following: existence of involuntary unemployment, upward sloping supply curve, existence of excess capacity in the consumption-goods industries, and comparatively elastic supply of the working capital, required for increased output. The paper brings out a path breaking result as follows: "a consequent blind application of the Keynesian formulae to the problems of economic development has inflicted considerable injury on the economies of underdeveloped countries and added to the forces of inflation that are currently afflicting the whole world. The old-fashioned prescription of 'work harder and save more' still seems to hold good as the medicine for economic progress, at any rate as far as the underdeveloped countries are concerned". The conclusions of this seminal paper have generated wide debate on the relevance of the Keynesian Multiplier Theory for development in the underdeveloped countries, like India.

It is convenient to begin by summarising the main content of the Keynesian theory on the subject, which, incidentally, makes no attempt to give a separate treatment to underdeveloped economies. The volume of employment and of income is determined by the level at which aggregate demand price is equal to aggregate supply price. The propensity to consume is such that when Y_w increases, C_w increases but not to the same extent. The gap has to be made up by I_w or investment. The nature of the propensity to consume is such that marginal propensity to consume declines with increasing income and unless investment increases sufficiently, aggregate demand price will fall short of aggregate supply price, so that income and employment will decline till equality is attained between the two. Savings and investment are always equal, but this equality is brought about because of appropriate changes in the volume of income and employment. Saving is a residual, while it is investment which is the crucial factor. Increase in investment results in increase in income and the increase in income leads to an increase in saving. The marginal propensity to consume determines the relation between an increment of investment and the appropriate increment of income such as will induce the increment of saving necessary to maintain the equality of saving and investment. This relationship between increment of investment and that of income is determined by k or what is called the multiplier, the formula being $\Delta Y_w = k \Delta I_w$, where $1 - \frac{1}{k}$ is equal to the marginal propensity to consume. As the marginal propensity to consume declines with increasing income, increasingly larger increments of investment become necessary for securing given increments of income at increasing levels of income. As the marginal propensity to consume is likely to be not far short of unity in the cases of poor communities, the multiplier has a high value in their case with the result that comparatively small increments of investment are likely to bring about full employment. At the same time, as their average propensity to consume is also high, investment accounts for a smaller portion of the value of their aggregate output which is the same thing as the volume of their income. Fluctuations in investment, therefore, account for smaller fluctuations in total employment than they do in the case of richer communities whose average propensity to consume is less and in whose case, therefore, investment accounts for a larger share of the value of the aggregate output. The paradoxical situation, therefore, arises that the poorer the community, the greater the ease of obtaining for it a condition of full employment and the smaller the fluctuations in its employment caused by changes in its net investment; while the richer the community, the more difficult it is to secure full employment, while the greater are the fluctuations in its total employment due to fluctuations in its net investment. Add to this the fact that fluctuations in net investment are more likely in a richer community, the conclusion seems to follow that instability in employment is a characteristic of increasing national income, and with it there is an increasing tendency towards the growth of involuntary unemployment unless offset by an increased investment that is possible only with the abandonment of both *laissez-faire* and balanced budgeting. Keynes is mainly concerned with the problem of involuntary unemployment in the richer communities, and his whole thesis relates to the question of how to secure full employment in the case of these countries. The remedies he puts forward, viz., cheap money, deficit financing, redistributive taxation, and public investment have all become current coin in national economic policies, with full employment as the major objective. Unfortunately, Keynes did not formulate the economic problem of underdeveloped countries, nor did he discuss the relevance to these countries of either the objective or the policy that he proposed for the more developed, i.e., the industrialised countries. The result has been a rather unintelligent application—not on Keynes's part—of what may be called Keynesian economics to the problems of the underdeveloped countries. Thus, it is common ground with most writers on the economics of underdeveloped countries that what was required for their economic development was an increase in the purchasing power of the people. Deficit financing and created money have figured in practically all the plans, both official and unofficial, that have been put forward, e.g., for the economic development of India, while cheap money seems to have become as much an article of financial faith in the underdeveloped countries as in the industrialised economies. It is, therefore, of some importance to examine the problem of investment, income and the multiplier in the special context of underdeveloped economies with a view to finding out how far Keynesian ideas on economic policy are relevant and applicable to the problems of economic development. I shall deal with this question with special reference to my own country, viz., India.

Take first the question of full employment. Everyone agrees that full employment is a major desired goal of economic policy. According to Keynes, in a poor country where the marginal propensity to consume is high and the multiplier, therefore, also high, comparatively small increments of investment are sufficient to secure full employment. It must be pointed out that, according to Keynes, an increase in employment is identical with an increase in real income whether measured in terms of wage units or of output. Full employment, therefore, involves the maximisation of output that is possible with the elimination of involuntary unemployment and the full utilisation of existing capacity and technical knowledge. Once this stage is reached, any attempt to increase investment sets up a tendency in money prices to rise without limit or leads to the emergence of a state of true inflation, where rising prices will no longer be associated with an increasing aggregate real income. Progress beyond this stage is not discussed in Keynes, the implicit assumption being that there is a unique level of full employment and when that is reached, the desired objective has been attained. Even when subsequent writers have discussed the next step by linking up the multiplier principle with that of acceleration, what is visualised is a change in the nature of employment, with a larger proportion now going into investment industries, rather than an increase in total employment. Let me now examine these concepts in the context of an underdeveloped economy like India.

To begin with, we have here a predominantly agricultural country, where capital equipment is low and the standard of technical knowledge applied to production, vastly inferior to that in the West. Moreover, the number of employees or workers employed on a wage is comparatively small, the vast majority of earners falling under the category of self-employees or household enterprises. Added to this is the fact that a significant proportion of the national output is not produced for the market but is intended for self-consumption. Under these circumstances, the multiplier principle does not work in the simple fashion visualised by Keynes primarily for the industrialised economies. An increase in investment leads to an increase in income and in employment. The next increase ought to come from a secondary increase in income, employment and output in the consumption-goods industries, to be followed by a tertiary increase and so on, till income, output, and employment have increased by *k* times the initial increase in investment, and saving has increased by an amount equal to the additional investment. I am aware that the investment multiplier and the employment multiplier are not identical, and that increase in output cannot be proportional either to the increase in money income, or to that in employment, but for purposes of argument, it is convenient to ignore these differences at this stage. Now in the case of a country like India, the secondary, tertiary and other increases in income output and employment visualised by the multiplier principle do not follow, even though the marginal propensity to consume is very high and the multiplier should, therefore, function in a vigorous fashion. This is because the consumption-goods industries to which the increased demand is directed are not in a position to expand output and offer effective additional employment. The most important reason for this is the technical nature of the chief consumption industry to which the additional demand would presumably be directed, viz., food. This means in most underdeveloped countries primarily the agricultural industry. Now, agriculture all over the world is notoriously an industry where the supply curve is steeply inelastic in the short period. Further, variations in agricultural output in a country like India, where irrigation accounts for less than 20 per cent of the cultivated area, are largely dominated by the vagaries of nature, and response to price increases is less effective in terms of aggregate output than in those of individual crop. Moreover, the belief is widely held, and not without justification, that the supply curve of agricultural industry as a whole is not only inelastic but also tends to be backward-rising, so that an increase in the value of output need not necessarily lead to a subsequent increase in the volume of output. The primary increase in income following on a given increment of investment does get spent to a large extent on the output of agriculture, and leads, therefore, to an appropriate increase in the income of the agricultural producers. But it is not followed up by these producers increasing their own output and thus, adding to both employment and real income.

Apart from the reasons mentioned above, the agricultural producer is rather reluctant to act in the way postulated for entrepreneurs by classical economists or even by Keynes himself in response to increase in profits. The presence of price control and governmental procurement both act as psychological disincentives, while uncertainty regarding the duration of high prices and their future also has the effect of dampening immediate response to price stimuli. Moreover, even to the extent to which agricultural producers want to increase output, they do not get the facilities necessary either by way of technique or of supplies to carry out their intentions. One may call all this either bottlenecks or shortages or inelasticity in the supply curves of the factors of production; the net result is the same, viz., that it is not possible significantly to increase output in the short period in spite of willingness to expend money on doing so. This means that while income increases, output does not increase in anything like the same measure in the agricultural sector. In other words, the income multiplier is much higher in money terms than in real terms, and to that extent prices rise much faster than an increase in aggregate real income.

The same conclusion also applies when we consider the behaviour of agriculturists as consumers in response to the increase in their money income resulting from the initial investment. Marginal propensity to consume being high, the larger proportion of the increased income will be sought to be spent on consumption goods. As the agriculturists are themselves producers of food, the increase that follows in their consumption of foodgrains—the increase in consumption may take the form of either increasing the quantity consumed or substitution of better quality grains for coarse grains—leads to a reduction in the marketable surplus of foodgrains. This means in turn that the non-agricultural sector of the economy now has to pay still higher prices for its foodgrains without an appropriate response on the part of production in the agricultural sector. The tendency, therefore, for prices to rise without a rise in aggregate real income is further strengthened by the working of the marginal propensity to consume on the part of the receiver of additional agricultural incomes. One may perhaps expect that the position would be different in respect of the increased consumption of non-agricultural goods on the part of the agriculturist consumers. But, even here, the position is not far different in the case of a country like India. This is due to many reasons such as the absence of effective excess capacity in industries, difficulty of obtaining raw materials and other ingredients for additional production, inelastic supply of skilled workers, and various bottlenecks arising out of controls and the general environment of a shortage-dominated economy. To the extent, therefore, that agriculturist consumers do spend a part of their additional income on non-agricultural goods, the tertiary increase in money income does take place, but not a corresponding or even a noticeable increase in either output or employment. To the extent that agriculturists find that they are unable to effect an increase in their real income in terms of non-agricultural goods in spite of expending a larger money income, the effect is to decrease the marginal utility of the additional income with the result that in terms of Keynes' second proposition in Chapter II of his *General Theory*, identity between utility of the wage—in this case the cultivator's income—and the marginal disutility of that amount of employment—in this case the cultivator's own labour—is reached at the existing level of the volume of labour in the agricultural industry, in spite of an increase in the money value of the output of that labour, and may even be reached at lower levels of the volume of labour expended in the agricultural industry. Thus, the primary increase in investment and, therefore, increase in income and employment leads to a secondary and a tertiary increase in income, but not to any noticeable increase in either output or employment in either the agricultural or the non-agricultural sector. The multiplier principle, therefore, works with reference to money income but not with reference either to real income or employment. To the extent that the increases in money income do not get absorbed by a rise in prices and leave a margin of additional real income in certain sections of the community such as agricultural producers and industrial producers, they are dissipated either by an increase in food consumption on the part of the former or by an increase in imports or in cash balances on the part of the latter; in neither case do they lead to an increase either in real income or in employment for the community as a whole.

The position may be summed up as under. In the Keynesian scheme of things, the supply curve of output as a whole is comparatively elastic in the short period, under conditions of involuntary unemployment. Therefore, there is a relation, if not of identity, of at least comparative identity in value between the multipliers relating increment of money investment to increment of money income, of increment of money investment in terms of wage units, of increment in investment output to increment in total output and of increment of employment in investment industries to increment in total employment. It is only on these assumptions that an increment of investment, operating on the basis of the multiplier principle, helps to increase output, real income, and employment, and leads to what may be called an automatic self-financing of the increased investment.

> An increment of investment in terms of wage-units cannot occur unless the public are prepared to increase their savings in terms of wage-units. Ordinarily speaking, the public will not do this unless their aggregate income in terms of wage-units is increasing. Thus their effort to consume a part of their increased incomes will stimulate output until the new level (and distribution) of incomes provides a margin of saving sufficient to correspond to the increased investment. The multiplier tells us by how much their employment has to be increased to yield an increase in real income sufficient to induce them to do the necessary extra saving, and is a function of their psychological propensities. If saving is the pill and consumption is the jam, the extra jam has to be proportioned to the size of the additional pill. Unless the psychological propensities of the public are different from what we are supposing, we have here established the law that increased employment for investment must necessarily stimulate the industries producing for consumption and thus lead to a total increase of employment which is a multiple of the, primary employment required by the investment itself. (Keynes, *The General Theory of Employment, Interest, and Money*, pp. 117–118).

Undoubtedly, the multipliers *k* and *k* would be smaller than the multiplier linking up increment in money investment to increment in money income, for the supply curve of output is not perfectly elastic but is, on the other hand, inelastic, though the inelasticity becomes marked and increasing only as one approaches full employment. But there is no doubt that all the multipliers mentioned above must be positive and moving in the same direction if the Keynesian thesis is to apply in practice. This implies, in turn that for the multiplier principle to work, there must exist the following:

a) Involuntary unemployment.
b) An industrialised economy where the supply curve of output slopes upwards towards the right but does not become vertical till after a substantial interval.
c) Excess capacity in the consumption-goods industries.
d) Comparatively elastic supply of the working capital required for increased output.

These assumptions do not hold in the case of an underdeveloped economy. Involuntary unemployment of the Keynesian type is necessarily associated with a free-enterprise wage economy where the majority of earners work for wages and where production is much more for exchange than for self-consumption. But this type of economy is of comparatively recent origin, which also explains the fact that over the whole range of human history, unemployment in the modern sense is, comparatively speaking, a rare and local phenomenon. Mrs. Robinson has pointed out that in a society in which there is no regular system of unemployment benefit, and in which poor relief is either non-existent or 'less eligible' than almost any alternative short of suicide, a man who is thrown out of work must scratch up a living somehow or other by means of his own efforts. Mrs. Robinson goes on to point out that such persons do not figure in the list of unemployed but take up some other work, subject however to the proviso that their productivity is less than in the occupations they have left. She continues: "Thus a decline in demand for product of the general run of industries leads to a diversion of labour form occupations in which productivity is higher to others where it is lower. The cause of this diversion, a decline in effective demand, is exactly the same as the cause of unemployment in the ordinary sense, and it is natural to describe the adoption of inferior occupations by dismissed workers *disguised unemployment*."[1] Mrs. Robinson has pointed out further that the existence of disguised unemployment introduces a complication into the formal scheme of the *General Theory of Employment*, the function relating total investment ceasing to be unique, since a given rate of investment will be accompanied by a greater rate of consumption the more unemployment is disguised. Underdeveloped economies are conspicuous for the extent to which they contain disguised unemployment. Only the kind of disguised unemployment they have is not of the type visualised by Mrs. Robinson, where it results from decline in effective demand and can exist in an industrialised economy only provided there is no unemployment dole or other not disagreeable social means for enabling the unemployed to exist. In an underdeveloped and agrarian economy with little capital equipment and a somewhat low state of technical knowledge like India, on the other hand, disguised unemployment is a normal feature of the economy. The term is not applied, as Mrs. Robinson applies it, to wage labour taking to less productive work on account of unemployment. It is applied in the case of India to persons who are employed in the sense that they are engaged in household enterprise but who are really in a state of disguised unemployment in the sense that no difference will be made to output by their withdrawal from the occupations concerned. As is pointed out in the recent report of the U.N. Committee of Experts on *Measures for the Economic Development of Underdeveloped Countries*, "the disguised unemployed are those persons who work on their own account and who are so numerous, relatively to the resources with which they work, that if a number of them were withdrawn for work in other sectors of the economy the total output of the sector from which they were withdrawn would not be diminished even though no significant reorganisation occurred in this sector, and no significant substitution of capital".[2] This kind of disguised unemployment makes a significant difference to the working of the theory of the multiplier. If unemployment in underdeveloped economies takes the form of disguised unemployment rather than that of involuntary unemployment, then the secondary, tertiary and other effects of the initial primary employment created by the initial increment of investment do not follow, apart from other reasons, for this reason that there is no labour force willing to accept employment at the current wage, and involuntarily unemployed because of lack of employment opportunities. By definition, involuntary unemployment implies an elastic supply of labour at the current wage level. Those who are suffering from disguised unemployment do not fall under this category. They are, first of all, not aware that they are unemployed and are not, therefore, on the look-out for employment. Secondly, they are already in receipt of a real income which presumably gives them at least the same satisfaction as they would get by taking up employment at the current wage level. In actual fact, a wage considerably higher than the income they are receiving in their existing occupations would be necessary in order to induce them to offer themselves for employment. In other words, they are not really involuntarily unemployed in the Keynesian sense, and yet they are unemployed in clearly economic sense in which we have defined disguised unemployment. The particular form which unemployment takes in the underdeveloped countries, viz., that of disguised unemployment makes the economy of Keynesian purposes practically analogous with one of full employment, and to that extent prevents the multiplier from working in the direction of an increase in either output or employment. The presence of disguised unemployment thus, prevents the working of the Keynesian law that "increased employment for investment must necessarily stimulate the industries producing for consumption and thus lead to a total increase of employment which is a multiple of the primary employment required by the investment itself".

Apart from the difficulties caused by the presence of disguised unemployment, the agrarian nature of the economy makes for a supply curve that, at best, is much more inelastic than that of an industrial ised economy such as Keynes primarily had in mind when formulating his theory of employment. This, in turn, tends to widen the difference between the multiplier linking up increments of money investment with increments of money income from that linking up increments of investment output with increments of total output, with the result that money incomes and prices rise much faster than real incomes and output. Savings, therefore, fail to rise to equality with investment, and with deficit financing, the inflationary process sets in earlier and proceeds faster in an agrarian or underdeveloped economy as compared with an industrialised or developed economy. The case for investment support by deficit-financing for the purpose of inducing a given increase in output is, therefore, much weaker in an underdeveloped economy as compared with that in a developed economy.

This conclusion gets further reinforcement when we look at the organisational nature of an underdeveloped economy. In an industrialised economy, the community consists of a small number of employers and a large number of employees, production for market is the rule, and consumers purchase the goods and services they require, with the result that when there is an increase in income, the marginal propensity to consume leads to an increase in the market demand for consumption goods and thereby to an increase in output and employment in the consumption-goods industries. In the case of an underdeveloped economy, however, household enterprises predominate, and production is much more for self-consumption than for the market with the result that when there is an increase in income the marginal propensity to consume leads to an increase in the demand for self-consumption rather than for purchases in the market. While this increased demand may partly be met by increased output on the part of the consumers themselves, at least a portion, if not actually the bulk, of the increased demand will be met by a diversion of output from the market to their self-consumption. Thus, a reduction in the marketable surplus rather than an increase in output makes available the extra quantity of consumption goods required by this class following an increase in their income, and to this extent the extra employment induced by their increased consumption is less than what it would have been if their increased consumption had been purchased in the market. In Keynesian terms, the effect of this is to reduce the value of the multiplier below the level calculable from the marginal propensity to consume. Such a conclusion would appear to undermine the theory of the multiplier, the whole basis of which is the marginal propensity to consume, and yet that seems inevitable in an underdeveloped economy dominated by household enterprises and production for self-consumption. It is, of course, possible to preserve the formal structure of the multiplier theory by regarding an increment of self-consumption as a leakage analogous to the leakage that takes place when the increased consumption resulting from increased income takes the form of increased imports. It may perhaps be added that the former type of leakage is more likely in underdeveloped economies while the latter is more likely in industrialised economies.

Another factor preventing the appropriate increase in the output of consumption-goods industries and the employment therein following an increase in income, arises from the absence of excess capacity in consumption-goods industries, coupled with a comparatively inelastic supply of the working capital needed for increasing production, which is characteristic of an underdeveloped economy. In effect, this is but analogous to the conditions that obtain in an industrialised economy as it approaches conditions of full employment; but there is this difference, viz., that it begins to operate much earlier and is quite consistent with the existence of disguised unemployment in the underdeveloped economy.

My conclusion, therefore, is that the multiplier principle as enunciated by Keynes does not operate in regard to the problem of diminishing unemployment and increasing output in an underdeveloped economy, an increment of investment based on deficit financing tending to lead more to an inflationary rise in prices than to an increase in output and employment. It would, however, be possible to give formal validity to the Keynesian law even in the case of underdeveloped economies by treating them as economies in a state of full employment or near-full employment. Full employment, however, is identified in the public mind with an optimum economic condition and carries with it the implication that it is accompanied by the maximum utilisation of labour, capital and natural resources in the economy. That is why it is regarded as the major objective of present day national and international economic policy and figures so prominently in the aims and objects of the U.N.O. and its specialised agencies. To describe underdeveloped economies as being in a state of full or near-full employment, therefore, is to do violence to the accepted connotation of that phrase even though it may satisfy the formal requirement of the Keynesian concept of full employment. Under the circumstances, I would prefer to say that the economic policy of deficit financing and disregard for thrift advocated by Keynes for securing full employment does not apply in the case of an underdeveloped economy. The policy that holds good for an underdeveloped economy is more on the lines formulated by the classical economists; and if the Keynesians would say that this is because of the existence of full employment in the underdeveloped economies, there can be no formal objection to their statement. In any case it would follow that the economic policy that would be advocated for underdeveloped economies for increasing incomes, output, and employment would be radically different from that so universally associated with Keynes and formulated by him primarily for application to the developed or industrialised economies. In that sense, the multiplier principle with its accepted relationship between increments of investment and increments of incomes, output, and employment does not hold for an underdeveloped economy like India.

The further conclusion also seems to follow that the existence of disguised unemployment, household enterprise, production for self-consumption, dominance of agriculture, and deficiency of capital equipment and of technical knowledge—all characteristic of an underdeveloped economy—creates conditions analogous to those of the full employment visualised by Keynes, when in actual fact there is no full employment in the economic, or even the popularly accepted, sense of the term. The formal effect of this on the *General Theory of Employment* still remains to be undertaken, but I have the feeling that the answer lies in giving up the assumption that there is one unique level of full employment. Apart from the level of full employment visualised by Keynes, there are as many levels of full employment as there are different stages of economic development. Indeed it is the transition from the level of full employment appropriate to a lower stage to another appropriate to a higher stage which constitutes the process of economic development. The economic process consists of two distinct categories, one where given the level of economic development, you move from low employment to full employment, and the other, where you move from full employment at a given level of economic development to full employment at the next level of economic development. The Keynesian thesis applies only to one of these categories, viz., where, given the level of economic development, you move from low employment to full employment. It is the classical thesis which is operative for the other category where you move from one level of economic development to a higher level of economic development. The mixing up of these two categories and a consequent blind application of the Keynesian formulae to the problems of economic development has inflicted considerable injury on the economies of underdeveloped countries and added to the forces of inflation that are currently afflicting the whole world. The old-fashioned prescription of 'work harder and save more' still seems to hold good as the medicine for economic progress, at any rate as far as the underdeveloped countries are concerned.

Notes

1 Joan Robinson, *Essays in the Theory of Employment*, p.84.
2 p. 7 of the Report.

21

Labor union resistance to economic liberalization in India

What can national and state level patterns of protests against privatization tell us?

Katrin Uba

Source: *Asian Survey*, 48:5 (September/October 2008), 860–84.

Introduction

Since the early 1990s, there has been heated debate among academics as well as politicians over the path and consequences of the Indian privatization process.[1] Although it is often accepted that organized labor played an obstructive role in this process, few scholars have paid systematic attention to the mobilization of this important interest group. Moreover, there is no scholarly agreement over the ability of labor to mobilize and resist liberalization after the decline of trade union membership during the 1980s.[2]

This article seeks to address these shortcomings by answering two broad sets of questions. First, how has the Indian labor movement reacted to liberal economic reforms since 1991? What mobilization strategies have been used and what organizations are behind the protests against privatization? Second, the inconsistency of prior studies on the relationship between a group's protest mobilization and the nature of its political allies raises an important question—namely, what role does a union's affiliation with political parties play in the labor movement's mobilization against privatization? Since there are observed differences in anti-privatization protests across states, this article also attempts to examine the reasons for this variation by using the framework of social movement theory.

These questions are answered by exploiting a unique data set that covers the vast majority of protests mobilized against the initiation of economic liberalization by the Indian federal and state governments from 1991 to 2003.[3] The empirical data for this article were collected from a broad set of Indian and international newspapers and combined with information presented in numerous earlier case studies on labor mobilization and economic policy in India. Taking into account the country's federal character, this analysis includes state level data on economic reforms and protests in 12 out of 28 Indian states.[4]

The theoretical framework for this largely descriptive study is derived from research on social movement theory, which is particularly relevant for studying the mobilization of different interest groups including labor movements. This strand of literature pays specific attention to the organizational and political conditions that facilitate mobilization.[5] Therefore, a central part of this study borrows conceptually from social movement theory by integrating the multifaceted discussions on Indian privatization policy (*trigger for mobilization*), membership of the India's labor movement (*resources for mobilization*), and trade unions' affiliation with political parties (*opportunities for mobilization*).

The results of this study show that workers in India, despite the relatively small trade union membership and declining number of officially reported strikes, have actively mobilized against privatization since the early 1990s. While the different major trade unions rarely cooperate with each other, there is, in contrast, significant collaboration with consumer and environmental organizations. The answer to the second set of questions is much more complex because the empirical cases analyzed in this study do not provide coherent support for the causal processes set forth by social movement theory. For example, policies, resources, and opportunities cannot fully explain why in West Bengal trade unions' affiliation with the governing Communist Party hindered protests against the state's privatization program, whereas it did not have the same effect in Kerala. The implications of this state level variation for Indian labor's mobilization against privatization in particular and social movement theory in general are discussed in the concluding part of this article.

This article begins with a brief introduction of the privatization process in India at both the federal and state levels. The second section provides an overview of the nature of India's labor movement and the relationship of labor unions to political parties. Third, I describe the collection of anti-privatization protest data used in this study and discuss its potential limitations. The fourth section describes protest mobilization at the federal level and compares the annual protest cycle with general trends of industrial disputes. The fifth section analyzes the varying patterns of protest at the state level and examines the role of the various unions' political party affiliation in anti-privatization protest mobilization.

Economic reforms at the central and state levels in India

Although initial attempts to liberalize India's economy were made in the 1980s, most scholars trace the start of liberalization to 1991 when the Congress Party-led government announced its New Economic Policy.[6] The aim of this policy was to restructure the inefficient, debt-burdened public sector and generate funds to fight the rising budget deficit. A year later in 1992, the government sold minority shares in 30 of its 244 public sector enterprises. Nonetheless, the privatization process in India has been comparatively slower than in Latin American, East European, and other Asian countries; the amount of revenue involved less; and the number of enterprises sold fewer. For example, the revenue generated from privatization in India totaled $11.5 billion from 1991 to 2003, compared to Poland—the largest East European reformer—which generated $16.9 billion during the same period.[7] Yet, the Indian privatization process has been similar to that in other countries: major decisions to initiate changes have been by executive order, and implementation has been handled by the specific government institutions—in India's case, the DD.

Interestingly, the term "privatization" was not used in Indian political discourse until the end of the 1990s. Instead, "disinvestment" was preferred because it was perceived as being less radical and thus more palatable to the general public.[8] Some members of the government, such as Minister of Civil Aviation Sharad Yadav from the Janata Dal Party and Minister of Heavy Industry Manohar Joshi from the Shiv Sena Party, used a strategy of "blame avoidance" while supporting privatization. To explain, they supported privatization as long as it did not involve their own areas of responsibility. As one anonymous minister said to the news magazine *India Today*, "As long [as] it is not my ministry and my PSU [public sector undertaking], I am all for reforms, disinvestment, and privatisation. When it comes to my turf I show my real colours."[9] Such a strategy of "reforming by stealth" left the public uninformed on important changes in economic policies. It is, therefore, not surprising that these issues did not become decisive for election results.[10]

Heated debate took place in the lower chamber of Parliament (the Lok Sabha House of the People), and also in the upper chamber, the Rajya

Sabha (Council of States) because the government needed parliamentary permission to sell enterprises that had been nationalized in the 1950s. Members of Parliament (MPs) from left-wing parties warned about the potential loss of jobs and workers' resistance. MPs from right-wing nationalist parties were concerned about the impact of foreign pressure from the World Bank (WB) and the International Monetary Fund (IMF).[11] Yet, left-wing rhetoric against privatization softened from 1996 to 1998, when the Communist parties became partners in governing coalitions in the center. The softening of the Communist parties' positions on economic liberalization created a general perception of a growing consensus on the need for economic reform in India.

The privatization process in the public sector continued even after the Hindu nationalist Bharatiya Janata Party (BJP) formed a coalition government with several regional parties in 1999. Although this led to an increased liberalization initiative, the Indian federal government had privatized only 10 enterprises and sold shares of only 47 others by 2004.[12] This slow pace of reform led to speculation that Indian politicians had non-ideological incentives for opposing privatization, such as defending the well-established patronage system. For example, studies have shown that the central government during this period did not privatize any enterprises in those states where its regional coalition partners had narrow electoral margins, nor in the home states of certain cabinet ministers. The gradualism of Indian reforms was also possibly related to opposition from workers.[13]

Still, restructuring of the economy took place below the federal level and state authorities were allowed to reform the state level public sector almost autonomously from New Delhi. Unfortunately, reports on state level privatization are inconclusive and provide only a general picture of significant variations in reform initiatives and implementation across India. For example, by 2002 Andhra Pradesh had privatized 13 state level public sector undertakings (SPSUs) and had marked 67% of all its SPSUs for further restructuring; in contrast, the much larger state of Uttar Pradesh had sold only two SPSUs and West Bengal had announced the goal of restructuring 15% of its undertakings.[14]

These variations were partly explained by the pro-privatization campaigns driven by these states' respective chief ministers. Perhaps the best example of this is the chief minister of Andhra Pradesh, Chandrababu Naidu, who governed the state from 1995 to 2004. Even though his party gained a majority in the state legislative assembly in 1994 after campaigning *against* liberal economic reforms, Naidu subsequently followed the liberalization policy of his predecessor and became an even more enthusiastic reformer than the central government.[15] Some other chief ministers used a variant of this "dual strategy" for attracting votes for their party in federal elections and making their state appealing for foreign investors. They opposed the privatization policies of the central government while simultaneously initiating reforms in their home states.[16]

Privatization involved not only the sale of government-owned factories but also wider reforms such as increasing the participation of private funds in the finance sector, restructuring health and education systems, and allowing the private sector to run public utilities (e.g., electricity and water distribution).[17] The major debate regarding the Indian financial and insurance sectors was over the amount of private and foreign funding to be allowed into publicly owned banks and insurance companies. Even though the initiative for reform in these sectors was undertaken in the early 1990s, important legislation allowing privatization and up to 26% foreign investment into the insurance and banking sectors was enacted later in 2000 despite active opposition from bank and insurance sector trade unions.

Reforming more-essential public utilities such as electricity and water proved more difficult and complicated because these sectors were mainly controlled by state governments with varying degrees of development and reform-mindedness. The central government did provide some general legal guidelines for electricity and water privatization after 2000, but many states had already moved much further with their reforms. For example, Orissa, one of the poorest states, was the first to fully privatize its electricity distribution, in 1996, whereas wealthy Maharashtra initiated electricity reform only after legal pressure from the center in 2003. Similarly, Karnataka initiated the privatization of its water systems in 1997, whereas the central government did not agree to privatize drinking water and sanitation, irrigation, and water transport until 2002.[18] Because these services so intimately affect the everyday lives of Indian citizens, state level reforms were vigorously debated, especially during campaigning for state assembly elections, and also sparked numerous protest campaigns by labor unions.

In order to mitigate the impact of labor retrenchment that so often accompanies privatization, the government launched specific voluntary retirement schemes (VRS) for redundant workers and offered them opportunities to buy equity in public enterprises. Trade union activists, however, called the VRS approach a "not-so-voluntary scheme" because management often aggressively pushed employees in select sectors to retire before they may have wanted to do so. Trade union activists also pointed out that the majority of employees lacked the money to buy the equity offered.[19] Much like labor movements in other countries, Indian labor perceived privatization as a process that would inevitably lead to higher unemployment and decreased union membership. For this reason, labor mobilization against privatization was not unanticipated, but the questions of real significance related to its scope and intensity.

The labor movement in India

The Indian labor movement is sometimes seen by scholars of industrial relations as being an exceptional case. Theoretically, it should be strong due to a supportive institutional framework, but, conversely, its relatively small membership points to a lack of mobilizing power.[20] These supportive institutions include protective labor legislation and Indian trade unions' affiliation with political parties. The law obligates an entrepreneur to ask for the government's permission before dismissing the labor force in an enterprise with more than 100 workers. The implementation of these restrictions is, however, irregular. Legislation also varies across states and it is suggested that restrictive labor laws hinder a state's economic development and investments.[21]

Moreover, reports of low trade union density and the small number of functioning unions in India are often considered to be inaccurate. On the one hand, the number of unions is underestimated because of the slow registration of unions' reports by state officials. On the other hand, self-reporting by unions can also lead to overestimated membership accounts. Existing files provide a complex set of numbers, and the level of unionization varies drastically across sectors. In general, the number of unionized workers forms 2% of the total work force, but it is up to 5.5% of non-agricultural labor and almost 20% of wage-earning labor. Reports show that about nine million workers were affiliated with trade unions in 1995 and that large enterprises tended to have higher rates of unionization.[22] Union membership in the public sector is shown to be much higher—almost 90%, a total of two million workers—in comparison to the private sector. Unionized workers in all sectors are divided between five major trade union federations and several independent trade unions. Most of the five major union federations are closely affiliated with different national political parties and have federal as well as state level branches. These branches, in turn, unite private and public unions across a wide spectrum of economic sectors from banking to mining. Thus, while labor movements in other countries are usually supported by left-wing parties, all major political parties in India—irrespective of their ideological leanings—have their "own" trade unions.

Table 1 shows that unions affiliated with the BJP and Congress Party have reported the largest number of members. These parties were also major initiators of the privatization process in India. This presents us with an interesting dilemma from the perspective of social movement research. On the one hand, proponents of resource mobilization theory suggest that groups with more resources are expected to mobilize more than others.[23] On the other hand, scholars favoring the political opportunity structure approach argue that protest mobilization is less likely under a government of political allies or when a union's "own" party is in power.[24] Although this last argument has not found coherent empirical support in studies on American and European movements, these tendencies could quite possibly be present in developing countries.[25] The research on economic liberalization in Latin America, in particular, suggests that unions allied with governing parties discard protest as being too costly. Those unions affiliated with opposition parties, however, mobilize protests with an aim to differentiate themselves from cooperative unions and thus hopefully attract more members.[26] Despite the significant political, socio-economic, and cultural differences with Latin America, one would expect a similar relationship to exist in India between unions' party affiliations and protest activism in anti-privatization mobilization. Hence, I ask whether a union's affiliation to an opposition party in India encourages its mobilization against privatization and how this relationship explains the variation of anti-privatization protests across states?

Unfortunately, there is a paucity of systematic empirical analysis that would allow us to answer these types of questions conclusively. Case studies exist that focus on individual states or a specific economic sector, but comparatively few assess the overall picture. The existing studies suggest that membership in Indian trade unions has declined during the past decade, diminishing their bargaining power.[27] Prior research also shows declining public support for trade union activism, spurred largely by the frequent strikes of the 1980s, malfunctioning public services, and several corruption scandals. This is why some authors have suggested that workers were able to show only limited resistance to liberal reforms, although there are also studies that argue that public sector unions did mobilize actively against privatization.[28] The reasons for these trends can be found using systematic information on labor mobilization since the early 1990s. This study attempts such an explication using a unique data set on anti-privatization protests in India from 1991 to 2003.

Table 1 Trade union membership and party affiliation

Union Federation	*Political Party*	*Members (in millions)*
Bharatiya Mazdoor Sangh (BMS)	BJP	3.117
Indian National Trade Union Congress (INTUC)	Congress	2.706
All India Trade Union Congress (AITUC)	Janata Dal, CPI	0.923
Center of the Indian Trade Unions (CITU)	CPI-M	1.798
Hind Mazdoor Sabha (HMS)	Non-affiliated	1.477

Source: Sinha (2004); Candland and Sil (2001).

Data collection and reliability concerns

The database of anti-privatization protests used for this study was compiled by building and analyzing a broad set of news reports. These news reports were collected and accessed through the electronic database Factiva, which includes many worldwide and Indian newspapers such as *The Hindu*, *The Economic Times of India*, and *Business Line*. This study is based on reports published between 1991 and 2003.[29] Although the central government controlled by the Congress Party implemented incipient economic reforms in the mid-1980s, more extensive liberalization plans—including privatization—were adopted later, in 1991, also under the Congress Party. The rationale for not including data beyond 2003 for this study is justified by two reasons. First, India's Supreme Court declared in August 2003 that government employees had no legal right and no moral justification to go on strike (Supreme Court Act, No. 5556). Even though some such strikes were considered to be "illegal" before, the Supreme Court's decision affected labor mobilization negatively, thus making comparison between the pre-decision and post-decision periods problematic. Second, there were parliamentary elections in 2004 that led to replacing the ruling BJP-led government with a Congress Party-led coalition, which relied on left-wing parties to maintain its majority. The nature of the incoming ruling coalition drastically changed the context for labor mobilization because left-wing unions that had been the major force in the anti-privatization movement got an opportunity to voice their dissatisfaction through internal governmental channels rather than by protesting. Moreover, the new government decided to temporarily stop the privatization process, thus removing the main reason for protesting. For these reasons, including data on these particular years would reduce the validity of comparison between the pre-2004 and post-2004 periods.

In order to capture as many reported protests as possible, the entire texts of all news reports archived in the Factiva database were searched, using a variety of relevant keywords.[30] Out of these searches, only those involving protests mobilized by groups other than political parties and only those clearly declared to be against privatization were included in the analysis. Below is a sample of the 226 events used for this study:

1 Millions of workers took part in a general nation-wide strike opposing the government's economic policy and privatisation of the public sector on 16th of June 1992. The action was mobilised by left-wing trade unions and 12,000 activists were detained before the strike. (Associated Press, June 16, 1992)
2 Women activists of All India Janawadi Mahila Sanghatane protested against the privatisation of Gulbarga city's [in Karnataka state] drinking water supply on 6th of July 1999. A large section of women gathered in front of the municipal council and demanded the reversal of the privatisation decision. (*Times of India*, July 7, 1999)
3 Unionised workers of the Metals and Mineral Trading Corporation observed one-day strike on 11th of January 2001 to protest against governments' moves to privatise their enterprise. The action was supported by workers from other public sector enterprises. (*The Hindu*, January 12, 2001)

All protests were carefully coded based on their mobilizing agency, the date and place of the protest, the target of the protest, and the number of people participating in it. There are, however, two major problems related to using media-based protest event data. The first is "description bias" and refers to the actual content of reported news events.[31] That is, news reports are often insufficiently accurate in determining the size and duration of a protest event. For example, discerning the number of participants in the cases presented above is problematic. A newspaper might also be sympathetic to a particular political party or ideology, and may thus give a "biased" account of the event. Yet, this type of bias can be somewhat minimized by using an electronic database such as Factiva, which includes many different sources reporting on the same event. This allows a researcher to compare the content of different sources and take an average of the size and duration of the reported protest event.

A second and more serious problem—selection bias—is related to the media's tendency to focus more on violent and large scale events rather than on smaller, peaceful ones.[32] Yet, the problem of case selection can be decreased by triangulating data sources. The news reports used as data for this study were complemented by official reports published by the central and state governments, trade unions' chronicles, scholarly literature on the Indian economy and industrial relations, and papers written by various civil society organizations.[33]

Irrespective of such measures, the compiled data might still be biased toward more-newsworthy events simply because of India's size and diversity. For example, we might still lack information about smaller protests or those in more remote areas. On the other hand, privatization is generally a well-monitored process and because Factiva is directed mainly toward an audience interested in the business environment, any action viewed as disturbing the investment climate would likely have been reported. Ways to comparatively assess the reliability data used in this study are limited because no similar data have been collected for other studies. Existing accounts of labor protests in India have tended to rely on events reported in the international media and as a result may omit many cases of collective action.[34] Thus, the protest data used in this study remain an important source for providing a systematic overview of protest mobilization against privatization in India.

National level trends of anti-privatization protests in India

Figure 1 puts mobilization against privatization in India into a broader context by comparing the number of these protests with the overall number of industrial disputes in India's public sector enterprises from 1991 to 2003.[35] Since the Ministry of Labor combines records of both strikes and lockouts under the collective umbrella of "industrial disputes," it tends to overestimate worker mobilization. In contrast to strikes, lockouts actually refer to the withdrawal of work by employees and have actually increased in the private sector since 1991.

Figure 1 clearly demonstrates that the annual number of disputes in the public sector has steadily declined, whereas the annual number of anti-privatization protests has significantly increased during the same period. Moreover, the reported number of worker-days [the commonly used official term is "man-days"] lost has remained relatively constant, suggesting that disputes tend to last longer than before.[36] Since official statistics do not report political strikes, it can be surmised that rising resistance to privatization and the declining rate of reported industrial disputes is indicative of changed inducements for protesting. Public sector workers seem to protest more over government policies than over salaries or working conditions. Thus, these trends suggest that prior studies might have underestimated the mobilization of the Indian labor movement because they relied only on the number of officially reported strikes.

The Indian labor movement has not only intensified its mobilization against privatization, but it has also employed a wide repertoire of protest tactics. As shown in Table 2, traditional *hartals* (strikes) are frequently combined with *morchas* (demonstrations), *rasta rokos* (traffic blockades), *gheraos* (surrounding the decisionmakers), *dharnas* (sit-in strikes), and marches. Only 40% of the studied protests were strikes, 24% were

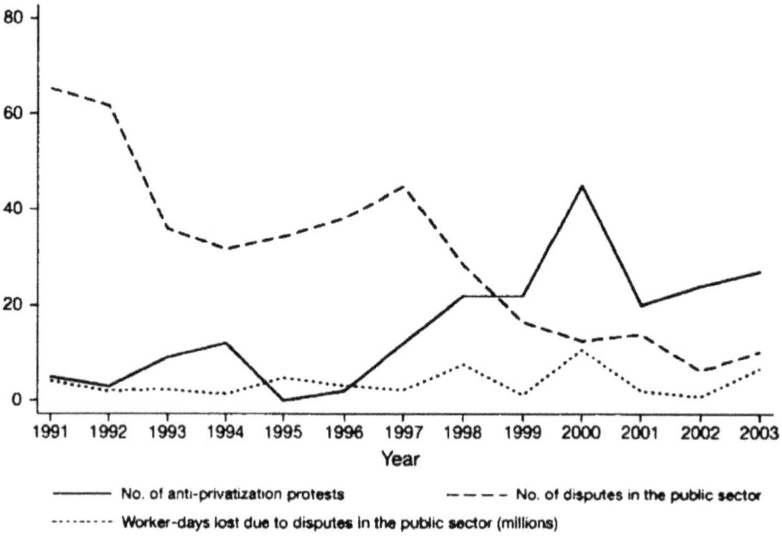

Figure 1 Growing resistance to privatization, declining number of disputes in the public sector, and the relatively stable number of worker-days lost in public sector disputes in India, 1991–2003

Source: Author's database; various annual reports published by the Ministry of Labor.

marches and demonstrations, and 14% nation-wide campaigns with multiple protest strategies. The size of protests varied from 10 workers on a hunger strike to a general demonstration with nearly 10 million participants.[37] Actions lasted from only a few hours to over three months, although the average did not exceed one and a half days. The method of data collection used in this study allowed for gathering information even on threats to protest. In fact, an estimated 7% of recorded events were "calls for strike" or "calls for mobilization." Even though such calls inform the government of labor resistance as do actual protests, the data on threats are less reliable than reports on actual events and are thus excluded from this analysis.

Table 2 Protests against privatization by type of action

Protest Tactics	*No. of Actions*	*Mean No. of Participants*	*Mean Duration in Days*
Blocking roads, occupying buildings	6	450	1.00
Demonstrations, marches, rallies	54	4,669	1.00
Strikes, slow-downs	91	161,385	2.68
Sit-ins	17	35,635	1.13
General nation-wide protests	32	768,256	1.08
Other	26	11,980	1.27

Source: Author's database.

Figure 2 presents the monthly number of protests and distinguishes between those targeting the central government and those against state governments. The figure shows that mobilization against privatization was modest during the early 1990s. Prime Minister Rajiv Gandhi of the Congress Party had, in fact, discarded attempts to liberalize the economy in 1986 because of minor protests at the time.[38]

The first major peaks in protest activity occurred in 1993 and 1994 when the central government under Congress Party Prime Minister Narasimha Rao decided to open India's oil exploration and refineries to private

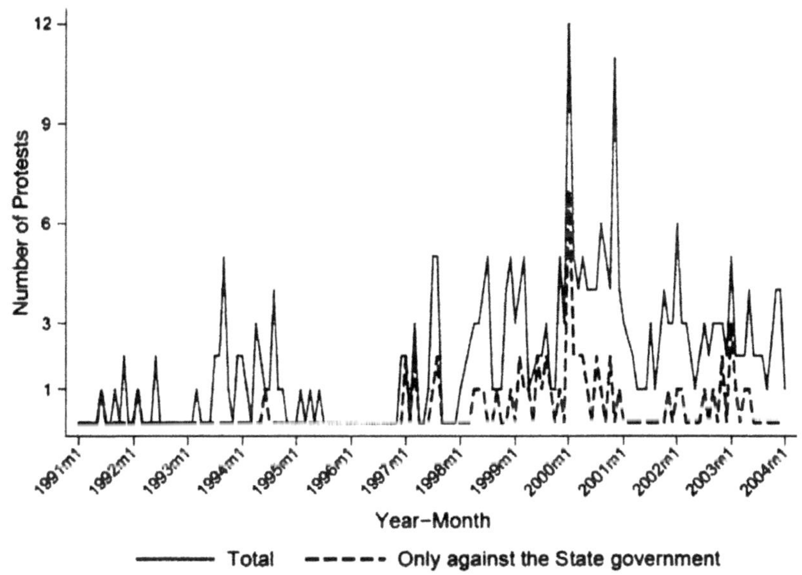

Figure 2 The monthly number of all and state governments' targeting anti-privatization protests in India, 1991–2003

Source: Author's database.

investment, and to sell some shares of public banks. Interestingly, the Indian National Trade Union Congress (INTUC)—the trade union affiliated with the Congress Party—even participated in some of these protest campaigns, although in a minor way. Prior to 1993, the federal-level leadership of INTUC had clearly distanced itself from any nationwide action against privatization, thus supporting the hypotheses set forth by classic social movement theory that unions associated with ruling political parties will tend not to mobilize. Yet, the INTUC continued to refrain from participating in anti-privatization protests targeting the central government, even after the BJP-led coalition came into power in 1998 and Congress became an opposition party. The INTUC's actions contrasted with those of the BJP-affiliated trade union—the Bharatiya Mazdoor Sangh (Indian Workers' Union, BMS). Surprisingly, the BMS significantly participated in nationwide strikes and demonstrations mobilized against the liberalization policies of the BJP-led government, although only until 2002.[39] However, the majority of anti-privatization protests directed against the policies of the central government were mobilized by the left-wing trade union federations—Center of the Indian Trade Unions (CITU) and All India Trade Union Congress (AITUC). For example, the BMS and INTUC were major organizers for three nationwide actions, whereas left-wing federations mobilized at least 37 campaigns.

The timeline in Figure 2 also demonstrates protest quiescence during the years 1995 and 1996. This relative quiet was probably related to deteriorating macroeconomic conditions and upcoming elections at the time. The Congress Party central government was preparing for upcoming Lok Sabha elections and did not want to discuss presumably unpopular privatization programs. Indeed, only 23.5% of respondents in one survey supported privatization, whereas 34% opposed it in 1996.[40] The lack of public debate on privatization was illustrated by the fact that 42% of the Indian public had no opinion regarding the process or had not even heard about the reforms.[41] Even though the elections resulted in the formation of a left-oriented government, the previous disinvestment policy continued under the new ruling coalition.[42] For example, this government allowed increased private investment into the banking sector, prompting massive protests in July 1997.

The government changed again in 1998 and the incoming BJP-led coalition government initiated drastic steps to reform India's public sector in 1999. The labor movement responded with increased protests, although it faced three significant setbacks to its efforts to mobilize. First, the government of the largest state, Uttar Pradesh, ignored the massive protest campaigns against its plans to trifurcate the state's electricity board in January 2000. This trifurcation entailed the creation of three separate parts of energy enterprises—generation, transmission, distribution. It was seen by energy workers' trade unions as a first step toward the full privatization of the state's energy sector. These protests against the Uttar Pradesh government also encouraged acts of solidarity by trade unions in other parts of India as well. This wave of protest is indicated by the peak of *state targeting protests* in Figure 2.[43] Second, the Indian Parliament approved the Insurance Regulatory and Development Bill in July 2000. This was a devastating blow to banking unions, which had managed to interrupt enactment of this legislation since the early 1990s. Unions saw the increased allowance of private investments into the finance sector as being a first step toward privatization and interpreted this defeat as a weakness of the anti-privatization movement. Third, the central government did not yield to labor unions in their 67–day strike protesting the sale of Bharat Aluminum Company (BALCO) to Sterlite Industries in March-May 2001. This unified action of all major trade unions took place after the enterprise was already sold and became a symbol of failed labor resistance to the central government's privatization policies.[44] These setbacks did not stop all mobilization; in fact, they encouraged further cooperation between the federal and state level union branches, although not between the different trade union federations affiliated with various political parties. Better coordination within unions and their increased collaboration with various consumer and environmental groups led to a massive protest campaign against the privatization of electricity systems in late 2001 and against the proposed privatization of Indian oil companies in 2003. Despite these actions, the governing BJP took up the question of economic reforms in upcoming parliamentary elections. It was defeated by the Congress Party in 2004. Even though the question of economic reforms was important during campaigning, this issue did not necessarily cause the loss. Nonetheless, public opposition to privatization increased from 34% in 1996 to 48% by 2004.[45] In contrast, the percentage of proponents remained almost the same.

Thus, this section shows that Indian labor's protest mobilization against privatization has clearly grown over the years and developed a wide repertoire of protest strategies. In contrast to the outcomes predicted by resource mobilization theories, left-wing trade union federations with relatively small official memberships have been more active than right-of-center-leaning unions. It can be hypothesized that the relative quiescence of these larger unions was related to the governing position of their allies (e.g., the Congress and BJP), but available data do not fully support this thesis. The INTUC's comparative restraint from mobilizing when Congress-led governments were in or out of power and, in contrast, the BMS's participation in national anti-privatization protests until 2002, even when the BJP was in power, points to more-complex mobilization patterns than classical resource mobilization theory suggests.

In order to better understand these complex processes, we need to move beyond federal level analysis. The following section focuses on anti privatization mobilization across 12 Indian states: Andhra Pradesh, Gujarat, Haryana, Karna-taka, Kerala, Maharashtra, Madhya Pradesh, Orissa, Rajasthan, Tamil Nadu, Uttar Pradesh, and West Bengal.

Variability of state level trends of anti-privatization protests in India

While exact annual data on privatization processes at the state level are not as readily available as at the federal level, some preliminary findings regarding patterns of anti-privatization protests can be extrapolated from the data at hand. For example, it is safe to conclude that the mobilization of Indian labor at the state level is weaker than at the federal level, partially because of the unions' geographical fragmentation.[46] Since state governments are often ruled by a different party than the central government, we can also assume that party affiliation plays an important role in explaining variants of mobilization against the central and state governments across Indian states. Figure 2 demonstrated that protests targeting state governments formed only a small portion of all anti-privatization protests. In order to make these accounts comparable across states, I have divided the number of protests by the number of workers in the public sector of each respective state and ranked the states according to their relative or "normalized" protest intensity.[47]

Figure 3 shows that there is a large variation in labor's targeting of central and state governments for protest across the 12 states included in this study. Certainly, the largest number of collective actions took place in Delhi—a Union Territory that includes the capital city of New Delhi. Since important governmental institutions including Parliament are located in the capital, Delhi is not comparable to other states and has thus been omitted from the analysis. Among the examined states, Kerala has the highest number of anti-privatization protests and Madhya Pradesh the lowest. Interestingly, no clear relationship appears to exist between labor legislation and the struggle against privatization. Kerala, Karnataka, Andhra Pradesh, Tamil Nadu, and Rajasthan have all approved legislation allowing the state government to prohibit strikes if doing so is considered to be in the larger public interest.[48] Mobilization against privatization is, as expected, higher in the first three states but lower than average in both Tamil Nadu and Rajasthan.

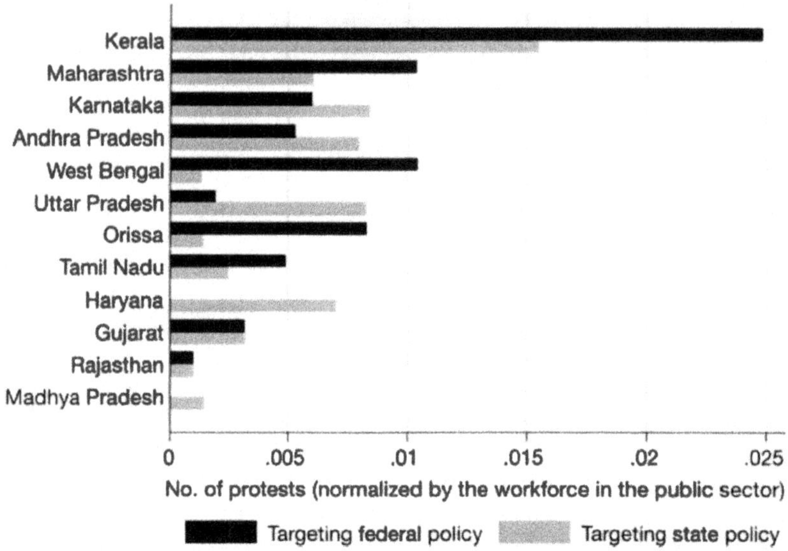

Figure 3 The difference between anti-privatization protests targeting the federal or state government, 1991–2003

Note: Number of protests is normalized by the public sector workforce of the state in 2001.

Source: Author's database; reports of the Planning Commission of India (2001).

One could conceivably hypothesize that the relative order of protest intensity reflects the general level of civil society activism in the states under examination. This hypothesis would be consistent with previous studies on individual level protest participation in Indian states.[49] However, Figure 3 also shows that protests initiated against the privatization policies of the central government and the respective state governments vary among the 12 states under examination. While in Haryana and Uttar Pradesh more protests were mobilized against the central rather than state governments, the situation is reversed in Orissa and West Bengal. This suggests that specific policy differences and the unions' affiliations with different political parties play a role at even the state level.

It is also reasonable to assume that protest activism against the central government is higher in those states where the central government decided to sell its public sector enterprises (PSEs). This was certainly the case in Orissa, where the BJP-led central government aimed to sell NALCO, an economically important aluminum company, and where even the state's chief minister supported a massive anti-privatization protest campaign in 2002.[50] Yet, the case of Orissa contrasts with that of Haryana and of Madhya Pradesh, where mobilization against the central government's privatization reforms was comparatively limited. This variation in patterns of mobilization across states suggests that other potential variables, such as trade union density or political party in power, were also at work.

The examples of Kerala and West Bengal leave an especially vexing puzzle unsolved. Both states are similar in that they are historic strongholds of Communist parties and the left-wing trade unions—CITU and AITUC—associated with them. Yet, both states have also witnessed significant economic reforms under their respective leftist governments. While the Communist Party of India (Marxist) (CPI-M)-led government in West Bengal has not directly privatized any of its enterprises, it has nonetheless engaged in privatization through the back door by extensively using the strategy of "joint ventures" for implementing economic reforms.[51] In fact, many scholars argue that West Bengal's political leadership under chief minister

Table 3 State level differences of public sector reforms

State	*No. of Protests against*		*No. of SPSUs (2003)*	*No. of Sold SPSUs*	*% of SPSUs Chosen for Reforms*	*Workers (in 1,000s) (2001)*
	Center	*State*				
Andhra Pradesh	8	12	128	13	67	1,509.65
Delhi*	54	7	15	1	0	–
Gujarat	3	3	50	3	48	949.67
Haryana	0	3	45	1	18	428.13
Karnataka	5	7	85	2	46	832.23
Kerala	16	10	111	1	49	645.02
Madhya Pradesh	0	2	26	1	54	1,376.44
Maharashtra	24	14	66	0	20	2,305.78
Orissa	6	1	72	9	46	723.14
Raj as than	1	1	28	1	36	1,014.77
Tamil Nadu	8	2	59	0	19	1,629.86
Uttar Pradesh	4	17	41	2	61	2,058.67
West Bengal	16	2	82	10**	15	1,530.71

* Delhi is Union Territory and includes the capital, New Delhi.
** Joint ventures.
Source: Author's database; Planning Commission of India, Department of Disinvestment (no. of workers in public sector, 2001).

Buddhadeb Bhattacharjee is even more liberal-minded than the highly touted pro-privatization authorities of Gujarat and Andhra Pradesh.[52] Kerala, on the other hand, has fully privatized one enterprise and earmarked 49% of its other PSEs for further reforms, as indicated in Table 3. Thus, trade unions in both states had the resources and motivation to mobilize against economic reforms, but the rate of anti-privatization protests targeting both levels of government was significantly higher in Kerala than in West Bengal. This was surprising because West Bengal has the highest rate of industrial disputes and largest number of unions in India. What explains this apparent difference in labor mobilization between these two states?

Applying the framework of political opportunity structures, classical social movement theory would surmise that trade unions' affiliation with political parties plays an important role in mobilization. However, prior empirical studies show that the CPI-M, which has governed West Bengal since 1977, strongly discouraged mobilization against the party's privatization policies by the state's largest trade union, CITU, while welcoming protests against the privatization policies of the central government.[53] Kerala has also been frequently governed by the CPI-M, although the Congress Party was in power for almost 10 years of our observation period, during 1991–96 and 2001–06. Therefore, it is not surprising that mobilization against privatization in Kerala was higher than in West Bengal, supporting the hypotheses set forth in social movement theory. However, counter to expectations, left-wing trade unions also mobilized against privatization policies under the CPI-M government from 1997 to 2000. While CITU protested against the West Bengal government's privatization policies only once, the left-wing unions in Kerala held several campaigns against the state government's attempt to liberalize the economy. These included protests against plans to allow private participation in the development of the Cochin (Kochi) port in 1999 and a general anti-privatization strike in 2000. AITUC and CITU affiliated employees of Kerala's State Electricity Board (KSEB) also mobilized a strike in support of the anti-privatization protests of Uttar Pradesh power unions in 2000. These collective actions sent a clear anti-privatization message to Kerala's state government.[54] The anti-privatization protests by AITUC and CITU against economic reforms initiated by the CPI-M state government in Kerala closely resemble federal-level activism of the BMS, which participated in protests against the BJP-led government's reform policies between 1998 and 2002.

Based on the analysis above, we can conclude that political opportunity structures (for example, the labor unions' affiliation with political parties) do not provide a conclusive explanation for the observed differences in protest mobilization in various Indian states. This suggests the need for further research; one potentially fruitful direction may be analyzing the comparative structure of civil society in the various Indian states including Kerala and West Bengal. Such contextual variables have not been sufficiently analyzed by scholars of social movements and woven into the theory's explanatory schema. Yet, prior studies on India do suggest, for example, that the relationship between the CPI-M and leftist trade unions, as well as the entire civil society of the state, is more open in Kerala than in West Bengal.[55] This includes the trade unions' cooperation across party lines and collaboration with various civil society organizations, including environmental and students' groups in Kerala, but not in West Bengal. However, more case study and comparative research must be done into these issues before we can extrapolate firm conclusions and potentially ascertain the precise causal processes that determine contrasting patterns of labor mobilization among Indian states.

Conclusion

The analytical goal of this article was to describe and analyze various patterns of trade unions' anti-privatization mobilization in India by using a unique set of protest data instead of the more commonly exploited strike statistics or the size of trade union membership. The results of this study have provided a picture of increased anti-privatization protests and an enlarged repertoire of labor movement mobilization approaches from 1991 to 2003. This shows that Indian labor was not as quiescent against liberal economic reforms as is often assumed. While unions organized few protests during the early 1990s, their mobilization intensified as successive central governments and their state-level counterparts accelerated the pace and scope of privatization. This increased mobilization took place despite a declining overall strike rate, demonstrating that future studies of Indian labor movement mobilization would benefit from using a broader set of data on protest campaigns rather than simply looking at officially reported strikes.

This study also shows that all major labor unions in India, regardless of their ideological leanings, took part in protests against privatization, although the leftist-oriented unions (AITUC and CITU) appeared to be more active than those affiliated with centrist or right-of-center political parties (the INTUC and BMS, respectively). Following the precepts set forth by social movement theory and prior research on Latin America, it was expected that protest activism would be related to the unions' affiliation with various political parties. But analysis at both the federal and especially state levels paints a more complex picture. For example, at the national level, INTUC tended to avoid mobilization, compared to other unions, whether its affiliated party—the Congress Party—was in power or not. In contrast, the BMS demonstrated more willingness to mobilize against privatization even when its affiliated party, the BJP, was in power.

Similarly, the leftist labor unions avoided protesting against the CPI-M state government in West Bengal while being willing to protest against the privatization policies of the central government. In contrast, these same labor unions protested actively against both the central government and also the CPI-M state government in Kerala. These examples suggest that the relationship between labor unions' resources, ideology and political affiliation, and their mobilization against privatization is more complex than previously assumed. The contrasting patterns of labor mobilization, especially in relation to Kerala and West Bengal, suggest that research on this question should, perhaps, focus on the local structure of civil society within states because this may play an important role in divergent patterns of union activism. There is much room for additional theory development and empirical testing when explaining labor mobilization against economic liberalization policies in India. This study has attempted to take a small but hopefully useful step in this direction.

Notes

Katrin Uba wishes to thank Hans Blomkvist, Sten Widmalm, Li Bennick-Björkman, Per Strömblad, and an anonymous reviewer for their help in preparing this article. This project was funded by the Swedish International Development Agency (project no. 22244050).

1 A detailed description of India's privatization process is beyond the scope of this article. Interested readers can find valuable information in Montek Ahluwalia, "Economic Reforms in India since 1991: Has Gradualism Worked?" *Journal of Economic Perspectives* 16:3 (Fall 2002), pp. 67–88; Sudhir Naib, *Disinvestment in India: Policies, Procedures, Practices* (New Delhi: Sage Publications, 2004); and Jos Mooij, ed., *The Politics of Economic Reforms in India* (New Delhi: Sage Publication, 2005).

2 There are several important case studies on the legislation of Indian labor laws and the labor movement's mobilization at the state level, but there is comparatively little systematic analysis on the protests against privatization in India. Some examples include Supriya Roychowdhury, "Public Sector Restructuring and Democracy: The State, Labor, and Trade Unions in India," *Journal of Development Studies* 29:3 (February 2003), pp. 29–50; and Rob Jenkins, *Regional Reflections: Comparing Politics across India's States* (Oxford: Oxford University Press, 2004). The most diverging arguments on the mobilization of trade unions in India are presented in Gopal Joshi, ed., *Privatization in South Asia: Minimizing Negative Social Effects through Restructuring* (Geneva: International Labor Organization, 2001), pp. 45–104; and Anil Sen Gupta and Prodip Kumar Sett, "Industrial Relations Law, Employment Security, and Collective Bargaining in India: Myths, Realities, and Hopes," *Industrial Relations Journal* 31:2 (2000), pp. 144–53.

3 The term "liberalization" refers to various types of market-oriented reforms. "Privatization" refers to the process of a state transitioning its economic and financial activities to the private sector.

4 The 12 states included for this study were selected according to their size and the availability of information on them. They are Andhra Pradesh, Gujarat, Haryana, Karnataka, Kerala, Maharashtra, Madhya Pradesh, Orissa, Rajasthan, Tamil Nadu, Uttar Pradesh, and West Bengal. These states cover 81% of the Indian population according to the Census of India (1991).

5 The scholarship on social movement theory is broad and constantly developing. Interested readers can find a valuable introduction in Donatella Della Porta and Mario Diani, *Social Movements: An Introduction* (Oxford: Blackwell Publishing, 2006). A good example of the use of "social movement" literature for studying collective action against liberal economic politics is Jeffrey M. Ayres, "Framing Collective Action against Neoliberalism: The Case of the 'Anti-Globalization' Movement," *Journal of World-Systems Research* 10:1 (2004), pp. 11–34.

6 For example, see Atul Kohli, "Politics of Economic Growth in India, 1980–2005. Part II: The 1990s and Beyond," *Economic and Political Weekly*, April 8, 2006, pp. 1361–70; and Sunila Kale, "The Political Economy of India's Second Generation of Reforms," *Journal of Strategic Studies* 25:4 (December 2002), pp. 207–25.

7 India's gross domestic product (GDP) was $461 billion in 2000, whereas Poland's was $171 billion. Information on privatization transactions can be accessed from the World Bank Privatization Databases, 1988–99, 2000–06, available at <http://rru.worldbank.org/privatization> accessed on May 1, 2006. The data on privatization in India used for this study was obtained from official publications of India's Department of Disinvestment (DD), available at <http://divest.nic.in>, last accessed on January 6, 2006; C. S. Venkata Ratnam, *Globalization and Labor-Management Relations: Dynamics of Change* (New Delhi: Response Books, 2001); and Naib, *Disinvestment in India*. Comparisons to Latin America are discussed in Hakan Tunc, "Privatization in Asia and Latin America," *Studies in Comparative International Development* 39:4 (December 2005), pp. 58–86.

8 In announcing liberal reforms over the years, various ministers of Finance spoke about "strategic sales" or the need to "open the economy for private sector participation," but tended to avoid the use of the word "privatization." See more in E. A. S. Sarma, "Disinvestment: What FMs [Financial Ministers] Have Said Since 1991," *Economic and Political Weekly*, May 29, 2004, pp. 2194–96.

9 Quoted in V. Shankar Aiyar, "Privatization. The Big Fight," *India Today*, July 17, 2000, available at

<http://indiatodaygroup.com/itoday/20000717/economy.html>, accessed on June 1, 2006.

10 See Rob Jenkins, *Democratic Politics and Reform in India* (Cambridge: Cambridge University Press, 1999).

11 These discussions are accessible on the Rajya Sabha's homepage, available at <http://rajyasabha.nic.in>, accessed last on October 16, 2006. During 1995 to 2005, members of the Rajya Sabha posed 28 questions regarding privatization and its related protests.

12 These formed 20% of federal government-owned enterprises; also see Naib, *Disinvestment in India*.

13 For example, see Serdar Dinc and Gupta Nandini, *The Decision to Privatize: The Role of Political Competition and Patronage*, Working Paper, University of Michigan (June 2005); and Geeta Gouri, "The New Economic Policy and Privatization in India," *Journal of Asian Economics* 8:3 (1997), pp. 455–79.

14 Exact measures for each state included in this study are given later in this article in Table 3. Scholars often use the measure on direct financial investments per capita (FDI) for gauging the level of liberalization in states, but this does not necessarily mirror the actual extent of privatization. For example, Kerala and Uttar Pradesh have privatized many SPSUs but have received much less FDI than Maharashtra, which has not sold any of its SPSUs. Also see Sadhana Srivastava and Rahul Sen, "Competing for Global FDI: Opportunities and Challenges for the Indian Economy," *South Asia Economic Journal* 5:2 (2004), pp. 233–60. The number of SPSUs I can discern for this study is an approximation because the DD only has information about those enterprises that had finalized their accounts for 2004. According to the *Economic Times*, February 17, 1996, Rajasthan and Haryana have privatized two SPSUs each, while the DD reports the sale of only one SPSU. The term "restructuring" refers to the process of splitting, closing, or selling state owned enterprises. Also refer to R. K. Mishra and J. Kiranmai, "Restructuring of SLPEs [State Level Public Enterprises] in India: A Macro-analysis," *Economic and Political Weekly*, September 30, 2006, pp. 4170–77.

15 This type of pattern has been more common with presidents of Latin American countries. For example, the former president of Peru, Alberto Fujimori, came to power with anti-reform arguments in 1991 but subsequently initiated reforms only months after being inaugurated into office. See Susan Stokes, "Economic Reform and Public Opinion in Peru, 1990–1995," *Comparative Political Studies* 29:4 (1996), pp. 544–65. For more on politics and reform in Andhra Pradesh, see Loraine Kennedy, "The Political Determinants of Reform Packaging," in Rob Jenkins, ed., *Regional Reflections: Comparing Politics across India's States* (Oxford: Oxford University Press, 2005), pp. 29–65.

16 For example, the chief minister of Orissa, Naveen Patnaik, was against privatizing the central government-owned National Aluminum Company, Ltd. (NALCO) in 2003 even though his own government had taken steps for selling many of its own state owned enterprises. See Mishra and Kiranmai, "Restructuring of SLPEs in India."

17 For example, see Devesh Kapur and Pratab Bhanu Mehta, *Indian Higher Education Reform: From Half-Baked Socialism to Half-Baked Capitalism*, Working Paper, no. 108, Center of International Development, Harvard University, 2004; Brijesh C. Purohit, "Private Initiatives and Policy Options: Recent Health System Experience in India," *Health Policy Plan* 16:1 (2001), pp. 87–97.

18 For more about reforms in the electricity and water sectors, see Thankom Arun and Fred Nixson, "The Reform of the Power Sector in India: 1991–1997," *Journal of International Development* 10:4 (1998), pp. 417–26; and Naunidhi Kaur, "Privatizing Water," *Frontline* 20:18 (August 30–September 12, 2003).

19 Also see Rob Jenkins, "Labor Policy and the Second Generation of Economic Reform in India," *India Review* 3:4 (October 2004), pp. 333–63.

20 Sarosh Kuruvilla, Subesh Das, Hyunji Kwon, and Soonwon Kwon, "Trade Union Growth and Decline in Asia," *British Journal of Industrial Relations* 40:3 (2002), pp. 431–61. A detailed overview of legal aspects of industrial relations in India is given in Venkata Ratnam, *Globalization and Labor-Management Relations*. Also see historical overview on the Indian labor movement in Debashish Bhattacherjee, *Organized Labor and Economic Liberalization in India: Past, Present, and Future*, ILO Discussion Paper Series, no. 105 (1999); and Ghanshyam Shah, "Social Movements in India: A Review of Literature" (New Delhi: Sage Publications, 2004).

21 Timothy Besley and Robin Burgess, "Can Labor Regulation Hinder Economic Performance? Evidence from India," *Quarterly Journal of Economics* 119:1 (2004), pp. 91–134. These results are, however, criticized in Alakh N. Sharma, "Flexibility, Employment, and Labor Market Reforms in India," *Economic and Political Weekly*, May 27, 2006, pp. 2078–85.

22 According to the Census India 2001, the Indian labor force consists of 402 million people, and 57% of them work in agriculture. Also see Christopher Candland and Rudra Sil, eds., *The Politics of Labor in the Global Age: Continuity and Change in Late-industrializing and Post-socialist Economies* (Oxford: Oxford University Press, 2001); and Shyam Sundar, "Official Data on Trade Unions: Some Comments," *Economic and Political Weekly*, October 2, 1999, pp. 2839–41.

23 Ashok Swain, *Social Networks and Social Movements: Are Northern Tools Useful to Evaluate Southern Protests?* Uppsala Peace Research Papers, no. 4 (2002). See also Sidney Tarrow, *Power in Movement: Social Movements and Contentious Politics* (Cambridge: Cambridge University Press, 1994).

24 Hanspeter Kriesi, "The Political Opportunity Structure of New Social Movements: Its Impact on Their Mobilization," in J. Craig Jenkins and Bert Klandermans, eds., *The Politics of Social Protest* (Berkeley, Calif.: University of California Press, 1995), pp. 167–98.

25 J. Craig Jenkins, David Jacobs, and Jon Agnone, "Political Opportunities and African-American Protest, 1948–1997," *American Journal of Sociology* 109:2 (2003), pp. 277–303.

26 Maria Victoria Murillo, *Labour Unions, Partisan Coalitions, and Market Reform in Latin America* (Cambridge: Cambridge University Press, 2001). Note that Murillo discusses all "market oriented reforms" rather than privatization alone.

27 Deepita Chakravarty, "Labor Arrangements and Bargaining Outcomes under Different Market Conditions," *Indian Journal of Labor Economics* 49:1 (2006), pp. 121–31.

28 Candland and Sil, *The Politics of Labor in the Global Age*.

29 Factiva also archives reporting from news agencies such as Dow Jones, Reuters, and even the Press Trust of India. Factiva is available at <www.factiva.com>. This source and method are often used in "social movement" research. For details, see Dieter Rucht, *Acts of Dissent* (Berlin: Sigma, 1998).

30 One of the search commands was (disinvestment OR privatization OR restructuring OR privatize OR disinvest) AND (protest OR strike OR resist OR oppose OR dharna OR sit-in OR demonstration); limiting the time frame from January 1, 1990, to January 1, 2004; and the geographical area to India. The codebook and data are available from the author upon request.

31 David G. Ortiz, Daniel J. Myers, Eugene Walls, and Maria-Elena Diaz, "Where Do We Stand with Newspaper Data?" *Mobilization: An International Quarterly* 10:3 (2005), pp. 397–419. These authors discuss three types of biases—description, selection, and ideological bias. I have neglected the last, although it is sometimes argued that the media in India became more pro-business and pro-BJP during the period from 1998 to 2004. See Smita Gupta, "Post-liberalization India: How Free is the Media?" *South Asia: Journal of South Asian Studies* 28:2 (August 2005), pp. 283–300.

32 For a general discussion about "selection bias," see Barbara Geddes, *Paradigms and Sand Castles: Theory Building and Research Design in Comparative Politics* (Ann Arbor: University of Michigan Press, 2003), pp. 89–130.

33 Some of the sources used include *Economic and Political Weekly;* India Labor Archive, available at <http://www.indialabourarchives.org>; websites of various trade union federations; and the author's personal correspondence with representatives of various trade unions.

34 Dean McHenry, "*What Is Left out When Events within a State Are Characterized Numerically? A Study of Democracy and Protest in India*," paper presented at the annual meeting of the American Political Science Association, August 27, 2003, available at <http://www.allacademic.com/meta/p63850_index.html>.

35 The data presented in Figure 1 are from the author's database, accumulated from annual reports published by the Ministry of Labor; and Bhattacherjee, *Organized Labor and Economic Liberalization in India.*

36 "Man-days lost" is an important indicator frequently used in official Indian statistics. This conceptual figure takes into account the number of workers involved and the duration of the collective action, and is usually measured in the millions. Since the number of participating workers has not necessarily increased, the relative stable trend in "worker-days lost" suggests longer industrial disputes. See also Bhattacherjee, *Organized Labor and Economic Liberalization in India.*

37 This data may underestimate the total number of hunger strikes because this method of protest tends to mobilize few active participants. Yet, my interviews with trade union activists in one of the first privatized enterprises in Andhra Pradesh (Allwyn Refrigerators) suggest that hunger strikes are very effective for gaining both the public and politicians' attention.

38 Candland and Sil, *The Politics of Labor in the Global Age.*

39 For example, the BMS took part in the strike against the privatization of the Indira Port in West Bengal in January 2000 and in the sit-in against the privatization of the Cochin Shipyard, Ltd., in Kerala in January 2002. In contrast, the union distanced itself from the protests opposing the sell-out of an aluminum corporation (NALCO) in Orissa in September 2002.

40 Subrata K. Mitra and V. B. Singh, *Democracy and Social Change in India* (New Delhi: Sage Publications, 1999), p. 76.

41 Ibid.

42 This United Front coalition was led by Janata Dal leader H. D. Deve Gowda, who became prime minister.

43 Every state in India has a state electricity board that controls generation, transformation, and distribution of power. Privatization of this enterprise has often involved the unbundling or trifurcation of its main functions. For more details, see Arun and Nixson, "The Reform of the Power Sector in India."

44 For details, see Devesh Kapur and Ravi Ramamurti, *Privatization in India: The Imperatives and Consequences of Gradualism*, Working Paper, no. 142, Stanford University (2002), at <http://scid.stanford.edu/pdf/credprl42.pdf>.

45 Y. Yadav, "Economic Reforms in the Mirror of Public Opinion," *The Hindu*, June 13, 2004.

46 For details, see Jenkins, *Regional Reflections*.

47 It would be more informative to normalize the protests by state-wide trade union membership, but there is no reliable data on this. Also, please note that the numbers presented do not include 20 nationwide campaigns because these actions were spread over many states. Protests against privatization also occurred in other states as well for which I lack sufficient information on the disinvestment process, including Punjab, Himachal Pradesh, Chattisghar, Assam, Bihar, and Manipur. More statistics on studied states are found in Table 3.

48 Besley and Burgess, "Can Labor Regulation Hinder Economic Performance?"

49 For example, a survey made in five states during 1998–99 showed that protest participation during the last half decade was highest in Kerala and lowest in Gujarat. Hans Blomkvist, "Social Capital, Civil Society, and Degrees of Democracy in India," in *Civil Society and Democracy in India*, ed. Carolyn Elliott (Oxford: Oxford University Press, 2003).

50 For details, see V. Sridhar, "Nalco—A Story of Resistance," *The Hindu*, January 17, 2003.

51 "Joint ventures" represent a more moderate form of privatization because no property rights or regulatory control are legally transferred to the private sector. Instead, the state government simply cooperates with a private company in running the operations of a public enterprise, and the private company can take shares of this enterprise via cash payments.

52 See AseemaSinha, *The Regional Roots of Developmental Politics in India* (Bloomington: Indiana University Press, 2005). For a discussion of Buddhadeb Bhattacharjee's strategies of economic reform in West Bengal, see Partha Pratim Basu, "Brand Buddha in India's West Bengal: The Left Reinvents Itself," *Asian Survey* (March/April 2007), pp. 288–306.

53 One rare case when CITU did protest against the West Bengal government was against the sale of the Great Eastern Hotel. See Anand Gupta, *The Political Economy of Privatization in India*, IRIS-India Working Paper, no. 17 (1996). Events in West Bengal are not unique. For example, the BMS withdrew from protests against the privatization of the state-owned cement company in Uttar Pradesh immediately after its ally, the BJP, formed the state government. See Mukul, "Uttar Pradesh: Workers Challenge Privatization," *Economic and Political Weekly*, January 4, 1992.

54 For more on Kerala's economic reforms, see P. D. Jeromi, "Economic Reforms in Kerala," *Economic and Political Weekly*, July 23, 2005, pp. 3267–77.

55 See Blomkvist (2003); and Manali Desai, "Party Formation, Political Power, and the Capacity for Reform: Comparing Left Parties in Kerala and West Bengal, India," *Social Forces* 80:1 (2001), pp. 37–60.

22

Labour and economic reforms

Disjointed critiques

Supriya Roychowdhury

Source: Jos Mooij (ed.), *The Politics of Economic Reforms in India* (New Delhi: Sage Publications, 2005), pp. 264–90.

1. Introduction: the changing context

Labour constitutes one of the most important arenas of restructuring during a process of adjustment and marketization. In India, however, the question of labour, at least in the first decade of economic reforms, drew more attention from academics and activists than from policy-makers. The reason for this is obviously political: organized labour commanded a unique position amongst major stakeholders in the limited welfaristic system that was introduced post-independence and constituted itself as a favoured client of the state in the decades that followed. As such, in the initial years after liberalization was introduced, there was a certain evasion of policy issues that might involve a significant overhauling of labour laws and labour institutions. Thus privatization, disinvestment, labour rationalization in public sector enterprises—all of these were placed on the back burner. Meanwhile, the policy apparatus went ahead with elements of liberalization that had no direct or immediate negative implications for labour, as in the sectors of finance, capital markets taxation and so on.

The most significant example of this shelving of the labour issue is, in fact, the Industrial Disputes (ID) Act, 1947—the essence of which remains unchanged to this day, despite several amendments. The central provision of the ID Act is that establishments employing more than 100 workmen can institute layoffs, retrenchment or closure, all of which affect labour, only after obtaining legal permission from the state government. Thus, the ID Act squarely placed the state in the management-labour negotiations arena. Organized labour, although constituting a small fraction of the total labour force, has nevertheless enjoyed significant political leverage. It was part of the ever-growing public sector and was organized in a dense network of trade unions with varying degrees of closeness to major political parties. Given this context, the element of worker protection built into the ID Act took on a sacrosanct and unyielding form—in the face of many challenges to its rationale in a marketizing economy.

Similarly, the Contract Labour (Abolition and Regulation) Act, 1970, makes illegal the use of contract labour in what was termed in the act as 'permanent' forms of employment. The thrust of the Contract Labour Act was to create a broader base for the absorption of labour into permanent employment and to narrow down the scope of contractual employment. Contract employment is an inherent part of market-based economies where employers wish to steer free of any long-standing commitment to workers, in terms of security of employment or other benefits that accompany permanent service. As economic liberalization began to take shape in India, the clamour for a market-oriented exit policy—enabling employers to hire and fire freely—and for a freer use of contract labour has been heard repeatedly. This demand has emerged not only from business circles but also from policy-makers impatient with what they perceive to be obsolete labour laws in a marketization/globalization context. The need for a new exit policy, which would allow for hiring and firing to be predominantly determined by the market, is widely acknowledged. Nevertheless, the ID Act, as well as the Contract Labour Act, remained essentially unchanged throughout the period of economic reforms up until the end of the nineties.

The National Democratic Alliance (NDA), which came into power at the centre in 1999 has made some efforts to change the framework of labour laws. The coalition government's union budget for 2001–02, proposed major changes in the ID Act. Firms with below 1,000 workers were sought to be defined as outside the ambit of the act; at the same time, contractual employment was sought to be made legal. While a cabinet committee on labour has endorsed these proposals, they are yet to become legislative acts. The proposals have drawn much public criticism, orchestrated by some of the major trade unions. Additionally, the so-called second-generation reforms have taken a more definitive approach towards the policies of privatization and disinvestment. These are, as yet, tendencies, rather than accomplished facts. However, the measures taken indicate that the state's patronage of organized labour has begun to decline, slowly but consistently.

Ironically, the reluctance to change labour laws is in marked contrast to the actual shifts that have been taking place in the realm of labour, both in the structures of industrial relations within firms and in the politics of labour. While market-driven hiring and firing still do not have legal sanction, there has been a great deal of labour retrenchment in the private sector through illegal closures, even in established industrial sectors such as textiles. The dislocation of labour from the formal sector has also taken place through indirect channels, such as outsourcing, subcontracting, setting up of small-scale units and so on, in order to evade the ID Act. More significantly, many public sector undertakings have taken to labour rationalization through voluntary retirement schemes and other measures, such as a freeze on recruitment, contract employment and so on. These shifts indicate that although the labour-friendly legal framework has remained in place, labour institutions and structures are undergoing rapid and significant changes.

In the context of public sector enterprises (PSEs), the move towards rationalization is mediated by their overall welfaristic posture. This makes it mandatory for PSEs to offer severance packages to laid-off workers and often forces them to ensure that jobs will not be lost subsequent to privatization. The historical legacy of state patronage for PSE unions also makes for a certain framework of closeness and communication, which rules out any dramatic confrontations. In turn, unions have offered ad hoc criticisms of privatization and labour rationalization. However; in a context where PSE losses and inefficiency have become a central theme of liberalization, unions have not provided any definitive alternative policy framework for addressing questions of PSE sickness and labour welfare. Thus, trade union and labour disquiet within public sector manufacturing remains inchoate rather than systematically articulated.

The domain of private enterprises includes a wide variety of contexts—be it the scale of the enterprise or the specific dynamics of regional politics. This diversity precludes any generalizations. In most cases, however, the numerical decline of the organized sector—attended by technological advances, outsourcing, contractual employment and so on—has underlined a certain weakening of the trade union movement. This is a worldwide trend, an inevitable aspect of the globalization process. In India, shifts are occurring in the realm of industrial relations—in terms of the institutions that define management—labour relations and the role of the state as a regulator of labour issues. Thus, for example, the erosion of the tripartite mode of conflict resolution and of consultation has been widely noted. Further, a process of decentralization in industrial relations bargaining systems has taken place, as collective bargaining becomes increasingly a plant-level exercise, rather than one at the industry or even enterprise level.

It is important to note that in the domain of private capital, direct and sustained conflicts are erupting in situations where labour is directly facing new forms of capital, i.e. multinational firms that have set up businesses in India in the last decade. The conventional understanding is that multinational companies (MNCs) provide better wages and working conditions compared to domestic firms and typically prefer to stay away from the rough and tumble of unions and politics. Surprisingly it is in these very domains that some of the most bitter industrial conflicts have broken out in recent times.

This chapter provides data drawn from case studies of three multinational companies in Bangalore city. The case studies draw attention to the following considerations: First, workers in multinational companies are engaged in conflict with the management over issues that are not radically different from those that have traditionally engaged the organized working class, i.e. wages, hours of work, production targets. Second, beyond these typical issues, a larger contestation is emerging over the effort by these companies to change the framework of industrial relations, away from organized bargaining to individual management–worker interactions. Although MNCs have in principle accepted unions and the 'law of the land', they have shown a sustained tendency to pin down workers to individual contracts and undertakings, to avoid the tripartite conciliation table and to marginalize the role of unions. This chapter highlights the role of the state in these conflicts. Finally, as these different levels of contestation between labour; management and governments emerge, within the framework of multinational companies, trade unions have focused on economic struggles. The broader policy framework, as also the structural context—which weakens the bargaining leverage of labour (for example, the availability of a large supply of contract workers)—has frequently slipped away from the everyday concerns of the trade unions.

What has emerged significantly from these processes is the weakening of trade unions as bargaining agents. The erosion of trade unionism as a consequence of marketization reforms is a widely-noted phenomenon across the world. There is, however, a tendency in the literature to generalize the causes of the weakening of trade unions into a cluster of underlying factors. Typically, these factors have to do with the numerical erosion of the organized sector workforce, the weakening of leftist political forces, and the enhanced power of capital in an era of state withdrawal from both economic activities and social commitments. These have become by now the staple of trade union studies in the context of marketization. This perspective has inserted an element of *fait accompli* in labour studies. The weakening of labour and unions is generally thought to be a dimension of the broadly irreversible processes unleashed by globalization. The specific nature of trade union erosion in varying contexts of marketization, and the broader implications of this phenomenon, has been rarely noted.

The underlying argument of this chapter is that it is important to highlight the specific dynamics of trade union struggles for the following reasons. First, trade unions constitute one amongst a wide range of sources from which the critique of marketization has emerged. However, by and large, trade unions are unable to connect, ideologically and organizationally, to other anti-marketization impulses, which have highly diverse constituencies and lack a common ideological/intellectual platform. Yet, in a context where trade unions have lost political leverage on account of declining numbers of organized sector workers, the key to newer forms of organization and empowerment may well lie in a more broad-based connection of the trade union movement to other forms of social struggle. In other words, once the structural factor of union erosion has been acknowledged, it is important to recognize that the weakness of unions is also a function of flaws in the movement itself, specifically in the inability or unwillingness to broaden its constituencies and discourse.

Second, the study of social conflicts in a context like India has moved very far away from capital–labour issues. Labour issues are placed in the specialized domains of labour studies or industrial relations. The underlying assumption has been that these labour studies cannot provide substantive analyses of broader political developments in India. Non-class perspectives have understandably provided more pertinent tools of social and political analysis in the highly complex and dense nature of identity politics and social movements that emerged in the last few decades. The relatively greater influence of North American, compared to Anglo-European, scholarship on Indian political scientists has underwritten the de-prioritization of capital–labour conflicts. The presence of a large public sector in industrial manufacturing has also diminished the relevance of class analysis in a context where labour faced a benevolent state rather than antagonistic capital. The chapter argues that in the new political economy framework created by liberalization policies, some of the most critical societal conflicts are actually occurring in the realm of capital–labour relations. Although encased within the microcosm of industrial relations, these conflicts in fact provide a vital clue to the unfolding nature of state–society relations in the rapidly changing context created by marketization reforms. The case studies in this chapter relate to trade union activities in specific situations of management–labour conflict, and thus highlight both the nature of such conflicts and the dynamics that define trade union activities.

2. Case studies

Pepsi: the struggle over wage

Pepsi Foods Ltd, whose head offices are in the United States, started its operations in India in 1989. It is in the business of producing snack food and soft drinks concentrate, which are also exported. The company operated through its Indian franchise bottlers. In 1993, the company decided to start a 100 per cent subsidiary, PepsiCo India Holdings, which would look after beverage bottling, soft funding to bottlers and joint venture exports. Pepsi has so far invested $500 million in its Indian operations. By 2002, it had 45 bottling plants in India; of these, 17 were company owned and the rest, franchise-owned bottling units. As of 2002, Pepsi had a turnover of Rs 25 billion, with an all-Indian employee force and a work force of 3,000 people. Out of these, 300 were managers.

In Bangalore, Pepsi has two plants—one set up in 1992 and the other in 1998. The crisis[1] discussed in this chapter began in the middle of 2001 in the second plant. The workers in this plant numbered around 200. In May 2001, these workmen joined the Karnataka Engineering and General Workers Union, affiliated to Centre for Indian Trade Unions (CITU, supported by the CPI[M]). They submitted a charter of demands in June 2001. The basic demand put forward by the union was a revision of the wage structure and uniformity in the payment of increments. The union pointed out that there were unexplained differences in the wages of workmen who were graduates of ITI of the same batch and who had joined the company on the same date. For 17 such workmen, the basic monthly wage varied from a low of Rs 1,450 to a high of Rs 2,600. In the middle of the range, too, there were unaccounted-for differences. There were similar differences in house rent allowance (HRA). Thus, the gross salary could be as low as Rs 3,430 and as high as Rs 4,900. The revised demand was for a uniform monthly basic of Rs 2,500; increase in dearness allowance (DA) from Rs 1,000 to Rs 2,000; increase in HRA from Rs 800 to Rs 1,250. The gross salary for ITI diploma holders would then be Rs 8,550 and for non-ITI workmen it would be Rs 6,330. The second issue related to increments. The increment offered ranged from Rs 350 to Rs 720, with an average of Rs 400. The union demanded uniformity in the payment of increments.

The charter of demands led to several rounds of meetings between the management and the union, but none of the issues could be resolved. The management offered a fixed increment for all employees—at Rs 400 for the first year and Rs 250 the following year. This was obviously unacceptable to the workers, as it was a reduction rather than an increase. With regard to salary structure, the management refused to grant a raise in any of the categories that had been asked for and ignored the issue of uniformity.

The response of the workers was to resort to 'work to rule', which was followed by several incidents of confrontation. During a period when maintenance work was being done, workers were withdrawn from skilled functions and asked to perform certain unskilled maintenance work, which earlier used to be typically done by contract workers. A worker was refused medical leave, which led to a scuffle between the union and the management. In the escalation of tensions that followed, five union office-bearers were suspended and the management insisted that each worker would sign an individual undertaking of good behaviour. Workers were stopped from going into the factory unless they were prepared to provide such an undertaking.

This confrontation was followed by a complete break in communication between the workforce and the management. The latter placed a complaint with the labour commissioner that the workers were on strike. The workers, on the other hand, insisted that they were prepared to resume work. Their argument was that since they were being prevented from doing so, this was a lockout. Under the union's leadership, however, the workmen refused to give individual undertakings of good behaviour. The leaders insisted that since there was a recognized union, any understanding with the management must be negotiated with the union, as the representative of workers.

In the meantime, the management at Pepsi sought to continue production by hiring a large number of contract workers. Previously, contract workers had typically been used only for security, housekeeping, and loading and unloading purposes. Due to an earlier conflict between the management and labour over the use of contract workers, an injunction was in place at the company that barred workers from preventing work by contract workers. The management used this injunction to get the workers' regular work done by contract workers. However, this was an unlawful measure. Under Clause 10 of the Contract Workers Regulation and Abolition Act, 1970, the use of contract workers to perform 'permanent and perennial forms of employment' has been made illegal. Workmen at Pepsi subsequently sought a counter-injunction to prevent the use of contract labour aimed at replacing them at the factory. They also stated that the management had no right to stop work unless they legally declared a lockout. When the workers insisted on resuming work and entered the factory, the police were brought in and several workers were arrested.

The office of the labour commissioner initiated conciliation proceedings. However, the management at Pepsi showed a sustained inclination to avoid tripartite meetings, failing to show up for most of the meetings. Finally, the labour department prohibited the lockout. The management, however, continued to insist on individual undertakings. Approximately, 40 workmen went back to work after signing the undertaking. Of these, 20 resigned from the union.

The onset of tensions between the management and labour at Pepsi began with a typical demand for higher wages and increments. The nature of the struggle, however, evolved in a manner that highlights the kind of industrial relations that are being sought to be inscribed by the management. They are somewhat atypical in the context of industrial relations practices pertaining to the organized sector in India. In the first place, the lack of uniformity in wages and the absence of a wage scale applicable to employees at similar positions within the organization, having similar qualifications and experience, is a significant departure from the organized sector wage practices in the country. It clearly indicates that the management preferred to keep wage negotiations at a purely individual level. In fact, the trouble at Pepsi began when workers unionized and put forward a charter of demands for the first time. Thereafter, as tensions escalated, the consistent approach of the management seemed to be to stick to interactions with individual workers, in effect bypassing the role of the union. As the struggle unfolded, the demand for higher, stages, ironically, receded from attention. What became the central focus of the dispute was the management's insistence on individual undertakings of good behaviour as a precondition for allowing workers to resume work.

The union challenged the demand for individual undertakings on two grounds. First, the management at Pepsi had insisted, both to the labour department and in public presentations of the case, that the workers were on strike. In view of this claim, the demand for a bond of good behaviour is an unlawful act. Under Clause 8 of the Fifth Schedule of the Industrial Disputes Act, 'to insist upon individual workmen who are on a legal strike, to sign a good conduct bond, as a precondition to allowing them to resume work' is subsumed under the category of 'unfair labour practices'. It may, of course, be pointed out that the strike was not, strictly speaking, a legal one in so far as the workers themselves had denied that it was a strike. The precise characterization of the struggle may be in doubt (whether strike or lockout). However, trade union leaders pointed out the following: first, the demand for higher wages was a legitimate ground on which to initiate a struggle; second, work to rule and stoppage of overtime work are recognized forms of struggle. In such a context, the insistence on an undertaking of good behaviour strongly suggests that the management was seeking to undermine the validity of established methods of workforce struggle. Finally, the management's insistence on individual undertakings went against the logic of collective bargaining. Where a union is engaged in a struggle, it alone can represent the workers; individual undertakings would negate the role of the union.[2]

Once the government asked the company to end the lockout, workers started returning to work. Several signed the bond and resigned from the union. According to union leaders, this was a consequence of several factors. First, the average age of the workers was 24. Workers here obviously lacked any experience in unionization. The company being new, the workforce did not have a history of union activities. Most of the workers came from neighbouring villages and were first-generation industrial workers. As such, union activities were not part of their social folklore. Second, the company had used a range of strategies to get its way—from putting pressure on the parents to send back their sons to work, to holding out the threat of job loss. Finally, and most important; the efficacy of the struggle was considerably weakened in the eyes of the workers because the company had access to a large number of contract workers who could be easily used to replace regular workers. That the company's production was not seriously affected by their struggle ultimately held out the most serious threat to the workers.

Bata, India, Bangalore: dispute over production targets

Bata is a Canadian company that has had a large presence in the Indian footwear market for several decades. At Bata, Bangalore workers have been waging, since 2000, a long struggle over production targets. Prior to 1998, the production target was 400 pairs of shoes per shift, based on four workmen per machine per shift. Two hundred extra pairs were produced on the payment of an incentive. In December 1998; a new machine with a higher capacity was introduced (machine no. 226 in company parlance). The normal production was raised to 720 pairs per shift, and the maximum production to 1,200 pairs per shift.

Workers resisted the introduction of the new machine on the following grounds.[3] The organization of work time in the earlier set of machines had allowed a 7-second dwell time (rest) between two cycles of 15 seconds each. With the introduction of the new machine, this dwell time was lost. Workers thus complained of additional work pressure. It became intolerable, particularly if the maximum production of 1,200 pairs of shoes was the target. The workmen did not accept the new production target and kept to the regular one of 400 pairs of shoes per shift.

In December 1999, another machine (no. 227), similar to machine no. 226, was introduced. At this time, the plant's union leadership was changed. While the earlier union (Bata Karmikara Sangha) had accepted the production targets set by the management, the newly elected union (Bata Employees Association) challenged these targets. Thus, a second union emerged. As tensions mounted between the new union leadership and the management, the general secretary of the union was suspended, and the organizing secretary and two other office-bearers were dismissed. The union took a stand that only the normal production target of the previous production arrangement would be adhered to, i.e. 400 pairs of shoes per shift.

In response, the management stated that the workers were deliberately slowing down production and it cut wages by 50 per cent. The workers' stand was that since the normal rate of production was being maintained, the management could justifiably refuse the payment of incentive (which is given only for maximum production) but that it was unlawful to offer half the wages. As tensions mounted, on 8 March 2000 all workers in the factory, including 90 women, were arrested. The company declared a lockout. The newer machine was taken out of the premises of the factory and lodged at a distant location, where it began to be operated with contract workers.

When the matter was referred to the government, the labour department recommended tripartite discussions to resolve the dispute. The management of Bata, however, showed a disinclination to participate in tripartite talks. In February 2001, the government prohibited the lockout. During the period of the lockout, 32 workmen were suspended and two union office-bearers were dismissed. However, as far as the central issues were concerned, nothing was resolved. The workers stuck to the normal production and refused to comply with the production targets of the new machinery. The management, in response, once slashed wages by 50 per cent and declared a lockout on 1 October 2001.

On 1 January 2002, the government prohibited the lockout and ruled that all workmen should work to contribute towards maximum production on all the machines. Further, all workmen would be required to provide an individual undertaking for maximum production. Following this directive, 40 workers returned to work, and provided the undertaking. All of them belonged to the older union, which had earlier signed, a bond with the management agreeing to the higher production targets. Workers affiliated to the Bata Employees Association did not return to work.[4]

In a remarkable similarity to the Pepsi case, the dispute at Bata highlights the inefficacy of a labour struggle in a context where a company's employees are easily replaceable by contract labourers. If the backbone of workers' bargaining strength lies in their capacity to hold up, reduce or stop production, then the potential availability and actual use of outside contract labour by employers significantly takes away the edge from the workers' bargaining leverage. At Bata, the management achieved this by shifting a machine to a different location, where it could be used by employing contract labour. Moreover, the Bata management demonstrated a sustained refusal to appear for tripartite talks, which were suggested by the government. Despite the management's refusal to negotiate with the state government, the latter's labour department appears to have played a role that clearly sought to affirm the management's position. Thus, not only did the government affirm the legitimacy of higher production targets, against the demands placed by labour, it also imposed a code of conduct, via an undertaking on individual employees. In a sense the labour department itself acted in a manner that diminished the trade union's role. These points will be taken up again in the concluding section.

Toyota Kirloskar Motors, Bangalore: dispute over work time and production targets

Toyota Kirloskar Motors (TKM) was set up at Bidadi, near Bangalore, as a joint collaboration between Toyota of Japan and Kirloskar—a Karnataka-based company with varied manufacturing interests— with 89 per cent and 11 per cent shares, respectively. The manufacturing of a range of standard, luxury and semi-luxury vehicles began in 1999, and sales started in January 2000. TKM began with a total investment of Rs 7 billion. Another Rs 4 billion was invested in the Toyota Technopark in the surrounding area for the development of automobile components industry.

TKM has a total employee strength of 1,500 of which around 500 are managers. The company believes in removing management–worker distinctions. As such, workers at TKM are referred to as team members. Managers and team members wear the same uniform and eat in the same canteen; and there are no closed office spaces. The management has also reiterated several times (over discussions) that there are no limits to vertical movement within the company. In Toyota's 50-year history, there have been many instances of team members reaching the rank of manager.

At the Bangalore branch, a large number of team members (almost 75 per cent) are on temporary contracts, without permanent placement within the company. They are known as trainees. Until 1999, the only organization of the workers was a team members' association, which had been sponsored by the management. Subsequently, the Toyota Kirloskar Motor Employees Union was formed. Initially, it was affiliated to INTUC (Indian National Tirade Union Congress, supported by the Congress [I]) and subsequently to CITU (Centre of Indian Trade Unions, supported by the CPI[M]).

An industrial relations crisis,[5] which erupted into a strike, began in the company in early January 2002. Initially, the central issues were production targets and shift timings: Subsequently, a more generalized struggle began over the management's suspension of two union office-bearers. Production at TKM is organized around a fixed target of one car per 8 minutes, 50 cars per shift and 100 cars per day. A major complaint of the workers has been that the shift time of 8 hours includes a half hour lunch break. As such, the 50 car per shift target actually has to be met within 7.5 hours. Workers complained that no minimum rest or fatigue time is allowed during the shift. Further, the shift timings are such that team members of the two shifts never meet. Workers have demanded continuous shifts rather than a morning one and another in the evening. Their major demand was that the shift timings and the production target should be adjusted after a proper evaluation via tripartite talks between the management, the union and the labour department of the government.

Another important issue was the regularization of trainees. Early in the company's history in Bangalore, there was a spontaneous movement of workers against their temporary status. The movement was brought under control fairly swiftly. Subsequently, the management entered into an MOU for a two-year training period, to be followed by regularization. In case a trainee failed to perform according to the company's standards, he would be placed in the Special Development Programme and subsequently either regularized or asked to leave. Despite the signing of the MOU, the criteria adopted for regularization have remained a matter of discontent for the workforce. The union has demanded a more open and standardized method of evaluation than what exists currently.

Early in January 2002, a trainee was placed in the Special Development Programme. The trainee challenged the management's decision and was subsequently dismissed. Tensions began to mount within the company over the demands being raised by the union. The workers demanded that the management must negotiate with the union and that the legal advisors of the union should be allowed to be part of the negotiations. Shortly afterwards, the services of two employees—the general secretary and the joint secretary of the union—were terminated and the president of the union was suspended. The workers went on strike from 10 January 2002. It was at this time that leadership of the union passed from INTUC to CITU.

The union, under the leadership of the CITU (Bangalore) general secretary (not a company worker), made an offer to the management that if the termination of employment of the union office-bearers were to be rescinded, the strike would be withdrawn and all other issues would be negotiated with the management. The management turned down the offer, stating their refusal to communicate with union leaders who were outsiders.

The labour commissioner provided the management with the option to convert the employment termination of the sacked employees to suspension orders, which could then be put through the process of enquiry, and to have the strike withdrawn on this condition. Once again, the management rejected the formula. Subsequently, a meeting was called by the labour minister. Here, the government suggested that the strike would be withdrawn unconditionally if the management agreed to reinstate the general secretary and the joint secretary after 15 days. In response, the management once again stated that they would not be part of any negotiations which involved union leaders who had been brought in from outside; and the workers could, if they wished, take the matter to court.

The management consistently took the stand that the demands put forward by the workers were based on false issues, which had been whipped up by external union leaders. In interviews and press statements, the company defended its compensation structure, claiming it was better than that of other companies in comparable areas. The termination and suspension orders were defended on grounds of indiscipline and misbehaviour. However, the central issues, that of work time and production target, were not substantively addressed in the management's statements.[6]

The strike continued. In the meantime, Section 144 of the Indian Penal Code (prohibiting public gatherings or meetings) was imposed on a 5 km area surrounding the company. A number of workers who had gathered at a bus stop close by were arrested on charges of violating the order; they were subsequently released on bail. In a surprise move, in late February 2002, the government declared the strike to be illegal. It referred three issues for adjudication to the labour court: employment termination of the two union office-bearers, whether the strike was justified or not, and change in shift timings. The other issues raised by the union were not referred to the court. Workers returned to work on 1 March 2002.

Workers at TKM returned to work in a context where the central issues raised in the dispute, i.e. an adjustment in the shift timings and production target, were not addressed. The following points are particularly noteworthy in this dispute. The management consistently refused to communicate with the union leadership. Union office bearers were suspended. The management at no time recognized the external leaders of the union as their legitimate interlocutors. In interviews, the management stated that it was prepared to hold talks with the company's union; in fact, it did so on a regular basis. In the management's perception, the demand for a revision of the work time and an adjustment in the production target was entirely the result of the intervention of external leaders in the company's union. It was therefore not prepared to consider this demand as one on which negotiations could be held.

There appeared to be a systematic effort to inscribe and institutionalize a pattern of industrial relations wherein negotiations for the collective interests of the workforce could be avoided. In interviews, the management stated that the majority of issues that arose were everyday problems pertaining to work or individual employee needs, which could be addressed through one-on-one interactions with the workers. Thus, the union's role was essentially limited. It needs to be underlined that in the initial years of the company, the management itself had floated and promoted a team workers' union. In doing so, it obviously saw a central role for itself in shaping the character and agenda of this union. The union's function, again, would be essentially to address problems related to minor adjustments on the shop floor, work assignment and so on. When the workers launched their own union under CITU's leadership, the management's response was hostile. Clearly, it considered vital issues, such as the reorganization of work time or a reduction in the production target, to be outside the purview of union activities.

More importantly, the TKM management was obviously confident of the state's support. The labour department at two stages did suggest methods of conciliation that would involve the trade union. However; the management easily rejected the government's suggestion that the two employees whose services had been terminated should be reinstated. The labour department's final act was to declare the strike illegal and to ignore the workers' demands for a revision of the production target and an adjustment in the shift timings.

3. Industrial policies and industrial relations strategies.

Sufficient evidence is available of the links between specific industrialization strategies and particular industrial relations (IR) regimes. In a context where states have an acknowledged need to provide space for multinationals, it is not unusual for government agencies to comply with MNCs' preferred pattern of IR. This has been particularly apparent in the East Asian economies, which have embarked on aggressive export-oriented growth models with the aid of foreign capital. Thus, in both the Philippines and Malaysia, the government enacted rules that restricted the amount of overtime payment; refused to legislate equal pay for equal work for men and women; and exempted foreign investors from considerable labour and employment legislation (Kuruvilla and Venkataratnam, 1996). Frederick Deyo's work (1989) has definitively established that the foundations of South Korea's industrial development lay in the highly autocratic labour practices within firms, supported by restrictive labour legislation. Deyo's later research on Thailand shows that with the onset of liberalized trade regimes and greater receptivity to multinational capital, employers in Thai manufacturing industries increasingly prefer to work with easier mechanisms for downsizing—flexible and contract-based—rather than permanent employment. Emerging industrial relations policies and institutions logically reflect these preferences (Deyo, 1995).

In India, the state's accommodation of multinationals' industrial relations practices raises a very different set of questions. Unlike the East Asian economies, which have achieved remarkable levels of development on the basis of foreign direct investment and export-oriented growth models, India's adoption of a marketized and internationally-oriented growth model is relatively recent. More importantly, in contrast to the authoritarian nature of most East Asian states, India has had a fairly long engagement with institutions of political democracy and strong traditions of leftism. In the first few decades of the republic, there was a pronounced commitment of the state to redistributive populism. As is well known, democracy and populist politics have had to be substantively accommodated to an increasingly pragmatic commitment to marketization policies. Economic reforms have revealed many apparent contradictions between marketization and democracy in a low income, highly inegalitarian context. These contradictions are apparent in a variety of spheres—from reservations to subsidies. Thus, state agencies have been embroiled in conflicting pulls and tensions, which are typically resolved via ad hoc political settlements and compromises, rather than by arriving at definitive, paradigmatic resolutions.

The three case studies of the industrial relations disputes of Bangalore-based MNCs underline the ways in which democratic institutions are being reframed in the context of economic reforms, without necessarily changing the legal–institutional framework in a manner that may have caused political ripples. The case studies reveal a uniform pattern. First, although each of the companies examined has a recognized union, the management consistently acted to bypass the process of arriving at negotiated settlements with the unions. In each of the three cases, the management refused to participate in tripartite discussions, did not acknowledge the external leaders of the union, and insisted on individual undertakings.

The role of external leaders in unions is a long accepted feature of union activities in the Indian scenario. External leaders typically act as advisors, often providing advice of a legal nature; or they stand for union elections in which they may be elected to the post of president of a company's union. The role of external leaders has often been critical in linking firm-level unions to the national trade union federations and to their allied political parties. Frequently, the office-bearers retain their positions within the firm's union long after they have retired as employees of the firm. Thus, the role of the external leader has been widely accepted in the history of unionization in the Indian context. In such a context, the TKM management's refusal to meet with the external leaders was a denial of the trade union practices of the land in which they had set up business.

Second, the Karnataka government's labour department has played a supportive role for MNCs. Karnataka has been one of the earliest and more robust supporters of the central government's liberalization policies. From the early nineties onwards, the state government has made efforts to facilitate private sector entry into business, to streamline the civil service and to create an enabling environment for privatization. The Karnataka Economic Restructuring Loan of $150 million, which was negotiated with the World Bank in May 2000, has further underscored the importance of creating a legal–institutional framework supportive of private investment. In such a context, the government's priority obviously has been to reassure MNCs of a non-problematic framework for labour relations.

Government officials acknowledge that the management in MNCs is unwilling to participate in tripartite negotiations and they bring in a set of industrial relations practices—possibly developed in their parent organizations—that may not be in keeping with the practices prevailing in India. Beyond this, state officials are not willing to confront the question that these IR practices are reshaping collective bargaining institutions in ways that are detrimental to workers' organizations.[7]

In each of the case studies discussed in the previous section, the government's decisions led to a situation where workers—at least a section of the workers—returned to work after signing individual undertakings and bypassing the union. In terms of the specific demands of the workers—wages, production targets, work time—the outcome of the dispute in each of the three cases went against the workers. More significantly, the actions of the management and the government created a context where the trade union was no longer a serious interlocutor in industrial disputes.

4. Trade unions

Responses to the changing environment

Trade union leaders do not necessarily see the developments described above as failures; instead, they are considered to be steps in a long line of struggles.[8] Despite the obvious defeat of the workers in the TKM dispute, a leading trade unionist saw the struggle as one which actually 'gave a serious warning to the management'.[9]

At the heart of the trade union movement, there appear to be serious ambiguities in conceptualizing the relationship between a political struggle and an economic one. National level trade unions have, throughout the period of economic reforms, kept up a sustained critique of liberalization policies. This critique has intensified during the tenure of the NDA government, particularly since 2001. As mentioned in the introduction, the 2001–02 budget was accompanied by proposals for wide-ranging changes in labour laws to suit a market-friendly economy. The thrust of the proposed amendments was to facilitate the process of easing workers out of presently permanent and secure employment; and to create a redefined framework wherein labour can be engaged for jobs that are flexible, time-bound, and can be easily terminated. In the wake of the announcement of the proposed changes, trade unions of different affiliations had come together in a rare demonstration of unity. The presentation of the 2002–03 budget drew similar critical responses from the trade unions.

Frequently, however, this critique has not had an effective impact on what is happening to labour and unions at the enterprise or plant levels. Earlier studies have shown that even within public sector enterprises (PSEs) that are assumed to be citadels of trade union strength, unions have been unable to resist restructuring processes, which in their perception negatively affect labour. Crook's work (1993) on steel plants shows that up to 20 per cent of labour in public sector steel units was employed on contractual terms and they were denied the facilities enjoyed by permanent workers. My own research on three large central public sector units in Bangalore city has revealed that through the increasing adoption of voluntary retirement schemes (VRS), labour is being removed from the public sector. The lack of growth in organized sector employment has meant that such labour is increasingly pushed into the uncertain world of the Unorganized sector. Public sector trade unions are by and large unable to stem this tide (RoyChowdhury, 2003). In the private sector, labour displacement without the payment of compensation and the relegation of labour to the informal sector are processes that are occurring across regions and industrial sectors.[10] The trade union movement has been largely unable to counter these tendencies. Thus, while the critique of liberalization was being sustained at the political level, struggles around specific economic issues at the micro-level were certainly characterized by many defeats and setbacks.

Union leaders acknowledge these features of the trade union movement. A senior leader of the CITU pointed out that the economic struggle of the working class and its leadership by the trade union movement was faltering to a great extent. 'The trade union movement became ineffective when it abandoned its own economic struggle. Political slogan is unrealistic devoid of economic struggle.'[11] According to one section of the CITU leadership there is now an urgent need for the trade union movement to turn towards the economic struggle, whereby its attention would be predominantly focused on rebuilding the power of the working class through gains at the workplace. Thus, if the critical rhetoric of trade unions at the national level can be termed the political struggle, then industrial action over work-related issues at the firm or industry level could be thought of as the economic struggle. There is now a growing awareness that the labour movement can be strengthened only by concentrated action on the latter front, i.e. by winning battles at the micro-level.

The case studies presented here show that an exclusive focus on firm-level issues is unlikely to be effective in addressing workers' problems unless these issues can be related to the broader changing economic policy environment. In the cases presented above, there appeared to be no clear conception of what would be the ideological/intellectual underpinnings of a conflict based on firm-level issues. In each of the three cases, the entire discourse of the struggle was defined in terms of the workers' specific demands—around higher wages, adjustment of production targets, or shift timings. Unionists and workers appeared to be entirely focused on firm-level issues. The broad context of these issues is determined by the fact that the government is inclined towards supplying MNCs with cheap, flexible and compliant labour.

However, the trade unions' struggle, by remaining confined to firm-level economic issues, appeared to be incapable of addressing the broader links between the state's industrial policy, which is supportive of MNCs, and the changing dynamics of industrial relations. In private conversations, trade unionists acknowledged that they do indeed have a critique of multinationals' entry into the economy; but given the rapidly deteriorating employment situation in the state, they were not, at the practical level, opposed to workers taking up jobs in MNCs. How, then, did they propose to protect workers, given that MNC industrial relations practices appear to go against the grain of negotiated settlements and collective bargaining institutions? There was no substantive answer to this question. The underlying thrust of the struggles thus remained ambiguously conceptualized and articulated.[12]

Apart from the level of conceptualization and discourse, in each of the three case studies, the trade unions' lack of leverage vis-à-vis the government and the management was obviously the function of a specific structural factor: the ample availability of contract labour, which could be used by management to replace regular employees. In a situation where the company's production schedule was not seriously disrupted by striking workers, it was difficult, if not impossible, to sustain the workers' confidence in strikes as effective tools of collective bargaining.

It would seem that there is an urgent need for the trade union movement to address issues involving contract labourers and, more broadly, the unorganized sector. While this need is in principle recognized by trade union leaders, no concrete steps have been taken to include unorganized workers in the activities of unions. The absence of such activities is particularly striking in the case of contract workers. They belong to the most exploited categories of the workforce, and their jobs are often insecure. Moreover, as the following cases illustrate, they often work in close contact with regular workers.

Unions and contract labour: informality within the formal sector

The highly exploitative and insecure nature of contract labour is widely recognized. It was this recognition that underlay the passage of the Contract Labour (Abolition and Regulation) Act, 1970, at the centre. The main objective of the act was to make illegal the use of contract labour in what was termed as 'permanent and perennial forms of employment' (Clause 10). Despite this act reaching the statute book, the regularization of the services of employees who work as contract labourers has proved to be elusive. I cite below cases from Karnataka.[13]

According to the Factories Act, 1948, all industrial establishments employing more than 250 employees are legally bound to maintain canteen services for employees. Based on this law, the Karnataka Industrial Canteens Act was passed in April 1997 by the then ruling Janata Dal. The act stipulates that workers in industrial canteens should not be employed as contract workers; they must be given permanent appointments, in so far as canteen service falls within the permanent and perennial forms of employment under the Contract Labour Act. Soon after the Karnataka Industrial Canteens enactment, industrial employers went to court seeking a stay of the order. The Bangalore High Court dismissed the employers' petition in March 1998. The employers then moved the Supreme Court. On 2 February 2001, the apex court upheld the Karnataka government's order. The petitioners then moved the Supreme Court for a review petition. This too was dismissed in April 2001.

However, in an extraordinary turn of events, the Congress (I) government in Karnataka withdrew the act on 1 August 2001. Thus, the Karnataka Industrial Canteens Act, upheld by successive Bangalore High Court and Supreme Court decisions, became null and void. CITU has once again taken the case to the High Court. In the meantime, the livelihoods of several thousand industrial canteen workers are on hold.

At the MICO (Motor India Company Ltd, a German firm) factory in Bangalore, of approximately 5,000 employees, 600 are contract labourers. On 19 September 2001, the MICO Contract Workers' Union organized a protest march to the chief labour commissioner's office with a charter of demands, which included better canteen services, a punching system to record their time at work, and a 25 per cent wage increase. Contract workers in MICO are not allowed to use the canteen services available for permanent workers. They have to eat and drink in a separate makeshift shed, where there are only stone slabs to sit on, amidst highly unhygienic surroundings. The food comes from a cheap outside hotel. The union demanded better, more humane canteen facilities for contract workers. Further, these workers are given a token at the gate every morning as a mark of their attendance. However, there is no mechanism to mark their overtime labour. As such, the contractor frequently denies them overtime pay. The union's second demand therefore was a time-punching system, which would record the contract workers' time at work. In response to these demands, the labour commissioner sent an inspection team. However, no action was taken on the team's report. Neither was the union allowed access to the report.

In situations where regular and contract labourers work together within the same company—in different, and sometimes similar, functions—the conflict of interests between the two sections, rather than commonalties, have featured centrally in industrial disputes. Trade union leaders acknowledge, in principle, that the organized workers' movement should address issues affecting contract labourers. However, in specific instances, trade unions have failed to provide support to contract labourers, as the following case highlights. Public sector firms now employ a significant proportion of their workers under contract appointments. At the Electronic City unit of ITI Bangalore, 125 contract workers were abruptly sacked on 10 October 2000. These men and women had worked for the company for 10–15 years. As such, they were not young enough to be immediately employable outside, even if such employment were to be readily available. The ITI Contract Workers' Union took up the matter with the state labour commissioner. The case is still pending, with the fate of the 125 employees whose services were terminated hanging in the air. At the time of termination, the ITI Employees Union refused to support the ITI Contract Workers' Union—in what was a dramatic demonstration of the division that plagues the relationship between the organized workforce and contract workers.[14]

The impermanent nature of contract employment places contract labourers outside the purview of conventional trade union activities. Management, for the most part, are unwilling to negotiate with contract workers' unions. Any threat of a strike leads to termination of employment. Thus, contract workers themselves are wary of unionized activities.[15] Moreover, the right to terminate employment gives enormous power to the employer in a situation where there is abundant labour in the market, and where the labour force is weak, unskilled, insecure economically and non-unionized.

As the case studies of the Bangalore-based multinationals showed, it is the easy availability of workers on contract, who are willing to work for lower wages and benefits, that significantly takes away the bargaining leverage of unionized workers. The crux of the matter; recognized by many trade unionists, is the trade union movement's preoccupation with protecting the wages and privileges of a small and shrinking organized workforce (employed in PSEs, multinationals and large private sector companies). On the other hand, a large and expanding unorganized sector functions on the margins of the economy, with inadequate wages and little access to any kind of social insurance.

Trade union leaders recognize that in such a context, organized workers are 'chasing an illusion'.[16] In the last decade, there have in fact been attempts by some trade unions, particularly by those with affiliations to the organized Left, to incorporate within their organizational structures workers belonging to the informal sectors. In Karnataka, CITU has a membership of 100,000, of which more than half belong to the informal sector—40,000 *bidi* workers, 5,000 anganwadi workers, 5,000–6,000 plantation workers, 5,000 hotel workers and 5,000 to 10,000 small-scale industry workers. Despite the formal linkages forged through such membership, the trade union movement has yet to substantively align itself with the interests and issues of unorganized sector workers. At the level of rhetoric, trade unionists have said that organized workers should close ranks with the unorganized sector; and that a minimum living wage should be the broad-based demand put forward on behalf of all workers. In practical terms, understandably, formal sector workers, who enjoy infinitely better wages and benefits, are unwilling to let go of their privileges. As such, the relationship between the formal and informal sectors, as outlined above, remains conflict-ridden.[17] While unions like CITU have committed themselves to informal sector workers, the issues affecting the two sectors are handled separately. Several unionists acknowledged that the political weakness of the trade union movement stems from its declining constituency and its inability to broaden its politics to incorporate the unorganized sector. At the level of practical politics, the struggle to broaden and unify the movement has yet to start.

5. Conclusion

While the decline of unions is acknowledged to be a worldwide phenomenon of recent origin, there has not been much systematic thinking on the specific dynamics of this decline or its possible reversal. The case studies examined here present a very narrow set of evidence on the dynamics of this decline. They allow us to raise some issues rather than to draw generalizations. In the first place, the kind of industrial relations systems that MNCs would naturally wish to inscribe is possibly out of keeping with the broader sociopolitical economic milieu of the country. For example, Japanese industrial relations are built on the notion of almost organic compatibility between the management and workers—with a workforce committed to cooperation rather than confrontation, unions adhering to the idea of 'enterprise as community' and, a culture where workers aspire for, rather than challenge, the superior status of managers (Gordon, 1993). This broad ambience of cooperation could emerge in the context of Japan's rapid post-war economic growth where the fruits of development have been widely shared in the form of high wages and high standards of living. In India, however, the context is one of poverty and stark inequalities in opportunities. This makes cooperation across classes an unrealistic goal, even within the reified atmosphere of a MNC. When companies attempt to limit institutionalized methods of expression of grievances and negotiations, the resulting labour relations may be marked by disharmony.

The second issue concerns the role of the state. In the period following independence, an important pillar of India's welfarist developmental model, as was the case in many other developing countries, was the state–labour pact—underwritten by the state's redistributive commitment to labour. The institutional anchoring of the state–labour pact was a form of corporatism; that is, the state became an arena for resolving disputes between capital and labour. Through public spending and sympathetic regulation, the corporatist state sought to mediate capital–labour relations (Cook et al., 1994). The process of globalization has largely diluted the state–labour pact. As mentioned in the introduction, while there have been very few changes in India's broadly worker-friendly labour legislation, in each of the cases discussed above, the state appeared to side with the management when conflicts arose. The withdrawal of the state's protection and patronage has occurred in a context where increasing legitimacy has been accorded to the adoption of market-friendly approaches towards industrial development. However, marketization has not spelt labour prosperity in the Indian context. Given this situation, labour's bargaining power in the unorganized sector is minimal and is declining even in the so-called organized sector, as highlighted by the case studies presented in this chapter. Thus while the state's patronage has declined, the market has not emerged as an alternative source of support for the workforce.

Yet, this is an undefined situation in many ways. If liberalization is predicated on a neo-liberal theory of individualism, this theory is difficult to sustain in a context of deep, structural inequalities. The role of the state—as a guarantor and protector of the weak, particularly as marketization processes intensify—remains an area of debate and contestation. This is particularly so in a democratic framework. Trade unions acknowledge the difficulties of battling MNCs in a context where state support for labour is declining and where large numbers of workers in the unorganized sector further weaken the bargaining leverage of those in the organized sector. The present moment of the working class struggle is therefore largely undefined, lacking a clear sense as to the direction in which the struggle is headed. It is for this reason that the question of workers' struggles and organizations, the need to redefine their forms and discourses, has as much relevance today as it did in an earlier era. Thus, economic reforms and globalization underline the critical importance of working class politics, rather than undermine it as is commonly thought.

Notes

1 Information on the Pepsi dispute was gathered from meetings with workers, union office-bearers as well as from e-mail communication with Mr Deepak Jolly, corporate vice president, Pepsi head office, Gurgaon.

2 Meeting with Pepsi workers and union leaders at a CITU convention in Bangalore on 1 March 2002.

3 Information on the Bata dispute was gathered from employees and union office-bearers.

4 This was the situation prevailing in March 2002 when research for the present chapter was conducted.

5 Information on the Toyota Kirloskar Motor dispute was gathered at a meeting with Dr Shripad Bhatt, corporate spokesperson for TKM; meetings with Mr Meenakshi Sundaram, CITU general secretary (Bangalore), who was in charge of the TKM case for CITU; and from press reports.

6 'Toyota Kirloskar Motor Clarifies' press information released on 9 February 2002.

7 Interview with Mr Narasimharaju, labour commissioner, Karnataka government, and the deputy labour commissioner on 11 March 2002.

8 Interview with Mr K. Subramanium, CITU leader, on 12 March, 2002, in Bangalore.

9 Interview with Mr Meenakshi Sundaram, general secretary of CITU, Bangalore, on 1 March 2002.

10 This process has been widely documented; for a sampling, see, Avachat (1978); Breman (1996); RoyChowdhury (1996; 1997).

11 Interview with Mr VJ.K. Naik, general secretary of CITU (Karnataka) on 28 February 2002.

12 For a discussion of the new trends in unionism, in which wider solidarities and larger issues are sacrificed for the pursuit of short-term and narrower interests, see Breman (1999).

13 The following section has been adapted from Supriya RoyChowdhury, 'The Law and Labour', *The Hindu*, Bangalore edition, 12 January 2002.

14 Interview with Mr N. Veeraswamy, general secretary of MICO Contract Employees Association, and president of the BEL Contract Labour Association on 3 January 2002.
15 Interview with Mr Veeraswamy.
16 Interview with Mr V.J.K. Naik, CITU.
17 Many scholars no longer accept the thesis of a strict duality between the formal and Informal sectors. Thus, not only are different segments of the labour force interlinked by broader social relationships, but there may be professional interconnections (such as moonlighting by formal sector waiters) as well. On this theme, see Holmstorm (1984); Breman (1999). However; there has been very little research on why these connections have not provided the foundations of a unified trade union movement across the formal and informal sectors. For an exploratory paper on this theme, see RoyChowdhury (2002).

References

Avachat, A. 1978. 'Bidi Workers of Nipani', *Economic and Political Weekly* 13(29–30): 1176–78 and 1203–5.

Breman, Jan. 1996. *Footloose Labour: Working in India's Informal Economy*. Cambridge: Cambridge University Press.

——. 1999. 'The Formal Sector: An Introductory Review' and 'The Informal Sector: A Concluding Review', in Jonathan Parry, Jan Breman and Karin Kapadia (eds), *The Worlds of Indian Industrial Labour.* Contributions to Indian Sociology, Occasional Studies No. 9, pp. 1–42 and 407–32, New Delhi: Sage.

Cook, Maria Lorena and Kevin J. Middlebrook. (eds). 1994. *The Politics of Economic Restructuring: State-Society Relations and Regime Change in Mexico.* San Diego: Center for U.S.–Mexican Studies.

Crook, N. 1993. 'Labour and the Steel Towns', in P. Robb (ed.), *Dalit Movements and the Meanings of Labour in India*, pp. 338–54, New Delhi: Oxford University Press.

Deyo, Frederick. 1989. *Beneath the Miracle: Labour Subordination in East Asian Development.* Berkeley: University of California Press.

——. 1995. 'Capital, Labour and State in Thai Industrial Restructuring: The Impact of Global Economic Transformations', in David Smith and Joseph Boroz (eds), *A New World Order: Global Transformations in the Late Twentieth Century*, pp. 131–43, Connecticut: Greenwood Press.

Gordon, Andrew. 1993. 'Conditions for the Disappearance of the Japanese Working Class Movement', in Elizabeth Perry (ed.), *Putting Class in Its Place: Worker Identities in East Asia*, Berkeley: Institute of East Asian Studies, University of California.

Holmstorm, M. 1984. *Industry and Inequality: The Social Anthropology of Indian Labour.* Cambridge: Cambridge University Press.

Kuruvilla, Sarosh and C.S. Venkataratnam. 1996. 'Economic Development and Industrial Relations: The case of South and South-East Asia' *Industrial Relations Journal* 27(1): 9–23.

RoyChowdhury, Supriya. 1996. 'Industrial Restructuring, Unions and the State: The Case of Ahmedabad Textile Labourers', *Economic and Political Weekly* 81(8): L7–L13.

——. 1997. 'The State, Private Sector and Labour: The Political Economy of Jute Industry Modernization, West Bengal, 1986–90', *Journal of the Indian School of Political Economy* 9(1): 119–27.

——. 2002. 'Old Classes and New Spaces: Unorganized Labour, New Unions, and India's Economic Reforms' Paper presented at Network of Scholars of South Asian Politics and Political Economy. 1–3 July 2002. Ann Arbor: Centre for South Asian Studies, University of Michigan.

——. 2003. 'Public Sector Restructuring and Democracy: The State, Labour and Trade Unions in India', *Journal of Development Studies* 39(3): 29–50.

23

Politics of exclusion

Jan Breman

Source: *The Poverty Regime in Village India: Half a Century of Work and Life at the Bottom of the Rural Economy of South Gujarat* (New Delhi: Oxford University Press, 2007), pp. 411–39.

The state and rural labour

The central planning and management of the national economy that was so prominent in the first decades following independence made way in the 1990s for cutting back on the presence of the state and its agencies in the economic process. This meant not so much that the government stopped supporting capital as a factor of production, but that it no longer intervened in the composition and operation of the labour market. At all levels and in all sectors, the bureaucracy stopped mediating between employers and employees. The advent of neoliberalism meant that the free play of social forces would no longer be harnessed by imposing obstacles on the dynamics of the private sector, while the expanded public sector was rigorously squeezed and streamlined. A fair deal for labour was no longer part of the repertoire of good governance, and the extensive legislation that had been built up over many decades in regulating and upgrading conditions of employment became obsolete. When Manmohan Singh, as Prime Minister of India, went on record saying that the days of the 'licence raj' were over for good, he basically confirmed that cheap labour would continue to be the cornerstone of economic policy, with the withdrawal of even minimal rights to protection and human dignity.

The regime change did not occur from one day to the next, but developed gradually and is in fact still in progress. Gujarat has been resolutely at the forefront of this trend since the end of the 1970s. Nowadays discussion is focused on the rearguard action by the trade unions to try and ensure that the legislation regulating formal sector employment remains intact. It is characteristic of the enormous difference in the articulation of interests that the erosion of the rights of the masses in the informal sector, which includes more than 90 per cent of the working population in India, has attracted much less attention. In the first place, the Minimum Wages Act for agricultural labour has slowly faded away from the policy agenda. The reluctant and delayed introduction of the Act, inadequate monitoring of compliance once it did become law, and unwillingness to concede an increase from time to time—the last revision in Gujarat dates back to 2002 when it was fixed at Rs 50—culminated in the decision to no longer implement the Act. The Contract Workers Act, which aimed to regulate and eventually abolish this form of employment, was repealed when employers were given permission to replace permanent labourers by contract workers. This trend is illustrated by the changed system of industrial relations in the Atul factories, as discussed in the preceding chapter. The authorities in Gujarat have never applied the Interstate Migrant Workers Act, which aimed to improve the lot of migrant workers, including the sugarcane cutters from Maharashtra who moved around the south Gujarat plain seeking work, the workers from Andhra Pradesh in the Chikhli quarries, and the Halpatis from south Gujarat who, for at least three generations, have migrated back and forth in the dry season to work in the brick kilns and saltpans near Mumbai. When I discussed these issues with the labour commissioner for Gujarat in the course of a meeting with him in Gandhinagar, I was told that all these changes were part of the government's policy to not intervene in the free movement of labour in any way. The Abolition of Bonded Labour Act, which was intended to remove the last remains of the traditional system of attached labour in agriculture, has not been used to combat the return of practices of neobondage, which particularly affect the massive armies of labour migrants. There is a widespread belief among politicians and policy-makers that the protection of labour benefits only a small privileged elite. Preserving the rights of a group considered the aristocrats of the working class is seen as an obstacle to flexibilization, which permits labour power to be hired and fired according to the needs of the moment. It is hard to believe that the neoliberal lobby, which advocates the unfettered working of the market and the transition to an informal labour regime, has so easily created an ideological climate in which it is possible to systematically ignore the brutal way in which the men, women, and children at the foot of the economy are dealt with. Protection and security, and the right to a minimum wage and decent work have become taboo words, and are seen as indications of politically incorrect thinking.

A new scheme to offer employment to people without work may mark a turning point in the low priority given to alleviating rural poverty in recent decades. The programme led to the adoption of the National Rural Employment Guarantee Act in 2005. A parallel package of social security benefits aims to protect the most vulnerable segments of the workforce. Both initiatives suggest that public intervention is necessary to halt the pauperization of the rural proletariat. Whether this really is a radical change of policy course will depend on the extent to which these proposals are genuinely implemented on a large scale. Impact studies have mainly focused on economic benefits while neglecting to find out how rural works schemes have given a boost to social assertion and collective action of the targeted beneficiaries (S. Patel 2006).[1]

Strong political opposition in the preparatory stage has resulted in compromises that jeopardize the achievement of the stated objective. The cautious start to the country-wide programme of public works is in itself understandable. None of the districts in which the four villages of my fieldwork are located have so far benefited from the first phase of the new Act. The choice of backward areas where the degree of rural poverty is highest suggests that policy-makers concur with the notion that underemployment is mainly found in the more remote hinterlands. This perception fails to take account of the displacement of local labour by migrants, which explains why the Halpatis are excluded from sufficient work and income although their habitat is in the zone of the high economic growth so characteristic of the central plain of south Gujarat. As shown in the preceding chapters, owners of agrarian and non-agrarian capital actually systematically prefer to employ labour from other regions, often from other states. The enormous circulation of labour throughout the whole subcontinent is facilitated by the fact that transport costs are borne by the migrants themselves. By paying an advance, employers or their agents ensure that the labourers are tied to them for as long as they are required.

Underlying the government's point of view is the assumption that poverty alleviation boils down to creating more, and more sustainable, employment. An altogether different approach would be to raise the productivity of the rural proletariat by a new round of land reforms. The way in which this operation was conducted in the mid-1950s strengthened the position of medium- and large-scale farmers, most of whom happened to be members of upwardly-mobile castes. In subsequent decades, a second wave of redistribution has been going on almost unnoticed: the privatization of waste land to which the land-poor and landless segments of the village population also traditionally had access. As these common property resources were withdrawn from the public domain, they came into the hands of the established landowners. The fact that agriculture lagged behind in the sectoral distribution of growth is linked to the extent to which the arable land has been utilized. The extremely uneven distribution of agrarian capital, the concentration of land-ownership among the rural minority belonging to the dominant castes, and the persistent landlessness of the bottom segments of the village population is counter-productive to more intensive agriculture. Making land accessible to households which had been made landless in the near or more distant past would put an end to their exclusion from rights to property.

A second public intervention of no less importance concerns two proposed bills aimed at improving the deprivation of the 300 million people in India who are made to work in the informal sector of the economy, and who earn less than Rs 5000 a month (later on raised to Rs 6500) per capita. The first is the 2005 Unorganised Sector Workers' Social Security Bill, which offers workers, on payment of a premium, the right to: (a) health insurance for self, spouse, and children younger than eighteen years; (b) maternity benefits for female workers or wives of male workers; (c) life insurance to cover death and disability arising out of accidents; and (d) old-age pension for workers above the age of sixty. A Social Security Fund is to be set up, to which the employee, the employer and the government will contribute equally. If the worker is unable to pay the one rupee a day contribution, that too will be paid by the government. An extensive apparatus, with social security boards at central and state levels, which are then further subdivided into district committees, will have to be set up to administer and provide the services. Workers must register themselves to participate in the scheme and each participant will be given a social security number and an identification card which can be used throughout the country.

This extensive and ambitious scheme has had its critics from the very beginning. In a first round of comments on the drafted bill, Hirway condemns the plan to bring all informal sector workers under the same authority (Hirway 2006). In her view, the targeted beneficiaries are far too heterogeneous for this to be a successful formula. She makes a number of proposals, including allowing contract workers and those employed temporarily by formal sector companies access to the same social security provisions as permanent employees. Hirway also questions whether all categories of informal workers have the same needs. Depending on the specific situation, the priority may lie with shelter, sanitation, or schooling. Why should this heterogeneity not be taken into account? She calls for a distinction to be made between informal sector workers at the foot of the economy and those who are slightly or even much better-off. By taking account of this variation, the level of the contributions can be adjusted depending on the degree of vulnerability of the different categories of workers. Hirway rejects the suggestion that BPL households should be exempt from the contribution, because their magnitude may have been inflated due to faulty registration. To avoid the problem of a top-heavy bureaucracy, she recommends a more participatory approach, in which the beneficiaries have a greater say in the delivery of the services. In this respect she refers to the important role that village councils, self-help groups, and trade unions can play. Her recommendation to strengthen the gender dimension of the social safety net is especially valuable. It is all too often forgotten that half the informal sector workers are women. Although the proposed act is long overdue, Hirway warns that unless the design and implementation is revised drastically, there is a chance that the social security of informal sector workers will get worse, rather than better.

In a similar argument, Dev (2006) also speaks of the agonizing reappraisal with which efforts are made, in opposition to the neoliberal ideology, to get the problem of the working poor back to the top of the political agenda. He is sceptical, however, of the efficacy of generating self-employment for the rural poor, an approach that is strongly advocated on many sides. Dev concludes that micro-entrepreneurs have trouble getting off the ground because of lack of cheap credit, and refers to critical assessments showing that the poorest of the poor are excluded from participation in self-help groups, while the somewhat better-off segments among the poor meet with resistance from the vested interests in their efforts to escape poverty. His conclusions are compatible with my own findings, as reported in the section of this book devoted to Chikhligam. Dev agrees with Hirway that the top-down approach that now characterizes the implementation of the social security package should be replaced by a more decentralized mode of operation. In that context he calls for panchayati raj institutions to be given a prominent role. Lastly, he correctly observes that a health insurance scheme is in itself no guarantee that all workers will indeed have timely and adequate access to doctors, clinics, and medicines.

Another package of measures, which perhaps promises to be of even greater significance and urgency, is the 2005 Unorganised Sector Workers (Conditions of Workers and Livelihood Promotion) Bill. This aims to improve the modalities of employment, not only by actually enforcing the existing bans on child labour and all forms of bonded labour, but also by combating the unbridled prolongation of the working day. Dev argues that it is also necessary to fix a minimum wage, as the guarantee of work alone is not enough to lift the poor above the poverty line. Without an increase in the excessively low pay, the measures will not achieve the desired effect. Among the list of entitlements which the working poor should acquire, Dev sees the right to organize themselves, the principle of non-discrimination in the payment of wages, safety at work, and absence of sexual harassment as essential. He is more optimistic than Hirway about the impact of the statutory measures, but calls for more discussion to improve the quality of their implementation. Both economists, who support their arguments with authoritative expertise, will undoubtedly continue to make a valuable contribution to the ongoing debate.

Bleak prospects for a new deal

While the comments made in the first round raised doubts about the practicalities of the proposed set of recommendations, even more critical reservations were voiced when the National Commission for Enterprises in the Unorganised Sector presented in 2006 its final report on the introduction of a national minimum social security scheme, ultimately covering all unorganized/informal workers (NCEUS Report 2006). The main provisions are the same as listed in the draft proposal, but wouldn't it make more sense—as several commentators argue—to opt for a gradualist and cautious approach? The suggestion coming from different corners is that the ambitions of the bill should be toned down to a more realistic level instead of reaching out to all informal sector workers for which the state simply lacks the administrative machinery as well as the political will. A.V. Jose has not minced words in expressing his misgivings about the course of action recommended by pointing out that the protective security systems which came about in the industrialized countries were the outcome, and not the cause, of improved living standards and productivity. His sweeping statement needs to be verified carefully. It is certainly misleading to say that labour rights and welfare benefits in western economies were only granted once the transition to an industrial economy was completed. Correcting the skewed balance between capital and labour was part and parcel of the process of industrialization itself. Jose further argues that the provisions for social protection against adversity cannot be imposed from above, but need to grow endogenously on their own. The transition to modern welfare institutions was historically preceded by experimentation with a number of promotional benefits initiated by a wide variety of social actors (cooperatives, trade unions, and other civil associations). While acknowledging that there is a compelling case for targeting assistance primarily towards the working poor in the rural hinterlands of India, he does not fail to notice the absence of adequate space for collective action in a landscape of labour which is highly fragmented, and based on casual and contractual rather than permanent employment. But then, what is the way out? According to Jose, not a legalistic scheme, which is bound to fail.

> Ensuring access to a basket of entitlements by the poor including primary education, public health, shelter, civic amenities and a clean environment can help set a minimum 'reserve price' of labour which would not be bid down by the market forces. Only by way of creating a social floor for wages, can there be a reduction in the volume of distress-induced migrations now taking place from the poorest regions of India. The least that can be done is to enable people to live in their natural habitats without being compelled to flee from poverty and deprivation (Jose 2006: 3483).

All this is very pertinent to the future fate of the people I have been writing about in south Gujarat. The predatory capitalism now dominating needs to be tamed by broad-based welfare policies resulting in inclusion rather than exclusion. I consider the prospects for a New Deal targeting the working poor of India at the beginning of the twenty-first century to be very meagre. While the drive towards further flexibilization of work and labour continues relentlessly, the proposed scheme for employment generation, together with the introduction of the most elementary social provisions and guarantees for payment of a fair wage and decent working conditions, should be understood as efforts to promote the well-being of the working poor. In this approach, informalization as the organizing principle on how to utilize labour power most efficiently, that is, at the lowest possible cost, is restrained by public interventions aiming to provide a safety net for the large segment of the workforce which has fallen through whatever social protection used to be available. The paradox is that to undo the vulnerability and insecurity that are the logical outcomes of the informalization doctrine, attempts to establish a floor of minimal well-being have to rely on arrangements that are essentially formal in nature. Such initiatives stand no chance in an economic policy frame that remains firmly based on cheap labour, which can be laid off without overhead costs at times of underemployment or unemployment.

The panel of experts set up to make wide-ranging proposals to improve the plight of informal sector labour has been designated the 'National Commission on Enterprises in the Unorganized Sector. 'Unorganized' is the synonym used in India for what has been labelled elsewhere as the informal sector. In fact, unorganized refers to a workforce unable to articulate its interests by resorting to collective action. The term is misconceived because the employers operating in this economic circuit have often managed to get organized not only in restricting market competition, but also in dealing either with labour problems or with the government. Even more problematic is the term 'enterprises'. The implied suggestion is that informal sector livelihoods are based on income gained from own-account work. This interpretation considers self-employment to be a distinct feature of the overwhelming majority of the workforce engaged in this circuit of the economy, which has rapidly grown in significance. Labelling them as a vast army of petty entrepreneurs ignores the fact that what is portrayed as own-account work are often barely disguised forms of waged labour. When the employer–employee nexus remains opaque, because of the casualization and contractualization of work practices, it would be misleading to conclude that these labouring lives survive and reproduce in modes of self-employment. Classification in these terms is, however, also inspired by the desire to hold the informal sector workforce accountable for its own welfare. The costs of achieving even a modicum of social protection and security should not be passed on to either employers or the government. The pretension of own-account labour as the overriding employment modality for the working poor in their search for income helps to defuse any such claims on all those who want to get work done at the lowest possible price.

Underlying my scepticism of the new public approach—which is intended to provide work, social security, and a wage that will allow the poor the fundamentals of a dignified life—are the results of the fieldwork I have conducted among the working poor in rural south Gujarat over the past half a century. Let me start by saying that there can be no doubt about the urgent need for interventions such as those now under consideration. They would require the restoration of a public domain which, in the relentless drive for privatization, has all but disappeared. I am deeply wary of the political context in which the new schemes are introduced. There is an enormous gap between the logic of the proposals and the economic policy currently being pursued in India. The Employment Guarantee Act and the two Social Security bills, all of which were announced during the last two years, assume that there is both the political will and the scope in the field of policy-making to reverse the dominant trend towards informalization of the economy in the past quarter of a century. The same assumption underlies a number of Hirway's suggestions, for example, her recommendation to give contract and temporary workers the same entitlements to social security as permanent employees. She proposes that:

> . . . sugar cane cutters who produce raw material and feed it to factories need to be considered as part of the factory workers, as they work exclusively for their factories and participate in the production process of manufacturing sugar. Legal fights are going on right now in several cases in Gujarat for a reasonably comparable level of benefits for such workers (Hirway 2006: 381).

She does not mention, however, the dismal results of the legal battles waged at the central and state levels on the basis of public interest litigations. I have reported on the discouraging state of affairs in these cases, with reference to the treatment of sugarcane cutters by the cooperative sugar factories in and around Bardoli, in a number of publications (see, for example, Breman 1994: ch. 5). It is precisely to defuse such claims in advance that the proponents of informalization press for the existing legislation to be dismantled. This constant political pressure, which has been successful and of which flexibilization is an integral part, aims to weaken rather than strengthen labour rights. The same can be said of the setting of a minimum wage, as included in the second Social Security Bill. Dev strongly supports this urgently needed improvement in the situation of informal sector workers.

> Some regulatory institutions are needed without having an inspection raj. Minimum wages have to be fixed keeping in view the various increasing expenditure of the poor and laws should be effectively implemented (Dev 2006: 1515).

Dev is, of course, absolutely right, but fails to address the crucial questions of why this has never happened before and, above all, what must be done to avoid a repeat of the earlier failure to impose a minimum wage. Hirway has quite correctly drawn attention to the dismal record of non-enforcement of labour laws in the past decades. However, both economists carefully avoid the issue of whether the chances of fair and just implementation have improved. Such a conclusion is mere wishful thinking, and does not do justice to the way power is distributed at the local level. Does the political will necessary to redress the severe imbalance between labour and capital in favour of the rural proletariat exist? After all, there can be no doubt that the provision of a social safety net is more a political than an economic issue.

It is understandable that Hirway and Dev express their fear of bureaucratization of the social security schemes intended to alleviate the suffering of the working poor. However, their plea to give the beneficiaries a greater say in identifying their needs and to encourage their active involvement in implementing the programmes is based on the assumption that there is sufficient political and social space for the masses at the base of the economy to take advantage of such opportunities. I have questioned this point of view in the preceding chapters. The landless proletariat is heavily under-represented on the village councils. Their voices are not heard in the decision-making process at this lowest level of political democracy. The main landowning caste, whether Anavil Brahmans or Kanbi Patidars, make up only a small part of the village population. They impose their dominance on the lower castes. In recent decades, as awareness of the world outside the village has increased, many younger Anavils and Patidars have left and in several instances they became truly globalized. The fact that relatively more members of the higher castes have left the village has led to a further shift in the demographic balance, adding to the numerical strength of the lower castes. Yet this change in the social composition of the population has not resulted in a loss of influence for the dominant caste. They have not given up their land, which has always been the source of their local hegemony. Their power has actually increased by utilizing the social capital they have acquired for the promotion of their interests outside the village. The members of the local elite have gained access to government agencies up to district level, are in the forefront of district political parties and religious organizations, and sit on the governing boards of cooperatives, schools, hospitals, and other civil institutions. This presence offers many advantages and privileges, but the results of my fieldwork make it clear that they rarely heed requests from their fellow villagers in the landless neighbourhoods to mediate on their behalf, and they provide direct help or support only in individual cases.

The contest for local power

The attitude of the village elite to the landless households appears to be based on a strategy intended to prolong the latter's marginality and hamper their advancement. It also confirms the public opinion of this underclass as a group of people cursed with a wide range of defects. In a case study of the murder of a Halpati farm labourer by local magnates in a village in Navsari district, I described the events leading up to the incident, the way outsiders responded, and the outcome of the trial of the perpetrators: acquittal on all charges (Breman 2003: 51–104). In two of the villages of my fieldwork—Gandevigam and Bardoligam—the village head is a Halpati woman. Neither can read or write. Their appointment is a result of positive discrimination, since in these villages the position of sarpanch is reserved for members of the tribal castes. They are puppets for the vice-sarpanch, who is an Anavil Brahman in Gandevigam and a Kanbi Patidar in Bardoligam. The latter in particular is well-known for the hard-handed way in which he treats Halpatis who come to him with complaints. He hits and kicks them and has been reported to the police on several occasions, once because a farm labourer died of his injuries. Yet he has never been charged with any crime. When I challenged N. Patel about his reputation, he laughed and told me that people who are beyond reason can only be kept under control with strict discipline.

The day before I arrived in Gandevigam in January 2006 the mamlatdar had paid a visit to inform the village council of the instruction he had received from the state capital Gandhinagar to close the BPL register. After an earlier decision to clean up the register by removing households that had allegedly been given BPL status erroneously, this latest instruction announced that no names could be added to the current list. The state Chief Minister Narendra Modi had decided to remove poverty from the political field of vision, and there was therefore no room for new cases in the government accounts. The Gujarat Human Development Report 2004 states that the incidence of income poverty has fallen sharply and that, at the end of the twentieth century (1999 2000), it affected less than 13 per cent of the total population (Hirway and Mahadevia 2004). Such an impressive figure is of course incompatible with village records such as those in Gandevigam, which has issued nearly all landless households with a card entitling them to subsidized food because they live below the poverty line. The discrepancy between macro-statistics and micro-reality can easily be solved by no longer registering cases of deprivation and destitution. This bureaucratic sleight of hand suggests that the figures in the next Human Development Report will be even more optimistic. Policy reports and official statistics present a facade of wishful thinking which conceal a reality of deep and widespread misery.

The procedure for conducting the panchayat business is that the talati, as secretary, draws up the agenda of the scheduled meetings. The idea is that the members come to the village office at the stated date and time to take part in the deliberations. But that is not how it goes in practice. In Bardoligam, for example, the talati bypasses the Halpati village head and confers only with the vice-sarpanch. The latter takes care of all correspondence, maintains contact with government offices in the sub-district, and deals with any visitors. The village council meetings take place only on paper. The talati writes down the list of decisions in a logbook, and sends the office peon to all the members to sign or place their thumbprint on the minutes. In this way all the prescribed formalities are fulfilled to ensure democracy at the local level. In reporting the findings of my fieldwork in the previous chapters, I have noted repeatedly the lack of collective action, solidarity, and leadership in the landless neighbourhoods. The caste panch of the landless communities in south Gujarat, who in the past used to mediate in disputes and promote cooperation in and beyond the village, has disappeared, and has not been substituted by any other form of neighbourhood consultation. The state of fragmentation into which the Halpatis, as the largest tribal caste, have now fallen makes them easy victims for the local power elite. The latter see to it that landless candidates for membership of the village council are those known to be docile, who cannot be expected to take any initiatives that might not serve the interests of the dominant castes.

As a senior staff member of the Centre for Social Studies in Surat, Satyakam Joshi has conducted research into the functioning of the panchayati raj system in Gujarat. The principle of representation at district, sub-district, and village levels was introduced here earlier than in most other states to deepen the working of democracy through the decentralization of governance and politics. What Joshi describes, confirms my own findings. This is illustrated by the passage below from his report on the situation in a village in south Gujarat, which is not far from Bardoligam and is therefore very similar in its economic and social fabric. The majority of farm labourers still exist in a state of subordination to the landowning minority. During the last elections, the Halpatis tried to put forward their own candidate for the position of sarpanch, but the Patidars succeeded in thwarting the attempt.

> The opposition candidate, Mr Bhanabhai Rathod, was an experienced and knowledgeable person and also used to fight for Halpati rights. The Patidars were aware that if Bhanabhai became the Sarpanch they (Patidars) probably might not be in a position to dictate him, hence they put up Naresh Rathod. During the discussion Bhanabhai said that 'Naresh is inexperienced and does not know anything about panchayat's functioning. He is mainly interested in his business. Apart from running a grocery shop he also distils country liquor, which is not legal. Our real problems are unemployment, proper minimum wages, and construction of good roads, rooms for school and regularizing our houses which are not on government land. Patidars do not want to solve all these problems because they are against their interest. Patidars believe that if Halpati children get educated then who will work in our field? Somehow they want us to remain under their mercy. Unfortunately, our people are not united and also succumb to the bad habit of liquor. Due to this we are not in a position to assert our rights. Today our children are going to school and get educated but there is no employment available to us. There are five to six Halpati boys in our village, who are graduates and diploma engineers, but they are eking out a miserable life as there is no job. In our area there are many private industries but they do not take our boys. On the other hand there is no vacancy in government. In such a situation they have to work as casual labourer. Most of us work as agricultural labourers in the fields of Patidars and Rajputs, today as per government prescribed rate daily wage is Rs 50, but we get only 30 to 35 rupees a day' (S. Joshi 2002: 37–8).

Dev based his comments on the proposed legislation to generate employment on the experience of the Employment Guarantee Scheme implemented in Maharashtra from the early 1970s. In this state the scheme not only had a positive impact in economic terms, such as a fall in unemployment, a rise in the incomes of the households taking part, and a general increase in wages for land labourers, but also gave the rural poor more political clout. I accept his argument, but with the reservation that a minimum of social and political room for manoeuvre is required for such programmes to be successful. Dev and Hirway identify the village panchayat as a platform for the target groups to have a say in the implementation of public works and bring them closer to the package of social security benefits. On the basis of my findings in south Gujarat, I predict that these interventions, which promise to put a stop to the exclusion of landless households, will be hampered by the indifference of local authorities and downright sabotage from the village elites. For those who advocate pressure from below, this is a deadly coalition of forces. The dominant landowning castes are only too well aware that reducing the vulnerability of the castes at the foot of the village economy will erode their power base. I was told time and again by Halpatis in the villages of my fieldwork that the Anavils/Patidars 'do not want us to improve our lives'. How about other stakeholders, such as trade unions and NGOs, who represent the interests of people who cannot themselves make their voices heard? Addressing this question gives me the opportunity to examine the role of civil society.

Initiatives from civil society

There can be no doubt that without considerable and persistent pressure from outside and from below, the government machinery is neither willing nor able to create the social safety net needed to successfully alleviate poverty. Disappointed with the incapacity of the state and its executive apparatus to ensure that economic growth benefits the deprived masses, many have set their hopes on NGOs, which have been given the responsibility and the corresponding mandate to achieve the inclusion of the poor in dividing up the spoils of development. Some advocates of this approach tend to sing the praises of private initiative and prove to be supporters of the free market, albeit if only in protest at the protectionism which has allowed the bureaucratic class to benefit more than the population living in misery.[2] Others adopt a less extreme standpoint and present themselves as the articulators of interests that receive insufficient attention in the public domain. Then there are social activists in search of a target group, which is their entry point in their efforts towards transformation of the social order. The range of civil associations is too large to do justice to all variations, and many are combined forms which serve multiple purposes. Gujarat is well-known as a state where civil society introduced emancipatory initiatives at an early stage. The social climate appeared to provide a fertile ground for the founding of many hundreds of NGOs aimed at putting a stop to backwardness, discrimination, deprivation, and bondage. In the light of this proud tradition, it is notable that in the past half a century, with one exception, not a single NGO has been active in the villages of my fieldwork in supporting the tribal caste of farm labourers in their struggle for economic and social progress.

In all those years, the HSS has had a monopoly in representing civil society among the rural proletariat of south Gujarat. I have repeatedly and extensively discussed the origins, approach, activities, and impact of this voluntary association in my village accounts. A summary will therefore suffice here. The core question is whether this social movement, originally set up under the guidance of Mahatma Gandhi, has ever been able to realize its promise of economic development and social emancipation. Drawing up the balance after half a century, there can be no other conclusion than that this Gandhian mission of upliftment has failed seriously and on all fronts. The movement made a discouraging start. The leaders of the struggle for national independence were convinced that they needed to win the support of the rural population for their cause. In that context, Gandhi took sides with the dominant farmers in Bardoli against an increase in land tax by the colonial authorities. The campaign that he initiated could not ignore the system of bonded labour on which agriculture was founded. During his tour of the region in the early 1920s, the father of the nation was shocked to learn from the landowners that the landless, then still known as Dublas, belonged to a category of *Untermenschen* who were not considered part of the population. Gandhi cancelled his first satyagraha in the region and when it resumed in 1928, called on his disciples to initiate a wide-ranging programme of social work to educate the landless underclass to be full-fledged citizens. With the clear disapproval of Sardar Patel, Gandhi persisted in this civilizing mission. Halipratha, he taught, was ignoble for both the farm labourers and their masters. The latter denigrated themselves by showing no feelings of humanity, compassion, or solidarity for their fellow villagers, who had to live their lives in ignorance and poverty.

After Gandhi's demise, many of his followers remained in the countryside around Bardoli and later throughout south Gujarat to continue the struggle for emancipation of the tribal castes. The Halpati Mahajan, founded in 1946, became the platform for a network of ashrams which served as a basis for the social work launched by Gandhian activists. Under the chairman Jugatram Dave, one of Gandhi's closest confidants, Arvind Desai became the secretary of the movement. He was then still a young man, the son of a disciple of the Gandhian school and member of the dominant Anavil Brahman caste. The main priority in the initially modest programme was education. The ashrams were boarding schools where the pupils not only learned to read and write, but also spinning and weaving. Classical Gandhian schooling included the promotion of a hygienic, regular, and orderly lifestyle as the only way to achieve liberation from all kinds of customs and practices that held the Halpatis backward and in a state of deprivation. Singing devotional songs was also part of the Hinduization of the children's way of life. This was motivated by a caste awareness that attributed the target group a place somewhere at the base of the social hierarchy. Bringing about a change in the enormous gap between landless and landowners, between high and low caste, could not be achieved overnight. The moment of emancipation and equality could only be achieved through patience and by not expecting an immediate response to the demand for a better life, no matter how justified that demand may be. This message was accompanied by the exhortation to the Halpatis to improve their own livelihood by, for example, not living beyond their means. The Surat Jilla Halpati Seva Sangh was set up in 1961 with the aim of pursuing this work of upliftment with even greater élan. The Congress government had pledged generous financial support. On the second anniversary of the organization, Morarji Desai, the Congress veteran who was minister of finance in the central government, addressed a gathering of some few hundred invitees in an orchard near the village of Sarbhon in the Bardoli sub-district. Social workers, recognizable by their khadi clothing and Congress cap, accounted for the largest part of the company and they responded enthusiastically to what the prominent guest had to say. But Desai looked over the heads of the social workers, aiming his words at the Halpatis, who had been encouraged to attend arid who stood at the back in total silence, as if to make it clear that the party had nothing to do with them. I summarized the tenor of his speech at the meeting, in which I participated, in my fieldwork diary.

> The *hali* system, he said, arose out of the loans contracted by the Halpatis for their marriages, and the system was maintained by their partiality for liquor. He called on them to free themselves from their bondage by avoiding indebtedness in future, and by abandoning bad habits, particularly drinking. The total amount of land was insufficient to allow Halpatis to profit from land reform. Therefore he counselled them to ask for higher wages. However, they were not to go on strike or even stage go-slows, since by doing so they would not only harm the farmers but also themselves, and he urged his audience to have patience and not to listen to agitators, but to put their trust in the Congress Party (Breman 1985: 146–7).

The HSS, which on its foundation had emphatically called itself an organization for social work rather than a trade union, had a board consisting of voluntary activists. From their names it is clear that about half came from the landowning classes: twelve Anavils and twelve Patidars. The target group itself provided only a quarter of the activists (eleven of the total of forty-eight). To be nominated to the board, candidates had to fulfil the following criteria: the wearing of khadi, abstention from alcohol, experience of having worked among Halpatis for at least five years, and an annual contribution of one day's wages and one days production of thread hand-spun by the applicant. Apart from two lifelong donors, one of whom was Morarji Desai, there were 7723 ordinary members who were supposed to pay 10 paise (cents) a year. Ten years later the membership was said to have risen to nearly 20,000 Halpatis to give the impression of a mass movement. In name the HSS was an association, but the contributions actually came from public and private donations. The large government subsidy covered all overheads, including staff salaries, and allowed the organization to open offices in the main towns of all sub-districts with a high percentage of Halpatis, to direct the social work in the surrounding villages. The price for these grants was paid gladly: the mobilization of the Halpatis to form a solid vote bank for the Congress party. In addition to education, the provision of shelter became an important point in the agenda. The activists, who were now salaried professionals, exercised pressure on the village panchyats and local bureaucrats to release land to the landless for house construction. The colonies that were built as a result of their efforts tend to lie on the outskirts of the villages, on bad, uneven land. They are difficult to access and remained for a long time without even the most elementary facilities. In this way, without being aware of the consequences of their actions, the Gandhian social workers in fact contributed to the segregation of the rural proletariat from mainstream society.

Patronizing the poor

As early as 1974 I described the Anavil leader of this social movement, highlighting his authoritarian behaviour (Breman 1974). He led the HSS with an iron hand, and young Halpatis who found jobs as teachers in one of the ashrams after having done well at school were ill-advised to cherish any ambitions towards leadership. Those that did were soon shown the door. In describing this top-down approach I qualified Arvind Desai as a typical boss, a dhaniyamo who demanded absolute loyalty and tolerated no initiative, let alone argument, from his subordinates. The landless labourers in south Gujarat watched from a distance and ignored directives from above. They showed no inclination at all to blindly follow the man who had proclaimed himself their leader.

Poverty reduction seemed to have become an important policy priority after Indira Gandhi came to power. When she discarded the conservative old guard of Congress in 1972, to which Morarji Desai also belonged, it led to a split in the party. It was clear from the beginning that the landless masses supported Indira, who made the eradication of poverty (garibi hatao) the main issue in the elections. Up to the present day, Mataji (as she is still referred to by the landless) enjoys a reputation among the Halpatis as a politician who took the side of the poor, subaltern classes. If she did not do what she promised, her followers saw this as a consequence of the opposition from the vested interests. After all, they stand in the way of any attempt to improve the lot of the deprived. In south Gujarat, it was Jhinabhai Darji who became the spokesman of the voiceless masses. He supported Indira Gandhi and represented her in the struggle for power that divided the Congress ranks. Jhinia emerged the victor and presented himself as the mouthpiece of the silent majority. As the key figure in the new course, which held out the prospect of a better life for the poor, this prominent reformer brought down on himself the hatred of the landowners. They vented on him all the anger that they were unable to express in the past about Mahatma Gandhi. In the words of a Patidar farmer:

> It was Gandhi's instigations that has made the Dublas braver and defiant now. Otherwise, in Gaekwadi, if the Dublas tried to disobey even a little, we used to cut them into pieces and bury them in the ground. Dublas were under our foot, but this Gandhi pulled them in the Independence struggle and made them fight against us, the benevolent care-takers of ignorant Dublas. Now, today they are stuck into worst economic conditions. Jhinia's instigations abolished *halipratha* and today they are rotting on daily wage system. They are getting twenty times less than what they got as a *hali* to a farmer like me. Today they are without employment. Now, they are waiting for our land to be distributed to them as Jhinia has promised them in return of their votes (P. Patel 1982: 10).

Without giving up its objective as a social welfare agency, the HSS increasingly conducted itself as a development organization. This enabled it to obtain funds for NGO activities from international donors. To allow the new generation of Halpatis to find alternative employment to farm work, vocational training courses were held for pupils who had attended the ashram school. Under the supervision of skilled craftsmen, a select number of candidates learned about tailoring, bricklaying, or diamond cutting/polishing, and took driving lessons to get a license. In addition, the leadership was aware that to maintain contact with the grassroots supporters in the villages, it was necessary to set up outposts in the landless neighbourhoods. It was the job of volunteers to make people aware of its activities and to get the local people to come to meetings where they would be addressed by outsiders, usually Congress politicians. The volunteers also kept a medicine chest at their homes with an assortment of the most common cures for Halpatis who suffered from illness or minor ailments. This was intended to stop them from going to the bhagat. The HSS wanted nothing to do with this traditional healer/exorcist, who they saw as a representative of the tribal culture that was an obstacle to their civilizing mission. To undertake this wide range of activities and to open sub-offices to expand the radius of action to the whole of south Gujarat required not only a lot of money, but also an extensive staff. In 1980, a large office building was completed opposite the Swaraj ashram in Bardoli. Morarji Desai was the guest of honour at the inauguration ceremony. Like many Gandhian veterans he had defected to the Janata Party in opposition to Indira Gandhi. At the end of his political career, Desai was for a short time prime minister at the head of a national government which the landowners had supported because of their disenchantment with the Congress party. The landless remained loyal to the Congress because its leader had solemnly promised to release them from poverty. Because the HSS boss refused to initiate the struggle for better conditions of employment in agriculture, the organization lost its way and its political credibility. In the diary of my field trip to south Gujarat at that time, I described the confusion and disillusionment that had taken hold of Arvind Desai.

> A.D. has withdrawn into his office and from there manages a number of projects for which he obtains financial support from an international organization. The last time I met him, in the spring of 1981, he had lost his earlier elan. He has no political ambitions any more, but no ideals either, he gave me to understand. Under his leadership the organization has acquired a markedly bureaucratic character (Breman 1985: 422).

This summary of the activities conducted by the HSS must also mention what is systematically omitted: the mobilization of farm labourers to articulate their demands for a minimum wage, and to pressurize the government and politicians to provide more and better employment. In 1966, Jugatram Dave became a member of the committee, set up by the government of Gujarat, to submit proposals for the introduction of a minimum wage for farm labourers. Although he stated during the deliberations that satisfying the labourers' basic needs required a higher wage than agreed upon by the majority, the HSS chairman gave in when the other members of the committee did not want to give in to his request for payment of a fair wage. He had voiced his opinion and desisted from any further action. As I already noted, on its foundation the organization made it clear that it had no ambitions to be a trade union. That was part of an ideological stance that resisted representing the interests of only one party. In the Gandhian approach, disputes had to be solved by seeking a compromise and thus by restoring harmony. The organization's main objective was to reconcile the differences between castes and classes and if relations between them became tense, the social workers acted as intermediaries who rejected the use of violence under any circumstances. If conflicts occurred—for example, when there was a strike for higher wages or clashes with landowners or their hirelings as a result of Halpati men or women being molested—they would rush to the scene and try to pacify the conflicting parties, immediately quashing any signs of militancy. I have reported on such incidents on several occasions (see, for example, Breman 1994: 312–13), and have concluded that HSS mediation more probably delayed rather than advanced the emancipation of the Halpatis. I would like to repeat my earlier comment that for half a century, by attributing them a place as 'semi-Hindus' at the bottom of the hierarchy, the

HSS social workers intensified—if not actually created—the caste awareness of their target group. Stimulating class awareness, on the other hand, was considered abominable and sinful in Gandhian teaching. Later events do not justify changing in any way the conclusions I drew after my first period of fieldwork (Breman 1974: 258).

Among the typical Anavil character traits displayed by Arvind Desai was his directness and his tendency to provoke the landowners in his public addresses for oppressing and exploiting the farm labourers. Once he went too far and was hauled from his house by a group of young Patidars, students at the college in Bardoli. They stripped him of all his clothes and forced him to walk through the streets naked to make him the object of scorn and humiliation (Breman 1985: 393–4). The abuse he had to suffer did not make the Halpatis any less cynical about the edifying sermons of the HSS boss and other Gandhian activists attributing their deprivation to their own failings.

> At an election meeting which I attended in 1977 in a Halpati colony, one of those present asked, in an ostensibly naïve way: 'how is it that we get no further? Morarji himself told us here that the Janata lot have the best of intentions because they are followers of Gandhi. And Congress has already governed a long time in the name of the poor, but we are still as poor as ever. Does the cause lie with ourselves, then?' (Loud laughter) (Breman 1985: 421).

During my last round of fieldwork I asked Arvind Desai what he thought about the current situation. The HSS leader has aged, and he told me he had given up all hope of seeing in his lifetime any real improvement in the lot of those for whom he had fought throughout his long career. He blames the BJP government of Narendra Modi for not letting him finish his work. When this hard-line Hindutva politician came to power in Gujarat, in the eyes of the dominant landowners as a worthy successor to Sardar Patel, he withdrew all subsidies for the social welfare work carried out by the HSS. The funds provided so generously were after all used to support a mass of people who had for many years voted for the Congress. Of the programme of activities, only the schools have survived, and it is very difficult to find sufficient funds to keep them open. In addition, there is no work outside agriculture for children who have completed a basic education. When I visited the HSS in 1995, there was a new sign on the door: Rural Labour Association. But even at that time, Arvind admitted that there was little going on inside. The once large staff of the HSS had disappeared. In his room, we talked about the outcome of half a century of Gandhian social activism. He agreed that indeed, the results were thin on the ground. But he defended himself by saying that that was not only the fault of the farmers for refusing to pay the minimum wage, but also of the Halpatis' reprehensible behaviour. After all, what keeps them poor and backward is their addiction to alcohol. These days women drink too, and their children start at an increasingly early age. Superstition is still rife in the landless milieu. Arvind gave me a leaflet instructing Halpatis how to leave behind the darkness of their tribal past and move forward towards the light of civilization.

When we met in 2005 he asked me what effects of the HSS' activities I had noticed in the villages of my fieldwork. In my reply I tried to tone down my firm opinion that the impact has been little or nothing. S., an inhabitant of one of the landless colonies in Gandevigam, was an HSS activist for a number of years. He operated from a branch office in the main town of the sub-district. The office was closed when the rent could no longer be paid. His job was to eradicate alcohol abuse, promote education, and submit applications for new houses to the government. In Chikhligam, there is a HSS boarding school where I stayed during my visit. A sign at the entrance to the school mentions the name of the organization. Yet, although all the pupils come from the tribal castes, very few of them are Halpati boys or girls. They are only allowed to attend the village school. The head of the HSS school has last year been caught tampering with the supplies of meal and oil provided by the government for the preparation of the children's noon meal. After complaints from parents he has been demoted to the status of teacher. In Atulgam, the HSS has disappeared completely and, more surprisingly, in Bardoligam too there is no sign of any presence now or in the past. The latter village is, after all, only a stone's throw from Bardoli town, and in the middle of the area in which Gandhi and his disciples first began their work of social upliftment.

Defiance and militancy

I therefore conclude that the engagement of civil society with the rural proletariat has continued to be extremely localized, and the performance of the social movement which took the lead in civil-society activities in south Gujarat was poor and perhaps even counter-productive. This critical judgement does not become much more positive if we look at the role played by trade unions. It is widely known that organized and sustainable collective action is relatively uncommon in the untransparent and fragmented landscape of the informal sector economy. Yet it is remarkable that the interests of the largest working class in India—the enormous mass of agricultural labourers—have rarely been represented in the political and economic arena. In the late-colonial era attempts in this direction in south Gujarat failed, not in the last instance because Gandhian activists strongly resisted the emergence of this form of mobilization on the left of the political spectrum.[3] A number of Congress leaders, including Jhina Darji, set up the Khet Vikas Parishad in 1977, but its main objective was again to win votes for the Congress party. There were no concrete plans to mobilize farm labourers to improve their lot. In response to the tense situation at that time in Bardoli, the organization's annual report had only this to say: '. . . those who believe in the struggle for social justice by violence will find fertile ground here. Khet Vikas Parishad, which believes in creating social justice by Gandhian means, will have a difficult time here to pass the test' (Khet Vikas Parishad Administrative Report 1978: 42). Other than this, the Halpatis have had little to do with trade unions. Those who worked as casual labourers in small workshops and factories in Bilimora or Navsari came into contact with unions, and a small number of my informants in Gandevigam and Chikhligam joined in the hope that their temporary jobs would become permanent, a hope that in most cases failed to materialize. Often those who do join fall into the hands of leaders who run the small-time unions like petty entrepreneurs, and use their members for their own private gain. They allow themselves to be bribed so as to not pursue their demands, which they might give added weight by organizing a short strike. The Halpatis from Atulgam who had found jobs in one of the factories of the nearby industrial complex seemed at first to be faring better. There were only a few dozen of them, but enough to keep the hope of a better future alive in the landless neighbourhoods. They joined the unions, which called for compliance with legislation that assured workers in the formal sector a decent wage, protected them against dismissal and other risks, and provided social services that increased the dignity of their lives. At least, until the policy of informalization put a stop to their involvement in collective action and excluded them once again from these benefits which they acquired in their formal sector employment. What then are the prospects for a better future?

In my view, the most important progress made at the bottom of the village economy is the Halpatis' demand for respect for their right to live and work in dignity. That attitude is expressed through moral indignation at being paid a wage that does not even allow them to meet their basic daily needs. The gradual monetization of their wages did not take account of the rising cost of living. The chronic indebtedness that is the inevitable outcome of this income deficit ensures that they remain confined in a state of dependence and vulnerability. The progressive transition to a capitalist economy has led to alienation between landowners and farm labourers, which I summarized in a previous study as follows.

> Growing consciousness among the landless has aroused the farmers' wrath. In the past the local landless were simply there, all the time at the beck and call of the Patidars (or Anavils), in exchange for which they had the right to a guaranteed subsistence. Labour had to be maintained at the behest of

> the employer, but was not something that had to be paid for. The dependent workforce, which was once not much more than an extension of the landowners' households, now emphasizes its independence and tries as far as possible to behave in an appropriate manner. This indicates a fundamental change in the interpretation of labour value. The farmers are reluctant to accept this change, which they themselves have created by ushering in a capitalist mode of production, because they rightly perceive this as an undermining of their social dominance (Breman 1985: 338–9).

Does the grudge shown by the farm labourers hark back to a better past that has now been lost? Most certainly not. Such statements express dissatisfaction with the situation in the present, but must not be explained in terms of a nostalgic desire to regain what has been lost. The view of halipratha as a harmonious work relationship, a cordial bond of mutual fondness between the landowning and landless families, is a myth. This presentation of the patron–client relationship exaggerates the generous and affectionate traits that bound master and servant. Jugatram Dave, a close associate of Gandhi to whom the leader of the independence movement entrusted the upliftment mission among the tribal population in the 1920s, pointed out in his monograph on this system of labour bondage the affection which the hali displayed for his dhaniyamo. The respect enjoyed by the latter reflected on his client, and he therefore shared in the status claimed by his master. This portrayal fits in with the characterization of a relatively closed village economy which may have been based on unequal power, property, and prestige, but in which common interests between the haves and have-nots took priority. In my first fieldwork study, I explicitly distanced myself from such an interpretation. In my analysis I defined the relationship between master and servant as one based on both patronage and exploitation (Breman 1974). Dave himself was not unaware of the fact that there was another dimension to the relationship between the landowners and their labourers, but he was unable to identify it as one of exploitation because such a term had no place in Gandhian ideology. He pointed out that the farm labourers did what the farmers considered betrayal—they collaborated with the colonial authorities, lending a hand to the authorities because they hated their masters.

> On the occasion of confiscation of the property of landowners, no one from this class was available to the government to carry away their belongings. But at this time it was very easy to use Halpatis as instruments by instigating their bitterness towards landowners (Dave 1946: 35–6).

This episode at the Bardoli satyagraha has been carefully removed from the hagiography of the movement. The official history holds resolutely to the image of unity between all the members of the village community. How inaccurate this was even at the time can be seen from a report by two colonial officials, which mentions the strikes that broke out in a number of villages, including Bardoligam, to add strength to the demands for a higher wage (Broomfield and Maxwell 1929). My Patidar informants in the village were not enamoured with this story, which was clearly in conflict with their own claim that mutual trust had reigned in the past. The Halpatis of today refuse to confirm this harmonious interpretation of their earlier state of bondage. In reply to my question why the new, generation no longer works as farm servants in the houses of the members of the dominant class, an elderly Halpati told me that the young men of today refuse to bow their backs in the house of a Patidar. He meant this both literally, in terms of bending to sweep the floor or do any number of other household chores, and metaphorically by avoiding work that so visibly demonstrates subordination.

The role of outsiders is always emphasized in explaining the disappearance of halipratha. In my opinion, this assessment exaggerates the role of civil society, especially that of the Gandhian activists who worked to bring it to an end, and the government's ban on the system under pressure from international conventions against bonded labour. I am inclined to attach greater significance to the increasing pressure from within, First, landowners gradually realized that it was much more expensive to employ permanent servants, with the obligation to ensure their survival even in slack seasons of the year, than to take on daily wage labourers who could be hired and fired instantly. Second, the farm labourers themselves were equally keen to escape from a regime that held them in a permanent state of dependence and took away their dignity as human beings. They had an explicit preference for free labour, albeit on the basis of other conditions than those they actually got. But their desire for a decent wage, regular employment, and equal status instead of subordination was not fulfilled.

Barriers to emancipation

There are few records of the historical past and those that do exist are coloured with a bias that assumes the internalization of subordination. Without any exact data to support this view, I doubt that the Halpatis ever accepted their lot with docility. The portrait of the grateful, loyal servant is an employers' myth. The landless did not respond with docility when they increasingly became redundant in agriculture. The complaints about their low productivity and their unwillingness to work can hardly be denied. The labour regime is not only unjust, but gradually saps the physical strength and mental resilience of the landless. People who live in a permanent state of malnutrition cannot work to their full potential and are susceptible to all kinds of ailments which make them even more vulnerable. The severe income deficit, which is the main feature of their way of life, also generates symptoms of pauperization that contribute to the downward spiral in which they live. These symptoms include an unpredictable tendency to stay at home and refuse to go to work because of fatigue, and not actively searching for work outside agriculture and beyond the village. Their availability for work is passive: 'anyone who is in need of labour can come to hire me'. Their pauperization is also evident from the alcohol addiction that affects both men and women, adults and children. In addition to the enormous burden this places on their meagre budget, it is also an indication of the loss of control over a regular and orderly life. Lastly, frequent conflict—violent or non-violent—is inherent to pauperization, not only with the neighbours, but also between the members of the same household. The anger and frustration that lies at the base of this lumpen behaviour is vented on those who are the most vulnerable: women, children, and the elderly.

Unwillingness to work is, however, not only a matter of incapacity or apathy, it is also a form of resistance to injustice. 'Why should we work for eight hours a day if we are paid a wage that is too low for the effort that is expected of us?' Starting late, going home early, and a long break in the middle of the day are the response of people who feel that they are being subjected to inhuman treatment. They have to ask for an advance to survive and the debt they accumulate is seen as a supplement to their inadequate wages and not as a generous gesture of goodwill for which they owe their employers. The payment of an advance is not in any case seen as an obligation to work in return. For their part, the members of the dominant castes respond to this work-shy behaviour with moral outrage. They see it as justifying their decision to refuse paying the minimum wage. In this way, both parties hold each other in a vicious circle of ill-will, but it is clear who has the worst of the arrangement. If the landowners are not prepared to alleviate the poverty of the landless from considerations of humanity or, in any case, their own enlightened self-interest in the long run, might they perhaps do so from fear that the tension will erupt into violence, of which they and their property will be the target? The landowners say that they are not afraid that this will happen. However, during my earlier stay in Bardoligam, the pseudonym I gave this village in my current study, I recorded the following passage in my diary.

> *10 August.* The village headman of A. spoke in respectful terms of the toughness and physical strength of specifically-named agricultural labourers of the previous generation. Their masters occasionally made use of these qualities to settle their mutual differences, but the work people of today are worth nothing any more, in this respect. The farmers' sons can manage them without difficulty.

> Nevertheless, however weakened through drink and complete wretchedness, the number of the landless is so great that the farmers are forced to fear for their possessions. After all, material progress has made the Patidars vulnerable to attacks from a mob (Breman 1985: 400).

The notion of a '*classe dangereuse*' is clearly not entirely absent. This awareness is kept alive by incidents which occur regularly, and which I recorded in my village accounts. The members of the dominant castes, however, see these as spontaneous, localized, and sporadic clashes, and expect them to stay that way. I consider this response wishful thinking. It is, however, too early to say when the resistance among the members of the labour reserve army will gather momentum and become more sustained and better organized.

In addition to polarization there is another trend observable in rural south Gujarat, which I have indicated as a process of growing divergence between the top and bottom of the village population. The landowning elite, more than in previous generations, prefer a way of life that is no longer anchored in agriculture and in the village. Young Anavils and Patidars choose to settle in the towns and cities, close by or further afield, and try to find access to occupations that have nothing to do with agriculture. They do this without giving up their agrarian property, but they do not invest in the land or in cultivating crops that might produce a higher yield. This management at a distance is one important reason for the loss of employment in this source of livelihood, which can no longer be seen as the primary sector of the economy. In contrast to the urban or even global orientation of the major employers, there has been little change at the foot of the village economy in the dependence on farm labour as the main source of income. With no schooling and other forms of social capital, only a relatively small part of the enormous landless mass has the opportunity to escape an agrarian regime that needs them much less than it used to. The occasional, rather than regular, use of their labour power in or outside agriculture is partly the consequence of migrant labour being brought in from elsewhere and sent away again in a never-ending circuit of circulation. The local and migrant proletariat together form an enormous army of reserve labour that is recruited for daily or seasonal work, close by or further afield, and then sent back to the slums in the villages that are their home bases.

The mobilization of the rural proletariat for temporary employment takes place with the aid of mechanisms that I have identified as neobondage. Such arrangements, which are expressed through the provision of a cash advance combined with delayed payment for work performed, contribute to the vulnerability of the rural underclasses. It results in a floating and fragmented existence that precludes the emergence of social consciousness based not on segmentation or alienation, but on solidarity. The neighbourhoods seem to be a better starting point for the collective action that is necessary to the development of such consciousness than drifting around a wide variety of work sites. Instead of offering an escape to the landless from the regime of poverty, the way the market mechanism operates helps them to remain stuck in misery. Piecework and contract labour, casual rather than permanent employment, and hire-and-fire have been raised to modes of organizing economic activity that favour capital above labour. The proletariat in the villages of south Gujarat finds itself subject to a policy of exclusion. Yet it would be incorrect to see the rigid pursuance of a neoliberal approach in the drive towards informalization as the only cause of poverty that turns into pauperization. When the supply of labour in the lower echelons of the economy is much larger than the demand for it, there can be little doubt that capitalism produces poverty rather than mitigating, let alone ending, massive misery (see Harriss-White 2006).

No less responsible for this situation, however, is the idea of natural inequality that continues to be the cornerstone of the social fabric. A hierarchical order in terms of superiority and inferiority justifies a regime founded not on equality, social justice, and equity, but on shoring up the privilege of the few at the expense of discriminating the many. Anyone listening to the language of the dominant castes/classes at the village level will hear of ideas and practices that bear witness to unveiled social Darwinism. Seen from the top of society, those at the bottom do not count, and rightly so as they simply do not have the qualities required to advance themselves. In a short essay on the advance and eclipse of social Darwinism in the West during the second half of the nineteenth century, I drew a parallel between the denigration of the poor then and now. The inferiority of the lower classes was an article of faith in this social doctrine.

> Nature and society were cruel only to those who did not possess the vitality and quality required to survive. The poor led incomplete and inadequate lives because they were incapable of taking control of the circumstances in which they were forced to maintain themselves. But the instinct among civilised people to sympathise with these wretches offered them unwarranted support and protection. By tempering the natural play of social forces instead of allowing them free rein, modern society had burdened itself with a parasitical underclass . . . For the better-off segment of the labouring poor, there was still the possibility of being uplifted at some time in the future. But for the riff-raff below them the only real remedy was social exclusion (Breman 2004: 3870).

What gives hope from a historical perspective is that the landless masses, now subject to the regime of poverty in the subcontinent of South Asia, have in the recent past insisted on their right to live and work in freedom. In the rural slums inhabited by them, there is no evidence at all of internalization of dependence and subordination, or a docile acceptance of deprivation. Poverty is made invisible in statistics, and the poor themselves are rendered invisible in society. But, in my view, the most important outcome of the research I have conducted in the villages of south Gujarat over the past half a century is that the poor claim the right, now more than ever before, to a decent and dignified life.

Notes

1 A team of researchers coordinated by S. Patel have analysed Maharashtra's Employment Guarantee Scheme, the state where this policy was already launched three decades ago, from a sociological and political perspective.

2 I see Kishwar as an exponent of this view. In a number of publications she displays her conversion to the neoliberal faith—see, for example, Kishwar (2005).

3 How and why is the subject of a historical study which I wrote as an introduction to the reports of my fieldwork. See Breman (2007).

Index

For Product Safety Concerns and Information please contact our EU representative GPSR@taylorandfrancis.com
Taylor & Francis Verlag GmbH, Kaufingerstraße 24, 80331 München, Germany

www.ingramcontent.com/pod-product-compliance
Ingram Content Group UK Ltd.
Pitfield, Milton Keynes, MK11 3LW, UK
UKHW050055200926
475702UK00019B/2849
* 9 7 8 1 0 3 2 6 5 2 9 7 9 *